21世纪国际经济与贸易学专业系列教材

"国际贸易实务"国家级双语教学示范课程参考教材

国际贸易实务双语教程

（第6版）

易露霞　尤彧聪　吕屹云◎主编

International Business Practice

清华大学出版社
北京

内 容 简 介

本书是为培养我国涉外经济部门所需的既能熟练掌握外贸专业知识，又能熟练运用专业英语从事进出口业务的复合型人才而专门编写的教材，旨在帮助具备一定英语基础并初步掌握国际贸易知识的专业人士，提高国际贸易英语水平，利用英语直接从事和研究对外经贸的实际与理论工作。

本书共十三章，每章包括四部分。第一部分是课文，按照外贸业务交易发展的规律，同时用中英文系统地阐述国际贸易中的各个重要环节的规律。第二部分是专业术语解释，对外贸业务中经常出现的重要术语进行简要、精确的解释，使读者能够正确、清晰地理解这些术语的含义。第三部分是专业词汇，紧扣课文内容，提供与课文内容相关的常用单词。第四部分是练习，充分体现双语特点，既有中文练习又有英文练习，便于读者自学。

本书既可作为普通高等院校经济管理类学生学习国际贸易实务的教材，也可作为从事国际贸易工作的专业人士的自学参考书。

图书在版编目（CIP）数据

国际贸易实务双语教程 / 易露霞，尤彧聪，吕屹云主编. --6 版.

北京：清华大学出版社，2025. 8.

(21 世纪国际经济与贸易学专业系列教材).

ISBN 978-7-302-70160-6

Ⅰ. F740.4

中国国家版本馆 CIP 数据核字第 2025V95W05 号

责任编辑：杜春杰
封面设计：刘　超
版式设计：楠竹文化
责任校对：范文芳
责任印制：丛怀宇

出版发行：清华大学出版社
　　　网　　址：https://www.tup.com.cn，https://www.wqxuetang.com
　　　地　　址：北京清华大学学研大厦 A 座　　　邮　编：100084
　　　社 总 机：010-83470000　　　邮　购：010-62786544
　　　投稿与读者服务：010-62776969，c-service@tup.tsinghua.edu.cn
　　　质量反馈：010-62772015，zhiliang@tup.tsinghua.edu.cn
印 装 者：北京同文印刷有限责任公司
经　　销：全国新华书店
开　　本：185mm×260mm　　　印　张：28.5　　　字　数：705 千字
版　　次：2006 年 9 月第 1 版　　　2025 年 8 月第 6 版　　　印　次：2025 年 8 月第 1 次印刷
定　　价：79.80 元

产品编号：107064-01

第 6 版前言

本书自 2006 年 9 月出版以来，因内容新颖、实用，中英文结合，受到了许多院校师生、学者的关注和认可，至今已经 6 次改版，多次印刷，收到了良好的社会效益和经济效益。

本次修订的主要原因是随着数字经济的发展，数字贸易成为一种新贸易模式。进入数字贸易时代，国际贸易与"互联网+"紧密联系，出现了数字贸易和跨境电商等新的业态，互联网和英语共同成为当前开展对外经济贸易业务和相关国际商务活动的最主要工具。因此，补充了数字贸易以及跨境电子商务的各个最新流程、专业实务环节、地道英语表达等知识，增加其对外进行数字贸易特别是跨境电子商务各项业务联系活动的竞争力。笔者结合多年的教学经验，通过与跨境电子商务公司和平台的相关人员的直接合作，并参考在欧洲做访问学者期间所获得的相关资料，经多年努力编写了此书。进行修订的另一个原因是，在本书第 1、2、3、4、5 版的使用过程中，广大读者、专家给出版社和笔者反馈了许多建议和意见。为了更好地紧跟形势发展，笔者对本书进行了修订，主要修订内容如下：

（1）在第一章中专门进行了数字贸易的专题介绍，以便读者了解数字贸易在世界贸易中的主要地位及其定义和具体范围（中英双语）。

（2）适当增加数字贸易特别是跨境电子商务各项业务所带来的贸易实务中的变化和更新部分的业务，以及对应的英文新的说法，如数字贸易交付与数字订购等新术语；添加数字化产品和跨境电商平台的一些新的英文表达。

（3）对书中有关的商品品质、合同、物流运输、支付方式等环节对应数字贸易的环节进行最新相关内容补充（中英双语）。

（4）练习题案例学习（case study）部分删除了一些旧的案例，更新为新的案例，特别结合了数字贸易平台、数字产品的案例，突出本书的时效性。

（5）作者结合这几年来从事教学和科研中积累的一些心得体会，对部分练习进行了修订，修订后的练习题更趋向于用英语学习国际贸易实务专业知识，更注重实务应用能力的培养。

修订后的教材主要体现以下特点：

（1）紧跟国际贸易实务发展变化的最新形势，特别是数字贸易和跨境电子商务发展的需求。

（2）补充完善前一版中不足的地方。

（3）更加注重应用性和操作性。

同时，本书也是"高等学校本科教学质量与教学改革工程"的成果之一。以本书为主要参考教材的国际贸易实务课程被评为国家级 2009 年度双语教学示范课程。

本书在修订过程中，参考了许多国内外出版社出版的相关著作和刊物，在此一并向这些著述的作者表示感谢。

由于作者水平有限，尽管倾心编写，也难免存在缺点和不足之处，恳请专家和读者不吝指正，以便再次修订时臻于完善。

编　者

2025 年 3 月

Contents

目　　录

Chapter One

Part A Text

A Brief Introduction to International Trade

Trading is one of the most basic activities of mankind. It exists in every society, every part of the world, and in fact every day since the caveman came into being. International trade is a business which involves the crossing of national borders. It not only includes international trade and foreign manufacturing, but also encompasses the growing services industry in areas such as transportation, tourism, banking, advertising, construction, retailing, wholesaling and mass communications. It includes all business transactions that involve two or more countries. Such business relationship may be private or governmental. In the case of private firms the transactions are for profit. Government-sponsored activities in international business may or may not have a profit orientation.

In order to pursue any of these objectives, a company must establish international operational forms, some of which may be quite different from those used domestically. The choice of forms is influenced not only by the objectives being pursued, but also by the environment in which the forms must operate. These environmental conditions also affect the means of carrying out business functions such as marketing. At the same time, the company operating internationally will, to a lesser degree, affect the environment in which it is operating.

贸易是人类最为基本的活动之一。它存在于每个社会，并遍及世界各地，事实上，从洞穴人开始就已经有了贸易交往活动。国际贸易就是人们跨越国界进行的商务活动。广义地说，它不仅包括国际贸易及国外生产，还包括新兴的服务行业，如交通运输业、旅游业、银行业、广告业、建筑业、零售业、批发业以及大众传播业等。它包括的商务活动涉及两个或两个以上的国家。这种商务活动，可能涉及私人间的关系，也可能涉及国家间的关系。私人企业为盈利从事国际商务活动，而带有国家色彩的国际贸易也可能不仅仅以盈利为目的。

不论是否盈利，企业必须建立起自己的国际贸易形式，其中有些形式与国内贸易形式完全不同。选择哪种形式不仅取决于企业所追求的目标，同时也受企业面临的环境制约。这些环境因素也影响着贸易活动的功能，如销售功能。同时，公司的活动也影响着国际贸易环境，只是这种影响不及环境对贸易影响那样深刻。

In the new era, a new round of scientific and technological revolution and industrial transformation based on the "Internet" and big data are advancing by leaps and bounds; at the same time, the global digital economy is booming, which has led to the birth of digital trade with "data" as the key factor of production. Furthermore, digital trade also takes digital services as its core factor, which is mainly characterized by digital ordering and digital delivery. Digitalization has formed the biggest difference between digital trade and traditional international trade. Digital trade is, as a matter of fact, a new trend in the development of international trade.

进入新时代，基于互联网和大数据的新一轮科技革命和产业变革突飞猛进，全球数字经济蓬勃发展，从而催生了以"数据"作为关键生产要素的数字贸易，同时，数字贸易以数字服务为核心，其主要特征体现为数字订购与数字交付，数字化形成了数字贸易与传统国际贸易的一个最大的不同，数字贸易也是国际贸易发展的一个新趋势。

The report of the 20th National Congress of the Communist Party of China proposed to accelerate the construction of a strong trading nation. Digital trade is a key component of the globalized digital economy. As a new form of trade, digital trade has become the latest trend in international trade development; it is also a brand-new growth point in the global economy. This has elevated the importance and significance of digital trade to new heights. China has the largest number of Internet users in the world, and the corresponding data resources are considerably rich. At the same time, the new model of "Internet + trade" has also created a wealth of digital application scenarios for international trade, while providing a solid foundation for the global development of digital trade.

党的二十大报告提出，要加快建设贸易强国。数字贸易是全球化数字经济的一个重要的组成部分，作为一种新的贸易业态，数字贸易已成为国际贸易发展的一个最新趋势，也是全球经济的一个新的增长点。这使得数字贸易的重要性提升到了新高度。中国拥有世界上最大规模的网民数量，相应的数据资源十分丰富，同时，"互联网+贸易"这一新的模式还创造了丰富的国际贸易数字化应用场景，同时为全球发展数字贸易提供了扎实的基础。

The Decision of the Third Plenary Session of the 20th Central Committee of the Communist Party of China stressed that opening up is a distinctive symbol of the Chinese path to modernization. China will continue to accelerate the development of digital trade in the new era. Therefore, it is necessary to learn about the latest developments in digital trade while studying international trade practices.

党的二十届三中全会《决定》强调，开放是中国式现代化的鲜明标识。我国将继续在新时代加快发展数字贸易。因此，有必要在学习国际贸易实务的同时，了解最新的数字贸易新进展。

So, what is digital trade? What is its definition and specific scope? At present, there is no complete consensus internationally on the specific definition of "digital trade". There is still a certain degree of disagreement amongst international organizations and major world economies regarding the definition and specific classification of "digital trade". According to the definitions and corresponding classifications of "digital delivery trade" and "digital ordering trade" jointly adopted by the Organization for Economic Cooperation and Development (OECD), the World Trade Organization (WTO), together with the International Monetary Fund (IMF), "Digital trade" mainly refers to service trade with digitalization-based delivery. In this regard, it can be clearly seen that digital trade belongs to a branch of service trade. On this basis, according to the dimension of "subject matter" in trading, "digital trade" can be further subdivided into four categories, namely: digital product trade, digital service trade, digital technology trade, and data trade. On the other hand, "digital ordering trade" is defined as a commodity trade based on digital ordering, and cross-border e-commerce is its main typical representative.

什么是数字贸易？它的定义和具体范围是什么呢？目前，国际上还未对"数字贸易"的具体定义达成完全一致的共识。国际组织和主要世界经济体对于"数字贸易"的定义及其具体的分类仍然存在一定程度的分歧。按照经济合作与发展组织（OECD）、世界贸易组织（WTO）、国际货币基金组织（IMF）所共同采取的有关"数字交付贸易"与"数字订购贸易"的概念界定和相应分类，"数字贸易"主要是指数字化交付的服务贸易。可见，数字贸易属于服务贸易的一个分支。在此基础上，按照"交易标的"的划分维度，"数字贸易"进一步细分为四个大类，即数字产品贸易、数字服务贸易、数字技术贸易以及数据贸易等。另一方面，"数字订购贸易"则被界定为一种基于数字化订购的商品贸易，跨境电商就是其典型代表。

Section One Reasons for International Trade（国际贸易的动机）

International trade, also known as foreign trade or overseas trade, is in essence the fair and deliberate exchange of commodities and services across national boundaries. It includes import and export operations. It arises for many reasons.

国际贸易又称对外贸易、世界贸易或海外贸易，从本质上说，即在平等的基础上，有意识地进行跨国界的商品和服务交换行为。它包括进口业务和出口业务两部分内容。国际贸易的兴起有多种原因。

1. Resource acquisition（寻求资源）

Manufacturers and distributors seek out products and services as well as components and finished goods produced in foreign countries. The different distributions of the world's resources determine the patterns of world trade. Some countries or regions are abundant in natural resources; elsewhere, reserves are scarce or nonexistent. For example, the United States is a major consumer of coffee, yet it does not have the climate to grow its own. So it has to import coffee from other countries that are rich in coffee, like Brazil, Colombia and so on. Britain possesses large reserves of coal but lacks many metals such as copper and aluminum. The world's raw materials are unevenly distributed, and both modern manufacturing and agriculture require many different resources. Thus, to obtain these through trading is an absolute necessity.

Climate and soil affect the cultivation of some agricultural products, which a nation can produce and trade internationally. Some South American countries, for instance, enjoy a favorable climate for growing coffee. However, the United States almost does not grow coffee, and has to import it. On the other hand, the climate and soil of some states of America are ideal for raising wheat. The wheat grown in the United States is so abundant that it is often exported to other countries.

制造商和经销商追求生产产品和服务，同时也在国外市场寻求配件和制成品，有时候这样做可以减少成本。资源在世界各地的不同分布状况决定着世界贸易的格局。有些国家或地区富有资源，而其他地方则相反，缺乏甚至没有资源。例如，美国是一个咖啡消费国，但由于气候的关系，它不能大量生产咖啡，因此，不得不从其他生产咖啡的国家，如巴西、哥伦比亚等地进口咖啡。英国拥有大量的煤炭资源，却严重缺乏像铜、铝之类的矿产资源。世界各地的原材料分布不均，而现代制造业和农业却都需要各种不同的资源。因此，通过贸易来获取这些资源是十分必要的。

气候和土壤影响着农产品的种植，这些农产品可以被该国用来生产和进行国际贸易。例如，一方面，一些南美国家的气候非常适宜咖啡的生长，而美国几乎不产咖啡，必须进口；另一方面，美国有些州的气候和土壤很适合小麦的生长，因此，美国的小麦产量非常高，经常出口到其他国家。

2．Benefits acquisition（追求利润）

With the development of manufacturing and technology, there has been another reason, namely, economic benefit, for nations to trade. It is found that a country benefits more by producing goods it can make most cheaply and buying those goods that other countries can make at lower costs than by producing everything it needs within its own border. This is often explained by the theory of comparative advantage, also called the comparative cost theory, which was developed by David Ricardo, John Stuart Mill, and other economists in the 19th century. The theory emphasizes that different countries or regions have different production possibilities. Trade between countries can be profitable for both, even if one of the countries can produce every commodity more cheaply. As long as there are minor, relative differences in the efficiency of producing a commodity, even a poor country can have a comparative advantage in producing it.

Comparative advantage has directed countries to specialize in particular products and to mass-produce. For example, the United States is relatively more efficient than Europe in producing food (using one third of the labor) and clothing (using half of the labor). Thus, while the United States has an absolute advantage in both forms of production, its efficiency in food production is greater. Consequently, a great deal of clothing is imported from Europe to the United States.

随着制造业和技术的发展，产生了另一个促进国家间进行贸易的原因，即经济效益。研究表明，相较于在本国境内生产所有所需商品，一个国家通过专注于生产其最具成本优势的商品，并进口其他国家能以更低成本生产的商品，将获得更大的经济利益。对于这一点，人们常用比较优势理论来解释。比较优势理论也称比较成本理论，是由大卫·李嘉图、约翰·斯图尔特·米尔和 19 世纪的其他一些经济学家发展而来的。比较优势理论强调不同国家和地区具有不同的生产可能性。国家之间的贸易对双方都有利，即使其中一方可用较低的成本生产所有的商品。只要两国在生产一种商品的效率上存在着微弱的相对差异，即便是穷国也可能具有生产这一商品的比较优势。

比较优势引导各国专门和批量生产某些特定产品。例如，美国生产食品的效率远高于欧洲。美国生产食品所需劳动力仅占欧洲所需劳动力的 1/3，制作服装所需劳动力只占欧洲所需劳动力的 1/2。可见，在食品业和服装业方面，美国都有绝对优势，但是生产食品的效率比制作服装的效率更高，所以，美国有大量服装从欧洲进口。

3．Diversification（多种经营）

Companies usually prefer to avoid wild swings in their sales and profits, so they seek out foreign markets as means to this end. Some film companies have to smooth their year-long sales somewhat because the summer vacation period (the main season for children's film attendance) varies between the northern and southern hemispheres. These companies have also been able to make large television contracts during different years for different countries. Many other firms take advantage of the fact that the timing of business cycles differ among countries. Thus while sales decrease in one country that is experiencing recession, they increase in another that is undergoing recovery. Finally, by depending on supplies of the same product or component from different countries, a company may be able to avoid the full impact of price swings or shortages in any country that might be brought about, for example, by a strike.

为尽量避免销售量和利润的剧烈波动,公司通常会寻找海外市场作为防止这种情况出现的措施。由于南北半球学校放暑假的时间不同（此时为放映儿童电影的主要时间）,电影制片公司将对其年度销售计划做精心策划。这些制片公司还在不同年份与不同的国家签订了拍摄电视的合同。其他许多公司则利用各国不同的经济周期,对其生产与销售进行调整。这样,当一国经济萧条而引起销售量减少时,在另一国则可因经济复苏而使销售量增加。最后,依靠来自不同国家的同一产品或配件,公司就可避免由于一国价格波动或资源短缺带来的损失,如由于罢工而引起的上述情况。

4. Sales expansion（扩大销售）

Sales are limited by the number of people interested in a firm's products and services and by customers' purchasing power. Since the global population and aggregate purchasing power exceed those of any single country, firms may increase their sales potentials by defining markets in international terms. Ordinarily, higher sales mean higher profits.

产品的销售量受制于潜在购买者的数量以及消费者的购买力。既然消费者人数及其购买力在世界范围内比在一国内大得多,企业就可以在全球范围内划分销售市场,以增加其销售量。通常,销售量越大则利润越高。

There are still several other reasons for international trade. Some nations are unable to produce enough products of a certain item. Thus, they must import these goods to meet domestic demand. Moreover, the preference for innovation or style also leads to international trade, which makes available a greater variety of products and offers a wider range of consumer choice of a certain product. Finally, some nations of the world trade with others mainly for political reasons. In that case, more considerations are given to political objectives rather than economic motivation.

还有其他一些进行国际贸易的原因。有些国家无法大量生产出某种产品,所以,必须从其他国家进口这类商品,以满足国内的大量需求。此外,国际贸易的发生有时也出自对产品创新和款式的追求,因为国际贸易能够提供花色品种更多的产品,并且能扩大消费者对某一产品的选择范围。最后,还有些国家进行贸易主要是出于政治原因。在这种情况下,政治目的的重要性超过了经济因素。

5. International balance of payments（国际收支平衡）

A nation's balance-of-payment account is the statistical record of all economic transactions taking place between its residents and the rest of the world. A balance of payments (BOP) sheet is an accounting record of all monetary transactions between a country and the rest of the world. It is not concerned with movement of money inside the country. It relates to the difference between the amount of money that has come into the country and the amount of money that has gone out of it. Trade in goods is known as visible imports and exports while in services, invisible. If imports and exports are not balanced, it is the job of the government to correct a deficit or adjust the trade policies. Sooner or later, all nations are compelled to remedy deficits in their balance of payments, whether through market adjustment or controls. When a nation's reserves are low and its balance of payments is weak, the objective of payments equilibrium may come to dominate other objectives of its foreign economic policy and even of its domestic policy. In the decade following World War II, the elimination of the dollar shortage occupied first place among the foreign economic policy objectives of Western European countries. In the 1960s and 1980s, the US balance of payments problem overshadowed other foreign economic issues.

一个国家的收支平衡账户表用于统计记录本地居民和世界其他地区发生的所有经济交易。国际收支平衡（BOP）表是一个国家与世界上其他地方所达成的所有货币交易的会计记录，它与国内货币流通无关。国际收支是一个国家外汇收入和支出的差额。商品进出口是有形贸易，而劳务进出口则是无形贸易。如果进出口不平衡，该国政府的工作就应该采取措施平衡逆差或调整外贸政策。所有国家迟早都必须通过市场调控弥补国际收支平衡表上的赤字。当一个国家的储备金少，收支平衡能力弱时，其对外的经济政策，甚至国内政策的主要目标就是收支平衡。第二次世界大战结束后的十年中，消除美元短缺成为西欧国家对外经济政策的首要目标。20世纪 60 年代及以后的 80 年代，美国收支平衡问题超过了其他对外经济问题。

Section Two　Problems Concerning International Trade（有关国际贸易的问题）

When engaging in international trade (exporting and importing), businesspeople face conditions that differ significantly from those they are accustomed to in domestic trade. The fact that the transactions are across national borders highlights the differences between domestic and international trade. Generally, there are certain differences which justify the separate treatment of international trade and domestic trade. In particular, these differences include cultural differences, monetary conversion, and trade barriers. Foreign traders must be aware of these differences because they often bring about trade conflicts in international trade.

在从事国际贸易（进口和出口）时，一个商人所面临的各种情况与他所熟知的国内贸易不太一样。实际上国内贸易和国际贸易的最大区别就是商品交易跨越了国界。一般来说，有几个差异要求我们必须对国内贸易和国际贸易分别对待。这些差异主要包括文化差异、货币兑换和贸易壁垒。从事国际贸易的商人必须了解这些差异，因为它们经常引起贸易摩擦。

1．Cultural differences（文化差异问题）

There are as many cultures as there are peoples on earth. When companies do business overseas, they come into contact with people from different cultures. They often speak different languages and have their own particular customs and manners. The people of all cultures are ethnocentric. This means that they judge the world from their own ways of looking at things. Therefore, in international trade, business people should be on alert against different local customs and business norms.

地球上的文化和民族一样数量众多。当公司在海外开拓业务时，它们必须同具有不同文化背景的人打交道。这些人说着不同的语言，有他们独特的风俗习惯和行为规范。具有各种文化背景的人都有种族中心倾向，也就是说，他们用自己看待事物的方式来判断世界。因此，在国际贸易中，商人应密切注意不同地方的风俗和商业准则。

2. Monetary conversion（货币兑换问题）

Monetary conversion is another major problem in international trade. If every country in the world used the same currency, the world trade would be much easier. But this is not the case: a Canadian beer producer wants to be paid in euros. Currencies, like other commodities such as beer, have a certain value. The only difference is that each currency's value is stated in terms of other currencies. Euro dollars have value in US dollars, which have a value in British pounds, or a value in Japanese yen. These exchange rates change every day and are constantly updated in banks and foreign exchange offices around the world.

Importing and exporting firms to whom the payment is made in foreign currency can be involved in significant foreign exchange risks because of the fluctuation in exchange rates. An importer, for example, does not receive a shipment immediately after ordering it, and is often given a short period of commercial credit. Suppose a Canadian importer must pay a certain amount of Canadian dollars in 60 days to a German exporter for the import of some equipment. This transaction leaves the Canadian firm open to substantial exchange rate risk because during those 60 days, the Canadian dollar may depreciate relative to the euro, forcing the Canadian firm to spend a large amount of Canadian dollars to satisfy its import commitment.

国际贸易中另外一个主要的问题就是货币兑换。如果世界上的每个国家都使用同样的货币，世界贸易将会变得容易得多。但事实并不如此，一个加拿大啤酒商人要求用欧元来支付货款。货币，如同啤酒或其他商品一样，具有一定的价值。唯一的区别是每种货币的价值是用另外的货币的价值表现出来的。欧元可以美元计价，美元也可以英镑、日元计价。汇率每天都在变化，全世界的银行和外汇交易所也在不断地更新汇率。

由于汇率波动，接受外币支付的进出口公司要面临很大的外汇风险。例如，一个进口商订购以后，不能马上收到货物，通常他会得到一段时间的商业信用。假设一个加拿大进口商 60 天内将付一定数目的加拿大元给一个德国出口商以进口一些设备。这个交易会使加拿大公司面临汇率风险，因为在这 60 天中，加拿大元对欧元可能会贬值，迫使这家加拿大公司支付大笔加拿大元来履行其进口承诺。

3. Trade barriers（贸易壁垒）

The third problem is trade barriers. It is generally assumed, as the famous economist David Ricardo stated in the 19th century, that the free flow of international trade benefits all who participate in. In actual practice, however, the world has never had a completely free trading system. This occurs because sovereign states impose trade barriers for three primary reasons:

1) To correct a balance-of-payment deficit

Such a deficit occurs when the total payments leaving a country are greater than money in receipt entering from abroad. The country then tries to limit imports and increase exports.

2) In view of national security

Nations sometimes restrict exports of critical raw materials, high technology, or equipment when such exports might harm its own security.

3) To protect their own industries against the competition of foreign goods

This is generally on the grounds that infant industries need to be shielded from foreign competition during their start-up periods. A country usually offers protection to its domestic industries by taxing imports of similar foreign goods. The tax may be levied as a percentage of the value of the imports, which is called an ad valorem tariff. When a tariff is added to the price of a foreign product, it raises the price of the item to the consumer.

Although tariffs have been lowered substantially by international agreements, countries continue to use other devices to limit imports or to increase exports.

第三个问题是贸易壁垒。正如著名经济学家大卫•李嘉图在 19 世纪所言，自由流动的国际贸易可以使贸易双方都获益。然而，在现实世界中，世界从来就没有真正意义上的自由贸易。这是因为每一个国家都会因为下列原因而设置贸易管制。

1）改善国际收支逆差

当一个国家的全部支出款项超过从国外收进的款项时，就会出现逆差。这时，该国就要限制进口，增加出口。

2）考虑国家安全

一些国家有时会限制出口关键原材料、高科技或设备，因为这种出口会影响其自身的安全。

3）保护本国产业免受国外商品竞争的影响

这一般是因为新兴产业在起步阶段需要保护，避免来自国外的竞争。一个国家经常对进口的类似产品征税来保护国内产业。税费可以按照进口商品价值的一定的百分比来征收，这称为从价关税。当关税计入进口商品的价格中时，消费者购买该商品的价格就会上涨。

虽然通过国际协定，关税已经大幅度下降，但各个国家仍继续使用其他策略来限制进口或增加出口。

There still exist other problems, but the above three are the most common problems in international trade.

在国际贸易中可能还存在着其他问题，但上述三种是最普遍的问题。

Section Three　Forms of International Trade（国际贸易的形式）

Since there are tremendous differences between international trade and domestic trade, companies face unique challenges when entering foreign markets. Although the same marketing concepts and strategies are utilized, cultural, political and economic differences make the task of entering an overseas market riskier. Thus, most companies proceed cautiously once they have decided to engage in international trade. They usually conduct research to have specific knowledge of foreign countries' economic, political, cultural, and social background as well as tariffs, quotas and foreign currencies, etc. Such researches will help the company choose the best form for dealing in international trade.

Companies must choose among different operational forms. In making their choices, the companies' own objectives and resources as well as the environment in which the firms operate should be considered. The following discussion introduces the major operating forms, which also correspond closely to the categories in which countries keep records of aggregate international transactions.

由于国际贸易和国内贸易存在着巨大的差异，当一家公司准备打入国外市场时，它必须面对一些特殊的困难。虽然它采用相同的营销理念和策略，但文化、政治和经济上的差异使其进入海外市场风险更大。所以，大多数公司一旦决定进入国际市场，就不得不谨小慎微，小心行事。他们通常通过调查来具体了解外国的经济、政治、文化和社会背景以及关税、配额和外币等方面的情况。这些研究将有助于公司选择从事国际贸易的最好方式。

公司在从事国际贸易时，必须选择适合自己的贸易形式。在选择形式时，公司必须考虑经营环境，也要考虑自身的目标及拥有的资源。在以下的探讨中，我们将介绍国际贸易的主要形式，这几种形式也符合各国总计的国际交易种类。

1. Merchandise exports and imports（商品进出口）

Merchandise exports are goods sent out of a country, whereas merchandise imports are goods brought in. Since these are tangible goods that visibly leave and enter countries, they are sometimes referred to as visible exports and imports. The terms exports and imports are used frequently, yet, in reality, the reference is only to the merchandise exports and imports.

商品出口指货物输往国外，而商品进口则指货物输入国内。因为这些有形物品的输出输入都是看得见摸得着的，所以商品进出口有时又可称作有形进出口。虽然人们经常使用出口与进口这两个词，实际上，进出口指的只是商品的进出口。

1) Exporting（商品出口）

Merchandise exports are goods sent out of a country. Exporting is an extension of trading with customers living in another country. This extension of the trade's domain is highly important, since it enables the vendee to make a choice between alternative goods in satisfying his needs. The need to acquire natural resources and capital equipment is vital to the well-being of all nations. Exporting is likely to be the simplest way to enter the international market. There are two types of exporting: direct exporting and indirect exporting.

商品出口指货物输往国外。出口是将贸易向外延伸到另一个国家客户的一种贸易形式，由于这种贸易外延可以满足买主对货物选择的需求而显得非常重要。对自然资源和资本设备的需求对一个国家的发展极为重要。出口或许是进入国际市场最简单的方法。出口分为两种：直接出口和间接出口。

(1) Direct exporting（直接出口）

Direct exporting involves establishing an export department or even an overseas sales branch. It provides a continuous presence and easier control for the exporter in the buyer's country but obviously means more expenses.

直接出口涉及建立出口部门甚至是国外销售分支机构。它能使出口商与买方国家长期接触，并易于控制，但显然也意味着需要支出较多的费用。

(2) Indirect exporting（间接出口）

A company can also sell its products abroad indirectly through middlemen, commonly called export agents. Export agents seldom produce goods themselves. Their purpose is to bring together buyers and sellers and help them handle international transactions. They make their money from commission of the sale price. Many agents specialize in specific kinds of products. The principal advantage of using an export agent is that the company does not deal with foreign currencies or the red-tape of international marketing. The major disadvantage is that because the export agent must make a profit, the price of the product must be increased or the domestic company must provide a larger discount than it would in a domestic transaction. Indirect exporting involves less investment and is therefore less risky, which enables small firms with limited capital and product diversification can export very easily.

公司还可以将其产品通过通常称之为出口代理商的中间商间接销往海外市场。出口代理商很少自己生产产品，它们的目的是把买卖双方联系到一起，并帮助它们处理国际贸易事务。它们通过收取佣金来赚钱。很多代理商只经营一些特定的产品。通过出口代理商的最大优点就是公司不必与外币打交道，避免国际营销的烦琐程序。这样做最大的弊端是由于出口代理商要盈利，产品的价格就要上涨，或者国内公司就要比在从事国内贸易时付出更大的折扣。间接出口投资少，因而危险性较小，它使那些资金有限、产品品种不多的小公司能很容易地出口。

2) Importing（商品进口）

Merchandise imports are goods brought in. One nation's imports are another nation's exports. Importing, opposite to exporting, is the process of purchasing goods and services from other nations. Like exporting, importing can be either indirect or direct. Indirect importing is the purchase of foreign goods through domestic middlemen, while direct importing is the direct purchase of goods from overseas market. Indirect importing is convenient but limited in selection of goods and less profit. Direct importing is economical but more complicated than buying from importing middlemen.

商品进口是指货物输入国内。一个国家的进口就是另外一个国家的出口。与出口相反，进口是从其他国家购买产品和服务的过程。和出口一样，进口可以是直接的，也可以是间接的。间接进口是通过国内的中间商购买国外产品，而直接进口则是直接从国外市场购买货物。通过间接进口比较便利，但商品的选择面较窄且利润较低。直接进口很经济，但比从进口中间商那里购买复杂。

2. Service exports and imports（服务进出口）

Service exports and imports refer to international earnings other than those from goods sent to another country. Receipt of these earnings is considered as a service export, whereas payment is considered as a service import. Services are also referred to as invisibletrade. International business comprises many different types of services.

服务进出口是指除去商品进出口以外的那部分国际收支。获得收入可看作服务出口，支出则可当作服务进口。服务这种商品，也被看作无形商品。国际贸易包括许多不同种类的服务。

1) Tourism and transportation（旅游业、交通运输业）

Earnings from transportation and from foreign travel can be an important source of revenue for international airlines, shipping companies, reservations agencies, and hotels. On a national level, such countries as Greece and Norway depend heavily on revenue collected from carrying foreign cargo on their ships. The Bahamas earns much more from foreign tourists than it earns from exporting merchandise.

交通运输业和旅游业是国际航空公司、航运公司、预约服务机构和旅馆收益的主要来源。就国家而言，像希腊和挪威这样的国家，收入的大部分要依赖航运业，巴哈马群岛的收入则更多来自海外游客，而不是商品出口。

2) Performance of activities abroad（国外商务活动）

Fees are payments for the performance of certain activities abroad, such as banking, insurance, rentals, engineering and management. Engineering services are often handled through turnkey projects, contracts for the construction of operating facilities that are transferred to the owner when the facilities are ready to begin operations. Fees for management services are often the result of management contracts, arrangements through which one firm provides management personnel to perform general or specialized management functions for another firm.

企业要为其在国外进行的某些活动支付服务费用，这些服务包括银行、保险、租赁、工程和管理等。工程服务常常是以交钥匙工程承包方式进行的，承建生产设施的合同规定工程完成时，将全部设施交付转让给物主。服务管理费用的支付以管理合同为依据，根据这一合同，其中某公司为对方公司提供管理人员进行一般管理或专门管理。

3) Use of assets from abroad（国外资产的运用）

Royalties are the payment for using assets from abroad, such as for trademarks, patents, copyrights, or other expertise under contracts known as licensing agreements. Royalties are also paid for franchising, a way of doing business in which one party (the franchisor) sells an independent party (the franchisee) the use of a trademark that is an essential asset for the franchisee's business. In addition, the franchisor assists on a continuing basis in the operation of the business, such as by providing components, managerial services, or technology.

Firms often move to foreign licensing or franchising after successfully building exports to a market. This move usually involves a greater international commitment than in the early stages of exporting. The greater involvement occurs because the firm commonly has to send technicians to the foreign country to assist the licensee or franchisee in establishing and adapting its production facilities for the new product.

特许使用费是使用国外资产所支付的费用，如商标、专利、版权或其他类似许可证协定那样的合同项目下的专业技术。特许使用费也可以用于特许经营。在这种经营方式中，一方当事人（特许人）将其商标的使用权出售给另一方独立的当事人（被特许人），该使用权即成为被特许人的基本资产。此外，特许人还要给予被特许人业务上的帮助，如提供零配件，提供管理服务或技术，等等。

企业在成功地建立起出口市场之后，往往倾向于采用国外许可证交易或特许经营。这种转移往往比早期单纯出口要承担更多的国际义务。这是因为企业通常需要向国外派遣技术人员以帮助被许可人或特许经营人建立和选择新产品的生产设施。

3. Licensing（许可证贸易）

Licensing refers to the business agreement in which the manufacturer (the licensor) of a product (or a firm with proprietary rights over certain technology trademarks, etc.) grants permission to some other group or individuals to manufacture that product (or make use of that proprietary material, trademark, manufacturing process, patent, etc.) in return for specified royalties or other payment for the firm granting the license.

Licensing is a simple way for a manufacturer to become involved in a market abroad. It can gain entry to a market at little risk. Under licensing, a producer (licensor) in one country enters into an agreement with a manufacturer(licensee) in another country offering the right to use the company's name, products, patents, brands and trademarks, as well as its raw material and manufacturing processes. In return, the licensee agrees to pay the licensor a flat fee or a royalty. Such fee, known as royalties, may consist of a lump sum royalty, a running royalty (royalty based on volume of production), or a combination of both. Companies frequently license their patents, trademarks, copyrights, and know-how to a foreign company that then manufacturers and sells products on the technology in a country or group of countries authorized by the licensing agreement. License agreements may be either exclusive or non-exclusive. An exclusive license forbids the licensor to sell the license to any other firm in some specific geographic areas. The main disadvantages of licensing are that the company may lose control of the manufacturer's products and right to sell them itself. Moreover, a new competitor may be created after the agreement expires.

许可证贸易指的是一种商业协定，产品（拥有某种技术商标的专利所有权企业）的生产商（许可人），允许其他组织或个人生产自己的产品（使用自己的材料、商标、生产工艺、专利等），并支付给自己指定的专利费或其他费用。

许可证贸易是制造商于海外销售的一种简单方法。它能以较小的风险进入市场。在许可证贸易中，一国的制造商（许可方）与另一国的制造商（被许可方）签订合同，授权它使用该公司的名称、产品、专利、品牌和商标以及原材料和生产工艺。作为交换，被许可方同意付给许可方一笔统一费用或特许权使用费。这种费用又称作特许使用权费，包括一次付清的总费用、浮动费用（基于生产数量的特许使用权费），或者两者结合而成。根据许可证贸易协定，企业通常将自己的专利、商标、版权、专有技术等使用权授予国外企业，允许其在当地或其他国家制造和销售基于这些技术的产品或服务。许可证可以是独占的形式，也可以是非独占的形式。独占许可证禁止许可方将许可证卖给特定地区内的其他公司。许可证贸易的主要弊端是公司可能会失去对其产品生产的控制和销售权。并且，在合同结束以后，还可能产生新的竞争者。

When we consider adopting the licensing agreement, it is very important to remember that foreign licensee may attempt to use the licensed technology to manufacture products that are marketed in the exporters' market or the third country in direct competition with the licensor or its other licensee. In many instances, licensors may wish to impose territorial restrictions on their foreign licensees, depending on antitrust laws and the licensing laws of the host country. Also, patent and trademarks laws can often be used to bar unauthorized sales by foreign licensee, provided that the licensor has valid patent, trademark, or copyright protection.

The prospective licensor must always take into account the host country's foreign patent, trademark, and copyright laws; exchange controls; product liability laws; possible countertrade or barter requirements; antitrust and tax laws; and attitudes toward repatriation of royalty and dividends. The existence of a tax treaty or bilateral investment treaties (BITs) between the licensors' country and the prospective host country is an important indicator of the overall commercial relationship. Because of the potential complexity of international technology licensing agreements, enterprises should seek professional legal advice before entering into such an agreement. In many instances licensors should also retain qualified legal counsel in the host country in order to obtain advice on applicable local laws and to receive assistance in securing the foreign government's approval of the agreement. Sound legal advice and thorough investigation of the prospective licensee and the host country increase the likelihood that the licensing agreement will be a profitable transaction and help decrease or avoid potential problems.

在采用许可证贸易时，需要记住的是，国外被许可人可能试图使用转让的技术生产产品并在出口商的市场或第三方国家销售，与许可人和其他被许可人直接竞争。在很多情况下，许可人希望对国外的被许可人设定地域限制，如东道国的反垄断法或者许可证合同法。同时，专利法、商标法、版权法也经常用于限制国外被许可人未经授权的销售，条件是许可人具有有效的专利、商标和受保护的版权。

有意向的许可人必须考虑到东道国的对外专利、商标以及版权法；外汇管制；产品责任法；可能存在抵偿贸易和易货贸易条件；反托拉斯法和税法；以及对于特许使用费和利息回笼的态度。许可人所在国家和有意向的被许可人的东道国之间签订的税收条约或双边投资条约是整体商业关系中重要的指南。由于许可证贸易协议潜在的复杂性，企业在签订协议前，应该寻求专业的法律咨询。大多数情况下，许可人应该在东道国聘请有资质的法律顾问，通过他们了解当地的法律，在获取国外政府对于合同的批准方面提供帮助。可靠的法律建议以及对未来被许可人和东道国的全面考虑提高了许可证贸易协议帮助企业获利并能够减少或者避免潜在问题的可能性。

4. Trading companies（贸易公司）

Trading companies are large international wholesalers, frequently larger and more powerful than the manufacturers they represent. They serve as a link between buyers and sellers in different countries to facilitate trade. They purchase goods at the best price they can obtain in one country and sell them to buyers in another. They handle all the details required to move goods from one country to another. They offer consulting, market research, advertising, insurance, product research and design, warehousing, and foreign exchange services to interested companies.

贸易公司是大型的国际批发商，其规模与实力通常比它们所代表的制造商强得多。作为分处不同国家的买卖双方的桥梁，贸易公司可以使贸易的操作便利。它们在一国以最优惠的价格购买商品，然后卖给另一国的购买者。它们处理将货物从一国运送到另一国所需的一切细节。它们为感兴趣的公司提供咨询、市场调查、广告、保险、产品研究和设计、仓储以及外汇服务。

5. Joint ventures（合资企业）

Joint venture is a form of business relations which involves pooling of assets, joint management and a sharing of profits and risks according to a commonly-agreed formula. Legally, the joint venture is a form of partnership, a pattern of business organization which can be adopted by every type of industrial cooperation; in other words, joint marketing, servicing, production, etc., separately or in combination, may be legally organized as a joint venture. It may be of either an equity or a non-equity type. If the former, a separate body is established whereby local interests purchase a share in the equity capital. If the latter, no additional body is set up; association is based entirely on a contract. Both equity and non-equity joint ventures are subject to risks and profits and risk sharing, as their common denominator. Joint ventures are more stable than exporting, importing, or licensing. Moreover, they are less expensive than wholly owned operations. However, joint ventures also encounter some problems such as control issues which arise because joint ventures require coordination across national boundaries, and problems concerning percentage of ownership, amount of investment, how much of the product will be exported, and how to equitably distribute profits.

合资企业是根据合资各方同意的规章而建立的一种商业关系，它涉及资产的统筹，共同经营管理，分享利润和分担风险。从法律上讲，合资企业是一种合伙关系，一种可以被各种产业合作所采取的商业组织形式；换句话说，就是以独立和联合的形式，把共同销售、服务、生产等方面按法律程序组织成一个合资企业。合资企业可以是股权式合营企业，也可以是非股权式合营企业。如果是前者，将建立一个独立的合资实体，当地合资者购买合资资本的部分股权。如果是后者，就不再建立另外的合资实体，合资完全建立在合同的基础上。不论是股权式合营企业，还是非股权式合营企业都要共同承担风险，分享利润。合资企业比出口贸易、进口贸易或许可证贸易更加稳定，比独资企业的费用低。然而，合资企业也面临一些问题，如控制问题，其原因是合资企业要求跨国合作，还有诸如所有权比例、投资数量以及出口量多少、如何公平分配利润等问题。

6. Investment（投资）

According to the definition of economics, investment refers to an economic activity, in which the value that is currently available is sacrificed or given up to obtain greater returns in the future. That is to say, investment is the act of allocating money into something with the expectation of profit. Investment can be divided into direct investment and indirect investment.

根据经济学的定义，投资是指牺牲或放弃现在可用于消费的价值以获取未来更大价值的一种经济活动。从金融和商业角度来看，投资是一项为盈利而进行的资产购买，这种购买可以通过收入、资本增值或其他组合来完成。也就是说，投资就是将钱投入某种活动以便获取利润。投资可以分为直接投资和间接投资。

1) Direct investment（直接投资）

Direct investment takes place when control follows the investment. This can amount to a small percentage of the equity of the company being acquired, perhaps even as little as 10% equity in foreign operations in the given country. Not only does it imply the ownership of an interest abroad, but also means the transfer of more personnel and technology abroad than when there is no controlling interest in the foreign facility. Because of the high level of commitment, direct investment usually (but not always) comes after a firm has experience in exporting or importing. Direct investment operations may be set up in order to gain access to certain resources or markets for the firm's product. Kenner, for example, uses its Mexican direct investment to assemble the Chewbacca Bandolier Strap because this gives access to a resource, cheap labor, for the product's manufacture. Kenner also has direct investments in Europe, which have been established as a means of gaining markets in the countries where the production occurs.

When two or more organizations share the ownership of a direct investment, the operation is known as a joint venture. In a special type of joint venture, a public-private joint venture, where a government is in partnership with a private company.

只有对企业享有控制权时，才会产生直接投资。但这种投资只占企业所获得的资产净值的一小部分，最少仅占 10%。在对外经营中控制股权的所有权是在该国进行国际经营所承担的一种最高义务。它不仅意味着对国外资产的所有权，还意味着要将更多的人力与技术进行海外转移，而如果这些缺少对海外企业的控制权是很难做到的。由于直接投资承担的是最高义务，企业一般是在进出口积累一定经验后才采用这种方式。经营者进行直接投资往往是为了便于获取某些资源的使用权或进入其产品的市场。例如，肯纳公司在墨西哥进行直接投资，装配 Chewbacca 子弹带，是为了靠近原料产地以及有廉价的劳动力；肯纳公司在欧洲市场进行的直接投资则是因为靠近产品的销售市场。

当两个或两个以上的组织联合进行直接投资时，可称作合资企业。若政府与私人联合投资，则是合资企业的一种特殊形式——混合企业。

2) Portfolio investment（间接投资，又称证券投资）

Portfolio investment can be either debt or equity, but the factor that distinguishes portfolio from direct investment is that control does not follow this kind of investment. For US firms as a whole, sales from output produced abroad are many times greater than sales from US production that is sent abroad as merchandise exports. Today most of the world's largest firms have substantial foreign direct investment encompassing every type of product, component, output distribution, and　service management.

Foreign portfolio investment is also important for nearly all firms operating extensively internationally. These investments are used primarily for financial purposes. Treasurers of companies, for example, routinely move funds from one country to another to get a higher yield on short-term investments. They also borrow funds in different countries.

间接投资可以以负债或资产的方式进行，它与直接投资是有区别的，它不享有对企业的控制权。就美国企业的总体情况看，企业在国外所生产的产品销售量远远大于美国产品以商品出口形式输出的销售量。事实上，世界上大多数大型公司对国外的直接投资有各种形式，如开采原材料、种植作物、生产成品或部件、销售产品以及从事各种服务。

国外间接投资对广泛开展国际贸易的企业来说也很重要。它们主要被用于金融方面。例如，企业按常规将资金以短期投资的形式从一个国家转到另一个国家以获取较高收益。同样，它们也会从其他国家借入资金用于周转。

For most nations, exports and imports are the most important international activities. Each country has to import the articles and commodities it does not produce itself, and it has to earn foreign exchange to pay for them. It does this by exporting its own manufactured articles and surplus raw materials. Thus the import and export trades are two sides of the same coin, and both can have beneficial effects on the home market. Imports create competition for home-produced goods; exporting gives a manufacturer a larger market for their products, so helping to reduce the unit cost. In each case the effect is to keep prices in the home market down.

But there may be factors that compel governments to place restrictions on foreign trade. Imports may be controlled or subjected to a customs duty to protect a home industry, or because the available foreign exchange must be allocated into buying more essential goods and exports. Exports may also be restricted, to conserve a particular raw material required by a developing home industry.

These factors mean that importing and exporting are subject to numerous formalities, such as customs clearance and exchange control approval, from which the home retail and wholesale trades are free. They also mean that the procedures of foreign trade are much more complicated than those of domestic trade, which requires specialized knowledge and highly trained personnel.

对大多数的国家来说，进出口贸易是最重要的国际经济活动。每个国家都必须进口本国所不能生产的货物和商品，还得创收外汇来支付货物，这要靠出口本国的制成品和剩余原料。因此，进出口贸易是同一件事物的两个方面，两者对国内市场都能产生有利影响。进口货物使国内产品有了竞争，而出口则为厂商的产品提供了更广阔的市场，有助于降低单位成本。无论是进口还是出口，其作用都是控制国内市场的价格。

但是，可能出于某些因素，政府不得不对对外贸易加以限制。为了保护国内的某一产业，或者由于需要外汇用于购买更为重要的物资，政府可能要控制进口或以关税制约进口。同样，为了保留发展中的国内产业所需要的某一种特殊的原料，出口也会受到限制。

这些因素意味着进出口贸易受许多手续的制约，如报关和外汇审批等，而国内的零售及批发业务则不受此限制。这说明对外贸易的程序比国内贸易的程序复杂得多，后者需要专业的知识以及受过良好训练的人才。

7. Visible and invisible trade（有形贸易和无形贸易）

International trade transactions can relate to the importation and exportation of goods or services from one country to another. Visible trade involves the importing and exporting of tangible goods, whereas invisible trade involves the service exchange between countries. For instance, Brazilian coffee is often transported by ocean vessels because these ships are the cheapest method of transportation. Nations such as Greece and Norway have large maritime fleets and provide transportation services. When an exporter arranges for this kind of transportation, they rent space in the cargo compartment of a ship for one voyage.

The prudent exporter buys insurance for their cargo's voyage. While at sea, every shipment has to run the risk of a long list of dangers: fire, storm, collision, theft, leakage, explosion, etc. To prevent these risks, marine cargo insurance is provided to protect the exporter or importer from financial losses. Thus, insurance is another service in which some nations specialize. Britain, because of the development of Lloyd's of London, is a leading exporter of this service, earning fees for insuring other nations' foreign trade.

国际贸易包括货物贸易的进出口或服务贸易的进出口。有形贸易是指国与国之间进行货物贸易的进出口，而无形贸易是指各国服务贸易的交换。例如，巴西出口的咖啡经常用远洋货轮来运输，因为其费用最低。像希腊和挪威这样拥有大规模海运船队的国家就可以为其提供运输服务。当出口商要安排这种运输时，就需要租船订舱。

谨慎的出口商往往为其货物买保险，因为在海上航行时货物会遭遇各种各样的危险，如起火、风暴、碰撞、偷窃、渗漏、爆炸等。海洋货物保险可以预防这些风险，保护出口商或进口商免受经济损失。因此，保险就成为一些国家专门经营的服务业。由于伦敦劳埃德保险公司的发展壮大，英国也因此成为这项业务的主要出口商，它通过为他国对外贸易提供保险而获取利润。

Some nations possess few exportable commodities or manufactured goods, but they have a mild and sunny climate. During the winter, the Bahamas attract large numbers of tourists, who spend money on hotel accommodations, meals, taxis, and so on. Tourism, therefore, is another form of invisible trade.

The United States has been described as a nation of immigrants. Many Americans send money back to families in the old country. Millions of workers from the countries of southern Europe have gone to work in Germany, Switzerland, France, the Benelux nations, and Scandinavia. The workers send money home to support their families. Such transactions are termed remittances. This is an extremely important kind of invisible trade for some countries, critical to balancing imports and exports. Invisible trade can be as important to some nations as the export of raw materials or commodities is to others. In both cases, the nations earn money to buy necessities.

有些国家几乎没有可供出口的商品和制成品，但气候温和、阳光充足。巴哈马在冬季能吸引大量的游客，他们要为住旅馆、吃饭和乘出租车等花费大笔的钱。所以，旅游业是另外一种无形贸易。

美国是一个移民国家。很多美国人把钱寄回他们原来国家的家人和亲戚。几百万来自南欧的工人到德国、瑞士、法国、比荷卢经济联盟以及斯堪的纳维亚半岛工作。他们寄钱回家，以养家糊口，这称为移民汇款。对于有些国家来说，作为进出口贸易，这是一种极为重要的无形贸易。无形贸易对于有些国家就如同出口原料或商品对于其他国家那样一样重要。这两种形式都可以为国家赚取外汇，以购买必需品。

Section Four　Cross-border E-Commerce（跨境电子商务）

1. Definition of cross-border e-commerce（跨境电子商务的定义）

Cross-border e-commerce is developed based on the network; the cyberspace is a new space, relatively speaking, to the physical space. Network space is a virtual reality defined by network addresses and passwords. Cyberspace's unique values and behavior patterns profoundly affect cross-border e-commerce, making it distinct from traditional trade methods and showing its own characteristics.

跨境电子商务是基于网络发展起来的，网络空间相对于物理空间来说是一个新空间，是一个由网址和密码组成的虚拟但客观存在的世界。网络空间独特的价值标准和行为模式深刻地影响着跨境电子商务，使其不同于传统的交易方式而呈现出自身的特点。

Cross-border e-commerce is a new form of trade that the digitalization and electronic platforms of exhibition, negotiation and conclusion of a business of the traditional trade by Chinese production and trade enterprises through e-commerce means to finally realize the import and export of products and at the same time also an effective way to expand overseas marketing channels, promote China's brand competitiveness and realize the transformation and upgrading of China's foreign trade.

跨境电子商务是我国生产和贸易企业通过电子商务手段将传统贸易中的展示、洽谈和成交环节数字化、电子化，最终实现产品进出口的新型贸易方式；同时，也是扩大海外营销渠道，提升我国品牌竞争力，实现我国外贸转型升级的有效途径。

2．Pattern of trade（贸易模式）

Buy-Ship-Pay reference model（See Fig.1-1）

In order to understand the complexity of international trade, this simple model provides a clear view of the key elements of a trade transaction, and consequently enabling proper compilation of the necessary trade facilitation measures. UN/CEFACT has developed this model of the international supply chain using an internationally accepted modeling technique to provide a reference model, which gives a view of the international supply chain in its entirety.

A simple view of the international supply chain based on the BSP model includes three main categories of processes which are buy, ship, and pay, and four key roles: customer, authority, intermediary and supplier.

Buy-Ship-Pay 参考模型（见图 1-1）

为了理解国际跨境电子商务贸易的复杂性，这个简单的模型可以清晰地了解贸易事务的关键要素，从而正确编制必要的贸易便利化措施。UN/CEFACT 运用国际公认的建模技巧，建构了跨境电子商务国际供应链模型，并为其他模型提供参考，使得跨境电子商务国际供应链的过程一目了然。

基于 BSP 国际供应链的一个简单的视图模型包括三个主要类别流程：购买、运输和支付，加上四种类型的角色，如客户、政府、中介和供应商。

As discussed above, the recommended measures, grouped into four categories, relate to the processes in this model.

• BUY—Covering all commercial activities related to the ordering of goods.

• SHIP—Covering all of the activities involved in the physical transfer of the goods, including official controls.

- PAY—Covering all of the activities involved in the payment for the goods.

After classifying the main categories of roles and processes in a cross-border supply chain, it is needed to have a closer view at the different types that each of these categories can support.

正如上面所讨论的，推荐的措施在这个模型与流程中可分为以下四类。

- 购买——包括所有与商业活动相关的商品的订购。
- 转移——包括所有的活动参与的货物的物理转移，包括官方控制。
- 支付——包括所有参与支付货物的活动。

在对跨境供应链中的主要角色和流程类别进行分类之后，需要仔细查看每一个类别可以在不同类型中所获得的支持。

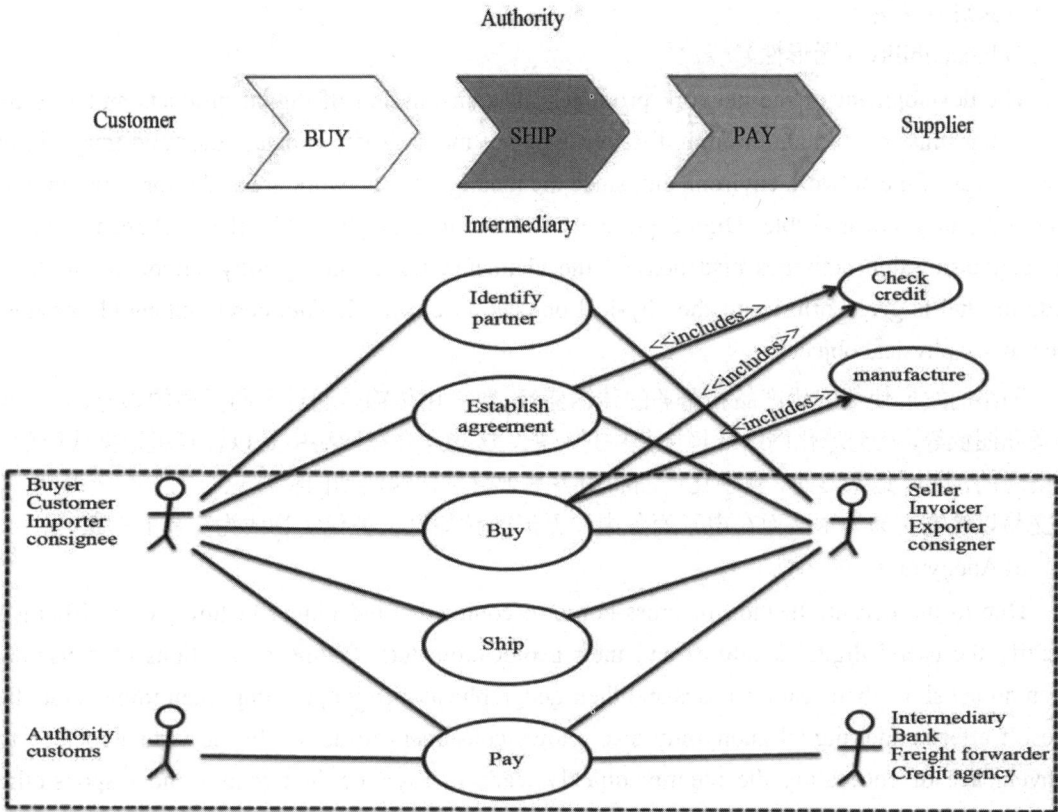

Fig.1-1　International supply chain（国际供应链）

3. Features of cross-border e-commerce（跨境电子商务的特征）

1) Global forum（全球性）

Network is a medium body with no boundary, sharing the characteristics of globalization and decentralization. Cross-border e-commerce, attached to the network, also has the characteristics of globalization and decentralization. E-commerce, compared with the traditional way to trade, boasts its important feature: a borderless trade, losing the geographical factors brought by the traditional exchanges. Internet users do convey products, especially high-value-added goods, and services to the market without crossing borders. The positive effect brought by features of network is the greatest sharing degree of information, whilst its negative impact is that the users confront risks due to different cultural, political and legal factors. Anyone, who has a certain technical means, can make information into the network, connecting with each other, at any time and in any place.

网络是一个没有边界的媒介体，具有全球性和非中心化的特征。依附于网络发生的跨境电子商务也因此具有了全球性和非中心化的特性。与传统的交易方式相比，电子商务的一个重要特点在于电子商务是一种无边界交易，丧失了传统交易所具有的地理因素。互联网用户能够不跨越国界就可以把产品，尤其是高附加值产品和服务提供给市场。网络的全球性特征带来的积极影响是信息的最大程度的共享，消极影响是用户必须面临因文化、政治和法律的不同而产生的风险。任何人只要具备了一定的技术手段，就可以在任何时候、任何地方让信息进入网络，相互联系进行交易。

2) Intangibility（无形性）

The development of the network promotes the transmission of digital products and services. Digital transmission is done through different types of media, such as data, voice and image in the global focus of the network environment, since the media in the network are in the form of computer data code, they are invisible. Digital products and services on the basis of the characteristics of digital transmission activities also possess the characteristic of intangibility, although traditional trade in kind is given priority to the physical objects, in electronic commerce, intangible products can replace physical objects.

网络的发展使数字化产品和服务的传输盛行。数字化传输是通过不同类型的媒介，如数据、声音和图像等，在全球化网络环境中集中进行的，这些媒介在网络中是以计算机数据代码的形式出现的，因而是无形的。数字化产品和服务基于数字传输活动的特性也必然具有无形性，传统交易以实物交易为主，而在电子商务中，无形产品却可以替代实物成为交易的对象。

3) Anonymity（匿名性）

Due to the decentralization of cross-border e-commerce and global features, it is difficult to identify the users' digital identities and their geolocation data. Online transactions of consumers often do not show their real identities and their geographical location, the important thing is that this doesn't affect trade; digital anonymity also allows consumers to do so. In the virtual society, the convenience of concealing the identity quickly leads to asymmetric freedom and responsibility. People here can enjoy the greatest freedom, but only bear the smallest responsibility, or even simply evading responsibility.

由于跨境电子商务的非中心化和全球性的特征，因此很难识别电子商务用户的身份和其所处的地理位置。在线交易的消费者往往不显示自己的真实身份和自己的地理位置，重要的是这丝毫不影响交易的进行，网络的匿名性也允许消费者这样做。在虚拟社会里，隐匿身份的便利性迅即导致自由与责任的不对称。人们在这里可以享受最大的自由，却只承担最小的责任，甚至干脆逃避责任。

4) Real-time（即时性）

In digital networks, the transmission speed is irrelevant to geographical distance. Traditional trading patterns, information communication, such as letter, telegraph, fax, etc., between the sending and receiving of information, are with a length in different time. With regard to the information exchange in e-commerce, regardless of the actual distance of time and space, one party sends a message to the other party who receives that information almost at the same time, just like talking face to face in life. Some digital products (such as audio and video products, software, etc.), can also get instant settlement, ordering, payment, delivery done in a flash.

对于网络而言，传输的速度和地理距离无关。传统交易模式，信息交流方式，如信函、电报、传真等，在信息的发送与接收间，存在着长短不同的时间差。而电子商务中的信息交流，无论实际时空距离远近，一方发送信息与另一方接收信息几乎是同时的，就如同生活中面对面交谈一样。某些数字化产品（如音像制品、软件等）的交易，还可以即时结清，订货、付款、交货都可以在瞬间完成。

5) Paperlessness（无纸化）

Electronic commerce mainly takes the way of the paperless operation, which serves as the main characteristic of trade in the form of electronic commerce. In e-commerce, electronic computer communication records files instead of a series of paper trading. Users send or receive electronic information. Now that the electronic information exists in the form of bits and transmission, the whole process is realized by paperless information. Paperlessness brings positive effect in terms of making information transferred without the limitation of paper, however, many specifications of the traditional law are with the standard "paper trades" as the starting point, therefore, paperlessness brings chaos in the law, to a certain extent.

电子商务主要采取无纸化操作的方式，这是以电子商务形式进行交易的主要特征。在电子商务中，电子计算机通信记录取代了一系列的纸面交易文件。用户发送或接收电子信息。由于电子信息以比特的形式存在和传送，整个信息发送和接收过程实现了无纸化。无纸化带来的积极影响是使信息传递摆脱了纸张的限制，但由于传统法律的许多规范是以规范"有纸交易"为出发点的，因此，无纸化带来了一定程度的法律混乱。

Section Five "Belt and Road" and Trade Facilitation（"一带一路"与贸易便利化）

1. Definition of the Belt and Road Initiative (BRI)（"一带一路"的定义）

In September 2013, President Xi Jinping proposed the initiative to jointly build the "Silk Road Economic Belt". In October 2013, President Xi Jinping proposed the initiative to jointly build the "21st Century Maritime Silk Road". Those two initiatives are referred to as the Belt and Road Initiative.

2013年9月，习近平主席提出了共同建设"丝绸之路经济带"的倡议，2013年10月，习近平主席提出了共同建设"21世纪海上丝绸之路"的倡议。这两个倡议简称"一带一路"倡议。

Since then, the Belt and Road Initiative (BRI) has received enthusiastic response from more and more countries. The Belt and Road Initiative is becoming China's participation program in global open cooperation, improving the global economic governance system, promoting global common development and prosperity, as well as promoting the building of a community of human destiny.

此后，"一带一路"倡议得到越来越多国家热烈响应，共建"一带一路"正在成为我国参与全球开放合作、改善全球经济治理体系、促进全球共同发展繁荣、推动构建人类命运共同体的中国方案。

The joint construction of the Belt and Road Initiative is conducive to building an open cooperation platform to maintain and develop an open world economy. Through the Belt and Road Initiative, China is likely to jointly create an environment conducive to open development, promote the establishment of a fair, rational and transparent international economic and trade investment rules system. It promotes the orderly flow of production factors, conducts efficient allocation of resources, and deepens the integration of markets. The Belt and Road Initiative invites countries in the world to, combined with their own national conditions, actively develop an open economy, participate in global governance and public goods supply, together with working together to build a broad community of interests.

共建"一带一路"倡议有利于打造开放型合作平台，维护和发展开放型世界经济。中国通过"一带一路"倡议共同创造有利于开放发展的环境，推动构建公正、合理、透明的国际经贸投资规则体系，促进生产要素有序流动，资源高效配置，市场深度融合。"一带一路"倡议世界各国结合自身国情，积极发展开放型经济，参与全球治理和公共产品供给，携手构建广泛的利益共同体。

2. Definition of trade facilitation（贸易便利化的定义）

Trade facilitation is a concept in international trade. Its primary goal is to simplify and coordinate trade procedures and accelerate the flow of factors across borders. Trade facilitation refers to the simplification of procedures and processes, the coordination of relevant laws and regulations, and the standardization of trade-related infrastructure. Trade facilitation creates a coordinated, transparent, and predictable environment for international trade transactions.

贸易便利化是国际贸易的一个术语，其基本精神是简化和协调贸易程序，加速要素跨境的流通。贸易便利化是指通过程序和手续的简化、适用法律和规定的协调、基础设施的标准化和改善，为国际贸易创造一个协调的、透明的、可预见的环境。

3. The Belt and Road Initiative improves trade facilitation（"一带一路"建设改善贸易便利化）

The Belt and Road Initiative helps maintain the multilateral trading system, promotes the development of a free trade zone, and advances trade and investment liberalization and facilitation. It also comprehensively improves China's trade facilitation conditions and enhances the quality and level of export trade in those countries and regions which are related to the "Belt and Road" . And those are essential contents and key points for further promoting the construction of the "Belt and Road".

"一带一路"建设有利于维护多边贸易体制，推动自由贸易区建设，促进贸易和投资自由化便利化。全面改善中国贸易便利化条件，提升与"一带一路"共建国家及地区出口贸易质量和水平，是深入推进"一带一路"建设的重要内容和关键所在。

(1) The Belt and Road Initiative optimizes and improves infrastructure construction, which is

conducive to improving the smoothness of trade facilitation. It increases investment in transportation, energy, communications and other infrastructure, while focusing on the development and improvement of hardware facilities such as trade port facilities and trade logistics services, which tend to better the smoothness of trade facilitation. In addition, the Belt and Road Initiative strengthens the support for information technology, implements e-commerce actions, and promotes e-government action plans, which functions as an important means to improve trade facilitation.

（1）"一带一路"优化完善基础设施建设，有利于提升贸易便利化的顺畅性。"一带一路"可以加大对交通、能源、通信等基础设施的投资力度，同时注重发展完善贸易口岸设施和贸易物流服务等硬件设施，这些都提升贸易便利化的顺畅性。另外，"一带一路"加大对信息技术领域的支持力度，实施电子商务行动，推动电子政府行动计划，也是提升贸易便利化的一个重要举措。

(2) The Belt and Road Initiative strengthens the coordination of trade facilitation by establishing a communication and coordination mechanism, which is the essential connotation of trade facilitation. It not only assists the traders to increase understanding and build up trust, but also achieves the purpose of properly solving the friction in trade. The cooperation and exchanges between various academic institutions and think tanks of relevant countries and regions in the "Belt and Road" can effectively realize the effective docking of different trade systems, leading to reducing the costs of institutional transactions, including adjustment of policies of customs clearance and import-export restrictions. Meanwhile, by eliminating the technical barriers to trade, facilitating the consistency and mutual recognition of inspection and quarantine standards, the coordination of trade facilitation is consolidated.

（2）"一带一路"构建沟通协调机制，强化贸易便利化的协调性。良好的沟通协调机制是贸易便利化的本质内涵要求，不仅有利于贸易双方增进了解、增加信任，更可以达到以妥善的方式解决贸易中的摩擦的目的。"一带一路"共建国家和地区的各类学术机构、智库之间的合作与交流，可以很好地实现不同贸易制度的有效对接，降低制度性交易成本，其中包括通关便利化、进出口商品限制政策的调整、贸易技术壁垒的消除、检验检疫标准的一致性和互认等，强化贸易便利化的协调性。

(3) The Belt and Road Initiative enhances the effectiveness of trade facilitation by lifting the customs clearance efficiency. The Belt and Road Initiative deepens the reform of customs modernization. Through the construction and establishment of a unified import and export business information system, the data distribution, reception and processing are comprehensively realized, so as to ensure the effectiveness, completeness and accuracy of information and data transmission. In addition, The Belt and Road Initiative vigorously guides the simplification of customs import and export procedures, thereby lifting customs administration efficiency and enhancing trade facilitation.

（3）"一带一路"提高海关通关效率，增进贸易便利化的实效性。"一带一路"可以深化海关现代化改革。通过建设和设立统一的进出口业务信息系统，综合实现数据的分发、接收和处理，保证信息和数据传递的时效性、完整性和准确性。另外，"一带一路"大力引导海关进出口流程和手续的简化，从而提高海关行政效率，增进贸易便利化。

Part B Terminology Practice

1. **Exporting**（出口）: Sending goods to another country for sale or trade.

2. **Importing**（进口）: Bringing goods from another country for sale or trade.

3. **Minerals**（矿产品）: Commodities obtained through mining.

4. **Comparative advantage**（比较优势）: Situation that exists when a country can produce a product or provide a certain service at a much lower cost than any other country.

5. **Absolute advantage**（绝对优势）: Situation that exists when only one country can produce a certain item, or can produce it more efficiently than any other country. Theory of comparative advantage: An economic theory stating that if one country can produce a product relatively more efficiently than another country, it is beneficial to both countries for the first country to export that product to the other. It is also called the comparative cost theory.

6. **Visible imports and exports**（有形进出口）: The import and export of tangible goods (not services).

7. **Invisible imports and exports**（无形进出口）: The import and export of services rather than actual goods, for example, banking, insurance, professional services, etc.

8. **Balance of trade**（贸易平衡）: The difference between the value of merchandise exports and the value of merchandise imports of a nation during a given period of time.

9. **Exchange rate**（汇率）: The amount of one country's currency that must be paid in order to obtain one unit of another country's currency.

10. **Tariff**（关税）: Duty or tax levied on a specific commodity when it crosses national boundaries.

11. **Quota**（配额）: The maximum quantity of a certain product that is allowed into a country during a given period of time. A quota is used to limit imports.

12. **Export agent**（出口代理商）: An agent who tries to find new markets for products manufactured in their own country.

13. **Patent**（专利）: An exclusive right granted by a government to an inventor to make, use or sell a new device, process, material, or other innovation for a specified period of time.

14. **Royalty**（特许权使用费）: A payment made for the right to use the property of another person for gain. This may be intellectual property, such as books (copyright) or an invention (patent).

15. **Balance-of-payment deficit**（国际收支逆差）: The amount by which money flowing out of the country exceeds the money flowing into the country during a given period of time.

16. **Infant industry**（幼稚产业）: An underdeveloped industry that, in the face of competition from abroad, may not be able to survive the early years of struggle before reaching maturity.

17. **Export subsidy**（出口补贴）: A payment by a government to an industry that leads to an expansion of exports by that industry.

18. **Ad valorem tariff**（从价关税）: A customs duty charged as a percentage of the value of goods rather than on a weight or quantity basis.

19. **Trade facilitation**（贸易便利化）：Refers to the simplification of procedures and processes, the coordination of applicable laws and regulations, and the standardization of infrastructure.

Part C Terms

1. foreign trade　对外贸易

2. overseas trade　海外贸易

3. international trade　国际贸易

4. to trade with...　和……进行贸易

5. to do business in a moderate way　做生意稳重

6. to do business in a sincere way　做生意诚恳

7. deal　交易，经营，处理，与……交往；to make a deal　做一笔交易

8. to deal in　经营，做生意

9. to explore the possibilities of...　探讨……的可能性

10. trade circles　贸易界

11. to handle　经营某商品

12. to trade in　经营某商品

13. business scope/frame　经营范围

14. trading firm/house　贸易行，商行

15. trade by commodities　商品贸易

16. visible trade　有形贸易

17. invisible trade　无形贸易

18. barter trade　易货贸易

19. bilateral trade　双边贸易

20. triangular trade　三角贸易

21. multilateral trade　多边贸易

22. countertrade　对销贸易，抵偿贸易

23. counter purchase　互购贸易

24. buy-back　回购贸易

25. compensation trade　补偿贸易

26. processing trade　加工贸易

27. assembling trade　装配贸易

28. leasing trade　租赁贸易

29. in exchange for...　用……交换……

30. trade agreement　贸易协议

31. global open cooperation　全球开放合作

32. governance system　治理体系

33. community with a shared future for mankind　人类命运共同体

34. be conducive to...　有利于……

35. community of interests　利益共同体

36. multilateral trading system　多边贸易体制

37. free trade zone　自由贸易区

38. infrastructure construction　基础设施建设

39. communication and coordination mechanism　沟通协调机制

40. customs clearance　海关通关

Part D Exercise

I. Answer the following questions in English.

1. What is international trade?

2. What are the major motivations for private firms to operate international business?

3. What is the most essential motive to pursue international trade?

4. What measures do most companies usually adopt to avoid wild swings in the sales and profits?

5. Please give the four major operation forms chosen by most companies.

6. What does balance of payments account mean?

7. What are the basic sources of international revenue and expenditure for most countries?

8. Could you find any differences between Direct Investment and Portfolio Investment? If you can, please tell the main reasons.

9. What is MNE? What are its synonyms?

10. Please give examples to explain "Services are earnings other than those from goods".

11. What influences the international operational forms which a company will choose?

12. What limits a firm's sales?

13. What are the advantages for firms to set up joint ventures in overseas market?

14. What does "royalties" mean?

15. What is "franchising"?

16. What is the Belt and Road Initiative?

17. How can the Belt and Road Initiative improve trade facilitation?

II. Match each one on the left with its correct meaning on the right.

1. motivation   A. to make continual efforts to gain sth.

2. pursue   B. the action of obtaining, esp. by efforts of careful attention

3. mark up   C. which by its nature can not be known by senses, not clear and certain, not real

4. procurement   D. the goods (freight) carried by a ship, plane or vehicle

5. intangible   E. the amount by which a price is raised

6. cargo   F. profit, interest

7. royalty   G. the net value of assets or interest, invest

8. equity   H. not needing other things or people, taking decisions alone

9. yield   I. a share of the profits

10. independent   J. need or purpose

1. (   )   2. (   )   3. (   )   4. (   )   5. (   )

6. (   )   7. (   )   8. (   )   9. (   )   10. (   )

III. Translate the following terms and phrases into Chinese.

1. purchasing power   2. potential sales

3. mark-up   4. domestic markets

5. finished goods   6. profit margin

7. market share   8. trade discrimination

9. timing   10. business cycles

11. recovery   12. economic recession

13. portfolio investment   14. tangible goods

15. visible exports and imports 16. revenue and expenditure

17. excess capacity   18. trade intermediary

19. turn-key operations   20. license agreement

IV. Case Study.

Batteries branded "White Elephant" exported from China gained popularity in Southeast Asia, but faced market rejection in the United States. Why?

V. Please try to find out some cases about cultural differences in doing international business.

VI. Please determine whether the following statements are True or False. Then put T for True or F for False in the bracket at the end of each statement.

1. When dealing in international trade(exporting and importing), a businessman has to face a variety of conditions which differ from those to which he has grown accustomed in domestic trade. (　　)

2. International trade includes import, export, direct selling and indirect selling trade operations. (　　)

3. The different distributions of the world's resources can not determine the patterns of world trade. (　　)

4. Every individual country puts controls on trade for the reasons: (1) To correct a balanced-of-payment deficit; (2) In view of national security; (3) To protect their own industries against the competition of foreign goods. (　　)

5. International trade transactions can refer to the importation and exportation of goods from one country to another. (　　)

6. There exists a variety of instruments for achieving the goals of foreign trade policy. (　　)

7. Licensing agreements could be a satisfactory method of exporting for small firms new to international business. (　　)

8. Compared with the joint venture, the wholly-owned subsidiary is a less risky mode of entering foreign markets. (　　)

9. Service exports and imports refer to international earnings other than those from goods sent to another country. (　　)

10. Services are also referred to as invisible. International business comprises many different types of invisible services. (　　)

11. If every country in the world use the same currency, the world trade would be much tougher. (　　)

12. Importing and exporting firms to whom the payment is made in foreign currency can be involved in significant foreign exchange risks because of the fluctuation in interest rates. (　　)

13. The free flow of international trade benefits all who participate in it. (　　)

14. Nations sometimes restrict exports of critical raw materials, high technology, or equipment when such export might harm its own security. (　　)

15. A country usually offers protection to its domestic industries by taxing imports of different foreign goods. (　　)

16. Digitalization has formed the biggest difference between digital trade and traditional international trade. (　　)

VII. Translate the following sentences into English.

1. 贸易常被说成是发展的"引擎"。这个比喻虽然过于简单，但它的确说明了对外贸易在经济发展中的重要性。虽然出口的健康增长并不总是快速、持久的经济增长的充分条件，但两者之间积极而密切的联系显然是不可否认的。贸易发展对经济增长的作用表现在很多方面。其中：专业分工带来的利益，国际竞争对国内经济效率的促进作用，提高对发展所需的进口商品的支付能力，而更为普遍的是鼓励投资和企业家精神。

2. 国际贸易是一个国家生产的商品和劳务与另一个国家生产的商品和劳务的交换。除了有形贸易，即商品和货物的进出口以外，还有无形贸易，这是指国家之间劳务的交换。希腊和挪威等国拥有庞大的海运船队，提供运输服务，这是无形贸易的一种。无形贸易对一些国家来说，就像原料和商品出口对其他一些国家那样重要。在这两种情况下，这些国家都能赚到钱去购买其所需要的商品。

3. 国际贸易的方式是多种多样的。包销是指卖方在特定地区和一定期限内给予国外客户独家销售指定商品的权力的贸易方式。在这种交往中，商品由包销商承购，自行销售，自负盈亏。这与只收取佣金的代理方式不同；也因为包销商在特定地区享有专营权，而与一般买卖合同有别。

4. 世界上没有任何一个国家能生产它所需的所有产品，所以各国参与国际分工，进行有效的生产和再生产。有时一个国家能够以易货方式从国外购买产品和服务，易货是指以一种货物交换另一种货物，而不是用钱交易。易货贸易本身并不足以满足一个国家的进口需要。但作为一种贸易方式，它对外汇短缺、外资流入远远无法满足外贸需求的发展中国家来说具有一定的吸引力。

5. "数字交付贸易"主要是指数字化交付的服务贸易。可见，数字贸易属于服务贸易的一个分支。在此基础上，按照"交易标的"的划分维度，"数字交付贸易"进一步细分为四个大类，即数字产品贸易、数字服务贸易、数字技术贸易以及数据贸易等。另一方面，"数字订购贸易"则被界定为一种基于数字化订购的商品贸易，跨境电商就是其典型代表。

VIII. Multiple Choices.

1. The international division of labor formed in the period of (   ) century.

    A. 11 to 12   B. 14 to 15

    C. 16 to 18   D. 18 to 19

2. The basis of the international division of labor and the development is (   ).

    A. natural conditions   B. population

    C. internationalization of capital   D. appearance of countries

3. The (   ) of each country determines its status in the international division of labor.

    A. productivity   B. market size

    C. natural conditions   D. social system

4. In the capital primitive accumulation period, the international division of labor is mainly between the (   ).

    A. developed countries and developing countries

    B. developed countries and developed countries

    C. developing countries and developing countries

    D. suzerain and colony

5. Which of the following world markets is characterized by free competition? (　　)

  A. Closed market   B. Free market

  C. Monopoly market   D. North America market

6. A few developed countries in professional collaboration, joint production, this is the (　　) international division of labor.

  A. horizontal   B. vertical

  C. hybrid   D. cross type

7. Different economic development level of vertical division of labor between countries is a (　　).

  A. vertical division of labor   B. horizontal division

  C. division of hybrid   D. three industrial division

8. The theory of absolute advantage and the relative theory of interest are the traditional theory claiming (　　).

  A. free trade   B. protection trade

  C. state intervention   D. state intervention combined with laissez faire

9. The theory of absolute advantage proposed by the international division of labor is based on the (　　) differences between countries.

  A. comparative cost   B. absolute cost

  C. factor endowments elements   D. factor combination proportion

10. In the interests of the relative theory, the division of labor between countries is based on the differences of (　　).

  A. products comparative advantage   B. products monopoly advantage

  C. products intensiveness   D. product protection

Chapter Two

Part A Text

General Procedures of Export and Import Transaction

Exports and imports have been crucial to the Chinese economy since the reform and opening up. In fact, international trade is essential for every country. Each country has to import goods it cannot produce domestically and earn foreign exchange through exports to fund these imports. Thus the import and export trades are two sides of the same coin, and both can have beneficial effects on the home market. Imports create competition for home-produced goods; exporting gives a manufacturer a larger market for his products, so helping to reduce the unit cost. In each case the effect is to keep prices in domestic markets.

But because of some reasons there may be factors that compel the government to place restrictions on foreign trade. Imports may be controlled or subjected to a customs duty to protect the home industry, or because the available foreign exchange ought to be paid for buying more essential goods and exports, too, may be restricted, to conserve a particular raw material required by the developing home industries.

自改革开放以来，外贸进出口一直是中国经济非常重要的组成部分。事实上，它对每一个国家经济来说都很重要。每一个国家都必须进口本国所不能生产的货物与商品，同时还要创收外汇，用于支付这些进口商品，这就要靠出口本国的制成品和富余的原材料。因此，进出口贸易是同一件事物的两个方面，两者对国内市场都能产生有利影响。进口货物使国内产品有了竞争，而出口则为厂商的产品提供了更广阔的市场，有助于降低单位成本。无论是进口还是出口，其作用都是控制国内市场的价格。

但是，由于这种或那种原因，政府不得不对对外贸易加以限制。为了保护国内的某一产业，或者由于需要外汇用于购买更为重要的物资，政府可能要控制进口或以关税制约进口。同样，为了保留发展中的国内产业所需要的某一种特殊的原料，出口也会受到限制。

Customs data indicate that China's digital-ordered trade will maintain strong growth momentum in 2024. In 2023, cross-border e-commerce import-export volume reached 2.4 trillion yuan. During the first half of 2024, this figure grew to 1.22 trillion yuan, a year-on-year increase of 10.5%, which is 4.4 percentage points higher than the overall growth rate of foreign trade during the same period. In order to promote the high-quality development of digital ordering trade, China vigorously encourages e-commerce platforms and related supporting service providers to become bigger and stronger, and accelerates the creation of cross-border e-commerce digital trade brands. Among them, promoting the construction of cross-border e-commerce comprehensive pilot zones is an important measure. The authorities support the development of "cross-border e-commerce+industrial belts" and promote the integration of domestic and foreign trade in the digital field. Therefore, it is necessary to understand the main differences between digital trade processes and traditional trade processes.

海关数据显示，2024 年我国数字订购贸易保持强劲发展势头。2023 年跨境电商进出口额达 2.4 万亿元，2024 年上半年跨境电商进出口额达到 1.22 万亿元，同比增长 10.5%，高于同期外贸整体增速 4.4 个百分点。为了推动数字订购贸易高质量发展，我国大力鼓励电商平台和相关配套服务商等主体做大做强，加快打造跨境电商数字贸易品牌。其中，推进跨境电商综合试验区建设就是一个重要举措。支持"跨境电商+产业带"发展，推进数字领域内外贸一体化。因此，有必要了解数字贸易流程与传统贸易流程的主要不同。

Section One　Procedures of Export and Import Transaction（进出口贸易的流程）

1. What is exporting（什么是出口）

In your lifetime, whether conscious of it or not, you engage in selling. Manufacturers sell the products they make and farmers sell the produce they grow. Theaters sell entertainment; insurance companies sell financial protection against future loss; action-driving ideas can be sold too. Selling is the process of assisting and/or persuading a prospective customer to buy a beneficial product or service or act upon an idea that has business significance to him. Later, selling extended its narrow meaning and crossed the border of other countries. Till now it has become a well-accepted form of exporting. A definition suitable for today is that exporting is the process of earning money by providing the right product at the right price, at the right time, in the right place beyond your home boundary. The ultimate goal is to make sure that the exporter is paid for the goods he sells.

Exporting is an orderly, methodical and a somewhat technical process of adapting Chinese products and exporting methods to the conditions in countries outside China. Export marketing has much in common with internal selling. But the business environment varies greatly because of differences in language, customs, and tradition. To some extent, this gap can be filled by export market research before real exporting is undertaken. In moving to the foreign market, the exporter who squarely confronts the problem of seeking a target, or locating the promising customer for his products finds himself facing many distinct but related problems, which involve using a variety of techniques and a whole set of procedures in a suitable and systematic way, making a series of right decisions about many different options that one has, and always bearing in mind the requirements and characteristics of the market itself. Above all, it all adds up to "marketing mix".

The procedures of an export or import business are so complicated that it may take quite a long time to conclude a transaction. Varied and complicated procedures have to be gone through in the course of an export or import transaction. From the very beginning to the end of the transaction, the whole operation generally undergoes four stages: preparing for exporting or importing, business negotiation, implementation of the contract, and settlement of disputes (if any). Each stage covers some specific steps. Since the export and import trades are two sides of the same coin, and one country's export is another country's import, hence, we will take the procedures of export transaction in the following diagram to illustrate the general procedures of export and import transaction. Before proceeding to the following units, we'd better keep this general picture in mind.

不管你是否意识到，你一生中都正在或将要进行推销。制造商出售它们制造的产品，农民出售他们种植的农产品，剧院推销它们的娱乐活动，保险公司则销售预防不测的金融保险，甚至督促人们采取行动的建议也可以出售。销售是帮助或说服潜在的顾客购买产品或劳务，或者使顾客按照对销售商有业务意义的某种想法采取行动。后来，销售的内涵扩大，范围也超出了国界。时至今日，销售作为出口的一种形式，指以合理的价格在适当的时间和适当的地点提供合适的产品以获得利润。

出口是一个有序、系统化且具有技术性的过程，旨在将中国产品及出口方式调整以适应海外国家的市场条件。出口推销和国内销售在很多地方有共同之处。但商业环境却因各国语言、习俗及传统的差异而有极大不同。从某种程度上说，这种不同可以在实际出口前通过对出口市场的调查来克服。在转向国外市场的过程中，正在寻找目标市场及有希望的顾客的出口商发现其面临着许多截然不同又密切相关的问题，其中包括采用各种技巧及一整套合适而有系统的措施，在多种不同的选择中制定一系列决策，同时还要牢记市场本身的要求及特点。最重要的是，这一切构成了"市场组合"。

进出口贸易的过程非常复杂，往往要花很长一段时间才能完成一笔交易。在一笔进出口交易中，要经历各种各样复杂的程序。从开始到结束，一笔交易一般要经历四个阶段：进口或出口的准备、商务谈判、执行合同、解决纠纷（如果有的话）。每个阶段包含一些具体的步骤。既然进口贸易和出口贸易是同一事物的两个方面，一个国家的进口就是另外一个国家的出口，那么在这里，我们用出口贸易步骤的流程图来说明进出口贸易的一般程序。在继续往下学习之前，读者的脑海里最好始终有这样一幅流程图。

2. Procedures of export transaction（出口贸易的程序）

The most difficult part of exporting is taking the first step. Different countries have different economic policies or systems. So before doing business with foreign countries, one has to understand the whole procedures of export transactions (See Fig.2-1).

对出口贸易来说，最困难的是迈出第一步。不同的国家有不同的经济政策或不同的经济体系。因此，任何想要做外贸出口的人都必须事先了解外贸出口的程序（见图 2-1）。

1) Making market research（做市场调研）

Any exporter who wants to sell his products in a foreign country must first conduct a lot of market research. Market research is a process of conducting research into a specific market for a particular product. Export market research, in particular, is a study of a given market abroad to determine the needs of that market and the methods by which the products can be supplied. The exporter needs to know which foreign companies are likely to use his products or might be interested in marketing and distributing the products in their country. He must think about whether there is a potential for making a profit. He must examine the market structures and general economic conditions in those places. If the economy is in a recession, the demand for all products is usually decreased. So the exporter's products might not sell well at such times.

任何一个想把货物销售到国外的出口商都必须首先做很多市场调研。市场调研是指对某一产品在某一特定市场条件下进行调研，具体到出口贸易的市场调研，它指的是对国外某一特定市场的调查研究，以确定其市场需求以及供给的方式。出口商必须了解有哪些国外公司可能使用其产品，有哪些公司对分销其产品感兴趣。其必须考虑是否有赚取利润的可能性。其必须调查那些国家的市场结构和总的经济形势。如果经济不景气，对产品的需求量通常会下降，那么，此时出口商的产品就会受到影响。

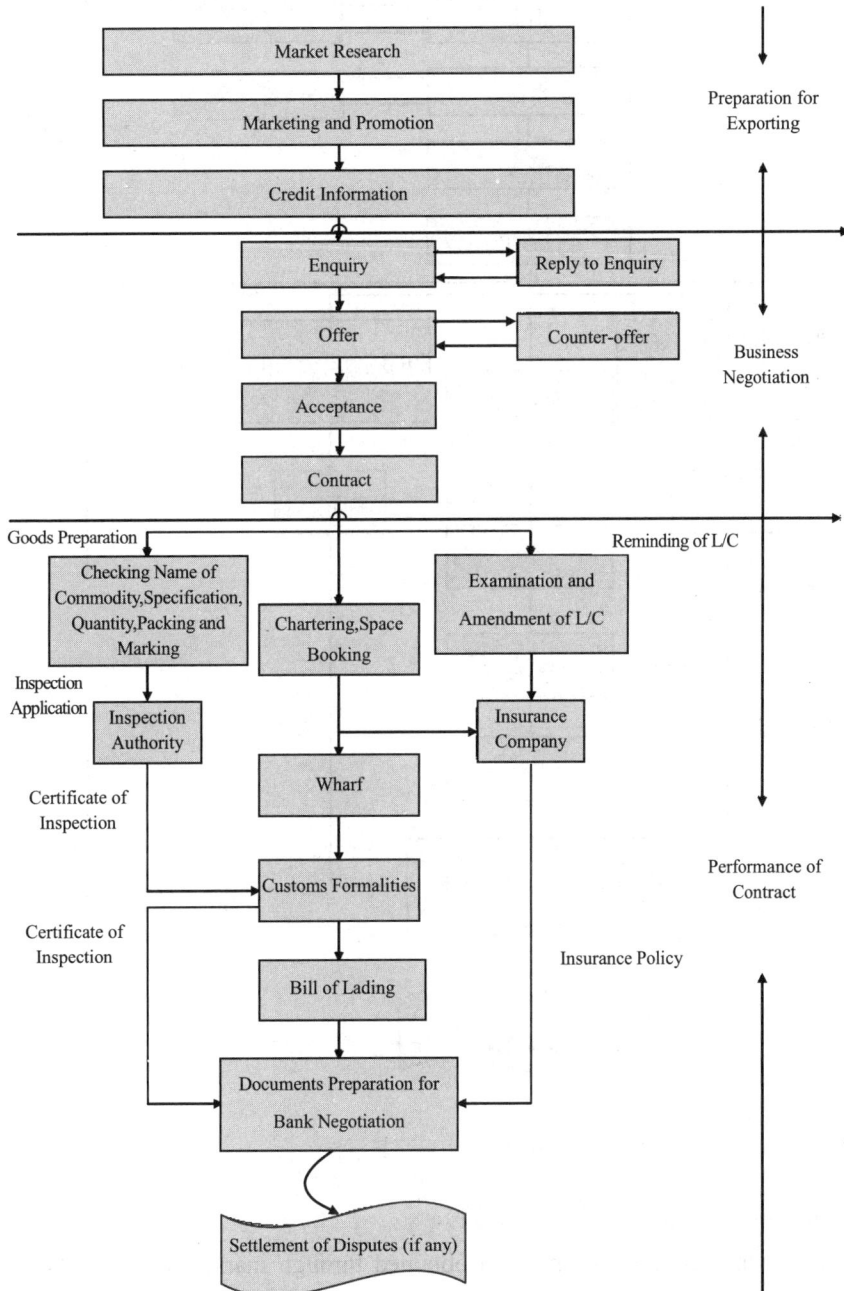

```
                    ┌──────────────────────────┐
                    │     Market Research      │                    ↓
                    └──────────────────────────┘           Preparation for
                    ┌──────────────────────────┐              Exporting
                    │  Marketing and Promotion │
                    └──────────────────────────┘
                    ┌──────────────────────────┐
                    │     Credit Information    │
                    └──────────────────────────┘
```

Fig.2-1 Procedures of Export Transaction

（流程图）

Preparation for Exporting

- Market Research
- Marketing and Promotion
- Credit Information

Business Negotiation

- Enquiry → Reply to Enquiry
- Offer → Counter-offer
- Acceptance
- Contract

Performance of Contract

Goods Preparation — Reminding of L/C

- Checking Name of Commodity, Specification, Quantity, Packing and Marking
- Chartering, Space Booking
- Examination and Amendment of L/C

Inspection Application
- Inspection Authority

Certificate of Inspection

- Wharf
- Insurance Company

Certificate of Inspection

- Customs Formalities
- Bill of Lading

Insurance Policy

- Documents Preparation for Bank Negotiation

- Settlement of Disputes (if any)

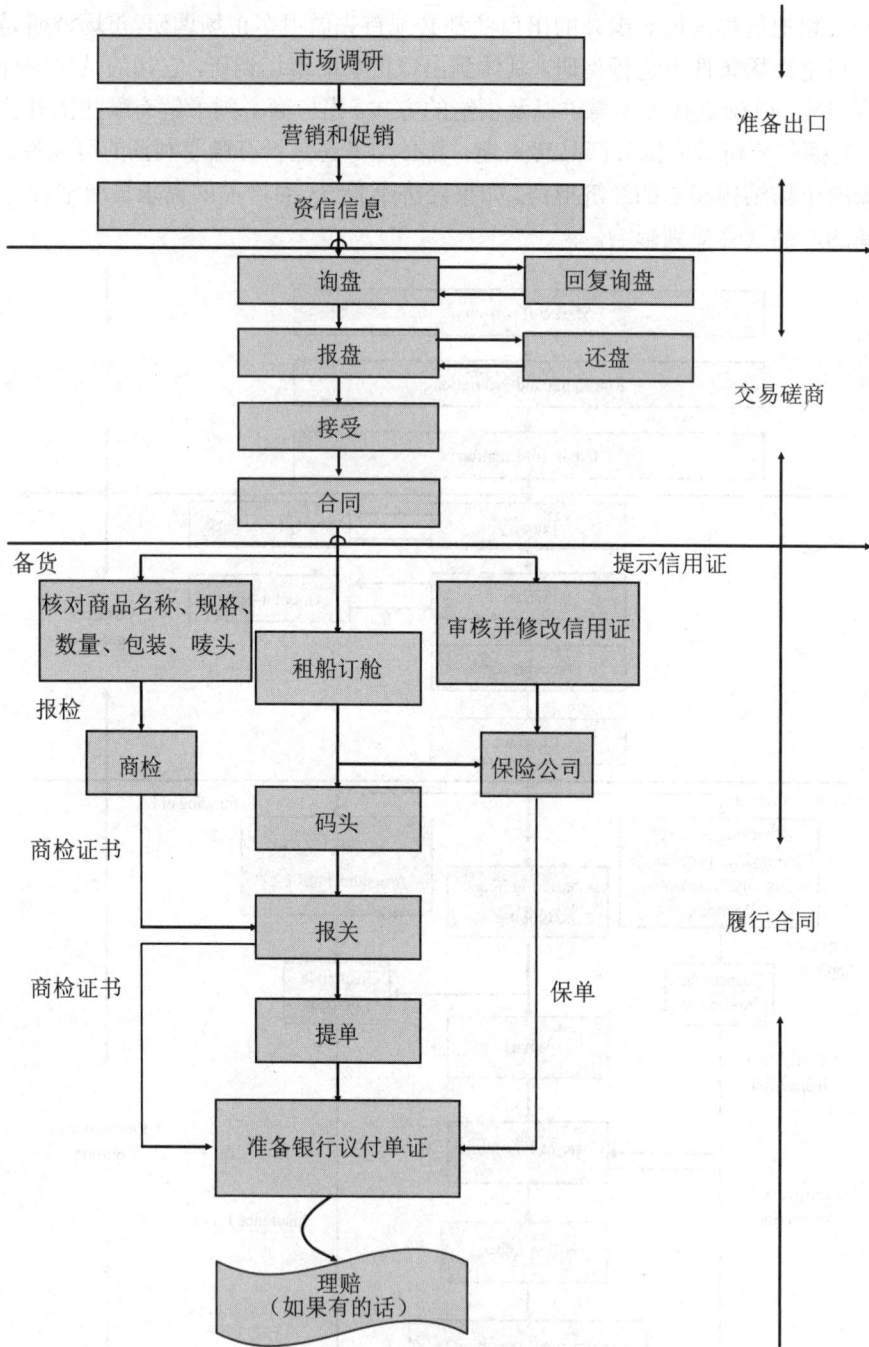

市场调研

营销和促销

资信信息

准备出口

询盘 → 回复询盘

报盘 → 还盘

接受

交易磋商

合同

备货　　　　　　　　　提示信用证

核对商品名称、规格、数量、包装、唛头

审核并修改信用证

租船订舱

报检

商检

保险公司

商检证书

码头

报关

履行合同

商检证书

提单

保单

准备银行议付单证

理赔
（如果有的话）

图 2-1　出口交易流程

2) Marketing and promotion（营销和促销）

After studying the information and data obtained through market research, the maker or the exporter may decide whether there are good prospects for their goods in the foreign market, and then take effective measures to promote the export of the goods to that market.

To help start an export business, the exporter may not only collect information or data from outside sources but also make their products known to others abroad on their own initiative. Nowadays, new equipment, new product developments and expanded research have brought about an entirely new stage in economic development. There is no longer a market waiting to consume everything the factories turn out. It has become evident that businessmen will have to sell and promote aggressively in order to develop and expand the markets necessary to consume all the things the factories produce. It means that businessmen have to determine beforehand what, how much, at what price and under what circumstances the ultimate consumers will purchase. Accordingly, various marketing strategies have been developed. Underlying all marketing strategies is the marketing concept which can be illustrated in the following diagram (See Fig.2-2).

经过分析市场调研结果,制造商或出口商可以判断出其商品在国外市场的前景,并采取有效的措施来促进对那个市场的出口。

为了出口业务,出口商不仅要从外部渠道收集信息或数据,而且还要发挥主动性以使产品为国外所知。今天,新设备、新产品开发和扩展的研究已给经济的发展带来了全新的意义,不再有一个等着消费工厂所生产的全部产品的市场。很明显,商家必须主动地去销售和促销,以发展和扩大必需的市场来消费工厂生产的一切产品。这就意味着商家必须事先确定最终消费者将购买什么、买多少,在什么价位以及在什么情况下购买。与之对应,其采取各种不同的营销策略的核心就是"营销理念"(见图 2-2)。

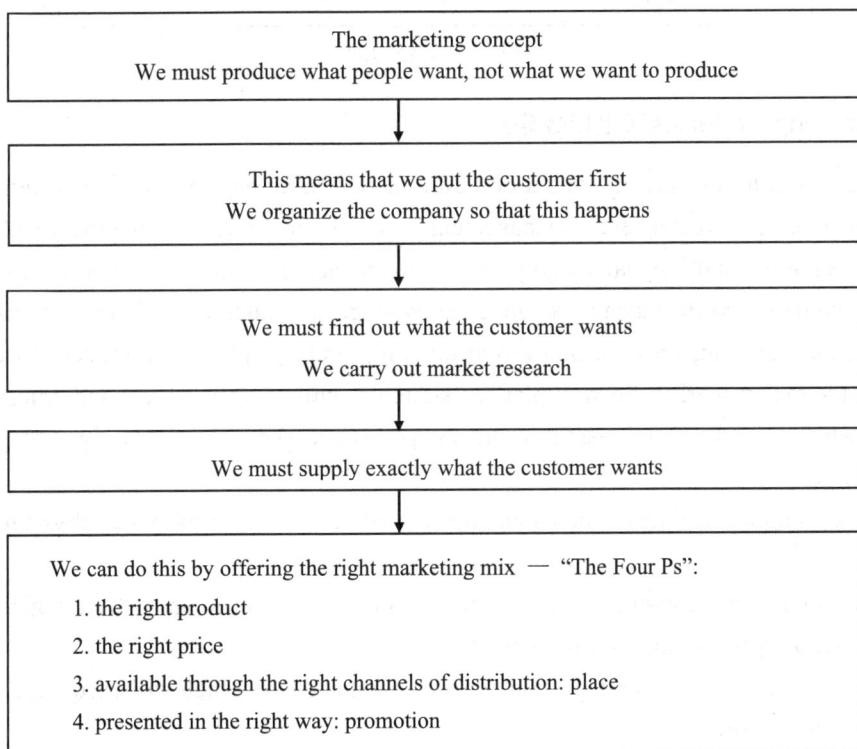

Fig.2-2 The Marketing Concept

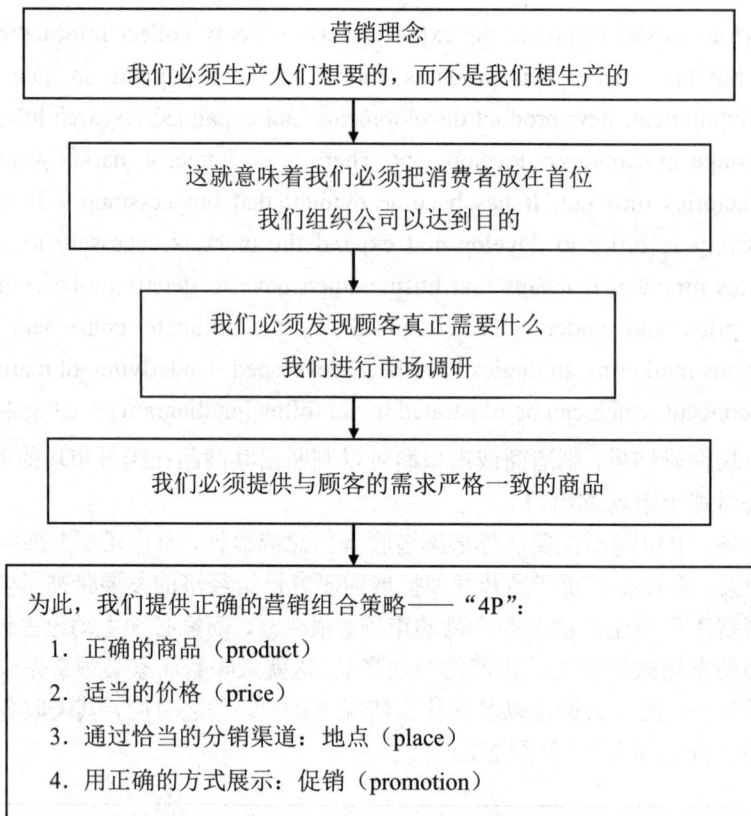

图 2-2　营销理念

3．Exporting strategies（出口战略）

The responsibility of moving from a domestic market to an export market and ultimately to a global market is a director-level management task. It involves an internationally focused management culture; multilingually equipped at all management levels; computer and logistical equipment; empathy with buyers; a good knowledge of international regulations and the international environment; creative innovative thinking; and complete commitment to developing and serving the export market. So well-planned strategies will be very critical and crucial for those enterprises which want to be successful in the competitive market. The following strategies can be paid attention to.

(1) The development of ideas and techniques should be seen as important as physical goods and services.

(2) Recognizing that growing global competition drives companies' growth strategies.

(3) Recognizing the importance of technology.

(4) Developing long-term strategies on a growth market basis, which will encourage a proactive rather than a reactive strategy.

(5) Striving to find new markets opening up new sales opportunities.

(6) Continuously reviewing and implementing internal company changes such as new manufacturing and disciplines dedicated to improving product specification.

(7) Exploiting new technology and new technological processes.

(8) Developing a strong service philosophy and empathy with the buyer.

(9) Undertaking continuous market research and being focused on logistics.

(10) Employ personnel who are experienced/educated in the products/services and have forward thinking international trade ideologies.

(11) Continuously reviewing world market changes.

(12) Developing a profound understanding of world cultures.

从国内市场转移到出口市场，最终扩展到全球化市场，都属于董事层的管理工作，这些职责包括：关注国际上的新管理文化，管理层懂多国语言，拥有计算机和物流设施，对买方需求的深刻同理心，熟悉有关国际规则和国际环境知识，富有创造力的创新思考，以及负责开发出口市场并为出口市场服务。因此，规划好出口战略对于希望在竞争激烈的出口市场上取得成功的企业来说就显得尤为重要。下列出口战略很有帮助。

（1）观念和技术的发展应该与实务和服务一样重要。

（2）认识到日益激烈的全球竞争能促使公司实施成长战略。

（3）认识到技术的重要性。

（4）以增长的市场为基础发展长期战略——这鼓励主动型战略而不是被动型战略。

（5）努力开发新市场。

（6）不断研究和实践公司内部新变化，如致力于改善产品规格的新生产方法和纪律。

（7）开发新技术和新技术处理过程。

（8）发展浓厚的服务意识和培养与客户的感情。

（9）不断进行市场研究，并关注物流发展情况。

（10）雇用那些在产品与服务上有经验或受过相关教育的人，并且这些人具有前瞻性的国际贸易意识。

（11）随时关注世界市场变化。

（12）熟知各国文化。

4．What is importing（什么是进口）

Importing refers to the purchase of foreign products produced on the world market or those services provided by foreign companies. Any business that brings goods or services into China from other countries is involved in importing. If you intend to import goods, you need to give careful consideration to the practicalities, such as how to get the goods into the country, as well as the legal requirements. Suppliers around the world offer a wide variety of goods that could suit your business. You might be able to find lower-priced goods, which could give you a competitive edge, or new supplies that allow you to sell a completely different product. Just as when you buy on the world market, it's important to find good suppliers, make sure they offer what you want and negotiate favorable terms.

Like exporting, importing presents complications, such as managing long-distance relationships and organizing international transport and customs clearance. It's important to be sure that you are ready to import before you commit yourself.

进口贸易是将外国所生产或加工的商品（包括外国拥有的服务）购买后输入本国市场的贸易活动。任何从国外将货物或服务引入中国市场的行为都是进口。如果你计划进口，必须认真考虑如何才能做到最好，例如如何把货物运到国内，以及相关的法律要求。世界各地的供销商备有各种各样的货物，其中总有适合你的货物。因此，最好找到最便宜的货物，这样可以有竞争优势，或者找一个可以让你销售一种全新产品的供货商。也就是说，在世界市场上采购任何商品时，找一个好的供货商非常重要，记住对方向你报价时，尽可能与对方进行贸易磋商。

与出口一样，进口也很复杂，如怎样与客户保持长久的业务关系，组织好国际长途运输，报关清关，进口前一定要确保已经做好了准备。

5. Procedures of import transaction （进口贸易的程序）

So far, we have studied the general procedures of export transactions and dealt with different stages and steps from the exporter's perspective. Having been familiar with the process of the export business, we find it much easier to understand how an importer handles his import business. After all, the export and import trades are two sides of one coin. When handling an import trade, the trade conditions and terms you are striving for are sometimes the opposite of those you do in an export trade. The terms of delivery remain the same meaning regardless of whether you work as an importer or an exporter. A bill of lading is a bill of lading no matter who uses it for some practical purposes. The knowledge we have acquired from the previous sections is also applicable to import procedures. With the fundamental knowledge of export procedures we can grasp the essential points of import procedures easily and manage import trade effectively.

The general procedures of import transaction can be summarized as follows.

(1) To conduct market investigations.

(2) To formulate import plans for a certain commodity.

(3) To send enquiries to the prospective sellers overseas.

(4) To compare and analyze the offers or quotations received.

(5) To make counter-offers and decide on which offer is most beneficial.

(6) To sign the purchase contract.

(7) To apply to a bank for opening a letter of credit.

(8) To book shipping space or charter a vessel to receive the cargo, if the contract is in terms of FOB.

(9) To effect insurance with the insurance company upon receipt of shipping advice.

(10) To apply for inspection if necessary.

(11) To attend to customs formalities to clear the goods through the customs.

(12) To entrust forwarding agents with all the transport arrangements from the port to the end user's warehouse.

(13) To settle disputes (if any).

See Fig.2-3 Procedures of Import Transaction.

```
                        ┌─────────────────┐
                        │   Acceptance    │
              ┌─────────┴──────┬──────────┴──────────┐
    ┌─────────┴─────────┐                  ┌──────────┴──────────────┐
    │  Signing Contract │                  │ Applying Import License │
    └─────────┬─────────┘                  └──────────┬──────────────┘
              └─────────┬──────┬──────────┬──────────┘
                    ┌───┴──────┴──────────┴──┐
                    │      Opening L/C        │
                    └────────────┬────────────┘
                    ┌────────────┴────────────┐
                    │ Chartering, Space Booking│
                    └────────────┬────────────┘
                    ┌────────────┴────────────┐
              ┌─────┤        Delivery         ├─────┐
    ┌─────────┴─────────┐   ┌─────────┐   ┌────┴────────────┐
    │     Insurance     │   │Checking L/C│  │   Track Goods   │
    └─────────┬─────────┘   └─────┬────┘   └────┬────────────┘
              └──────────┬────────┴────────┬────┘
                    ┌────┴────────────┴────┐
                    │       Arrival         │
                    └──────────┬────────────┘
                    ┌──────────┴────────────┐
                    │ Declare and Discharge │
                    └──────────┬────────────┘
                    ┌──────────┴────────────┐
              ┌─────┤       Discharge       ├─────┐
    ┌─────────┴─────────┐              ┌──────────┴──────────┐
    │    Settlement     │              │  Claims, Adjustment │
    └─────────┬─────────┘              └──────────┬──────────┘
              └──────────┬──────────────┬────────┘
                    ┌────┴──────────────┴────┐
                    │      Conclusion         │
                    └─────────────────────────┘
```

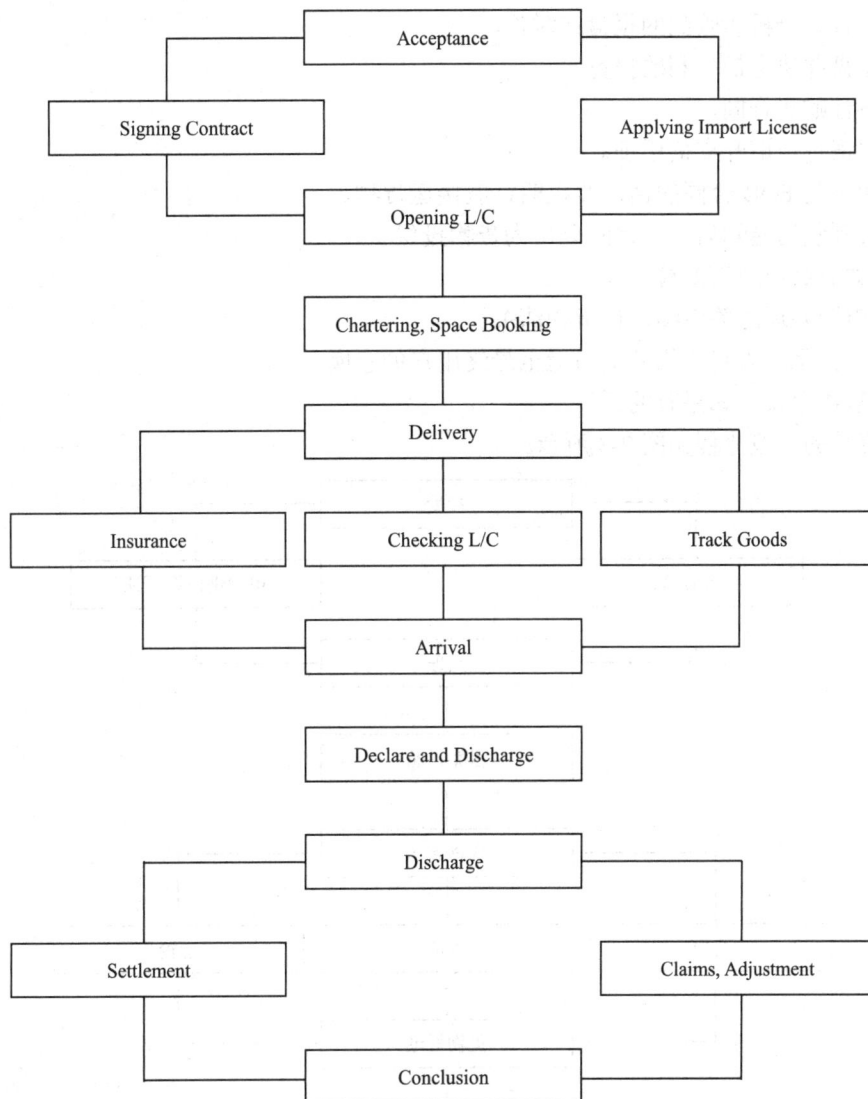

Fig.2-3 Procedures of Import Transaction

现在我们已经学习了出口贸易的一般程序,并从出口商的角度简要地了解了其各个阶段和步骤。因为已经熟悉了出口贸易的过程,我们就可以很容易理解进口商是如何进行进口交易的。毕竟,出口贸易和进口贸易是同一件事物的两个方面。在进口贸易中,进口商竭力争取的交易条件很可能与其在出口贸易中争取的条件恰恰相反。不管是作为出口商还是进口商,交货术语的意思是一样的。不管是谁出于什么样的目的,提单还是提单。我们前面获得的关于出口贸易的知识同样适用于进口贸易。具备了出口程序的基本知识后,我们很容易就可以掌握进口程序的要点,从而顺利地进行进口贸易。

进口贸易的一般程序如下。

(1)进行市场调查。

(2)制订某一商品的进口计划。

(3)向海外可能的卖方发出询盘。

（4）比较、分析所收到的报盘或时价。

（5）还盘并决定最有利的报盘。

（6）签订购买合同。

（7）向银行申请开立信用证。

（8）如果是 FOB 合同的话，要租船订舱接运货物。

（9）收到装运通知后，让保险公司为货物投保。

（10）如有必要申请商检。

（11）申请办理海关手续，让货物清关。

（12）委托承运人将货物从港口运至最终用户的仓库。

（13）解决争议（如果有的话）。

进口贸易的一般流程如图 2-3 所示。

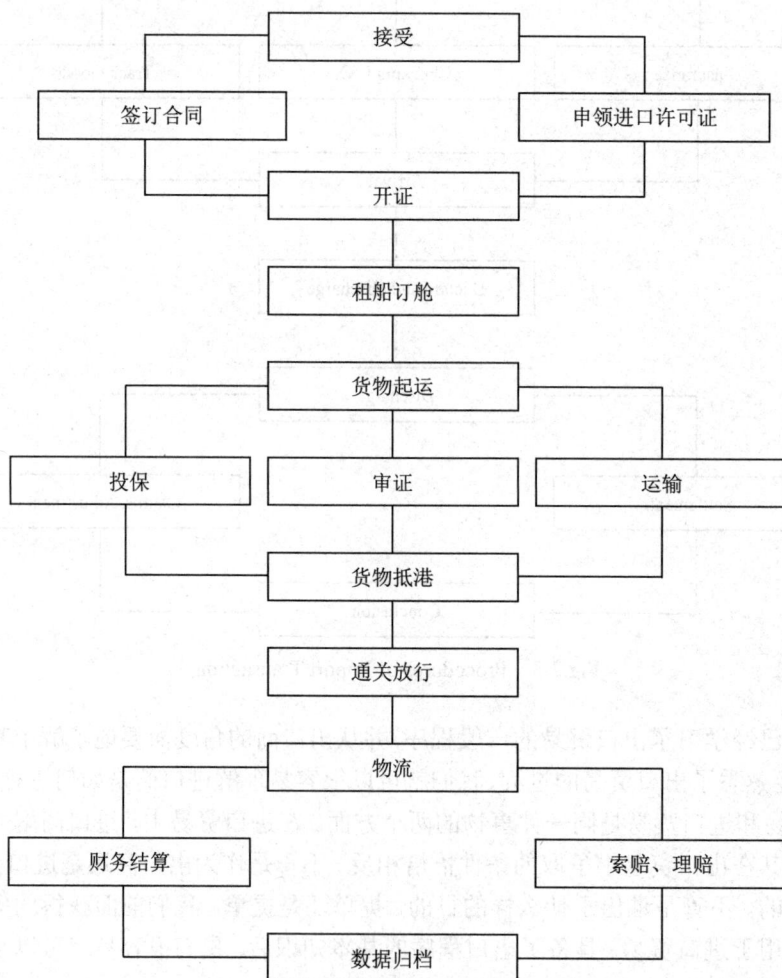

图 2-3　进口流程

6．Importing strategies（进口战略）

The following suggestions are very helpful when you are preparing to import goods from foreign countries into your domestic country.

(1) Importing should fit in with your overall business strategy. For example, importing low-cost goods might be part of a cost-control strategy, but you should be sure that this does not compromise your reputation for quality.

(2) It's worth thinking about how much time, money and effort you want to devote to setting up and managing your importing activities.

(3) You also need to decide how much involvement you want to have in the import process.

(4) Importing requires special skills and extra resources. Before you start importing, you should assess whether you have the right skills and resources and decide how to cope with any shortcomings.

(5) Strive to find new markets and to open up new sales opportunities.

(6) Keeping continuously informed of your financial conditions. If your finances are limited, you may prefer to deal with suppliers who offer credit. On the other hand, agreeing to pay promptly could help you negotiate a competitive price.

(7) Understanding your own strengths and weaknesses, and what your supplier's priorities are, helps you negotiate the best deal.

(8) Developing empathy with the suppliers.

(9) Undertaking continuous market research and being focused on logistics.

(10) Employ personnel who are experienced/educated in the products/services and have forward thinking international trade ideologies.

(11) Continuously reviewing the world market changes.

(12) Developing a profound understanding of world cultures.

当你准备从国外进口商品到国内销售时，下列建议会有帮助。

（1）进口业务必须符合整个发展战略要求。例如，进口低价商品可能是成本控制的一部分，但是，切记不能因此而牺牲商品质量。

（2）应该想清楚需要付出多少时间、金钱和努力才能建立并很好地经营进口业务。

（3）必须清楚知道整个进口过程。

（4）从事进口业务需要具备特殊技能与丰富资源，因此，进口货物前，应该明白你是否已经具备这些技能与资源，并知道如何处理所有问题。

（5）不断开发新市场。

（6）随时掌握公司财务状况。如果公司有资金困难，你可以与能够给予赊账的供应商进行交易，换句话说，同意即期付款可以赢得具有竞争力的价格。

（7）知道自己的优势与弱势，了解供应商的实际情况，可以帮助你赢得最好的进口业务。

（8）不断发展与客户的感情。

（9）不断进行市场研究，并关注物流发展情况。

（10）雇用那些在产品与服务上有经验或受过相关教育的人，并且这些人具有前瞻性的国际贸易意识。

（11）随时关注世界市场变化。

（12）熟悉各国文化。

7. Parties involved in export and import transaction（进出口贸易所涉及的当事人）

The parties who are involved in export and import transactions are numerous and can be described in various ways. The basic parties are the buyer who purchases the goods and the seller who provides the goods. The main parties involved in an export and import transaction are as follows:

(1) The exporters.

(2) The shipping agents at the port or airport of loading.

(3) The railway (in some cases) in the exporter's country.

(4) The road hauler (in some cases) in the exporter's country.

(5) The port authority.

(6) The shipping company (for sea freight).

(7) The airline (for air freight).

(8) The insurance company or brokers.

(9) The exporter's bank.

(10) The importer's bank.

(11) The railways (in some cases) in the importer's country.

(12) The road haulier (in some cases) in the importer's country.

(13) The shipping agents at the port or airport of unloading.

(14) The importers.

进出口贸易活动中所涉及的当事人有许多，最主要的有货物买方和货物卖方。主要涉及的当事人如下。

（1）出口商。

（2）装运港或机场的运输经纪人。

（3）出口商所在国家的铁路部门（在一些情况下）。

（4）出口商所在国家的陆路承运人（在一些情况下）。

（5）港口当局。

（6）船务公司（对海洋运输）。

（7）航空公司（对航空运输）。

（8）保险公司或经纪人。

（9）出口商银行。

（10）进口商银行。

（11）进口商所在国家的铁路部门（在一些情况下）。

（12）进口商所在国家的陆路承运人（在一些情况下）。

（13）装卸港或机场的运输经纪人。

（14）进口商。

8. Specialists involved in export and import transactions（出口和进口贸易所涉及的专业人员）

Many specialists may be involved in export and import transactions, including:

(1) A shipping agent and /or foreign forwarder (forwarding agent) will take responsibility for the documentation and arrange for the goods to be shipped by air, sea, rail or road. These services may be carried out by the supplier's own export department, if they have the expertise.

(2) Airlines, shipping lines, railway companies or haulage contractors will actually transport the goods.

(3) Both the importer's and exporter's banks will be involved in arranging payments if a letter of credit or bill of exchange is used.

(4) Customs and Excise officers may need to examine the goods, check import or export licensing and charge duty and /or VAT.

(5) A chamber of commerce may need to issue a certificate of origin, if this is required by the importer's country.

(6) An insurance company insures goods in transit.

(7) A lawyer may be involved if a special contract has to be drawn up.

出口和进口贸易中要涉及很多专业人员，包括以下方面。

（1）运输经纪人或货物转运商负责制单并安排货物的空运、海运、铁路运输或公路运输。如果有专门人才的话，这些服务将由供货商自己的出口部门实施。

（2）航空公司、船运公司、铁路公司或货物承运人实际运输货物。

（3）如果进出口贸易使用信用证或汇票来支付，则涉及进口商银行和出口商银行。

（4）海关和征税官员要检查货物和核查进出口许可证，征收关税和/或增值税。

（5）如果进口国要求，商会将颁发原产地说明书。

（6）保险公司为运输中的货物保险。

（7）如果要起草特殊合同的话，还需要律师。

9. Basic documents needed in export and import transactions（进出口贸易所需的主要单证）

An import/export transaction usually requires a lot of complicated documents because it is difficult to make many different arrangements when one firm is dealing with another on the other side of the world. The number and type of documents needed depend on the specific requirements of the exporter and importer. Generally, the documents needed include:

(1) Bill of Lading

(2) Commercial Invoice

(3) Pro Forma Invoice

(4) Consular Invoice

(5) Packing List

(6) Weight Memo

(7) Certificate of Inspection

(8) Certificate of Origin

(9) Insurance Policy (Certificate)

(10) Sales Contract

(11) Sales Confirmation

进出口贸易通常需要许多复杂的单证。因为在交易中，要做出很多安排，而这些安排由于同另外一国打交道而变得复杂。所需要单证的数量和种类取决于进口商和出口商的具体要求。一般来说，所需要的单证包括以下方面。

（1）提单。

（2）商业发票。

（3）形式发票。

（4）领事发票。

（5）装箱单。

（6）重量单。

（7）检验证书。

（8）原产地证书。

（9）保险凭证（合同）。

（10）销售合同。

（11）销售确认书。

Many of these documents can be replaced with computerized procedures. Standard "aligned" export documents are often used, where the required information is entered on a "master" document, and then photocopied to produce all the required documents.

以上很多单证可用计算机化的过程取而代之，标准"统一"的出口单证经常使用。在这种单证中，把所需要的信息输入"母"单证中，再复印成所有所需要的单证。

10．Basic characteristics of digital trade process（数字贸易流程的主要特点）

The differences between digital trade processes and traditional trade processes are mainly reflected in the following aspects:

The trading methods and platforms differ. Digital trading activities mainly rely on the "Internet+" e-commerce platform and online markets to complete trading activities. Traditional trade activities rely on offline physical storefronts, especially exhibitions and other venues (such as trade fairs) for displaying goods. The digital trade e-commerce platform provides a virtual display space, allowing trade customers to browse anytime and anywhere so as to place orders to purchase goods online. In traditional trade processes, buyers and sellers need to negotiate face-to-face, negotiate various transaction terms. In addition, the digital trade transaction process has been fully digitized, including online inquiries, quotations, contract signing, payments, etc. The traditional transaction process involves various paper documents and supporting materials (such as commercial invoices, certificates of origin, packing lists, bills of lading), and usually requires a fixed trading venue.

数字贸易流程与传统贸易流程的不同主要体现在以下几个方面：

交易方式与平台不同。数字贸易活动主要是依靠"互联网"电子商务平台以及在线市场等完成交易活动。传统的国际贸易活动则依赖于线下实体店面，特别是展览等场所（如交易会）进行商品展示。数字贸易电子商务平台提供了虚拟的展示空间，使得贸易客户可以进行随时随地的浏览，并且在线上下单购买商品。而传统贸易流程的买卖双方需要面对面地进行谈判，磋商、协商各种交易条件。另外，数字贸易交易流程实现全面电子化，包括在线询盘、报价、合同签订、支付等。而传统交易流程涉及多种纸质单据和证明材料（如商业发票、原产地证书、装箱单、提单等，且通常传统交易流程需要在固定的交易场所进行。

From the perspective of transaction efficiency and cost, the transaction process involved in digital trade activities is simplified, and customers can quickly place orders, make online payments, and cross-border logistics delivery on e-commerce platforms. Therefore, it greatly improves the efficiency of the transaction process in digital trade activities and reduces the cost of digital transactions. At the same time, digital trade can also conduct data analysis through the Internet and artificial intelligence to achieve precise trade marketing and further improve the trade sales effect. The transaction process involved in traditional international trade is complex and cumbersome, and therefore time-consuming. The process mainly includes multiple links such as inquiry, quotation, sample confirmation, contract signing, deposit payment, production arrangement, customs declaration and shipment. These links increase the time and operational costs of traditional international trade.

从交易效率与成本的视角看，数字贸易活动所涉及的交易流程简单化，客户可以在电商平台实现快速下单、进行在线支付和跨境物流配送。因此，很大程度上提高了数字贸易活动的交易过程效率，降低了数字交易成本。同时，数字贸易还可以通过互联网和人工智能进行数据分析，实现精准贸易营销，进一步提高贸易销售效果。而传统国际贸易所涉及的交易过程烦琐，因此，耗时较长，其流程主要包括询盘、报价、样品确认、签订合同、支付定金、生产安排、报关发货等多个环节。这些环节增加了传统国际贸易的时间成本和物力成本。

Section Two　Business Negotiation（交易的磋商）

Negotiation is a voluntary process of giving and taking where both parties amend their offers and modify their expectations so as to come closer to each other and they can quit at any time. It is an essential part of each transaction. It can be a very trying process that is full of confrontation and concession. For the most part, it comes to the interaction between two sides with a common goal but divergent methods. These methods must be negotiated to the satisfaction of both parties. Business negotiations proceed through four stages.

(1) Non-task sounding.

(2) Task-related exchange of information.

(3) Persuasion.

(4) Concessions and agreement.

Despite the consistency of this process across cultures, the content and duration of the four stages differ substantially between the two cultures.

谈判是一个自发给予和获取的过程，有关双方为了接近对方而调整其报价和期望值，甚至随时可以退出。谈判是每一笔交易的核心，它是非常艰辛的过程，充满了冲突与妥协。多数情况下，双方共同的目的和不同的交易方式都要经过谈判来达成。谈判中所采取的种种方法必须获得双方认可。商务谈判分为以下四个阶段。

（1）开局前的试探。

（2）交换与谈判目标有关的信息。

（3）说服。

（4）让步与同意。

尽管各国的谈判阶段都比较一致，但这四个阶段的具体内容和持续时间在各国谈判中表现各不相同。

If a foreign company is interested in buying the exporter's products, negotiations should be organized. Business negotiations play a very important role in the conclusion and implementation of a sales contract. It has a great bearing on the economic interests of the parties concerned. No matter how the negotiations are conducted, they generally consist of the following links: enquiry, offer, counter-offer, acceptance and the conclusion of a sales contract. Of these, offer and acceptance are two indispensable steps for reaching an agreement and concluding a contract. Negotiations work wonders. This is particularly so in international business since it is mostly through negotiations that exporters and importers bridge their differences and reach a fair and mutually satisfactory deal.

In order to improve the success rate of the transaction, the following preparations should be made before the business negotiation.

(1) Arrange competent trade negotiation personnel.

(2) Select a target market.

(3) Select a transaction object.

(4) Work out an import and export management plan.

What should be negotiated while negotiating includes all the terms based on which the contract is going to be concluded: the name of the commodity, quality or specifications, quantity, packing, price, shipment, insurance, payment, inspection, claims, arbitration, force majeure, etc. Among all these terms, the name of the commodity, quality or specifications, quantity, packing, price, shipment, payment are usually considered as the essential terms in a transaction. The rest are general transaction terms, which can be printed on the back of the contract.

如果外国公司有兴趣购买出口商的产品，就应安排磋商。交易的磋商在销售合同的签订及以后的履行中起着重要的作用，它与交易双方的经济利益密切相关。不管磋商以什么方式开始，它通常包括下列几个环节：询盘、发盘、还盘、接受和签订销售合同。其中，发盘和接受是达成协议和签订合同不可缺少的环节。谈判出奇迹，在国际贸易中更是如此，因为出口商和进口商要消除分歧、达成一项公平和相互满意的交易，大多是通过谈判才能做到的。

为了提高交易的成功率，在交易磋商开始前应该做好以下几个方面的准备工作。

（1）配备交易治谈人员。

（2）选择目标市场。

（3）选择交易对象。

（4）制订进出口商品经营方案。

交易磋商的内容涉及拟签订合同中的各项条款，包括品名、品质或规格、数量、包装、价格、运输、保险、支付、商检、索赔、仲裁和不可抗力等。其中品名、品质或规格、数量、包装、价格、运输、支付等一般被认为是交易的主要条件。而其他条件，如商检、索赔、仲裁和不可抗力等常常被事先印在合同的背面。

1. Market research（市场调研）

The most difficult part of exporting is taking the first step. Any exporter who wants to sell their products in foreign markets must first conduct extensive market research. Market research is a process of gathering and analyzing data about a specific market for a particular product. In the broadest terms, market research is the process of investigating a market in order to find out the sales prospects for a particular product or group of products, and how to achieve success with that product or group of products. Export market research, in particular, is a study of a given market abroad to determine the needs of that market and the methods by which the products can be supplied. The exporter needs to know which foreign companies are likely to use his products or might be interested in marketing and distributing the products in their country. He must think about whether there is a potential for making a profit. He must examine the market structures and general economic conditions in those places. If the economy is in a recession, the demand for all products usually declines. So the exporter's products might not sell well at such times.

Market research can be carried out either before or after an attempt has been made to penetrate a market. It can be conducted by, or for, an individual company, a group of companies or a government agency. It may be concerned with physical products or with services, such as after-sale services. Generally, there are two kinds of research: desk research and field research. Desk research is just as demanding as field research. It requires just as much professional knowledge, experience, and skill. It is often a tedious process, and can take a long time to carry out as well. It requires patience, ingenuity and persistence.

对出口贸易来说，最困难的是迈出第一步。任何一个想把货物销售到国外的出口商都必须首先做大量的市场调研，市场调研是指对某一产品在某一特定市场条件下进行调研。从广义上讲，市场调研是针对一个市场进行的调查过程，目的在于为某个特定产品或一系列产品寻求潜在市场及促其成功的营销方式。具体到出口贸易的市场调研，它指的是对国外某一特定市场的调查研究，以确定其市场需求以及供给的方式。出口商必须了解有哪些国外的公司可能使用其产品，有哪些公司对在它们所在国销售和分销其产品感兴趣。出口商必须考虑是否有赚取利润的可能性。其必须调查那些国家的市场结构和总的经济形势。如果经济不景气，对产品的需求量通常会下降。那么，此时出口商的产品就会受到影响。

市场调研既可以在商品进入市场前进行，也可以在商品进入市场后展开。单个公司、多个公司集团或某个政府机构都可以开展市场调研或成为市场调研的对象。市场调研对象既可以是物质产品，也可以是服务类产品，如售后服务。一般来说，市场调研可以分为两种：文案调研和实地调研。文案调研和实地调研一样，对市场调研人员要求很高。与做实地调查一样，文案调研人员也要具备相关的专业知识、实践和技能。文案调研经常是一个枯燥的过程，而且需要很长时间来开展。所以，调研人员要有耐心、创造力及恒心。

2. Enquiry（询盘）

An enquiry is a request for business information, such as price lists, catalogues, samples, and details regarding the goods or trade terms. It can be made by either the importer or the exporter. On receiving an enquiry, it is standard practice for the exporter to respond promptly. In foreign trade, enquiries are usually made by the buyers without engagement to get information about the goods to be ordered, such as price, catalogue, delivery date and other terms. Enquiries may be either dispatched by mail, email, telex, fax, or handed to the suppliers through personal contact. So, that is to say an enquiry (enquiry) is, in fact, a request for information on price, trade terms, etc. An importer may send out an enquiry to an exporter, inviting a quotation or an offer for the goods he wishes to buy or simply asking for some general information about these goods.

According to content or purpose, an enquiry may be either general or specific. If the importer wants to have general information about the products or commodities, which the exporter is in a position to supply, they may request catalogs, brochures, price lists, and samples. This is a general enquiry. If the importer intends to purchase a certain product or commodity, he may ask the exporter to make an offer or a quotation on this product. This kind of enquiry is called a specific enquiry.

There are two forms of enquiry: oral and written. For the written enquiry, there will be fax, telex, email, letters and enquiry sheet. Nowadays, with the fast development, telex is not so much used, and the cable is no longer utilized. An enquiry is an exploratory business contact, so there is no legal binding for both the buyer and the seller. As per the customary practice, the enquiree party should answer the coming enquiry at the time when he receives it.

询盘是要求提供有关交易的信息，如商品的价格单、目录、样品以及贸易条件。询盘可由进口商或出口商发出。收到询盘以后，作为惯例卖方应立即回复以便开始交易磋商。在对外贸易中，询盘通常由买方提出，不受约束，主要是了解进口商品的基本信息，如价格、目录、交货期等交易条款。因此，询盘信事实上就是要求获得有关价格和贸易条款的信函。进口商向出口商发出询盘信，希望得到想要购买商品的报价或报盘，但有时只是了解商品的基本信息。

根据内容或目的，询盘信可以分为一般询盘信和具体询盘信。如果进口商想要了解出口商可以供货的某种产品或商品的一般信息，可以要求出口商寄给其商品目录、产品宣传册、价目表和样品，这就是一般询盘信。如果进口商想要购买某种产品或商品，会要求出口商报盘或报价，这类询盘信被称为具体询盘信。

询盘有两种形式：口头询盘和书面询盘。如果是书面形式的询盘，常常有传真、电传、电子邮件、书信和询价单。随着社会的发展，电传已经很少用，而电报也已经不用了。询盘属于试探性的业务联系，对于买卖双方都无法律约束力。但是，按照商业习惯，当被询盘一方接到询盘后，应尽快予以回复。

Sample of Enquiry（询盘实例）

Penang, June 20th, 2019

Dear Sirs,

We are in the market for melon seeds of the first and second grades, and would appreciate it if you could let us have your offers with some representative samples by airmail. When offering the seeds, please state the earliest possible time of shipment and quantity available.

Yours faithfully,

敬启者：

我方拟购甲、乙级瓜子，请予报盘，并请航邮具有代表性的样品为感。报价时，请说明最早装运期及可供量。

……启

2019 年 6 月 20 日

3. Offer and counter-offer（发盘和还盘）

1) Offer（发盘）

An offer is a proposal made by sellers to buyers in order to enter into a contract. In other words, it refers to trading terms put forward by offerors to offerees, on which the offerors are willing to conclude business with the offerees. An offer can be made by a seller, called a selling offer; it can also be made by a buyer, called a buying offer or bid. In practice, most offers are made by the seller. It becomes effective when it reaches the offeree. It may be withdrawn if the withdrawal reaches the offeree before or at the same time as the offer even if it is irrevocable. Until a contract is concluded an offer may be revoked if the revocation reaches the offeree before he has dispatched an acceptance. However, an offer cannot be revoked: ① if it indicates, whether by stating a fixed time for acceptance or otherwise, that it is irrevocable; ② if it was reasonable for the offeree to rely on the offer as being irrevocable and the offeree has acted in reliance on the offer. An offer, even if it is irrevocable, is terminated when a rejection reaches the offeror.

There are two kinds of offers, one is the firm offer, the other is a non-firm offer. A reply to an offer which purports to be an acceptance but contains additions, limitations or other modifications is a rejection of the offer and constitutes a counter offer.

As to in which conditions an offer can be made, there are clear stipulations in the United Nations Convention on Contracts for the International Sale of Goods: Article 14 (1), A proposal for concluding a contract addressed to one or more specific persons constitutes an offer if it is sufficiently definite and indicates the intention of the offeror to be bound in case of acceptance. A proposal is sufficiently definite if it indicates the goods and expressly or implicitly fixes or makes provision for determining the quantity and the price. Article 14 (2), A proposal other than one addressed to one or more specific persons is to be considered merely as an invitation to make offers, unless the contrary is clearly indicated by the person making the proposal.

According to the United Nations Convention on Contracts for the International Sale of Goods, a lawful offer should include the following parts.

(1) There must be a specified offeree.

(2) All the contents in the offer should be very clear.

(3) In the offer, the binding terms of the transaction for both parties should be clearly expressed.

(4) The offeree should receive the offer within its validity.

发盘是卖方向买方提出的签订合同的建议。换句话说，它指的是发盘人向受盘人提出的交易条件。按此条件，发盘人愿意与受盘人进行交易。发盘可以是卖方的行为，称为售货发盘；也可以是买方的行为，称为购货发盘或递盘。在实际业务中，一般以卖方的发盘居多。发盘于送达受盘人时生效。如果撤回通知于发盘送达受盘人之前或同时，那么这项发盘即使是不可撤销的，也可以撤回。在未订立合同之前，如果撤销通知于受盘人发出接受通知之前送达受盘人，发盘可以撤销。但在下列情况下，发价不得撤销：① 发价写明接受发价的期限或以其他方式表示发价是不可撤销的；② 被发盘人有理由信赖该项发盘是不可撤销的，而且被发盘人已本着对该项发价的信赖行事。一旦发盘，即使是不可撤销的，于拒绝通知送达发盘人时终止。

发盘有两种：一种是实盘，另一种是虚盘。对发盘表示接受但载有添加、限制或其他更改的答复，即为拒绝该项发盘并构成还盘。

关于发盘的构成条件，《联合国国际货物销售合同公约》有明确的说明：第 14 条（1）款，向一个或一个以上特定的人提出的订立合同的建议，如果十分确定并且表明发价人在得到接受时承受约束的意旨，即构成发价。一个建议如果写明货物并且明示或暗示地规定数量和价格或规定如何确定数量和价格，即为十分确定；第 14 条（2）款，非向一个或一个以上特定的人提出的建议，仅应视为邀请做出发价，除非提出建议的人明确地表示相反的意向。

根据《联合国国际货物销售合同公约》的规定，一个有效的发盘应包括以下内容。

（1）发盘要有特定的受盘人。

（2）发盘内容必须十分确定。

（3）发盘必须表明承受约束的意旨。

（4）发盘必须在有效期内送达受盘人。

The validity period of an offer refers to the binding time of the offeror over the offeree, which is the time limit for the offeree to accept. When the offeree accepts the offer within its validity, the offeror should assume all the responsibilities in the contract stipulated by the offeror; if the offeree does not accept the offer within its validity, the offeror needn't bear any obligations stated in the contract. So the time validity of an offer is a binding condition for the buyer and the seller. There is time validity for any offer; some have specific and clear expressions for time validity, others are not so clear. The stipulations for expressing time validity can be either firm or non-firm. There are ways for stipulating firm offer:

(1) Stipulating the latest acceptance time, such as: The offer is subject to your reply reaching here by March 20, 2019.

(2) Stipulating a period of acceptance time, such as: The offer is valid/open/effective for 5 days.

Because of the time differences in the world, there should be a very clear stipulation for the time limitation regarding the applicable time zone. In practice, the offeror prefers to adopt his end.

The withdrawal of an offer refers to the fact that before the offer reaches the offeree, which is to say before it begins to come into effect, the offeror withdraws it. As to when a withdrawal of an offer can be effected, there are stipulations in the United Nations Convention on Contracts for the International Sale of Goods: Article 15(1): An offer becomes effective when it reaches the offeree. Article 15(2): An offer, even if it is irrevocable, may be withdrawn if the withdrawal reaches the offeree before or at the same time as the offer.

发盘的有效期是指发盘对发盘人约束的期限，也是受盘人接受发盘的期限。受盘人在有效期内接受发盘，发盘人就要承担按发盘条件与之订立合同的责任；而受盘人超过有效期做出的接受无效，发盘人不必承担按发盘条件与之订立合同的义务。因此，发盘的有效期是对双方的一种限制，也是对双方的一种保障。凡是发盘都有有效期，有的发盘对有效期做出明确规定，也有的不做明确规定。有效期有以下两种规定方法：

（1）规定最迟接受期限，例如：发盘限 2019 年 3 月 20 日回复至此。

（2）规定一段接受时间，例如：发盘 5 天有效。

由于不同国家之间往往有时差，因此发盘中应明确以何方时间为准。实际业务中，发盘人大多规定以其所在地时间为准。

发盘的撤回是指一项发盘在尚未送达受盘人之前，即尚未生效之前，由发盘人将其取消。关于何时可以撤回发盘，《联合国国际货物销售合同公约》第 15 条（1）款规定：发价于送达被发价人时生效；第 15 条（2）款规定：一项发盘，即使是不可撤销的，得予撤回，如果撤回的通知于发盘送达受盘人之前或同时到达受盘人。

The revocation of an offer refers to the fact that when the offer reaches the offeree, that is to say, it begins to come into effect, the offeror revokes the offer. As to the revocation of an offer, each country has different expressions in law. We should pay attention to these differences. Regarding when a revocation of an offer can be effected, there are stipulations in the United Nations Convention on Contracts for the International Sale of Goods: Article 16 (1): Until a contract is concluded an offer may be revoked if the revocation reaches the offeree before they have dispatched an acceptance. Article 16 (2): However, an offer cannot be revoked: a. if it indicates, whether by stating a fixed time for acceptance or otherwise, that it is irrevocable; or b. if it was reasonable for the offeree to rely on the offer as being irrevocable and the offeree has acted in reliance on the offer. According to the Convention we can infer the information that in most cases an offer cannot be revoked. So when we make offers we should take care in order to avoid getting into disputes.

发盘的撤销是指一项发盘在已经送达受盘人之后，即开始生效之后，由发盘人将其取消。对于发盘的撤销，各国的法律规定存在较大差异。我们一定要注意这些不同之处。关于何时可以撤销发盘，《联合国国际货物销售合同公约》在第 16 条中做了规定：（1）在未订立合同之前，发盘得予撤销，如果撤销通知于被发盘人发出接受通知之前送达被发盘人。（2）但在下列情况下，发盘不得撤销：a. 发盘写明接受发盘的期限或以其他方式表示发盘是不可撤销的；或 b. 被发盘人有理由信赖该项发盘是不可撤销的，而且被发盘人已本着对该项发盘的信赖行事。由此规定可见，发盘在大多数情况下是不可撤销的，因此我们在对外发盘时要采取谨慎的态度，以免引起纠纷。

As per the termination of an offer, the United Nations Convention on Contracts for the International Sale of Goods states in Article 17: An offer, even if it is irrevocable, is terminated when a rejection reaches the offeror. In addition, the following can also be regarded as termination of an offer:

(1) The offeree has already made a counter-offer.

(2) The offer has been lawfully withdrawn or revoked by the offeror.

(3) The offer has expired.

(4) A force majeure event occurs, such as war, government prohibition, incapacitation of the party, bankruptcy or death.

有关发盘失效的问题，《联合国国际货物销售合同公约》第17条规定：一项发盘，即使是不可撤销的，于拒绝通知送达发盘人时终止。除此之外，下列情况也可造成发盘的失效：

（1）受盘人做出还盘。

（2）发盘人依法撤回或撤销发盘。

（3）发盘过了有效期。

（4）出现人力不可抗拒的意外事故或事件，如战争、政府禁令、当事人丧失行为能力或破产、死亡等。

2) Counter-offer（还盘）

A counter-offer means that the offeree doesn't accept the offer wholly and puts forward some additions, modifications, limitations, etc. to the basic terms and conditions contained in the offer. Once a counter is made, the original offer made by the offeror loses its effectiveness.

Article 19 of the United Nations Convention on Contracts for the International Sale of Goods stipulates:

(1) A reply to an offer which purports to be an acceptance but contains additions, limitations or other modifications is a rejection of the offer and constitutes a counter-offer.

(2) However, a reply to an offer which purports to be an acceptance but contains additional or different terms that do not materially alter the terms of the offer constitutes an acceptance, unless the offeror, without undue delay, objects orally to the discrepancy or dispatches a notice to that effect. If the offeror does not object, the terms of the contract are the terms of the offer with the modifications contained in the acceptance.

(3) Additional or different terms relating, among other things, to the price, payment, quality and quantity of the goods, place and time of delivery, extent of one party's liability to the other or the settlement of disputes are considered to alter the terms of the offer materially.

还盘是指受盘人不能完全接受发盘的内容，提出了一些补充、修改、限制等基本条款和条件。一经还盘，原发盘即失效。

《联合国国际货物销售合同公约》第19条对还盘的规定如下：

（1）包含了附加条件、限制和其他修改是对发盘的拒绝，构成了还盘。

（2）但是，对发盘表示接受但附有添加或不同条件的答复，如所附的添加或不同条件在实质上并不变更该项发盘的条件，除发盘人在未不当迟延的期间内以口头或书面通知反对期间的差异外，仍构成接受。如果发盘人不做出这种反对，合同的条件就以该项发盘的条件以及接受通知内所附的更改为准。

（3）有关货物价格、付款、货物质量和数量、交货地点和时间、一方当事人对另一方当事人的赔偿责任范围或解决争端等的添加或不同条件，均视为在实质上变更发盘的条件。

Sample of offer（发盘实例）

Your Ref: 216 BW

Our Ref: ST/GW

5th May, 2019

China National Import & Export Corp.

Beijing

China

Dear Sirs,

We have recently received a number of enquiries for your light-weight raincoats and have good reasons to believe that we could place regular orders with you if your prices are competitive.

From the description in your catalogue we learn that your "D.D." range is the one most suitable for these clients and we would be glad if you would send us your quotation for men's and women's coats, in both small and medium size, delivered on CIF Kuwait basis. If your prices are reasonable, we should place a first order for 400 raincoats, namely 100 raincoats each of the four qualities. Shipment would be required within four weeks of order.

We would particularly stress the importance of price since the principal market here is for mass-produced goods at popular prices.

Yours sincerely,

Abdullah Samith & Co.

Manager

中国进出口公司

先生：

我们最近收到许多来信，要求购买你们的薄型雨衣。假如你们的价格是有竞争性的，我们有理由相信能经常向你们订购。

根据你们的目录说明，我们得知"D.D."系列雨衣是最适合这些客户的。如你方能寄男式和女式雨衣的报价，我们将非常高兴。两者的尺码都要小号及中号，以 CIF 科威特交货。如价格合适，我们首批将订购 400 件，即 4 种各 100 件。订货后须在四星期内装运。

我们要特别强调价格的重要性，因为这里的主要市场是那些大批量生产而价格又比较大众化的产品。

Abdullah Samith & Co.

经　　理

2019 年 5 月 5 日

Reply to the offer（回复发盘）

Messrs. Abdullah Samith & Co.

P. O. Box No. 2231

Kuwait

Dear Sirs,

Thank you for your letter of 5 May. We are glad to learn of the enquiries you have had from your customers for our raincoats. Our "D.D." range is particularly suitable for warm climates, and in recent years we have supplied this range to dealers in several tropical countries, from many of whom we have already had repeated orders. This range is popular not only because it is light in weight, but also because the material used has been specially treated to prevent excessive condensation on the inside surface.

For the quantities you mentioned in your letter we are pleased to quote as follows:

"D.D." Raincoats

100 men's medium	at USD14.50	USD 1 450
100 men's small	at USD14.00	USD 1 400
100 women's medium	at USD13.20	USD 1 320
100 women's small	at USD12.70	USD 1 270

CIF Kuwait USD 5, 440

Payment: By irrevocable L/C at sight

Shipment: Within three to four weeks upon receipt of the L/C.

This offer is subject to our final confirmation. You may be interested in our other products and enclose some pamphlets for your reference.

We are awaiting your early orders.

Yours sincerely,

×××

先生：

感谢你方 5 月 5 日来信。我们很高兴得悉你方收到了客户要购买我们雨衣的一些询价。我们的"D.D."系列雨衣特别适合暖热的气候，而且在过去几年中，已经供应给几个热带国家的商人。他们中的许多人已经重复订购，有些复订不止一次。这个商品之所以受到欢迎不只因为重量轻，而且也因为所用原料已经过特殊处理，可以防止在衬里上凝结过多的水汽。

按你方信中所说的数量，我们报价如下：

"D.D." 雨衣

100 件男式中号	每件 USD14.50	USD1 450
100 件男式小号	每件 USD14.00	USD1 400
100 件女式中号	每件 USD13.20	USD1 320
100 件女式小号	每件 USD12.70	USD1 270

CIF 科威特净价 USD5 440

支付条款：即期不可撤销信用证

装运条款：收到信用证后 3～4 星期。

本报价以我方最后确认为准。我们认为你方可能对我们的其他产品也有兴趣，今附上一些说明小册子和供你方客户参考的推销说明书。

等候你方订单。

Sample of counter-offer（还盘实例）

Messrs. Wright & Co.

2901 Thames House

London E. C. 3

England

Dear Sirs,

We wish to thank you for your letter of the 10 June offering us 3,000 kg of Walnut Meat at USD50.00 per kilogram.

We regret to say that we find your price appears uncompetitive, and we believe we'll have a hard time convincing our clients at your price.

Furthermore, there's keen competition from supplies in South Korea and Thailand. You can't very well ignore that. Should you reduce your price by 5%, we might come to business.

In view of our long-standing business relationship, we submit this counter-offer. As the market is declining, we hope you will consider our counter-offer most favorable and fax us as soon as possible.

Yours faithfully,

先生：

感谢你方 6 月 10 日函，给我方 3 000 千克核桃仁，50 美元/千克。

我们抱歉地奉告，贵方价格偏高。我们认为很难说服客户接受你方的价格。况且，来自韩国和泰国的供应商的竞争是很激烈的。你方不能忽视这一点。如你方能减价 5%，也许能达成交易。

只是鉴于双方长期的业务关系，我们才给予上述还盘。市价正在下跌，希望你方采取积极态度加以考虑，并早日来电回复我方的还盘。

……启

4．Acceptance（接受）

Acceptance is a statement made by or other conduct of the offeree indicating unconditional consent to an offer. A contract is concluded once the offer is accepted.

An acceptance of an offer becomes effective at the moment the indication of assent reaches the offeror. An acceptance is not effective if the indication of assent does not reach the offeror within the time fixed by the offeror or, if no time is fixed, within a reasonable time, due account being taken of the circumstances of the transaction, including the rapidity of the means of communication employed by the offeror.

As to acceptance, the United Nations Convention on Contracts for the International Sale of Goods stipulates Article 18:

(1) A statement made by or other conduct of the offeree indicating assent to an offer is an acceptance. Silence or inactivity does not in itself amount to acceptance.

(2) An acceptance of an offer becomes effective at the moment the indication of assent reaches the offeror. An acceptance is not effective if the indication of assent does not reach the offeror within the time fixed by the offeror or, if no time is fixed, within a reasonable time, due account being taken of the circumstances of the transaction, including the rapidity of the means of communication employed by the offeror. An oral offer must be accepted immediately unless the circumstances indicate otherwise.

(3) However, if, by virtue of the offer or as a result of practices which the parties have established between themselves or of usage, the offeree may indicate assent by performing an act, such as one relating to the dispatch of the goods or payment of the price, without notice to the offeror, the acceptance is effective at the moment the act is performed, provided that the act is performed within the period of time laid down in the preceding paragraph.

接受是指受盘人声明或做出其他行为表示无条件同意一项发盘。发盘接受以后，合同随即达成。

受盘人声明或做出其他行为表示同意一项发盘，即接受，缄默或不行动本身不等于接受。发盘人收到受盘人表示接受发盘的通知书时，发盘开始生效。如果表示同意的通知书在发盘人所规定的时间内，如未规定时间，在一段合理的时间内，未曾送达发盘人，接受就无效，但须适当地考虑到交易的情况，包括发盘人所使用的通信方法的迅速程度。

关于接受，《联合国国际货物销售合同公约》第 18 条规定：（1）被发价人声明或做出其他行为表示同意一项发价，即接受。（2）接受发价于表示同意的通知送达发价人时生效。如果表示同意的通知在发价人所规定的时间内，如为规定时间，在一段合理的时间内，未曾送达发价人，接受就无效，但需要适当地考虑到交易的情况，包括发价人所使用的通信方法的迅速程度。对口头发价必须立即接受，但情况有别者不在此限。（3）但是，如果根据该项发价或依照当事人之间确立的习惯做法或惯例，被发价人可以做出某种行为，例如与发运货物或支付价款有关的行为，来表示同意，而无须向发价人发出通知，则接受于该项行为做出时生效，但该项行为必须在上一款所规定的期间内做出。

But sometimes the acceptance is a conditional acceptance. The Convention also stipulates in Article 19 as follows: (1) A reply to an offer which purports to be an acceptance but contains additions, limitations or other modifications is a rejection of the offer and constitutes a counter-offer. (2) However, a reply to an offer which purports to be an acceptance but contains additional or different terms which do not materially alter the terms of the offer constitutes an acceptance, unless the offeror, without undue delay, objects orally to the discrepancy or dispatches a notice to that effect. If the offeror does not object, the terms of the contract are the terms of the offer with the modifications contained in the acceptance. (3) Additional or different terms relating, among other things, to the price, payment, quality and quantity of the goods, place and time of delivery, extent of one party's liability to the other or the settlement of disputes are considered to materially alter the terms of the offer.

Sometimes, due to various reason, the acceptance will be late, which is called a late acceptance. It refers to an acceptance by the offeree that exceeds the time fixed by the offeror or, if no time is fixed exceeds the reasonable time for acceptance. Regarding late acceptance, please refer to Article 21 of the United Nations Convention on Contracts for the International Sale of Goods.

When the offer is withdrawn before it comes into effect in order that the acceptance can be stopped. Regarding withdrawal, please refer to Article 22: An acceptance may be withdrawn if the withdrawal reaches the offeror before or at the same time as the acceptance would have become effective. What we should take notice of is that when the acceptance becomes effective, the contract has been made. In this case, the acceptance cannot be withdrawn. Withdrawal of an effective contract means withdrawal of a lawful contract, which is breaching.

但是有时候接受是有条件的接受，《联合国国际货物销售合同公约》第 19 条对此规定如下：（1）对发价表示接受但载有添加、限制或其他更改的答复，即为拒绝该项发价，并构成还价。（2）但是，对发价表示接受但载有添加或不同条件的答复，如所载的添加或不同条件在实质上并不变更该项发价的条件，除发价人在不过分迟延的期间内以口头或书面通知反对其间的差异外，仍构成接受。如果发价人不做出这种反对，合同的条件就以该项发价的条件以及接受通知内所载的更改为准。（3）有关货物价格、付款、货物质量和数量、交付地点和时间、一方当事人对另一方当事人的赔偿责任范围或解决争端等的添加或不同条件，均视为实质上变更发价的条件。

有时因为各种原因接受可能会延迟，这就是逾期接受或延迟接受。逾期接受是指受盘人的接受通知超过发盘规定的有效期或发盘未明确规定有效期而超过合理时间才到达发盘人。关于逾期接受，请参看《联合国国际货物销售合同公约》第 21 条。

接受在生效之前可以被撤回，以阻止其生效。《联合国国际货物销售合同公约》第 22 条认为：接受得予撤回，如果撤回通知于接受原应生效之前或同时送达发价人。值得注意的是，由于接受一旦生效，合同即告成立，所以接受是不能撤销的。撤销一项已生效的接受，相当于撤销已成立的合同，属于毁约行为。

Sample of acceptance（接受实例）

Guangzhou, 13 February, 2019

Dear Sirs,

We refer to your fax of 12 February and are pleased to confirm having sold to you 50 long tons of Gum Rosin on the terms and conditions agreed upon.

We enclose our Sales Confirmation No. CF123 in two copies, a copy of which please countersign and return to us for our file.

Yours sincerely,

敬启者：

你方 2 月 12 日传真收悉，现按双方同意的条款确认售予你方 50 长吨松香。

兹随函附寄第 CF123 号销货确认书一式两份，其中一份请签退我方，以便存档。

……启
2019 年 2 月 13 日

5. Investigation of credit-worthiness of customers（顾客的信用调查）

After an overseas market has been found, what the exporter should know before starting trade includes the credit worthiness of the foreign buyers or importers. Obviously, customers of sound reputation are advantageous. The question is whether the exporter has known such customers. Thus, assessing credit worthiness is one of the chief factors to consider at the time of setting up a new business connection.

Credit worthiness is the lifeblood of trade. Modern commerce has been built up on it and it has in recent years penetrated the retail market to such an extent that today many people spend half of their income on credit purchases. Large consumer finance companies have sprung up to finance this kind of spending.

In international trade, credit is of even greater importance than in domestic trade, partly because of the time lag between receiving regular orders by businesses which will want credit terms, and also orders made by buyers who may want to place a single but very large order. Here, we will deal only with the credit given by the exporter or seller himself.

海外市场开辟以后，出口商在进行贸易之前还应了解外国买方或进口商的信用状况。显然，有良好信誉的客户对出口商来说颇为有益。但问题是出口商是否已了解这样的客户。所以，了解信用状况是开始建立商业联系的重要因素之一。

信用是贸易的命脉。现代商业已经建立在信用的基础之上。近年来信用已如此深入地渗透到零售购买者，以至于今天很多人把收入的一半用于信用购买上，并且大规模的信用金融公司也应运而生，为这种消费提供资助。

在国际贸易中信用比在国内贸易中更为重要。部分原因是以记账贸易进行的一般的订货与一笔非常大的一次性订单之间有时间间隔。在这里，我们只讨论出口商或卖方提供的信用。

Samples of credit enquiry（信用调查实例）

CREDIT ENQUIRY

(THROUGH A FIRM)

12 November 2019

(CONFIDENTIAL)

Dear Sirs,

We have received an order valued at USD56,500 from Ocean Electronic Co. Ltd, U.S.A.. The company has given us the name of your firm as a reference. We wish to know whether, in your opinion, they are good for this amount and in every way trustworthy and reliable. We shall be most grateful for any information you are able to give us.

We should of course treat as strictly confidential any advice you give us and be only too pleased to perform a similar service for you should the opportunity ever arise. We enclose a stamped, addressed envelope for your reply.

Yours faithfully,

敬启者：

我公司现收到大西洋电子有限公司的订单一份，订货总值达 56 500 美元。该公司提供你方商号作其资信证明人。为此，我们想知道该公司是否可靠、是否值得信任。请提供这方面的资料，不胜感激。

你方所提供的任何信息都将严予保密。如有机会，我们将乐意回报类似服务。现随附回邮信封一个，供复信之用。

······启

2019 年 11 月 12 日

CREDIT INFORMATION FROM A FOREIGN FIRM

(FAVOURABLE REPLY)

23 November 2018

(STRICT PRIVATE AND CONFIDENTIAL)

Dear Sirs,

We are pleased to state that the firm referred to in your letter of 12 November is a well-known and highly respectable firm who has been established in this town for over two decades.

We ourselves have now been doing business with them for more than five years under quarterly account terms and although they have not as a rule taken advantage of our cash discounts, they have always paid their accounts promptly on time. The credit we have allowed the firm has at times been well above USD56 500 that you mentioned.

We hope this information will be helpful and understand that you will treat it confidentially.

Yours faithfully,

（有利的回复）

敬启者：

你们 11 月 12 日来函所提到的这家公司是一家颇有名气、很受尊敬的商号。该公司自从在本市创建以来已有二十多年的历史。

5 年来，我商号与该公司一直按季度结账，有业务往来。虽然该公司不和我们做现金交易，不享受我们现金结账折扣的优惠，但其总是准时清账。我们给该号赊账信用额总是超过你们所说的 56 500 美元。

希望这些资料对你们有用，并予以保密。

……启

2019 年 11 月 23 日

(UNFAVORABLE REPLY)

Dear Sirs,

We have completed our enquiries concerning the firm mentioned in your letter of 12 November and regret that we must advise you to exercise caution regarding their request for credit.

About one year ago, a legal action was brought against the firm by one of its suppliers for recovery of outstanding debts, though payment was later recovered in full.

Our enquiries reveal nothing to suggest that the firm is not straight forward. On the contrary, the firm's difficulties seem to be due to bad management and in particular to overtrading. Consequently, most of the firm's suppliers either give only very short credit for limited sums, or make deliveries on a cash basis.

The information is provided under the strictest confidentiality.

Yours faithfully,

（不利的回复）

敬启者：

你们 11 月 12 日的来函中所提到公司的资信，我方已予查询，十分遗憾，对该公司的赊账要求应谨慎。

约在 1 年前，该公司由于欠款问题曾受其供货商的投诉，事后才全数付清。

从我方查询所得资料来看，该公司并不是不诚实可靠，似乎是由于该公司管理无方，尤其是由于盘子放得太大，以至于近年来多数供货商对其减少供货的赊欠额度，并缩短其赊欠期限，甚至要求付现供货。

以上资料应予保密，自不待言。

……启

2019 年 11 月 23 日

6. Implementation of contract（合同的履行）

Under a CIF contract with terms of payment by L/C, the implementation of an export contract usually goes through the steps of goods preparation, inspection application, urging establishment of L/C, examination and amendment of L/C, chartering and booking shipping space, shipment, customs formalities, insurance, preparation of documents for bank negotiation and the settlement of claims, etc.

当出口合同为 CIF 合同，采用信用证为付款方式时，出口合同的履行一般包括备货、报检、催证、审证和改证、租船和订舱、装运、办理报关手续、保险、制单结汇和理赔等。

1) Preparing goods for shipment（备货）

After a contract is made, it is the main task for the exporter to prepare the goods for shipment and check them against the terms stipulated in the contract. The quality, specifications, quantity, marking and the packing should be in line with the contract or the L/C, the date for the preparation should be in agreement with the shipping schedule.

合同签订以后，出口商的主要任务就是为装船准备货物，并按合同条款对货物进行核查。货物的品质、规格、数量、唛头和包装必须与合同或信用证一致。备货时间应结合船期安排。

2) Inspection application（报检申请）

If required by the stipulations of the state or the contract, the exporter should obtain a certificate of inspection from the institutions concerned where the goods are inspected. Usually, the commodity will be released only after the inspection certificate is issued by the inspection organization.

如有国家或者合同的规定要求，出口商的货物应经有关的商检部门检验并获取商品检验证。通常，只有在取得商检部门发给的合格检验证书后，货物才能被海关放行。

3) Reminding, examining and modifying L/C（催证、审证和改证）

In international trade, a banker's L/C is commonly used for the payment of the purchase price. In the course of the performance of the contract, one of the necessary steps for the seller is to urge the buyer to establish the L/C. According to the contract, the buyer should establish the L/C on time, but sometimes they may delay establishing it for various reasons. For the safe collection of payment, the seller has to urge the buyer to expedite the opening of the L/C. Upon receipt of the letter of credit, the seller must examine it very carefully to ensure all terms and conditions are in accordance with the contract. If any discrepancies exist, the seller should contact the buyer immediately for L/C amendments to guarantee smooth execution of the contract.

在国际贸易中，银行信用证被广泛用来支付货款。在执行合同时，其中一个重要的步骤就是卖方应催促买方按时开立信用证。按合同规定，买方应该及时开立信用证，但有时由于各种原因而迟开。为了安全收汇，卖方应催促买方开证。当卖方收到信用证后，必须对照合同逐条进行严格审核。审核时发现的任何不符点，应该立即联系买方尽快修改，以保证合同的顺利进行。

4) Chartering and booking shipping space（租船和订舱）

After receiving the relevant L/C, the exporter should contact the ship's agents or the shipping company for chartering and booking shipping space, and prepare for shipment in accordance with the importer's shipping instructions. Chartering is required for goods in large quantities that require a full shipload; for goods in small quantities, space booking is sufficient.

收到有关的信用证后，出口商必须马上与轮船代理人或船运公司联系租船和订舱，并按照进口人的装船要求准备装运。如果货物数量较大，需要整船载运，则需要办理租船手续；如果数量不大，办理订舱手续即可。

5) Customs formalities（报关手续）

Before the goods are loaded, certain procedures in customs formalities have to be completed. As required, completed forms giving particulars of the goods exported together with a copy of the contract of sale, invoice, packing list, weight memo, commodity inspection certificate and other relevant documents, have to be lodged with customs. After the goods are on board, the shipping company or the ship's agent will issue a bill of lading which is a receipt evidencing the loading of the goods on board.

在货物装运前还应完成一些海关手续。按照规定，必须把填写出口货物细节的报关单连同合同、发票、装箱单、重量单、商检证书和其他相关单证报关。货物一装上船，船运公司或轮船代理人将开出提单，它是证明货物已装上船的收据。

6) Insurance（保险）

The export trade is subject to many risks. For example, ships may sink or consignments may be damaged in transit, exchange rates may fluctuate, buyers may default, or governments suddenly announce an embargo, etc. It is customary to insure goods sold for export against the perils of the journey. The cover paid for will vary according to the type of goods and the circumstances. If the exporter has bought insurance for the goods, they will be reimbursed for the losses.

出口贸易要面临很多危险。例如，船舶可能沉没，货物可能在运输途中受损，外汇兑换率可能有变动，买主可能违约或者政府部门突然宣布禁运，等等。为避免旅途中的风险，通常要为出口货物购买保险。所购的险种应根据货物的种类和环境的不同而不同。如果出口商购买了保险，出险后就会得到赔偿。

7) Preparing documents for bank negotiation（制单结汇）

After the shipment, all kinds of documents required by the L/C shall be prepared by the exporter and presented within the validity period of the L/C to the bank for negotiation. As to the shipping documents, they include commercial invoice, bill of lading, insurance policy, packing list, weight memo, certificate of inspection, and in some cases, a consular invoice, certificate of origin, etc. Documents should be correct, complete, concise and clean. Only after the documents are verified to fully conform with the L/C terms will the issuing bank effect payment. Payment will be refused by the bank for any discrepancies in the documents.

出口货物在装运后，出口商应立即按照信用证的规定编制各种单据，并在信用证规定的交单有效期内交银行办理议付结汇手续。其要求的单据包括商业发票、提单、保险单、装箱单、重量单、商检证书。在有些情况下，还包括领事发票、原产地证书等。编制的单据必须正确、完整、简明和整洁。开证行只有在审核单证与信用证完全相符后才付款。单证中任何不符点都会遭到银行的拒付。

7．Settlement of disputes（解决争议）

Sometimes complaints or claims inevitably arise in spite of the careful performance of a contract by the exporter and importer. They are likely to be caused by various reasons such as delivery of incorrect quantities, wrong goods delivered, poor packing, inferior quality, discrepancy between the samples and the goods that were actually delivered, delay in shipment, etc. In accordance with the specific conditions, complaints and claims may be made to the exporter, importer, insurance company or shipping company. Once disputes arise, it is advised that arbitration is preferable to litigation, and conciliation is preferable to arbitration.

有时尽管进出口双方小心谨慎地履行合同，但抱怨和索赔可能由于各种原因引起，如交货数量或多或少、发错货、包装粗劣、质量低劣、样品和实际到货存在差异、发运迟误等。根据具体情况，抱怨和索赔可向出口商、进口商、保险公司或运输公司提出。一旦发生争议，明智的选择是仲裁比诉讼好，而调解又比仲裁好。

Section Three　Basic Qualities for Good Negotiators（优秀谈判人员的基本素质）

It is well-known that business negotiation is a profession. Therefore, all the foreign trade companies and international economic and financial organizations place great emphasis on the careful selection of business negotiators. How can one be good negotiators? The basic qualities for a good negotiator are listed below:

(1) Good business negotiators should be familiar with the business and financial environments of their own country. If they work in a foreign country, they must not only know the local language, but also adapt themselves to local customs, and generally feel at home in the host country.

(2) Negotiation is absorbing, complex, and challenging work, and it is not confined to one or a few product lines, market areas, types of buyers, marketing management skills, or financial specialties. They will have to acquire knowledge of many aspects of business activities. They must understand government laws, policies and regulations, both at home and in the host country. They must gain an insight into international trade practices and at least the fundamentals of commercial law.

(3) They must be able to identify and assess barriers to trade affecting their country. They will have to analyze such matters as international physical distribution (shipping services, freight rates), financial terms, and other aspects of trade facilities. They must learn about export documentation, terminology, packing, costing and pricing for export and product adaptation, and appreciate the importance of quality control.

Besides the work regulations concerning foreign affairs, good business negotiators shall also comply with the following principles.

(1) They must plunge into their work with the greatest zeal and at the same time keep a cool head; they should adopta sincere and friendly attitude while being cautious, resolute and pleasant.

(2) Before negotiations, talks or meetings, they must be prepared thoroughly. They should clearly understand the topic and content to be covered in the talk, the intention and purpose they are to achieve, deliberate over the problems that might crop up in the process of the negotiations and tactics to be adopted to tackle the opponents.

(3) In case they encounter any baffling problems or the decision-making is beyond their power, they must tell the truth and report to their competent authority for instruction.

众所周知，商务谈判作为一种职业已为我们认可很多年了。外贸公司和国际财经组织十分重视选择商务谈判人员。如何做一名优秀的谈判人员呢？以下是谈判人员应具备的基本素质。

（1）优秀谈判人员应对本国的商务及财经形势十分了解。如果是在国外，则不仅应懂当地语言，还要接受当地的风俗习惯，如在本国一样适应自如。

（2）谈判工作本身错综复杂，且具有挑战性，因为它不只限于几类商品、几个市场，买方身份多变，营销技巧各异，金融制度不一。这就要求谈判人员应具备商贸活动方方面面的知识。他们必须了解本国政府和驻在国政府的法律、政治和规章；必须对国际贸易惯例，至少是商法的有关内容，有透彻的了解。

（3）他们必须有能力对影响本国的贸易壁垒进行判断和分析。他们要对国际物流（航运服务、运费）、金融术语以及其他贸易条款进行深入研究。他们必须熟悉出口文件、术语、包装、出口商品的成本核算、定价以及产品适用性，充分了解质量控制的重要性。

除了应遵守涉外工作和各项规定，商务谈判人员还应努力做到以下几点。

（1）谈判人员应满腔热忱，全身心投入工作，同时应保持冷静的头脑。他们应处事谨慎、果断而待人诚恳、友好及和颜悦色。

（2）在谈判、会谈及会议之前，他们应做好充分准备。应充分了解会谈的议题及内容、谈判意图及要达到的目的。对在谈判中可能出现的问题要充分考虑，并准备好应对策略。

（3）万一碰到难以处理的问题或要做的决定超出权限，谈判人员应如实说明并向上级汇报。

Section Four　Procedures of Cross-border E-commerce（跨境电子商务的流程）

In this scenario a communication between two trade points over borders, and the role of each of the model components are being discussed. These four phases are:

Phase 1: Exporter signs in to the system and submits an application record.

Phase 2: Interaction between exporter and exporter's national single window.

Phase 3: Interaction between exporter and importer's national single windows.

Phase 4: Interaction between importer and importer's national single window.

Now, the above phases through each of the following subsections are discussed. In each subsection, the functionality of each component in the cross-border model was discussed according to the schemas of messaging and content layers. (see Fig.2-4)

在这个流程中，两个跨境电子商务贸易点边界之间的通信，以及每个模型组件的作用被分成如下四个阶段。

阶段1：出口国签到记录系统和应用程序。

阶段2：出口国之间的交互和出口商国家单一窗口。

阶段3：出口国和进口国之间的交互单窗口。

阶段4：进口国之间的交互和进口国单一窗口。

上述阶段通过图2-4部分进行了讨论。在每个阶段，将根据消息层和内容层对跨境模型中各组件的功能性进行论述。

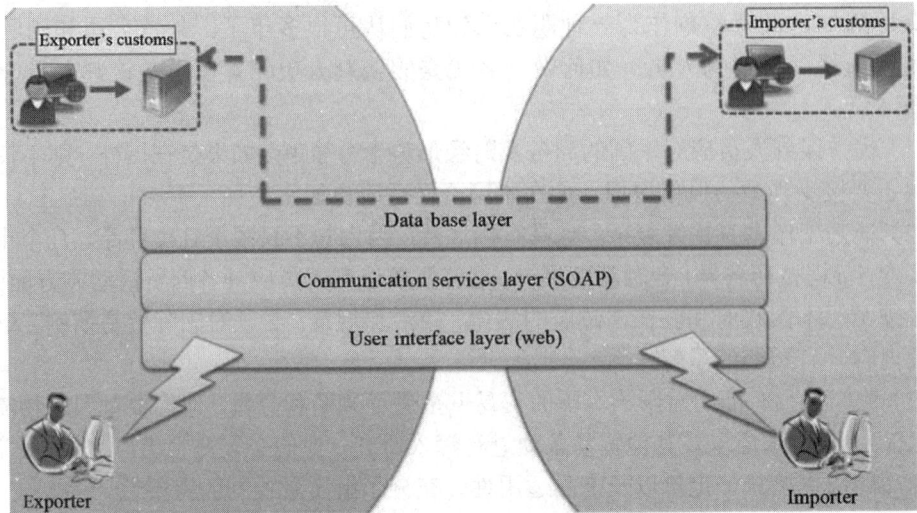

Fig.2-4　Model implementation schema（模型的实现方案）

Section Five　Policy Defects of Cross-border E-commerce（跨境电子商务面临的政策缺陷）

1. The ownership management problems of e-commerce transactions（电子商务交易归属管理问题）

Based on the analysis of e-commerce transactions modes, pure electronic trading, to a great extent, belongs to the category of services trade, which is under the rule of GATS rules according to the trade in services. Those orders by electronic commerce, contract, etc., while are transported by the traditional modes of transportation, are classified as trade in goods category, which belongs to the category of the management of the GATT. In addition, for special types of e-commerce, trade in services is neither service trade nor goods trade, such as electronic products provided by means of electronic commerce (such as cultural products, software, entertainment, etc.), whether this kind of e-commerce trade belongs to services trade or trade in goods is still under discussion.

从电子商务交易形式上分析，纯粹的电子交易在很大程度上属于服务贸易范畴，国际普遍认可归入 GATS 的规则中，按服务贸易进行管理。对于只是通过电子商务方式完成定购、签约等，但要通过传统的运输方式运送至购买人所在地的情形，则归入货物贸易范畴，属于 GATT 的管理范畴。此外，对于特殊的电子商务种类，既非明显的服务贸易也非明显的货物贸易，如通过电子商务手段提供电子类产品（如文化、软件、娱乐产品等），国际上对此类电子商务交易归属服务贸易或货物贸易仍存在较大分歧。

2. The market access issue of trading body（交易主体市场准入问题）

Cross-border e-commerce and payment businesses can break through space and time limits, making the business reach every corner of the world, while the economic and financial information and capital chain are increasingly focused on data platforms. Once the trading body lacks adequate financial strength or faces problems such as irregular operations, credit crisis, system failures, information leakage, will cause the risk of customers' foreign exchange funds.

跨境电子商务及支付业务能够突破时空限制，将商务辐射到世界的每个角落，使金融信息和资金链日益集中在数据平台。一旦交易主体缺乏足够的资金实力或出现违规经营、信用危机、系统故障、信息泄露等问题，便会引发客户外汇资金风险。

Part B Terminology Practice

1. **Unit cost**（单位成本）：The cost of a single, mass-produced article. In general, the greater the quantity produced of an article, the lower will be its unit cost.

2. **Customs entry**（报关）：The submission of certified documents to the customs for the purpose of import or export, declaring that all regulations have been complied with.

3. **Exchange control**（外汇管制）：The regulations governing all transactions involving foreign currencies, and especially the transmission of funds to, or from foreign countries.

4. **Foreign exchange**（外汇）：The currencies of foreign countries. Foreign exchange is bought and sold in foreign exchange markets. Firms or organizations require foreign exchange to purchase goods from abroad or for the purpose of investment or speculation.

5. **Shipping agent**（船舶代理商）：A shipowner's representative whose job is to find cargoes for the ships to carry.

6. **Freight forwarder**（货运代理）：A common carrier that transports or provides transport of property by assembling or consolidating of shipments, performs break-bulk or distributing operations in regard to such consolidated shipments, and assumes responsibility for the transportation of such goods from the point of receipt to the point of destination.

7. **Hauler (haulage contractor)** [运输商（运输承包商）]：Person or firm that owns lorries and contracts to carry goods by road.

8. **Exporter license**（出口许可证）：A license required before goods can be exported from a country.

9. **Import license**（进口许可证）：A permit allowing an importer to bring a stated quantity of certain goods into a country.

10. **VAT (valued-added tax)**（增值税）：Type of national sales tax paid by manufacturers and merchants on the value contributed to a product at each stage of its production and distribution.

11. **Chamber of commerce**（商会）：An association of businessmen whose purpose is to promote commerce and industry in the community.

12. **Certificate of origin**（原产地证书）：A document in which certification is made as to the country of origin of the merchandise.

13. **Consular invoice**（领事发票）：A customs invoice certified, in the exporting country, by the consulate of the country to which the goods are destined. The invoice is usually designed and issued by the consulate, and a fee is charged for certification.

14. **Documentation**（单据）：The documents involved in import/export, such as invoices,

insurance policies or insurance certificates, bills of lading, drafts, etc.

15. **Landed price**（到岸价）: The cost of goods when all charges have been paid, including delivery ex-docks in the country of destination; such charges include freight, insurance, unloading, and import duty, if any.

16. **Market price**（市场价格）: The price at which supply and demand are in a state of equilibrium.

17. **Confirming house**（保兑行）: A buying agency which guarantees payment to the supplier in the event that the buyer defaults.

18. **Marketing mix**（营销组合）: The combination of product, price, promotion, and distribution strategies a company uses to reach a specific target market.

19. **Total product**（整体产品）: The promotion of a product involves considering it as a "total product": its brand name, presentation, labeling, packaging, instructions, reliability, and after-sales service are all part of the total product.

20. **Profit margin**（利润率）: The difference between what it costs to make something and its net price, (real price) on which discount is not allowed.

21. **Distribution channels**（分销渠道）: The means by which goods are distributed.

22. **End-user**（最终用户）: The ultimate user for whom a machine, product, or service is designed.

23. **Middlemen**（中间商）: Dealers (such as agents, merchant brokers, wholesalers, etc.) who are neither producers nor consumers, but buy from one or sell to the other, or to other middlemen, or act as agents between producers, and consumers.

24. **Mail order**（邮购）: A system of direct selling through the post. Catalogues are sent to potential customers, who order goods to be sent to them.

25. **Credit**（信贷）: A promise by one party to pay another for money borrowed or for goods and services received.

26. **Credit enquiry**（信用查询）: An enquiry into the reputation of a business house and its ability to meet financial commitments.

27. **Trade association**（行业协会）: A nonprofit organization of professionals in related businesses and industries, established to serve the common interests of its members.

28. **Feasibility study**（可行性研究）: An analysis of whether or not a proposed course of action is possible.

Part C Terms

1. business association 业务联系，交往
2. business connection 业务联系
3. close relationship 密切的关系
4. closer ties 更密切的关系
5. to establish (enter into, set up) business relationship 建立业务关系
6. to continue business relationship 继续业务关系
7. to present business relationship 保持业务关系

8. to improve business relationship 改善业务关系

9. to promote business relationship 促进业务关系

10. to speed up business relationship 加快业务关系的发展

11. to enlarge (widen) business relationship 扩大业务关系

12. to restore (resume) business relationship 恢复业务关系

13. to interrupt business relationship 中断业务关系

14. to cement business relationship 巩固业务关系

15. quantity 数量

16. packing 包装

17. time of shipment 装运期

18. price 价格

19. discount 折扣

20. terms of payment 支付条款

21. insurance 保险

22. commodity inspection 商品检验

23. acceptance 接受

24. to sign a contract 签订合同

25. claim 索赔

26. agency 代理

27. commission 佣金

28. exclusive sales 包销

29. joint venture 合资企业

30. be of the latest style 最新式样

31. financial position 财务状况

32. meet with great favor 受欢迎

33. credit standing 信用地位

34. currency, Chinese currency, British currency 货币，中国货币，英国货币

35. firm offer 实盘

36. order, indent 订单

37. book, booking 订货，订购

38. fax reply 传真回复

39. bid, bidding 递盘

40. counter-offer 还盘

41. offer 发盘（发价）

42. reply immediately 速复

43. reference price 参考价

44. usual practice 习惯做法

45. without engagement 不受约束

46. sponsorship 赞助

47. desk research 案头调研

48. quantitative research 定量研究

49. qualitative research 定性研究

Part D Exercise

I. Answer the following questions in English.

1. Please tell us the procedures of international trade.

2. What are the parties involved in export and import transactions?

3. What are the specialists involved in export and import transactions?

4. What are the documents needed in export and import transactions?

II. Filling in the blanks with the suitable words in the text.

1. What is marketing? Marketing is the creative process of _____ customer needs profitably.

2. In Britain an intermediary called a commission _____ or export commission house acts on behalf of the _____ importers.

3. Agents are paid _____ on the amount of goods purchased.

4. An agent may receive goods in his ____ name, and stock them in anticipation of sale.

5. A few shares for assistance in ____ up the company will be issued. We'll issue some founder's shares.

6. We have developed an excellent product and obtained from the government the sole right to manufacture and sell it. We have obtained ____.

7. When our production and marketing expenses have been paid, we hope to have quite a lot of money left over as earnings. We expect to make good ____.

8. We had to find other people through whom to make sales. We had to find other sales ____.

9. The licensee wanted us to invest some money with him in a new company. He wanted to set up a ____ with us.

10. We used to have a smaller part of our company located abroad, but we don't now. We have no ____ abroad.

III. Judge the following statements, mark T (True) or F (False).

1. According to the CISG, once the offeror stipulates the validity of the offer, the offeror can still cancel the offer. (   )

2. Offer and acceptance are two indispensable links for reaching an agreement and concluding a contract. (   )

3. During the negotiation, the offer is made by the seller and acceptance is made by the buyer. (   )

4. 在国际贸易中，一项合同的有效成立必须经过询盘、发盘、还盘、接受和签约五个环节。（   ）

5. Enquiry, offer and acceptance are indispensable parts of a negotiation. (   )

6. An advertisement on paper is an effective offer. (   )

7. 如果发盘人在发盘中没有受约束的意思，则不构成发盘，而只是邀请对方发盘。（   ）

8. If an offer remarks "irrevocable", it means the offeror has no right to withdraw the offer. (   )

9. Same to the offer, acceptance also can be cancelled. (   )

10.《联合国国际货物销售合同公约》规定，发盘生效的时间为发盘送达受盘人时。（   ）

11. Good business negotiators should be familiar with the business and financial environments of their own country. (   )

12. If business negotiators work in a foreign country, they can ignore the local customs in the host country. (   )

13. Customs entry is the submission of certified documents to the customs for the purpose of import or export, declaring that all regulations have been complied with. (   )

14. An export license is a permit allowing an importer to bring a stated quantity of certain goods into a country. (   )

15. VAT refers to a type of national sales tax paid by manufacturers and merchants on the value contributed to a product at each stage of its production and distribution. (   )

16. The transaction process involved in digital trade activities is simplified, and customers can quickly place orders, make online payments, and cross-border logistics delivery on e-commerce platforms. (   )

IV. Explain the meaning of the words or phrases below as requested.

1. Offer

2. Withdrawal

3. Enquiry

4. Acceptance

5. Shipping agent

V. Compose a letter of enquiry with the following particulars.

1. The addressee: Messrs. Arthur Grey & Son, 19 Cheapside, London, E. C. 2.

2. You have the addressee's name and address from China Council for the Promotion of International Trade.

3. You wish to buy 100 sets of Ice Box.

4. State clearly price terms, payment terms, time of shipment, packing conditions, etc.

5. Ask for illustrated catalogues.

VI. Please make your offer according to the following particulars.

1. You have got the enquiry of May 5th for "D.D." Raincoats.

2. Quantity: 100 for men and 100 women.

3. Specifications: medium and small size, each 100 pieces.

4. Unit price: at USD14.50 for men's medium; 14.0 for men's small; 13.2 for women's medium; 12.7 for women's small.

5. Payment: irrevocable L/C at sight.

6. Shipment: Shipment will be effected within three or four weeks after receiving the L/C.

7. In your offer, some comments on the goods can be illustrated.

VII. Write a counter-offer according to the following particulars.

1. 回复对方 5 月 10 日关于 1 000 台海尔冰箱的来信。

2. 对价格和装运期满意，但要求变更付款方式。

3. 以前用的都是不可撤销的保兑信用证付款，花费很大。

4. 资金吃紧达 4 个月，再加上银行前所未有的高利率，资金问题特别突出。

5. 建议对方接受"货到后凭单付款"或者"见票后 60 天付款"的汇票。

VIII. Case study.

Company A made an offer for a farm product to Company B stating: "Packing in sound bags". Within the validity, Company B replied "Refer to your telex first accepted, packing in new bags". On receiving the reply, Company A began to purchase the goods for export. Days later, as the market price of the commodity was falling, Company B wrote to Company A "No contract is entered between us, as you failed to confirm our changing of the packing requirement." Company A argued that Company B's acceptance was effective and the contract was established then.

Questions:

(1) What is your opinion? Give the reasons to support your opinion.

(2) How to prevent such dispute?

IX. Multiple Choices.

1. The case when total imports over exports could be called (　　).
   A. trade surplus　　　　　　　　B. trade deficit
   C. deficit　　　　　　　　　　　D. surplus

2. Which of the following indicators can reflect the direction of international trade geography?
   (　　)
   A. proportion of a country's exports in the world's total exports
   B. proportion of a country's imports in the world's total imports
   C. the manufactured goods exports accounted for the proportion of world exports
   D. countries imports of manufactured goods accounted for the proportion of total imports of the world
   E. Countries' total import and export proportion of the total import and export

3. According to the direction of movement of goods, international trade can be divided into
   (　　).
   A. direct trade　　　　　　　　B. import trade
   C. export trade　　　　　　　　D. transit trade
   E. entrepot trade

4. A country's trade scale in 1992 is: exports of \$38 billion, imports \$31.2 billion, the country's trade conditions is (　　).
   A. a. surplus of \$6.8 billion　　　B. \$6.8 billion in net exports
   C. deficit of \$6.8 billion　　　　D. a net \$6.8 billion income
   E. total trade volume of \$69.2 billion

5. According to whether the trade involves a third country, international trade can be divided into: (　　)
   A. direct trade　　　　　　　　B. import trade
   C. export trade　　　　　　　　D. indirect trade
   E. entrepot trade

6. Which of the following belongs to the invisible trade? (　　)
   A. clothing trade　　　　　　　B. technical service
   C. labor export　　　　　　　　D. transportation
   E. insurance

7. According to the members , the international trade can be divided into (　　).
   A. one party trade　　　　　　　B. Multi-party trade
   C. bilateral trade　　　　　　　D. multilateral trade
   E. unilateral trade

8. Foreign trade dependence indicators include (　　).
   A. total of foreign trade dependency　　B. export dependence
   C. import dependency　　　　　　D. import proportion
   E. export proportion

9. Which of the following statements are true about the terms of trade? (　　)

　　A. also called exchange value

　　B. is also called trade terms

　　C. its value is greater than 100 when better terms of trade occur

　　D. its value is less than 100 when trade conditions are better

　　E. its value is equal to 100 when terms of trade are better

10. Compensation trade is in the way of (　　).

　　A. buyback 　　　　　　　　B. mutual purchase

　　C. partly compensation 　　　D. stock exchange

　　E. collaborative production

Chapter Three

Part A Text

Contracts for the Sale and Purchase of International Commodity

Business as we know it today would be impossible if there were no agreement or contract to bind the contracting parties. A long time ago, people devised a means for bargaining for the conduct of others by exchanging promises. The exchange of promises came to be known as "agreements" and gradually became very important in the lives of people and in the field of business. A promise or an agreement is reached as a result of the process of an offer and acceptance. When an agreement is reached, a contract is formed, which creates legal obligations enforceable by law. Contracts can be long or short, formal or informal, simple or complicated, and verbal or written, of which the most popular is the written contract for pre-printed contracts. The importance of a contract in an international sales transaction cannot be underestimated. Often it is the only document between the parties to which they may refer for clarification of mutual responsibilities, resolution of disputes, or in the event of disagreement. And such a contract serves as a "living document" that may well survive the relationship it defines. Therefore, the exporter should avoid viewing the contract merely as a document that initiates transactions and subsequently is filed and forgotten. Contracts must be drafted with an awareness of the background of the law in which the transaction takes place, with a clear conception of the various services they may be called upon to render, etc.

It is best to obtain legal advice as to the best set of contractual terms appropriate to the product and type of business. Pre-printed contracts can be utilized to meet the specialized needs of certain categories of commodities such as textiles, cereals, and steel products. Though most of the contracts have many provisions in common, each is different from the others owing to the nature of the goods. For example, there may be a clause protecting the exporter against claims if the goods deteriorate because of delays outside their control, and a clause protecting the exporter against libel, obscenity, or other charges that might arise in another country for printed materials.

Whether we are dealing with a pre-printed form, or a long form of the contract, there are certain key provisions that every contract should contain to avoid ambiguity and possible future conflicts. Other provisions, while desirable and even essential in some contracts, may be entirely superfluous in others. Whether to include them depends on the type of goods, shipping and insurance complexities, and the degree of trust and mutual confidence existing between buyer and seller. An initial contract will invariably take more time to work out than a repeat order after a certain pattern has already been established.

假如没有合同或协议去约束买卖双方，我们今天所说的商业就不可能成立。很久以前，人们发明了"互换承诺"作为一种引导其他人讨价还价的方法。这种"互换承诺"演变成了我们现在众所周知的"合同"，并且逐渐在人们的生活和商业活动中变得非常重要。一个承诺或者协议就是报盘和承诺达成一致的结果。当一个协议达成或一个合同形成，就意味着产生了强制性的法律责任。一个合同可短可长，可以正式或非正式，可以简单或复杂，可以是口头的或书面的，但最流行的是书面的并已印刷好的合同。合同的重要性在国际销售活动中不可轻估。这份合同通常是双方提及各自清晰的责任、在争议时的解决方法等的文件。这份合同同时也是维持双方所定义的关系的一种"存在证明"。所以出口商应该避免将合同仅仅看作交易开始和开展的文件而忽略了合同的重要性。合同应该由一个在当地有熟悉法律背景的人起草，并且要对不同服务的实施等有一个清晰的概念。

关于交易合同条款是否符合商品交易的类型和要求可以请教相关法律顾问。已印刷好的合同可以用于满足纺织品、谷类、钢铁等特定类型的日用品的特殊要求。尽管合同一般都有很多不同的规定，但每一项的差异由商品不同的特性所决定。例如，合同会有一个条款保护出口商免于索赔，如果该商品的变化是由于出口商不能控制的原因而引发的，同时，还有另一个条款保护出口商因其他国家的印刷资料而引起的免于赔偿或责任或其他诉讼。

假如我们在处理已印刷好的合同，或是一个全式的合同时，有几个关键的地方必须注意，即合同条款尽量避免模棱两可，这样可以避免以后产生摩擦。有些规定，在某些合同里我们认为是值得注意的，甚至是重要的，而在其他人的眼里可能完全是多余的。是否应该包含这些条款则取决于商品类型、运输和保险的复杂性，和买卖双方之间的信任程度以及对对方的信心。相比一份建立了确定的模式的重复订单，一份新的合同总是需要花更多的时间去商定。

Section One　Definition of Contract（合同的定义）

A contract is an agreement between two or more competent parties in which an offer is made and accepted, and each party benefits. It is an agreement which sets forth binding obligations of the relevant parties. The agreement can be formal, informal, written, oral or just plainly understood. Some contracts are required to be in writing in order to be enforceable. This term, in its more extensive sense, includes every description of agreement, or obligation whereby one party becomes bound to another to pay a sum of money, or to do or omit to do a certain act. In its more confined sense, it is an agreement between two or more persons, concerning something to be done, whereby both parties are bound to each other, or one is bound to the other.

A contract proper includes: (1) the full name and address of the buyer and the seller; (2) the commodities involved; (3) all the terms and conditions agreed upon; (4) indication of the number of original copies of the contract, the language used, the term of validity, and possible extension of the contract. In international trade, export and import contracts vary in both names and forms. The names that often appear are contracts, confirmation, agreement and memorandum.

A contract or confirmation can be drawn up either by the seller or the buyer. Respectively, they are called a sales contract/confirmation or a purchase contract/confirmation. Whatever they are named, they are equally binding on the parties. The sales or purchase contract is more formal than the sales or purchase confirmation. Furthermore, the former contains more details than those in the latter. The former usually consists of commodities, specifications, quantity, packing, marking, price, shipment, port of shipment and port of destination, and payment, as well as those clauses concerning insurance, commodity inspection, claims, arbitration and force majeure, etc.; while the latter only includes several main items. What's more, the former is appropriate for transactions of large amounts and huge quantities because of its detailed clauses, which can prevent the occurrence of disputes. If the amount is not large or the business is done by means of agency arrangement, or exclusive-sale agreement, the sales or the purchase confirmation is often used.

国际货物买卖合同是指营业地处于不同国家或地区的当事人之间所订立的货物买卖契约，合同双方都可受益。合同是对有关当事人规定了约束性责任的一种协定。这种协定可以是正式的、非正式的、书面的、口头的，应明了易懂。有些合同需要以书面形式呈现以便执行。从广义的角度看，国际货物买卖合同包括协议的各个方面，根据该契约，一方有义务向另一方支付一定数额的货款，或必须履行某种义务，或可以免除某种义务。从狭义的角度看，合同是两个或两个以上的法人之间为某一经济目的而确定相互的权利和义务所达成的关系。

合同正文部分包括：（1）买卖双方的全名和地址；（2）所涉及的商品；（3）双方同意的所有条款；（4）合同正本的份数、所使用的语言、有效期和合同可能的延期。在国际贸易中，进出口贸易书面合同的名称和形式均无特定的限制。经常出现的名称有合同、确认书、协议书和备忘录。

合同和确认书可以由双方任何一方起草，分别称为售货合同/确认书、购货合同/确认书。不管它们有怎样的叫法，对双方都有约束力。销售或购货合同比销售或购货确认书更正式，并且含有更多的细节。前者通常包含商品名称、规格、数量、包装、唛头、价格、运输、装运港、目的港、付款方法以及有关保险、商检、索赔和不可抗力等条款，而后者只包含几项主要条款。再者，售货或购货合同对价值和数量较大的交易较为合适，因为合同制定了详细的条款以避免产生争议。如果数量不大或交易是通过代理或独销协议来进行的，人们经常使用销售或购货确认书。

Samples of contracts（合同样本）

Agreement of compensation trade
补偿贸易协议

This contract is hereby made and entered into between Guangdong Jiaxing Industrial Co., Ltd.(hereinafter referred to as Party A) and Tailong Electronics(Singapore) Co., Ltd.(hereinafter referred to as Party B) on October 12, 2012 in Guangzhou, China, through amicable negotiation on the basis of equality and mutual benefit.

下列双方在平等互利的基础上，通过友好协商，于 2012 年 10 月 12 日在中国广州订立本合同。

Party A: Guangdong Jiaxing Industrial Co., Ltd.
Add: 317 Huanshi East Road, Guangzhou, China
Tel: (020) 87786162

Fax: (020) 87619503

甲方：广东嘉兴实业有限公司

地址：中国广州环市东路 317 号

电话：（020）87786162

传真：（020）87619503

Party B: Tailong Electronics (Singapore) Co., Ltd.

Add: 111 North Bridge Road, Singapore

Tel: (65) 3324951

Fax: (65) 3324928

乙方：泰隆电子（新加坡）有限公司

地址：新加坡北桥路 111 号

电话：（65）3324951

传真：（65）3324928

Article 1　Contents of transactions（交易内容）

(1) Party A agrees to buy from Party B and Party B agrees to sell to Party A the Assembly Lines for Color TV Sets, of which the specifications, technical requirements, price, and delivery schedule shall be specified in an additional contract to be made between both the parties, which shall serve as an integral part of this contract.

甲方同意从乙方购买、乙方同意向甲方出售彩电装配线，其规格、技术要求、价格和交货日程安排由双方另行签订合同，作为本合同不可分割的一部分。

(2) Party B shall buy from Party A Color TV Sets manufactured on the Assembly Lines supplied by Party B in a quantity approximately equal to that of the Assembly Lines. The quality, quantity, unit price, packing, and delivery schedule shall also be specified in an additional contract, which shall constitute an integral part of this contract.

乙方从甲方购买乙方提供的装配线生产的彩色电视机，其金额与装配线的金额相等。彩电的质量、数量、单价、包装和交货日程安排亦由双方另行签订合同，作为本合同不可分割的一部分。

Article 2　Terms of payment（支付条件）

Payment of the transactions stipulated in Article 1 shall be effected by reciprocal L/C. Party A shall open a usance L/C in favor of Party B to pay by installments the entire cost of the Assembly Lines to be supplied by Party B; whereas Party B shall open a sight L/C in favor of Party A to pay for each shipment of Color TV Sets to be delivered by Party A. The tenor of the usance L/C shall be consistent with the term of compensation stipulated in Article 3. The total proceeds received by Party A from selling Color TV Sets to Party B within the duration of this contract shall be equal to the total value of the Assembly Lines and used to cover such total value of the Assembly Lines. In case the total proceeds received by Party A from selling Color TV Sets to Party B are not enough to cover the total value of the Assembly Lines, the balance shall be made up by Party B with a down payment before the usance L/C opened by Party A expires, thus enabling Party A to effect payment due under the usance L/C.

第一条所订交易的支付通过对开信用证进行。甲方开出以乙方为受益人的远期信用证，分期支付乙方所供装配线的全部价款；乙方开出以甲方为受益人的即期信用证，支付甲方交付的每一批彩电。远期信用证的期限应与第三条所订补偿期限相一致。甲方在本合同期限内向乙方出售彩电的全部收入应等于并用于支付装配线的价款，假使甲方向乙方出售彩电的全部收入不足以支付装配线的全部价款，余额由乙方在甲方开出的远期信用证到期前用预付款补足，以使甲方能够履行远期信用证项下的付款。

Article 3　Period of compensation（补偿期限）

Party A shall pay the total cost of the Assembly Lines by exporting Color TV Sets to Party B within 10 months commencing from the fourth month after all parts of the Assembly Lines have been delivered. In principle, the amount to be paid by Party B for its imports from Party A monthly shall be 10 percent of the total amount due to be paid for the Assembly Lines. Party A can make payment ahead of schedule by providing party B with a one-month prior notice.

从装配线的所有部分交付以后第 4 个月起，甲方应在 10 个月内通过向乙方出口彩电支付装配线的全部价款。原则上，乙方为每月自甲方的进口货物应支付的金额是装配线应付总金额的 10%。甲方可提前付款，但须提前 1 个月通知乙方。

Article 4　Currency for pricing（计价货币）

Both the Assembly Lines and the Color TV Sets shall be priced in terms of US Dollars. If the Color TV Sets are also to be sold in the home market within the term of compensation and thus have a price in RMB, their export price shall be the equivalent in US Dollars according to the exchange rate prevailing at the time.

装配线与彩色电视机均使用美元计价。如果彩电在补偿期内也在国内市场上销售，而具有人民币价格，其出口价格应为按当时汇率折算的美元价格。

Article 5　Interest Rate（利率）

Party A shall bear the interest on the usance L/C and Party B's down payment. The annual interest rate is agreed at 7.5%.

甲方负担远期信用证及乙方预付款的利息。年利率双方同意按 7.5%计。

Article 6　Technical service（技术服务）

After arrival at the destination, the Assembly Lines shall be installed by Party A. When Party A believes it is necessary, Party B shall send its technicians to provide on-site instructions and other technical assistance in the course of installation. Party B shall be liable for the expenses of its technicians and any losses incurred in the course of installation as a result of technical default on its part.

装配线运达目的地后，由甲方安装，当甲方认为必要时，乙方应派遣技术人员在安装过程中提供现场指导和其他技术协助。乙方负担技术人员的花费及安装过程中由于技术人员的过失造成的损失。

Article 7　Insurance（保险）

(1) The buying and selling of the Assembly Lines and the Color TV Sets shall be on an FOB basis, thus the marine cargo insurance on them shall be effected by Party A and Party B respectively.

装配线与彩色电视机的买卖均在 FOB 基础上进行，其海运保险分别由甲方和乙方办理。

(2) During the duration of this contract, the Assembly Lines shall be insured by Party A. Should any loss or damage occur, Party A shall lodge claims against the insurer and pay a part of the indemnification received from the insurer to Party B, which shall be in proportion to the payment Party A has not made for the part of machinery involved in the loss or damage.

在本合同期限内，装配线由甲方投保。如果发生损失或损坏，由甲方向保险人提出索赔，并将从保险人处获得的赔偿的一部分付给乙方,这部分应与受损机械设备中甲方未支付的部分成比例。

Article 8　Liability for breach（违约责任）

Either party shall be liable for its breach of contract and shall indemnify the other party for all losses there by incurred by the other party. In addition, the breaching party shall pay the other party a fine, which shall account for 15% of the total amount involved.

任何一方均要对其违约行为负责，并赔偿由此给另一方造成的损失。此外，违约方须向另一方支付一笔罚金，其金额占违约金额的 15%。

Article 9　Performance guarantee（履约保证）

To guarantee the implementation of the contract, each party shall submit to the other a performance guarantee issued by a bank agreed upon by both parties. The guarantee bank of Party A is the Bank of China, Guangzhou Branch, while that of Party B is Sanhe Bank.

为保证本合同的履行，任一方须向另一方提交由双方同意的银行签发的履约保函。甲方的保证银行是中国银行广州分行，乙方的保证银行是三和银行。

Article 10　Force majeure（不可抗力）

(1) Either party shall not be held responsible for failure or delay to perform all or any part of the contract due to flood, fire, earthquake, drought, war or any other events which could not be predicted at the time of conclusion of this contract, and could not be controlled, avoided or overcome by the relevant party. However, the party affected by the event of Force Majeure shall inform the other party of its occurrence in writing as soon as possible and thereafter shall send a certificate of the event issued by the relevant authorities to the other party within 15 days of its occurrence.

由于水灾、火灾、地震、干旱、战争或合同一方在签约时无法预见且无法控制、避免和克服的其他事件导致不能或暂时不能履行全部或部分合同义务，该方不负责任。但是，受不可抗力事件影响的一方须尽快将发生的事件通知另一方，并在不可抗力事件发生后 15 天内将有关机构出具有不可抗力事件的证明寄交对方。

(2) If the event of force majeure lasts over 120 days, both parties shall have the right to terminate the contract.

如果不可抗力事件持续 120 天以上，那么任何一方有权终止合同。

Article 11　Arbitration（仲裁）

(1) All disputes arising from the performance of this contract shall be settled through friendly negotiations. Should no settlement be reached through negotiation, the case shall then be submitted to the China International Economic and Trade Arbitration Commission (Beijing) for arbitration, and the rules of this Commission shall apply. The award of the arbitration shall be final and binding upon both parties. The arbitration fee shall be borne by the losing party unless otherwise awarded by the Commission.

因履行本合同所发生的一切争议应通过友好协商解决；如协商不能解决争议，则应将争议提交中国国际经济贸易仲裁委员会（北京），依据其仲裁规则进行仲裁。仲裁裁决是终局的，对双方都有约束力。除非仲裁委员会另有裁定，仲裁费由败诉方承担。

(2) During the course of the arbitration, the contract shall be performed except for the part under arbitration.

仲裁期间，除仲裁部分以外的合同条款应继续执行。

Article 12　Amendment to the contract（合同的变更）

The contract can be amended only after the amendment is agreed upon by both parties.

只有经双方一致同意，合同方可变更。

Article 13　Language and validity（文字、生效）

(1) The contract shall be written in Chinese and English. Both versions are equally authentic. In the event of any discrepancy between the two versions, the Chinese version shall prevail.

本合同用中文和英文写成，两种文字具有同等效力。上述两种文字如有不符，以中文文本为准。

(2) The contract shall come into effect as soon as it is duly signed by both parties and shall remain effective for two years.

本合同经双方签字生效，有效期为两年。

Party A: Guangdong Jiaxing Industrial Co., Ltd.　Party B: Tailong Electronics (Singapore) Co., Ltd.
(Signature)　(Signature)

甲方：广东嘉兴实业有限公司　乙方：泰隆电子（新加坡）有限公司
（签字）　（签字）

Sales contract
销售合同

No.:
编号：

Date:
日期：

Signed at:
签约地点：

Sellers:
卖方：

Address: Postal Code:
地址：   邮政编码：

Tel: Fax:
电话：   传真：

Buyers:
买方：

Address: Postal Code:
地址：   邮政编码：

Tel: Fax:
电话：   传真：

The sellers agree to sell and the buyers agree to buy the undermentioned goods on the terms and conditions stated below.

买卖双方同意按下列条款由卖方出售、买方购进下列货物：

(1) Article No.:
货号：

(2) Description & Specification:
品名及规格：

(3) Quantity:
数量：

(4) Unit Price:
单价：

(5) Total Amount:
With _____% more or less both in amount and quantity, allowed at the sellers' option.
总值：
数量及总值均有_____%的增减，由卖方决定。

(6) Country of Origin and Manufacturer:
生产国和制造厂家：

(7) Packing:
包装：

(8) Shipping Marks:
唛头：

(9) Time of Shipment:
装运期限：

(10) Port of Loading:
装运口岸：

(11) Port of Destination:
目的口岸：

(12) Insurance: To be effected by buyers for 110% of full invoice value covering _____ up to _____ only.

保险：由买方按发票全额 110%投保至_____为止的_____险。

(13) Payment:

By confirmed, irrevocable, transferable and divisible L/C to be available by sight draft to reach the sellers before _____/_____/_____ and to remain valid for negotiation in China until 15 days after the aforesaid time of shipment. The L/C must specify that transshipment and partial shipments are allowed.

付款条件：

买方须于_____年_____月_____日将保兑的、不可撤销的、可转让和可分割的即期信用证开到卖方。信用证议付有效期延至上列装运期后 15 天在中国到期，该信用证中必须注明允许分运及转运。

(14) Documents:

单据：

(15) Terms of Shipment:

装运条件：

(16) Quality/Quantity Discrepancy and Claim:

品质与数量（重量）的异议与索赔：

(17) Force Majeure:

Neither party shall be held responsible for failure or delay to perform all or any part of this agreement due to flood, fire, earthquake, drought, war or any other events which could not be predicted, controlled, avoided or overcome by the relevant party. However, the party affected by the event of Force Majeure shall inform the other party of its occurrence in writing as soon as possible and thereafter shall send a certificate of the event issued by the relevant authorities to the other party within 15 days after its occurrence.

不可抗力：

由于水灾、火灾、地震、干旱、战争或协议一方无法预见、控制、避免和克服的其他事件导致不能或暂时不能全部或部分履行本协议，该方不负责任。但是，受不可抗力事件影响的一方须尽快将发生的事件通知另一方，并在不可抗力事件发生 15 天内将有关机构出具的不可抗力事件的证明寄交对方。

(18) Arbitration:

All disputes arising from the execution of this agreement shall be settled through friendly consultations. In case no settlement can be reached, the case in dispute shall then be submitted to the Foreign Trade Arbitration Commission of the China Council for the Promotion of International Trade for arbitration in accordance with its Provisional Rules of Procedure. The decision made by this Commission shall be regarded as final and binding upon both parties. Arbitration fees shall be borne by the losing party, unless otherwise awarded.

仲裁：

在履行协议过程中，如产生争议，双方应友好协商解决。若通过友好协商未能达成协议，则提交中国国际贸易促进委员会对外贸易仲裁委员会，根据该会《仲裁程序暂行规定》进行仲裁。该委员会决定是终局的，对双方均有约束力。仲裁费用，除另有规定外，由败诉一方承担。

(19) Remark:

备注：

Sellers:	Buyers:
卖方：	买方：
（Signature）	（Signature）
（签字）	（签字）

Sales confirmation
售货确认书

Date:

日期：

No.:

编号：

Signed at:

签约地点：

The undersigned sellers and buyers have agreed to close the following transactions according to the terms and conditions stipulated below.

经买卖双方同意成交下列商品订立条款如下。

(1) Commodity:

商品：

(2) Specification:

规格：

(3) Quantity:

数量：

(4) Unit Price:

单价：

(5) Total Value:

总值：

(6) Time of Shipment:

装运期：

(7) Packing:

包装：

(8) Loading Port and Destination:

装运口岸和目的地：

(9) Shipping Marks:

唛头：

(10) Terms of Payment:

Terms of payment: by 100% value confirmed irrevocable letter of credit by draft at sight with transhipment and partial shipments allowed, to reach the Sellers _____ days before the month of shipment, with shipment validity arranged till the 15th day after the month of shipment, and remain valid for negotiation in the loading port until the _____ day after the shipment validity.

付款条件：

凭 100%保兑的、不可撤销的信用证附带即期汇票付款，允许分批装运和转船，要求在装船期前_____天到达卖方，有效期至装船期后 15 天，且在装船有效期后_____天在装货港议付仍然有效。

(11) Insurance:

保险：

The Buyers   The Sellers

买方   卖方

                                          China National Textiles

                                          Import & Export Corporation

                                          Shanghai Silk Branch

                                          中国纺织品进出口公司

                                          上海丝绸分公司

Section Two   Formation of Contract（合同的格式）

A business contract is an agreement, enforceable by law. It may be formal or informal. The business contract which is generally adopted in international trade activities is the formal written one. Generally speaking, a business contract is usually made up of three parts, i.e., the preamble, the body and the witness clause.

The preamble usually includes title, number, date of signing, signing parties, place of signing, each party's authority, recitals (whereas clauses) and so on.

The body of a business contract usually includes definition clause, general terms and conditions, basic conditions, duration, termination, assignment, force majeure, governing law, arbitration, jurisdiction, notice, entire agreement clause, amendment and so on.

The witness clause usually includes language validity, copies, presence of witnesses, annex, signature, seal and so on.

贸易合同是一份具有法律效力的协议书。它可以是正式的，也可以是非正式的，但在国际贸易活动中采用的贸易合同则是正式的文字合同。一般来说，一份正式的合同通常由约首、约文和约尾三部分组成。

约首通常包括合同名称、合同号码、缔约日期、缔约当事人、缔约地点、当事人的合法依据、缔约缘由等。

约文通常包括定义条款、一般条款、基本条款、有效期、终止、让与、不可抗力、适用的法律、仲裁、诉讼管辖、通知手续、完整条款、修改等。

约尾通常包括文字效力、份数、见证人、附件、当事人签字、盖印等。

The contents involved in a business contract can be summed up as follows（贸易合同的内容如下）：

Title and Reference	合同名称及其编号
Preamble	序言（约首）
Name of Commodity	商品名称
Quality Clause	品质条款
Quantity Clause	数量条款
Price Clause	价格条款
Packing Clause	包装条款
Delivery Clause	交货条款
Payment Clause	支付条款
Insurance Clause	保险条款
Inspection Clause	检验条款
Claim Clause	索赔条款
Arbitration Clause	仲裁条款
Force Majeure Clause	不可抗力条款
Breach and Cancellation of Contract Clause	违约及解除契约条款
Miscellaneous Clause	其他条款

In international trade, there are a great variety of business contracts, which mainly include（贸易合同的种类如下）：

Agreement	协议书
Sales Note	售货单
Sales Agreement	销售协议
Sales Contract	销售合同
Sales Confirmation/Confirmation of Sales/Acknowledgement of Sales	销售确认书
Confirmation of Order	订货确认书
Purchase Agreement Contract	购货合同
Purchase Note	购货单
Order Sheet/Purchase Order	订单
Purchase Confirmation/Confirmation of Purchase	购货确认书
Trade Agreement	贸易协议
Bilateral Trade Agreement	双边贸易
Multilateral Trade Agreement	多边贸易
Import Contract	进口合同
Export Contract	出口合同
Consignment Contract	寄售合同
Agency Agreement	代理协议
Agency Contract	代理合同
Compensation Trade Contract	补偿贸易合同

Sample of exclusive agency agreement（独家代理协议书样本）

Exclusive agency agreement
独家代理协议书

This agreement is made and entered into by and between the parties concerned on September 20, 2019 in Qingdao, China on the basis of equality and mutual benefit to develop business on terms and conditions mutually agreed upon as follows:

本协议于 2019 年 9 月 20 日在中国青岛由有关双方在平等互利基础上达成，按双方同意的下列条件发展业务关系：

Article 1　The parties concerned（协议双方）

Party A: Qingdao Hongda Industrial Co., Ltd.

Add: 25 Qutangxia Road, Qingdao, China

Tel: (0532)2877932

Fax: (0532)2876415

甲方：青岛宏达实业有限公司

地址：中国青岛瞿塘峡路 25 号

电话：（0532）2877932

传真：（0532）2876415

Party B: Huaxing Trading Company (Pte) Ltd.

Add: 126 Waterloo Street, Singapore (0718)

Tel: 3366436

Fax: 3397862

乙方：华兴贸易私人有限公司

地址：新加坡滑铁卢街 126 号（0718）

电话：3366436

传真：3397862

Article 2　Appointment（委任）

Party A hereby appoints Party B as its Exclusive Agent to solicit orders for the commodity stipulated in Article 3 from customers in the territory stipulated in Article 4,and Party B accepts and assumes such appointment.

甲方指定乙方为其独家代理，负责在第 4 条规定的区域内向顾客招揽所规定商品的订单，乙方接受上述委任。

Article 3　Commodity（代理商品）

"Golden Fish" Brand Washing Machines

"金鱼"牌洗衣机

Article 4　Territory（代理区域）

In Singapore only

仅限于新加坡

Article 5　Minimum turnover（最低业务量）

Party B shall undertake to solicit orders for the above commodity from customers in the above territory during the effective period of this agreement for not less than USD 100,000.00.

乙方同意，在本协议有效期内从上述代理区域内的顾客处招揽的上述商品的订单价值不低于 10 万美元。

Article 6　Price and payment（价格与支付）

The price for each individual transaction shall be fixed through negotiations between Party B and the buyer, and shall be subject to Party A's final confirmation. Payment shall be made by confirmed, irrevocable L/C opened by the buyer in favor of Party A, which shall reach Party A 15 days before the date of shipment.

每一笔交易的货物价格应由乙方与买主通过谈判确定，并须经甲方最后确认。付款使用保兑的、不可撤销的信用证，由买方开出，以甲方为受益人。信用证须在装运日期前 15 天到达甲方。

Article 7　Exclusive rights（独家代理权）

In consideration of the exclusive rights granted herein, Party A shall not, directly or indirectly, sell or export the commodity stipulated in Article 3 to customers in Singapore through channels other than Party B; Party B shall not sell, distribute or promote the sales of any products competitive with or similar to the above commodity in Singapore and shall not solicit or accept orders for the purpose of selling them outside Singapore. Party A shall refer any enquiries or orders for the commodity in question received by Party A from other firms in Singapore to Party B during the validity of this agreement.

基于本协议授予的独家代理权，甲方不得直接或间接地通过乙方以外的渠道向新加坡顾客销售或出口第 3 条所列商品，乙方不得在新加坡经销、分销或促销与上述商品相竞争或类似的产品，也不得招揽或接受以到新加坡以外地区销售为目的的订单，在本协议有效期内，甲方应将其收到的来自新加坡其他商家的有关代理产品的询价或订单转交给乙方。

Article 8　Market report（商情报告）

In order to keep Party A well informed of the prevailing market conditions, Party B should undertake to supply Party A, at least once a quarter or at any time when necessary, with market reports concerning changes in the local regulations in connection with the import and sales of the commodity covered by this agreement, local market tendency and the buyer's comments on quality, packing, price, etc. of the goods supplied by Party A under this agreement. Party B shall also supply Party A with quotations and advertising materials on similar products of other suppliers.

为使甲方充分了解现行市场情况，乙方承担至少每季度一次或在必要时随时向甲方提供市场报告，内容包括与本协议代理商品的进口与销售有关的地方规章的变动、当地市场发展趋势，以及买方对甲方按协议供应的货物的品质、包装、价格等方面的意见。乙方还承担向甲方提供其他供应商类似商品的报价和广告资料。

Article 9　Advertising and expenses（广告及费用）

Party B shall bear all expenses for advertising and publicity in connection with the commodity in question in Singapore within the validity of this agreement, and shall submit to Party A all audio and video materials intended for advertising for prior approval.

乙方负担本协议有效期内在新加坡销售代理商品做广告宣传的一切费用，并向甲方提交用于广告的声像资料，供甲方事先核准。

Article 10　Commission（佣金）

Party A shall pay Party B a commission of 5% on the net invoiced selling price on all orders directly obtained by Party B and accepted by Party A. No commission shall be paid until Party A receives the full payment for each order.

对乙方直接获取并经甲方确认接受的订单，甲方按净发票售价向乙方支付 5% 的佣金。 佣金在甲方收到每笔订单的全部货款后才会支付。

Article 11　Transactions between governmental bodies（政府部门间的交易）

Transactions concluded between governmental bodies of Party A and Party B shall not be restricted by the terms and conditions of this agreement, nor shall the amount of such transactions be counted as part of the turnover stipulated in Article 5.

在甲、乙双方政府部门之间达成的交易不受本协议条款的限制，此类交易的金额也不应计入第 5 条规定的最低业务量。

Article 12　Industrial property rights（工业产权）

Party B may use the trade-marks owned by Party A for the sale of the Washing Machines covered herein within the validity of this agreement, and shall acknowledge that all patents, trademarks, copyrights or any other industrial property rights used or embodied in the Washing Machines shall remain the sole property of Party A. Should any infringement be found, Party B shall promptly notify Party A and assist Party A to take steps to protect the latter's rights.

在本协议有效期内，为销售有关洗衣机，乙方可以使用甲方拥有的商标，并承认使用或包含于洗衣机中的任何专利商标、版权或其他工业产权为甲方独家拥有。一旦发现侵权，乙方应立即通知甲方并协助甲方采取措施保护甲方权益。

Article 13　Validity of agreement（协议有效期）

This agreement, when duly signed by both parties concerned, shall remain in force for 12 months from October 1st, 2018 to September 30th, 2019, and it shall be extended for another 12 months upon expiration unless notice in writing is given to the contrary.

本协议经有关双方如期签署后生效，有效期为 1 年，从 2018 年 10 月 1 日至 2019 年 9 月 30 日。除非做出相反通知，本协议期满后将延长 12 个月。

Article 14　Termination（协议的终止）

During the validity of this agreement, if either of the two parties is found to have violated the stipulations herein, the other party has the right to terminate this agreement.

在本协议有效期内，如果一方被发现违背协议条款，另一方有权终止协议。

Article 15　Force majeure（不可抗力）

Either party shall not be held responsible for failure or delay to perform all or any part of this agreement due to flood, fire, earthquake, drought, war or any other events which could not be predicted, controlled, avoided or overcome by the relevant party. However, the party affected by the event of Force Majeure shall inform the other party of its occurrence in writing as soon as possible and thereafter send a certificate of the event issued by the relevant authorities to the other party within 15 days after its occurrence.

由于水灾、火灾、地震、干旱、战争或协议一方无法预见、控制、避免和克服的其他事件导致不能或暂时不能全部或部分履行本协议，该方不负责任。但是，受不可抗力事件影响的一方须尽快将发生的事件通知另一方，并在不可抗力事件发生 15 天内将有关机构出具的不可抗力事件的证明寄交对方。

Article 16　Arbitration（仲裁）

All disputes arising from the performance of this agreement shall be settled through friendly negotiation. Should no settlement be reached through negotiation, the case shall then be submitted for arbitration to the China International Economic and Trade Arbitration Commission (Beijing) and the rules of this Commission shall be apply. The award of the arbitration shall be final and binding upon both parties.

因履行本协议所发生的一切争议应通过友好协商解决。如协商不能解决争议，则应将争议提交中国国际经济贸易仲裁委员会（北京），依据其仲裁规则进行仲裁。仲裁裁决是终局的，对双方都有约束力。

Party A: Qingdao Hongda Industrial Co., Ltd. 　　Party B: Huaxing Trading Company (Pte) Ltd.
(Signature) 　　(Signature)
甲方：青岛宏达实业有限公司 　　乙方：华兴贸易私人有限公司
（签字） 　　（签字）

Sample of purchase note（购货单样本）

**Purchase note
购货单**

Date:
日期：
The Buyers:
买方：
The Sellers:
卖方：
The Buyers agree to buy and the Sellers agree to sell the following goods on terms and conditions as set forth below:
双方同意按下列条款由卖方售出下列商品：
(1) Name of Commodity, Specifications and Packing:
商品名称、规格及包装：
(2) Quantity:
数量：

(3) Unit Price:

单价：

(4) Total Value:

总值：

(Shipment Quantity _____% more or less allowed)

（装运数量允许有_____%的增减）

(5) Time of Shipment:

装运期限：

(6) Port of Loading:

装运口岸：

(7) Port of Destination:

目的口岸：

(8) Insurance:

Insurance to be covered by the seller for 110% of the invoice value against_____.

保险：

由卖方负责，按本合同总额的 110%投保_____险。

(9) Terms of Payment：

By confirmed, irrevocable, transferable and divisible L/C in favour of _____ payable at sight with T/T reimbursement clause/_____ days'/sight/date allowing partial shipments and transshipment. The covering L/C must reach the sellers before _____ and is to remain valid in _____, China until the 15th day after the aforesaid time of shipment, failing which the sellers reserve the right to cancel this Sales Contract without further notice and to claim from the buyers for losses resulting therefrom.

付款条件：

凭保兑的、不可撤销的、可转让的、可分割的即期有电索汇条款，出票_____天即期付款信用证，信用证以_____为受益人并允许分批装运和转船。该信用证必须在_____前开到卖方，信用证的有效期应为上述装船期后第 15 天，在中国_____到期，否则卖方有权取消本售货合约，不另行通知，并保留因此而发生的一切损失的索赔权。

(10) Inspection:

The Inspection Certificate of Quality/Quantity/Weight/Packing/Sanitary issued by_____of China shall be regarded as evidence of the sellers' delivery.

商品检验：

中国_____所签发的品质/数量/重量/包装/卫生检验合格证书作为卖方的交货依据。

(11) Shipping Marks:

唛头：

Other Terms:

其他条款：

(1) Discrepancy: In case of quality discrepancy, claim should be lodged by the buyers within 30 days after the arrival of the goods at the port of destination, while for quantity discrepancy, claim

should be lodged by the buyers within 15 days after the arrival of the goods at the port of destination. In all cases, claims must be accompanied by Survey Reports of Recognized Public Surveyors agreed to by the sellers. Should the responsibility of the subject under claim be found to rest on the part of the sellers, the sellers shall, within 20 days after receipt of the claim, send their reply to the buyers together with a suggestion for settlement.

异议：品质异议须于货到目的口岸之日起 30 天内提出，数量异议须于货到目的口岸之日起 15 天内提出，但均须提供经卖方同意的公证行出具的检验证明。如责任属于卖方，卖方应于收到异议后 20 天内答复买方并提出处理意见。

(2) The covering L/C shall stipulate the sellers' option of shipping the indicated percentage more or less than the quantity hereby contracted and be negotiated for the amount covering the value of quantity actually shipped. (The buyers are requested to establish the L/C in the amount with the indicated percentage over the total value of the order as per this Sales Contract)

信用证内应明确规定卖方有权可多装或少装所注明的百分比，并按实际装运数量议付。（买方所开信用证的金额按本售货合约金额增加相应的百分比）

(3) The contents of the covering L/C shall be in strict conformity with the stipulations of the Sales Contract. In case of any variation thereof necessitating amendment of the L/C, the buyers shall bear the expenses for effecting the amendment. The sellers shall not be held responsible for possible delay of shipment resulting from awaiting the amendment of the L/C and reserve the right to claim from the buyers for the losses resulting therefrom.

信用证内容须严格符合本售货合约的规定，否则修改信用证的费用由买方负担，卖方并不负因修改信用证而延误装运的责任，并保留因此而发生的一切损失的索赔权。

(4) Except in cases where the insurance is covered by the buyers as arranged, insurance is to be covered by the sellers with a Chinese insurance company. If insurance for additional amount and /or for other insurance terms is required by the buyers, prior notice to this effect must reach the sellers before shipment and is subject to the sellers' agreement, and the extra insurance premium shall be for the buyers' account.

除经约定保险归买方投保者外，由卖方向中国的保险公司投保。如买方需增加保险额或需加保其他险，可于装船前提出，经卖方同意后代为投保，其费用由买方负担。

(5) The sellers shall not be held responsible if they fail, owing to Force Majeure cause or causes, to make delivery within the time stipulated in this Sales Contract or cannot deliver the goods. However, the sellers shall inform the buyers immediately by cable. The sellers shall deliver to the buyers by registered letter, if it is requested by the buyers, a certificate issued by the China Council for the Promotion of International Trade or by any competent authorities, attesting the existence of the said cause or causes. The buyers' failure to obtain the relevant Import License is not to be treated as Force Majeure.

因不可抗力事故使卖方不能在本售货合约规定期限内交货或不能交货，卖方不负责任，但是卖方必须立即以电报通知买方。如果买方提出要求，卖方应以挂号函向买方提供由中国国际贸易促进委员会或有关机构出具的证明，证明事故的存在。买方不能领到进口许可证，不能被认为属于不可抗力范围。

(6) Arbitration: All disputes arising in connection with this Sales Contract or the execution thereof shall be settled by way of amicable negotiation. In case no settlement can be reached, the case at issue shall then be submitted for arbitration to the China International Economic and Trade Arbitration Commission in accordance with the provisions of the said Commission. The award of the said Commission shall be deemed as final and binding upon both parties.

仲裁：凡因执行本合约所发生的或与本合约有关的一切争执，双方应以友好方式协商解决；如果协商不能解决，应提交中国国际经济贸易仲裁委员会，根据该会的仲裁规则进行仲裁。仲裁裁决是终局的，对双方都有约束力。

(7) Supplementary Condition(s): (Should the articles stipulated in this Contract be in conflict with the following supplementary conditions, the supplementary condition(s) shall be taken as valid and binding).

附加条款（本合同其他条款如与本附加条款有抵触，以本附加条款为准）。

Sellers:	Buyers:
卖方：	买方：
（Signature）	（Signature）
（签字）	（签字）

Section Three Performance of Contract（合同的履行）

A sales contract or sales confirmation is binding on both parties. Nothing in it can be altered without mutual consent. During its performance, however, various unforeseen problems may arise. In that case, it will be necessary to find through consultations some arrangements acceptable to both sides.

Such consultation is not always plain sailing because modification of terms and conditions already agreed upon will naturally affect in some way the interests of one side or the other. Careful handling at this stage will prevent the matter from developing into a serious dispute. In trade practice, usually, we should follow the principle of "honor the contract and maintain commercial integrity" and fulfill seriously and honestly the obligations set forth in the contract. At the same time, we are entitled to the rights granted therein against any acts which are inconsistent with the contract stipulations.

The performance of the contract involves many working links, and the procedures are also very complicated. In order to ensure the smooth implementation of the contract, scientific management of the contract must be strengthened and a management system that can reflect the process of execution of the contract should be established.

销售合同或销售确认书对进出口双方都具有约束力，如果没有经过双方的同意，任何一方都不能随意修改。然而，在执行合同的过程中，各种意想不到的问题都有可能出现，此时一定要经过双方协商，寻找双方都能接受的解决途径。

这种协商肯定不会是一帆风顺的，原因是要修改双方已经同意了的条款肯定会在一定程度上影响其中一方的利益，因此，在明确修改时，总不会是一帆风顺的。谨慎而稳妥地对待和处理这些问题可以避免使问题进一步转化成严重的争端。在做外贸业务时，切记"重合同，守信用"的原则，认真忠实地履行合同规定的责任和义务。同时，合同也赋予我们权利，反对一切违背合同规定的行为。

出口合同的履行涉及的工作环节较多，手续也繁杂，为了保证出口合同的顺利履行，要加强对合同的科学管理，建立能反映合同执行情况的管理制度。

Section Four   Components of a Typical Successful Cross-border E-commerce Transaction（典型跨境电子商务事务的成功要素）

Cross-border e-commerce does not refer merely to a firm putting up a website for the purpose of selling goods to buyers over the Internet. For cross-border e-commerce to be a competitive alternative to traditional commercial transactions and for a firm to maximize the benefits of e-commerce, a number of technical as well as enabling issues have to be considered. A typical cross-border e-commerce transaction loop involves the following major players and corresponding requisites.

跨境电子商务并不仅仅指公司为在互联网上出售商品给买家设置一个网站。跨边界的电子商务竞争替代传统的商业交易，使得公司电子商务的好处最大化，这就需要考虑很多技术以及使用问题。典型的跨边界的电子商务交易循环包括以下主要参与者和相应的条件。

The Seller should have the following components:

• A corporate website with e-commerce capabilities (e.g., a secure transaction server);

• A corporate intranet so that orders are processed in an efficient manner;

• IT-literate employees to manage the information flows and maintain the e-commerce system.

卖方应该具有以下条件：

• 具有电子商务功能的企业网站（如安全事务服务器）；

• 公司内部网络，订单在一个有效的方式下进行处理；

• 具备信息技术知识的员工，管理信息流并维护电子商务系统。

Transaction partners include:

• Banking institutions that offer transaction clearing services (e.g., processing credit card payments and electronic fund transfers);

• National and international freight companies to enable the movement of physical goods within, around, and out of the country. For business-to-consumer transactions, the system must offer a means for cost-effective transport of small packages (such as purchasing books over the Internet, for example, so that it is not prohibitively more expensive than buying from a local store); and

• An authentication authority that serves as a trusted third party to ensure the integrity and security of transactions.

交易的合作伙伴包括：

· 银行机构（如提供交易结算服务，处理信用卡支付和电子资金转账）；

· 国内及国际货运公司，以确保实体货物在境内、跨区域及出境运输的畅通。B2C 交易，系统必须提供有成本效益的小包装运输方式（例如，通过互联网购买书籍，不比从当地的商店购买贵）；

· 权威认证作为受信任的第三方来保证交易的完整性和安全性。

Consumers (in a business-to-consumer transaction) who:

· Form a critical mass of the population with access to the Internet and disposable income enabling widespread use of credit cards; and

· Possess a mindset for purchasing goods over the Internet rather than by physically inspecting items.

消费者（B2C）：

· 形成一个一定规模的上网人口和可支配收入，使信用卡得以广泛使用；

· 拥有在互联网上购买货物的心态而不是通过亲自检查物品。

The government, to establish:

· A legal framework governing e-commerce transactions (including electronic documents, signatures, and the like); and

· Legal institutions to enforce the legal framework (i.e., laws and regulations) and protect consumers and businesses from fraud, among others.

政府需建立：

· 电子商务法律框架管理事务（包括电子文档、签名等）；

· 法律机构执行法律框架（即法律法规）和保护消费者和企业免受欺诈等。

China's E-commerce Law, newly enacted on August 31, 2018, made clear provisions on promoting e-commerce and cross-border e-commerce trade. The authorities firmly support credit evaluation agencies established according to law, to conduct e-commerce credit evaluation and provide such services to society. The authorities promote the establishment of cross-border e-commerce exchanges and cooperation between different countries and regions, participate in the formulation of international e-commerce rules, and promote international mutual recognition of electronic signatures and electronic identities. At the same time, the authorities promote the establishment of cross-border e-commerce dispute resolution mechanisms with different countries and regions.

我国 2018 年 8 月 31 日新制定的《电子商务法》在促进电子商务和跨境电子商务贸易方面做出了明确的规定。国家支持依法设立的信用评价机构开展电子商务信用评价，向社会提供电子商务信用评价服务。国家推动建立与不同国家、地区之间跨境电子商务的交流合作，参与电子商务国际规则的制定，促进电子签名、电子身份等国际互认。同时，国家推动建立与不同国家、地区之间的跨境电子商务争议解决机制。

The newly enacted E-Commerce Law also makes clear provisions on the legal liability of e-commerce operators. If an e-commerce operator, who sells goods or provides services, fails to perform its contractual obligations adequately, or fails to conform to the agreement, or causes damage to others, the operator shall bear civil liability according to law.

《电子商务法》也在电子商务经营者的法律责任方面做出了明确的规定。电子商务经营者销售商品或者提供服务,不履行合同义务或者履行合同义务不符合约定,或者造成他人损害的,依法承担民事责任。

最后,互联网的成功使用取决于以下两方面:

• 一个健全和可靠的网络基础设施;

• 一种不会因消费者在线消费时长及网购行为而施以惩罚性收费的定价结构(例如:包含网络服务商接入费与本地通话费的统一固定月费)。

The Internet, the successful use of which depends on the following:

• A robust and reliable Internet infrastructure; and

• A pricing structure that doesn't penalize consumers for spending time online and buying goods over the Internet (e.g., a flat monthly charge for both ISP access and local phone calls).

Section Five　Digital Trade Contracts（数字贸易合同）

China is promoting institutional openness in digital trade to facilitate and regulate cross-border data flow. It is imperative to establish a sound data export security management system, improve relevant mechanisms and procedures, and carry out data export security assessments in a standardized and orderly manner. On the premise of ensuring the security of important data and personal information, it is imperative to establish an efficient, convenient, and secure cross-border data flow mechanism to promote orderly cross-border data flow. For digital trade activities, it is necessary to accelerate the construction of a digital trust system, including accelerating the construction of a digital trade certification system, promoting the development, innovation, and application of cutting-edge digital trust technologies, and cultivating a digital trust ecosystem. It is also required to promote international mutual recognition of digital certificates, electronic signatures, and other technologies, meanwhile, and encourage the international development of third-party service providers such as data security, data assets, and digital credit. So, what are the differences between digital trade contracts and traditional trade contracts?

我国正在推进数字贸易制度型开放,促进和规范数据跨境流动。健全数据出境安全管理制度,完善相关机制程序,规范有序开展数据出境安全评估。在保障重要数据和个人信息安全的前提下,建立高效、便利、安全的数据跨境流动机制,促进数据跨境有序流动。对于数字贸易活动而言,需要加快构建数字信任体系,其中包括加快数字贸易认证体系建设,促进数字信任前沿技术的开发创新与应用推广,培育数字信任生态。推动数字证书、电子签名等国际互认。鼓励数据安全、数据资产、数字信用等第三方服务机构国际化发展。那么,数字贸易合同与传统贸易合同有什么不同呢?

There are significant differences between digital trade contracts and traditional trade contracts in multiple aspects.

From the perspective of the environment and mode of trade contract signing, the digital trade contract signing environment is virtual, and the contract signing is mainly completed through the

Internet platform. The traditional environment for the formation of trade contracts is in the real world, where both parties engage in face-to-face negotiations and sign contracts. The formation of digital trade contracts is often negotiated and confirmed through electronic data interchange (EDI), emails, or other online tools. The traditional way of concluding trade contracts is through paper documents, which are signed and stamped by both parties for confirmation.

From the perspective of contract signing and authentication, the main signing methods for digital trade contracts are electronic signatures or digital signatures, which are often based on specific encryption techniques to ensure the authenticity and integrity of the signatures. In addition, the authentication method for digital trade contracts involves third-party authoritative authentication agencies to ensure the legal validity of electronic signatures. Compared to traditional trade contracts, the signature method is handwritten or stamped.

The performance and payment of digital trade contracts are also different from traditional trade contracts, reflected in the fact that the performance of digital trade contracts relies on online electronic trading platforms or third-party service providers to deliver goods and provide services. The traditional way of fulfilling trade contracts is to deliver goods and provide services through physical locations such as storefronts and warehouses. Correspondingly, the payment methods for digital trade contracts mainly involve electronic payment methods such as online payment and electronic transfer. Unlike traditional trade contracts, which use methods such as cash, letters of credit, draft, and bank transfer.

数字贸易合同与传统贸易合同在多个方面存在显著差异。

从贸易合同订立的环境与方式看，数字贸易合同的订立环境是虚拟空间，其合同签订主要通过互联网平台完成。传统贸易合同的订立环境是现实世界，合同双方进行面对面协商和签约。数字贸易合同的订立往往通过电子数据交换（EDI）、电子邮件或其他在线工具进行协商和确认。传统贸易合同的订立通过纸质文件，双方签字并盖章进行确认。

从合同的签名与认证方面看，数字贸易合同主要采用电子签名或数字签名，这些签名往往基于特定的加密技术，以保证签名的真实性和完整性。此外，数字贸易合同的认证方式是通过第三方权威认证机构进行认证，确保电子签名的法律效力。相比较而言，传统贸易合同采用手写签名或盖章的方式。

数字贸易合同的履行与支付也与传统贸易合同不同，数字贸易合同的履行方式是依托在线电子交易平台或第三方服务提供商进行货物的交付和服务的提供。传统贸易合同的履行方式则是通过实体店面、仓库等物理场所进行货物的交付和服务的提供。相应地，数字贸易合同的支付方式主要采用在线支付、电子转账等电子化支付方式。不同于传统贸易合同的支付方式，即采用现金、信用证、汇票、银行转账等传统支付方式。

Part B Terminology Practice

1. **Acceptance**（接受）：The unconditional agreement to an offer. This creates the contract. Before acceptance, any offer can be withdrawn, but once accepted the contract is binding on both sides. Any conditions have the effect of a counter-offer that must be accepted by the other party.

2. Agent（代理人）：Somebody appointed to act on behalf of another person — known as the principal. The amount of authority to deal that the agent has is subject to agreement between the principal and the agent. However, unless told otherwise, third parties can assume the agent has full authority to deal.

3. **Breach of contract**（违约）：A failure by a party to a contract to perform its obligations in that contract or an indication of an intention not to do so.

4. Consumer（消费者）：A person who buys goods or services but not as part of their business. A company can be a consumer for contracts not related to its business — especially for goods or services it buys for its employees. Charities are also treated as consumers.

5. Collective agreement（指导建议）：Term used for agreements made between employees and employers, usually involving trade unions. They often cover more than one organization. Although these can be seen as contracts, they are governed by employment law, not contract law.

6. Conditions（合同条件）：Major terms in a contract. Conditions are the basis of any contract and if one of them fails or is broken, the contract is breached. These are in contrast to warranties, the other type of contract term, which are less important and will not usually lead to a breach of contract — but rather an adjustment in price or a payment of damages.

7. **Due diligence**（尽职调查）：The formal process of investigating the background of a business, either prior to buying it or engaging with it as another party in a major contract. It is used to ensure that there are no hidden details that could affect the deal.

8. **Exclusion clauses**（免责条款）：Clauses in a contract that are intended to exclude one party from liability if a stated circumstance occurs. They are types of **exemption clauses.** The courts tend to interpret them strictly and, where possible, in favour of the party that did not write them. In customer dealings, exclusion clauses are governed by regulations that render most of them ineffective, but note that these regulations do not apply to business dealings.

9. **Exemption clauses**（豁免条款）：Clauses in a contract that try to restrict the liability of the party that writes them. These are split into exclusion clauses that try to exclude liability completely for specified outcomes, and limitation clauses that try to set a maximum on the amount of damages the party may have to pay if there is a failure of some part of the contract. Exemption clauses are regulated very strictly in consumer dealings but don't apply to business-to-business.

10. **Joint and several liability**（连带和个别责任）：Where parties act together in a contract as partners they have joint and several liability. In addition to all the partners being responsible together, each partner is also liable individually for the entire contract — so a creditor could recover a whole debt from any one of them individually, leaving that person to recover their shares from the rest of the partners.

11. **Household goods**（个人物品）：The commodity we have authority to handle. The term "household goods" embraces not only personal effects and property transported from residence to residence, but also relocations of offices, museums, or the transportation of displays.

12. **Household goods carrier**（个人物品运输承运人）：A carrier granted authority by the Interstate Commerce Commission to transport household goods in interstate or foreign commerce.

13. **Household goods transportation act**（个人物品搬运监管公共法律）：Public Law 96-454 (1980) which was designed to increase competition and reduce regulation of the Household Goods Moving Industry, by the Federal Government.

14. **ICC (Interstate Commerce Commission)**（监管州际运输业联邦机构）：The Federal Agency regulating the interstate transportation industry, including movers of household goods.

15. **Interstate commerce**（州际贸易）：Interstate commerce means commerce between any place in a state and any place in another state, or between places in the same state through another state, whether such commerce moves wholly by motor vehicle or partly by motor vehicle, rail, express, or water.

16. **Interstate commerce commission**（州际贸易委员会）：The regulatory body established by Congress to administer the Interstate Commerce Act and related amendments.

17. **Intrastate**（州内移动）：A move with its origin and destination within the same state.

18. **Intrastate commerce**（州内贸易）：Commerce that originates, is destined for, and is entirely transported within one state.

19. **Lease**（出租）：This type of lease is a fee for the use of equipment. Responsibility for maintenance, upgrades, etc. may vary, but generally remain with the lessor. Title is maintained by the supplier.

20. **Lease to own, lease/purchase**（租赁）：A lease agreement for the lessee (user) to pay the lessor (owner) for use of an asset.

21. **Letter of authority**（授权信）：If no purchase order or order for service is used, the commercial account paying for a credit account move must write a letter authorizing or giving permission to move their employee, and assuring the mover that they will pay for said move.

22. **Low bidder**（低报价供应商）：A supplier submitting the lowest bid that meets and/or exceeds minimum specifications, delivery requirements, etc. This does not always mean that the lowest price received is the low bidder.

23. **Order for service**（授权搬家公司运输家庭物品的文件）：The document authorizing the moving company to transport household goods.

24. **Origin agent**（代理人）：The agent supervising the packing and loading of a shipment.

25. **Purchase**（购买）：To acquire goods or services by paying money or its equivalent.

26. **Purchase order**（购买合同）：A legally binding document for goods or services.

27. **Quote**（报价）：To state the current price for a good or service. Quotes may be either verbal or written and are generally non-binding.

28. **Sole source**（唯一来源）：Sole sourcing exists when only one source is available. Local telephone and electric companies are examples. Sole sourcing also exists when only one source makes the item.

29. **Standing microphone**（固定麦克风）：A mike attached to a metal stand on the floor. Adjustable to the height of the speaker.

30. **Surcharge**（额外收费）：Additional charge, over and above an established rate of service.

31. **Terms**（条款）：Specific agreed payment terms to vendor. Examples: Net 30 Days; Net 10

Days; 2% 10 Days.

32. **Unit of measure**（测量标准单位）: A determined quantity adopted as a standard of measurement. Example: Box, Case, Each, Gallon, Pound, etc.

33. **Valuables**（贵重物品）: Documents, currency, jewelry, watches, precious stones and metals, articles of extraordinary or irreplaceable value, accounts, bills, deeds, evidence of debt, securities, notes, postage stamps or coin collections, etc.

34. **Value season**（淡季）: A term used by some suppliers to indicate off-peak season when prices are lower.

Part C Terms

1. agency agreement 代理协议

2. agreement on general terms and conditions on business 一般经营交易条件的协议

3. agreement on loan facilities up to a given amount 商定借款协议

4. agreement fixing price 固定价格协议 5. agreement in writing 书面协议

6. agreement of reimbursement 偿付协议

7. agreement on import licensing procedure 进口许可证手续协议

8. agreement on reinsurance 再保险协议 9. agreement to resell 转售协议

10. bilateral agreement 双边协议 11. bilateral trade agreement 双边贸易协议

12. commercial agreement 商业协议 13. distributorship agreement 分销协议

14. exclusive distributorship agreement 独家销售协议

15. joint venture agreement 合资协议 16. licensing agreement 许可证协议

17. loan agreement 贷款协议 18. partnership agreement 合伙协议

19. supply agreement 供货协议 20. barter contract 易货合同

21. binding contract 有约束力合同 22. blank form contract 空白合同

23. commercial contract 商业合同 24. cross license contract 互换许可证合同

25. exclusive license contract 独家许可证合同 26. formal contract 正式合同

27. illegal contract 非法合同 28. installment contract 分期合同

29. vice-president of sales 销售副总裁 30. senior customer manager 高级客户经理

31. sales manager 销售经理 32. regional sales manager 地区销售经理

33. merchandising manager 采购经理

34. marketing and sales director 市场与销售总监

35. director of subsidiary rights 分公司权利总监

36. sales assistant 销售助理

37. assistant customer executive 客户管理助理

38. wholesale buyer 批发采购员 39. tele-interviewer 电话调查员

40. real estate appraiser 房地产评估师 41. marketing consultant 市场顾问

42. market research analyst 市场调查分析员 43. manufacturers representative 厂家代表

44. sales representative 销售代表 45. marketing intern 市场实习

46. marketing director 市场总监   47. insurance agent 保险代理人
48. customer manager 客户经理   49. vice-president of marketing 市场副总裁
50. regional customer manager 地区客户经理 51. sales administrator 销售主管
52. telemarketing director 电话销售总监   53. advertising manager 广告经理
54. travel agent 旅行代办员   55. sales executive 销售执行者

Part D Exercise

I. Translate the followings from Chinese into English.

1. 支付方式   2. 书面合同
3. 合同的执行   4. 销售合同
5. 购货确认书   6. 交易条件
7. 贸易伙伴   8. 合同的构成
9. 贸易协定   10. 寄售合同
11. 合同正文   12. 合同延期
13. 合同缔约方   14. 特约条款
15. 一般条款

II. Answer the following questions in English.

1. What is the definition for a contract? What may happen if any party fails to fulfill his contractual obligations?

2. What are the two parties of business negotiations? And give examples as you can.

3. Why do the trading parties usually prefer a written contract? What is the difference between a sales contract and a sales(purchase) confirmation?

4. What does the setting up of a contract generally contain?

5. What does the contract proper usually include?

III. Translate the following English into Chinese.

The contract is based on agreement, which is the result of business negotiation. There are two types of business negotiations: oral and written. The former refers to the direct discussion conducted at trade fairs or by sending trade groups abroad or by inviting foreign customers. Business discussions through international trunk class are also included in this category.

IV. Case Study.

1. Mr. Smith, an American businessman, sold a batch of IBM computers to a Hong Kong importer, Mr. Chen. The sales contract was concluded in the United States of America on the terms of CIF Hong Kong. During execution of this contract, disputes arose between the seller and the buyer on the form and interpretation of the contract.

Question:

In such a case, did the law of the U.S.A. or the law of Hong Kong apply to the disputes? Why?

2. Mr. Anderson intended to sell a plane to Mr. Johnson. In his cable, Mr. Anderson offered: "Confirm sale of a plane ... Please send 5 000 pounds by telegraphic transfer." Mr. Johnson cabled

back immediately: "Confirm purchase of your plane, terms and conditions same as your cable. I've sent the 5000 pounds to your Account Bank who keeps your money on your behalf until delivery of the plane. Please confirm delivery within 30 days from the date of this cable." Mr. Anderson did not reply and sold the plane to another buyer at a much higher price. Disagreements occurred between the two parties about whether the contract was concluded effectively.

Question:

In such a case, was the contract concluded? Why?

V. Please fill in the Sales Contract according to the letters between LONDON GREEN TRADE CORP. and GUANGDONG LIGHT ELECTRICAL APPLANCES CO., LTD.

英国伦敦格林贸易公司业务员 DAVID CURTIS 在广州春交会上获知广东轻工家电公司经营 DESK LIGHT，遂于 2019 年 6 月 2 日发来询盘。

函 1

敬启者：

在 2019 年春交会上，获悉贵公司生产 HALOGEN FITTING，我方对 J201 号产品感兴趣，请报 6 000PCS CIF LONDON。

我方渴望了解你公司最优惠的交易条件和有关的资信情况，我公司业务往来银行是伦敦商业银行。

盼早复。

DAVID CURTIS

2019 年 6 月 2 日

广东轻工家电公司接到英国伦敦格林贸易公司的信后，业务员李牛即于 6 月 4 日发盘并建议增加订货数量以便凑成一整集装箱货柜。

函 2

敬启者：

很高兴收到你方 6 月 2 日询价，我公司经营 DESK LIGHT 已有二十多年的历史，该产品在欧洲深受欢迎。建议你方将产品数量增加到 9 600PCS，以便我们装成 40×1 整柜。现报价如下：

（1）商品：DESK LIGHT

（2）包装：箱包装，每箱 12 件

（3）数量：9 600 件

（4）型号：J201

（5）价格：每件 3.5 美元 CIF 伦敦

（6）支付方式：不可撤销的即期信用证，做成以我方为受益人

（7）装运：收到信用证后 3~4 周内装运

我公司业务往来银行为中国银行广州分行，有关我公司的资信情况，请洽询中国银行伦敦分行。

盼早来首次订单。

李牛

2019 年 6 月 4 日

英国伦敦格林贸易公司接信后，认为价格太高，于 6 月 8 日来信说明该公司的经营优势，希望广东轻工家电公司降低价格。

函 3

敬启者：

你方 6 月 4 日信已收到，谢谢你方要求将数量增加到 9 600PCS，我方没有异议。但价格偏高，我方难以接受。

我方对本地区市场有充分的了解并在芬兰拥有广泛的销售组织，我们有信心推广贵公司该型号产品，请你方报最优惠价。

盼早复。

DAVID CURTIS

2019 年 6 月 8 日

广东轻工家电公司李牛接对方信后，经研究同意降低价格，以便打开伦敦的市场。于是 6 月 12 日去信英国伦敦格林贸易公司。

函 4

敬启者：

你方 6 月 8 日信收悉，谢谢。

我方在欧洲销售该产品的价格均不低于 3.5 美元/件。但考虑到贵公司首次与我方合作，并对我方产品有信心，我方愿降低价格，现报价如下：

（1）商品：DESK LIGHT

（2）包装：箱包装，每箱 12 件

（3）数量：9 600 件

（4）型号：J201

（5）价格：每件 3.00 美元 CIF 伦敦

同时，我方要求以不可撤销即期信用证支付，若你方能在本月底前下订单并开立信用证，我方可保证在 6 月交货。

正像你方所看到的那样，我方产品在欧洲地区享有盛名。由于我方产品物美价廉，无疑有助于你方开拓市场。

请贵方尽快答复。

李牛

2019 年 6 月 12 日

英国伦敦格林贸易公司接到广东轻工家电公司的降价信函后，即于 6 月 15 日来信表示接受。

函 5

敬启者：

我方接受你方 6 月 12 日的发盘。由于我方急需此货，望你方按报盘许诺的 2019 年 6 月装运，不允许分批装运。装船通知必须在装船后 2 天内寄给开证申请人，告知毛重和净重、船名、提单号码、提单日及合同号码。请你方准备好合同并寄我方签署。一旦签订合同，我方即申请开证。

希望很快收到合同。

DAVID CURTIS

2019 年 6 月 15 日

销售合同
SALES CONTRACT

卖方： Contract No.: _____

Seller: _____ Date: _____

地址： Signed at: _____

Address: _____ Telephone: _____

Fax: _____

Buyer: _____ Telephone: _____

Address: _____ Fax: _____

This Sales Contract is made by and between the Seller and the Buyer, whereby the Seller agrees to sell and the Buyer agrees to buy the under-mentioned goods according to the terms and conditions stipulated below:

(1) 货号、品名及规格 Name of Commodity and Specifications	(2) 数量 Quantity	(3) 单位 Unit	(4) 单位价格 Unit Price	(5) 数量 Amount
_____% more or less both in amount and quantity allowed				
	Total Amount			

(6) Packing: _____

(7) Delivery from _____ to _____

(8) Shipping Marks: _____

(9) Time of Shipment: Within _____ days after receipt of L/C allowing transshipment.

(10) Terms of Payment: By 100% confirmed irrevocable L/C in favor of the seller to be available by sight draft to be opened and to reach China before _____ and to remain valid for negotiation in China until the 15th days after the aforesaid time of shipment.

L/C must mention this contract number L/C advised by Bank of China Guangzhou Branch.

TLX: 444U4K GZBC, CN. All banking charges outside China (the mainland of China) are for the account of the Drawee.

(11) Insurance: To be effected by the seller for 110% of full invoice value covering _____ up to _____

(12) Arbitration: All disputes arising from the execution of or in connection with this contract shall be settled amicably by negotiation. If a settlement can not be reached through negotiation, the case shall then be submitted to China International Economic and Trade Arbitration Commission in Shenzhen (or in Beijing) for arbitration in accordance with its procedures rules. The arbitral award is final and binding upon both parties for settling the dispute. The fee for arbitration shall be borne by the losing party unless otherwise awarded.

The Seller: _____ The Buyer: _____

VI. Please make out a Sales Confirmation according to the following particulars.

1. We are interested in the plush toys of your company. Please make an offer.
2. Plush toys: bear 20 US Dollars each; cat 30 US Dollars each. CIF Osaka, irrevocable L/C at sight. Each is packed in a plastic pocket and twenty are in a carton. The delivery time should not be after August, 2009.
3. We are interested in the plush toys (bear, cat). Other terms can be accepted except the high price. If you can decrease 5 US Dollars each, we are willing to order 10 000 each kind.
4. We agree with your requirements of price, other trade terms continue.

VII. Multiple Choices.

1. We feel sure that they will be glad to furnish you (   ) any information you require.
   A. for　　　　　　B. at　　　　　　C. on　　　　　　D. with
2. We look forward to (   ) your catalogue and price list for women's sweater.
   A. receive　　　B. receiving　　　C. received　　　D. being received
3. Quotations and samples will be sent (   ) receipt of your specific enquiries.
   A. for　　　　　　B. upon　　　　　C. with　　　　　D. to
4. As this article falls (   ) the scope of our business activities, we take this opportunity to express our wish to conduct some transactions with you in the near future.
   A. with　　　　　B. in　　　　　　C. within　　　　　D. at
5. We assure you (   ) our full cooperation.
   A. for　　　　　　B. at　　　　　　C. with　　　　　D. of
6. We thank you for your letter dated May 6th (   ) our silk blouses of various styles.
   A. enquiry for　　B. enquiring for　　C. enquired for　　D. enquire for
7. They are seriously considering (   ) a complete plant for the production of cutting tools.
   A. import　　　　B. importing　　　C. to import　　　D. imported
8. Will you please send us your prices for the items (   ) below.
   A. listing　　　　B. being listed　　C. to list　　　　D. listed
9. If you can supply us the goods immediately, we shall (   ) to place a prompt trial order.
   A. preparing　　　B. be preparing　　C. prepare　　　D. be prepared
10. These leather handbags are fully illustrated in the catalogue and are (   ) the same high quality as our gloves.
    A. for　　　　　B. of　　　　　　C. to　　　　　　D. in

VIII. Please determine whether the following statements are True or False. Then put T for True or F for False in the bracket at the end of each statement.

1. A contract is an agreement between two or more competent parties in which an offer is made and accepted, and each party benefits. (   )
2. A contract is an agreement which sets forth binding obligations of the relevant parties. (   )
3. A contract or confirmation can be drawn up only by the seller. (   )
4. The sales or purchase contract is less formal than the sales or purchase confirmation. (   )
5. A business contract is enforceable by the community. (   )

6. A business contract may be formal or informal. (   )

7. Generally speaking, the business contract is usually made up of three parts, i.e., the preamble, the body and the witness clause.(   )

8. Conditions are the basis of any contract and if one of them fails or is broken, the contract is breached. (   )

9. Exemption clauses are regulated very strictly in consumer dealings. (   )

10. Exemption clauses apply to those who deal in the course of their business. (   )

Chapter Four

Part A Text

Trade Terms

The buying and selling of goods internationally are conducted around the contract. Both buyers and sellers not only enjoy the rights conferred by the contract, but also assume various obligations under the contract. As a seller, they should send the goods to the buyer as well as the documents related to the goods according to the stipulations set forth in the contract and the provisions stated in the relative law and rules. The ownership of the goods, thus, is transferred. The buyer's reciprocal obligations are to accept the goods and pay for them. During the handover process of the goods, how to partition the responsibilities, costs and risks should be dealt with very carefully by the buyers and sellers in the negotiation and signing of the contract.

In international trade, price terms lie at the core of the terms and conditions of a contract and often result in some of the key problems for which the exporter and the importer have to strive. What's more, sending goods from one country to another, as part of a commercial transaction, can be a risky business. If they are lost or damaged, or if delivery does not take place for some other reasons, the climate of confidence between the parties may degenerate to the point where a lawsuit is brought. Thus, the pricing problems an exporter and an importer deal with are far more complicated than those in domestic trade. Besides the cost covered in the calculation of export price, the price quotation of export trade should also indicate which party is to bear the expenses of freight, insurance and other relevant charges, and which party is to bear the risks in case of the goods being damaged. In order to complete their deals successfully, the sellers and the buyers in international contracts should, at the very beginning of the deal, make clear to each other their respective obligations and find the full expression of those in the trade terms.

国际货物买卖业务都是围绕合同进行的，买卖双方既享受合同赋予的各种权利，同时也要承担合同规定的各种义务。作为卖方，其基本义务是按照合同和法律、惯例的规定，交付货物，移交一切与货物有关的单据，并转移货物所有权；买方的对等义务则是接受货物和支付货款。在货物交接的过程中，有关责任、费用和风险的划分问题，是买卖双方在谈判和签约时要加以明确的重要内容。

在国际贸易中，价格条款是合同中所有条款的核心，经常引发一些进口商和出口商不得不为之力争的问题。并且，作为一笔商业交易的一部分，从一国运输货物到另一国，可能是一种有风险的业务。如果货物丢失或损坏，或由于某种原因货物未予交付，则当事人之间的信任可能会降低到引起法律诉讼的程度。因此，进口商和出口商所要解决的价格问题比国内贸易中的价格问题复杂得多。出口报价除了要包括成本，还要指明由哪一方承担运费、保险费和其他相关费用，由哪一方承担货物受损的风险。因此，为顺利地完成交易，国际货物买卖合同的卖方和买方最好在交易的一开始就明确双方的责任，并通过贸易术语（又称价格术语）充分体现出来。

What is trade terms（什么是贸易术语）

When quoting prices to their overseas buyer, an exporter will naturally take into account paying of the various expenses involved in getting the goods from the factory or warehouse in their own country to the buyer's premises. For example, an exporter, in calculating their export price, works out dock charges, clearing and forwarding charges, freight and insurance, and certainly also adds its profit margin, to the price paid to the manufacturer, to make it a CIF Hamburg. What is "CIF Hamburg"? It is one of the trade terms, or delivery terms as we usually call them.

When an exporter and an importer enter into a contract, they may not know the differences in the different trading practices in their respective countries. This can give rise to misunderstandings, disputes and litigations with all the waste of time and money that this entails. What is more, sending goods from one country to another, as part of an international transaction, can be a risky business. If they are lost or damaged, or if delivery does not take place for some other reason, the climate of confidence between the contracting parties may degenerate to the point where a lawsuit is brought. However, if the sellers and the buyers in international contracts want their deals to be successfully completed, they must, at the very beginning of the deal, make clear to each other their respective obligations and find the full expression of those in the trade terms.

出口商在向国外买主报价时，自然要考虑把货物从本国国内的工厂或仓库运输到买方所在地所涉及的各种费用包括在内。例如，出口商在计算出口价格时，还要计算出码头费用、运输报关费用、运费和保险费，并把这些费用，当然还有它们的利润，加到已经支付给生产厂家的价格上，使其成为比如说 CIF 汉堡价。什么是"CIF 汉堡价"呢？这就是我们通常所说的贸易术语，或者叫作交货条件。

进出口商双方在签订合同时，可能还不知道各自国家中存在着不同的贸易习惯做法。这样就可能引起误会、纠纷和诉讼，并由此造成时间和金钱的浪费。另外，作为国际贸易的一部分，把货物从一个国家发送到另一个国家，可能是一件需承担风险的事情。如果货物灭失或损坏，或者由于某种原因没有交货，缔约双方之间的相互信任感可能就会降低到提起诉讼的地步。国际贸易中的买卖双方如果想要顺利达成交易，就必须在交易的一开始讲明各自的责任，并且用贸易术语充分表达清楚。

In order to avoid, or at least reduce to a considerable degree, the uncertainties of different interpretations of such terms in different countries, the International Chamber of Commerce (ICC) first published a set of international rules for the interpretation of the most commonly used trade terms in foreign trade. These rules were known as "Incoterms 1936". Amendments and additions were later made in 1953, 1967, 1976, 1980, 1990, 2000, 2010 and currently 2020 in order to bring the rules in line with current international trade practices.

It should be stressed that the scope of Incoterms is limited to matters relating to the rights and obligations of the parties to the contract of sale with respect to the delivery of goods sold (in the sense of "tangible", not including "intangibles" such as software).

While it is essential for exporters and importers to consider the practical relationship between the various contracts needed to perform an international sales transaction — where not only the contract of sale is required, but also contracts of carriage, insurance and financing — *Incoterms* relate to only one of these contracts, namely the contract of sale.

为了避免在不同的国家对这类术语可能产生的歧义，或者至少把产生歧义的可能性减少到最低程度，国际商会于 1936 年首次出版了一套国际通则，解释对外贸易中最常用的贸易术语，即《1936 年国际贸易术语解释通则》（简称《1936 年通则》）。为了使这些通则符合现实的国际惯例，后来曾于 1953 年、1967 年、1976 年、1980 年、1990 年、2000 年、2010 年和最近的 2020 年对其进行修改和补充。

需要强调的是，《通则》涵盖的范围只限于销售合同当事人的权利义务中与已售货物（指"有形货物"，不包括"无形货物"，如电脑软件）交货有关的事项。

做一笔国际贸易业务不仅需要销售合同，而且需要运输合同、保险合同和融资合同。对进出口商来说，虽然考虑到各种合同之间的实际关系十分必要，但是《通则》涉及的只是其中的一种合同，即销售合同。

Nevertheless, the parties' agreement to use a particular Incoterm would necessarily have implications for the other contracts. For example, a seller having agreed to a CFR or CIF contract cannot perform such a contract by any other mode of transport than carriage by sea, since under these terms the seller must present a bill of lading or other maritime document to the buyer which is simply not possible if other modes of transport are used.

In addition, Incoterms deal with a number of identified obligations imposed on the parties, such as the seller's obligation to place the goods at the disposal of the buyer or hand them over for carriage or deliver them at destination and with the distribution of risk between the parties in these cases. Furthermore, they also deal with the obligations to clear the goods for export and import, the packing of the goods, the buyer's obligation to take delivery as well as the obligation to provide proof that the respective obligations have been duly fulfilled.

Generally, Incoterms do not deal with the consequences of breach of contract and any exemptions from liability due to various impediments. These questions must be resolved by other stipulations in the contract of sale and the applicable law.

尽管如此，当双方当事人同意使用某一具体贸易术语时，必然会暗示到其他合同。例如，卖方同意在合同中使用 CFR 或 CIF 术语时，就只能以海运方式履行合同，根据这两个术语的规定，其必须向买方提供提单或其他海运单据，而如果使用其他运输方式，这是根本办不到的。

另外，《通则》讲的是为当事人规定的若干特定义务，如卖方将货物交由买方处置或者将货物交付运输或者在目的地交货的义务，以及当事人在这些情况下的风险划分。再者，《通则》还规定了进出口货物清关的包装和义务，买方提货的义务，以及提供证明各项义务已履行无误的证据。

《通则》一般不涉及违约的后果或由于各种障碍导致的免责事项，这些问题必须通过销售合同中的其他条款和适用的法律解决。

Incoterms 2020 came into effect on January 1, 2020. The International Chamber of Commerce (ICC) aims to make Incoterms 2020 more accessible, and the updated rules specify the costs and risks associated with the delivery of goods that sellers and buyers need to bear. We should be familiar with the 11 accepted terms, which are divided into two categories.

《国际贸易术语解释通则 2020》于 2020 年 1 月 1 日起生效。国际商会（ICC）旨在让《国际贸易术语解释通则 2020》更易于理解，更新的通则规定了卖方和买方需要承担的与货物交付相关的成本和风险。我们应当熟悉被分成两个类别的 11 个公认术语。

适用于所有运输方式的术语如下。

EXW: 工厂交货

FCA: 货交承运人

CPT: 运费付至

CIP: 运费、保险费付至

DAP: 目的地交货

DPU: 卸货地卸货交付（新）〔原 DAT 终点（目的）地交货这个术语不再使用〕

DDP: 完税后交货

适用于海运及内河运输方式的术语如下。

FAS: 船边交货

FOB: 船上交货

CFR: 成本加运费

CIF: 成本、保险加运费

The amendments made by the International Chamber of Commerce to Incoterms 2010 to Incoterms 2020 are mainly focused on five aspects:

(1) Amendments to bill of lading terms and FCA terms. Incoterms 2020 provides, in effect, for demonstrated market need in relation to bills of lading (BL) with an on-board notation and the Free Carrier (FCA) Incoterms rule.

(2) Insurance-related clauses in CIF and CIP. Incoterms 2020 align the different levels of insurance coverage in Cost Insurance and Freight (CIF) and Carriage and Insurance Paid To (CIP).

(3) In FCA, DAP, DPU, and DDP, the relevant individual terms and conditions for transportation allowing either the seller or buyer to choose their own specific means of transport. Incoterms 2020 includes arrangements for carriage with their own means of transport in FCA, Delivery at Place (DAP), Delivery at Place Unloaded (DPU), and Delivered Duty Paid (DDP).

(4) There is a change in the three-letter name from Delivered at Terminal (DAT) to DPU.

(5) Incoterms 2020 include security-related requirements within carriage obligations and costs.

相比较《国际贸易术语解释通则 2010》而言，国际商会对《国际贸易术语解释通则 2020》所做的修改主要体现在五个方面：

（1）提单条款和 FCA 条款的修改。《国际贸易术语解释通则 2020》规定了与提单有关的已证明的市场需求，即在 FCA 货交承运人术语下添加已装船批注。

（2）CIF 和 CIP 中与保险有关的条款。《国际贸易术语解释通则 2020》调整了 CIF 成本加保险费加运费以及 CIP 运费和保险费付至的不同保险范围。

（3）在 FCA、DAP、DPU 和 DDP 中，与卖方或买方选择自己的运输工具运输的相关条款。《国际贸易术语解释通则 2020》包括 FCA 货交承运人，DAP 目的地交货，DPU 卸货地交（付）货，DDP 完税后交货等术语下可用卖方或买方自有的运输工具安排拖车。

（4）将 DAT 改为 DPU。DAT 终点（目的）地交货这个术语不再使用，而改为 DPU 卸货地交（付）货。

（5）《国际贸易术语解释通则 2020》在运输义务和成本中与安全相关的要求。

Section One　Components of Trade Terms（贸易术语的构成）

In international trade, the price terms of a sales contract include unit price and total price. Total price is the total amount of a deal. The price of a commodity usually refers to the unit price. The unit price consists of the type of currency, price per unit, measurement unit and trade terms. For example: a price term, "USD100 per dozen FOB New York", may be understood as follows.

USD　　　100　　　per dozen　　　FOB New York

在国际贸易中，合同中的价格条款包括商品的单价和总价。总价是指一笔交易的货款的总金额。商品的价格通常指的是商品的单价。单价是由计价货币、单位价格金额、计价数量单位和贸易术语构成的。例如，一项价格条款"每打 100 美元 FOB 纽约价"可以解释如下。

每打	100	美元	FOB 纽约
↓	↓	↓	↓
计价数量单位	单位价格金额	计价货币	贸易术语

1.　Type of currency（计价货币种类）

Prices for exports may be quoted in the buyer's currency, the seller's currency or a third currency. Since the change in value of the selected currency may directly affect their financial interests, the parties concerned should choose the currency favorable to them during pricing. In general, hard currency (e.g. US dollars, British sterling or euro) should be chosen for export and soft currency for import.

出口商品可用买方国家的货币、卖方国家的货币或第三国的货币报价。由于计价货币的币值变化会直接影响到进出口双方的经济利益，因此买卖双方在确定价格时应该注意选择对自己有利的计价货币。一般来说，出口应选择硬通货（如美元、英镑、欧元等），而进口应选择软通货。

2.　Price per unit（单位价格金额）

While quoting an export price, first of all, the exporters should take into account the various costs and charges involved in getting the goods from the factory or warehouse in their own country to the buyer's premises. Generally speaking, they consist of the purchasing cost of the goods, inland freight, packing expenses, warehousing, commodity inspection fees, export tariffs and entry fees, agent's commissions, etc. In some cases, ocean freight and insurance premiums should be covered in the quotation. Additionally, the profit margin, of course, should also be considered when a price is quoted.

在出口报价时,出口商首先要考虑的是把这些商品从自己国家的工厂或仓库运到买方所在地所要涉及的各种成本和费用。一般来说，主要包括购买商品的费用、内陆运输费、包装费、仓储费、商检费、出口关税、报关手续费、佣金以及其他各种费用。在有些情况下，海洋运输费和保险费也包括在出口商品报价里。当然，在计算报价时，还应考虑利润。

3. Measurement unit（计价数量单位）

The specified measurement unit should also be mentioned, because many countries use different systems of weights and measures. For example, if "ton" is used as the measurement unit, it should be clearly indicated whether it is "metric ton", "long ton" (British) or "short ton" (American).

报价中应指明具体的计价数量单位，因为很多国家使用不同的度量衡体系。例如，如采用"吨"作为计价数量单位，应明确指出它是"公吨"、"长吨"（英制）或"短吨"（美制）。

4. Trade terms（贸易术语）

Under no circumstance can a buyer get a quotation without trade terms in international trade. Trade terms are short forms and abbreviations which are used to explain the components of the price, to define the delivery of the goods, to indicate which party bears the freight, insurance and other relevant charges, and to assume the liability in case damage or loss of the goods occurs. Trade terms ensure both exporter and importer know their own responsibilities. In foreign trade, there are various prices for the same commodity. Granted that the cost of certain commodities is the same ex-factory, the prices quoted by the seller will vary with the place of delivery. For example, in the case of a contract based on CIF terms such as "CIF London", that means the seller bears all the cost, freight and insurance up to the named port of destination, here being "London".

在国际贸易中，买方收到的报价绝对不能没有贸易术语。贸易术语用简单的概念或外文缩写来表明价格的构成，规定所售货物的交货方法，指明由哪方负担运费、保险费和其他相关费用，由哪方承担货物损坏或灭失的责任。贸易术语使进出口双方明确各自的责任。在对外贸易中，相同的商品有不同的价格。某种商品在出厂价格都一样的情况下，卖方将随着交货地点的不同而报出不同的价格来。例如，以 CIF 签订的合同（如 CIF 伦敦）就意味着卖方承担所有的成本、运费和保险费直至指定的目的港，在这里是"伦敦"。

Section Two　Incoterms（《国际贸易术语解释通则》）

Under some legal systems, trade terms have, at least traditionally, been used only to determine the division of costs between the parties. However, in present international custom, the main purpose of trade terms is to determine at what points the seller has fulfilled their obligations so that the goods in the legal sense could be said to have been delivered to the buyer.

Uncertainty about these obligations could be very harmful to the contracting parties. Lack of precision would almost inevitably lead to disputes, including litigation, and to a considerable increase in overhead expenditures in everyday operations.

Moreover, the parties in different countries would be very unwilling to subject themselves to the laws and practices of the other party. They would probably feel secure under the laws of their own country but would find it difficult to assess the consequences of rules of interpretations used in a foreign country. In order to be truly useful, trade terms should have universal application and should make explicit the obligations of both parties. This is the aim of Incoterms (International Rules for the Interpretation of Trade Terms).

In 1936, the International Chamber of Commerce first published a set of international rules for the interpretation of trade terms in foreign trade. These rules were known as "Incoterms 1936". Amendments and additions were later made in 1953, 1967, 1976, 1980, 1990, 2000, 2010 and currently 2020 in order to bring the rules in line with current international trade practice (See Table 4-1, Table 4-2, and Table 4-3).

Table 4-1　Main Trade Terms of Incoterms 2000

Group E Departure	EXW		Ex Works
Group F Main Carriage Unpaid	FCA FAS FOB	Shipment Contract	Free Carrier Free Alongside Ship Free on Board
Group C Main Carriage Paid	CFR CIF CPT CIP		Cost and Freight Cost, Insurance and Freight Carriage Paid to Carriage and Insurance Paid to
Group D Arrival	DAF DES DEQ DDU DDP	Arrival Contract	Delivered at Frontier Delivered Ex Ship Delivered Ex Quay Delivered Duty Unpaid Delivered Duty Paid

在某些法律制度下，贸易条款只用来确定如何划分双方的费用，至少从传统上来讲一直如此。不过，在当前的国际贸易中，贸易术语的主要目的是确定卖方在哪些方面已经履行了义务，也就是从法律的意义上来说，货物已经交付买方。

这些义务若不明确，会对契约双方十分有害。缺乏准确性就几乎不可避免地会导致纠纷，包括诉讼，并且会使日常业务的"经营性"开支大量增加。

此外，处在不同国家的买卖双方很不愿意受对方国家种种法律和习惯的制约。它们对使用本国的法律可能会感到放心，但是对外国使用其规则与解释得出的后果就难以估计。为了使贸易术语发挥作用，条款应具有普遍的适用性，并应使双方的义务明确。这就是制定"国际贸易术语"的目的。

在 1936 年，国际商会出版了一套有关贸易术语解释的国际规则，定名为《1936 国际贸易术语解释通则》（即《1936 年通则》），以后于 1957 年、1967 年、1976 年、1980 年、1990 年、2000 年、2010 年和 2020 年分别对其做了修改和补充，以便使这些术语更加符合现行的国际贸易实践的要求。表 4-1 为《2000 年通则》的主要贸易术语，表 4-2 为《2010 年通则》的主要贸易术语，表 4-3 为《2020 年通则》的主要贸易术语。

表 4-1 《2000 年通则》主要贸易术语

E 组（启运）	EXW	出口地交货贸易术语，合同为装运合同	工厂交货
F 组（主运费未付）	FCA		货交承运人
	FAS		船边交货
	FOB		船上交货
C 组（主运费已付）	CFR		成本加运费
	CIF		成本、保险费加运费
	CPT		运费付至
	CIP		运费、保险费付至
D 组（到达）	DAF	到达合同	边境交货
	DES		目的港船上交货
	DEQ		目的港码头交货
	DDU		未完税交货
	DDP		完税后交货

Table 4-2 Main Trade Terms of Incoterms 2010

（《2010 年通则》主要贸易术语）

Group 1. Incoterms that apply to any mode of transport are:
第一组：适用于任何运输方式的术语

EXW	Ex Works	工厂交货
FCA	Free Carrier	货交承运人
CPT	Carriage Paid to	运费付至
CIP	Carriage and Insurance Paid to	运费、保险费付至
DAT	Delivered at Terminal	运输终端交货
DAP	Delivered at Place	目的地交货
DDP	Delivered Duty Paid	完税后交货

Group 2. Incoterms that apply to sea and inland waterway transport only:
第二组：适用于海上和内陆水上运输方式的术语

FAS	Free Alongside Ship	船边交货
FOB	Free on Board	船上交货
CFR	Cost and Freight	成本加运费
CIF	Cost, Insurance and Freight	成本、保险费加运费

Table 4-3 Main Trade Terms of Incoterms 2020

（《2020 年通则》主要贸易术语）

Group 1. Incoterms that apply to any mode of transport are:
第一组：适用于任何运输方式的术语

EXW	Ex Works	工厂交货
FCA	Free Carrier	货交承运人
CPT	Carriage Paid to	运费付至
CIP	Carriage and Insurance Paid to	运费、保险费付至
DAP	Delivered at Place	目的地交货
DPU	Delivery at Place Unloaded	卸货地卸货交货
DDP	Delivered Duty Paid	完税后交货

Group 2. Incoterms that apply to sea and inland waterway transport only: 第二组：适用于海上和内陆水上运输方式的术语		
FAS	Free Alongside Ship	船边交货
FOB	Free on Board	船上交货
CFR	Cost and Freight	成本加运费
CIF	Cost, Insurance and Freight	成本、保险费加运费

Section Three　Six Main Trade Terms in Incoterms 2020 (《2020 年通则》的 6 个主要贸易术语）

In international trade, of the 11 trade terms, FOB, CFR, CIF, FCA, CPT and CIP are the most important. FOB, CFR and CIF are suitable for sea and inland waterway transport; FCA, CPT and CIP are used regardless of modes of transportation.

在 11 个国际贸易术语中，FOB、CFR、CIF、FCA、CPT 和 CIP 是 6 个最常用的贸易术语，其中，FOB、CFR 和 CIF 适合海上和内河运输，而 FCA、CPT 和 CIP 适合任何运输方式。

1．FOB: Free on Board (… named port of shipment)［FOB：船上交货（……指定装运港）］

This rule is to be used only for sea or inland waterway transport.

"Free on Board" means that the seller delivers the goods on board the vessel nominated by the buyer at the named port of shipment or procures the goods already so delivered. The risks of loss or damage to the goods pass when the goods are on board the vessel, and the buyer bears all costs from that moment onwards. The seller is required either to deliver the goods on board the vessel or to procure goods already so delivered for shipment. The reference to "procure" here caters to multiple sales down a chain (string sales), particularly common in the commodity trades.

FOB may not be appropriate where goods are handed over to the carrier before they are on board the vessel, for example goods in containers, which are typically delivered at a terminal. In such situations, the FCA rule should be used. FOB requires the seller to clear the goods for export, where applicable. However, the seller has no obligation to clear the goods for import, pay any import duty or carry out any import customs formalities.

FOB = EXW + risks and expenses before the cargo is loaded on the named ship

　　　　+ risks and expenses for export customs clearance

　　　　+ charges for commodity inspection before loading as stipulated by the government

When adopting the FOB terms, one should pay attention to the following points.

(1) Delivery of the goods on board the vessel.

(2) Link-up of vessel and goods.

(3) Expense for loading the goods on board the vessel.

(4) The transfer of the risks.

Under the FOB terms, in case the buyer charters a liner to carry the goods, since liner charges contain loading and unloading expenses, the loading cost is actually borne by the buyer. In case the goods are carried by a chartered vessel, the two parties shall negotiate who is to bear the loading expense and stipulate it clearly in the contract.

该术语仅用于海运或内河水运。

"船上交货"是指卖方以在指定装运港将货物装上买方指定的船或通过取得已交付至船上货物的方式。货物灭失或损坏的风险在货物交到船上时转移，同时买方承担自那时起的一切费用。卖方应将货物运至船边或取得已经这样交运的货物。此处使用的"取得"一词适用于商品贸易中常见的交易链中的多层销售（链式销售）。

FOB 可能不适合货物在上船前已经交给承运人的情况，例如用集装箱运输的货物通常是在集装箱码头交货。在此类情况下，应当使用 FCA 术语。FOB 要求卖方出口清关。但卖方无义务办理进口清关、支付任何进口税或办理任何进口海关手续。

$$FOB = EXW + 货物装上货船前的风险和费用 + 出口清关的风险和费用$$
$$+ 出口国政府规定的装船前检验费用$$

使用该术语时要注意以下四点。

（1）船上交货的要求。

（2）船货衔接问题。

（3）货物装船的费用问题。

（4）风险转移的问题。

在 FOB 术语下，如果是买方负责派船到装运港去接货，由于租船费用包括装货和卸货费用，那么，实际上装货费用由买方负责。如果是以班轮条件办理，那么买卖双方可以协商由买方还是卖方承担装货费用，并在合同中明确规定。

A THE SELLER'S OBLIGATIONS

A1　General obligations of the seller

The seller must provide the goods and the commercial invoice in conformity with the contract of sale and any other evidence of conformity that may be required by the contract.

Any document to be provided by the seller may be in paper or electronic form as agreed or, where there is no agreement, as is customary.

A2　Delivery

The seller must deliver the goods either by placing them on board the vessel nominated by the buyer at the loading point, if any, indicated by the buyer at the named port of shipment or by procuring the goods so delivered.

The seller must deliver the goods

(1) on the agreed date, or

(2) at the time within the agreed period notified by the buyer under B10, or

(3) if no such time is notified, then at the end of the agreed period, and

(4) in the manner customary at the port.

If no specific loading point has been indicated by the buyer, the seller may select the point within the named port of shipment that best suits their purpose.

A3　Transfer of risks

The seller bears all risks of loss or damage to the goods until they have been delivered in accordance with A2,with the exception of loss or damage in the circumstances described in B3.

A4　Carriage

The seller has no obligation to the buyer to make a contract of carriage. However, the seller must provide the buyer, at the buyer's request, risk, and cost, with any information in the possession of the seller, including transport-related security requirements, that the buyer needs for arranging carriage. If agreed, the seller must contract for carriage on the usual terms at the buyer's risk and cost. The seller must comply with any transport-related security requirements up to delivery.

A5　Insurance

The seller has no obligation to the buyer to make a contract of insurance. However, the seller must provide the buyer, at the buyer's request, risk, and cost, with information in the possession of the seller that the buyer needs for obtaining insurance.

A6　Delivery/transport document

The seller must provide the buyer, at the seller's cost, with the usual proof that the goods have been delivered in accordance with A2.

Unless such proof is a transport document, the seller must provide assistance to the buyer, at the buyer's request, risk, and cost, in obtaining a transport document.

A7　Export/Import clearance

a) Export clearance

Where applicable, the seller must carry out and pay for all export clearance formalities required by the country of export, such as:

- Export Licence
- Security Clearance for Export
- Pre-Shipment Inspection; and
- any other official authorisation

b) Assistance with import clearance

Where applicable, the seller must assist the buyer at the buyer's request, risk, and cost, in obtaining any documents and/or information related to all transit/import clearance formalities, including security requirements and pre-shipment inspection, needed by any country of transit or the country of import.

A8　Checking/Packing/Marking

The seller must pay the costs of those checking operations (such as checking quality, measuring, weighing, counting) that are necessary for the purpose of delivering the goods in accordance with A2.The seller must, at their own cost, package the goods, unless it is usual for the particular trade to transport the type of goods sold unpackaged. The seller must package and mark the goods in the manner appropriate for their transport, unless the parties have agreed on specific packaging or marking requirements.

A9　Allocation of costs

The seller must pay:

a) all costs relating to the goods until they have been delivered in accordance with A2, other than those payable by the buyer under B9;

b) the costs of providing the usual proof to the buyer under A6 that the goods have been delivered;

c) where applicable, duties, taxes and any other costs related to export clearance under A7(a); and

d) to the buyer for all costs and charges related to providing assistance in obtaining documents and information in accordance with B7(a).

A10　Notices

The seller must give the buyer sufficient notice either that the goods have been delivered in accordance with A2 or that the vessel has failed to take the goods within the time agreed.

A 卖方义务

A1　卖方一般义务

卖方必须提供符合销售合同的货物和商业发票，以及合同可能要求的任何其他符合性证据。

卖方提供的任何文件可以按照协议以纸质或电子形式提供，或者在没有协议的情况下按惯例使用。

A2　交货

卖方必须在指定的装运港内的装货点（如有的话），将货物置于买方指定的船舶上，或以买方指定的方式交货。

卖方必须交付货物

（1）在约定的日期，或

（2）在买方根据 B10 规定的约定期限内的时间，或

（3）如果未通知此类时间，则在约定期限结束时，并且

（4）按照该港的习惯方式交货。

如果买方没有指定特定的装货地点，卖方则可在指定装运港选择最适合其目的的装货点。

A3　风险转移

除按照 B3 的灭失或损坏情况外，卖方承担按照 A2 完成交货前货物灭失或损坏的一切风险。

A4　运输

卖方对买方无订立运输合同的义务。但若买方要求，卖方必须根据买方的要求向买方提供卖方所拥有的协助买方安排运输所需的任何信息，包括风险和费用，包括与运输有关的安全要求信息。如果达成协议，卖方必须按照通常的条款订立运输合同，但买方承担风险和费用。卖方必须遵守与运输有关的所有安全要求，直到交货为止。

A5　保险

卖方对买方无订立保险合同的义务。但应买方要求并由其承担风险和费用（如有的话），卖方必须向买方提供后者取得保险所需的信息。

A6 交货/运输文件（凭证）

卖方必须自付费用，向买方提供凭证，以证明该货物已按照 A2 规定交付。

除非上述证据是运输凭证，否则，应买方要求并由其承担风险和费用，卖方必须协助买方取得运输凭证。

A7 出口/进口清关

a）出口清关

在适用的情况下，卖方必须执行并支付出口国要求的所有出口清关手续，例如：

· 出口许可证

· 出口安全通关

· 装运前检查；和

· 其他任何官方授权

b）协助进口清关

如适用时，应买方要求并由其承担风险和费用，卖方必须及时向买方提供或协助其取得相关货物进口和/或将货物运输到最终目的地所需要的任何单证和/或信息，包括过境或进口国安全要求和装运前检查。

A8 查对/包装/标记

卖方必须支付为了按照 A2 交货所需要进行的查对费用（如查对质量、丈量、过磅、点数的费用），以及出口国有关机构强制进行的装运前检验所发生的费用。除非在特定贸易中，某类货物的销售通常无须包装，卖方必须自付费用包装货物。除非买方在签订合同前已通知卖方特殊包装要求，卖方可以适合该货物运输的方式对货物进行包装。包装应做适当标记。

A9 费用划分

卖方必须支付：

a）按照 A2 交货前与货物相关的一切费用，但按照 B9 应由买方支付的费用除外；

b）根据 A6 向买方提供通常的凭证以证明货物已经交付的费用；

c）在适用的情况下，根据 A7（a）货物出口所需海关手续费用，以及出口应缴纳的一切关税、税款和其他费用；和

d）买方承担与根据 B7（a）获得凭证和信息的协助有关的所有费用。

A10 通知

卖方必须就其已经按照 A2 交货或船舶未在约定时间内收取货物给予买方充分的通知。

B THE BUYER'S OBLIGATIONS

B1　General provision of the buyer

The buyer must pay the price of the goods as provided in the contract of sale.

Any document to be provided by the buyer may be in paper or electronic form as agreed or, where there is no agreement, as is customary.

B2　Taking delivery

The buyer must take delivery of the goods when they have been delivered under A2.

B3　Transfer of risks

The buyer bears all risks of loss of or damage to the goods from the time they have been delivered under A2.

If:

a) the buyer fails to give notice in accordance with B10; or

b) the vessel nominated by the buyer fails to arrive on time to enable the seller to comply with A2, fails to take the goods, or closes for cargo earlier than the time notified in accordance with B10; then the buyer bears all risks of loss of or damage to the goods:

(i) from the agreed date, or in the absence of an agreed date,

(ii) from the date selected by the buyer under B10, or, if no such date has been notified.

(iii) from the end of any agreed period for delivery.

provided that the goods have been clearly identified as the contract goods.

B4　Carriage

The buyer must contract at their own cost for the carriage of the goods from the named port of shipment, except when the contract of carriage is made by the seller as provided for in A4.

B5　Insurance

The buyer has no obligation to the seller to make a contract of insurance.

B6　Delivery/Transport document

The buyer must accept the proof of delivery provided under A6.

B7　Export/Import clearance

a) Assistance with export clearance

Where applicable, the buyer must assist the seller at the seller's request, risk, and cost in obtaining any documents and/or information related to all export clearance formalities, including security requirements and pre-shipment inspection, needed by the country of export.

b) Import clearance

Where applicable, the buyer must carry out and pay for all formalities required by any country of transit and the country of import, such as:

• Import Licence and any licence required for transit;

• Security Clearance for Import and any transit;

• Pre-Shipment Inspection; and

• any other official authorisation.

B8　Checking/Packing/Marking

The buyer has no obligation to the seller.

B9　Allocation of costs

The buyer must pay:

a) all costs relating to the goods from the time they have been delivered under A2, other than those payable by the seller under A9;

b) to the seller all costs and charges, related to providing assistance in obtaining documents and information in accordance with A4, A5, A6 and A7(b);

c) where applicable, duties, taxes and any other costs related to transit or import clearance under B7(b); and

d) any additional costs incurred, either because:

(i) the buyer has failed to give notice under B10, or

(ii) the vessel nominated by the buyer under B10 fails to arrive on time, fails to take the goods, or closes for cargo earlier than the time notified in accordance with B10,

provided that the goods have been clearly identified as the contract goods.

B10　Notices

The buyer must give the seller sufficient notice of any transport-related security requirements, the vessel name, loading point and, if any, the selected delivery date within the agreed period.

B　买方义务

B1　买方的一般规定

买方必须按照销售合同中的规定支付货款。

买方要提供的任何文件可以按照协议以纸质或电子形式提供，或者在没有协议的情况下按惯例提供。

B2　受领货物

当货物按照 A2 交付时，买方必须受领。

B3　风险转移

买方承担按照 A2 交货时起货物灭失或损坏的一切风险。

如果：

a）买方未按照 B10 发出通知；或

b）买方指定的船舶未按 B10 通知的时间准时到达，使得卖方未能按 A2 装载货物或早于 B10 通知的时间停止装货；买方则按下列情况承担货物灭失或损坏的一切风险：

（i）从约定日期开始，或在没有约定日期的情况下，

（ii）从买方根据 B10 选择的日期开始，或者，如果尚未通知该日期。

（iii）自任何约定交货期限届满之日起。

但以该货物已清楚地确定为合同项下之货物者为限。

B4　运输

买方必须自付费用订立合同，从指定的装运港运输货物，除非卖方按照 A4 的规定订立运输合同。

B5　保险

买方无义务与卖方订立保险合同。

B6　交货/运输凭证

买方必须接受 A6 规定的交货凭证。

B7　出口/进口清关

a）协助出口清关

在适用的情况下，如卖方要求协助出口清关，买方必须自负风险和费用，取得任何进口许可证或其他官方授权，办理货物进口和在必要时从他国过境所需的任何文件和/或信息，包括安全要求和装运前检验。

b）进口清关

在适用的情况下，买方必须执行并支付任何过境国和进口国要求的所有手续，例如：

• 进口许可证和过境所需的任何许可证；

- 进口和任何过境的安全检查；
- 装运前检查；和
- 任何其他官方授权。

B8 检查/包装/标记

买方对卖方没有此义务。

B9 费用划分

买方必须支付：

a）自按照 A2 交货之时起与货物相关的一切费用，但卖方根据 A9 应付的费用除外；

b）卖方承担与根据 A4、A5、A6 和 A7（b）协助获取文件和信息有关的所有费用；

c）适用时，根据 B7（b）征收关税和与过境或进口清关有关的任何其他费用；和

d）由于以下原因之一而产生的任何额外费用：

（i）买方未按照 B10 给予卖方相应的通知，或

（ii）买方根据 B10 所指定的船只未按 B10 通知的时间准时到达，不能装载货物或早于 B10 通知的时间停止装货，但以该货物已清楚地确定为合同项下之货物者为限。

B10 通知

买方必须在约定的期限内充分通知卖方任何与运输有关的安全要求、船舶名称、装载点以及（如果有）选定的交货日期。

2. CFR: Cost and Freight (…named port of destination)［CFR：成本加运费（……指定目的港）］

This rule is to be used only for sea or inland waterway transport.

"Cost and Freight" means that the seller delivers the goods on board the vessel or procures the goods already so delivered. The risk of loss or damage to the goods passes when the goods are on board the vessel. The seller must contract for and pay the costs and freight necessary to bring the goods to the named port of destination.

When CPT, CIP, CFR or CIF are used, the seller fulfils their obligation to deliver when they hand the goods over to the carrier in the manner specified in the chosen rule and not when the goods reach the place of destination.

This rule has two critical points, because risk passes and costs are transferred at different places. While the contract will always specify a destination port, it might not specify the port of shipment, which is where risk passes to the buyer. If the shipment port is of particular interest to the buyer, the parties are well advised to identify it as precisely as possible in the contract.

The parties are well advised to identify as precisely as possible the point at the agreed port of destination, as the costs to that point are for the account of the seller. The seller is advised to procure contracts of carriage that match this choice precisely. If the seller incurs costs under their contract of carriage related to unloading at the specified point at the port of destination, the seller is not entitled to recover such costs from the buyer unless otherwise agreed between the parties.

The seller is required either to deliver the goods on board the vessel or to procure goods already so delivered for shipment to the destination. In addition, the seller is required either to make a contract of carriage or to procure such a contract. The reference to "procure" here caters to multiple sales down a chain (string sales), particularly common in the commodity trades.

CFR may not be appropriate where goods are handed over to the carrier before they are on board the vessel, for example goods in containers, which are typically delivered at a terminal. In such cases, the CPT rule should be used.

CFR requires the seller to clear the goods for export, where applicable. However, the seller has no obligation to clear the goods for import, pay any import duty or carry out any import customs formalities.

CFR = FOB + responsibilities of shipping space and charter + main freight

When adopting the CFR term, one should pay attention to the following points.

(1) Bearing unloading expenses.

(2) Responsibilities of chartering.

(3) Shipping advice.

该术语仅用于海运或内河水运。

"成本加运费"是指卖方在船上交货或以取得已经这样交付的货物的方式交货，货物灭失或损坏的风险在货物交到船上时转移。卖方必须签订合同，并支付必要的成本和运费，将货物运至指定的目的港。

当使用 CPT、CIP、CFR 或者 CIF 时，卖方按照所选择术语规定的方式将货物交付给承运人时，即完成其交货义务，而不是货物到达目的地之时。

由于风险转移和费用转移的地点不同，该术语有两个关键点。虽然合同通常都会指定目的港，但不一定都会指定装运港，而这里是风险转移至买方的地方。如果装运港对买方具有特殊意义，那么特别建议双方在合同中尽可能准确地指定装运港。

特别建议双方应尽可能准确地指定约定目的港的交付点，因为将货物运至该交付点的费用由卖方承担。建议卖方取得的运输合同应能与做出的这个选择准确吻合。如果卖方按照运输合同在目的地交付点发生了卸货费用，则除非双方事先另有约定，卖方无权向买方要求补偿该项费用。

卖方需要将货物在船上交付，或以取得已经这样交付运往目的港的货物的方式交货。此外，卖方还需签订一份运输合同，或者取得一份这样的合同。此处使用的"取得"一词适用于商品贸易中常见的交易链中的多层销售（链式销售）。

CFR 可能不适合于货物在上船前已经交给承运人的情况，例如用集装箱运输的货物通常在集装箱码头交货。在此类情况下，应当使用 CPT 术语。

如适用时，CFR 要求卖方办理出口清关。但卖方无义务办理进口清关、支付任何进口税或办理任何进口海关手续。

CFR = FOB + 租船订舱责任 + 主运费

使用该术语时要注意以下几点。

（1）卸货费用的负担。

（2）租船或订舱的责任。

（3）关于装船通知。

A THE SELLER'S OBLIGATIONS

A1   General obligations of the seller

The seller must provide the goods and the commercial invoice in conformity with the contract of sale and any other evidence of conformity that may be required by the contract.

Any document to be provided by the seller may be in paper or electronic form as agreed or, where there is no agreement, as customary.

A2   Delivery

The seller must deliver the goods either by placing them on board the vessel or by procuring the goods so delivered. In either case, the seller must deliver the goods on the agreed date or within the agreed period and in the manner customary at the port.

A3   Transfer of risks

The seller bears all risks of loss or damage to the goods until they have been delivered in accordance with A2, with the exception of loss or damage in the circumstances described in B3.

A4   Carriage

The seller must contract or procure a contract for the carriage of the goods from the agreed point of delivery, if any, at the place of delivery to the named port of destination or, if agreed, any point at that port. The contract of carriage must be made on usual terms at the seller's cost and provide for carriage by the usual route in a vessel of the type normally used for the transport of the type of goods sold.

The seller must comply with any transport-related security requirements for transport to the destination.

A5   Insurance

The seller has no obligation to the buyer to make a contract of insurance. However, the seller must provide the buyer, at the buyer's request, risk, and cost, with information in their possession of the seller that the buyer needs for obtaining insurance.

A6   Delivery/Transport document

The seller must, at their own cost, provide the buyer with the usual transport document for the agreed port of destination. This transport document must cover the contract goods, be dated within the period agreed for shipment, enable the buyer to claim the goods from the carrier at the port of destination and, unless otherwise agreed, enable the buyer to sell the goods in transit by the transfer of the document to a subsequent buyer or by notification to the carrier.

When such a transport document is issued in negotiable form and in several originals, a full set of originals must be presented to the buyer.

A7   Export/Import clearance

a) Export clearance

Where applicable, the seller must carry out and pay for all export clearance formalities required by the country of export, such as:

- Export Licence
- Security Clearance for Export

- Pre-Shipment Inspection; and
- any other official authorisation

b) Assistance with import clearance

Where applicable, the seller must assist the buyer at the buyer's request, risk, and cost, in obtaining any documents and/or information related to all transit/import clearance formalities, including security requirements and pre-shipment inspection, needed by any country of transit or the country of import.

A8 Checking/Packing/Marking

The seller must pay the costs of those checking operations (such as checking quality, measuring, weighing, counting) that are necessary for the purpose of delivering the goods in accordance with A2.

The seller must, at their own cost, package the goods, unless it is usual for the particular trade to transport the type of goods sold unpackaged. The seller must package and mark the goods in the manner appropriate for their transport, unless the parties have agreed on specific packaging or marking requirements.

A9 Allocation of costs

The seller must pay:

a) all costs relating to the goods until they have been delivered in accordance with A2, other than those payable by the buyer under B9;

b) the freight and all other costs resulting from A4, including the costs of loading the goods on board and transport-related security costs;

c) any charges for unloading at the agreed port of discharge that were for the seller's account under the contract of carriage;

d) the costs of transit that were for the seller's account under the contract of carriage;

e) the costs of providing the usual proof to the buyer under A6 that the goods have been delivered;

f) where applicable, duties, taxes and any other costs related to export clearance under A7(a); and

g) to the buyer all costs and charges related to providing assistance in obtaining documents and information in accordance with B7(a).

A10 Notices

The seller must notify the buyer that the goods have been delivered in accordance with A2.

The seller must give the buyer any notice required to enable the buyer to receive the goods.

A 卖方义务

A1 卖方一般义务

卖方必须提供符合销售合同的货物和商业发票，以及合同可能要求的任何其他符合性证据。

卖方提供的任何文件可以按照协议以纸质或电子形式提供，或者在没有协议的情况下按惯例使用。

A2 交货

卖方必须以将货物装上船，或者以取得已装船货物的方式交货。无论哪种情况，卖方都必须在约定日期或期限内按照该港的习惯方式交货。

A3 风险转移

卖方承担货物灭失或损坏的一切风险，直到按照 A2 规定交货为止，但 B3 中所述情况下的灭失或损坏除外。

A4 运输

卖方必须签订合同或促成合同，将货物自交货地内的约定交货点（如有的话）运送至指定目的地或指定目的地内的约定的地点（如有约定）。必须按照通常条件订立运输合同，由卖方支付费用，经由通常航线，由通常用来运输该类商品的船舶运输。

卖方必须遵守任何与运输有关的安全要求，才能运输到目的地。

A5 保险

卖方对买方无订立保险合同的义务。但应买方要求并由其承担风险和费用（如有的话），卖方必须向买方提供后者取得保险所需的信息。

A6 交货/运输凭证

卖方必须自付费用，不得延迟向买方提供到约定目的港的通常的运输凭证。

此运输凭证必须载明合同该项货物，且其签发日期应在约定运输期限内，并使买方能在指定目的港向承运人索取货物。同时，除非另有约定，该项凭证应能使买方在货物运输途中以向下家买方转让或通知承运人的方式出售货物。

当此类运输凭证以可转让形式签发并有数份正本时，则必须将整套正本凭证提交给买方。

A7 出口/进口清关

a）出口清关

在适用的情况下，卖方必须执行并支付出口国要求的所有出口清关手续，例如：

• 出口许可证

• 出口安全通关

• 装运前检查；和

• 其他任何官方授权

b）协助进口清关

如适用时，应买方要求并由其承担风险和费用，卖方必须及时向买方提供或协助其取得相关货物进口和/或将货物运输到最终目的地所需要的任何单证和信息，包括过境或进口国安全相关信息。

A8 检查/包装/标记

卖方必须支付为按照 A2 规定交付货物所需的检查操作费用（例如检查质量、测量、称重、计数）。

卖方必须自付费用包装货物，除非特定行业将未包装出售的货物运输。除非双方已就特定的包装或标记要求达成协议，否则卖方必须以适合其运输的方式包装和标记商品。

A9 费用划分

卖方必须支付：

a）按照 A2 交货前与货物相关的一切费用，但按照 B9 应由买方支付的费用除外；

b）按照 A4 所产生的运费和所有其他费用，包括在船上装载货物的费用和与运输有关的安保费用；

c）根据运输合同由卖方承担的在约定卸货港卸货的任何费用；

d）按照运输合同规定，由卖方支付的货物从他国过境运输的费用；

e）根据 A6 向买方提供通常的证据以证明货物已经交付的费用；

f）在适用的情况下，根据 A7（a）进行出口清关的关税、税金和任何其他费用；和

g）买方承担与根据 B7（a）获得文件和信息的协助有关的所有费用。

A10 通知

卖方必须通知买方已按照 A2 规定交货。

卖方必须给买方任何必要的通知，以使买方能够接收货物。

B THE BUYER'S OBLIGATIONS

B1　General obligations of the buyer

The buyer must pay the price of the goods as provided in the contract of sale.

Any document to be provided by the buyer may be in paper or electronic form as agreed or, where there is no agreement, as is customary.

B2　Taking delivery

The buyer must take delivery of the goods when they have been delivered under A2 and receive them from the carrier at the named port of destination.

B3　Transfer of risks

The buyer bears all risks of loss of or damage to the goods from the time they have been delivered under A2.

If the buyer fails to give notice in accordance with B10, it bears all risks of loss of or damage to the goods from the agreed date or the end of the agreed period for shipment, provided that the goods have been clearly identified as the contract goods.

B4　Carriage

The buyer has no obligation to the seller to make a contract of carriage.

B5　Insurance

The buyer has no obligation to the seller to make a contract of insurance.

B6　Delivery/Transport document

The buyer must accept the transport document provided under A6 if it is in conformity with the contract.

B7　Export/Import clearance

a) Assistance with export clearance

Where applicable, the buyer must assist the seller at the seller's request, risk and cost in obtaining any documents and/or information related to all export clearance formalities, including security requirements and pre-shipment inspection, needed by the country of export.

b) Import clearance

Where applicable, the buyer must carry out and pay for all formalities required by any country of transit and the country of import, such as:

• import licence and any licence required for transit;

- security clearance for import and any transit;
- pre-shipment inspection; and
- any other official authorisation.

B8　Checking/Packing/Marking

The buyer has no obligation to the seller.

B9　Allocation of costs

The buyer must pay:

a) all costs relating to the goods from the time they have been delivered under A2, other than those payable by the seller under A9;

b) the costs of transit, unless such costs were for the seller's account under the contract of carriage;

c) unloading costs including lighterage and wharfage charges, unless such costs and charges were for the seller's account under the contract of carriage;

d) the seller for all costs and charges related to providing assistance in obtaining documents and information in accordance with A5 and A7(b);

e) where applicable, duties, taxes and any other costs related to transit or import clearance under B7(b); and

f) any additional costs incurred if it fails to give notice in accordance with B10, from the agreed date or the end of the agreed period for shipment, provided that the goods have been clearly identified as the contract goods.

B10　Notices

The buyer must, whenever it is agreed that the buyer is entitled to determine the time for shipping the goods and/or the point of receiving the goods within the named port of destination, give the seller sufficient notice.

B　买方义务

B1　买方一般义务

买方必须按照销售合同中的规定支付货款。

买方要提供的任何文件可以按照协议以纸质或电子形式提供，或者在没有协议的情况下按惯例提供。

B2　受领货物

买方必须按照 A2 规定受领货物，然后从指定目的地的承运人处接收货物。

B3　风险转移

买方承担按照 A2 交货时起货物灭失或损坏的一切风险。

如果买方未按照 B10 通知卖方，则自约定的交货日期或交货期限届满之日起，承担货物灭失或损坏的一切风险，但以该货物已清楚地确定为合同项下的货物为限。

B4　运输

买方没有义务与卖方订立运输合同。

B5　保险

买方无义务与卖方订立保险合同。

B6　交货/运输凭证

如果符合合同规定，则买方必须接受 A6 提供的运输单据。

B7　出口/进口清关

a）协助出口清关

如适用时，应卖方要求并由其承担风险和费用，买方必须及时向卖方提供或协助其取得货物运输和出口及从他国过境运输所需要的任何单证和信息，包括安全相关信息和装运前检验。

b）进口清关

在适用的情况下，买方必须执行并支付任何过境国和进口国要求的所有手续，例如：

- 进口许可证和过境所需的任何许可证；
- 进口和任何过境的安全检查；
- 装运前检查；和
- 任何其他官方授权。

B8　检查/包装/标记

买方对卖方没有义务。

B9　费用划分

买方必须支付：

a）自货物按照 A2 交付之日起与货物有关的所有费用，但卖方根据 A9 应付的费用除外；

b）过境费用，除非这些费用是根据运输合同由卖方承担的；

c）包括卸货和码头费在内的卸货费用，除非这些费用是根据运输合同由卖方承担的；

d）卖方承担与根据 A5 和 A7（b）协助获取文件和信息有关的所有费用；

e）在适用的情况下，与 B7（b）项下的过境或进口清关相关的关税、税金和任何其他费用；和

f）如果买方未按照 B10 发出通知，则自约定运输之日或约定运输期限届满之日起，所发生的一切额外费用，但以该货物已清楚地确定为合同项下的货物为限。

B10　通知

买方一旦决定装运货物的时间和/或指定的目的港卸货点，买方必须向卖方发出充分的通知。

3.　CIF: Cost, Insurance and Freight (…named port of destination)（成本、保险费加运费（……指定目的港））

This rule is to be used only for sea or inland waterway transport.

"Cost, Insurance and Freight" means that the seller delivers the goods on board the vessel or procures the goods already so delivered. The risk of loss of or damage to the goods passes when the goods are on board the vessel.

The seller must contract for and pay the costs and freight necessary to bring the goods to the named port of destination.

The seller also contracts for insurance cover against the buyer's risk of loss of or damage to the goods during the carriage. The buyer should note that under CIF the seller is required to obtain insurance only on minimum cover.

Should the buyer wish to have more insurance protection, it will need either to agree as much expressly with the seller or to make its own extra insurance arrangements.

When CPT, CIP, CFR, or CIF are used, the seller fulfills its obligation to deliver when it hands the goods over to the carrier in the manner specified in the chosen rule and not when the goods reach the place of destination.

This rule has two critical points, because risk passes and costs are transferred at different places. While the contract will always specify a destination port, it might not specify the port of shipment, which is where risk passes to the buyer. If the shipment port is of particular interest to the buyer, the parties are well advised to identify it as precisely as possible in the contract.

The parties are well advised to identify as precisely as possible the point at the agreed port of destination, as the costs to that point are for the account of the seller. The seller is advised to procure contracts of carriage that match this choice precisely. If the seller incurs costs under its contract of carriage related to unloading at the specified point at the port of destination, the seller is not entitled to recover such costs from the buyer unless otherwise agreed between the parties.

The seller is required either to deliver the goods on board the vessel or to procure goods already so delivered for shipment to the destination. In addition the seller is required either to make a contract of carriage or to procure such a contract. The reference to "procure" here caters for multiple sales down a chain (string sales), particularly common in the commodity trades.

CIF may not be appropriate where goods are handed over to the carrier before they are on board the vessel, for example goods in containers, which are typically delivered at a terminal. In such circumstances, the CIP rule should be used.

CIF requires the seller to clear the goods for export, where applicable. However, the seller has no obligation to clear the goods for import, pay any import duty or carry out any import customs formalities.

该术语仅用于海运或内河水运。

"成本、保险费加运费"是指卖方在船上交货或以取得已经这样交付的货物的方式交货。货物灭失或损坏的风险在货物交到船上时转移。

卖方必须签订合同，并支付必要的成本和运费，将货物运至指定目的港。

卖方还要为买方在运输途中货物的灭失或损坏风险办理保险。

买方应注意到，在 CIF 下，卖方仅需投保最低险别。如买方需要更多保险保护的话，则需要与卖方明确达成协议，或者自行做出额外的保险安排。

当使用 CPT、CIP、CFR 或者 CIF 时，卖方按照所选择的术语规定的方式将货物交付给承运人时，即完成其交货义务，而不是货物到达目的地之时。

由于风险转移和费用转移的地点不同，该术语有两个关键点。虽然合同通常都会指定目的港，但不一定都会指定装运港，而这里是风险转移至买方的地方。如果装运港对买方具有特殊意义，特别建议双方在合同中尽可能准确地指定装运港。

特别建议双方应尽可能准确地指定约定目的港的交付点，因为将货物运至该交付点的费用由卖方承担。建议卖方取得的运输合同应能与做出的这个选择准确吻合。如果卖方按照运输合同在目的地交付点发生了卸货费用，则除非双方事先另有约定，卖方无权向买方要求补偿该项费用。

卖方需要将货物在船上交货，或以取得已经这样交付运往目的港的货物的方式交货。此外，卖方还需签订一份运输合同，或者取得一份这样的合同。此外使用的"取得"一词适用于商品贸易中常见的交易链中的多层销售（链式销售）。

CIF 可能不适合于货物在上船前已经交给承运人的情况，例如用集装箱运输的货物通常是在集装箱码头交货。此类情况下，应当使用 CIP 术语。

如适用时，CIF 要求卖方办理出口清关。但卖方无义务办理进口清关、支付任何进口税或办理任何进口海关手续。

A THE SELLER'S OBLIGATIONS

A1 General obligations of the seller

The seller must provide the goods and the commercial invoice in conformity with the contract of sale and any other evidence of conformity that may be required by the contract.

Any document to be provided by the seller may be in paper or electronic form as agreed or, where there is no agreement, as is customary.

A2 Delivery

The seller must deliver the goods either by placing them on board the vessel or by procuring the goods so delivered. In either case, the seller must deliver the goods on the agreed date or within the agreed period and in the manner customary at the port.

A3 Transfer of risks

The seller bears all risks of loss of or damage to the goods until they have been delivered in accordance with A2, with the exception of loss or damage in the circumstance described in B3.

A4 Carriage

The seller must contract or procure a contract for the carriage of the goods from the agreed point of delivery, if any, at the place of delivery to the named port of destination or, if agreed, any point at that port. The contract of carriage must be made on usual terms at the seller's cost and provide for carriage by the usual route in a vessel of the type normally used for the transport of the type of goods sold.

The seller must comply with any transport-related security requirements for transport to the destination.

A5 Insurance

Unless otherwise agreed or customary in the particular trade, the seller must obtain, at its own cost, cargo insurance complying with the cover provided by Clauses (C) of the Institute Cargo Clauses (LMA/IUA) or any similar clauses. The insurance shall be contracted with underwriters or an insurance company of good repute and entitle the buyer, or any other person having an insurable interest in the goods, to claim directly from the insurer.

When required by the buyer, the seller must, subject to the buyer providing any necessary information requested by the seller, provide at the buyer's cost any additional cover, if procurable, such as cover complying with the Institute War Clauses and/or Institute Strikes Clauses (LMA/IUA) or any similar clauses (unless such cover is already included in the cargo insurance described in the preceding paragraph).

The insurance shall cover, at a minimum, the price provided in the contract plus 10% (i.e. 110%) and shall be in the currency of the contract.

The insurance shall cover the goods from the point of delivery set out in A2 to at least the named port of destination.

The seller must provide the buyer with the insurance policy or certificate or any other evidence of insurance cover.

Moreover, the seller must provide the buyer, at the buyer's request, risk, and cost, with information that the buyer needs to procure any additional insurance.

A6　Delivery/Transport document

The seller must, at its own cost, provide the buyer with the usual transport document for the agreed port of destination. This transport document must cover the contract goods, be dated within the period agreed for shipment, enable the buyer to claim the goods from the carrier at the port of destination and, unless otherwise agreed, enable the buyer to sell the goods in transit by the transfer of the document to a subsequent buyer or by notification to the carrier.

When such a transport document is issued in negotiable form and in several originals, a full set of originals must be presented to the buyer.

A7　Export/Import clearance

a) Export clearance

Where applicable, the seller must carry out and pay for all export clearance formalities required by the country of export, such as:

- Export Licence
- Security Clearance for Export
- Pre-Shipment Inspection; and
- Any other official authorisation

b) Assistance with import clearance

Where applicable, the seller must assist the buyer at the buyer's request, risk, and cost, in obtaining any documents and/or information related to all transit/import clearance formalities, including security requirements and pre-shipment inspection, needed by any country of transit or the country of import.

A8　Checking/Packing/Marking

The seller must pay the costs of those checking operations (such as checking quality, measuring, weighing, counting) that are necessary for the purpose of delivering the goods in accordance with A2.

The seller must, at its own cost, package the goods, unless it is usual for the particular trade to transport the type of goods sold unpackaged. The seller must package and mark the goods in the manner appropriate for their transport, unless the parties have agreed on specific packaging or marking requirements.

A9　Allocation of costs

The seller must pay:

a) all costs relating to the goods until they have been delivered in accordance with A2, other than those payable by the buyer under B9;

b) the freight and all other costs resulting from A4, including the costs of loading the goods on board and transport related security costs;

c) any charges for unloading at the agreed port of discharge that were for the seller's account under the contract of carriage;

d) the costs of transit that were for the seller's account under the contract of carriage;

e) the costs of providing the usual proof to the buyer under A6 that the goods have been delivered;

f) the costs of insurance resulting from A5;

g) where applicable, duties, taxes, and any other costs related to export clearance under A7(a); and

h) the buyer for all costs and charges related to providing assistance in obtaining documents and information in accordance with B7(a).

A10　Notices

The seller must notify the buyer that the goods have been delivered in accordance with A2.

The seller must give the buyer any notice required to enable the buyer to receive the goods.

A 卖方义务

A1 卖方一般义务

卖方必须提供符合销售合同的货物和商业发票，以及合同可能要求的任何其他符合性证据。

卖方提供的任何文件可以按照协议以纸质或电子形式提供，或者在没有协议的情况下按惯例使用。

A2 交货

卖方必须按以下方式交货：将货物装上船，或者以取得已经这样交付的货物的方式交货。无论哪种情况，卖方都必须在约定日期或期限内，按照该港的习惯方式交货。

A3 风险转移

卖方承担货物灭失或损坏的一切风险，直到按照 A2 规定交货为止，但 B3 中所述情况下的灭失或损坏除外。

A4 运输

卖方必须签订合同或促成合同，将货物自交货地内的约定交货点（如有的话）运送至指定目的地或指定目的地内的约定的地点（如有约定）。必须按照通常条件订立运输合同，由卖方支付费用，经由通常航线，由通常用来运输该类商品的船舶运输。

卖方必须遵守任何与运输有关的安全要求，才能运输到目的地。

A5 保险

除非在特定行业中另有约定或惯例，否则卖方必须自费购买符合保险协会货物条款（LMA/IUA）条款（C）或任何类似条款规定的承保范围的货物保险。保险应与承销商或信誉良好的保险公司签订合同，并赋予购买者或在货物中具有可保权益的任何其他人直接向保险人索赔的权利。

当买方要求时，卖方必须在向买方提供任何必要信息的前提下，提供任何额外的承保范围（如果可以购买的话），例如符合协会战争条款和/或协会的承保范围罢工条款（LMA / IUA）或任何类似条款（除非前款所述货物保险中已包含此类保险）。

保险应至少涵盖合同中规定的价格再加 10%（即 110%）的价格，并应以合同货币为准。

保险应涵盖从 A2 中规定的交货地点到至少指定的目的地港口的货物。

卖方必须向买方提供保险单或证明或任何其他保险证明。

此外，卖方必须根据买方的要求向买方提供风险和成本，以告知买方需要购买其他保险的信息。

A6　交货/运输凭证

卖方必须自付费用，不得延迟向买方提供到约定目的港的通常的运输凭证。

此运输凭证必须载明合同该项货物，且其签发日期应在约定运输期限内，并使买方能在指定目的港向承运人索取货物。同时，除非另有约定，该项凭证应能使买方在货物运输途中以向下家买方转让或通知承运人的方式出售货物。

当此类运输凭证以可转让形式签发并有数份正本时，则必须将整套正本凭证提交给买方。

A7　出口/进口清关

a）出口清关

在适用的情况下，卖方必须执行并支付出口国要求的所有出口清关手续，例如：

· 出口许可证

· 出口安全通关

· 装运前检查；和

· 其他任何官方授权

b）协助进口清关

如适用时，应买方要求并由其承担风险和费用，卖方必须及时向买方提供或协助其取得相关货物进口和/或将货物运输到最终目的地所需要的任何单据和信息，包括过境或进口国安全相关信息。

A8　检查/包装/标记

卖方必须支付为按照 A2 规定交付货物所需的检查操作费用（例如检查质量、测量、称重、计数）。

卖方必须自付费用包装货物，除非特定行业将未包装出售的货物运输。除非双方已就特定的包装或标记要求达成协议，否则卖方必须以适合其运输的方式包装和标记商品。

A9　费用划分

卖方必须支付：

a）按照 A2 交货前揽物相关的一切费用，但按照 B9 应由买方支付的费用除外；

b）按照 A4 所产生的运费和所有其他费用，包括在船上装载货物的费用和与运输有关的安保费用；

c）根据运输合同由卖方承担的在约定卸货港卸货的任何费用；

d）根据运输合同由卖方承担的过境费用；

e）根据 A6 向买方提供通常的证明已交付货物的费用；

f）A5 产生的保险费用；

g）在适用的情况下，根据 A7（a）进行出口清关的关税、税金和任何其他费用；和

h）买方承担与根据 B7（a）获得文件和信息的协助有关的所有费用。

A10 通知

卖方必须通知买方已按照 A2 规定交货。

卖方必须给买方任何必要的通知，以使买方能够接收货物。

B THE BUYER'S OBLIGATIONS

B1 General obligations of the buyer

The buyer must pay the price of the goods as provided in the contract of sale.

Any document to be provided by the buyer may be in paper or electronic form as agreed or, where there is no agreement, as is customary.

B2 Taking delivery

The buyer must take delivery of the goods when they have been delivered under A2 and receive them from the carrier at the named port of destination.

B3 Transfer of risks

The buyer bears all risks of loss of or damage to the goods from the time they have been delivered under A2.

If the buyer fails to give notice in accordance with B10, then it bears all risks of loss of or damage to the goods from the agreed date or the end of the agreed period for shipment, provided that the goods have been clearly identified as the contract goods.

B4 Carriage

The buyer has no obligation to the seller to make a contract of carriage.

B5 Insurance

The buyer has no obligation to the seller to make a contract of insurance. However, the buyer must provide the seller, upon request, with any information necessary for the seller to procure any additional insurance requested by the buyer under A5.

B6 Delivery/Transport document

The buyer must accept the transport document provided under A6 if it is in conformity with the contract.

B7 Export/Import clearance

a) Assistance with export clearance

Where applicable, the buyer must assist the seller at the seller's request, risk, and cost in obtaining any documents and/or information related to all export clearance formalities, including security requirements and pre-shipment inspection, needed by the country of export.

b) Import clearance

Where applicable, the buyer must carry out and pay for all formalities required by any country of transit and the country of import, such as:

• import licence and any licence required for transit;

- security clearance for import and any transit;

- pre-shipment inspection; and

- any other official authorisation.

B8   Checking/Packing/Marking

The buyer has no obligation to the seller.

B9   Allocation of costs

The buyer must pay:

a) all costs relating to the goods from the time they have been delivered under A2, other than those payable by the seller under A9;

b) the costs of transit, unless such costs were for the seller's account under the contract of carriage;

c) unloading costs including lighterage and wharfage charges, unless such costs and charges were for the seller's account under the contract of carriage;

d) the costs of any additional insurance procured at the buyer's request under A5 and B5;

e) the seller for all costs and charges related to providing assistance in obtaining documents and information in accordance with A5 and A7(b).

f) where applicable, duties, taxes, and any other costs related to transit or import clearance under B7(b); and

g) any additional costs incurred if it fails to give notice in accordance with B10, from the agreed date or the end of the agreed period for shipment, provided that the goods have been clearly identified as the contract goods.

B10   Notices

The buyer must, whenever it is agreed that the buyer is entitled to determine the time for shipping the goods and/or the point of receiving the goods within the named port of destination, give the seller sufficient notice.

B 买方义务

B1 买方一般义务

买方必须按照销售合同中的规定支付货款。

买方要提供的任何文件可以按照协议以纸质或电子形式提供,或者在没有协议的情况下按惯例提供。

B2 受领货物

买方必须按照 A2 规定受领货物,然后从指定目的地的承运人处接收货物。

B3 风险转移

买方承担按照 A2 交货时起货物灭失或损坏的一切风险。

如买方未按照 B10 通知卖方,则买方必须从约定交货日期或交货期限届满之日起,承担货物灭失或损坏的一切风险,但以该货物已清楚地确定为合同项下之货物者为限。

B4 运输

买方没有义务与卖方订立运输合同。

B5 保险

买方无义务与卖方订立保险合同。但是，买方必须应要求向卖方提供卖方购买 A5 规定的买方要求的任何其他保险所需的任何信息。

B6 交货/运输凭证

如果符合合同规定，则买方必须接受 A6 规定的运输单据。

B7 出口/进口清关

a）协助出口清关

如适用时，应卖方要求并由其承担风险和费用，买方必须及时向卖方提供或协助其取得货物运输和出口及从他国过境运输所需要的任何单证和信息，包括安全相关信息和装运前检验。

b）进口清关

在适用的情况下，买方必须执行并支付任何过境国和进口国要求的所有手续，例如：

• 进口许可证和过境所需的任何许可证；
• 进口和任何过境的安全检查；
• 装运前检查；和
• 任何其他官方授权。

B8 检查/包装/标记

买方对卖方没有义务。

B9 费用划分

买方必须支付：

a）自货物按照 A2 交付之日起与货物有关的所有费用，但卖方根据 A9 应付的费用除外；

b）过境费用，除非这些费用是根据运输合同由卖方承担的；

c）包括卸货和码头费在内的卸货费用，除非这些费用是根据运输合同由卖方承担的；

d）根据买方要求根据 A5 和 B5 购买的任何其他保险的费用；

e）卖方承担与根据 A5 和 A7（b）协助获取文件和信息有关的所有费用。

f）在适用的情况下，与 B7（b）中的过境或进口清关相关的关税、税金和任何其他费用；和

g）如果未能明确按照合同 B10 的规定自通知之日或约定的装运期限起发出通知，则产生的任何额外费用。

B10 通知

买方一旦决定装运货物的时间和/或指定的目的港卸货点，买方必须向卖方发出充分的通知。

4. FCA: Free Carrier (...named place of delivery)［FCA：货交承运人（……指定交货地点）］

This rule may be used irrespective of the mode of transport selected and may also be used where more than one mode of transport is employed.

"Free Carrier" means that the seller delivers the goods to the carrier or another person nominated by the buyer at the seller's premises or another named place. The parties are well advised to specify as clearly as possible the point within the named place of delivery, as the risk passes to the buyer at that point.

If the parties intend to deliver the goods at the seller's premises, they should identify the address of those premises as the named place of delivery. If, on the other hand, the parties intend the goods to be delivered at another place, they must identify a different specific place of delivery.

FCA requires the seller to clear the goods for export, where applicable. However, the seller has no obligation to clear the goods for import, pay any import duty, or carry out any import customs formalities.

Compared to FOB, because it can be used in any kind of transportation, there are some differences in delivery by the seller and notice to the seller by the buyer. As for the remaining obligations of the buyer and the seller, please refer to FOB.

In FCA, the seller's obligation for delivery is as follows:

A6　Delivery/Transport document

The seller must provide the buyer, at the seller's cost, with the usual proof that the goods have been delivered in accordance with A2.

The seller must provide assistance to the buyer, at the buyer's request, risk, and cost, in obtaining a transport document.

Where the buyer has instructed the carrier to issue to the seller a transport document under B6, the seller must provide any such document to the buyer.

A10　Notices

The seller must give the buyer sufficient notice either that the goods have been delivered in accordance with A2 or that the carrier or another person nominated by the buyer has failed to take the goods within the agreed time.

For the buyer's obligations, they are as follows:

B6　Delivery/Transport document

The buyer must accept the proof that the goods have been delivered in accordance with A2.

If the parties have so agreed, the buyer must instruct the carrier to issue to the seller, at the buyer's cost and risk, a transport document stating that the goods have been loaded (such as a bill of lading with an on-board notation).

B10　Notices

The buyer must notify the seller of:

a) the name of the carrier or another person nominated within sufficient time as to enable the seller to deliver the goods in accordance with A2;

b) the selected time, if any, within the period agreed for delivery when the carrier or person nominated will receive the goods;

c) the mode of transport to be used by the carrier or the person nominated, including any transport-related security requirements; and

d) the point where the goods will be received within the named place of delivery.

该术语可适用于任何运输方式，也可适用于多种运输方式。

"货交承运人"是指卖方在卖方所在地或其他指定地点将货物交给买方指定的承运人或其他

人。由于风险在交货地点转移至买方，特别建议双方尽可能清楚地写明指定交货地内的交付点。

如果双方希望在卖方所在地交货，则应当将卖方所在地址明确为指定交货地。如果双方希望在其他地点交货，则必须确定不同的特定交货地点。

如适用时，FCA 要求卖方办理货物出口清关手续。但卖方无义务办理进口清关，支付任何进口税或办理进口的任何海关手续。

相对于 FOB 术语来说，由于 FCA 术语适用于任何运输方式，因此，在有关卖方交货及买方的通知义务方面，它与 FOB 术语有差别。其他买方与卖方的责任与义务，请参阅 FOB。

在 FCA 中，卖方的交货义务如下：

A6 交货/运输凭证

由卖方承担费用，卖方必须向买方提供通常的证明，证明货物已按照 A2 规定交付。

卖方必须根据买方的要求为买方提供协助，承担风险和费用，以获取运输单据。

如果买方已指示承运人根据 B6 向卖方签发运输单据，则卖方必须向买方提供任何此类单据。

A10 通知

卖方必须给买方充分的通知，即货物已按照 A2 规定交付，或者买方指定的承运人或其他人未在约定的时间内取走货物。

买方的义务如下：

B6 收货/运输证据

买方必须接受证明已按照 A2 规定交货的证据。

如果双方同意，则买方必须指示承运人向卖方出具运输凭证，由买方承担费用和风险，以表明货物已装好（例如添加已装船批注提单）。

B10 通知

买方必须通知卖方

a）在足够的时间内指定的承运人或另一人的姓名，以使卖方能够按照 A2 的规定交付货物；

b）被指定的承运人或个人将在约定的交货期限内选定的时间（如果有的话）接收货物；

c）承运人或被提名人使用的运输方式，包括任何与运输有关的安全要求；和

d）在指定的交货地点范围内的接收货物的具体地点。

5．CPT: Carriage Paid To (…named place of destination) ［CPT：运费付至（……指定目的地）］

This rule may be used irrespective of the mode of transport selected and may also be used where more than one mode of transport is employed.

"Carriage Paid To" means that the seller delivers the goods to the carrier or another person nominated by the seller at an agreed place (if any such place is agreed between the parties) and that the seller must contract for and pay the costs of carriage necessary to bring the goods to the named place of destination.

When CPT, CIP, CFR or CIF are used, the seller fulfils its obligation to deliver when it hands the goods over to the carrier and not when the goods reach the place of destination.

This rule has two critical points, because risk passes and costs are transferred at different places. The parties are well advised to identify as precisely as possible in the contract both the place of delivery, where the risk passes to the buyer, and the named place of destination to which the seller must contract for the carriage. If several carriers are used for the carriage to the agreed destination and the parties do not agree on a specific point of delivery, the default position is that risk passes when the goods have been delivered to the first carrier at a point entirely of the seller's choosing and over which the buyer has no control. Should the parties wish the risk to pass at a later stage (e.g., at an ocean port or airport), they need to specify this in their contract of sale.

The parties are also well advised to identify as precisely as possible the point within the agreed place of destination, as the costs to that point are for the account of the seller. The seller is advised to procure contracts of carriage that match this choice precisely. If the seller incurs costs under its contract of carriage related to unloading at the named place of destination, the seller is not entitled to recover such costs from the buyer unless otherwise agreed between the parties.

CPT requires the seller to clear the goods for export, where applicable. However, the seller has no obligation to clear the goods for import, pay any import duty or carry out any import customs formalities.

该术语可适用于任何运输方式，也可适用于多种运输方式。

"运费付至"是指卖方将货物在双方约定地点（如果双方已经约定了地点）交给卖方指定的承运人或其他人。卖方必须签订运输合同并支付将货物运至指定目的地所需费用。

在使用 CPT、CIP、CFR 或 CIF 术语时，当卖方将货物交付给承运人时，而不是当货物到达目的地时，即完成交货。

由于风险转移和费用转移的地点不同，该术语有两个关键点。特别建议双方尽可能确切地在合同中明确交货地点，风险在这里转移至买方，以及指定的目的地（卖方必须签订运输合同运到该目的地）。如果运输到约定目的地涉及多个承运人，且双方不能就交货点达成一致时，可以推定：当卖方在某个完全由其选择，且买方不能控制的点将货物交付给第一个承运人时，风险转移至买方。如双方希望风险晚些转移的话（例如在某海港或机场转移），则需要在其买卖合同中注明。

由于卖方需承担将货物运至目的地内的该点的费用，特别建议双方尽可能确切地注明约定的目的地内的该点。建议卖方签订的运输合同应能与所做选择确切吻合。如果卖方按照运输合同在指定的目的地卸货发生了费用，除非双方另有约定，卖方无权向买方要求偿付。

如适用时，CPT 要求卖方办理货物的出口清关手续。但是卖方无义务办理进口清关，支付任何进口税或办理进口相关的任何海关手续。

Compared with CFR, because it can be used in any kind of transportation, there are some differences in A3 a) contract of carriage, A4 delivery by the seller. As per the remaining obligations of the buyer and the seller, please refer to CFR.

In CPT, the seller's obligation for contract of carriage is as follows:

A4　Carriage

The seller must contract or procure a contract for the carriage of the goods from the agreed point of delivery, if any, at the place of delivery to the named place of destination or, if agreed, any point at that place. The contract of carriage must be made on usual terms at the seller's cost and provide for carriage by the usual route in a customary manner of the type normally used for the carriage of the type of goods sold. If a specific point is not agreed or is not determined by practice, the seller may select the point of delivery and the point at the named place of destination that best suit its purpose.

The seller must comply with any transport-related security requirements for transport to the destination.

相对于 CFR 术语来说，由于 CPT 术语适用于任何运输方式，因此，在有关运输合同以及卖方交货方面，它与 CFR 术语有差别。其他买方与卖方的责任与义务，请参阅 CFR。

在 CPT 术语中，卖方对运输合同的义务如下。

A4 运输合同

卖方必须签订或取得运输合同，将货物自交货地内的约定交货点（如有的话）运送至指定目的地或该目的地的交付点（如有约定）。必须按照通常条件订立合同，由卖方支付费用，经由通常航线和习惯方式运送货物。如果双方没有约定特别的点或按照惯例也无法确定，卖方则可根据合同需要选择最适合其目的的交货点和指定目的地内的交货点。

卖方必须遵守任何运输相关的安全要求运输至目的地。

In CPT, the seller's obligation for delivery is as follows.

A2　Delivery

The seller must deliver the goods by handing them over to the carrier contracted in accordance with A4 or by procuring the goods so delivered. In either case, the seller must deliver the goods on the agreed date or within the agreed period.

在 CPT 术语中，卖方的交货义务如下。

A2 交货

卖方必须在约定日期或期限内，将货物交给按 A4 签订合同的承运人。无论哪种情况，卖方都必须在约定的日期或约定的期限内交付货物。

6. CIP: Carriage and Insurance Paid to (…named place of destination)［CIP：运费和保险费付至（……指定目的地）］

This rule may be used irrespective of the mode of transport selected and may also be used where more than one mode of transport is employed.

"Carriage and Insurance Paid to" means that the seller delivers the goods to the carrier or another person nominated by the seller at an agreed place (if any such place is agreed between the parties) and that the seller must contract for and pay the costs of carriage necessary to bring the goods to the named place of destination.

The seller also contracts for insurance cover against the buyer's risk of loss of or damage to the goods during the carriage. The buyer should note that under CIP the seller is required to obtain insurance only on minimum cover. Should the buyer wish to have more insurance protection, it will need either to agree as much expressly with the seller or to make its own extra insurance arrangements.

When CPT, CIP, CFR, or CIF are used, the seller fulfills its obligation to deliver when it hands the goods over to the carrier and not when the goods reach the place of destination.

This rule has two critical points, because risk passes and costs are transferred at different places. The parties are well advised to identify as precisely as possible in the contract both the place of delivery, where the risk passes to the buyer, and the named place of destination to which the seller must contract for carriage. If several carriers are used for the carriage to the agreed destination and the parties do not agree on a specific point of delivery, the default position is that risk passes when the goods have been delivered to the first carrier at a point entirely of the seller's choosing and over which the buyer has no control. Should the parties wish the risk to pass at a later stage (e.g., at an ocean port or an airport), they need to specify this in their contract of sale.

The parties are also well advised to identify as precisely as possible the point within the agreed place of destination, as the costs to that point are for the account of the seller. The seller is advised to procure contracts of carriage that match this choice precisely. If the seller incurs costs under its contract of carriage related to unloading at the named place of destination, the seller is not entitled to recover such costs from the buyer unless otherwise agreed between the parties.

CIP requires the seller to clear the goods for export, where applicable. However, the seller has no obligation to clear the goods for import, pay any import duty, or carry out any import customs formalities.

该术语可用于任何运输方式，也可用于多种运输方式。

"运费和保险费付至"是指卖方将货物在双方约定地点（如双方已经约定了地点）交给其指定的承运人或其他人。卖方必须签订运输合同并支付将货物运至指定目的地所需的费用。

卖方还必须为买方在运输途中货物的灭失或损坏风险签订保险合同。买方应注意到，CIP只要求卖方投保最低险别。如果买方需要更多保险保护的话，则需与卖方明确就此达成协议，或者自行做出额外的保险安排。

在使用 CPT、CIP、CFR 或 CIF 术语时，当卖方将货物交付给承运人时，而不是当货物到达目的地时，即完成交货。

由于风险转移和费用转移的地点不同，该术语有两个关键点。特别建议双方尽可能确切地在合同中明确交货地点，风险在这里转移至买方，以及指定目的地（卖方必须签订运输合同运到该目的地）。如果运输到约定目的地，涉及多个承运人，且双方不能就特定的交货点达成一致时，可以推定：当卖方在某个完全由其选择，且买方不能控制的点将货物交付给第一个承运人时，风险转移至买方。如双方希望风险晚些转移的话（例如在某海港或机场转移），则需要在其买卖合同中注明。

由于卖方需承担将货物运至目的地内的该点的费用，特别建议双方尽可能确切地注明约定的目的地内的该点。建议卖方签订的运输合同应能与所做选择确切吻合。如果卖方按照运输合同在指定的目的地卸货发生了费用，除非双方另有约定，卖方无权向买方要求偿付。

如适用时，CIP 要求卖方办理货物的出口清关手续。但是卖方无义务办理进口清关，支付任何进口税或办理进口相关的任何海关手续。

Compared with CIF, because it can be used in any kind of transportation, there are some differences in "A2 Delivery" and "A6 Delivery/Transport document" by the seller. As per the remaining obligations of the buyer and the seller, please refer to CIF.

A2   Delivery

The seller must deliver the goods by handing them over to the carrier contracted in accordance with A4 or by procuring the goods so delivered. In either case, the seller must deliver the goods on the agreed date or within the agreed period.

A6   Delivery/Transport document

If customary or at the buyer's request, the seller must provide the buyer, at the seller's cost, with the usual transport documents for the transport contracted in accordance with A4.

This transport document must cover the contract goods and be dated within the period agreed for shipment. If agreed or customary, the document must also enable the buyer to claim the goods from the carrier at the named place of destination and enable the buyer to sell the goods in transit by the transfer of the document to a subsequent buyer or by notification to the carrier.

When such a transport document is issued in negotiable form and in several originals, a full set of originals must be presented to the buyer.

相对于 CIF 而言，由于该术语适用于任何运输方式，因此，在"A2 交货"和"A6 交货/运输凭证"方面，它与 CIF 术语有差别。其他买方与卖方的责任与义务，请参阅 CIF。

A2 交货

卖方必须在约定日期或期限内，将货物交给按照 A4 签订合同的承运人。无论哪种情况，卖方都必须在约定的日期或约定的期限内交付货物。

A6 交货/运输凭证

依惯例或应买方要求，卖方必须承担费用，向买方提供其按照 A4 订立的运输合同通常的运输凭证。

此项运输凭证必须载明合同中的货物，且其签发日期应在约定运输期限内。如已约定或依惯例，此项凭证也必须能使买方在指定目的地向承运人索取货物，并能使买方在货物运输途中以向下家买方转让或通知承运人方式出售货物。

当此类运输凭证以可转让形式签发，且有数份正本时，则必须将整套正本凭证提交给买方。

Incoterms 2020 aligns different levels of insurance coverage in Cost Insurance and Freight (CIF) and Carriage and Insurance Paid To (CIP).

《国际贸易术语解释通则 2020》调整了 CIF 成本加保险费加运费以及 CIP 运费和保险费付至的不同保险范围。

A5   Insurance

Unless otherwise agreed or customary in the particular trade, the seller must obtain, at its own cost, cargo insurance complying with the cover provided by Clauses (A) of the Institute Cargo Clauses (LMA/IUA) or any similar clauses as appropriate to the means of transport used. The insurance shall be contracted with underwriters or an insurance company of good repute and entitle the buyer, or any other person having an insurable interest in the goods, to claim directly from the insurer.

When required by the buyer, the seller must, subject to the buyer providing any necessary information requested by the seller, provide at the buyer's cost any additional cover, if procurable, such as cover complying with the Institute War

Clauses and/or Institute Strikes Clauses (LMA/IUA) or any similar clauses (unless such cover is already included in the cargo insurance described in the preceding paragraph).

The insurance shall cover, at a minimum, the price provided in the contract plus 10% (i.e 110%) and shall be in the currency of the contract.

The insurance shall cover the goods from the point of delivery set out in A2 to at least the named place of destination.

The seller must provide the buyer with the insurance policy or certificate or any other evidence of insurance cover.

Moreover, the seller must provide the buyer, at the buyer's request, risk, and cost, with information that the buyer needs to procure any additional insurance.

A5 保险

除非特定行业另有约定或惯例，否则卖方必须自费购买符合保险协会货物条款（LMA/IUA）条款（A）或适用于该条款的任何类似条款提供的承保的货物保险。保险应与承销商或信誉良好的保险公司签订合同，并赋予购买者或在货物中具有可保权益的任何其他人直接向保险人索赔的权利。

当买方要求时，卖方必须在向买方提供要求的任何必要信息的前提下，提供买方提供的任何额外保险（如果可以购买的话），例如，符合协会战争的保险条款和/或协会罢工条款（LMA / IUA）或任何类似的条款（除非上一段所述的货物保险中已包含此类保险）。

保险应至少涵盖合同中规定的价格再加 10%（即 110%）的价格，并应以合同货币为准。

保险应涵盖从 A2 中规定的交货地点到至少指定的目的地的货物。

卖方必须向买方提供保险单或证明或任何其他保险证明。

此外，卖方承担风险和成本，根据买方的要求向买方告知需要购买其他保险的信息。

B5 Insurance

The buyer has no obligation to the seller to make a contract of insurance. However, the buyer must provide the seller, upon request, with any information necessary for the seller to procure any additional insurance requested by the buyer under A5.

B5 保险

买方无义务与卖方订立保险合同。但是，买方必须应要求向卖方提供卖方购买 A5 规定的买方要求的任何其他保险所需的任何信息。

Section Four　EXW and FAS in Incoterms 2020 (《2020 年通则》中的 EXW 和 FAS 术语）

1. EXW: Ex Works (…named place of delivery) [EXW：工厂交货（……指定交货地点）]

This rule may be used irrespective of the mode of transport selected and may also be used where more than one mode of transport is employed. It is suitable for domestic trade, while FCA is usually more appropriate for international trade.

"Ex works" means that the seller delivers when it places the goods at the disposal of the buyer at the seller's premises or at another named place (i.e. works, factory, warehouse, etc.). The seller does not need to load the goods on any collecting vehicle, nor does it need to clear the goods for export, where such clearance is applicable.

The parties are well advised to specify as clearly as possible the point within the named place of delivery, as the costs and risks to that point are for the account of the seller. The buyer bears all costs and risks involved in taking the goods from the agreed point, if any, at the named place of delivery.

EXW represents the minimum obligation for the seller. The rule should be used with care as:

a) The seller has no obligation to the buyer to load the goods, even though in practice the seller may be in a better position to do so. If the seller does load the goods, it does so at the buyer's risk and expense. In cases where the seller is in a better position to load the goods, FCA, which obliges the seller to do so at its own risk and expense, is usually more appropriate.

b) A buyer who buys from a seller on an EXW basis for export needs to be aware that the seller has an obligation to provide only such assistance as the buyer may require to effect that export: the seller is not bound to organize the export clearance. Buyers are therefore well advised not to use EXW if they cannot directly or indirectly obtain export clearance.

c) The buyer has limited obligations to provide the seller with any information regarding the export of the goods. However, the seller may need this information for, e.g., taxation or reporting purposes.

该术语可适用于任何运输方式，也可适用于多种运输方式。它适合国内贸易，而 FCA 一般则更适合国际贸易。

"工厂交货"是指当卖方在其所在地或其他指定地点（如工厂、车间或仓库等）将货物交给买方处置时，即完成交货。卖方无须将货物装上任何前来接收货物的运输工具，需要清关时，卖方也无须办理出口清关手续。

特别建议双方在指定交货地范围内尽可能明确具体交货地点，因为在货物到达交货地点之前的所有费用和风险都由卖方承担。买方则需承担自此指定交货点（如有的话）受领货物所产生的全部费用和风险。

EXW（工厂交货）术语是卖方承担责任最小的术语，使用时需注意以下问题：

a）卖方对买方没有装货的义务，即使实际上卖方也许更方便这样做。如果卖方装货，也由买方承担相关风险和费用。当卖方更方便装货物时，FCA 一般更为合适，因为该术语要求卖方承担装货义务，以及与此相关的风险和费用。

b）以 EXW 为基础购买出口产品的买方需要明白，卖方只有在买方要求时，才有责任协助办理出口，即卖方无义务安排出口通关。因此，在买方不能直接或间接地办理出口清关手续时，不建议使用该术语。

c）买方仅有限度地承担向卖方提供货物出口相关信息的责任。但是，卖方则可能出于交税或申报等目的需要这方面的信息。

2. FAS: Free Alongside Ship (...named port of shipment)［FAS：船边交货（……指定装运港）］

This term can only be used for sea or inland water transportation.

"Free Alongside Ship" means that the seller delivers when the goods are placed alongside the vessel (e.g., on a quay or a barge) nominated by the buyer at the named port of shipment. The risk of loss of or damage to the goods passes when the goods are alongside the ship, and the buyer bears all costs from that moment onwards.

The parties are well advised to specify as clearly as possible the loading point at the named port of shipment, as the costs and risks to that point are for the account of the seller and these costs and associated handling charges may vary according to the practice of the port.

The seller is required either to deliver the goods alongside the ship or to procure goods already so delivered for shipment. The reference to "procure" here caters for multiple sales down a chain (string sales), particularly common in the commodity trades.

Where the goods are in containers, it is typical for the seller to hand the goods over to the carrier at a terminal and not alongside the vessel. In such situations, the FAS rule would be inappropriate, and the FCA rule should be used.

FAS requires the seller to clear the goods for export, where applicable. However, the seller has no obligation to clear the goods for import, pay any import duty, or carry out any import customs formalities.

该术语仅用于海运或内河水运。

"船边交货"是指当卖方在指定的装运港将货物交到买方指定的船边（例如，置于码头或驳船上）时，即为交货。货物灭失或损坏的风险在货物交到船边时发生转移，同时买方承担自那时起的一切费用。

由于卖方承担在特定地点交货前的风险和费用，而且这些费用和相关作业费可能因各港口惯例不同而变化，特别建议双方尽可能清楚地注明指定的装运港内的装货点。

卖方应将货物运至船边或取得已经这样交运的货物。此处使用的"取得"一词适用于商品贸易中常见的交易链中的多层销售（链式销售）。

当货物装在集装箱里时，卖方通常将货物在集装箱码头移交给承运人，而非交到船边。这时，FAS 术语不适合，应当使用 FCA 术语。

如使用时，FAS 要求卖方办理出口清关手续。但卖方无义务办理出口清关、支付任何进口税或办理任何进口海关手续。

Under FAS terms, the seller's obligations are fulfilled when the goods have been placed alongside the vessel on the quay or in lighters. This means that the buyer has to bear all costs and risks of loss or damage to the goods from that moment.

FAS = EXW + all risks and expenses before the goods are placed alongside the vessel on the quay

This term is used for waterway transport, and when adopting this term, the name of the port of shipment should be stated clearly after FAS. This term requires the seller to clear the goods for export.

这一术语是指卖方在装运港将货物放置在码头买方所指派的船只的船边，即完成了交货。买方必须自该时刻起，负担一切费用和货物灭失或损坏的一切风险。

FAS = EXW + 将货物交至装运港船边的一切费用和风险

它仅适用于水上运输方式，采用此术语时要在 FAS 后面注明装运港名称。

FAS 术语要求卖方办理货物出口清关。

Section Five　D Group in Incoterms 2020（《2020 年通则》中的 D 组术语）

In Incoterms 2020, D group has been greatly altered.　First of all, Incoterms 2020 include arrangements for carriage with own means of transport in FCA, Delivery at Place (DAP), Delivered at Place Unloaded (DPU), and Delivered Duty Paid (DDP). That is, when FCA, DAP, DPU, and DDP terms are used for trade, buyers and sellers can use their own means of transport according to their respective transportation obligations, and there is no longer a presumed need to use third-party carriers for transportation as in the Incoterms 2010. The transportation obligations assumed by both parties remain unchanged and still follow Incoterms 2010 standards. Apart from that, the three-letter name for Delivered at Terminal (DAT) has been changed to DPU. This means that the DAT delivery term has been replaced by DPU.

在《国际贸易术语解释通则 2020》中，D 组术语改变很大，首先，《国际贸易术语解释通则 2020》包括 FCA 货交承运人、DAP 目的地交货、DPU 卸货地交货、DDP 完税后交货术语下可用自有运输工具安排拖车。

即当采用 FCA、DAP、DPU 和 DDP 术语进行贸易时，贸易买卖双方可以根据各自的运输义务使用自有运输工具，而不再需要像 2010 版术语那样推定适用第三方承运人进行运输。双方承担的运输义务不变，仍旧遵循 2010 版的规定。另外，DAT 终点地交货术语成为历史，现使用 DPU 卸货地交货，这意味着 DAT 终点地交货术语被 DPU 卸货地交货所替代。

1．DPU: Delivered at Place Unloaded（DPU：卸货地交货）

"DPU-Delivered at Place Unloaded" means that the seller delivers the goods, and simultaneously, the risks and costs are both transferred to the buyer of trade when the goods are physically unloaded from the arriving means of transport and subsequently handed over to the buyer of trade. The place of delivery is the destination indicated in the contract or at an agreed point.

In this case, the place or point of delivery and destination refer to the same place or venue. DPU is, as a matter of fact, the only Incoterms rule that requires the seller of trade to unload goods at the place of delivery. Taking this into account, the seller bears the responsibility to ensure that the buyer can organize unloading at the place specified in the relevant contract.

This rule may be used irrespective of the mode of transport selected and may also be used where more than one mode of transport is employed.

The parties are well advised to specify as clearly as possible the terminal and, if possible, a specific point within the terminal at the agreed port or place of destination, as the risks to that point are for the account of the seller. The seller is advised to procure a contract of carriage that matches this choice precisely.

Moreover, if the parties intend the seller to bear the risks and costs involved in transporting and handling the goods from the terminal to another place, then the DAP or DDP rules should be used.

DPU requires the seller to clear the goods for export, where applicable.

However, the seller has no obligation to clear the goods for import, pay any import duty, or carry out any import customs formalities.

DPU——在卸货地点交货，是指卖方实际交付了货物，同时，当货物从到达的运输工具中实际卸下后，风险和成本都转移给了买方。交货地点在合同中指定的目的地或约定的地点进行。

在这种情况下，交货地点或交货点与目的地指向完全相同的地点或场所。实际上，DPU是唯一要求卖方在交货地点卸货的规则。考虑到这一点，贸易卖方有责任确保贸易买方能够在相关合同规定的地点组织卸货。

该术语可适用于任何运输方式，也可适用于多种运输方式。

由于卖方承担在特定地点交货前的风险，特别建议双方尽可能确切地约定运输终端，或如果可能的话，在约定港口或目的地的运输终端内的特定的点。建议卖方取得的运输合同应能与所做选择确切吻合。

此外，如果双方希望由卖方承担将货物由运输终端运输和搬运至另一地点的风险和费用，则应当使用 DAP 或 DDP 术语。

如适用时，DPU 要求卖方办理出口清关手续。

但卖方无义务办理进口清关，也没有义务支付任何进口税或办理任何进口海关手续。

2．DAP: Delivered At Place (…named place of destination)［DAP：目的地交货（……指定目的地）］

This rule may be used irrespective of the mode of transport selected and may also be used where more than one mode of transport is employed.

"Delivered At Place" means that the seller delivers when the goods are placed at the disposal of the buyer on the arriving means of transport, ready for unloading at the named place of destination. The seller bears all risks involved in bringing the goods to the named place.

The parties are well advised to specify as clearly as possible the point within the agreed place of destination, as the risks to that point are for the account of the seller. The seller is advised to procure contracts of carriage that match this choice precisely. If the seller incurs costs under its contract of carriage related to unloading at the place of destination, the seller is not entitled to recover such costs from the buyer unless otherwise agreed between the parties.

DAP requires the seller to clear the goods for export, where applicable. However, the seller has no obligation to clear the goods for import, pay any import duty, or carry out any import customs formalities. If the parties wish the seller to clear the goods for import, pay any import duty, and carry out any import customs formalities, the DDP term should be used.

该术语可适用于任何运输方式，也可适用于多种运输方式。

"目的地交货"是指当卖方在指定目的地将还在运输工具上可供卸载的货物交由买方处置时，即为交货。卖方承担将货物运送到指定地点的一切风险。

由于卖方承担在特定地点交货前的风险，特别建议双方尽可能清楚地注明指定的目的地的交货点。建议卖方订立的运输合同应能与所做选择确切吻合。如果卖方按照运输合同在目的地发生了卸货费用，除非双方另有约定，卖方无权向买方要求偿付。

如适用时，DAP 要求卖方办理出口清关手续。但是卖方无义务办理进口清关、支付任何进口税或办理任何进口海关手续。如果双方希望卖方办理进口清关、支付所有进口关税，并办理所有进口海关手续，则应当使用 DDP 术语。

3. DDP: Delivered Duty Paid (...named place of destination)［DDP：完税后交货（……指定目的地）］

This rule may be used irrespective of the mode of transport selected and may also be used where more than one mode of transport is employed.

"Delivered Duty Paid" means that the seller delivers the goods when the goods are placed at the disposal of the buyer, cleared for import, on the arriving means of transport ready for unloading at the named place of destination. The seller bears all the costs and risks involved in bringing the goods to the place of destination and has an obligation to clear the goods not only for export but also for import, to pay any duty for both export and import, and to carry out all customs formalities.

DDP represents the maximum obligation for the seller.

The parties are well advised to specify as clearly as possible the point within the agreed place of destination, as the costs and risks to that point are for the account of the seller. The seller is advised to procure contracts of carriage that match this choice precisely. If the seller incurs costs under its contract of carriage related to unloading at the place of destination, the seller is not entitled to recover such costs from the buyer unless otherwise agreed between the parties.

The parties are well advised not to use DDP if the seller is unable, directly or indirectly, to obtain import clearance.

If the parties wish the buyer to bear all risks and costs of import clearance, the DAP rule should be used.

Any VAT or other taxes payable upon import are for the seller's account unless expressly agreed otherwise in the sales contract.

该术语可适用于任何运输方式，也可适用于多种运输方式。

"完税后交货"是指当卖方在指定目的地将仍处于抵达的运输工具上，但已完成进口清关，且可供卸载的货物交由买方处置时，即为交货。卖方承担将货物运至目的地的一切风险和费用，并且有义务完成货物出口和进口清关，支付所有出口和进口的关税。

DDP 代表卖方的责任最大。

由于卖方承担在特定地点交货前的风险和费用，特别建议双方尽可能清楚地注明在指定目的地内的交货点。建议卖方订立的运输合同应能与所做选择确切吻合。如果按照运输合同卖方在目的地发生了卸货费用，除非双方另有约定，卖方无权向买方索要。

如卖方不能直接或间接地完成进口清关，则特别建议双方不使用 DDP。

如双方希望买方承担所有进口清关的风险和费用，则应使用 DAP 术语。除非买卖合同中另行明确规定，任何增值税或其他应付的进口税款由卖方承担。

Section Six Clauses Commonly Used about the Trade Terms in Contract（合同中的通用贸易术语）

1. USD 100 per dozen CFR New York.

每打 100 美元，CFR 纽约价。

2. USD 150 per MT CIF London including our 2% commission.

每公吨 150 美元，CIF 伦敦价，包括给我方 2%的佣金。

3. RMB ￥25 per case CFR Singapore less 1% discount.

每箱 25 元人民币，CFR 新加坡价，减 1%的折扣。

4. USD 4.5 per dozen FOB Shanghai.

每打 4.5 美元，FOB 上海净价。

5. Unless otherwise specified, prices are FOB Ex Works with freight allowed to US port of Westinghouse choice.

除非另有规定，价格采用 FOB 工厂交货价，运费付至威斯汀豪斯选定的美国港口。

6. Fluctuation in the freight and contingent imposition of export levies and changes therein, after the date of sale, to be for buyer's account regardless of CIF or FOB term.

合同签订后，不管合同采用 CIF，还是 FOB，运费的变化与出口税的增加变化均由买方负责。

7. In case the quotation is made on CIF basis, the freight is estimated and calculated to the best of the ability of the seller on prevailing rates at the time of quoting. Any increase in freight rate and/or insurance premium rate at the time of shipment shall be for the buyer's risks and account. The seller reserves the right to adjust the quoted price, if prior to delivery there is any substantial variation in the cost of raw materials or component parts.

如果按 CIF 报价，那么运费尽可能根据卖方的能力以现行的价格估价、核算。买方负担装运时运费及保险费增加所带来的风险和/或损失。如果交货前其原材料或组件成本大幅度涨价，卖方可调整合同价格。

8. The purchase price shall be … dollars per unit FAS Vessel, … place. The price is … charged alongside the vessel designated by the buyer at … place, the port of shipment.

购买价格为_____（地点）FAS 船边交货价格，每单位_____美元，此价格为买方指定在_____港装货的船边交货价。

9. In the case of EXW contract, insurance is to be effected by the end users after loading. In the case of CIF contract, insurance is to be effected by the seller for 110% percent of invoice value on All Risks basis.

在工厂交货合同条件下，货物装运后由买方负责投保。在 CIF 合同条件下，卖方应负责按货物价值的 110%投保综合险。

10. The Letter of Credit shall permit payment of 100 percent of the CIF price on presentation of shipping documents stipulated within the delivery date specified in the Letter of Credit.

在信用证规定的交货期内，（向银行）提交规定的装船单据后，信用证允许支付 CIF 价格的 100%。

11. USD 1 230.00 per ton CIF Shanghai including 3% commission. The commission shall be payable only after the seller has received the full amount of all payment due to the seller.

每吨 1 230 美元，CIF 上海价，含 3%佣金，佣金以卖方收讫全部货款为交付条件。

12. Any advance in freight at time of shipment shall be for buyer's account.

装运期间运费的上涨由买方支付。

Section Seven   Terminology Relating to International Trade and International Practices（有关国际贸易术语的国际惯例）

The rules and conventions of international trade refer to those customary practices and explanations of universal significance in international trade, which are formed through long-term practice. Therefore, there is a development process for the meaning and interpretation of each term. In trade practice, although there have been formed several explanations for various trade terms and the terms have won popular acceptance in the world, yet the explanation contents are not in strict conformity with each other. So disputes often emerge. The International Chamber of Commerce, the International Law Association and some well-known business groups in the United States worked out those rules and conventions to explain the international trade terms respectively after long efforts. These rules and conventions are widely used and accepted in the world and have become part of international trade practice. Nowadays, the most important rules and conventions are the following three.

(1) Revised American Foreign Trade Definition 1990

(2) Warsaw-Oxford Rules 1932

(3) Incoterms 2020

所谓国际贸易惯例，是指在国际贸易中具有普遍意义的一些习惯性的做法和解释，它是在长期的国际贸易实践中形成的。所以，每个术语的含义和解释都有一个发展过程。在贸易实践中，虽然形成了对各种贸易术语的习惯解释，而且得到了广泛承认，但内容并不完全一致，容易引起纠纷。于是，国际商会、国际法协会等国际组织以及美国一些著名商务团体经过长期努力，分别制定了解释国际贸易术语的规则，这些规则在国际上被广泛采用，因此成为一般的国际贸易惯例。其中，在国际上影响较大的主要有以下三种。

（1）《1990 年美国对外贸易定义修订本》

（2）《1932 年华沙—牛津规则》

（3）《2020 年国际贸易术语解释通则》

Section Eight   Declaration No. 56 on Cross-border E-commerce Goods Supervision by General Administration of Customs of the People's Republic of China（海关总署公告 2014 年第 56 号关于跨境贸易电子商务进出境货物、物品有关监管事宜的公告）

In order to better supervise the imported or exported cargoes and goods in cross-border e-commerce trade (hereinafter referred to as e-commerce) and promote the healthy growth of e-commerce, GACC hereby makes the following declaration on cross-border e-commerce cargoes and goods supervision:

1. Supervision requirement

(1) E-commerce enterprises or individuals, conducting cross-border transactions for imported or exported cargoes and goods through e-commerce sites approved by and connected with the customs, shall be under the supervision of GACC in accordance with this declaration.

(2) E-commerce enterprises shall submit the Declaration List of Cargoes for import or Export Through Cross-border E-commerce Trade of the People's Republic of China (hereinafter referred to as Declaration List of Cargoes) and handle the declaration procedures for e-commerce imported or exported goods by way of "List Approval & Collective Declaration"; individuals shall submit Declaration List of Articles for import or Export Through Cross-border E-commerce Trade of the People's Republic of China (hereinafter referred to as Declaration List of Articles) and handle the declaration procedures for e-commerce imported or exported goods by way of "List Approval".

The Declaration List of Cargoes, Declaration List of Articles and Customs Declaration for imports and Exports have the same legal force.

(3) Operators at the customs supervision organs shall handle the filing procedures for conducting e-commerce business such as storage of imported or exported cargoes and goods through e-commerce trade. Otherwise, the operators shall not conduct e-commerce business.

(4) E-commerce enterprises or individuals, payment companies, operators at the customs supervision organs as well as logistics companies shall submit the transaction, payment, storage and logistics data to the E-commerce declaration administration platform through the E-commerce declaration service platform in accordance with relevant regulations.

2. Corporate registration and filing management

(5) When it is necessary for E-commerce business enterprises to handle the customs declaration, the relevant party shall be registered at the customs in accordance with the relevant provisions of the customs registration management for declaration units. If these companies need to change or cancel registration information, they shall be handled in accordance with the relevant provisions of the registration management.

(6) The operator of customs supervision area of e-commerce business shall establish a perfect electronic warehouse management system and deliver warehouse management accounts data to the customs network via e-commerce clearance service platform; the E-commerce trading platform shall deliver electronic records data to the customs networking via e-commerce clearance service platform; The E-commerce enterprises, payment companies, logistics enterprises shall deliver raw data of entry and exit goods and articles to the customs networking via e-commerce clearance service platform.

(7) E-commerce enterprises shall in advance be registered at the customs in terms of imported and exported goods and items information, which shall include customs-recognized 10-digit HS code and 8-digit tariff code.

3. Customs management of e-commerce export and import goods and articles

(8) E-commerce enterprises or individuals, payment and logistics enterprises shall respectively submit information of orders, payments and logistics to the customs before the declaration of goods and articles in E- commerce import and export.

(9) E-commerce enterprise or its agent shall complete the customs clearance formalities within 14 days after the declaration of means of transport and 24 hours prior to the loading when the goods arrive in customs supervision areas of E-commerce, all these are according to the order payment, logistics and other information which has been sent to the customs. Individual inbound or outbound articles should be truthfully filled in the list of items by themselves or their agent and complete the customs clearance formalities for each ticket.

In addition to the special circumstances, the cargo list, the list of goods, the import and export goods customs declaration should be taken to declaration paperless.

(10) The E-electronic commerce enterprise or its agent shall declare the clearance of the goods list of last month on the basis of the same content on the listing head before 10th each month (if it is a legal holiday during the month, it will be automatically postponed to the following first working day. The collective clearance list of December should be completed before the last working day during the month.): the same business unit, the same mode of transportation, the same delivery country and arrival country, the same ports, the same 10 customs commodity code, the same unit of measurement of declaration, the same legal measurement units, the same monetary rules of merge, the declaration should be offered respectively according to the import and export goods customs declaration formed by the sort of import or export.

If an E-commerce enterprise or its agent fails to collect the list of goods needed to offer the declaration to the customs, the customs will no longer accept the relevant enterprises which would need the E-commerce inbound and outbound goods customs declaration formalities in the way of cargo list check and collective declaration, until the related collective declaration work is accomplished.

(11) E-commerce enterprises who need the declaration formalities by the way of the list of goods shall be in accordance with the relevant provisions of the general import and export goods tax formalities, and submit the relevant certificates; It is not needed the formalities related to tax-free or to submit certificates when enterprises declare to the customs in collective form of the import and export goods customs declaration.

For individual who needs the declaration formalities in the item listing way, their tax exemption formalities should be completed in accordance with the relevant provisions of the export and import personal postal articles levy, it is needed to submit the approval documents of the relevant department if the items are under customs control.

(12) If the E-commerce enterprises or individuals need to modify or cancel the cargo list, the list of items shall refer to the current customs import and export goods declaration form. After modification of the list of goods or cancellation, the corresponding "import and export goods

declaration form" should be accordingly modified or canceled.

(13) The date of import and export on the import and export goods declaration list should be the date when the customs accepts the declaration forms of import and export goods.

(14) After release of E-commerce export and import goods and articles, E-commerce enterprises should still be under the follow-up supervision of customs according to the relevant provisions.

4. The monitoring of E-commerce import&export goods and articles logistics

(15) The inspection and release of the e-commerce import and export goods and articles should be done within the customs surveillance area.

(16) The customs supervision site operator should manage the E-commerce import and export goods and articles through the established electronic storage management system. Every month before 10th (when the 10th is a national statutory holiday, it will be postponed to the following first workday), the operator should transmit the total lists and the detail lists of the E-commerce goods and articles passing in and out of the customs supervision area to the Customs.

(17) The Customs in accordance with the customs regulations, shall carry out the risk control and inspection on the E-commerce import and export goods and articles. During the inspection, the E-commerce enterprises, individuals and the customs supervision site operator should facilitate the action according to the current Customs import and export goods inspection regulations and other relevant provisions, and the E-commerce enterprises or the individuals shall attend or entrust others to cooperate with the customs inspection.

Once the suspected violations or smuggling are found, the E-commerce enterprises, logistics companies and the customs supervision site operator should take the initiative to report to the Customs.

(18) The E-commerce import and export goods and articles which need to be transferred to other customs supervision sites for inspection and release shall go through procedures according to the current provisions on the relevant provisions of the goods transition between customs offices.

5. Other business

(19) China customs implements E-commerce statistics according to the customs declaration for imports and exports and inventory.

(20) The meanings of terms in this notice:

E-commerce enterprise means domestic enterprises which develop E-commerce business of cross-border trade through building themselves by themselves or using the E-commerce transaction platform of a third party, or provide the cross-border trade and E-commerce platform of a third party for transaction services.

Individual means domestic residents.

E-commerce transaction platform means the platform for E-commerce inbound and outbound goods of cross-border trade and articles which can be traded, paid, distributed, approved by China customs and connected with the China customs Internet.

E-commerce customs clearance services platform means the platform which is built by the Electronic Port for data exchange and information sharing among enterprises, customs, and relevant administrative departments.

E-commerce customs clearance management platform means the platform which is built by China Customs for the transaction, storage, logistics, and customs clearance of cross-border trade of e-commerce to be supervised and enforced by law electronically.

(21) Except as otherwise herein provided, areas under special customs supervision and bonded areas under supervision supervise the goods and articles of cross-border E-commerce trade according to the provisions of this notice.

This notice shall be applied from August 1th, 2014, and matters not mentioned herein shall be dealt with according to current rules of China Customs.

Notice is hereby given.

General Administration of Customs

July 23rd, 2014

为做好跨境贸易电子商务（以下简称电子商务）进出境货物、物品监管工作，促进电子商务健康发展，现就电子商务进出境货物、物品监管问题公告如下：

一、监管要求

（一）电子商务企业或个人通过经海关认可并且与海关联网的电子商务交易平台实现跨境交易进出境货物、物品的，按照本公告接受海关监管。

（二）电子商务企业应提交《中华人民共和国海关跨境贸易电子商务进出境货物申报清单》（以下简称《货物清单》），采取"清单核放、汇总申报"方式办理电子商务进出境货物报关手续；个人应提交《中华人民共和国海关跨境贸易电子商务进出境物品申报清单》（以下简称《物品清单》），采取"清单核放"方式办理电子商务进出境物品报关手续。

《货物清单》、《物品清单》与《进出口货物报关单》等具有同等法律效力。

（三）存放电子商务进出境货物、物品的海关监管场所的经营人，应向海关办理开展电子商务业务的备案手续，并接受海关监管。未办理备案手续的，不得开展电子商务业务。

（四）电子商务企业或个人、支付企业、海关监管场所经营人、物流企业等，应按照规定通过电子商务通关服务平台适时向电子商务通关管理平台传送交易、支付、仓储和物流等数据。

二、企业注册登记及备案管理

（五）开展电子商务业务的企业，如需向海关办理报关业务，应按照海关对报关单位注册登记管理的相关规定，在海关办理注册登记。

上述企业需要变更注册登记信息、注销的，应按照注册登记管理的相关规定办理。

（六）开展电子商务业务的海关监管场所经营人应建立完善的电子仓储管理系统，将电子仓储管理系统的底账数据通过电子商务通关服务平台与海关联网对接；电子商务交易平台应将平台交易电子底账数据通过电子商务通关服务平台与海关联网对接；电子商务企业、支付企业、物流企业应将电子商务进出境货物、物品交易原始数据通过电子商务通关服务平台与海关联网对接。

（七）电子商务企业应将电子商务进出境货物、物品信息提前向海关备案，货物、物品信息应包括海关认可的货物 10 位海关商品编码及物品 8 位税号。

三、电子商务进出境货物、物品通关管理

（八）电子商务企业或个人、支付企业、物流企业应在电子商务进出境货物、物品申报前，分别向海关提交订单、支付、物流等信息。

（九）电子商务企业或其代理人应在运载电子商务进境货物的运输工具申报进境之日起 14 日内，在电子商务出境货物运抵海关监管场所后、装货 24 小时前，按照已向海关发送的订单、支付、物流等信息，如实填制《货物清单》，逐票办理货物通关手续。个人进出境物品，应由本人或其代理人如实填制《物品清单》，逐票办理物品通关手续。

除特殊情况外，《货物清单》《物品清单》《进出口货物报关单》应采取通关无纸化作业方式进行申报。

（十）电子商务企业或其代理人应于每月 10 日前（当月 10 日是法定节假日或者法定休息日的，顺延至其后的第一个工作日，第 12 月的清单汇总应于当月最后一个工作日前完成），将上月结关的《货物清单》依据清单表头同一经营单位、同一运输方式、同一启运国/运抵国、同一进出境口岸，以及清单表体同一 10 位海关商品编码、同一申报计量单位、同一法定计量单位、同一币制规则进行归并，按照进、出境分别汇总形成《进出口货物报关单》向海关申报。

电子商务企业或其代理人未能按规定将《货物清单》汇总形成《进出口货物报关单》向海关申报的，海关将不再接受相关企业以"清单核放、汇总申报"方式办理电子商务进出境货物报关手续，直至其完成相应汇总申报工作。

（十一）电子商务企业在以《货物清单》方式办理申报手续时，应按照一般进出口货物有关规定办理征免税手续，并提交相关许可证件；在汇总形成《进出口货物报关单》向海关申报时，无须再次办理相关征免税手续及提交许可证件。

个人在以《物品清单》方式办理申报手续时，应按照进出境个人邮递物品有关规定办理征免税手续，属于进出境管制的物品，需提交相关部门的批准文件。

（十二）电子商务企业或个人修改或者撤销《货物清单》《物品清单》，应参照现行海关进出口货物报关单修改或者撤销等有关规定办理，其中《货物清单》修改或者撤销后，对应的《进出口货物报关单》也应做相应修改或者撤销。

（十三）《进出口货物报关单》上的"进出口日期"以海关接受《进出口货物报关单》申报的日期为准。

（十四）电子商务进出境货物、物品放行后，电子商务企业应按有关规定接受海关开展后续监管。

四、电子商务进出境货物、物品物流监控

（十五）电子商务进出境货物、物品的查验、放行均应在海关监管场所内完成。

（十六）海关监管场所经营人应通过已建立的电子仓储管理系统，对电子商务进出境货物、物品进行管理，并于每月 10 日前（当月 10 日是法定节假日或者法定休息日的，顺延至其后的第一个工作日）向海关传送上月进出海关监管场所的电子商务货物、物品总单和明细单等数据。

（十七）海关按规定对电子商务进出境货物、物品进行风险布控和查验。海关实施查验时，电子商务企业、个人、海关监管场所经营人应按照现行海关进出口货物查验等有关规定提供便利，电子商务企业或个人应到场或委托他人到场配合海关查验。

电子商务企业、物流企业、海关监管场所经营人发现涉嫌违规或走私行为的，应主动报告海关。

（十八）电子商务进出境货物、物品需转至其他海关监管场所验放的，应按照现行海关关于转关货物有关管理规定办理手续。

五、其他事项

（十九）海关依据《进出口货物报关单》《物品清单》对电子商务实施统计。

（二十）本公告有关用语的含义：

"电子商务企业"是指通过自建或者利用第三方电子商务交易平台开展跨境贸易电子商务业务的境内企业，以及提供交易服务的跨境贸易电子商务第三方平台提供企业。

"个人"是指境内居民。

"电子商务交易平台"是指跨境贸易电子商务进出境货物、物品实现交易、支付、配送并经海关认可且与海关联网的平台。

"电子商务通关服务平台"是指由电子口岸搭建，实现企业、海关以及相关管理部门之间数据交换与信息共享的平台。

"电子商务通关管理平台"是指由中国海关搭建，实现对跨境贸易电子商务交易、仓储、物流和通关环节电子监管执法的平台。

（二十一）海关特殊监管区域、保税监管场所跨境贸易电子商务进出境货物、物品的监管，除另有规定外，参照本公告规定办理。

本公告内容自2014年8月1日起施行，未尽事宜按海关现行规定办理。特此公告。

海关总署

2014年7月23日

Part B Terminology Practice

1. **Hard currency**（硬通货）：Currency that is strong and unlikely to fall in value, and can be converted into other currencies. For example, the US dollar is a hard currency.

2. **Soft currency**（软通货）：Currency that is subject to sharp fluctuations in value.

3. **Commission**（佣金）：Money paid to salespeople or agents. Commission is usually a percentage of the money received from the sales made.

4. **Premium**（保费）：Money paid by the insured to the insurer in exchange for insurance coverage.

5. **Duty**（关税）：The tax imposed by a government on merchandise imported from another country to standardize the interpretation of commonly used terms in foreign trade. The aim is to avoid disagreement resulting from differences in trading practice in various countries by describing clearly the duties of the seller and the buyer.

6. **International Chamber of Commerce**（国际商会）: An international organization that seeks to improve trading conditions among nations by supporting the free movement of people, goods, and services and by sponsoring a court of arbitration, services to help standardize business practices and documents, and publications.

7. **Roll-on/Roll-off**（滚装/滚卸）: Designed to allow vehicles to be driven onto or off it.

8. **Freight**（运费/货运）: Refers to cargo or space reserved by a shipper on a carrying vessel, or the charge made by a shipping company.

9. **Waybill**（运单）: A document prepared by a carrier of cargo that describes the shipment, states the charges, names the consignee and consignor, and specifies the origin, route, and destination.

10. **Lighterag**（驳运费）**e:** The unloading of cargo by means of small boats or lighters that ferry between a freighter and the quay; or the charge for such a service.

11. **Wharfage**（码头使用费）: The charge made by a wharf owner for the use of a wharf for loading or unloading cargo onto or from a ship.

12. **EDI (Electronic Data Interchange)**（电子数据交换）: The main reason for the 1990 revision of Incoterms was the desire to adapt terms to the increasing use of electronic data interchange (EDI). Through, the parties may provide various documents such as commercial invoices, documents needed for customs clearance, documents in proof of delivery of the goods, and transport documents.

13. **Variance**（差异/偏差）: A change in a process or business practice that may alter its expected outcomes.

14. **Defects**（缺陷）: Sources of customer dissatisfaction. Defects are costly to both customers and to manufacturers or service providers. Eliminating defects offers cost benefits.

15. **Control**（控制）: The state of stability, normal variation and predictability. It is the process of regulating and guiding operations and processes using quantitative data.

Part C Terms

1. HACCP 危害分析关键环节控制点
2. CAC (Codex Alimentarius Commission) 食品法典委员会
3. OIE 世界动物卫生组织
4. IPPC 国际植物保护公约
5. SPS 实施动植物卫生检疫措施协议
6. TBT 技术性贸易壁垒协定
7. FAO 联合国粮食及农业组织
8. ANSI 美国国家标准协会
9. ASTM 美国材料与试验协会
10. IEEE 美国电气电子工程师学会
11. UL 美国保险商实验室
12. FDA 美国食品药品监督管理局
13. FSIS 美国食品安全检验局
14. ISO 国际标准化组织
15. IEC 国际电工委员会
16. ITU 国际电信联盟
17. ICAO 国际民航组织
18. WHO 世界卫生组织
19. ILO 国际劳工组织
20. IWTO 国际毛纺织组织

21. OIE 国际动物流行病学局　　　22. CQC 中国质量认证中心
23. CIQ 中国检验检疫局　　　　　24. WTO 世界贸易组织
25. CCC 中国强制性产品认证

Part D Exercise

I. Please illustrate the Incoterms 2010.

II. True or False. For the false statement, please state the specific reasons.

1. Price terms are mainly applied to determine the prices of commodities in international trade. (　　)

2. Warsaw-Oxford Rules clearly explain the thirteen kinds of trade terms in current use. (　　)

3. As an exporter, you concluded a deal with an American on the basis of EXW; then your transaction risk is reduced to the minimum degree. (　　)

4. According to the interpretation of the Revised American Foreign Trade Definition, FAS is suitable for all kinds of transportation. (　　)

5. On CIP terms, the seller must pay the freight and insurance premium as well as bear all the risks until the goods have arrived at the destination. (　　)

6. The common feature of an FOB contract and an FAS contract is that the seller must load the goods onto a named ship. (　　)

7. With "Delivered Duty Paid", the buyer bears all the costs and risks involved in bringing the goods to the place of destination. (　　)

8. With "Delivered Duty Paid", the buyer does not have an obligation to clear the goods not only for export but also for import, to pay any duty for both export and import and to carry out all customs formalities. (　　)

9. "Free Alongside Ship" means that the seller delivers when the goods are placed alongside the vessel nominated by the buyer at the named port of shipment. (　　)

10. With "Free Alongside Ship", the risk of loss of or damage to the goods passes when the goods are alongside the ship, and the buyer bears all costs from that moment onwards. (　　)

III. Suppose you are an exporter and your business place is in China; judge if the following statements are correct or not and give your reasons.

1. Offer 1 000 bales of Cotton Price Goods at USD 150 per bale FOB New York.

2. We accept your offer for 500 paper cases of Chinese Black Tea at USD 400 per case CIF Shanghai.

3. Your order for Bitter Apricot Kernels at USD 15 per kilo CPT Liverpool has already been delivered.

4. We appreciate your quotation for D.D. Raincoats at USD 100 per dozen CIP Guangzhou, but the price is rather high.

5. Your counter-offer for Fairy Brand Leather Shoes at CAD 50 per pair CFRC2 Vancouver has been well received.

6. We shall execute your order for 1 000 sets of Flying Fish Typewriters at USD 30 per set FCA Beijing.

7. We confirm having sold to you 2 000 dozen Pillow Cases at Euro 50 per dozen FOB Marseilles.

8. Referring to your enquiry of July 15th, we quote as follows: Sharp Vacuum Cleaner 500 sets USD 120 per set.

9. We offer Chinese Tin Plate (马口铁) DDP Shanghai. Reply here July 10th.

10. Our Sales Confirmation No. 9405 for 1 000 Sewing Machines at USD 45 CIF Hong Kong is being airmailed today.

IV. Translate Chinese into English in the parenthesis with given English words or phrases.

1. As the risks and obligations involved on CIF terms, _____ （请参考《2020 年通则》）. (refer to)

2. As our business is concluded on the basis of CFR, _____ （按照 Incoterms 2020 的规定，你方必须将货物装上船）. (in accordance with)

3. _____ （关于贵方 6 月 5 日交到的货），we are pleased to inform you that we have today remitted USD15 000 by a promissory note issued by us payable not later than 15 days after its issuance. (in reference to; consignment)

4. Thank you for your order, which we wish to execute at once, _____ （但是我们做生意的宗旨，不论新旧客户一律交现金）. (on cash payment)

5. However, in view of your long patronage, we propose _____ （双方各让一步，并给你方 10%的折扣）. We trust to have your appreciation of our doing so. (meet halfway)

6. Thank you for your cable of June 5th. Please let us know by return of cable _____ （下列货物在 Liverpool 船上交货 FOB 的最低价格）. (lowest FOB)

7. _____ （价格有变动，不另行通知）. Please confirm when placing your order and refer to the catalogue Model Number and specifications concerning design and capacity. (subject to)

8. _____ （因为这是大订单，希望你方照列表价格打 5%的特别折扣）. If our request is agreeable, we will be most anxious to place an order with you. (discount)

9. _____ （由于市场价格经常变动，要保持价格一星期有效是不可能的）. Therefore, they are subject to change without notice and without engagement. (keep the prices open)

10. We are pleased to _____ （接到贵方 7 月 15 日电报报价，样品 1302 号衬衫 300 打，到纽约运费、保险费在内价，每打 35 美元）for immediate shipment. (cable offer)

V. Cloze.

Fill in the blanks with the words and phrases given below, and change the form when necessary.

offer	under	upon receipt of	enter	through	know
enjoy	acquaint	in the market for	learn	fall/come	effort

We _____(1)_____ from the Chamber of Commerce that you are _____(2)_____ silk products. Since this article _____(3)_____ within the scope of our business activities, we take this opportunity to express our wish to _____(4)_____ into business relations with you.

Good Luck brand silk products are ___(5)___ for their good quality and fine workmanship. They have enjoyed great popularity in the US market. We are sure that ___(6)___ our joint ___(7)___ they will ___(8)___ fast sale in your market.

In order to ___(9)___ you with our products, we are airmailing to you ___(10)___ separate cover several brochures together with a price list. ___(11)___ your specific inquiry, we shall send you our ___(12)___ without delay.

VI. Case Study.

1. A Chinese import and export company concluded a Sales Contract with a Holland firm on August 5th, 2000, selling a batch of certain commodity. The contract was based on CIF Rotterdam at USD 2 500 per metric ton. The Chinese company delivered the goods in compliance with the contract and obtained a clean-on-board Bill of Lading. During transportation, however, 100 metric tons of the goods got lost because of rough sea. Upon arrival of the goods, the price of the contracted goods went down quickly. The buyer refused to take delivery of the goods and effect payment and claimed damages from the seller.

Question:

How would you deal with this case?

2. A Chinese trading company A concluded a transaction in steel with a Hong Kong company B on the basis of FOB China Port. Company B immediately resold the steel to Company H in Libya on the terms of CFR Liberia. The L/C from B required the price terms to be FOB China Port and the goods to be directly delivered to Liberia. The L/C also required "Freight Prepaid" to be indicated on the Bill of Lading.

Question:

Why did Company B perform so? What should we do about it?

Chapter Five

Part A Text

Quality of Commodity

The quality of goods is indispensable to international trade. Whether it is visible trade or invisible trade, the goods sold have their own qualities, and the quality of a certain kind of goods determines, to a great degree, its market and price. Therefore, the quality of the goods is among the main terms upon which a sales contract is based and constructed.

Commodities provides the material basis for international trade. All commodities present certain qualities. Therefore, the quality of commodities is not only one of the major terms of a sales contract, but also the first item which should be agreed upon by the exporter and the importer while the business is being negotiated. The seller must deliver the goods that are of the quality required by the contract, the failure of which will result in disputes between the seller and the buyer. Thus, due consideration should be given to the matters of quality of the commodity transacted. That's to say that the seller must deliver goods that are of the quality required by the contract. If the goods do not conform to the contract, the buyer will be entitled to lodge a claim for damages. Therefore, at the time of the conclusion of the contract, the quality should be clearly stipulated.

In export trade, the superior or inferior quality of a certain commodity has an immediate bearing not only on the use and price of the commodity, but also on the sale and reputation of it. With the intensifying competition in the international market, manufacturers in different countries make great efforts to promote the sale of their products by improving the quality of them. The commodity with superior quality always enjoys a good market. On the other hand, the importer would only purchase those goods of certain quality in which he is particularly interested. Both the seller and the buyer express deep concern about the quality of commodity.

The quality of goods refers to the intrinsic attributes and the outer form or shape of the goods, such as modeling, structure, color, luster, taste, chemical composition, mechanical performance, biological features, etc. In another sense, a certain kind of goods possesses both natural and social attributes. From a narrow point of view, it possesses natural attributes, while from a broad point of view, it also includes its social attributes, which is how it meets the subjective requirements and different tastes of its customers.

In the import and export trade of e-commerce, the quality of goods has special characteristics. Therefore, the newly issued E-commerce Law on August 31, 2018 has made relevant regulations on the quality of e-commerce import and export trade goods. First of all, the goods or services provided by e-commerce operators shall comply with the requirements for the protection of personal and property safety as well as environmental protection requirements, and they shall not sell or provide goods or services prohibited by law or administrative regulations. Secondly, e-commerce operators who sell goods or provide services should issue paper invoices or electronic invoices, together with other purchase vouchers or service documents. Electronic invoices have the same legal effect as paper invoices. In addition, for the e-commerce platform, if the e-commerce platform operator spots that the goods or service information on the platform violates the relevant provisions of the E-commerce Law, it shall take necessary disposal measures, according to law, and report to the relevant competent authorities. At the same time, the e-commerce platform operators should record and save the goods and services information as well as transaction information published on the platform, and ensure the integrity, confidentiality and availability of the information. The storage time of goods and services information and transaction information shall not be less than three years from the date of completion of the transaction; if otherwise provided by laws and administrative regulations, such provisions shall be followed.

商品的品质是国际贸易不可缺少的部分。无论是有形贸易还是无形贸易，所销售的货物都有其自身的品质，并且该品质决定着该商品的市场占有率和市场价格。因此，品质是销售合同中最主要的条款，也是签订合同的基础。

商品是进行国际贸易的基础，而所有商品都表现出一定的品质。因此，商品的品质不仅仅是国际货物销售合同的主要条件，同时也是进出口商进行交易磋商时首先要取得一致意见的事项。卖方必须按照合同规定的品质交货，如果不符就会引起买卖双方的纠纷，因此，特别要注意交易商品的品质。也就是说，卖方必须按照合同规定的品质交货，如果货物不符合合同要求，进口商将有权提出索赔。

在出口贸易中，商品品质的优劣不仅关系到商品使用效能和销售的价格，还关系到商品的销路和声誉。在竞争激烈的国际市场上，各个国家的生产厂家都会以努力提高产品的质量来促销自己的产品。质地优良的商品总会有良好的销路。同时，各国进口商也只愿购买那些他所感兴趣的并且具有某种品质的产品。无论是买方还是卖方关心的都是商品的质量。

商品的品质指的是商品本身所具有的内在特性和商品的外观形态，如造型、结构、颜色、光泽、味道、化学成分、机械性能和生物特征等。换句话说，商品具有自然和社会属性，从狭义上说，商品具有自然属性，从广义上说，商品具有社会属性，因而能满足各种不同消费者的需要。

在电子商务进出口贸易中，商品的品质具有特殊性，因此，2018 年 8 月 31 日新颁布的《电子商务法》对电子商务进出口贸易商品的品质做出了相关规定。首先，电子商务经营者销售的商品或者提供的服务应当符合保障人身、财产安全的要求和环境保护要求，不得销售或者提供法律、行政法规禁止交易的商品或者服务。其次，电子商务经营者销售商品或者提供服务应当依法出具纸质发票或者电子发票等购货凭证或者服务单据。电子发票与纸质发票具有同等法律效力。另外，对于电子商务平台来说，电子商务平台经营者如果发现平台内的商品或者服务信息存在违反《电子商务法》相关规定情形的，应当依法采取必要的处置措施，并向有关主管部门报告。同时，电子商务平台经营者应当记录、保存平台上发布的商品和服务信息、交易信息，并确保信息的完整性、保密性、可用性。商品和服务信息、交易信息保存时间自交易完成之日起不少于三年；法律、行政法规另有规定的，依照其规定。

Section One Methods of Stipulating Quality of Commodity（货物品质的表示方法）

The quality of a commodity is the combination of the intrinsic quality and external form or shape of the commodity, such as modeling, structure, color, luster, chemical composition, mechanical performance, biological features, etc. The qualities of different commodities can be expressed in different ways. The methods of stipulating the quality of a commodity depend on the quality, characteristics, and the customary usage in practice. In international trade, there are two ways to indicate the quality of the goods either by description or by sample.

商品的品质是商品的外观形态和内在质量的综合，如造型、结构、颜色、光泽、化学成分、机械性能和生物化学特征等。不同种类的商品可以用不同的方法表示品质。确定商品品质的方法主要取决于商品的性质、特点及其在国际贸易中长期以来形成的习惯做法。在国际贸易中，表示商品品质的方法可分为用样品表示和用文字说明表示两个大类。

1. Sale by description（凭文字说明买卖）

In international trade, most goods are sold by the method of sale by specification, grade or standard except in some special cases. This method may be further classified into the following types.

在国际货物买卖业务中，除某些特殊情况外，大部分是采用凭规格、等级或标准表示商品品质的方法。具体可以分为以下几种。

1) Sale by specification, grade or standard（凭规格、等级、标准买卖）

The specification of the goods refers to certain main indicators that indicate the quality of the goods, such as composition, content, purity, size, length, thickness, etc. Sale by specification is a sales way of convenience and accuracy. So in practice it is the most widely used. Goods with different qualities should have different standards, and for those with different applications there are also different standards.

The grade of the goods refers to the classifications of the commodities of one kind which is indicated by words, numbers or symbols. The classifications are usually decided by different qualities, weights, compositions, appearances, properties, etc. For example, Chinese raw silk is sold by standard and its standard consists of 12 grades: 6A, 5A, 4A, 3A, 2A, A, B, C, D, E, F, and G. In practice, we often have Special Grade, First Grade, Second Grade, Large, Medium, Small.

When the method of "sale by grade" is used, the quality clause in business is simplified. The quality of the goods can be known by simply stating its grade. However, the seller and the buyer should reach a consensus on the "grades". When the goods are sold by grade, it is okay when the grade of goods is stated clearly. However, different countries have their own different grades to illustrate the goods, so when the buyer and the seller cannot understand each other's grade standard, it is better for both parties to stipulate which grade should be accepted in great detail. For example, in the U.S.A., there is "American Industrial Materials Inspection Association Standards (ASTM)", in Germany there is "German Industrial Standards (DIN)", in the UK there is "The British Standard Association Standards", in Japan there is "Japanese Industry Standard (JIS)". When the goods are dealt with this term, the goods delivered by the seller should be in exact conformity with the stipulations such as grade, specifications and standard in the contract. Otherwise the buyer has the right to ask for the price difference to be reduced, or to refuse to take the goods, even to cancel the contract and declare for compensation.

规格是指表达商品质量的一些主要指标，如成分、含量、纯度、大小、长度、厚度等。凭规格买卖比较方便、准确，在国际货物买卖中应用最广。商品不同，表示商品品质的指标亦不同；商品的用途不同，要求的品质指标也会有所不同。

等级是指对同类商品按照规格中若干主要指标的差异，用文字、数字或符号所做的分类。"凭等级买卖"只需说明其级别，即可明确买卖货物的品质。例如：中国生丝就是按标准销售的，共分 12 个等级：6A、5A、4A、3A、2A、A、B、C、D、E、F、G。实际业务中，常有特级、一级、二级、大号、中号、小号等。

当采用"凭等级买卖"时，简化了交易中表示品质的条款。只要说明其等级，就可了解所要买卖的商品的品质。然而，买卖双方必须对"等级"有共同的认识。凭等级买卖时，只需说明商品的等级，即可明确商品品质。由于不同国家等级的划分原则各不同，如果双方不熟悉等级内容，则最好列明每一等级的具体规格。例如，在美国就有"美国工业材料检验协会标准"，在德国有"德国工业品标准"，在英国有"英国标准协会标准"，在日本有"日本工业标准"等。凡按这类方式成交时，卖方所交货物必须与合同规定的规格、等级、标准相符。否则，买方有权要求扣减品质差价，甚至可以拒收货物、撤销合同并要求赔偿损失。

The standard refers to the specifications or grades that are stipulated and announced (laid down and proclaimed) in a unified way by government departments or commercial organization of a country such as the chamber of commerce, etc.

It is important to note that the standard of a commodity is subject to change or amendment and a new standard often takes the place of the old one. Therefore, in case of sales by standard, it is important and necessary to also mention in the terms also the name of the publication in which the standard of the commodity appears.

e.g.: Tetracycline HCL Tablets (Sugar Coated) 250mg. B.P. 1973

B.P. = British Pharmacopoeia

标准是指政府机关或商业团体，如商业协会等统一制定和公布的规格或等级。

值得注意的是，某种商品的标准或等级经常会进行变动和修改，新的标准常常代替旧的标准。因此，如果按"标准"买卖的话，就必须注明是按照哪个版本的标准，并标明援用标准的版本年份。

如：四环素糖衣片，250 毫克，1973 年英国药典

B.P.是英国药典的缩写

For those agricultural products and by-products that are easy to change in quality and difficult to stipulate the standard, the following ways would be preferred: 1) Fair Average Quality (F.A.Q.); 2) Good Merchantable Quality (G.M.Q.).

对于某些品质变化较大而难以规定统一标准的农副产品，通常采用以下两种方法来表示其品质：（1）"良好平均品质"；（2）"上好可销售品质"。

In the international agricultural product and by-products market, there is a commonly adopted standard, i.e., fair average quality (F.A.Q.). According to the explanation of some countries, F.A.Q. refers to the average quality level of the export commodity within a certain period of time. This kind of standard is quite ambiguous. In fact, it does not represent any fixed, accurate specification.

For example:

Chinese Groundnut, 2018 crop, F.A.Q.

Moisture : (max.) 13%

Admixture: (max.) 5%

Oil content: (min.) 44%

"良好平均品质"即"大路货"（F.A.Q.），是国际农副产品市场上通用的标准。据有些国家解释，"大路货"指的是出口商品在某一特定的时期内所具有的中等平均水平。这种解释含糊不清，模棱两可，事实上它不代表任何固定的、准确的规格。

如：

中国花生仁，2018 年产，大路货

水分：（最高）13%

杂质：（最高）5%

含油量：（最低）44%

For the trading of wood and aquatic products, good merchantable quality (G.M.Q.) is employed to indicate the quality. G.M.Q. means the goods are free from defects and are good enough for use or consumption. G.M.Q. is usually not supplemented with specifications, and when disputes arise due to the quality of the goods, exporters may need to be invited for arbitration.

在买卖木材和水产品时，可以采用凭"上好可销售品质"方式。凭"上好可销售品质"是指卖方必须保证其交付的货物品质良好，适合销售，在成交时无须以其他方式证明商品的品质。但如果出现纠纷，卖方将卷入纠纷的仲裁。

ISO 9000 series standards are the international quality assurance standards formulated by the International Standard Organization (ISO) to meet the need for international trade development, which can function as an international pass to the world market. While ISO14000 "Environmental Management" series standards are environmental management standards for standardizing enterprise environmental behavior, controlling and reducing the damage or environmental contamination caused by the production process. The ISO14000 certificate means that the products produced are in accordance with the requirements of international environmental trends. The enterprises with ISO 14000 certificate can be called green enterprises, whose products can be referred to as environmental products. The products with these two certificates are of great competitive capabilities.

With the development of technology and the change of situations, the standard of a commodity is always subject to change or amendment and a new standard often takes the place of the old one. Therefore, the standard of the same commodity formulated by a country usually has several editions with some different contents. So in the contract, the standards based on which copy should be specified very clearly.

ISO 9000 系列标准是国际标准化组织为适应国际贸易发展的需要而制定的国际品质保证

标准，ISO 9000 证书具有国际通行证的作用。ISO14000 "环境管理"系列标准是国际标准化组织为规范企业的环境行为，控制和减少企业在生产经营过程中对环境造成的破坏而制定的环境管理标准。ISO14000 证书是表明产品符合国际环保潮流的环保证书，符合 ISO14000 系列标准的企业称为绿色企业，其生产的产品经认可成为环保产品。两证齐全的产品在国际市场上具有较强的竞争力。

随着技术的发展和情况的变化，某种商品的标准经常要进行变动和修改，新的标准规则常常代替旧的标准。因此，某个国家颁布的同一商品标准通常有几个内容不尽相同的版本。在合同中，应该尽量明确说明应采用哪个版本的标准。

2) Sale by brand name or trade mark（凭牌号或商标买卖）

Brand name or trade mark is based on high quality, which is used by the manufacturers to distinguish their high quality goods from others of the like. A brand is the name of the goods, while a trade mark is the tag. They are closely related to each other. As to the goods whose quality is stable, reputation is sound and with which the customers are quite familiar, we may sell it by brand name or trade mark. For example, "Maxam Dental Cream", "Haier Air Conditioner", "Toyota Automobile", etc. Since these goods with the same brand name or trade mark possess the same quality and their quality remains unified and unchanged, their brand names or trademarks are often used to indicate the quality of these goods. Such a method is called "sale by brand name or trade mark".

牌号或商标都是以品质为基础的，是生产者或销售者用以区别其他同类商品的一种标志。牌号是商标的名称，商标是牌号的标记，两者不能脱离对方而单独存在。用牌号或商标表示品质，一般都是在国际市场上有良好信誉、品质稳定的商品，它们被广大客户所喜爱，因而可以凭牌号或商标买卖。例如，"美加净牙膏""海尔空调""丰田汽车"等。由于这些同一牌名或商标的商品具有相同的品质，且品质统一、稳定，所以这些牌名或商标经常用来表示商品的品质。这种方法称为"凭牌号或商标"买卖。

3) Sale by name of origin（凭产地名买卖）

Some goods, just like some agricultural products and by-products subject to the influence of nature and traditional production techniques, are well known for their origins due to their excellent quality all over the world. As to these products, the origins may well indicate their qualities. These goods can be sold by name of origin.

e.g.: Longjing Green Tea

Jingdezhen Chinaware

有些货物，特别是农副产品，受产地自然条件和传统的生产技术影响较大，一些历史较长、条件较好地区的产品，由于品质优良并具有一定的特色，产地名称也成为该项产品品质的重要标志。这类产品可凭产地名进行买卖，如龙井茶、景德镇瓷器。

4) Sale by description and illustration（凭说明书和图样买卖）

The quality of some commodities, such as large-sized machines, technological instruments, electric machines, etc. can not be simply indicated by quality indexes; instead, it is quite necessary to explain in detail the structure, material, performance, as well as the method of operation. Thus, the specific descriptions of products are required to indicate the quality of the goods. If necessary, pictures, photos, etc. must also be provided.

有些商品，如大型机电、仪器产品，无法用几个简单的指标来表示其品质，必须用说明书详细地说明其结构、用材、运转性能及操作方法。如果有必要的话，还要提供图片和照片等。

2．Sale by sample（凭样品买卖）

Sale by sample refers to the transaction method based on a sample agreed by both the buyer and the seller.

The sample refers to the article that can be used to represent the quality of the whole lot. In merchandising, a sample is a small quantity of a product, often taken out from a whole lot or specially designed and processed, to encourage prospective customers to buy the product. The transaction concluded based on a sample representing the quality of the whole lot is called sale by sample. This method is used when the transaction is hard to conclude by standard, grade or words, such as certain arts and crafts products, garments, local specialties, light industrial products, etc.

Sale by sample includes three cases, i.e., sale by the seller's sample, sale by the buyer's sample and sale by the counter sample.

凭样品买卖是指买卖双方约定以样品作为交货品质依据的买卖方式。

所谓样品是指能够代表整批货物质量的实物，通常是指从一批货物中抽取出来或由生产和使用部门设计加工出来的能够代表出售货物品质的少量实物，用于向客户推广自己的产品。凡以样品表示商品品质并以此作为交货依据的，称为凭样品买卖。凭样品买卖的方法一般适用于难以标准化、规格化，难以用文字说明其品质的商品，如部分工艺品、服装、土特产品、轻工产品等。

凭样品买卖主要有凭卖方样品、凭买方样品和凭对等样品三种成交方式。

1) Sale by the seller's sample（凭卖方样品买卖）

Seller's samples are the samples which are usually sent by the seller to the buyer, which is also called original sample.

In this case, the seller shall supply a representative sample which will possess the moderate quality among a large quantity of the physical goods, and at the same time keep a duplicate sample, which shall be in quality as the same as or on the whole as the same as the standard sample. The sample dispatched and the duplicate sample/file sample kept shall have the same article-number so as to make it convenient for delivery, verification when handling quality disputes or future transactions.

凭卖方样品是指由卖方向买方提供货物的样品，即原样。

如果采用凭卖方样品的话，通常卖方要提供能够代表整批货物质量的实物，同时，卖方要自留与这些样品质量一致的复样。一般来说，发出的样品和复样具有相同的编号，以备交货或处理品质纠纷时核对之用。

2) Sale by the buyer's sample（凭买方样品买卖）

(1) In this case, the seller shall first take into consideration the availability of the new material and the possibility of providing the processing technology.

(2) In order to take the initiative, the seller may reproduce the buyer's sample, i.e., counter sample, and send it back to the buyer as a type sample. After the buyer confirms the counter sample, sale by the buyer's sample is changed into sale by the seller's counter sample.

(3) The two parties shall stipulate that in case the buyer's sample results in any disputes regarding infringement of industrial property, the seller will have nothing to do with it.

（1）如果按这种方式交易，卖方首先要考虑的是能否满足所提供的新材料和加工工艺的要求。

（2）有时为了采取主动，卖方按买方来样复制，并回寄给买方确认，经确认后作为交货品质依据的样品，即对等样品。这种做法实际是把交易的性质由"凭买方样品买卖"转变为"凭卖方样品买卖"。

（3）买卖双方应在合同中明确指出如果买方样品出现了工业产权侵权，卖方不承担责任。

3) Sale by the counter sample（凭对等样品买卖）

Samples can also be provided by the buyer. They are given as the quality standard for the goods to be produced and delivered by the seller. Under such circumstances, to avoid future disputes over the quality of the goods, the seller usually first duplicates the samples and then sends the duplicate to the buyer for confirmation. This sample is called a counter sample.

样品可以由买方提供，作为卖方生产和交货的产品质量标准。为了避免有关商品质量方面的纠纷问题，卖方通常会复制样品，然后将复制样品寄给买方确认。这种样品就是对等样品。

In international trade practice, if sale by samples is adopted, the following should be paid attention to:

(1) We should try to conduct business by "sale by the seller's sample".

(2) When the seller sends out the sample, it is better for the seller to keep the "original" or "duplicate" sample, to facilitate verification when handling quality disputes or future transactions.

(3) If the transaction is done by "sale by the buyer's sample", we should pay attention to the fact that whether the sample of the buyer has something to do with the problems of politics, society and religion, such as color, pattern and design. We should also take into consideration the availability of the new material and the possibility of providing the processing technology in order to avoid unnecessary trouble in delivery. For the sake of caution, import and export enterprises usually make it clear in the remarks in the contract that "For any cotton price goods produced with the designs, trade marks, brands and/or stampings provided by the buyers, should there be any dispute arising from infringement upon the third party's industrial property right, it is the buyer who is held responsible for it".

(4) When we get the sample of the buyer, it is better to make it as counter sample.

(5) Whether the sale is by the buyer's sample or the seller's sample, if it is difficult to keep the goods contracted in strict accordance with the sample, the seller should write some flexible terms in the sales contract as follows:

* Shipment shall be similar to the sample;

* Quality to be about equal to the sample;

* Quality to be nearly the same as the sample.

(6) Whether the sale is by the buyer's sample or the seller's sample, if it is necessary, sometimes "sealed sample" can be adopted.

在出口业务中，如采用凭样品成交时，应注意做好以下工作：

（1）应争取凭卖方样品成交。

（2）卖方寄出样品（原样）时应留存"原样"或"复样"，以备将来交货或处理品质纠纷时核对之用。

（3）如凭买方来样成交，应考虑对方来样在政治、社会、宗教方面敏感的色彩、造型、图案等问题，是否有不良影响；还应注意我方在原材料、生产技术条件和工艺水平上能否落实，以免在交货时陷入被动；特别要注意，按买方所提供的样品生产的产品是否会涉及第三者的工业产权。为慎重起见，外贸企业在签订合同时常在"一般交易条件"中写入相应说明，如：凡根据买方提供的式样、商标、牌号及（或）印记等生产的任何棉布织物，如因侵犯第三者的工业产权而引起纠纷，概由买方负责。

（4）买方来样时，最好将来样成交改为凭对等样品成交。

（5）无论是凭买方还是凭卖方样品买卖，对于某些因制造技术原因等确实难以保证货、样完全一致的，卖方往往可在合同中订明一些弹性品质条款。例如：

* 交货与样品近似；

* 品质与样品大致相同；

* 品质接近样品。

（6）无论是凭买方还是凭卖方样品买卖，必要时可使用"封样"的做法。

Section Two   Quality Latitude & Quality Tolerance（品质机动幅度条款和品质公差条款）

In international trade, the seller should strictly abide by the terms specified in the contract. The quality delivered by the seller should be in strict conformity with the terms and conditions in the contract. But because for some goods there will be natural consumption during production, production craft influence and the goods' own characteristics, it is very hard to deliver the goods exactly as per the terms and conditions stated in the contract. For such goods, if the stipulations are too rigid or quality criteria too fixed, it brings the seller into trouble in delivery. Consequently, when the two parties negotiate the terms and conditions of the contract, flexible clauses may be adopted. If the quality delivered by the seller is within the limits of the contract, this delivery can be considered compliant with the contract. The buyer cannot refuse to take the delivery. The following are the two ways often used in practice: (1)Quality Latitude/Quality Flexible Allowance; (2)Quality Tolerance.

在国际贸易中，卖方必须严格遵守合同条款。卖方交货品质必须严格与买卖合同规定的品质条款相符。但是，某些商品由于生产过程中存在自然消耗，以及受生产工艺、商品自身特点等诸多方面原因的影响，难以保证交货品质与合同规定的内容完全一致，对于这些商品，如果条款规定过死或把品质指标定得绝对化，必然会给卖方的顺利交货带来困难。为此，订立合同时可以规定一些灵活条款，卖方所交商品质量只要在规定的灵活范围内，即可以认为交货质量与合同相符，买方无权拒收。常见的规定有以下两种：（1）品质机动幅度条款；（2）品质公差条款。

（1）Quality latitude/Quality flexible allowance（品质机动幅度）：Quality latitude/quality flexible allowance refers to flexibility for those specific quality indications in a certain range. The following three methods are often used in practice:

a. Specification of range: moisture 5%~10%.

b. Specification of limitation: maximum or minimum, wool 98% min.

c. Specification of more or less: Eiderdown content 16%, 1% more or less.

品质机动幅度是指对特定品质指标在一定幅度内有灵活性。具体有以下三种规定方法：

a. 规定范围：湿度5%~10%。

b. 规定极限：最大或最小，如羊毛最少98%。

c. 规定上下差异：羽绒含绒量16%，允许上下误差1%。

（2）Quality tolerance（品质公差）：In trading agricultural products, industrial raw materials, or some products of light industry, a tolerance clause is usually stipulated in the sales contract. Quality tolerance means the permissible range within which the quality supplied by the seller may be either superior or inferior to the quality stipulated in the contract. The tolerance may be pre-agreed between the seller and the buyer, or generally recognized by trade associations. Such tolerance can be compensated by price adjustments proportional to the degree of the tolerance. Sometimes, price adjustment is not needed if the tolerance is within a certain limit.

If there is a specific and popular quality tolerance for some line or standard for the goods about to be transacted, it is not necessary for this quality tolerance to be stated in the contract. However, if there is no clear or popular "quality tolerance" for the goods in the world market, or there is no definite understanding of the "quality tolerance" by the seller and the buyer, or there is a need to extend the "quality tolerance" because of production needs, the quality tolerance, in the case, can be specified clearly in the contract. This is the quality tolerance range agreed upon by both parties.

When the allowance of the quality tolerance delivered by the seller or the quality tolerance falls in line with the agreed range, the price of the quality tolerance can be calculated over the contract. There is no need to make adjustment.

在农副产品、工业原料或部分轻工业品的交易中，合同里经常要订立品质公差条款。品质公差是指允许卖方交付商品的品质可以高于或低于合同所规定的幅度。品质公差可由买卖双方事先共同商订，也可采用行业公会所公认的误差。品质公差可以按比例计算增减价格，也可以在公差内不计算增减价格。

对于国际同行业或标准有公认的品质公差，可以不在合同中明确规定。但如果国际同行业对特定指标并无公认的品质公差；或者买卖双方对品质公差理解不一致；或者由于生产原因，需要扩大公差范围，也可在合同中具体规定品质公差的内容，即合同约定买卖双方共同认可的允许范围。

卖方交货品质在品质机动幅度或品质公差允许的范围内，一般均按合同单价计价，不再按品质高低另作调整。

Section Three Examples of Quality Clauses in Contract（合同中的品质条款实例）

The quality clauses in an export contract, in general, include the name, specification or grade, standard and brand name, etc. of the subject goods. In the case of sale by sample, the reference number and the dispatch date should be included; sometimes a brief specification may also be attached.

For example:

(1) Sample No. 210 Man's T-Shirt.

(2) Brazilian Coffee Beans 2018 New Crop, F.A.Q.

(3) Tetracycline HCI Tablets (sugar coated) 250mg B.P. 1993.

(4) Cotton Grey Shirting, 30s×36s 72×69 No. of threads 38"×121.5yds.

(5) Chinese Northeast Rice, Moisture 25% (max.), Admixture 0.25% (max.).

(6) Red Nylon Cloth Umbrellas for Ladies, 18"×8 ribs, Stainless Steel Shaft, Plastic Handles.

一般来说，出口合同中的品质条款应列明商品的品名、规格或等级、标准和牌名等。凭样品销售时，则应列明样品的参考编号或寄送日期，有时也附列简要的规格。

例如：

（1）样品号为 210 的男士衬衫。

（2）巴西咖啡豆 2018 年产，良好平均品质。

（3）盐酸四环素糖衣片 250 毫克，按 1993 年版英国药典。

（4）棉坯布，30 支×36 支，72×69（纱线密度），38 英寸×121.5 码。

（5）中国东北大米，水分含量最高 25%，杂质含量不超过 0.25%。

（6）女士红色尼龙布雨伞，18 英寸×8 伞骨，不锈钢伞轴，塑料伞柄。

Section Four General Catalog of E-commerce Platform（电子商务平台的产品目录及分类）

C001 Electronics 数码电子产品

C001001 Computer & Networking C001 计算机&网络设备

C001001001 Tablets C001001 平板电脑

C001001002 Laptops C001001 笔记本电脑

C001001003 Desktops C001001 台式电脑

C001001004 Storage C001001 内存条

C001001005 Networking C001001 网络设备

C001001006 Tablet Accessories C001001 平板电脑配件

C001001007 Laptop Accessories C001001 笔记本电脑配件

C001001008 Computer Peripherals C001001 计算机外设

C001001009 Computer Components C001001 计算机部件

C001002 Consumer Electronics C001 消费电子产品

C001002001 Camera & Photography C001002 相机&摄影器材

C001002002 Home Audio & Video C001002 家庭影音设备

C001002003 TV Stick C001002 电视网络播放器

C001002004 Accessories & Parts C001002 相关配件&部件

C001002005 Video Games C001002 游戏机&配件

C001002006 Portable Audio & Video C001002 便携式影音设备

C001002007 Earphones & Headphones C001002 耳机&头戴式耳机

C001002008 Mini Camcorders C001002 微型摄像机

C001002009 Memory Cards C001002 内存卡

C001003 Phones & Accessories C001 手机&配件

C001003001 Mobile Phones C001003 手机

C001003002 Bags & Cases C001003 手机套&手机壳

C001003003 Batteries C001003 电池

C001003004 Chargers & Docks C001003 充电器

C001003005 Backup Powers C001003 充电宝

C001003006 Cables C001003 数据线

C001003007 Lenses C001003 手机镜头

C001003008 Parts C001003 手机部件

C001003009 LCDs C001003 手机屏

C001003010 Holders & Stands C001003 手机座

C001003011 Stickers C001003 手机贴

C002 Apparel & Accessories 服装&配饰

C002001 Women C002 女装

C002001001 Dresses C002001 连衣裙

C002001002 Coats & Jackets C002001 大衣&外套

C002001003 Blouses & Shirts C002001 上衣&衬衫

C002001004 Tops & Tees C002001 短袖&T 恤

C002001005 Hoodies & Sweatshirts C002001 卫衣&运动衫

C002001006 Intimates C002001 内衣

C002001007 Swimwear C002001 泳衣

C002001008 Pants & Capris C002001 长裤&紧身裤

C002001009 Sweaters C002001 毛衣

C002001010 Skirts C002001 半身裙

C002001011 Leggings C002001 打底裤

C002001012 Accessories C002001 配饰

C002002 Men C002 男装

C002002001 Tops & Tees C002002 短袖&T 恤

C002002002 Coats & Jackets C002002 大衣&外套

C002002003 Underwear C002002 内衣

C002002004 Shirts C002002 衬衫

C002002005 Hoodies & Sweatshirts C002002 卫衣&运动衫

C002002006 Jeans C002002 牛仔裤

C002002007 Pants C002002 长裤

C002002008 Suits & Blazer C002002 套装&西装

C002002009 Shorts C002002 短裤

C002002010 Sweaters C002002 毛衣

C002002011 Accessories C002002 配饰

C002003 Wedding & Events C002 婚礼&特殊场合礼服

C002003001 Wedding Dresses C002003 婚纱

C002003002 Evening Dresses C002003 晚礼服

C002003003 Homecoming Dresses C002003 校友返校日礼服

C002003004 Ball Gown C002003 舞会礼服

C002003005 Cocktail Dresses C002003 鸡尾酒会礼服

C002003006 Casual Party Dresses C002003 聚会礼服

C002003007 Celebrity-Inspired Dresses C002003 明星款礼服

C002003008 Quinceanera Dresses C002003 成人礼礼服

C002003009 Communion Dresses C002003 圣餐礼服

C002003010 Graduation Dresses C002003 毕业礼服

C002003011 Wedding Accessories C002003 婚纱配饰

C002003012 Wedding Party Dress C002003 婚礼礼服

C003 Bags & Shoes 箱包&鞋子

C003001 Luggage & Bags C003 行李箱&包

C003001001 Women's Shoulder Bags C003001 女式单肩包

C003001002 Women's Wallets C003001 女式钱包

C003001003 Women's Crossbody Bags C003001 女式长带包

C003001004 Women's Totes C003001 女式手提包

C003001005 Women's Clutches C003001 女士手包

C003001006 Women's Backpacks C003001 女式双肩包

C003001007 Men's Wallets C003001 男式钱包

C003001008 Men's Backpacks C003001 男式双肩包

C003001009 Men's Briefcases C003001 男式公文包

C003001010 Men's Crossbody Bags C003001 男式长带包

C003001011 School Bags C003001 书包

C003001012 Travel Duffle C003001 旅行包

C003002 Shoes C003 鞋子

C003002001 Women's Fashion Sneakers C003002 女式帆布鞋

C003002002 Women's Sandals C003002 女式凉鞋

C003002003 Women's Flats C003002 女式平底鞋

C003002004 Women's Pumps C003002 高跟鞋

C003002005 Women's Boots C003002　女靴

C003002006 Women's Slippers C003002　女式拖鞋

C003002007 Men's Fashion Sneakers C003002　男式帆布鞋

C003002008 Men's Flats C003002　男式平底鞋

C003002009 Men's Sandals C003002　男式凉鞋

C003002010 Men's Boots C003002　男靴

C003002011 Men's Loafers C003002　男式便鞋

C003002012 Men's Slippers C003002　男式拖鞋

C003003 Children's Shoes C003　童鞋

C003003001 Girls' Sneakers C003003　平底女童鞋

C003003002 Boys' Sneakers C003003　平底男童鞋

C003003003 Girls' Sandals C003003　女童凉鞋

C003003004 Boys' Sandals C003003　男童凉鞋

C003003005 Children's Boots C003003　童靴

C003003006 Girls' Leather Shoes C003003　女童皮鞋

C003003007 Boys' Leather Shoes C003003　男童皮鞋

C003003008 Baby First Walkers C003003　学步鞋

C003003009 Baby Leather Shoes C003003　婴儿皮鞋

C003003010 Baby Sneakers C003003　婴儿平底鞋

C003003011 Baby Boots C003003　婴儿靴子

C003003012 Baby Sandals C003003　婴儿凉鞋

C004 Home & Garden　家居&园艺

C004001 Home & Garden C004　家居用品

C004001001 Home Decor C004001　家居饰品

C004001002 Home Textile C004001　家纺

C004001003 Kitchen, Dining & bar C004001　厨具、餐具&酒具

C004001004 Bathroom Products C004001　卫浴用品

C004001005 Festive & Party Supplies C004001　节日&聚会用品

C004001006 Home Storage & Organization C004001　收纳用品

C004001007 Household Cleaning Tools & Accessories C004001　清洁用品

C004001008 Pet Products C004001　宠物用品

C004001009 Bedding Set C004001　床上用品

C004001010 Curtains C004001　窗帘

C004001011 Painting & Calligraphy C004001　装饰书画

C004001012 Furniture C004001　家具&配件

C004002 Outdoors & Garden C004　户外&花园用品

C004002001 Garden Pots & Planters C004002　花盆

C004002002 Garden Landscaping & Decking C004002　花园造景&美化

C004002003 Garden Tools C004002　园艺工具

C004002004 Watering & Irrigation C004002　浇水灌溉用具

C004002005 Temperature Gauges C004002　温度计&测温仪

C004002006 Fertilizer C004002　花肥

C004002007 BBQ C004002　烧烤用具

C004002008 Shade C004002　遮阳用具

C004002009 Mailboxes C004002　信箱

C004002010 Garden-Buildings C004002　篱笆&温室

C004002011 Outdoor Furniture C004002　户外家具

C004002012 Bonsai C004002　盆景

C004003 Home Improvement C004　灯具&杂货

C004003001 Lighting C004003　灯具

C004003002 Home Security C004003　家用安全装置

C004003003 Home Appliances C004003　小家电

C004003004 Hardware C004003　小五金件

C004003005 Hand Tools C004003　家用小工具

C004003006 Kitchen & Bath Fixtures C004003　厨房&卫浴设施

C004003007 Faucets, Mixers & Taps C004003　水龙头&花洒

C004003008 CCTV Product C004003　闭路电视设备

C004003009 Indoor Lighting C004003　室内灯具

C004003010 Outdoor Lighting C004003　室外灯具

C004003011 Lighting Bulbs & Tubes C004003　灯泡&灯管

C004003012 LED Lighting C004003　LED 灯具

C005 Toys, Kids & Baby　玩具&婴幼用品

C005001 Clothing & Accessories C005　童装&配饰

C005001001 Girls C005001　女童装

C005001002 Boys C005001　男童装

C005001003 Baby Girls C005001　女婴装

C005001004 Baby Boys C005001　男婴装

C005001005 Clothing Sets C005001　童装套装

C005001006 Girls' Dress C005001　女童连衣裙

C005001007 Boys' T-shirts C005001　男童 T 恤

C005001008 Baby Rompers C005001　婴儿背带裤

C005001009 Children's School Bags C005001　儿童书包

C005001010 Baby First Walkers C005001　学步鞋

C005001011 Children's Shoes C005001　儿童鞋

C005001012 Children's Accessories C005001　儿童配饰

C005002 Toys C005　玩具

C005002001 Stuffed Animals & Plush C005002　毛绒玩具

C005002002 RC Helicopters C005002　遥控玩具直升机

C005002003 Action Figures C005002 卡通人偶玩具

C005002004 Balloons C005002 气球

C005002005 Model Building C005002 拼装玩具

C005002006 Blocks C005002 积木玩具

C005002007 Dolls & Accessories C005002 洋娃娃&配饰

C005002008 Electronic Toys C005002 电子玩具

C005002009 Learning & Education C005002 益智玩具

C005002010 Baby Toys C005002 婴儿玩具

C005002011 Outdoor Fun & Sports C005002 户外玩具&体育用品

C005003 Baby & Maternity Products C005 母婴用品

C005003001 Nappy Changing C005003 妈咪包

C005003002 Activity & Gear C005003 出行用品

C005003003 Baby Care C005003 婴儿护理

C005003004 Safety Gear C005003 安全用品

C005003005 Feeding C005003 喂养用品

C005003006 Bedding C005003 婴儿床上用品

C005003007 Swimming Pool C005003 婴儿游泳池

C005003008 Baby Monitors C005003 婴儿监视器

C005003009 Maternity Dress C005003 孕妇裙

C005003010 Intimates C005003 孕妇内衣

C005003011 Maternity Tops C005003 孕妇上衣

C006 Automotive 汽车

C006001 Car Electronics C006 车用电子产品

C006001001 Motor Electronics C006001 车用小电子产品

C006001002 Car DVD C006001 车载 DVD

C006001003 Alarm Systems & Security C006001 报警系统&安全装置

C006001004 DVR/Camera C006001 行车记录仪

C006001005 Radar Detectors C006001 测速仪

C006001006 GPS C006001 GPS 导航仪

C006001007 Car Video Players C006001 车载播放器

C006001008 Motorcycle C006001 摩托车用品

C006001009 Motorbike Brakes C006001 摩托刹车片

C006001010 Protective Gears C006001 摩托车手保护装备

C006001011 Electrical System C006001 摩托车电气装置

C006002 Replacement Parts C006 汽车配件

C006002001 Car Parts C006002 汽车部件

C006002002 Car Lights C006002 车灯

C006002003 External Lights C006002 外灯

C006002004 Car Light Source C006002 车用 LED 灯

C006002005 Interior Lights C006002 内灯

C006002006 Engine C006002 引擎

C006002007 Fuel Injector C006002 喷油嘴

C006002008 Car Accessories C006002 汽车配件

C006002009 Car Stickers C006002 车饰

C006002010 Chromium Styling C006002 车身保护条

C006002011 Bumpers C006002 保险杠保护条

C006002012 Car Covers C006002 车罩

C006003 Tools Maintenance & Care C006 汽车保养工具

C006003001 Tools & Equipment C006003 车用工具&装置

C006003002 Diagnostic Tools C006003 汽车诊断仪

C006003003 Code Readers & Scan Tools C006003 汽车扫描仪

C006003004 Car Washer C006003 洗车用具

C006003005 Car Chargers C006003 车载充电器

C006003006 Steering Covers C006003 方向盘套

C006003007 Seat Covers C006003 汽车座椅套

C006003008 Floor Mats C006003 汽车置物防滑垫

C007 Sports & Outdoor 运动&户外

C007001 Sports Clothing C007 运动服装

C007001001 Hiking Jackets C007001 登山服

C007001002 Hiking T-shirts C007001 登山 T 恤

C007001003 Hiking Pants C007001 登山长裤

C007001004 Rucksacks C007001 登山包

C007001005 Running T-Shirts C007001 跑步 T 恤

C007001006 Running Bags C007001 跑步包

C007001007 Cycling Jersey C007001 自行车骑行服

C007001008 Cycling Jackets C007001 自行车骑行外套

C007001009 Cycling Shorts C007001 自行车骑行短裤

C007001010 Cycling Eyewear C007001 自行车骑行眼镜

C007001011 Skiing Jackets C007001 滑雪服

C007001012 Soccer Jersey C007001 足球球衣

C007002 Sport Shoes C007 运动鞋

C007002001 Running Shoes C007002 跑步鞋

C007002002 Basketball Shoes C007002 篮球鞋

C007002003 Soccer Shoes C007002 足球鞋

C007002004 Hiking Shoes C007002 登山鞋

C007002005 Skateboarding Shoes C007002 滑板鞋

C007002006 Tennis Shoes C007002 网球鞋

C007002007 Walking Shoes C007002 健走鞋

C007002008 Dance Shoes C007002 舞鞋

C007002009 Skate Shoes C007002 轮滑鞋

C007002010 Fitness Shoes C007002 健身鞋

C007003 Sport Equipment C007 运动装备

C007003001 Bicycle C007003 自行车

C007003002 Bicycle Parts C007003 自行车部件

C007003003 Bicycle Helmet C007003 自行车头盔

C007003004 Bicycle Light C007003 自行车灯

C007003005 Bicycle Bags & Panniers C007003 自行车骑行包&车筐

C007003006 Fishing Reels C007003 鱼线轮

C007003007 Fishing Rods C007003 钓竿

C007003008 Fishing Lines C007003 鱼线

C007003009 Fishing Lures C007003 鱼饵

C007003010 Tent C007003 帐篷

C007003011 Yoga C007003 瑜伽用品

C007003012 Guitar C007003 吉他

C008 Jewelry & Watches 首饰&手表

C008001 Fashion Jewelry C008 时尚饰品

C008001001 Necklaces & Pendants C008001 项链&吊坠

C008001002 Bracelets & Bangles C008001 手镯&手链

C008001003 Earrings C008001 耳饰

C008001004 Rings C008001 戒指

C008001005 Jewelry Sets C008001 首饰套装

C008001006 Hair Jewelry C008001 发饰

C008001007 Tie Clips & Cufflinks C008001 领带夹&袖扣

C008001008 Brooches C008001 胸针

C008001009 Charms C008001 小饰品

C008001010 Body Jewelry C008001 鼻饰&肚脐饰品

C008001011 Anklets C008001 脚链

C008001012 Jewelry Findings & Components C008001 饰品小配件

C008002 Watches C008 手表

C008002001 Sports Watches C008002 运动手表

C008002002 Wristwatches C008002 腕表

C008002003 Fashion & Casual Watches C008002 时尚休闲手表

C008002004 Pocket & Fob Watches C008002 怀表

C008002005 Women's Fashion Watches C008002 女式时尚手表

C008002006 Men's Casual Watches C008002 男士休闲手表

C008002007 Lover's Wristwatches C008002 情侣手表

C008002008 Watch Accessories C008002 手表配件

C008003 Fine Jewelry C008 高档首饰

C008003001 Diamond Series C008003 钻石首饰

C008003002 Pearl Collection C008003 珍珠首饰

C008003003 Ruby Jewelry C008003 红宝石首饰

C008003004 Sapphire Jewelry C008003 蓝宝石首饰

C008003005 Silver C008003 银饰

C008003006 Necklaces & Pendants C008003 项链&吊坠

C008003007 Rings C008003 戒指

C008003008 Earrings C008003 耳饰

C008003009 Jewelry Sets C008003 首饰套装

C008003010 Charms C008003 小饰品

C008003011 Bracelets & Bangles C008003 手镯&手链

C009 Beauty & Health 美容美发&保健

C009001 Beauty C009 美发

C009001001 Hair Styling C009001 美发用品

C009001002 Hair Rollers C009001 卷发器

C009001003 Straightening Irons C009001 直发器

C009001004 Hair Trimmers C009001 电动理发器

C009001005 Hair Dryers C009001 吹风机

C009001006 Hair Scissors C009001 理发剪刀

C009001007 Hair Color C009001 一次性染发粉

C009001008 Hair Loss Products C009001 防脱发产品

C009001009 Shaving & Hair Removal C009001 剃须&脱毛用品

C009001010 Combs C009001 梳子

C009001011 Mirrors C009001 镜子

C009002 Hair C009 假发

C009002001 Human Hair C009002 真人发假发

C009002002 Hair Weaves C009002 织发补发片

C009002003 Hair Extension C009002 驳发

C009002004 Wigs C009002 假发片

C009002005 Closure C009002 一片式假发

C009002006 Synthetic Hair C009002 合成纤维假发

C009002007 Blended Hair C009002 真发与合成纤维混合制假发

C009002008 Feather Hair C009002 羽毛假发

C009002009 Accessories & Tools C009002 假发配件&工具

C009003 Additional Categories C009 美容用品及其他

C009003001 Makeup C009003 美妆用品

C009003002 Nail & Tools C009003 美甲用品

C009003003 Skin Care C009003 护肤用品

C009003004 Health Care C009003 保健用品
C009003005 Oral Hygiene C009003 口腔保健
C009003006 Tattoo & Body Art C009003 文身与人体艺术用品
C009003007 Sex Products C009003 成人用品
C009003008 Fragrances & Deodorants C009003 香水&香体露
C009003009 Bath & Shower C009003 沐浴用品
C009003010 Sanitary Paper C009003 尿片

Section Five　Characteristics of Digital Products（数字产品的特点）

Currently, China is vigorously developing digital product trade, including strengthening innovation in digital application scenarios and models, improving both the quality and level of digital content production, as well as cultivating and expanding cross-border digital delivery channels to enhance the international competitiveness of digital products.

Digital trade weakens the impact of geographical distance on international trade, reduces intermediate links in trade, and achieves direct contact between producers and consumers to provide customized services while reducing trade costs, which is also conducive to improving the quality of export products. So, what are the characteristics of digital products, the main objects of digital products?

当前，我国正在大力发展数字产品贸易，其中，包括加强数字应用场景和模式创新，提升数字内容制作质量和水平，以及培育、拓展跨境数字交付渠道，从而提升数字产品的国际竞争力。

数字贸易减弱了地理距离对国际贸易的影响，减少贸易的中间环节，在降低贸易成本的同时实现生产者和消费者的直接接触以提供定制式服务，这也有利于促进出口产品质量的提升。那么数字贸易的主要对象，即数字产品具有什么特点呢？

Firstly, from its conceptual definition, digital products refer to products or services represented in digital format, that is, encoded into binary bytes and can be transmitted through computer networks. Second, digital products are significantly different from ordinary international trade goods products, and their characteristics are mainly reflected in the following aspects: firstly, their physical properties are completely different from ordinary international trade goods products, reflected in the non-material attributes of digital products. This stems from the fact that digital products fail to have a fixed material form, therefore, they are different from material products in the industrial economy or traditional goods trade. Therefore, digital products belong to intangible products. Secondly, digital products have replicability in that digital products can be replicated in bulk at extremely low or even close to zero cost, and the replicated products have no economic difference from the original. Replicability trait makes the dissemination and distribution of digital products extremely convenient compared to commodity products. This also gives rise to the third characteristic of digital products, which is the speed of dissemination. Digital products can be transmitted anywhere in the world in a very short period of time through the online world, and the speed of dissemination is unique to virtual digital products.

From the perspective of economic characteristics, it can be found that digital products have the characteristics of high fixed costs and low marginal costs. From the perspective of marginal analysis in economics, the cost of digital products is mainly concentrated in the early research and development stage of the product, whist the marginal cost generated by the replication and distribution of digital products in the later stage is extremely low. This diminishing marginal cost effect enables digital products to have economies of scale, meaning that the more digital products are produced, the lower the average cost of digital products. Additionally, digital products have externalities, meaning that their value often increases with the number of users using them. For example, the more people use a certain operating system or app mini program, the better the evaluation of its corresponding utility by new buyers.

首先，从其概念界定看，数字产品指的是用数字格式进行表示，即编码成一段二进制的字节，并可通过计算机网络传输的产品或服务。其次，数字产品明显不同于普通的国际贸易货物产品，其特点主要体现在以下几个方面：第一是其物理特性与普通的国际贸易货物产品截然不同，体现在数字产品的非物质属性。这一点源自数字产品没有固定的物质形态，因此，它不同于工业经济或传统货物贸易中的物质产品，所以，数字产品属于无形产品。第二，数字产品具有可复制性。即数字产品能够以极低甚至接近于零的成本进行批量复制，且复制后的产品与原件在经济效用上并无差异。这种可复制性使得数字产品的传播和分发比起货物产品，显得极为便捷。这也产生了数字产品的第三个特点，即传播的快捷性。数字产品能够通过网络世界在极短的时间内传送至世界任何地方，这种传播的快捷性是虚拟的数字产品所特有的。

从经济特性角度分析，可以发现数字产品具有高固定成本、低边际成本的特点。从经济学的边际分析看，数字产品的成本主要集中在该种产品前期的研发阶段，而后期的数字产品复制和分发所产生的边际成本极低。这种边际成本递减效应使得数字产品具有规模经济效应，即数字产品生产得越多，数字产品的平均成本就越低。另外，数字产品具有外部性，即数字产品的价值往往随着使用它的用户数量的增加而增加。例如，使用某种操作系统或 App 小程序的人越多，新购买者对它们的相应效用的评价就越好。

The specific examples of digital products are vast, covering multiple fields such as information and entertainment, symbols and signs, processes and services in daily life and economic activities. Here are some specific classifications and examples:

数字产品的具体例子非常丰富，涵盖了日常生活和经济活动中的信息和娱乐、象征和符号、过程和服务等多个领域。以下是一些具体的分类及例子：

1. Information and entertainment products（信息和娱乐产品）

Digital products of paper-based information, such as e-books, electronic manuals, electronic journals (magazines), electronic newspapers, electronic reports, electronic push news, etc. These digital products digitize traditional paper content, information enabling online users to read, download, and transmit.

Digital products of video images, say, movies, microfilms, TV programs, short video clips, electronic photos, electronic maps, electronic images, electronic cards, electronic calendars, and electronic promotional posters. These digital products present image information in digital three-dimensional form and in digital video form, providing users with a rich and good visual experience.

纸上信息数字产品：如电子书、电子说明书、电子期刊（杂志）、电子报纸、电子报告、电子推送新闻等。这些信息数字产品将传统的纸质内容进行了数字化，有利于用户的在线阅读、下载和传输。

视频图像的数字产品：如电影、微电影、电视节目、短视频、电子照片、电子地图、电子影像、电子卡片、电子日历、电子宣传海报等。这些数字产品以数字化的三维形式呈现图像信息，并以数字视频形式展示，为用户提供丰富的视觉体验。

2. Symbols and symbolic concepts（象征和符号概念）

Ticket booking services: such as electronic ticketing for flights, hotel stays, high-speed rail transportation, ferries, concerts, and international sports events. These products have clear symbols and symbolic concepts, that is, they are not physical objects, but present and represent ticketing information in digital form, which is conducive to facilitating users' online booking and digital payment.

Financial tools: such as electronic invoices, electronic currency, online credit cards, electronic bills, etc. These products have clear symbols and symbolic concepts, that is, they are not actual currency, but process financial information in digital form, thereby improving the convenience of trade and financial transactions, and ensuring the security of financial transactions through network encryption technology and blockchain technology.

In addition, digital products also include other forms such as software, App mini-programs, games, digital artworks, etc. Those products present software functionality, gaming entertainment content, and artistic aesthetic value in digital form, which furnish a rich digital experience for various users.

订票服务：如飞行航班、入住旅馆、高铁运输、轮渡、音乐会以及国际体育赛事等的电子票务。这些产品具有明显的象征和符号概念，即不是实物，而是以数字化形式呈现，方便用户在线预订和数字化支付。

财务工具：如电子发票、电子货币、网上信用卡、电子账单等。这些产品具有明显的象征和符号概念，即不是实际货币，而是以数字化形式处理财务信息，从而提高了贸易、金融交易的便捷性，并借助网络加密技术和区块链技术确保金融交易的安全性。

此外，数字产品还包括一些其他的形式，如软件、App 小程序、游戏、数字艺术品等。这些产品以数字形式呈现软件功能、游戏娱乐内容和艺术审美价值，为各种用户提供丰富的数字体验。

Part B Terminology Practice

1. **Spread**（价差）：The price difference between two related markets or commodities. For example, the April-August live cattle spread.

2. **Speculator**（投机者）：A market participant who tries to profit from buying and selling futures

and option contracts by anticipating future price movements. Speculators assume market price risk and add liquidity and capital to the futures markets. They do not hold equal and opposite cash market risks.

3. **Option**（期权）：A contract that conveys the right, but not the obligation, to buy or sell a futures contract at a certain price for a specified time period. Only the seller (writer) of the option is obligated to perform.

4. **Maintenance margin**（维持保证金）：A set minimum margin (per outstanding futures contract) that a customer must maintain in a margin account.

5. **Cash (spot) market**（现货市场）：A place where people buy and sell the actual (cash) commodities, that is, a grain elevator, livestock market, or the like.

6. **Adding value**（增值）：Adding something that the customer wants that was not there before.

7. **Benchmarking**（标杆管理）：Comparing your product to the best competitors.

8. **Bring to the table**（提出意见/贡献）：Refers to what each individual in a meeting can contribute to a meeting, for example, a design or brainstorming meeting.

9. **Concurrent (or simultaneous) engineering**（并行工程/同步工程）：Integrating the design, manufacturing, and test processes.

10. **Continuous improvement**（持续改进）：The PDSA (Plan-Do-Study-Act) process of iteration which results in improving a product.

11. **Customer satisfaction**（顾客满意度）：Meeting or exceeding a customer's expectations for a product or service.

12. **Design**（设计）：The creation of a specification from concepts.

13. **Flow charting**（流程图）：Creating a "map" of the steps in a process.

14. **Manufacturing**（制造）：Creating a product from specifications.

15. **Metrics**（指标）：Ways to measure: e.g., time, cost, customer satisfaction, quality.

16. **Process**（流程）：What is actually done to create a product.

17. **Six-sigma quality**（六西格玛质量）：Meaning 99.999 997% perfect; only 3.4 defects in a million.

18. **Statistical Process Control (SPC)**（统计过程控制）：used for measuring the conformance of a product to specifications.

19. **Test**（测试）：A procedure for critical evaluation; a means of determining the presence, quality, or truth of something, e.g., testing the product for defects.

20. **Total Quality Management (TQM)**（全面质量管理）：Controlling everything about a process.

Part C Terms

1. sales conditions 销售条件	2. special orders 特殊订货
3. confirmation 确认	4. in duplicate 一式两份
5. in triplicate 一式三份	6. above the average quality 中等以上质量

7. below the average quality 中等以下质量

8. to execute the order 执行订单

9. plain sailing 一帆风顺

10. Fair Average Quality (F.A.Q.) 良好平均品质，大路货

11. mutual consent 双方同意

12. Sales Confirmation 销售确认书

13. conclude a deal 达成交易

14. offer is subject to… 报盘以……为准

15. make a ××% reduction 减价××%

16. market condition 市场状况

17. market fluctuation 市场波动

18. market information 市场情报

19. market price 市场价格

20. market report 市场报告

21. market risk 市场风险

22. market survey 市场调查

23. domestic market 国内市场

24. foreign market 国外市场

25. money market 货币市场

26. product market 产品市场

27. spot market 即期市场

28. stock market 股票市场

29. market glut 市场饱和

30. market structure 市场结构

31. market shortfall 市场供应不足

32. market value 市场价

33. full range of samples 全套样品

34. representative sample 有代表性样品

35. sample book 样品册

36. sample pad 样品

37. counter sample 对等样，回样

38. sample of no value 无价样品

39. free sample of no charge 免费样品

40. sample free of charge 免费样品

41. free sample 免费样品

42. as per sample 按照样品

43. equal to sample 和样品相同

44. sample post 样品邮寄

45. sample for reference 参考样品

46. sample invoice 样品发票

47. up to sample 达到样品，比得上样品

48. inferior quality 低劣质量

49. superior quality 优等质量

50. prime quality tip-top quality 一流质量

51. quality shipped 装船品质

52. quality landed 卸岸品质

53. pattern sample 型式样品

54. duplicate sample 复样

Part D Exercise

I. Give the Chinese equivalents for the following English terms.

1. intrinsic attribute_____

2. luster, modeling, structure_____

3. endurability_____

4. marketability_____

5. social attributes_____

6. disinfected_____

7. serviceability_____

8. hygiene_____

9. specifications_____

10. aquatic products_____

11. transnational corporation_____

12. life of quality assurance_____

II. Two columns are given for you to decide which method is best suited for a certain commodity, please match them.

（　　）1. mineral ore　　　　　　　　　　A. sample

（　　）2. ordinary garments　　　　　　　B. manual

（　　）3. fish　　　　　　　　　　　　　　C. F.A.Q.

（　　）4. Haier washing machines　　　　　D. G.M.Q.

（　　）5. medical apparatus　　　　　　　E. famous brand

（　　）6. wheat　　　　　　　　　　　　　F. specification

（　　）7. calligraphic works　　　　　　　G. origin

（　　）8. power plant generator　　　　　　H. drawing or diagram

III. Monomial Choice.

1. Quality latitude is used for（　　）.

　A. 初级产品　　　　　　　　　　B. 工业制成品

　C. 机械产品　　　　　　　　　　D. 机电产品

2. 凡货、样不能做到完全一致的商品，一般都不适宜凭（　　）买卖。

　A. specification　　　　　　　　B. size

　C. standard　　　　　　　　　　D. sample

3. 我国出口大豆一批，合同规定大豆的水分为最高 14%、含油量为最低 18%、杂质为最高 1%，这种规定品质的方法是（　　）。

　A. sale by specification　　　　　B. sale by grade

　C. sale by standard　　　　　　　D. sale by instruction

4. Plain Satin Silk:

Width (inch)	Length (YDS)	Weight (m/m)	Composition
55	38/42	16.5	100% Silk

　The content above refers to the quality of plain silk is sale by（　　）.

　A. sample　　　　　　　　　　　B. grade

　C. standard　　　　　　　　　　D. specification

5. F.A.Q. is used for（　　）.

　A. agricultural and by-product products　B. industrial products

　C. mechanical products　　　　　D. wood and aquatic products

6. G.M.Q. is used for（　　）.

　A. agricultural and by-product products　B. wood and aquatic products

　C. industrial products　　　　　　D. man-made products

7. 在我国花生出口合同中规定：水分每增减 1%，则（　　）。

　A. 合同价格增减 0.5%　　　　　B. 合同价格减增 0.5%

　C. 合同价格增减 1%　　　　　　D. 合同价格减增 1%

8. "四川榨菜"中用来表明商品品质的方法是（　　　　）。

    A. sale by brand or trade mark   B. sale by standard

    C. sale by specification   D. sale by origin

9. "Description of Goods"条款就是合同的（　　　　）。

    A. 品质条款   B. 数量条款

    C. 品名条款   D. 说明条款

10. Grey Duck Feather Soft Nap 18% allowing 1% more or less，此处文字表明了品质指标（　　　　）。

    A. 差异的范围   B. 变动的上下限

    C. 上下变动幅度   D. 误差

11. 凡货、样难以达到完全一致的，不宜采用（　　　　）。

    A. 凭说明买卖   B. 凭样品买卖

    C. 凭等级买卖   D. 凭规格买卖

12. 在交货数量前加上"约"或"大约"字样，按惯例《UCP600》的规定这种约定可解释为交货数量不超过（　　　　）的增加幅度。

    A. 10%   B. 5%   C. 2.5%   D. 1.5%

13. 在品质条款的规定上，对某些比较难掌握其品质的工业制成品或农副产品，我们多在合同中规定（　　　　）。

    A. 溢短装条款   B. 增减价条款

    C. 品质公差或品质机动幅度   D. 商品的净重

14. 凭卖方样品成交时，应留存（　　　　）以备交货时核查之用。

    A. 回样   B. 复样   C. 参考样   D. 对等样品

15. 对于价值较低的商品，往往采取（　　　　）计算其重量。

    A. 以毛作净   B. 法定重量   C. 净重   D. 理论重量

16. 对于大批量交易的散装货，因较难掌握商品的数量，通常在合同中规定（　　　　）。

    A. 品质公差条款   B. 溢短装条款

    C. 立即装运条款   D. 仓至仓条款

17. 合同中未注明商品重量是按毛重还是净重计算时，则习惯上应按（　　　　）计算。

    A. 毛重   B. 净重   C. 以毛作净   D. 公量

18. 某公司与外商签订了一份出口某商品的合同，合同中规定的出口数量为 500 吨。在溢短装条款中规定，允许卖方交货的数量可增减 5%，但未对多交部分货物如何作价给予规定。卖方依合约规定多交了 20 吨，根据《公约》的规定，此 20 吨应按（　　　　）作价。

    A. 到岸价   B. 合同价   C. 离岸价   D. 议定价

19. 我方某进出口公司拟向马来西亚出口服装一批，在洽谈合同条款时，就服装的款式可要求买方提供（　　　　）。

    A. 样品   B. 规格   C. 商标   D. 产地

20. 我国现行的法定计量单位制是（　　　　）。

    A. 公制   B. 国际单位制   C. 英制   D. 美制

IV. Fill in the blanks with below with the most appropriate terms from the box.

samples	vivid	outdated	marked	rejected material
qualify	outturn samples	official seal	regular orders	as per

1. If the quality of your products is satisfactory, we may place_____.

2. There is no _____qualitative difference between the two.

3. The new varieties have very _____designs and beautiful colors.

4. The quality is all right, but the style is a bit _____.

5. No doubt you've received the _____of the inferior quality goods.

6. You know we sell our tea according to our _____.

7. We sell goods _____the sales sample, not the quality of any previous supplies.

8. If you find the quality of our products unsatisfactory, we're prepared to accept return of the _____within a week.

9. The quality of this article cannot _____for first-class.

10. Our Certificate of Quality is made valid by means of the _____.

V. Briefly answer the following questions.

1. 我国对于品质增减价条款有何种不同的规定方法？

2. 数量机动幅度是什么？它的规定方法有哪些？

3. 数字产品具有哪些特点？

4. 简述溢短装条款的计价方法。

5. 品质条款的内容有哪些？

VI. Case Study.

1. One China Foods Co., Ltd. exports a batch of cider. The name of the goods is written as "APPLE WINE" on the coming letter of credit by the foreign importing company. In order to be identical with the L/C, in all the documents the Chinese company also give the name of the goods as "APPLE WINE". Unexpectedly, when the goods arrived at the importing company's port, they were detained by the importing country's customs and fined, because on both the inner and outer package of this batch of wine, the name of the goods was "CIDER" instead of "APPLE WINE". As a result, the foreign company asked the Chinese company for compensation for the loss of the fines.

Question:

Does the Chinese company have any responsibility?

2. In February, 2018, A and B companies signed a purchase and sale contract of aluminum profiles worth USD4 million. The contract term for operation was agreed to the fact that Party B provided 4 million of aluminum profiles to Party A. The delivery date was in April, 2018, and the delivery mode was for the supply-side delivery. Party A made the down payment of USD8 000 and liquidated damages of 5% according to the contract requirements. In the contract there were very clear stipulations of the aluminum profiles about the specifications, quality requirements and so on. After the signing of the contract, Party A met its contractual delivery of the deposit. But Party B

failed to make the delivery when it was the time for it to deliver the goods. Party A sent staff to hold talks with Party B on several occasions (including travel spending USD2 000). Both the two sides agreed to postpone the delivery until June, 2018. In June, 2018, Party B only delivered USD2 million profiles. After receiving the goods, Party A stored the goods in the warehouse and at the same time continued urging for the rest of the delivery. In August, Party A picked the profiles up from the warehouse for use. Party A found that the profile did not meet the contract specification requirements, so Party A requested to return the goods, and demanded the lifting of non-compliance with part of the contract. Party B did not agree to the requirement of the return by Party A, and did not agree to lift the unperformed portion of the contract, either. Party A was in urgent need of the goods, so they had to purchase from other resources $4 million of the same kinds of type material. After that Party A took action in court.

Questions:

(1) Party B has fulfilled part of its ability, which can be returned? Why?

(2) Can the unperformed part of the contract be lifted? Why?

(3) How to deal with the deposit?

(4) Should Party B bear responsibility for the breach of contract or not?

VII. Please determine whether the following statements are True or False. Then put T for True or F for False in the bracket at the end of each statement.

1. Electronic invoices bear a different legal effect from paper invoices. (   )

2. The quality of a certain kind of goods determines its market and price. (   )

3. The quality of the goods is among the main terms upon which a sales contract is based and constructed. (   )

4. Commodity provides the material basis for international trade. (   )

5. Not all commodities have certain qualities. (   )

6. The quality of goods refers to the intrinsic attributes and the outer form or shape of the goods. (   )

7. The e-commerce platform operators should record and save the goods and services information as well as transaction information published on the platform, and generally the storage time shall not be less than one year from the date of completion of the transaction. (   )

8. The quality of goods includes its social attributes, which refer to how it meets the subjective requirements and different tastes of its customers. (   )

9. In international trade, most goods are sold by the method of sale by specification, grade or standard except some special cases. (   )

10. Sale by specification is convenient and accurate. (   )

Chapter Six

Part A Text

Quantity of Goods

Any business deal consists of a certain quantity of goods supplied by the seller and a certain sum of money paid by the buyer. Without a certain quantity of goods, any business deal would be groundless. Thus, the quantity clause is one of the essential terms and conditions for the conclusion of a transaction in the contract. The United Nations Convention on Contracts for the International Sale of Goods requires that the quantity of goods delivered should be identical to that called for in the contract, otherwise the buyer is entitled to reject the portion of goods excessive in quantity, and to claim against the seller if the quantity is found to be less than that called for in the contract. If the seller delivers a quantity of goods greater than that provided for in the contract, the buyer may take delivery or refuse to take delivery of the excess quantity. If the buyer takes delivery of all or part of the excess quantity, he must pay for it at the contract rate.

任何一笔交易都是由卖方提供一定数量的货物和买方支付一定数目的货款构成的。没有一定量的商品，交易就无法进行。因此，商品的数量是交易中一个不可缺少的因素。《联合国国际货物销售合同公约》规定所交付的货物必须与合同中所签订的数量一致，买方有权拒收多余部分的货物，如果所交付的货物少于合同中规定的数量，买方可以向卖方提出索赔。如果卖方交付的货物多于合同规定的数量，买方可以提货，也可以拒收多余部分，但如果买方收下全部货物或多余部分货物，则必须按合同价格付款。

Section One   Calculating Units of the Goods Quantity（货物数量的计量单位）

Because different countries have different systems for calculating units such as length, capacity and weight, the units of measurement vary from one country to another. Furthermore, the same unit of measurement may represent different quantities. Take the example of "ton". There are various "tons" with different weights in different systems such as Long ton/English ton (2 240 lbs), Short ton/American ton (2 000 lbs) and Metric ton/French ton (about 2 204 lbs). Therefore, it is greatly important for traders to know the units of measurement in different systems and the way they are converted from one to another. The commonly used systems in the world are the Metric System, the British System and the US System. The unit of measurement should be chosen in the contract should go in accordance with the nature of goods. The units of measurement generally used in international trade are listed in the following table (See Table 6-1 Units of Measurement).

Table 6-1　Units of Measurement

	Units of Measurement
Weight	gram (g), kilogram (kg), ounce (oz), pound (lb), metric ton (MT), long ton(LT), short ton(ST), etc.
Number	piece (pc), package (pkg), pair, set, dozen (doz), gross (gr), ream (rm), etc.
Length	meter (m), centimeter (cm), foot (ft), yard (yd), etc.
Area	square meter (sq m), square foot (sq ft), square yard (sq yd), etc.
Volume	cubic-meter (cu m), cubic centimeter (cu cm), cubic foot (cu ft), cubic yard (cu yd), etc.
Capacity	liter (L), gallon (gal), pint (pt), bushel (bu), etc.

由于各国度量衡制度的不同，所使用的计量单位也不一样，即使同样的计量单位所表示的数量也不尽相同。如"吨"，不同的度量衡制度里有不同的"吨"，有长吨/英吨（2 240 磅）、短吨/美吨（2 000 磅）和公吨/法吨（约 2 204 磅）。由此可见，了解不同制度中的计量单位以及它们之间的换算关系对从事国际贸易的业务员来说就显得非常重要。目前，国际上通常使用的度量衡制度有公制、英制和美制。合同中选择何种度量衡单位应根据商品的性质而定。国际贸易中经常使用的计量单位如表 6-1 所示。

表 6-1　常用计量单位

	计 量 单 位
重量	克、千克、盎司、磅、公吨、长吨、短吨等
数量	只、件、双、套、打、罗、令等
长度	米、厘米、英尺、码等
面积	平方米、平方英尺、平方码等
体积	立方米、立方厘米、立方英尺、立方码等
容积	公升、加仑、品脱、蒲式耳等

Usually the following measuring units are adopted in China.

我国通常采用下列计量单位。

1. Weight（重量）

It is usually used for mineral products, agricultural and by-products such as wool, cotton, grains and ore products. When it is used in the contract, there are metric ton or kilo ton, long ton or gross ton, short ton or net ton, gram(g), kilogram(kg), ounce(oz), pound(lb), quintal, hundredweight(cwt), etc.

重量单位多应用于矿产品、农副产品，如羊毛、棉花、谷物、矿产品等。按重量交易时，其常用的单位有公吨、长吨、短吨、克、千克、盎司、磅、公担、英担等。

2. Number（数量）

Constantly used for measurement of industrial products and general products such as ready-made clothes, stationery, paper, toys and so on, such as piece(pc), package(pkg), pair, set, dozen(doz), gross(gr), ream(rm), roll or coil, etc.

一般杂货和工业制品，如服装、文具、纸张、玩具、五金工具等习惯于按数量进行买卖，如只、件、双、套、打、罗、令、卷等。

3. Length（长度）

It is mostly used for textile products, metal cords, electric wires, ropes and so on, such as meter(m), foot(ft), yard(yd), etc.

有些商品如金属绳索、布匹、绸缎、钢管、电线、电缆等常采用长度计量，如米、英尺、码等。

4. Area（面积）

It is often used in trade of glass, textile products such as carpets, etc. like square meter, square foot, square yard and the like. Often we add thickness in the contract.

面积多用于皮革、木板、玻璃、地毯等商品的交易。其表示单位有平方米、平方英尺、平方码等。有的还另列厚度。

5. Volume（体积）

It is generally used for timber, wood, chemical gases, etc., and includes cubic meter, cubic foot, cubic yard, etc.

按体积表示多用于木材、天然气、化学气体等的交易。计量单位如立方米、立方英尺和立方码等。

6. Capacity（容积）

It is mostly used for grain, petroleum/oil, etc. The commonly used capacity units are liter, gallon, bushel and so on.

常用于谷类、石油等。常见的容积单位有公升、加仑、蒲式耳等。

7. Package（包件）

It is often used in the packing of cement, cotton, tinned food and so on, such as bag, carton, case, bale, etc.

这种表示方法常用于水泥、棉纱、罐头食品等商品交易，如袋、箱、包等。

The followings (see Table 6-2, 6-3, 6-4, and 6-5) are the main measurement conversion often used in international trade practice.

Table 6-2　Length conversion（长度换算）

Metric System （公制）		Chinese System（中国市制）	Britain/American System （英美制）		
Meter（米）	Centimeter（厘米）	Chi（尺）	Yard（码）	Foot（英尺）	Feet（英寸）
1	100	3	1.094	3.280 8	39.370 1
0.01	1	0.03	0.010 94	0.032 81	0.393 7
0.333 3	33.33	1	0.364 6	1.094	13.123
0.914 4	91.44	2.743	1	3	36
0.304 8	30.48	0.914 4	0.333 4	1	12
0.025 4	2.54	0.076 2	0.027 8	0.083 3	1

Table 6-3　Area conversion（面积换算）

Metric System（公制）		Britain/American System（英美制）			Chinese System（中国市制）
Square meter（平方米）	Square centimeter（平方厘米）	Square yard（平方码）	Square foot（平方英尺）	Square feet（平方英寸）	Square Chinese meter（平方尺）
1	10 000	1.196	10.763 9	1 550	9
0.000 1	1	0.000 12	0.001 08	0.155	0.000 9
0.836 1	8 361	1	9	1 296	7.525
0.092 9	929	0.111 1	1	144	0.836
0.000 65	6.45	0.000 77	0.006 94	1	0.005 8
0.111	1 111	0.133	1.196	172.2	1

Table 6-4　Capacity conversion（容积换算）

Metric System（公制）	Chinese System（中国市制）	Britain System（英制）	American System（美制）
Liter（升）	Chinese liter（升）	Britain gallon（英制加仑）	American gallon（美制加仑）
1	1	0.22	0.264
4.546	4.546	1	1.201
3.785	3.785	0.833	1

Table 6-5　Capacity conversion（体积换算）

Metric System（公制）		Britain/American System（英美制）			Chinese System（中国市制）
Cubic-meter（立方米）	Cubic centimeter（立方厘米）	Cubic yard（立方码）	Cubic foot（立方英尺）	Cubic feet（立方英寸）	Cubic Chinese meter（立方尺）
1	1 000 000	1.303	35.314 7	61 024	27
0.000 001	1	0.000 001 3	0.000 04	0.061 02	0.000 027
0.763 6	764 555	1	27	46 656	20.643
0.028 32	28 317	0.037	1	1 728	0.764 6
0.000 016	16.387	0.000 02	0.000 58	1	0.000 44
0.037	37 037	0.048 4	1.308	2 260	1

Section Two　Methods of Calculating Weight（计算重量的方法）

In international trade, goods are most often measured in units of weight. The methods to measure the weight of goods are stated as follows.

国际贸易中，大多数商品的买卖通常是按重量计算的，计算重量的方法一般有下列几种。

1. Weight calculation（重量的计算）

1) By Gross Weight（按毛量）

Gross weight is the sum of the total weight of the commodity itself and the tare (the package weight). That's to say it refers to the net weight plus the tare weight of the goods.

毛重是指商品本身的重量加上皮重（包装的重量），也就是净重和皮重的总重量。

2) By net weight（按净重）

Net weight is the actual weight of a commodity without the addition of the tare. In international trade if goods are sold by weight, the net weight is often used.

$$\text{Net weight} = \text{gross weight} - \text{tare weight}$$

There are four ways to calculate tare weight:

(1) By actual tare: The actual weight of packages of the whole commodities.

(2) By average tare: In this way, the weight of packages is calculated on the basis of the average tare of a part of the packages.

(3) By customary tare: The weight for standardized package has a generally recognized weight which can be used to represent the weight of such packages.

(4) By computed tare: The weight of package is calculated according to the tare previously agreed upon by the seller and the buyer instead of actual weight.

It is customary to calculate the weight by net weight if the contract does not stipulate definitely by gross weight or by net weight. Occasionally, the weights of some commodities are usually calculated by conditioned weight and theoretical weight. Conditioned weight is obtained with the moisture content of the commodity removed by scientific methods and the standardized moisture added. It is often applicable to such commodities as raw silk and wool, which are of high economic value and with unsteady moisture content. Commodities with regular specifications and regular sizes, such as galvanized iron and steel plates, are suitable to be weighed by theoretical weight which is computed by the total number of sheets.

净重即货物自身的实际重量，不包括皮重。国际贸易中，以重量计算的商品，大部分以净重计价。净重的计算方法是用货物的毛重减去皮重，即：

$$净重 = 毛重 - 皮重$$

衡量皮重一般有以下四种方法。

（1）实际皮重：整批商品包装的实际重量。

（2）平均皮重：按部分商品的实际皮重，取其平均值，然后计算出全部皮重。

（3）习惯皮重：比较规格化的包装，已为市场所公认，可以代表这种包装的重量。

（4）约定皮重：即无须经过实际衡量，而是以买卖双方事先协商约定的皮重为准。

如果合同中没有明确规定是用毛重计量还是用净重计量，按惯例应按净重计量。有些商品的重量可以用公量和理论重量计算。公量即用科学方法抽出商品所含的水分，再加标准水分求得的重量。这种按公量计算的方法经常用于经济价值较大而水分含量极不稳定的商品，如生丝、羊毛等。理论重量适用于固定规格和尺寸的商品，如马口铁和钢板。它们的重量只要根据张数就可以推算出来。

3) Conditioned weight（公量）

This refers to the kind of weight derived from the process, with which the moisture content of the commodity is removed and standardized moisture added both by scientific methods. This kind of calculating method is suitable for those cargoes, which are of high economic value and have unsteady moisture content (whose water contents are not stable), such as wool, raw silk, etc.

The formula for calculating the conditioned weight is:

$$\text{Conditioned Weight} = \frac{\text{actual weight} \times (1 + \text{standard regaining rate of water})}{1 + \text{actual regaining rate of water}}$$

$$= \text{Dried Weight} + \text{Standard Moisture}$$

有些商品如羊毛、生丝等，吸湿性较强，实际重量随空气湿度变化，其价格较高而水分含量不稳定，因此，要以公量计算，即采用科学方法抽出商品中的水分后，再加上标准含水量所求的重量。其计算公式如下：

$$\text{公量} = \frac{\text{实际重量} \times (1 + \text{标准回潮率})}{1 + \text{实际回潮率}}$$

$$= \text{干量} + \text{标准含水量}$$

4) Theoretical weight（理论重量）

Commodities that have regular specifications and fixed sizes, such as galvanized iron, tin plate and armor plate are often subject to the use of theoretical weight. So long as the specifications and size of such commodities are the same, their theoretical weight is calculated by the number of sheets put together. Some fixed cargoes, such as tin plate, steel plate, etc. have unified shapes and measurement, as long as the specification is identical, the size is conformable, the weight will be about the same, and we can calculate the weight according to the number of pieces.

某些有固定规格、形状和尺寸的商品，如镀锌铁、马口铁、钢板等，只要规格一致，尺寸相符，其重量大致相等，根据其件数计算出来的重量，称为理论重量。由于这些商品的规格和大小尺寸相同，根据其数量就能计算出实际重量，这就是理论重量。对于诸如镀锌铁、马口铁、钢板这样有规定规格的商品，只要规格一致，大小合适，重量很容易计算，完全可以按照其数量来计算。

5) Legal weight（法定重量）

Legal weight is the weight of the goods and the immediate package of the goods. Such kinds of goods include cans, small paper boxes, small bottles, etc.

法定重量是指货物和销售包装加在一起的重量，像罐、小纸盒、小瓶这样的商品常常采用法定重量计算方法。

2. More or less clause（溢短装条款）

At the time of the conclusion of a contract, the quantity clause should be clearly and definitely stipulated so as not to give rise to disputes thereafter. Expressions like "about or approximate 10 000 metric tons" are not allowed because "about or approximate" may be given several ambiguous interpretations: some refer to 2% more or less, and some 5%, and some 10%. However, it is very difficult to measure accurately those bulk goods of agricultural and mineral products like corn, soybean, wheat, coal, etc. In some cases, because of the change of goods resources or the limitation of processing, the quantity of the goods last delivered may not be in accordance with the stipulations in the contract. What's more, influenced by natural conditions, packing patterns, loading and unloading methods, the quantity of goods delivered by the seller usually doesn't conform to the quantity definitely stipulated in the contract. To facilitate the processing of the contract, the seller and the buyer, generally, agree to use a "more or less" clause. It means over load and under load are permitted but should not surpass a certain percentage of the stipulated quantity. That's to say both the seller and the buyer agree to allow some more or less of the goods delivered, but not to exceed the fixed quantity agreed upon. For example, "20 000 metric tons, 5% more or less at seller's option". "Plus or minus" or the sign "±" may also be used to take the place of "more or less". Under the "more or less" clause, the payment for the over load or under load will be made according to the contract price or at the market price at the time of shipment.

A complete "more or less" term should include the following three parts: First, there is a certain proportion. Secondly, who has the right to decide the more or less quantity. Generally speaking, it is decided by the seller, but when the buyer is responsible for renting the entire ship for the goods, in order to be linked with the charter party, sometimes it can be decided by the buyer. Thirdly, pay attention to the calculation of more or less clause. Under the more or less clause, the payment for the over load or under load will be made according to the contract price, and it can also be made according to the goods and the market situation at the market price at the time of shipment. If there are no comments on more or less clause, as a usual practice, it can be understood as the payment for the over load or under load will be made according to the contract price.

在签订合同时应明文规定交货时商品的数量，以避免因商品数量问题而引起的纠纷。像"大约 10 000 公吨"这样的表达就应尽量避免，因为这样的表达可能会引起理解上的差异，有的理解为2%左右的差额幅度，有的理解为5%的上下幅度，有的理解为10%的误差幅度。但是，有些大宗散装农产品和工矿业产品，如玉米、大豆、小麦、煤等很难计算其准确数量，此外，某些商品由于货源变化、加工条件限制等，往往在最后出货时，实际数量与合同规定数量有所出入。并且，由于受自然条件、包装方式、装卸货方法等因素的影响，卖方所交货物往往很难与合同中规定的数量一致。为了顺利履行合同，买卖双方同意使用"溢短装条款"，其意思是允许多装或少装，但以不超过合同规定数量的百分之几为限。即规定交货数量可在一定幅度内增减。例如"20 000 公吨，卖方可溢短装 5%，由卖方选择"，也可采用"增加或减少"，或用"±"符号代替"溢短装"条款。在此条款下，溢短装部分按合同规定的价格计价，或按装船时的市价计算价格。

一个完整的溢短装条款应包括以下三项内容：第一，允许溢装或短装的比率。第二，实际交货时由谁决定溢短装。一般都是规定由卖方决定，但在由买方负责租整船接货的情况下，为便于同租船合同衔接，也可规定由买方决定。第三，溢短装部分的价格计算。通常按合同价格计算，但也可根据商品和市场情况按交货时的市价计算。如果溢短装条款中未订明第三项内容，应理解为溢短装部分按合同价格计价。

Section Three　Quantity Terms in the Contract（合同中的数量条款）

1．Attentions when making quantity terms（订立数量条款的注意事项）

Important points that should be taken into account when making quantity terms.

(1) Understanding very clearly the whole quantity to be delivered both for import and export.

(2) The supply conditions in the domestic market.

(3) The supply conditions in foreign markets.

(4) The financial standing and management capability of the foreign customers.

(5) The price fluctuation in both global and domestic both on the world market and home markets.

在规定数量条款时，要注意下列事项。

（1）正确掌握进出口成交数量。

（2）国内货源供应情况。

（3）国外市场的供求情况。

（4）国外客户的资信情况和经营能力。

（5）国内外价格波动情况。

As for the quantity terms in the contract, we should make them very specific and clear.

In order to avoid unnecessary disputes, the quantity terms in the contract should be made very specific and clear. It is better not to use the words like "about", "approximate". This is because there is different understanding for these words, which will cause ambiguity. It should also be very clear for quantity units. For example, if it is calculated by tons, there will be MT, LT, or ST. For the goods calculated by weight, the specific calculating method should be stipulated, such as "gross for net".

在规定数量条款时，必须明确清晰。

为了避免争议，合同中数量条款要明确具体。在数量上不要用"大约""左右"等词语，因为对这些词语的解释可能不一致，从而引起歧义。对计量单位的使用要完整，如用吨（ton），则要明确是公吨（MT），还是长吨（LT）或短吨（ST）。对按重量计算的商品，还应规定计算重量的具体方法，如"以毛作净"。

2．Sample quantity terms　（数量条款实例）

(1) Bleached cotton clothing 25 000 yds, with 5% more or less at seller's option.

漂白棉布 25 000 码，卖方可溢装或短装 5%。

(2) Chinese northeast soybean: 6 000MT, gross for net, 3%more or less at seller's option.

中国东北大豆：6 000 公吨，以毛作净，卖方可溢装或短装 3%。

(3) 500 metric tons, 5% more or less at seller's option.

500 公吨，卖方可溢装或短装 5%。

(4) The seller is allowed to load 3% more or less, the price shall be calculated according to the unit price in the contract.

允许卖方在装货时溢装或短装 3%，价格按照本合同所列的单价计算。

(5) To be packed in double gunny bags containing about 100 kgs and each bag shall weigh 1.15 kgs with allowance of 0. 1kg more or less.

双层麻袋装 100 千克，每包 1.15 千克，误差为 0.1 千克。

(6) It is agreed that a margin of 10 per cent shall be allowed for over or short count.

溢短装时允许 10%的差额。

(7) For printed, dyed and yarn-dyed goods, a maximum of 10% of two-part pieces with the short part not less than 10yds is permissible if necessary and for each two part pieces an additional length of 1/2 yd (half yard) will be supplied free. Also a tolerance of plus or minus 10% in quantity for each colorway (for each shade in case of dyed goods) shall be permitted.

花色、色布及色织布必要时可有不超过 10%的 2 段拼匹，其短的一段应不低于 10 码，拼匹免费另加半码。此外，每一配色，在数量上可有 10%上下的差额。

(8) A usual trade margin of 5% plus or minus of the quantities confirmed shall be allowed. When shipment is spread over two or more periods, the above-mentioned trade margin of plus or minus 5% shall, when necessary, be applicable to the quantity designated by the Buyers to be shipped each period.

本确认书所确定的数量，卖方可有 5%的增减。如果分批装运，每批装运数量必要时卖方亦得在买方规定范围内增减 5%。

Part B Terminology Practice

1. **Tare weight**（皮重）**：** The weight of a container and/or packing materials without the weight of the goods it contains.

2. **Shipping weight**（装货重量）**：** Shipping weight represents the gross weight in kilograms of shipments, including the weight of moisture content, wrappings, crates, boxes, and containers (other than cargo vans and similar substantial outer containers).

3. **Related parties**（关联方）**：**

* Members of the same family, spouse, and lineal descendants.

* Officers or directors if each individual is also an officer or director of the other organization.

* Partners.

* Person owning, controlling or holding with power to vote 5% or more of the outstanding stock.

* Person who is an officer or director in both organizations.

4. **Movement certificate**（原产地证书）**：** Required when goods are being exported from the EU to a country covered by EU trade agreements. These certificates ensure preferential duty rates for an exporter's goods.

5. **Open General Import Licence (OGIL)**（一般进口许可证）**：** Available from the Department of Trade and Industry, this allows the import of most goods from outside the European Union (EU) without licensing formalities. However some goods require a special licence and are listed in the schedule to OGIL.

6. **Pre-Shipment Inspection (PSI)**（装运前检验）**：** A few countries require goods and documents to be examined before export by an independent agency. In some cases it's optional but can be requested by the customer. Usually, countries where PSI applies have appointed one dedicated

agency to perform the pre-shipment inspection. Normally, your freight forwarder or customer will be able to advise on the necessary arrangements.

7. **Payment in advance**（预付货款）：An exporter may be able to negotiate these terms for all or part of a shipment. The exporter bears no risks or financing costs. Payment or part-payment in advance is typically used for low-value sales to individuals or new customers.

8. **Reduced rates of duty**（优惠税率）：Some goods can be imported into the UK at zero or reduced rate of customs duty because they originated in a preference country or are from a non-EU country and qualify for a temporary suspension of customs duty.

9. **Terms of delivery**（交货条款）：Define the division of responsibility for the costs of an export or import sale and for the risk of loss or damage in transit.

10. **Tariff quotas**（关税配额）：An EU system to allow the importation of limited amounts of certain goods (sometimes from specified countries) at a rate of duty lower than would otherwise apply.

Part C Terms

1. reduction 降价
2. allowance 补贴
3. rebate 回扣
4. cash discount 即期付款折扣
5. quantity discount 数量折扣
6. special discount 特别折扣
7. trade balance 贸易平衡
8. business activities 经济活动
9. trading center 贸易中心
10. quality clause 品质条款
11. good merchantable quality 全销质量
12. fair average quality 大路货
13. first-class 一等品
14. sampling 抽样
15. colour sample 色彩样品
16. subject to the counter sample 以对等样品为准
17. sales by sample 凭样品买卖
18. grade 等级
19. Sales by Description 凭说明书买卖
20. Sales by Trade Mark or Brand 凭商标和名牌买卖
21. quality as per seller's sample 凭卖方样品质量交货
22. quality as per buyer's sample 凭买方样品质量交货
23. quality control 质量管理
24. Sales by specification, grade, or standard 凭规格、等级或标准买卖
25. Fair Average Quality (F. A. Q.) "良好平均品质"（国际上买卖农副产品时常用此标准）
26. quality to be considered as being about equal to the sample 品质与样品大致相同
27. huge quantity 或 enormous quantity 巨大的数量
28. maximum quantity 最大数量
29. minimum quantity 最小数量
30. small quantity 小量
31. entire quantity 整个数量
32. total quantity 总量
33. further quantity 更多的数量
34. sufficient quantity 足够的数量
35. liberal quantity 充足的数量

36. shipment quantity 够装运的数量　　37. equal quantity 等量

38. reasonable quantity 相当的数量　　39. corresponding quantity 相应的数量

40. large quantity 大数量

41. considerable quantity 大数量（可观的数量）

42. substantial quantity 大数量　　43. useful quantity 较大数量

44. average quantity 平均数量　　45. moderate quantity 中等数量

Part D Exercise

I. Here given in the following are short forms for some units of measure and weight. Please give the complete form of each.

1. t _____　2. oz_____

3. lb _____　4. pt_____

5. yd _____　6. gal_____

7. rm _____　8. kg _____

9. g _____　10. sqm _____

II. Please fill in the blanks with what you have learnt in this unit.

1. If the seller delivers a quantity of goods greater than that provided for in the contract, the buyer may _____ or _____ of the excess quantity.

2. Gross weight refers to the _____ of the goods.

3. There are _____ ways to calculate tare weight: _____, _____, _____, _____.

4. If the buyer takes delivery of all or part of the excess quantity, he must pay for it at_____ _____.

5. Conditioned weight refers to the kind of weight _____ , with which the _____ of the commodity is removed and _____ both by scientific methods.

6. Legal weight is the weight of the goods and the _____ of the goods.

7. A complete more or less term should include three parts: (1) _____;

(2) _____;

(3) _____.

8. At the time of the conclusion of a contract, the quantity clause should be _____ stipulated so as _____.

III. Please give the following definitions for the names in English.

1. gross weight

2. net weight

3. actual tare

4. average tare

5. customary tare

6. computed tare

IV. Briefly answer the following questions.

1. 简述订好数量条款的意义。

2. 简述各计量单位适用的范围。

3. 重量的计算方法有哪些？

V. Please determine whether the following statements are True or False. Then put T for True or F for false in the bracket at the end of each statement.

1. The quantity term of goods is one of the conditions of an effective sales contract.(   )

2. In international trade, only the Metric System is allowed to indicate the quantity of goods.(   )

3. If the parties to a sales contract do not in advance agree upon whether the quantity of goods is determined by gross weight or net weight, it will be determined by gross weight. (   )

4. Net weight refers to the actual tare of all the packing materials. (   )

5. Conditioned weight is, in fact, the actual weight of the moisture of a certain commodity. (   )

6. According to the CISG, if the quantity delivered by the seller is greater than that of the contract, the buyer can refuse all the goods. (   )

7. If a buyer has taken delivery of the excess quantity, he holds the right of not paying for it. (   )

8. The More or Less Clause in a sales contract allows the seller to deliver as many or as few goods as possible. (   )

9. The only weakness of delivering fewer goods than stipulated is that the seller gets less paid. (   )

10. Usually we can learn from shipping marks the destination and weight of the goods in transit. (   )

11. Indication marks are to show the capacity and place of origin of the goods in transit. (   )

12. Warning marks are to warn those who move goods of possible danger. (   )

VI. Case Study.

1. In 2010, a certain export company in China sent a group of businessmen to the United States for the purchase of equipment. In New York both parties reached an oral agreement on such items as specifications, unit price, and quantity. Upon leaving, the group indicated to the other party that, when they got back to Beijing, they would draw up a contract, which would become effective after being signed by both parties. After going back to Beijing, the group found that the clients withdrew their import of the equipment, and thus the contract was not signed and the L/C was not opened, either. The US side urged the Chinese side to perform the contract; otherwise they would lodge a claim with the Chinese side in the US.

Question:

How did the Chinese export company deal with this case in your opinion? why?

2. A Chinese export company sent on June 1st an offer to a businessman living in Italy, stipulating for the reply to reach them before June 10th. The Italian businessman cabled his acceptance of the offer on June 8. Because of the delay by the post office, the acceptance did not reach the Chinese company till on the morning of June 11th. And before receiving the acceptance,

the Chinese company was informed that the prices of the said products were rising rapidly.

Question:

What do you think is the best way for the Chinese company to deal with this case? Why?

3. A company purchased four kinds of steel plate: 420MT, and the type is 6 inch, 8 inch, 10 inch and 12 inch. The quantity is 100MT each size, and the contract marked that: "5% more or less for each size, at seller's option" When the seller delivered the goods, the quantity was: 6 inch-70MT; 8 inch-80 MT; 10 inch-60 MT;12 inch-210 MT. And the total quantity is 420 MT. When the exporter submits the full set of document, the importer refuses to receive the goods owing to quantity problems.

Question:

Do you think the importer's action is reasonable? List your reasons.

4. 我国某出口公司以 CIF 条件与意大利客商签订了一份出口 500 公吨大豆的合同，合同规定：双线新麻袋包装，每袋 50 千克，外销价为每公吨 200 美元 CIF 悉尼，即期信用证支付方式付款。我公司凭证出口并办妥了结汇手续。货到后买方来电称：我公司所交货物扣除皮重后不足 500 公吨，要求我方退回因短量而多收的货款。

问：

对方的要求是否合理，为什么？

5. 有一年我国外贸公司向德国出口大麻一批，合同规定水分最高 15%，杂质不超过 3%。但在成交前，我方曾向对方寄过样品，合同订立后我方又电告对方"成交货物与样品相似"。货到德国后，买方出具了货物品质比样品低 7%的检验证明，并要求赔偿 600 英镑的损失。我方拒绝赔偿，并陈述理由说：我方这批商品在交货时是经过挑选的，因为是农产品，不可能做到与样品完全相符，但也不至于品质比样品低 7%。

问：

我方失误在哪里？我方是否可以该商品并非凭样成交为由而不予理赔？

VII. Calculate and answer questions.

We import 20 MT wool from New Zealand. In the S/C, it indicated "20 MT". When we receive the wool, we find that the actual regaining rate of water is highly up to 33%. How much do we lose in this transaction? In the S/C, what kind of quantity clause is suitable for us to avoid such unnecessary losses?

VIII. Multiple Choices.

1. Contracts must be renewed one week (   ) their expiration.
     A. on   B. against   C. the moment of   D. before

2. The commodities you offered are (   ) line with the business scope of our clients.
     A. outside   B. out of   C. out   D. without

3. We are arranging for an inspection tour of (   ) the material was processed.
     A. place   B. the place   C. where   D. there

4. We are reconsidering those trade terms (   ) might be adverse to the interest of our principals.
     A. what   B. that   C. when   D. where

5. We find that there is no stipulation of transshipment (　　) in the relative L/C.

    A. allowing   B. which allows   C. which allowed   D. being allowed

6. After unpacking the case we found that the goods did not (　　) with the original sample.

    A. match   B. come up   C. agree   D. measure

7. If the first shipment (　　), we guarantee that we will send you many repeat orders.

    A. match   B. come up   C. agree   D. measure

8. It is necessary that an arbitration clause (　　) in the contract.

    A. will be included   B. must be included

    C. be included   D. has been included

9. Please see that your written confirmation (　　) by the end of this month, otherwise we will be free from the obligation for this offer.

    A. reaches us   B. will reach us   C. reach us   D. reached us

10. That helps to explain (　　) businesses are setting up net sites even though profits aren't yet very big.

    A. that   B. the reason for   C. why   D. why that

Chapter Seven

Part A Text

Packing and Marking of Goods

Whatever mode of transport is used, the product will require packing. Packing is a part of export business. In recent years, the significance of packing has been increasingly recognized, and today the widespread use of packing is truly a major competitive force in the struggle for markets. Sound packing will help promote the export sales; poor or insufficient packing affects both the exporter and the importer—and probably, in the long run, the exporter more than the importer. In practice, exporters are often confused between these two words: packing and packaging. Packaging refers to the job of providing specialized containers or wrapping materials for packaging of goods. Packing is used for the general operation of putting goods into containers for shipment and storage, i.e., transportation. These two words are sometimes used interchangeably in business.

Packing, in business practice, is one of the most important problems facing merchants engaged in foreign trade. It needs more care in export trade than domestic trade. The real art of packing is to get the contents into a nice, compact shape that will stay in perfect condition with nothing missing during the roughest journey. Every buyer expects that his goods will reach him in perfect condition. Nothing is more infuriating to a buyer than to find his goods damaged or part missing on arrival. It has been estimated that up to 70% of all cargo loss could be prevented by proper packaging and marking. Hence, in this respect, suitable packing is of great necessity and importance.

不论以何种方式运输，产品都需要包装，包装是出口贸易的一部分。近些年来，人们越来越意识到包装的重要性。今天，包装的广泛使用更成为争夺市场的一个重要竞争手段。出口商品的良好包装能够促进其销售，拙劣包装或包装不充分对进出口商品都会造成不良影响——从长远来看，对出口商更为不利。在实践中，出口商经常混淆这两个词：包装和包装方法。包装方法是指用特殊的装货容器或包装材料给货物打包。包装是指货物装船运输及库存的一般过程。在商业上，这两个词有时可以交换使用。

按照商业惯例，包装是从事国际贸易的商人所要面临的最重要的问题之一。出口贸易中的包装必须比国内贸易中的包装更为仔细。真正的包装艺术是把货物摆放成良好的、紧凑的形状，并能在颠簸的旅途中保持原状，不丢失。买方都希望货物完整无缺地到达自己手中，如果货物到达时，买方发现货物受损或部分丢失，这是很令人恼火的。据估计，大约 70%的货物损失可以通过恰当的包装和标记得以预防。所以，适当的包装是非常必要和重要的。

Section One　The Function of Packing（包装的作用）

Packing has become more and more important in competing for overseas markets. One of its basic purposes is to protect the product. This is important because the product may have to withstand rough handling during transportation between the factory and the consumer. The second purpose of packaging is to make the product look appealing to the buyer. Products that are packed in such a way as to catch the consumer's eyes will help to sell. Other common purposes of packing are to provide information about the product inside, make it easy to carry the product, and provide convenience in using the product. Therefore, more and more people, not only manufacturers, have come to realize the importance of packaging.

When thinking of the goods to be packed for shipment, exporters should try to anticipate the damages that are likely to occur in the transportation. We all know that the goods shipped to overseas destinations may involve greater damage than the shipment in the domestic country. So exporters should know well the common shipping problems such as rough handling, mishap at transshipment, excessive humidity or dryness and pilferage.

在争夺国外市场的过程中，包装变得越来越重要。包装的基本目的之一是保护产品。这一点很重要，因为在从工厂到用户手中的运输过程中，产品必须经历若干次的搬运。包装的第二个目的是使产品的外观能取悦买家。这样的产品包装能引起消费者的注意从而有助于销售。包装的另外一个常见目的是提供内在产品的信息，便于携带产品和使用产品。所以，不仅仅是生产厂家，越来越多的人开始意识到包装的重要性。

出口商在考虑货物包装运输时，必须考虑运输途中可能出现的各种风险。众所周知，运往国外目的港的货物比在国内运输的货物要冒更大的风险。因此，出口商必须了解运输途中的一般问题，如野蛮装卸、转船发生的灾难、过于潮湿或干燥、盗窃等问题。

1．Problems in transport（运输中的问题）

Generally speaking, goods sent by air are usually handled more carefully, although there are occasionally examples of mishaps such as goods arriving at the wrong destination or fresh vegetables arriving frozen. During the process of shipment, the packing cases in which the export goods are traveling may not be properly unloaded from the truck and may in fact be dropped. The crate may suffer from dragging, tumbling and lifting; it may be placed the wrong way up. If the crate is damaged at this stage, it will be vulnerable throughout the rest of its journey to the entry of dirt and to the attention or would-be pilferage. At the stage of loading the goods aboard a ship, slings, grabs and nets used may not be properly located, causing crushing from without and pressures from within. In the ship's hold, the crate may be subject to further dropping, tumbling, leveling or hooking. During the voyage, the movement of ships may cause fastenings of boxes or crates to become loose, the interior blocking and bracing to be dislocated, the walls of the boxes or crates to become punctured, and even some of the markings to become obliterated. The ship's constant movement causes the friction within the hold. When the box or crate is unloaded at the port of destination, the stevedores may be illiterate, and unable to read cautionary signs "This Side Up", even if printed in their own language. There may not be adequate covered storage available for the goods, sometimes even no proper unloading equipment. Numerous unexpected problems at any stage of the journey may occur. If the packing provided by the exporter is proper, sound and strong enough to sustain any rough and improper handling, all these can be avoided considerably.

一般来说，尽管偶尔会发生运输灾难，如货物运错目的港，或新鲜蔬菜到港时被冻坏了等问题，但航空运输的货物受到的保护会好很多。在装运码头装货的过程中，出口货物包装箱有可能没有从卡车上合适地搬运下来，而是从卡车上被扔下来；板条箱可能被拖来拖去，在地上翻滚或被高高吊起；如果此时板条箱破损，那么在整个运输途中，板条箱就会很容易被弄脏，或容易引起盗贼的注意而使货物被盗。在把货物装上货船的过程中，可能会由于对吊索、抓具、网子等装船工具使用不当而导致货物从外部受挤压，以至于内部货物受损变形的情况发生。在货仓里，板条箱可能会受到进一步的抛掷、滚动，或用杠杆搬移，或用挂钩吊起。在航行途中，船体的震动可能会使捆扎货箱的绳子松动，箱内固定货物的装置脱离原位，箱子的四壁被刺穿，甚至一些箱子的标记被毁掉。船体不停地颠簸也会引起仓内货物的相互碰撞，因而损坏货箱外部的标记。当这些包装箱运到目的港卸下货船时，装卸工人由于不识字而看不懂"此端向上"这样的注意事项。即使标有他们自己的文字说明，他们也有可能不认识这些字。而港口有可能没有足够或合适的地方存储这些货物，有时甚至连合适的装卸设备也没有。在货物的整个装运过程中或运输途中，都有可能出现这样或那样数不清的意想不到的问题。然而，如果货物的包装非常坚固、合适、完好，那么，所有这些问题都可以避免。

2. Purpose of packing（包装的目的）

It is because of all the problems that may occur during transportation that we have to pay great attention to packing. Before goods are packed, exporters should consider the purpose of the packing. In general, there are several objectives facing all exporters. So they have to make sure what objectives the goods are to be packed.

(1) Packing can be used to protect the goods and keep them as good and complete as they are shipped in the circulation field. Generally speaking, only packed commodities can enter into the circulation field, and attain the commercial value and use value of the goods.

(2) It makes the commodities convenient for storing, taking care of, transportation, loading, unloading, and calculating them. Cargo packing in design, namely dimension and configuration, should facilitate the most economical method of handling. This is particularly relevant to awkward shaped cargo. Moreover, it applies from the time the goods are packaged, which may be in the factory, until it reaches the importer's warehouse/distribution centre. Mechanical and computerized and high-tech cargo handling equipment is now in extensive use to reduce labor cost and speed up cargo handling.

(3) Strong packing can prevent the goods from being stolen and damaged. It can be used to improve standards to reduce risk of damage and pilferage. This in turn encourages competitive cargo insurance premiums and maintains good relations with the importer. Cargo received in a damaged condition seriously impairs the exporter's product overseas market prospects as it loses goodwill with the importer. Moreover, the exporter is ultimately obliged to replace the damaged goods, which can be a costly task.

(4) Reasonable packing can reduce shipping space and save freight. Good packing can ensure the lowest insurance premium.

(5) Marketing packing makes it convenient for consumers to select, carry, or use the goods.

(6) Marketing packaging can also beautify the commodity, attract consumers, expand sales and increase the gains on foreign exchange.

In addition to all those mentioned above, packing of the goods, in a sense, incarnate the level of a country's economic construction, science and technology, culture and art, etc.

正是由于货物在运输途中有可能遭遇各种风险，所以要特别重视货物的运输包装。在对货物进行包装之前，出口商应该仔细考虑包装的目的。一般来说，在包装时出口商可针对几种目的进行选择，其必须决定包装的主要目的是什么。

（1）包装可以保护商品免遭运输途中的损坏，一般来说，只有包装好的商品才能进入流通领域，并达到商品保值的目的。

（2）包装可以使商品方便存储、保管、运输、装卸和统计数量。货物的包装设计、尺寸以及结构应该有助于使用最经济的装卸方法。这对于形状不规则的货物运输尤其重要。此外，从货物最初在工厂包装的时候开始一直到货物抵达进口商的仓库/物流中心，这种做法一直贯穿其中。机械化、计算机化和高科技化的货物装卸设备现在已经广泛使用以减少劳动力成本并加速装卸速度。

（3）坚固的包装可以保护商品被盗和损坏，并可以提高减少损坏和盗窃风险的标准。这一点相应地促进了货物保险费的竞争力，并促进出口商与进口商保持良好的合作关系。如果收到受损货物，会严重损坏出口商海外市场销售的前景，因为这将使出口商丧失商誉。此外，出口商不得不替换受损的货物，这也需要付出很大的代价。

（4）合理的包装可以节省空间，节约运费，而良好的包装可以确保最低的保险费。

（5）销售包装可以方便客户挑选、搬运或使用。

（6）销售包装同样可以方便商品的美化，以吸引消费者，扩大销售量，有利于创汇。

除了上述功能外，从某种意义上说，包装的好坏体现了一个国家的经济、科学和技术的发展水平。

3. Practical suggestions for packing methods（包装方法的实质性建议）

There are three steps in export packing. The first step is to determine the hazards involved in shipping the goods to the foreign destination. The second step is to choose the type of box, crate, or container which is most suitable for the goods. Whenever possible, the package should be kept as small and light as you can make it. The third step is to ensure that certain guidelines are observed when the goods are actually packed.

(1) Protection from corrosion: Before goods are packed, materials which are liable to deterioration during transit should be properly treated with protection.

(2) Protection from damage: Poor packing may result in damage to goods in transit and cause annoyance and inconvenience to customers.

(3) Cartons should not be overfilled.

(4) Sharp edges on packages should be avoided.

(5) Measures of security against hazards and pilferage, fire, containerization corrosion, etc. should be attended to.

(6) Goods like tea must be carefully packed not only against the usual climate risks, but must also be sealed tightly so as to prevent it from absorbing odors and smells from the surrounding cargo.

(7) Food articles have to be packed very carefully and in sanitary cans.

(8) Cargoes shipped in bulk require little or no packing.

(9) As to the highly dangerous materials, the shipping companies do lay down specifications for packages.

(10) As for the goods packed in cases, it is better to line with waterproof material or cloth inside the cases.

出口包装有三个步骤。第一步，预测货物在运至国外目的地的过程中可能遭遇哪些危险。第二步，选择适合货物的盒子、箱子或集装箱。无论何时，包装都应尽量小而轻。第三步，在包装货物时应遵守准则。

（1）保护货物免遭损坏。包装之前，对那些在运输途中易变质的货物应该采取妥当的保护措施。

（2）保护货物以防破损。包装不当会导致货物在运输途中破损，给客户带来烦恼和不便。

（3）纸箱不能超量装载，必须按设计规定的重量装箱。

（4）包装避免边缘尖锐（否则，尖锐的边缘会磨损或割断绳子，甚至会损伤其他包裹）。

（5）应注意采取安全措施预防海上意外风险、偷窃、火灾、集装箱腐蚀等。

（6）有些商品，如茶叶必须仔细地密封包装起来。这不仅是为了使它免受气候变化的影响，而且可以防止它吸收周围货物的气味。

（7）对于食品的包装必须非常认真，应装在卫生的罐头盒中。

（8）散装物不需要什么包装。

（9）对于危险品的包装，船公司应有特殊的包装要求。

（10）包装箱必须用防水纸或防水布作为衬垫。

Section Two　Kinds of Packing（包装的种类）

1. Nude cargo, cargo in bulk/bulk cargo and packed cargo（裸装货、散装货及包装货）

The kinds of cargoes are various in international trade, from the point of view of whether they need packing, they fall into three kinds.

贸易中的货物是多种多样的，根据包装的不同可以分为以下三种。

1) Nude cargo（裸装货）

Nude cargoes or nude packed commodities refer to those kinds of cargoes whose qualities are more stable and to be shipped without packaging or in simple bundles. They are not easy to be influenced by outside circumstances and they become single pieces of their own. They are difficult to be packed or do not need any packing, such as steel products, lead ingot, timber, rubber, automobile, etc.

所谓裸装货是指有些商品的品质比较稳定，只要将商品略加捆扎或以其自身进行捆扎的货物。裸装方式适用于一些形态上自然成件，能抵抗外界影响，或品质稳定，难以包装的货物，如钢材、铅锭、木材、橡胶、车辆等。

2) Cargo in bulk/Bulk cargo（散装货）

Cargo in bulk refers to goods which are shipped or even sold unpackaged on the conveyance in bulk, such as oil, ore, grain, coal, etc. Cargoes in bulk can be transported, loaded and unloaded by conveyance and loading and unloading equipment designed particularly. Bulk shipment is usually applicable for large quantity of commodities that are to be shipped by means of transport with special purposed shipping equipment. Bulk shipment has the advantages of space saving, quick handling and lower freight.

所谓散装货是指未加任何包装、直接付运直至销售的货物，通常适用于不需要包装即可直接进入流通领域，或不容易包装或不值得包装的货物，如石油、煤炭、矿砂、粮食等。散装货的装卸和运输可以通过专门的散装货运输工具和设备进行。散装货运输通常适用于经由特别装运设备装运的大宗商品的运输和装卸。散装货的优点是节约舱位、装运快捷、运费低廉。

3) Packed cargo（包装货）

Most commodities in international trade need a certain degree of packing during the shipping, storing and sales process. Packed cargoes refer to those which need shipping packing, marketing packing or both.

国际贸易中大多数货物都需要某种程度的包装以便于运输、仓储和销售。所谓包装货是指需要运输包装、销售包装或两者都需要的货物。

2．Transport/Shipping packing and sales /marketing packing（运输包装和销售包装）

In international trade, according to the functions of the goods in the process of circulating and the packing materials and methods, packing can be divided into transport/shipping packing(also called outer packing) and sales/marketing packing (also called inner packing). A third kind of packing, neutral packing is also often used in international trade.

在国际贸易中，根据商品包装在流通过程中作用的不同、包装材料和包装方法的不同，包装可分为运输包装（又称外包装）和销售包装（内包装）。另一种包装——中性包装，也经常在国际贸易中使用。

1) Transport/shipping (Outer packing)（运输包装）

Transport/shipping is also called big packing or outside packing, or outer packing or giant packing. It is used mainly to keep the goods safe and sound during transportation. It must not only be solid enough to prevent the packed goods from any damage, but also be burglarproof, easy to store, convenient to load and unload and discharge. On the basis of packing materials and packing methods, transport packing includes the following types. See Table 7-1 Types of Packing Containers.

Table 7-1 Types of Packing Containers

Bag	May be made of strong paper, linen, canvas, rubber, etc.
Sack	A larger bag usually made of jute
Carton	Made of light but strong cardboard, or fiberboard with double lids and bottoms, fixed by glue, adhesive tapes, metal bands or wire staples. Sometimes a bundle of several cartons is made up into one package, held by metal bands
Case	A strong container made of wood. For extra strength it may have battens. Sometimes thinner wood may be used with metal bands or wires passed around the case. The inside of the case may be lined with various materials, e.g. damp-resisting paper, tin foil, etc. to prevent damage by water, air or insects
Box	A small case, which may be of wood ,cardboard or metal, and may have a folding (hinged) lid
Crate	This is a case, but one not fully enclosed. It has a bottom and a frame, sometimes open at the top. Crates are often built for the particular things they have to carry. Machinery packed in crates needs a special bottom(a skid) to facilitate handling
Drum	A cylinder-shaped container for carrying liquids, for carrying liquids, chemicals, paints, etc. It is usually made of metal. Certain dry chemicals(non-inflammable) or powders are sometimes packed in wood or cardboard drums
Bale	A package of soft goods (e.g. cotton, wool, sheepskin) tightly pressed together and wrapped in a protective material. Usually size30×15×15 inches. May be strengthened by metal bands
Can/Tin	A small metal container in which small quantities of paint, oil, or certain foodstuffs are packed
Carboy	A large glass container protected in a metal or wicker cage with soft packing between glass and cage. It is used for chemicals
Bundle	Miscellaneous goods packed without a container. A number of small cartons fixed together could be called a bundle
Container	A very large metal box for transport of goods by road, rail, sea or air. Packing goods in a large container facilitates loading and unloading by mechanical handling; thus time is saved
Pallet	A large tray or platform for moving loads (by means of slings) e.g. from a lorry into a train or onto a ship, and so save time for handling of separate items

　　运输包装又称外包装或大包装，它的作用主要在于保护运输途中的商品，同时使之便于防盗、运输、装卸、储存和分配。根据包装材料和包装方法，运输包装的容器分类如表7-1 所示。

表 7-1　包装容器的分类

袋	可用硬纸、亚麻布、帆布、橡胶等制成
麻袋	通常是由黄麻制成的大袋
纸箱	用轻且坚固的纸板或纤维板，双盖双底，用胶水、胶带、金属带或骑马钉固定。有时几个纸箱为一组，用金属带绑起来形成一个包装
箱	用木材做成的坚固容器。为使其更为坚固，可以加上板条。有时可用较薄的木材制成，并用金属带或金属丝缠绕箱子。箱内可用各种材料（如防湿纸、锡箔等）加衬，以保护商品免受由水、空气或虫子造成的损坏
盒	小箱子，用木材、纸板或金属制成，可带折叠盖
板条箱	一种没有完全封闭的箱子。它有一个底和一个框架，有时顶部敞开。板条箱通常是为运输某种特定的物品制作的。用板条箱包装的机械设备需要一个特制的底（滑动枕木）以便于操作

桶	用来装运液体、化学品、油漆等的圆柱状容器。通常用金属制成。一些干燥的化学品（不易燃烧）或粉末有时用木制或纸板桶包装
包	紧压在一起并用保护性材料包裹起来的柔软货物（如棉花、羊毛、羊皮）的包装。通常的尺寸是30×15×15英寸，可用金属带加固
罐/听	一种小的金属容器，用于包装少量的油漆、油或特定的食品
玻璃瓶	一种大的有金属或柳条罩防护的玻璃容器，玻璃与罩之间有软包装，用于装运化学品
捆	没有容器的混杂货物的包装。大量的小纸板箱放置在一起称为捆
集装箱	一种非常大的金属盒，用于陆路、铁路、海上或空中运输货物。用大集装箱装运货物便于用机械装卸，从而节省时间
托盘	一种大的盘子或平台，其通过吊索转移货物，如从卡车上转送到火车或货船上，以便节省单个货物的处理时间

The methods of transport/shipping packing usually fall into two kinds:

运输包装通常分为以下两种：

(1) Single piece packing（单件运输包装）

The cargoes are packed as a single unit, i.e., a measuring unit, in the transportation process. Single piece packing can be sub-divided into the following two kinds:

According to style: cases, drums, bags, bales, bundles, etc.

According to material: cartons, wooden cases, iron drums, wooden casks, plastic casks, paper bags, gunny bags, plastic bags, etc.

单件运输包装是指货物在运输过程中作为一个计件单位的包装，常被细分为以下两种。

按包装造型分有箱、桶、袋、包、瓶罐、捆等。

按使用材料分有纸箱、木箱、铁桶、木桶、塑料桶、纸袋、麻袋和塑料袋等。

(2) Collective packing（集合运输包装）

Collective packing is also called group shipping packing by which a certain number of single pieces are grouped together to form a big packing or are packed in a big container. Collective packing can be classified into.

集合运输包装是指在单件运输包装的基础上，为了适应运输、装卸作业现代化的要求，将若干单件包装组合成一件大包装。目前常见的组合包装有以下几种。

a. Container（集装箱）. The container is a kind of tool used for transportation which can be thought of as a particular shipping packing of the cargo, usually provided by the shipping companies to go around. At present, the specifications of containers in common use in the world are: those of the first series in ISO, including 1A, 1AA, 1B, 1C, 1D, 1E and 1F. When calculating the circulating quantity of container, we often take the 20-foot container as a measuring unit, i.e., TEU (Twenty-foot Equivalent Unit) to indicate it, it means "being equal to a 20-foot unit".

集装箱是指一种运输工具，被认为是一种特殊的运输包装，它一般由运输公司提供以便周转。目前，国际上普遍采用的集装箱是ISO的第一系列规格，包括1A、1AA、1B、1C、1D、1E和1F型号的集装箱。最常用的规格为8×8×20英尺（1C）的集装箱，其实际最大载货重量为 18 公吨，一般计算集装箱流通量时，都以这种规格为一个标准单位，称为 TEU（Twenty-foot Equivalent Unit），意为："20 英尺相当单位"。

b. Pallet（托盘）. The pallet is a kind of single-layer or double-layer flat carrier which is made according to a certain specification. Certain quantities of single pieces are packed collectively on the flat carrier and tied up in the light of the requirements to form a shipping unit, which makes it convenient to load, unload, lift and pile the goods by using machinery in the shipping process.

The pallet is usually made of wood, but it may also be made of plastic, or metal. The commonly used pallets are: flat pallets, box pallets, post pallets, etc.

A typical size is 1 000×1 200 (mm²), has a capacity of two metric tons, and in appearance, is like a platform on which the cargo is placed. An aperture is provided at each side to enable the fork lift truck to mobilize or handle the pallet.

Other size includes: 800×1 000, 800×1 200, 1 200×1 600, 1 200×1 800 (mm²).

这是一种单层或双层的平板载货工具，有其固定的尺寸大小规格。将货物堆放在托盘上，并根据装运要求加以固定，以方便装货、卸货、吊货、堆放货物等工作。托盘通常由木材制成，也可用塑料或金属等制作。常用的托盘有平板型、箱型、邮件型等类型。最典型的托盘是 1 000×1 200（平方毫米），装载量为 2 吨。从外表看，它像一个平台，上面可以堆放货物，托盘下面有插口，供铲车装卸使用。

其他推荐使用的尺寸有 800×1 000、800×1 200、1 200×1 600 和 1 200×1 800（平方毫米）。

c. Flexible container（集装包和集装袋）. The flexible container is a kind of round-shaped or square-shaped bag woven with synthetic fiber or compound material. The capacity varies with the material and production techniques used, usually from 1-4 MT. The maximum capacity can reach about 13 MT. The flexible container is suitable for powder or grain cargoes such as fertilizer, flour, sugar, cement, etc.

集装包和集装袋一般是指用合成纤维或复合材料编织成的圆形大口袋或方形大包。其容量一般为 1～4 公吨，最高可达 13 公吨。集装包和集装袋适用于粉状货物，如化肥、面粉、糖、水泥等。

2) Sales/Marketing packing (Inner packing)（销售包装）

Sales/marketing packing (also called inner packing, small packing, or immediate packing) is not only adopted as a form of protection to reduce the risks of goods being damaged in transit and prevent pilferage, but primarily to promote sales. It is now universally recognized as a decisive aid in selling household consumer goods. It can be realized in various forms and with different materials as long as it is nice to look at, easy to handle and helpful to the sales. The sales packing can be decided as wholesale package(package) and retail package(small package).

销售包装又称内包装、小包装或直接包装。它除了保护商品免受损坏和防盗以外，主要起促销的作用。现在，作为一种非常重要的辅助手段，它广泛应用于家庭消费品的销售。只要美观，便于操作和有利于销售，销售包装可采用各种形式和材料。销售包装可分为批发包装（包装）和零售包装（小包装）两类。

3) Neutral packing and brand designated by the buyer（中性包装和定牌）

(1) Neutral packing（中性包装）

The neutral packing means that there is neither a name of the origin, nor a name and address of the factory/manufacturer, nor a trade mark, a brand, nor any words on the (outer or inner) packing of the commodity or the commodity itself. The purpose of using neutral packing by exporters is to break down the tariff and non-tariff barriers of some countries or regions, or meet the special demand of the transaction (such as entrepot). It may also help the manufacturers in exporting countries to increase the competitiveness of their products, expand the exports, and market profitably in the importing countries. It is, sometimes, used as a strategy to a. achieve profitable marketing and b. to increase the competitiveness and c. expand sales. At present, using the neutral packing for the marketing packing of some exported commodities has become common practice in international trade.

中性包装是一种既不标明生产国、厂商的地名和名称，也不标明商标和牌子的包装。出口商采用中性包装的目的是打破某些进口国家和地区的关税或非关税壁垒，或适应交易的特殊需要（如转口销售）。它还能帮助生产厂商提高产品的竞争能力，对进口国扩大出口并赚取外汇。采用中性包装的目的可以是：a. 获利；b. 提高竞争力；c. 扩大销售。目前，某些出口商品中的销售包装形式采用中性包装已经成为许多贸易实务中比较常用的方法之一。

(2) Brands designated by the buyer（定牌）

Brands designated by the buyer refer to the packing goods according to the buyer's trademarks and brands by the buyer. As to the goods to be ordered regularly in large quantities for a long time by foreign customers, in order to expand sales, we can accept buyer-designated trademarks while indicating the manufacturing country mark, that is, the neutral packing with brands designated by the buyers.

Sometimes we may accept trade marks or brands designated by foreign buyers, but under the trade marks and brands, we indicate "Made in the People's Republic of China" or "Made in China". In some other cases, we may accept the designated trade marks or brands while indicating that the goods are made by a factory in the buyer's country, i.e., trade marks or brands and origins designated by the buyers.

定牌是指按买方要求在出口国商品和包装上使用买方指定的商标或牌名的做法。为了扩大销售，对于那些长期大量订购的外国客户，我方常按其要求接受其指定的商标，并根据其要求不加注生产国别标志，即定牌中性。

有时接受客户指定的商标，但在商标、牌名下标明"中华人民共和国制造"或"中国制造"字样；有时定牌可以用"××公司进口""××公司经销""××公司特制"等字样。

Section Three　Marking of Package（包装标志）

Classification of marking of package（包装标志的分类）

When talking about transport packing, packing marks(or marking of package) of course has to be referred to. Packing marks or recognition mark refers to different diagrams, words and figures which are written, printed, or brushed on the outside of the shipping packing in order that it is easy and convenient for goods' loading, unloading, storage, inspection and discharge. Packages should not be marked with crayons, tags, or cards. The best method of marking is stenciling the marks on the outside of the package. Some exporters paint the marks with a brush and indelible ink. All in all, the mark should be permanent and easily read at a glance.

According to the uses of the packing mark, it can be divided into shipping marks, indicative marks, warning marks and supplementary/additional marks, See Fig.7-1 kinds of packing marks.

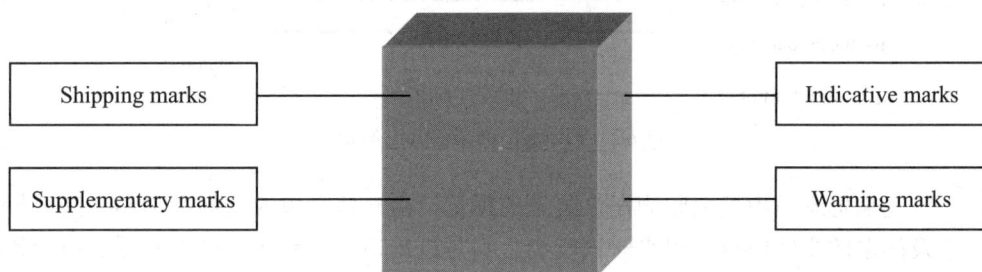

Fig.7-1 Kinds of Packing Marks

在运输包装上有时要涉及包装标志的问题。包装标志是指在商品的包装上书写、压印、刷制各种有关的标志，如图形、文字、数字等，以便识别货物，有利于装卸、运输、仓储、检验和交接工作的顺利进行。不能用粉笔、标签或卡片做包装标志。有的出口商用易保持的墨水刷运输标志，总之，无论如何，要使货物包装上的运输标志易于识别，一目了然。

包装标志根据用途可分为运输标志、指示性标志、警告性标志和附加标志四种，如图 7-1 所示。

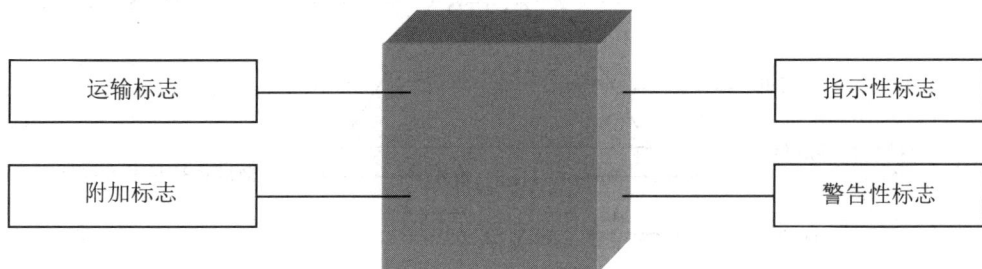

图 7-1 包装标志的分类

1. Shipping marks（运输标志）

Shipping marks are marks of simple designs, including letters, numbers and simple words on packages, often stenciled, that serve as identification of the consignment to which they belong. It is one of the most important elements which are agreed upon by the exporter and the importer in a sales contract. The shipping mark consists of.

(1) Name or code of destination.

(2) Code of consignee or consignor.

(3) Piece number, serial number, contract number or license number.

An example of shipping marks is illustrated as follows (See Fig.7-2).

```
The consignee ——————→       ABC         ←—————— Triangle-shaped
                             Co. LTD,              shipping mark

Destination ——————→
                             New York

The first one of the
total 600 packages ——————→   Nos.1-600    ←—————— The total 600
                                                  packages
The contract number ——————→  80MST-6997
```

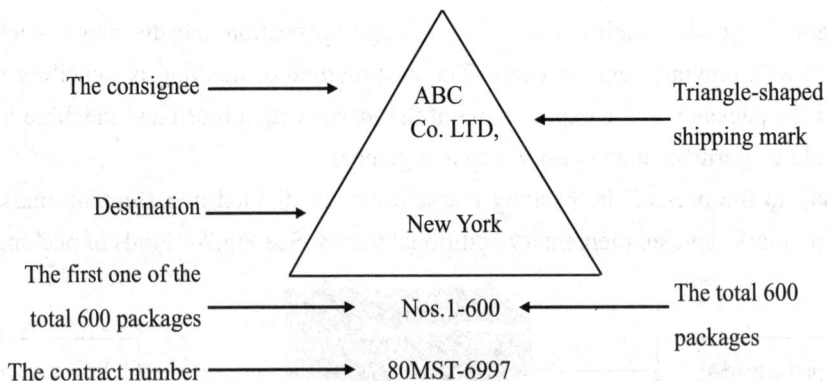

Fig.7-2   Example of Shipping Marks

　　运输标志是用模板印刷在包装上的标记，由一些简单的几何图形和一些字母、数字及简单的文字组成，用来辨识货物。它是进出口商在销售合同里必须达成一致的几个最重要的事项之一。运输标志由以下几部分构成。

（1）目的地的名称或代号。

（2）收货人和发货人的代号。

（3）件号、批号、合同号或许可证号。

下面是运输标志的一个例子，如图 7-2 所示。

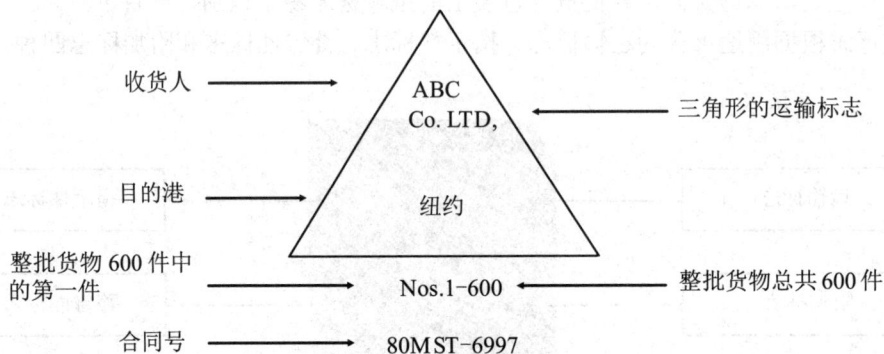

```
收货人 ——————→        ABC          ←—————— 三角形的运输标志
                      Co. LTD,

目的港 ——————→
                      纽约

整批货物 600 件中
的第一件 ——————→      Nos.1-600     ←—————— 整批货物总共 600 件

合同号 ——————→        80MST-6997
```

图 7-2   运输标志举例

Simple shipping marks are generally made up of four parts.

(1) Consignee's code

The consignee's codes are usually indicated by different geometrical diagrams, such as triangles, diamonds, circles, squares, etc. with letters inside them as the main marks.

(2) Consignor's code

Letters are usually printed inside or outside the diagrams to represent the consignor's code.

(3) Name or code of destination

To avoid ambiguity, full destination names are used. If there happen to be two same names of different destinations in the world, the name of the country must also be printed after the name of the destination in order to avoid wrong delivery.

e.g.: ARATRA CO.

    S/C NO.: 975530

    L/C NO.: 601225

    TRIPOLI

    (LIBYA)

    CTN/NO. 1-1 000

If transshipment is needed, the port of transshipment must be indicated.

e.g.: In Transit Hong Kong

e.g.: London Via Hong Kong

(4) Package number/piece number

Below the name of the destination is usually placed the package number. Packages may be numbered consecutively or marked merely with a total number.

运输标志通常由以下四部分内容组成。

（1）收货人的代码

一般为自己设计的图形和收货人的代号，如三角形、菱形、圆形或方形，里面刷有主要标识。

（2）发货人的代码

一般刷在几何图形的里面或外面，表示发货人的代码。

（3）目的港（地）的名称或代码

一般来说，表示目的港的标识都不用缩写，以免引起歧义。如果碰巧有两个相同的目的港，那么就要把国家全名表示出来，以免出错。

如：ARATRA 公司（收货人英文缩写）

    S/C NO.: 975530（合同号）

    L/C NO.: 601225（信用证号）

    的黎波里（利比亚）（目的地）

    件号 1-1 000（货物件号）

如果需要转船，那么转船地点也要写清楚。

如：经由香港转船

如：经香港转运至伦敦

（4）件号标志

件号标志一般放在目的港下面。件号数字可以是从 1 到最后总数这样一个连贯的数字，也可以是最后的一个总数。

2. Indicative marks（指示性标志）

We usually make use of the simple, noticeable design, remarkable diagrams and simple words on the packages to remind the relevant workers to pay attention to the items when they load, unload, carry and store the goods, such as: HANDLE WITH CARE,THIS SIDE UP(See Fig.7-3), etc. These are printed in black color generally.

人们通常会在包装上使用简单、醒目的图形和文字标出货物在运输、装卸、搬运、保管过程中应注意的事项，如"小心轻放""此端朝上"等（如图7-3所示）。指示性标志一般应印成黑色。

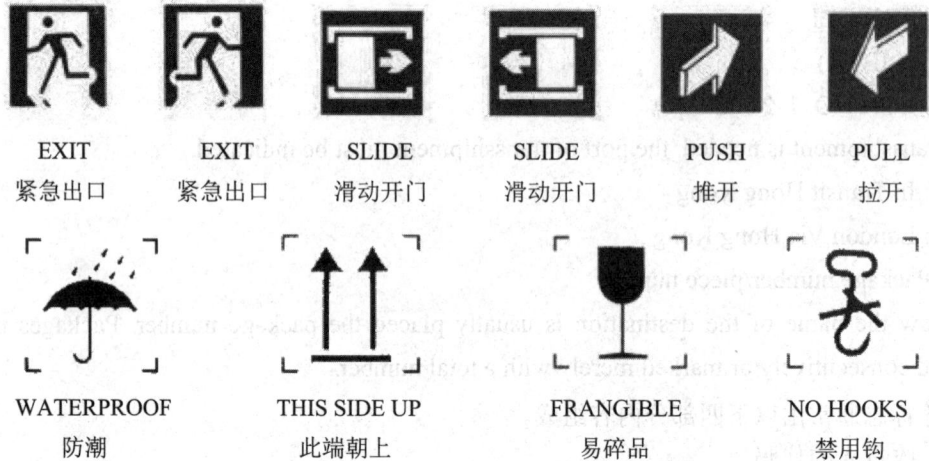

EXIT 紧急出口	EXIT 紧急出口	SLIDE 滑动开门	SLIDE 滑动开门	PUSH 推开	PULL 拉开

WATERPROOF 防潮	THIS SIDE UP 此端朝上	FRANGIBLE 易碎品	NO HOOKS 禁用钩

Fig.7-3　Some Indicative Marks（一些指示性标志）

The following are some common markings and phrases:
以下是一些常见的标志和用语：
NEW YORK IN TRANSIT　运往纽约
DO NOT DROP　切勿乱摔
NOT TO BE LAID FLAT　切勿平放
USE NO HOOKS　请勿用钩
STOW AWAY FROM HEAT　切勿受热
NO TURNING OVER　切勿倒置
OPEN HERE　此处打开
THIS SIDE UP　此端向上
PORCELAIN, WITH CARE　小心，瓷器
INFLAMMABLE　易燃品
CANADA VIA HONG KONG　经香港运往加拿大
CENTER OF GRAVITY　重心点
LIQUID　液体
NO DUMPING　切勿投掷
DO NOT CRUSH　切勿挤压
HANDLE WITH CARE　小心轻放
PERISHABLE GOODS　易腐物品
FRAGILE　易碎物品
GUARD AGAINST DAMP　防潮
KEEP FLAT　必须平放

SLIDING HERE　从此处吊起

KEEP IN DARK PLACE　暗处存放

KEEP DRY　保持干燥

3. Warning marks（警告性标志）

The warning mark is also called the dangerous cargo mark or shipping mark for dangerous commodities, which is brushed/printed clearly and prominently on the shipping packaging of the inflammable, explosive, poisonous, corrosive or radioactive goods, so as to provide warnings to the workers/dockers/crew.

Warning marks are usually made up of simple geometric diagrams, word descriptions, and specific pictures. Regarding this, every country usually has its own stipulation. For example, China has promulgated Indicative Marks for Packing, Storage and Transportation and Warning Marks for Packing Dangerous Cargoes.

警告性标志又称危险货物包装标志，是指凡在运输包装内装有爆炸品、易燃物品、有毒物品、腐蚀物品、氧化剂和放射性物质等危险货物时，都必须在运输包装上标明用于各种危险品的标志，以示警告，使装卸、运输和保管人员按货物特性采取相应的防护措施，以保护物资和人身的安全。

警告性标志是由文字和特定的图案组成的，各国都有自己国家的规定，如我国已颁布了《包装储运指示标志》和《危险货物包装标志》。

The common warning marks printed on the outer package are:

外包装上常印制的警告性标志有：

INFLAMMABLE COMPRESSED GAS　易燃压缩气体

EXPLOSIVES　爆炸品

CORROSIVES　腐蚀剂

POISON　有毒品

MATERIAL RADIOACTIVES　放射物品

HAZARDOUS ARTICLE　危险物品

OXIDIZING MATERIAL　氧化剂

See Fig. 7-4

DANGER OF FIRE-
HIGHLY FLAMMABLE
MATERALS
当心火灾——易燃物质

DANGER OF FIRE-
OXIDIZING MATERALS
当心火灾——氧化物

DANGER OF EXPLOSION-
EXPLOSIVE MATERALS
当心爆炸——爆炸性物质

Fig.7-4　Examples of Warning Marks（警告性标志举例）

4. Supplementary (or Additional) marks（附加标志）

Supplementary marks are any official marks required by authorities. Some countries require the country of origin to be marked on every package, and weight and dimensions may also be required.

附加标志是有关当局所要求的正式标志。一些国家要求商品的包装上标明原产地、重量和尺寸。

Recently, packing has been developing rapidly. To catch up with the packing trend, management has two parts for considering a package change: to combat a decrease in sales, and to expand a market by attracting new groups of customers. Packing terms in the contract are extremely important for the exporter. They are often written in this way: "Goods must be packed in…". Sometimes the buyer may ask the exporter to pack the goods according to his design. If his requirements can be met by you, you can accept his terms. Otherwise, try to persuade the buyer to adopt your own or traditional packing instead. Sometimes neutral packing is offered.

近些年来，包装业在迅速地发展，为了赶上世界包装新趋势，在考虑改进包装时，管理部门要注意两点：挽回逐渐下降的销售额以及吸引新顾客来扩大市场。合同中的包装条款对出口商极为重要，它经常以这种形式写在合同中："货物必须装在……。"有时，买方可要求出口商按其设计包装货物。如果能做到，你可以答应其条件。否则，尽量劝说买方使用你自己设计或是传统的包装。有时也使用中性包装。

Section Four   Factors Influencing Types of Cargo Packing（影响包装形式的各种因素）

1. Value of goods（货物价值）

In general, high-value consignment usually attracts more extensive packing than the low-value merchandise. Much, of course, depends on the nature of the commodity. If packing is inadequate, bearing in mind transit and declared cargo valuation, problems could be experienced with carriers' liability, acceptance and adequate cargo insurance coverage. Moreover, high-value consignments, such as a valuable painting, require adequate security and likewise attract higher freight rates. Such packing must be done professionally.

大体上说，价格昂贵的商品其包装费用要比低价商品贵很多，当然在很大程度上这要取决于商品类型。值得注意的是，如果包装不妥，在转运、货物申报估价的过程中，承运人的责任范围、验收及其是否有足够的保费等都可能出现问题。此外，对于高价值的货物托运，例如贵重的油画，保安工作十分重要，同样也会带来更高的运费。这样的包装非常专业化。

2. Nature of the transit（运输类型）

The type and length of transit is another factor that can influence packing. Is the movement national or transglobal? What form of transport will be used during the transit—road, rail, short-sea, deep-sea, or air? All have varying characteristics which make varying demands of the packaging of the goods. Furthermore, one must consider the method of shipment; it may be break-bulk, LCL, or FCL.

运输类型及距离是影响包装的因素。运输范围是国内的还是国际的呢？在运输过程中将使用什么形式——公路、铁路、近海、深海还是航空？所有这些运输形式都具有不同特点，所以对货物的包装形式都有不同要求。另外，还必须考虑装运方法，它可以是非集装箱化、拼装集装箱和整装集装箱。

3. Nature of cargo（货物类型）

This concerns the characteristics of the goods concerned and their susceptibility to various loss/damage. This factor, together with item 2, are the two major factors which determine the type of packing for an individual consignment. Cargo shipped in bulk requires little or no packing, while general merchandise needs adequate packing. For example, apples can be consigned in cases, boxes, cartons or pallet boxes. Grain, ores and coal are all shipped in bulk.

这涉及所装运货物的特征以及它们对于各种损失/损坏的敏感程度。本条因素和上面的第2条因素是决定单独托运需要采取哪种包装类型的主要因素。散装货的运输只需要少量的包装或者无包装，而普通商品则需要足够的包装。例如，苹果可用箱子、盒子、纸箱或托盘集装箱来运输；粮食、矿石及煤炭都是散装运输的。

4. Compliance with customs or statutory requirements（符合海关法或法规要求）

This is particularly relevant to dangerous cargoes where strict regulations apply both by air and sea concerning the carriers' acceptance, packing, stowage, documentation, marking and carriers' liability. In the EU, stringent regulations exist under the European Packaging Waste Legislation of 2001. This embraces a high proportion of packaging to be recovered and recycled after use.

In some countries, straw is an unacceptable form of packing due to the risk of insects being imported. Quarantine regulations are particularly extensive in Australasia, where materials such as wood products, rice husks, straw, and similar plant materials may not be used as packing materials or dunnage. This ensures that all packing materials are free from soil and contamination from animal products which can harbor pests, particularly insects, which are capable of causing wholesale devastation in forests. If the exporter does use wood, it is advisable to have it suitably treated, namely by fumigation, kiln drying, or impregnation, and to obtain a certificate to this effect for dispatch to the importer. If in doubt, the exporter is advised to consult their agent.

这一点尤其与危险物品运输有关，这类货物的空运和海运在承运人验收、包装、装载、单证、标记和承运人的责任方面都有严格规定。由于在 2001 年颁布实施了《欧洲包装废弃物法》，欧盟有着严格的法律法规。这其中规定了很大比例的包装废弃物要重新包装并循环使用。

在一些国家，由于存在昆虫入境的风险，麦秆是一种不被接受的包装形式。检疫规定在澳大利亚使用得特别广泛，因为诸如木材制品、稻壳、麦秆和类似的植物材料不能被用作包装材料或垫舱物料。这一点是为了保证所有的包装材料不受到土壤和畜产品的污染，因为畜产品可能会携带有害物，尤其是昆虫，它可能会引起森林的整体毁坏。如果出口商一定要使用木材包装，则建议对其进行适当的处理，即烟熏、窖干或浸渍，从而获得准许货物发送到进口商的证明。如果拿不定主意，建议出口商咨询其代理人。

5. Resale value, if any, of packaging material in the importer's country（进口商国家包装材料的转卖价值）

In some developing countries, large drums, wooden cases, or bags have a modest resale value. This helps to offset the packaging cost.

在一些发展中国家，大的圆桶、木质箱或袋子都拥有一定的转卖价值，这一点有利于降低包装成本。

6. General fragility of cargo（货物的整体易碎性）

In most cases, the more fragile the cargo is, the greater amount of packaging required.

大多数情况下，货物越容易碎，需要的包装程度就越高。

7. The international consignment delivery terms of sale （国际委托运送货物的销售条款）

Again, the actual packing specification may be contained therein and it is important to take into account who will bear the cost. The traders can refer to packaging in Incoterms 2010.

又一次将实际的包装规格包含其中，而且考虑谁将承担这项费用是十分重要的。贸易双方可参考 Incoterms 2010 中的有关包装的内容。

8. Variation in temperature during the course of transportation（运输途中温度变化）

During transportation, temperature variation can be quite extensive, so packaging must take account of this to permit the cargo to breathe and avoid excessive condensation/sweating.

在运输过程中，温度会发生很大变化，所以包装时必须考虑这一点，从而使货物保持通风并避免冷凝、返潮。

9. Easy handling and stowage（易于处理和装卸）

Awkwardly shaped cargoes packed in cartons or containers can greatly facilitate stowage, particularly in containers and using mechanical cargo handling equipment. Cargo stowage and obtaining the maximum practical utilization of available transport unit capacity are areas worthy of study to lower unit distribution cost. Likewise, if awkwardly shaped cargoes are conveniently packed this will speed cargo handling. Moreover, cargoes of awkward shapes can attract additional handling charges and freight surcharges in some circumstances. Furthermore, such cargoes are more vulnerable to damage and could therefore attract higher cargo insurance premiums.

形状不规则的货物使用纸箱或集装箱能够极大地方便装卸，尤其是在使用集装箱和机械化货物处理设备的时候。为了降低单位货物成本，货物的装载以及如何最切合实际地使用可用运输单元的装载能力，都是值得研究的领域。同样，如果形状不规则的货物能很合适地进行包装，这样也能加快货物处理速度。另外，此类货物更易于损坏，因此还需要收取更高的货物保险费。

10. The size of the cargo and its weight（货物尺寸及重量）

Basically there are three main considerations to consider when determining the form that a package should take: size, shape, and strength.

在确定应该采用何种包装形式时，要注意三个方面：尺寸、形状和强度。

11．Marketing consideration（营销因素）

An overriding consideration, certainly for consumer goods and increasingly so for industrial products, is that the package should fit into the overall marketing concept.

这对于日用消费品肯定如此，对于目前越来越多的工业产品来说，一个首要考虑的因素就是包装应该适合总体营销的概念。

12．Marking of cargo packaging（货物包装标志）

Each package must bear a marking code and use symbols to ease handling.

每个包装都必须印有标记代码，并且使用易于处理的符号。

13. Cost of packaging（包装成本）

This has become an increasingly important aspect in deciding on the type of packaging. In a world where overseas markets are becoming more competitive, the exporter is constantly exploring ways and means of reducing distribution cost and improving marketing techniques. Packaging features very much in this evaluation.

这一点正日益成为决定包装类型的一个重要方面。当海外市场竞争越来越激烈的时候，出口商一直在寻找缩减物流成本和提高营销技巧的方式方法，包装在成本评估过程中起着非常重要的作用。

Section Five　Elements Concerning Cross-border E-commodity Packaging and Platform Requirements（跨境电子商务时代商品包装应该考虑的要素和平台包装要求）

1. Elements concerning cross-border e-commodity packaging（跨境电子商务包装设计考虑因素）

In the era of cross-border e-commerce, merchants tend to carry out the commodity (product) packaging design from three aspects: the protective function of the goods, the convenience function, and the sales function.

在跨境电子商务时代，商户在进行商品（产品）包装设计时，通常从商品的保护性功能、便利性功能和销售性功能三个方面进行考虑。

1) "Special positioning" for online shopping goods（网购商品的"专供"定位）

Now that online shopping goods have already become a form of consumer behavior in the 21st century, occupying   more and more market shares, from the stage of packaging at the place of the manufacturers, the feature of "online shopping goods" should be considered. That means the packaging of online shopping goods should be separated from traditional commodities (off line) packaging when they are delivered by the factory. So with "special positioning" for online shopping goods, commodity packaging design will be of clear purpose and direction, also avoiding unnecessary charges for packaging.

既然网购商品已经是 21 世纪消费行为中的一种形式，而且所占份额越来越大，那么从生产厂家出产产品进行包装的时刻，就要考虑部分产品是"专供"网购的。即网购商品从产品出厂时的包装就与传统商品（网下）包装分开。这样有了网购商品的"专供"定位，商品的包装设计目的与方向就会很明确，也避免了不必要的包装费用的支出。

2) The "function first" principle（"功能至上"的原则）

In e-commerce, customers do goods shopping in a direct contact manner with the goods (image) and instructions about the goods, and thus they do not need to contact packaging or understand the goods from the packaging, therefore, this fails some of the functions of the packaging such as the beautification function, the display function, etc.. At this point, the commodity packaging design principle is "function first". The "function" mainly refers to the security protection function design, which is separated from "promotion", "beautification", "display" and other decorative designs. The all-around security of online commodity packaging design includes the security in the aspects of production, transportation, loading and unloading, storage, distribution, as well as in the links of secondary packaging, such as express.

顾客网购商品是直接接触商品（图片）和商品的有关说明，无须接触包装或从包装上了解商品，因此包装促销性功能中的美化功能、展示功能、吸引功能等毫无作用了。此时，商品包装设计原则就是"功能至上"。这个"功能"主要是指安全保护性功能设计，是针对"促销""美化""展示"等装饰性设计而言的。网购商品包装设计一切围绕商品的安全性，包括出厂、运输、装卸、储存、分发、二次包装、快递送货等环节中的安全性。

3) Identification of product and customer information（商品与顾客信息识别）

The currently adopted online packing is mostly plastic bags, corrugated cartons, plastic foam boxes and paper tape, etc. Some packaging like packages, is wrapped in a layer of a layer with adhesive tape paper, with a form almost like trash. Again, the above product information and customer information on the box are handwritten or copied, which is very vague. Due to the similar size and shape, the same material, the packing bags of approximate colour and lustre, even the couriers find it difficult to identify the goods. Customers identify the goods basically based on their memory of the purchase, or else they have to open the package to know what's inside. How to use colour and shape of the packing box (bag), marks and clear information program design to better assist the customers identify the goods is a vital issue for cross-border e-commerce.

目前采用的线上包装主要为塑料袋、瓦楞纸箱、泡沫塑料盒和纸胶带等。有些包装（如包裹）会用胶带纸层层缠绕，外观几乎像垃圾。此外，包装箱上的上述产品信息和客户信息多为手写或复印，内容非常模糊。由于尺寸形状相近、材质相同、包装袋色泽相近，甚至快递员都难以识别货物。消费者识别货物基本依赖购买时的记忆，否则必须拆开包装才能知道里面装的是什么。如何通过包装箱（袋）的颜色与形状、标识及清晰的信息方案设计，更好地辅助消费者识别货物，是跨境电商的一个关键问题。

2. Differences between packaging of digital trade products and packaging of traditional trade products（数字贸易产品包装与传统货物贸易的产品包装的差异）

The packaging of digital trade products is different from that of traditional goods trade products. Digital trade product packaging refers to the combination of advanced digital technology and traditional packaging concepts to meet the special needs of digital products. Currently, digital product packaging is widely used in digital trade, especially in cross-border e-commerce platforms, and it is also different from the innovation of digital technology.

Firstly, Augmented Reality (AR) packaging is designed for digital trade products. Consumers of digital trade, especially cross-border e-commerce platforms, can interact with digital trade product packaging using their mobile phones or tablets, with the aim of obtaining more information about digital trade products or experiencing virtual reality effects of digital trade products, enhancing the connection between digital trade brands and consumer groups.

Secondly, digital trade products emphasize sustainable and environmentally friendly packaging. With the promotion of a low-carbon economy, digital trade products use renewable materials, reduce packaging waste, and promote a circular green economy to meet consumers' concerns about the environmental commitments of digital trade brands and cross-border e-commerce platforms.

Thirdly, personalized intelligent packaging is needed for digital trade products. Through data analysis, especially in combination with Internet of Things (IoT) technology, personalized intelligent packaging for digital trade products can not only track product status and location, improve transportation safety, but also understand consumer preferences and timely needs of digital trade products, provide customized and unique packaging for the consumer end, increase the brand's sense of technology, and enhance the emotional marketing effect between the brand and consumers.

数字贸易产品包装与传统货物贸易的产品包装有着不同点,数字贸易产品包装是指将先进的数字技术与传统包装理念相结合,以满足数字产品的特殊需求的产品包装。当前,数字产品包装在数字贸易特别是跨境电商平台中得到广泛应用,同时也随着数字技术创新而不同。

第一,数字贸易产品增强现实（AR）包装。数字贸易特别是跨境电商平台的消费者可使用自己的手机或平板电脑端与数字贸易产品包装进行互动,目的是获取更多的数字贸易产品信息或数字贸易产品体验虚拟现实效果,增强数字贸易品牌与消费群体的连接。

第二,数字贸易产品重视可持续环保包装。随着低碳经济的推进,数字贸易产品使用可再生材料、减少包装废物,并提倡循环绿色经济,满足消费者对数字贸易品牌、跨境电商平台环保承诺的关注。

第三,数字贸易产品的个性化智能包装。通过数据分析,特别是与物联网（IoT）技术结合,数字贸易产品的个性化智能包装不仅可以追踪产品状态和所处位置,提高运输安全性,还可以了解数字贸易产品的消费者偏好和及时需求,提供面向消费端的定制化独特包装,增加品牌的科技感,同时增强品牌与消费者间的情感营销效果。

3. Amazon platform requirements for product packaging（亚马逊平台对产品包装的要求）

The packaging of cross-border e-commerce products needs to comprehensively consider multiple aspects such as platform requirements for product packaging, material selection, design considerations, environmental trends, and technological innovation. Taking the requirements for product packaging on Amazon, the world's largest cross-border e-commerce platform, as an example, Amazon platform has quite strict requirements for product packaging. Here are some related packaging requirements and precautions.

跨境电子商务产品的包装需要综合考虑平台对产品包装的要求、材料选择、设计注意事项以及环保趋势与技术创新等多个方面。以全球最大跨境电子商务平台亚马逊平台对产品包装的要求为例，亚马逊平台对产品包装的要求相当严格。以下是一些相关的包装要求和注意事项梳理。

1) General packaging requirements（一般包装要求）

(1) Protect platform products: The packaging should be sturdy enough to prevent unnecessary product damage during transportation, distribution, and storage.

(2) Labels and barcodes: Each packaging unit on the Amazon platform should be accompanied by clear and accurate labels and barcodes for Amazon FBA warehouse employees to accurately identify and scan.

(3) Compliance: The packaging should comply with all relevant legal and regulatory requirements, including but not limited to environmental and safety regulations.

（1）保护平台产品：包装应足够坚固，以防止在运输、配送和存储过程中造成不必要的产品损坏。

（2）标签和条码：每个亚马逊平台包装单元都应附有清晰准确的标签和条形码，以便亚马逊 FBA 仓库员工准确识别和扫描。

（3）合规性：包装应符合所有相关的法律法规要求，包括但不限于环保、安全等方面的规定。

2) Packaging requirements for specific categories of products（特定类别的包装要求）

(1) Sharp products（尖锐商品）

Starting from April 14, 2025, the Amazon platform has put forward new requirements for the packaging of sharp products:

a. Anti-cut and anti-puncture materials: Anti cut and anti-puncture packaging materials must be used, such as hardened plastic or vacuum formed packaging, to ensure that sharp parts are completely covered. Do not use bubble wrap, regular cardboard boxes, or other easily punctured materials.

b. Packaging design standard: The packaging must be completely sealed, stable, and not easily damaged and must pass the 1.2-meter drop test and 50kPa compression test.

c. Packaging responsibility: The seller is responsible for the entire packaging of the product, including the entire process from production to delivery to the Amazon logistics center. Amazon no longer provides supplementary packaging services. If the packaging is not compliant, the product will be directly destroyed, and the cost of destruction will be borne by the seller.

自 2025 年 4 月 14 日起，亚马逊平台对尖锐商品的包装提出了全新要求：

a. 防割、防刺穿材料：必须使用防割、防刺穿的包装材料，如硬化塑料或吸塑包装，确保尖锐部分被完全覆盖。禁止使用气泡膜、普通纸箱或其他易刺穿材料。

b. 包装设计标准：包装需完全封闭，稳固且不易破损。必须通过 1.2 米跌落测试和 50kPa 抗压测试。

d. 包装责任：卖家需全程负责商品的包装，包括从生产到送达亚马逊物流中心的全程包装。亚马逊不再提供补充包装服务。若包装不合规，商品将被直接销毁，且销毁费用由卖家承担。

(2) Other specific products（其他特定商品）

a. Liquids, pastes, gels or creams: sealed containers should be used to prevent leakage.

b. Paint and coatings: Ensure container sealing to avoid contamination.

c. Clothing, fabrics, and textiles: Use dust-proof bags or plastic bags for packaging.

d. Fluffy products: Wrap with bubble wrap to prevent deformation.

e. Infant and toddler products: Use non-toxic and odorless packaging materials.

f. Granular, powdery, and granular products: Seal with plastic bags to prevent scattering.

g. Small commodities: Package in hard boxes or plastic bags.

h. Batteries: Use a dedicated battery packaging box to prevent short circuits.

i. Jewelry category: Wrap with soft materials to avoid scratching.

j. Glass, ceramics, fragile products: Use bubble film and foam pad for multi-layer protection.

a. 液体、糊剂、凝胶或膏霜类：应使用密封容器，防止泄漏。

b. 油漆涂料：确保容器密封，避免污染。

c. 服饰、布料及纺织品：使用防尘袋或塑料袋包装。

d. 绒毛商品：用气泡膜包裹，防止变形。

e. 婴幼儿用品：使用无毒、无味的包装材料。

f. 颗状、粉状和粒状产品：用塑料袋密封，防止散落。

g. 小型商品：使用硬质盒子或塑料袋包装。

h. 电池：使用专用电池包装盒，防止短路。

i. 珠宝首饰类：用软质材料包裹，避免刮擦。

j. 玻璃、陶瓷、易破易碎品：使用气泡膜和泡沫垫多层保护。

(3) Packaging size and weight restrictions（包装尺寸和重量限制）

a. Carton size: The size of any side of the carton in North America, Europe, the Middle East, India, Australia, and Singapore cannot exceed 63.5 centimeters, unless the size of the product itself exceeds this limit.

b. Carton weight: The maximum load-bearing capacity of cartons is also specified, and cartons exceeding a certain weight need to be labeled accordingly.

a. 纸箱尺寸：北美、欧洲、中东、印度、大洋洲、新加坡站的纸箱任意一边尺寸不能超过 63.5 厘米，除非商品本身尺寸超出此限制。

b. 纸箱重量：纸箱的最大承重也有具体规定，超过一定重量的纸箱需贴上相应的标签。

(4) Pre shipment inspection（发货前检查）

Before shipment, the seller should conduct a strict inspection of the packaging to ensure compliance with the packaging requirements of the Amazon platform. This includes checking the integrity, stability, and accuracy of the packaging and labels.

在发货前，卖家应对包装进行严格检查，确保符合亚马逊平台的包装要求。这包括检查包装的完整性、稳固性以及标签的准确性等。

Part B Terminology Practice

1. **Acquisition**（采购）：The process through which resources are obtained to meet determined requirements, methods include purchase, rent, lease, or borrowing.

2. **Certificate of packing and unpacking**（装卸证明）：The document showing the extent of packing and unpacking performed by the agent.

3. **Container (carton)**[集装箱（纸箱）]：A sturdily constructed box used in packing.

4. **Equipment**（设备）：Any item with a unit price of USD500 or more (including freight and installation) that does not lose its identity by incorporation into a larger unit and has an expected life of over two years.

5. **Hospitality**（招待室）：A room used for entertaining, i.e., cocktail party, etc. Usually a function room or parlor.

6. **Gas packing**（气体包装）：Packaging in a gas-tight container in which any air has been replaced by a gas that contains practically no free oxygen, such as commercial carbon dioxide or nitrogen.

7. **Grading**（分级）：The selection of produce for certain purposes. Produce is sorted for size, color, quality, ripeness, etc. and may be done manually or mechanically on sizing belts.

8. **Cubic Feet(CF)**（立方英尺）：Volume of a shipment using the most extreme dimensions in inches. The formula is: length(in) × width(in) × height(in)/1 728 = CF.

9. **Certified lumber**（认证木材）：Lumber that has been treated for parasites either through heat or chemicals, and then inspected to meet certification requirements. Non-coniferous (hardwood) and manufactured (plywood) lumber generally do not need to be certified.

10. **Class**（类别）：All items that are shipped are divided into various classifications that play a part in determining the cost to ship them. Different "Class" examples are electronics, machinery, and household goods. Each Class is assigned its own number (See "NMFC Number and Class").

11. **Crate**（板条箱）：A wooden box built around the product being shipped. Provides the best protection for items being shipped.

12. **Declared value**（申报价值）：Amount the shipper assigns any item or shipment. Not a declaration of insurance value. As with Release Value, insurance must be arranged for in advance of the shipment.

13. **Dimensional Weight (DW)**（体积重量）：Typically used for "air" or "international" shipments. Dimensional Weight is also considered "Billable Weight" (minimum charge) regardless of actual weight, if less than DW. The formula is: length(in) × width(in) × height(in)/194 = DW.

14. **Fulfillment**（订单货运履行）：The act of storing product, filling orders, and shipping for an outside company.

15. **Full Truck Load (FTL)**（整车运输）：Any shipment that takes up more than half a trailer

full, or the trailer is used for one shipment no matter how much room is used.

16. **Inside delivery**（室内交货）：The carrier will deliver the product inside the first room encountered through the closest ground-floor door to the street.

17. **Less Than Load (LTL)**（零担运输）：Any shipment that is less than half a trailer full, and can be moved with other shipments.

18. **Lift-gate service**（吊门服务）：A hydraulic platform on the rear of the trailer or truck that lifts items up or down. Typically used when item is very heavy (more than one person can safely handle) and there is no forklift or dock available to unload. Lift-gate services often incur additional charges.

19. **National Motor Freight Classification (NMFC)**（美国国家机动车货运分类）：Rules, regulations, and classifications pertaining to freight transported by a motor carrier.

20. **NMFC Number and Class**（分配给物品的分类号码）：Classification numbers assigned to an item dealing mostly with density. The class determines the level of pricing for an item.

21. **Pallet**（托盘）：A flat wooden structure used to stack items to be shipped on. Allows a forklift or pallet jack to safely move the product around.

22. **Pro-number**（货运单号）：Number assigned to a shipment for tracking purposes.

23. **Pup**（短途货运拖车）：A freight trailer that is 28-foot long.

24. **Reefer**（冷藏拖车）：Nickname for a refrigerated freight trailer. This term has nothing to do with any controlled substance.

25. **Release value**（免责价值）：Not considered a declaration of insurance value. Typically expressed in terms of value per pound. Based on classification rules governed by the NMFC. If damage occurs happen, a claim can be filed on a customer's behalf up to the release value, but a settlement is not guaranteed.

26. **Residential delivery**（住宅送货）：Delivery in a residential area, including businesses operated from home. This service is to the sidewalk or driveway only. Also known as curbside delivery. Residential deliveries may incur an additional charge. The consignee must have the means to handle the item after it is removed from the truck.

27. **Stretch film**（拉伸膜）：A protective barrier used to hold a collection of goods together, and to keep dust and moisture off the product. In some cases, a black stretch film is used for UV protection and security.

Part C Terms

1. neutral packing　中性包装
2. customary packing　习惯包装
3. cargo in bulk　散装货
4. nude cargo　裸装货
5. shipment packing　运输包装
6. consumer packing　消费包装
7. packaging industry　包装工业
8. packaging test　包装试验
9. package design　包装设计
10. package engineering　打包工程
11. package in damaged condition　破损包装
12. waterproof　防水

13. actual weight 实际重量

14. actual tare 实际皮重

15. average tare 平均皮重

16. customary tare 习惯皮重

17. computed tare 约定皮重

18. weight shortage 短重

19. a shortage of 50 kilos 短重 50 千克

20. gross weight 毛重

21. net weight 净重

22. "gross for net" 以毛作净

23. tare 皮重

24. conditioned weight 公量

25. circa or approximate "约"量

26. theoretical weight 理论重量

27. more or less clause 溢短装条款

28. additional words and phrases 补充词汇和短语

29. quantity delivered 供给量，交付数量

30. quantity shipped 装船数量

31. quantity buying 大量购买，定额购买

32. quantity production 大批生产，批量生产

33. quantity of shipment 货运量，发运量

Part D Exercise

I. Please determine whether the following statements are True or False. Then put T for True or F for False in the bracket at the end of each statement.

1. Packing is not a competitive factor in seeking a new market. (   )

2. Sound packing will help push the sales. (   )

3. Insufficient packing can only affect the exporter. (   )

4. During different stages of the journey, the goods become extremely vulnerable. (   )

5. Packing is a kind of job of providing packing materials for the goods. (   )

6. Different types of goods require different types of packing. (   )

7. Most cargo is shipped with freight charged by weight rather than by volume. (   )

8. Customs duties levied by the importing country are based on the weight of the packing materials. (   )

9. Materials liable to deterioration should be treated with protective measures. (   )

10. Packing is not only designed to protect the goods, but also to preserve the quality of the goods. (   )

11. A container is a sturdily constructed box used in packing. (   )

12. Full Truck Load is any shipment that takes up more than 1/3 trailer full, or the trailer is used for one shipment no matter how much room is used. (   )

13. Less Than Load is any shipment that is less than 1/4 trailer full, and can be moved with other shipments. (   )

14. Pup is a freight trailer that is 28 feet long. (   )

15. Lift-gate service refers to the hydraulic platform on the rear of the trailer or truck that lifts items up or down. (   )

II. Translate the followings into English.

1. 消费品位

2. 礼品式包装

3. 美化商品

4. 便捷式包装

5. 民族习俗　　　　　　　　　　6. 透明式包装

7. 创意设计　　　　　　　　　　8. 悬挂式包装

III. Please made the best choice from the four choices A, B, C and D.

1. Gross weight of the commodities refers to (　　).

    A. the packing weight of the commodities

    B. commodity's weight plus the inner packing weight

    C. commodity's weight

    D. commodity's weight plus the inner and outer packing weight

2. The packing of ring-pull can is a kind of packing of (　　).

    A. stacked type packing　　　　　　　B. portable packing

    C. complete packing　　　　　　　　　D. easy open packing

3. Some foreign importers require that there should be no any origin indications or trade marks on the packing of the goods we provide. This requirement of the foreign importer is (　　).

    A. unlicensed neutral packing　　　　　B. brand designated packing

    C. transportation packing　　　　　　　D. sales packing

4. Large packing can also be called (　　).

    A. whole packing　　　　　　　　　　B. transport packing

    C. sales packing　　　　　　　　　　　D. neutral packing

5. According to international business practice, if there is no indication in the contract, usually it is the (　　) who should take responsibility for the transport marks.

    A. opening bank　　　B. seller　　　C. buyer　　　D. transport party

6. Cargo in bulk means (　　).

    A. 裸装货　　　　　B. 散货　　　　C. 单件包装　　D. 集合运输包装

7. The basic purpose of packing is to (　　).

    A. protect the product　　　　　　　　B. offer decent service

    C. produce side-product　　　　　　　D. manufacture product

8. As for the goods packed in cases, it is better to line with (　　) or cloth inside the cases.

    A. waterproof　　　B. fireproof　　　C. thief proof　　　D. idiot-proof

9. Transport/shipping is also called (　　) packing.

    A. inside　　　　　B. outside　　　　C. small　　　　D. middle

10. The (　　) is a kind of single-layer or double-layer flat carrier which is made according to a certain specification.

    A. pallet　　　　　B. container　　　　C. box　　　　D. carton

11. (　　) please finds our price list.

    A. Enclose　　　B. Enclosed　　　C. Enclosing　　　D. Be enclosed

12. We don't know that canned goods (　　) the scope of your business activities.

    A. meet　　　　B. fall within　　　C. reach　　　D. get into

13. Type 1 is (　　), so its price is considerably higher than that of last year.

    A. in short supply　　B. in free supply　　C. out of supply　　D. for supply

14. Pens are packed 12 pieces (　　) a box and 200 boxes (　　) a wooden cases.

　　A. to, in 　　　　　　B. in, to 　　　　　C. to, to 　　　　　D. to, of

15. We would suggest that you (　　) the carton with double straps.

　　A. will secure 　　　　B. securing 　　　　C. secure 　　　　D. are secured

16. Packing charges (　　) in the price, and we can make delivery whenever you wish.

　　A. is included 　　　　B. are included 　　C. include 　　　D. included

17. This container can be easily opened (　　) both ends.

　　A. by 　　　　　　　　B. on 　　　　　　　C. at 　　　　　　D. in

18. We are confident that the package of our products will (　　) the roughest handling in transit.

　　A. stand up to 　　　　B. stand to 　　　　C. suffer from 　　D. put up

19. The overall (　　) of the case are 100cm×50cm×50cm.

　　A. volumes 　　　　　　B. weights 　　　　C. capacities 　　　D. dimensions

20. It was found upon examination that nearly 20% of the (　　) had been broken, obviously due to improper (　　).

　　A. packing, packages 　　　　　　　　　B. packages, packing

　　C. packing, packing 　　　　　　　　　　D. packages, packages

IV. Please give the definition to the followings in English.

　　1. Transport packing 　　　　　　　　2. Container

　　3. Sales packing 　　　　　　　　　　4. Neutral packing

　　5. Packing marks 　　　　　　　　　　6. Shipping marks

V. Briefly answer the following questions.

　　1. 简述国际贸易中包装的重要性及约定包装条件的意义。

　　2. 国际贸易中商品运输包装的要求有哪些？

　　3. 简述运输包装的分类情况。

　　4. 国际贸易中商品销售包装的要求有哪些？

　　5. 设计和制作销售包装时，应做好哪些工作？

　　6. 影响定牌生产的原因有哪些？其具体做法是什么？

　　7. 联合国制定标准运输标志的原因是什么？其作用有哪些？

　　8. 买卖双方制定合同中包装条款时应注意哪些问题？

VI. Case study.

　　1. 我国某公司出口一批冻鸡，货物抵达目的港后经海关检验发现因包装不良导致部分冻鸡变质，外商据此向我方提出索赔。

　　问题：

　　外商的做法是否合理？

　　2. 某公司向国外出口一批仪器，合同规定由买方提供码头，但截至买方提供时间届满为止，仍未见其通知设计情况，而该公司货已备好。

　　问题：

　　该公司应如何处理此事？

3. 我国某公司从国外进口一批手套，合同上规定每箱 60 双，共 100 箱。货物运抵大连海关后，经检验发现外商擅自改为每箱 50 双，共计 120 箱。

问题：

我方若据此提出拒收和索赔是否合理？

4. 英国环球公司以 CIF 伦敦的条件，从兰陀公司购买 300 箱澳大利亚苹果罐头。合同的包装条款规定：“箱装，每箱 30 听。”卖方所交货物中有 150 箱为每箱 30 听装，其余 150 箱为每箱 24 听，买方拒收。卖方争辩说，“每箱 30 听”字样并非合同的重要部分，不论是 24 听还是 30 听，其品质均与合同相符，因此，买方应接受。

问题：

卖方的要求合理吗？

5. 2002 年世界杯期间，日本一进口商为了促销运动饮料，向中国出口商订购 T 恤衫，要求以红色为底色，并印制“韩日世界杯”字样，此外不需印制任何标识，以在世界杯期间作为促销手段随饮料销售赠送现场球迷，合同规定 2002 年 5 月 20 日为最后装运期，我方组织生产后于 5 月 25 日将货物按质按量装运出港，并备齐所有单据向银行议付货款。然而货到时由于日本队止步于 16 强，日方估计到可能的积压损失，以单证不符为由拒绝收单，在多次协商无效的情况下，我方只能将货物运回国内销售以减少损失，但是在货物途经海关时，海关认为由于“韩日世界杯”字样及英文标识的知识产权为国际足联所有，而我方外贸公司不能出具真实有效的商业使用权证明文件，因此海关以侵犯知识产权为由扣留并销毁了这一批 T 恤衫。

请分析：

海关的处理是否正确？

6. A British company purchased 300 cases of fruit cans from an Australian company. The contract is stipulated as follows: "Pack in cases of 30 cans each". When the buyer picked up the goods, they found half the quantity was packed as stipulated. But the other part was packed in 90 cases with 60 cans each. The buyer refused the goods immediately. But the seller informed that 30 cans each case is not the core part of the contract, the total quantity is correct and the quality is similar to the stipulation in the contract, so the buyer should accept it.

Question:

Which party breached the contract? Why?

7. Company A is an electronic product brand enterprise that sells its smart electronic earphones globally through the Amazon cross-border e-commerce platform. The packaging of company A 's smart electronic earphones has distinct characteristics. Firstly, the electronic earphones are packaged with environmentally friendly, recyclable, and biodegradable materials. At the same time, the R&D department of Company A, together with the marketing department, invited customers to participate in designing a simple and stylish appearance. The packaging of its smart electronic earphones is made of shockproof and pressure resistant materials, ensuring the safety of the earphones during cross-border transportation on Amazon. In addition, the design department of Company A has also attached a QR code to the packaging of the smart electronic earphones, making it convenient for Amazon cross-border e-commerce platform consumers to scan the QR code after purchase to further understand the detailed product information and specific product usage methods of the smart

electronic earphones.

Question:

What innovative applications of digital trade product packaging are reflected in the packaging characteristics of company A 's intelligent electronic earphones, based on this case analysis?

8. Company A is a cultural product company that mainly sells its unique cultural products, such as stationery, calligraphy and painting, and ceramics, to international market consumers through the cross-border e-commerce platform of AliExpress. The company attaches great importance to the cultural connotation and aesthetic value of packaging. The R&D department and marketing department of the company have invited customers to participate in the design of packaging materials and designs that incorporate traditional Chinese cultural elements. At the same time, detailed introductions of related products and the background of craftsmanship are also attached to the packaging of company's stationery, calligraphy, painting, and ceramics, allowing international market consumers on cross-border e-commerce platforms to better understand the cultural value, historical heritage, and Eastern artistic charm of company's stationery, calligraphy, painting, and ceramics products.

Question:

What innovative applications of digital trade product packaging are reflected in the packaging characteristics of the company's stationery, calligraphy, painting, ceramics, etc., based on this case analysis?

Chapter Eight

Part A Text

Price of Goods

In international trade practice, the price term is one of the most important terms of a contract. Thus, the price of goods is certainly among the chief terms. Pricing is a complex and generally unscientific activity in most firms involved in business negotiations. Actual practice is much more difficult than following the theories and simple suggestions of economists. Therefore, pricing becomes trial and error and hard calculations in decision making. Pricing in international trade markets becomes even more problematic because the complexities of domestic pricing are compounded by the idiosyncrasies of individual foreign markets with their own competitive, legal, and buyer behavior environments. Therefore, setting the price level is not just a question of determining the lowest possible price that will achieve the optimum balance between the performance desired by customers and the costs incurred by the exporter. Pricing refers to a series of techniques relating to a single product or a group of products. Price is the amount of money (plus possible some goods) that is needed to acquire some combination of a product and its accompanying services. In practice, this indicates that price is simply an offer or an experiment to test the pulse of the market. If the market rejects it, the price will usually be changed quickly, or the product may even be withdrawn from the market. In managing the price portion of a firm's marketing mix, the exporter must, first of all, decide on its pricing objectives or targets, and then set the base price for a product or service.

在国际贸易实践中，价格条款是合同最重要的条款之一。因此，商品价格必然属于核心条款。定价对大多数企业而言是一项复杂且非科学化的商业谈判活动。实际操作远比遵循经济学家的理论和简单建议困难得多。因此，定价成为决策过程中反复试错与精密计算的结合。国际市场营销中的定价问题更为棘手，因为国内定价的复杂性叠加了各个海外市场特有的竞争环境、法律体系及买方行为特性。因此，设定价格水平不仅需要确定最低可行价格，还需在客户期望的性能与出口商承担的成本之间实现最优平衡。定价是指针对单一产品或产品组合的一系列技术手段。价格是为获取产品及其配套服务组合所需支付的金额（可能包含部分实物）。实践表明，价格本质上是对市场反应的试探性提案。若市场拒绝接受，价格通常会被迅速调整，甚至可能导致产品退出市场。在管理企业营销组合中的价格环节时，出口商首先需明确定价目标，随后为产品或服务设定基准价格。

Section One Contents of Price Term（价格条款的构成）

1．Pricing strategy（定价策略）

Pricing strategy is part of the process of developing an overall marketing strategy. According to the objectives of a company, the pricing strategy may be demand-oriented or competition-oriented. Demand-oriented pricing examines the intensity of demand as expressed by consumers. Price varies with the intensity of demand for a product, with a high price charged where there is a high degree of interest in the product and a low price when demand is weak. Competition-oriented pricing examines the pricing behavior of competitors. Firms which rely entirely on the competitive element to determine a price will set it at a level which is just above or below the prices prevailing in the market.

Three well-known pricing strategies are penetration pricing, skimming pricing, and early cash recovery pricing, which are often used by firms introducing new products to a market. The first two are direct opposites, while the third can incorporate features of the other two. These may be used as a promotional device, or as a contributory element in developing a company image.

定价策略是整个营销策略制定过程中的一部分。根据公司的目标，定价策略可以分为需求型和竞争型两种。需求型定价策略考虑的是消费者表现出的对商品的强烈需求愿望。由于消费者对商品需求愿望的不同，价格也随之不同。如果对某种商品的需求特别强烈，其价格也高很多；如果需求量小，该商品的价格很低。竞争型价格策略考虑的是竞争对手的问题，如果公司完全依靠竞争决定价格，那么该价格高于或低于市场预期。

三个广为人知的定价策略是渗透定价法、撇脂定价法和资金速期回收定价法，公司向市场推销新产品时常使用这些定价法。前两种策略针锋相对，而第三种是前两种策略的结合。这些定价策略可以作为经销方式，也可助力塑造公司形象。

1) Penetration pricing（渗透定价法）

A very important way to achieve a large share of the market for a new product is to set a relatively low price initially to stimulate demand and attract more buyers. If the market appears to be highly price sensitive, setting a low price will bring additional buyers into the market. It is helpful to unlock markets that may not have even been anticipated. A low initial price strategy also has the benefit of discouraging actual and potential competition and is consequently an important protective element in the firm's armory. When a product is being produced under conditions which give rise to scale economies and unit production and distribution costs decline with increased output, this strategy will be workable.

使某一新产品占据较大市场份额的一种方法就是在最初阶段以相对低价刺激需求。如果该市场显示出很大的价格弹性，那么定低价能吸引更多的买主进入市场。渗透定价策略可以开拓预料之外的市场。初期定低价策略也有益于降低实际和潜在的竞争，进而也是保护公司的重要因素。当出现大量订单积压时，公司不能调整价格。只有对能促成规模经济、单位生产和经销成本随产量的增加而降低的情况下生产的产品，此策略方可奏效。

2) Skimming pricing（撇脂定价法）

This strategy is designed to gain a premium from those buyers who want to take advantage of readiness of a market. After a time, when the premium segment is saturated, the firm gradually reduces prices to draw in the more price sensitive segments of the market. Typically a price skimming strategy works well where there are significant entry barriers such as patents, high development costs, raw material advantages sometimes accrue to the firm setting a high initial price. The firm setting a high initial price sometimes has two other edges: this strategy leaves room for a price reduction if a miscalculation has been made; it is always easier to reduce price than to raise it once a product has been established on the market. A high price may also create an impression of a superior product in the minds of consumers.

这种策略目的在于从这类买主身上赚取高额利润。经过一段时间,当高价市场部分趋于饱和时,公司逐渐减价以吸引价格敏感群体。特别是在有重要市场壁垒,如专利权、高开发成本、原材料控制或促销成本长期偏高的情况下,撇脂定价策略才能充分发挥效应。初定高价的公司有时还有另外两方面的优势:如有定价失误,这种策略还有减价的余地;一旦某产品打开了市场,减价总比涨价容易。高价也可在消费者和用户心中留下优质产品的印象。

3) Early cash recovery pricing（资金速期回收定价法）

Companies sometimes do not believe that the market for their products will exist for a long period, or they face cash shortages, or survival may be the overriding objective facing them. In such circumstances they tend to set a price which will bring in cash at an earlier stage rather than in the longer term. Market conditions dictate whether the price should be high or low. The firm can maximize immediate cash flow through a high price strategy because of the presence of a low demand elasticity and constant unit cost of production and distribution, and through a low price strategy because of the presence of a high demand elasticity and declining unit cost. The choice of strategy depends on the firm's objectives and its view of market condition.

有时公司相信它们的产品市场不会持久,或者会经受缺少现金的困难,或者正面临着公司能否生存的困境。在这种情况下,公司倾向于制定一个在短期内而不是较长期限内收回现金的价格。市场条件决定价格应高还是应低。在需求弹性较低且单位生产和经销成本不变时,公司可采取高价策略;需求弹性较高且单位生产成本下降时,公司可采用低价策略。这样做公司可以最大限度地迅速收回现金。策略的选择取决于公司的目标及其对市场情况的了解。

2. Pricing objectives（定价目标）

Every market task, especially pricing, must be directed toward the achievement of a goal, in other words, management should decide on its pricing objectives before determining the price itself. The objectives can be divided into two kinds: long-term objectives and short-term objectives.

Long-term objectives are usually concerned with profitability and market share. Firms which consider price as a strategic marketing weapon will devote more attention to long-term price objectives than those which view price as a tactical instrument to gain short-term advantage in the market. Short-term objectives are usually specified in annual budgets developed by the firm for a number of items including profits, sales volume and market share. The main objectives whether long-term or short-term, established by the company are oriented either toward profits, toward sales, or toward maintaining the status quo.

市场上每一项工作，尤其包括定价，必定是为了达到某种目标。换言之，经营者在决定价格本身之前，必须首先明确定价目标。定价目标可分为两类：长期目标和短期目标。

长期目标通常与盈利情况和市场份额相关。有些公司把价格作为一种战术手段以求在市场上取得短期优势，与此相比，那些将价格作为战略性的营销武器的公司，则更重视定价的远期目标。短期目标一般体现在公司的年度预算中，包括利润、销售额和市场份额等几个方面。公司所确定的主要目标，无论是长期的还是短期的，都是为了取得利润、扩大销量或维持现状。

3. Pricing principles（定价原则）

It is very complicated to set a reasonable price for a product in the import and export business. In order to do it well, we should carry out correctly our pricing principles and be sure to master the changing trend of the international market. All the factors that may influence pricing should be taken into account. The calculation of cost, profit and loss must be reinforced.

In order to pricing properly, the following three principles should be adhered to.

(1) To price according to the international market. The international market price is made on the basis of international merits and formed in the international market competition, which can be accepted both by the buyer and the seller.

(2) To price based on the situations of different policies of various countries and regions. In order to let the foreign trade work in with the diplomatic policies, we should consider the policies of different countries and regions in the reference with the international market.

(3) To price based on the purpose of purchasing. The price of goods to be imported and exported can be made according to the international market, and be made based on the purpose of purchasing. That's to say, the price can be a little higher or lower than the international market.

在进出口业务中，确定一个合理的价格是一项十分复杂的工作。为了做好这项工作，必须正确贯彻我国进出口商品的定价原则，切实掌握国际市场价格的变动趋势，充分考虑影响价格的各种因素，加强成本和盈亏的核算。

在确定进出口商品价格时，必须遵循下列三项原则。

（1）按照国际市场价格水平定价。国际市场价格是以商品的国际价值为基础并在国际市场竞争中形成的，它是交易双方都能接受的价格。

（2）要结合国别、地区政策定价。为了使外贸配合外交，在参照国际市场价格水平的同时，也可适当考虑国别、地区政策。

（3）要结合购销意图定价。进出口商品价格在国际市场价格水平的基础上，可根据购销意图确定，即可略高于或略低于国际市场价格。

4. Pay close attention to the ups and downs of the international market（注意国际市场价格动态）

The international market price is subject to supply and demand, so it is not so stable. Therefore, in making the price of the goods, we should pay great attention to the ups and downs of the international market, make good prediction, and avoid blindness by the making correct use of pricing.

国际市场价格因受供求关系的影响而经常波动，不断变化。因此，在确定进出口价格时，必须注意市场供求关系的变化,对国际市场价格走势做出正确判断,避免价格掌握上的盲目性。

5. Take various cost factors into account（考虑影响价格的各种成本费用因素）

To negotiate price with foreign traders is not an easy job at all as for the glib-tongued peddler traveling on horseback selling to domestic consumers. Quoting export price is even more difficult and includes meticulous cost calculation prepared well in advance. In the contract, price is usually quoted in this way: USD100 per metric ton FOB Shanghai. That means the complete price term consisting of currency, measuring unit, unit price, price terms, delivery port or destination. Now the question is how the unit price is worked out.

One of the exporter's tasks is to make the decision on what price to set for a product. The price setting relates to product costs, market demand, and competitive prices. But first the exporter or manufacturer has to take into account the different costs: fixed cost and variable cost. Fixed cost is an element, such as rent, executive salaries, or property tax that remains constant regardless of how many items are produced. The more units that are produced the more these fixed costs can be spread, thus reducing the fixed cost per unit. On top of these fixed costs are variable costs, which rise as the quantity produced rises. Variable cost is an element, of the cost of inputs such as cost of materials, direct labor, fuel and power, and that is directly related to production. When production stops, all variable production costs become zero. The distinction between these two costs has to be made clear before price determination, having determined the total cost for producing and selling any given quantity of product, it is equally important for the exporter to make it clear how much the foreign buyer is asked for the product and how many different kinds of costs are involved in your quoted price. The best solution is to use a costing sheet. Its purpose is to check that every expense has been covered in arriving at the selling price. The following is the detailed illustration of the costing sheet.

与外商谈判价格不像能说会道的小商贩骑在马背上向国内消费者兜售那样简单。出口报价的难度更大,它需要事先做精心的成本计算。合同中常报价"上海港 FOB 每公吨 100 美元"。这就意味着,完整的价格条款应包括货币名称、计价单位、单价、价格术语以及装运港或目的港。而问题是: 单价是怎样制定出来的?

出口商的工作之一是决定产品定多高的价格。制定价格要考虑产品成本、市场需求和竞争性价格。但出口商或制造商首先要考虑的是各种成本: 固定成本和可变成本。固定成本不随产量变化而变化,如租金、管理人员工资、财产税。即使生产完全停顿下来,这种消耗仍然存在。生产的产品越多,这些固定成本越能分散到更多的产品中,从而减少了单位产品的固定成本。除了固定成本,还有可变成本。可变成本随产量的增加而增加。它是一种与生产直接相关的因素或者说是投入的消耗,如原料消耗、直接劳动、燃料和动力等。生产一停止,全部可变成本就变成零。在确定价格之前,首先要弄清这两种成本的区别。确定了生产或销售一定数量产品的总成本之后,同样重要的是出口商须明确国外买主付多少钱购买此产品,以及所报的价格中包含多少不同种类的费用。最好的办法是利用成本核算表。采用这种表格的目的在于查对售价中是否包含了所有的开支。以下是关于成本核算表的详细说明。

1) Unit cost of product（产品的单位成本）

It is simply the domestic price per unit of the product. The exporter should subtract any cost not directly related to export sales—for example, advertising—to arrive at its base price. This price is also the factory price.

这是指产品的国内单价。出口商应扣除任何与外销无直接联系的费用——例如广告——形成一个基价，这个价格就是出厂价。

2) Profit（利润）

Normally, profit will have already been included in the domestic price. However, if it is insufficient for the risk involved in selling abroad, an extra allowance for profit can now be added.

一般来说，产品的国内市场价格中已经包括了利润。但如果这仍不足以与外销的风险相符的话，则可以附加一部分特别利润。

3) Agent's commission abroad（国外代理人的佣金）

It depends on which channel the goods are sold through. If an overseas agent is employed, as a rule, his commission is usually given on a percentage basis. In the contract, it is always expressed as CIFC5%—C5% means five percent commission is given to the middlemen.

这要视商品的销售渠道而定。如果有海外代理，则通常付其一定百分比的佣金。在合同中以"CIFC5%"表示支付5%的佣金给中间人。

4) Packing cost（包装费）

The goods may need to be repacked if they are not up to the contract stipulations. Export packing calls for a great deal of money. The cost of packing for overseas shipment will vary according to the product, destination, and means of transportation. The exporter must include a reasonable price to cover the cost.

如果商品包装不符合合同规定的话，可能需要重新包装。出口包装的费用很高。海上运输货物包装费用因产品、目的港、运输方式而不同。出口商须合理加价以补偿这些费用。

5) Labeling cost（标签费用）

Labels may have to be printed in a foreign language, perhaps containing information not included in the labels used in the home market. From the sales point of view, they must include sufficient allowance for these extra labeling costs.

标签必须用外文印制，上面可能包括一些国内市场的标签所没有的内容。为销售起见，标签必须符合外国消费者的要求。所报的价格中必须包含额外的标签费用。

6) Marking cost（刷唛费用）

A small cost is involved in stenciling an identification mark on each package for export.

在出口的每一包货上刷唛头也要涉及一笔费用。

7) Strapping cost（加固费用）

Each carton must be strapped to help prevent it from being accidentally or intentionally opened in route to its destination. Small packages must be handled or strapped together to discourage pilferage and other loss.

每箱货物必须加固以防在运往目的港途中有意或无意的破损。小件货物须捆在或连在一起，以防失窃或其他损失。

8) Cost of taking goods to the seaport（将货物运到港口的费用）

The cost includes: taking goods from factory to local railway station or container depot, next comes the cost of transporting the goods to the seaport for shipment abroad.

这些费用包括：货物从工厂运到火车站或集装箱货运站的费用，以及再运到装运港的费用。

9) Unloading cost（卸货费）

This cost will be incurred when the goods arrive at the seaport.

卸货费指货到港口后的卸货费用。

10) Terminal cost（终点费用）

This includes handling, wharfage and harbor dues that must be paid by the exporter to the port authorities.

包括出口商必须向港务局缴纳的管理费、码头费和停泊费。

11) Cost of documents（单证费用）

It mainly refers to consular documents which can be quite expensive particularly in the case of exports to the Latin American countries. Initially, the exporter may wish to quote to the foreign customer a price, plus the cost of consular documents. Other documents are also very costly, such as license or inspection certificate, etc. but not in all countries.

主要指领事发票。这笔费用也会很高，尤其在对拉丁美洲国家的出口中。报价时，出口商有时可以向外国客户要求外加"领事票据费"。其他票据如许可证或商检证书费用也很高，但不是所有国家都如此。

12) Ocean freight（海上运输费用）

This usually takes up a large proportion of the total quoted price if it is the exporter's responsibility to make all the shipping arrangements.

如果出口商负责安排运输，海运运费在所报价格中常占很大比例。

13) Freight forward's fee（发运代理费）

If the exporter uses the services of a freight forwarder to handle all the export documentation and book the shipping space required, allowance must be made for the fee involve.

如果出口商请发运代理人帮助办理出口手续、租船订舱，则应在成本核算表中包括这笔费用。

14) Export credit insurance（出口信贷保险）

The exporter may decide to take out insurance on its credit sales abroad. Export credit is always given by the exporter's bank.

出口商可能决定办理对外赊销的保险。出口信贷由出口方银行提供。

15) Marine insurance（海运保险）

The exporter must choose the coverage most suitable for the shipments as stipulated in the contract while they are being shipped abroad. Usually ocean shipments are insured for 110 percent of their total costs. If he wishes, the exporter may include the insurance premium in the amount on which insurance is taken on certain for basis.

出口商必须按合同规定，为正在运输途中的货物选择适当的险别进行投保。通常，海运货物按其总价值的 110% 投保。如果出口商愿意，也可以在投保的总量中溢价投保。

16) Financial charges（财务费用）

Until he receives payment, the exporter will have part of his working capital tied up in the export merchandise. Even if no credit is given, he will give credit to the foreign customer, he may have to wait for several months for payment. Consequently, the export price should include an amount to cover the cost of this working capital as well as the interest.

在收到贷款之前，出口商总有部分流动资金被压在出口的货物上。即使没有出口信贷，其也要向国外客户提供信用，有时甚至要等好几个月才能收取货款。因此，出口价格中还应包括补偿这部分流动资本的费用和这部分利息。

17) Other charges（其他费用）

Here, space is left for the inclusion of unexpected additional expenses such as the cost of overseas telegrams or phone calls, fax charges, extra storage charges, and even "gifts" to the foreign customers.

The above separate costs are now available for consolidation into a properly printed price list. These are the ones being used by most of the Chinese trading companies. To guard against complications, it is advisable to print on all price lists the words: "All prices are subject to change without notice". In the case of certain countries, there are special charges which have to be paid for the legalization and certification of export document or for having B/L visited and for certificates of origin. It is well to make the situation quite clear by having the following words printed on the list "free for certification and legalization of documents are not included in the above prices". The export price is a multi-dimensional variable. Whether or not you can export your merchandise with price calculated from the above costing sheet, the foreign consumer is always the final controller of your price. Accurate calculation does not imply right exporting. That is dependent upon your pricing strategies and policies.

这里还应考虑那些意想不到的附加开支，如国际电报或电话、传真费用、附加的仓储费，甚至还要算上给外商的"礼物"。

报价单就是在以上各种费用基础上合计而成的。绝大部分中国的贸易公司都使用这些项目。为避免麻烦，报价单上最好写明"如无意外变动，以上报价有效"字样。在某些国家，对出口票据的合法化及证明书、提单签证、原产地证明书等，还要收缴特别费用。为清楚起见，报价单上可以注上文字："上述价格不含票据合法化及证明费用。"出口价格是个多元的变量。是否能以上述成本核算出的价格成功地进行出口，最后还得由外国消费者决定。精确的计算并不意味着出口一定成功，还取决于定价策略和措施。

18）Some other factors that should be considered （其他一些必须考虑的因素）

(1) the quality and classification of the goods（考虑商品质量与档次）

(2) the quantity for transaction（考虑成交数量）

(3) the distances of transportation（考虑运输距离）

(4) the delivery destination（考虑交货地点）

(5) the seasonal demand alteration（考虑季节性需求变化）

6. Formulas（计算公式）

1) Profit-loss rate for export goods　（出口商品盈亏率）

$$\text{The profit-loss rate of export goods} = \frac{\text{export distribution net RMB incoming} - \text{export total cost}}{\text{export total cost}} \times 100\%$$

$$\text{出口商品盈亏率} = \frac{\text{出口销售人民币净收入} - \text{出口总成本}}{\text{出口总成本}} \times 100\%$$

The profit-loss rate of export goods refers to the ratio between the export profit-loss amount and the total export cost. The export profit-loss amount is the balance between the RMB net income and export total cost. If the former is greater, there will be profit, otherwise, loss.

它是指出口商品盈亏额与出口总成本的比率。出口盈亏额是指出口销售人民币净收入与出口总成本的差额，前者大于后者为盈利，反之为亏损。

2) Exchange cost of export products（出口商品换汇成本）

$$\text{The exchange cost of export products} = \frac{\text{total export cost (RMB)}}{\text{export sale net income (USD)}}$$

$$\text{出口商品换汇成本} = \frac{\text{出口总成本（人民币）}}{\text{出口销售外汇净收入（美元）}}$$

The exchange cost of export products refers to the ratio between the total cost of export goods and the foreign exchange net income. That is to say how much RMB can be exchanged for 1 US dollar, or the total RMB cost needed for exporting goods worthy of net 1 US dollar. It is also an important index to show the profits and losses of the export business. If the exchange cost of export goods is greater than the exchange rate quotation when making settlement, there will be losses, conversely, there will be profits.

There is an inner link between the exchange cost and the profit-loss ratio, the higher the export loss ratio, the higher the exchange cost. On the contrary, a lower loss rate or a small profit corresponds to lower exchange cost.

$$\text{Profit-loss ratio} = \frac{\text{conversion rate} - \text{exchange cost}}{\text{exchange cost}} \times 100\%$$

它是指某种商品的出口总成本与出口所得的外汇净收入之比，得出用多少人民币换取 1 美元，即该商品每出口净收入 1 美元所需要的人民币总成本。它也是用来反映出口商品盈亏的一项重要指标。出口商品换汇成本如高于结汇时银行的外汇牌价，则出口为亏损；反之，则说明出口有盈利。

换汇成本与盈亏率有着内在联系，即出口商品亏损率越大，换汇成本越高；反之，亏损率越小或有盈利，则换汇成本就越低。

$$\text{盈亏率} = \frac{\text{折算率} - \text{换汇成本}}{\text{换汇成本}} \times 100\%$$

7. Prices of digital trade goods and services（数字贸易商品和服务价格）

The scope of goods and services covered by digital trade, especially cross-border e-commerce, is extensive (including but not limited to e-books, digital music, short videos, software applications, game software, cloud computing services, big data mining, analysis and decision-making services, etc.). The goods and services involved in digital trade are diverse, and their prices vary significantly due to their nature, functions, attributes, brands, and other factors, digital trade products and services have significant price differences. The prices of digital trade products are mainly influenced by the following factors:

The first one is the relationship between demand and supply in the digital trade product market. The digital economy is a branch of economics. Therefore, digital trade products and services are also influenced and dominated by supply and demand relationships. The prices of digital goods or services worldwide are often directly influenced by actual trade market demand and supply relationships. For example, when the demand for a certain digital commodity or service increases in the global market, the supplier of its product or service may use price increases to obtain higher marginal profits. On the contrary, if there is an oversupply of their products or services, suppliers may lower prices to attract more buyers.

The second is the pricing strategy of digital trade product trading platforms. This is very evident on cross-border e-commerce platforms, as different cross-border e-commerce trading platforms may adopt different pricing strategies for digital trade product transactions. Some cross-border e-commerce trading platforms may adopt fixed pricing models, while others may use dynamic pricing methods such as auctions and bidding. In addition, some cross-border e-commerce platforms may also adopt 4P strategies in their marketing mix, such as offering coupons, discounts, and other promotional activities, which can affect the final price of digital goods or services in cross-border e-commerce trading platforms.

The third factor is the inherent cost of digital trade products. The cost factors of digital trade will also directly affect prices. This mainly includes the direct production costs of digital goods or services, as well as various indirect costs such as digital information transmission costs, cross-border e-commerce transaction platform maintenance costs, etc. If this indirect cost is high, digital suppliers may pass on some of the cost to digital product consumers, thereby increasing the price of digital trade products.

数字贸易特别是跨境电子商务所涵盖的商品和服务范围非常广泛（包括但不限于从电子书、数字音乐、短视频、软件应用、游戏软件到云计算服务、大数据挖掘、分析决策服务等）。数字贸易所涉及的这些商品和服务具有多样性，而且因其性质、功能、属性、品牌等因素，使得数字贸易产品和服务在价格上存在显著差异。数字贸易产品的价格主要受以下几大因素的影响：

一是数字贸易产品的市场需求与供应关系。数字经济属于经济学的一个分支。因此，数字贸易产品与服务也受供需关系的影响与支配。全球的数字商品或服务的价格往往受到实际贸易市场需求和供应关系的直接影响。比如，当某种数字商品或服务在全球的市场上需求量变大时，其产品或服务的供应商可能会借助提高价格获取更高的边际利润。相反，如果其产品或服务的供应过剩，供应商可能会降低价格以吸引更多买家。

二是数字贸易产品交易平台的定价策略。这一点在跨境电商平台十分明显，不同的跨境电子商务交易平台可能采用不同的数字贸易产品交易定价策略。一些跨境电子商务交易平台可能采用固定的价格模式，而另一些跨境电子商务平台则可能采用拍卖、竞价等动态定价方式。此外，一些跨境电子商务平台还可能采用市场营销组合里面的4P策略，如提供优惠券、折扣等促销活动，从而影响跨境电子商务交易平台中的数字商品或服务的最终价格。

三是数字贸易产品的自身成本因素。数字贸易的成本因素也会直接影响价格。这主要包括数字商品或服务的直接生产成本，以及各类间接成本，如数字信息传输成本、跨境电子商务交易平台维护成本等。如果这种间接成本较高，那么数字供应商可能会将部分成本转嫁给数字产品消费者，从而提高数字贸易产品价格。

Section Two　Pricing Methods（定价方法）

In the course of business negotiation and contract conclusion, appropriate trade terms, reasonable price and favorable money of account should be chosen. Detailed method of pricing should be included in the clause of price, and price adjustment clauses should also be added in the price term if necessary. In addition, commissions and discounts could be used as a flexible way of motivating the initiatives of the supplier and expanding the sales.

在对外磋商交易和签订合同时，应采用适当的贸易术语，合理确定商品的价格，选择有利的计价货币，价格条款中应列明具体的作价办法，必要时订立价格调整条款，还应灵活运用佣金和折扣，以调动采购商的积极性和扩大销路。

1．Pricing（定价）

In international sales of goods, the following methods of pricing can be used.

(1) Fixed pricing. The Seller delivers and the Buyer accepts the commodities at a fixed price agreed by both parties, neither party shall have the right to change the agreed price.

(2) Flexible pricing. The pricing time and the pricing method are specified in the price terms, for instance: "The price will be negotiated and decided by both parties 60 days before the shipment according to the international price level". Or only the pricing time is fixed，for instance: "To be priced on July 1st, 2018 by both parties".

(3) Partial fixed price and partial unfixed price. The parties concerned only fix the price for the commodities to be delivered recently, and leave the price of the commodities to be delivered in the long term open.

(4) Floating pricing. At the time of pricing, the price adjustment is also stipulated, for instance: "If the concluded price for other buyers is 5% higher or lower than the contract price, both parties will negotiate to adjust the contract price for the quantity of the contract".

在国际货物买卖中，可采取下列几种作价办法。

（1）固定价格。买卖双方按约定价格交接货物和收付货款，任何一方无权要求对约定价格进行变更。

（2）暂不固定价格。在价格条款中明确规定定价的时间和定价方法，如"在装船前 60 天，参照国际市场价格水平，协商议定正式价格"。或只规定作价时间，如"由双方在 2018 年 7 月 1 日商定价格"。

（3）价格部分固定，部分不固定。交易双方只约定近期交货部分的价格，远期交货部分的价格则待以后商定。

（4）浮动价格。在规定价格的同时，还规定价格调整条款，如"如果卖方对其他客户的成交价高于或低于合同价 5%，对本合同的数量，双方协商调整价格"。

In order to master the pricing well, three pricing techniques are illustrated here.

(1) Cost-plus pricing approach is one in which the exporter calculates his "costs" and adds the desired markup to cover unassigned costs either in total or per unit. The chief merit of this approach is its simplicity.

(2) Break-even pricing is a method in use by a number of firms which extends the cost approach somewhat along the road to considering the market, and also the method of determining the quantity of sales at which the firm's revenues will equal its costs identifying a break-even point at a specific price. Thus, there is a different break-even point for different selling price. Sales of quantities above the break-even output result in a profit on each unit. The further the sales are above the break-even point, the higher the total and unit profits. Sales below the break-even point result in a loss to the seller.

(3) Marginal price is another approach. Sometimes the export price set is much lower than the domestic price because of the complexities of the market and different policy-making considerations. In many cases, the company has more production capacity than the home market can absorb. Businessmen are naturally reluctant to reduce their prices. But the key to marginal pricing is to view home sales and export sales as separate compartments and to consider your export sales as extra sales. If you are recovering your fixed cost with your home sales, you can consider the extra cost of the additional products made for export to be only the variable costs involved.

Before determining prices and going into exporting, an exporter should carefully consider using these three alternative pricing approaches.

为了把握好商品的定价，这里介绍三种定价技巧。

（1）成本加成定价法就是出口商计算出成本，再加上预期的加成，以弥补总产或单产中的未分摊成本。这种方法的主要优点是简单方便。

（2）收支平衡定价法是许多公司采用的方法。它在考虑市场因素的基础上对成本法进行了延伸，并通过确定在特定价格下企业收入与成本相等的销售量（即损益平衡点）来实现定价。因此，每一不同的售价都有其不同的损益平衡点。超过该点销售量的每个单位产品都产生利润。销售量超过损益平衡点越多，总产和单产带来的利润就越高。低于该点的销售量，会使卖方产生亏损。

（3）边际成本定价法是定价技巧的另一种方法。有时由于市场的复杂性及制定政策时考虑的不同，所定的出口价格比国内价格低得多。在多种情况下公司生产能力大于国内市场容量，商人自然不愿意降低其价格。边际成本定价法的关键在于视国内销售与出口销售为分离的"隔室"，而把出口销售视为"额外销售"。如果在国内销售就可收回固定成本，那么就可以认为出口产品的额外成本只是可变成本。

出口商在定价和出口前，要仔细考虑采用这三种可供选择的定价法。

2. Selection of money of account（计价货币的选择）

In international trade, the money of account can be the currency of the export country, the currency of the import country, or the currency of a third country agreed by both parties, it can also be a unit of account agreed upon by both parties. As the change in value of the selected currency may directly affect the financial interests of both parties, the parties concerned should choose the currency favorable to them during pricing. Theoretically, hard currency should be chosen for exports and soft currency for imports. In practice, however, the selection of money of account depends on the business practices and intentions of both parties. If an unfavorable currency has to be adopted for the conclusion of a deal, the following two remedies may be taken: to make corresponding adjustment to the quotation according to the possible trend of the currency in the future and to get the price protected against the currency risks.

在国际贸易中，用来计价的货币可以是出口国家的货币，也可以是进口国家的货币或双方同意的第三国货币，还可以是某一记账单位，由买卖双方协商确定。由于计价货币的币值变化会直接影响到进出口双方的经济利益，因此买卖双方在确定价格时应注意选择对自己有利的计价货币。从理论上来说，出口应选用硬货币计价，进口则应选择软货币计价。但在实际业务中，以什么货币作为计价货币，还应视双方的交易习惯、经营意图而定。如果为达成交易而不得不采用对我方不利的货币，则可以采用以下两种方法补救：一是根据该种货币今后可能的变动幅度，相应调整对外报价；二是争取订立保值条款，以避免计价货币汇率变动的风险。

3. Construction of the price of a contract（合同中的价格组成）

The price term of a sales contract includes unit price and total price. Unit price includes the measuring unit, unit price amount, money of account, and trade terms. For instance, a price term can be worded like this: "USD1 500 per metric ton CIF London including 3% commission". Total price refers to the total amount of a deal.

国际货物买卖合同中的价格条款一般包括单价和总价两项基本内容。商品的单价通常包括计量单位、单位价格金额、计价货币和贸易术语。如在价格条款中规定："每公吨 1 500 美元 CIF 伦敦，折扣 3%。"总价是一笔交易的货款总金额。

4. Price conversion（价格换算）

When the buyer and seller negotiate the price, they often adjust their offered trade terms according to the requirement of the other party, likely they may change the original offer of FOB into CIF or CFR as required. This concerns the price conversion.

(1) FOB converts into CIF or CFR.

① CFR = FOB + F

② $CIF = \dfrac{FOB+F}{1-(1+insurance\ bonus\ rate)\times premium\ rate}$

(2) CFR into converts into FOB or CIF.

① FOB = CFR − F

② $CIF = \dfrac{CFR}{1-(1+\text{insurance bonus rate})\times\text{premium rate}}$

(3) CIF converts into FOB or CFR.

① FOB = CIF × [1−(1 + insurance bonus rate) × premium rate]−F

② CFR = CIF × [1−(1 + insurance bonus rate) × premium rate]

Note: F= freight

买卖双方在洽谈交易时，经常会根据对方要求改变原报价的贸易术语，如原按 FOB 报价，对方要求改报 CIF 价或 CFR 价，这就涉及价格换算问题。

(1) FOB 价换算为 CFR 或 CIF 价。

① CFR = FOB + F

② $CIF = \dfrac{FOB+F}{1-(1+\text{投保加成率})\times\text{保险费率}}$

(2) CFR 价换算为 FOB 或 CIF 价。

① FOB = CFR−F

② $CIF = \dfrac{CFR}{1-(1+\text{投保加成率})\times\text{保险费率}}$

(3) CIF 价换算为 FOB 或 CFR 价。

① FOB = CIF × [1−(1+投保加成率)×保险费率]−F

② CFR = CIF × [1−(1+投保加成率)×保险费率]

5. Commission and Discount（佣金和折扣）

Commission is the service fees charged by the agents or brokers for the transactions made for their principals. For example, the commission paid by the exporter to its sales agent, and the commission paid by the importer to its purchasing agent. Discount is the price deduction allowed by the seller to the buyer. Different methods are used for specifying commission and discount in the price terms. Usually the rate of commission or discount is either clearly stated in the price, such as: USD 1 200 per MT CIFC3% New York, or expressed as a specific amount, such as: USD 4 discount per MT Sometimes at the time of negotiation, both sides have reached agreement on the commission or discount which will not be stated in the contract, and the commission or discount will be paid according to the method agreed by the parties concerned.

佣金是代理人或经纪人为委托人进行交易而收取的报酬。例如，出口商付给销售代理人、进口商付给购买代理人的酬金。折扣是卖方给予买方的价格减让。在价格条款中，对于佣金或折扣可以有不同的规定办法。通常是在规定具体价格时，用文字明示佣金率或折扣率，如每公吨 CIF 纽约 1 200 美元，佣金 3%；或用绝对数表示，如每公吨折扣 4 美元。但有时在洽谈交易时，双方对佣金或折扣的给予已达成协议，并不在合同中表示出来，佣金或折扣由一方当事人按约定另付。

Part B Terminology Practice

1. **Annual carrier's performance report**（承运人年度业绩报告）：A yearly report giving statistics on a carrier's performance in areas such as estimates, claim settling, and on-time delivery. At the time of estimate (household goods survey), you should be given a copy of this report, for which you must sign a receipt.

2. **Appliance servicing**（电器维修服务）：The preparation of major electrical appliances for shipment, such as adding special braces to secure the tub and motor of automatic washer.

3. **Auction**（拍卖）：A public sale of items sold to the highest bidder. Used in enforcement of a warehouseman's lien covered by the Uniform Commercial Code.

4. **Bailee**（受托人）：A public warehouseman is considered a "bailee for hire"—person who holds or stores goods for another.

5. **Bailor**（托运人）：The owner of goods being stored, typically the shipper.

6. **Barrels**（纸板桶）：Cardboard cartons used for packing odd dishes, glassware, lamp bases, and anything breakable.

7. **Bid**（报价）：A statement of what a vendor will take for a good or service. A vendor may bid either verbally or in writing and the bid is generally good for a defined period of time.

8. **Binding estimate**（约束性估价）：An agreement which specifies in advance the exact cost of moving, including all services requested and/or needed at the time the computation is made.

9. **Booking agent**（订舱代理）：The agent who accepts the order for service and registers it with the van lines. He is not necessarily at either origin or destination.

10. **Brand name only**（仅指定品牌）：Requirement calling for a specific brand name item because of unique features, quality of performance that has been demonstrated and proven to be reliable for a particular application.

11. **Buy**（购买）：The outright purchase (cash to seller) of goods or services.

12. **(Mirror) Cartons**（镜框纸箱）：Pre-made, heavy-duty cartons for mirrors and/or pictures. They are usually long, wide and narrow.

13. **Competitive bid**（竞争性报价）：The effort of two or more vendors acting independently to secure the business of the University by offering the most favorable terms (price, quality and service).

14. **Confirmation**（确认）：A confirmed reservation exists when a supplier acknowledges, either orally or in writing, that a booking has been accepted. Most confirmations are subject to certain conditions.

15. **Confirming order**（确认订单）：A type of PO used when there is a rush to place an order.

16. **Connecting rooms**（连通房）：Connecting rooms or cabins enable guests to move from one room to another without going outside.

17. **Continental breakfast**（欧陆式早餐）：A light breakfast or coffee, roll and juice.

18. **Corkage**（开瓶费）**:** Charge for beverages brought into a facility, usually includes glasses, ice, and openers.

19. **Declared valuation**（申报价值）**:** A system for establishing the van line's maximum liability for loss or damage to the shipment.

20. **Direct Pay Request (DPR)**（直接付款请求）**:** A type of payment request. Used for employee reimbursement, petty cash, and other types of payments that do not require Purchasing approval.

21. **Duties**（关税）**:** Are taxes levied by governments on the importation, exportation, or use of goods.

22. **Express**（快递）**:** A system for the prompt and safe transportation of goods at rates higher than standard freight charges. Examples: 2-Day Air, Overnight Delivery, etc.

23. **Free trade**（自由贸易）**:** Trade based on the unrestricted international exchange of goods with tariffs used only as a source of revenue.

24. **Group function**（团体活动）**:** Event planned for groups of more than ten people.

Part C Terms

1. rock-bottom price 最低价
2. type 型号
3. specification 规格
4. quality 品质
5. weight 重量
6. quantity 数量
7. domestic subsidy 国内补贴
8. domestic support （农产品）国内支持
9. electronic commerce 电子商务
10. ex ante 采取措施前
11. ex post 采取措施后
12. export performance 出口实绩
13. export subsidy 出口补贴
14. free-rider 免费搭车者（享受其他国家最惠国待遇而不进行相应减让的国家）
15. *Lisbon Agreement* 《里斯本协定》（地理标志保护及国际注册）
16. direct payment valuation request 直接支付估价申请
17. direct payment valuation 直接支付估价单
18. provisional payment valuation 临时支付估价单
19. payment valuation 支付估价单
20. quantity valuation 数量估价单
21. quantity valuation request 数量估价申请
22. contract bill of quantities-BOQ 合同数量单
23. No pricing tender BOQ 不计价投标数量单
24. priced tender BOQ 标价投标数量单
25. stores requisition 领料单
26. average price 平均价
27. base price 底价
28. maximum price 最高价
29. buying price 买价
30. bedrock price 最低价
31. ceiling price 最高价
32. closing price 收盘价
33. cost price 成本价
34. current price 现行价格
35. exceptional price 特别价
36. extra price 附加价
37. floor price 最低价
38. gross price 毛价
39. nominal price 名义价格
40. opening price 开盘价

41. original price 原价

42. popular price 大众化的价格

43. present price 现价

44. prevailing price 通行价格

45. reserve price 保留价格

46. retail price 零售价

Part D Exercise

I. Multiple Choice—Select one answer choice.

1. The core clause of the international sales of goods contract is (   ).

   A. packing terms
   B. transportation terms
   C. price clause
   D. quality terms

2. The determinants of export price usually are (   ).

   A. international price movement
   B. the international market price level
   C. exporters operating intentions
   D. importers business intentions

3. The important indicators of foreign trade enterprises and import and export trading profit and loss are (   ).

   A. export foreign exchange income
   B. export cost price
   C. export profit and loss rate
   D. export swap costs

4. The total cost of goods for export is RMB 55 000, foreign exchange net income after export is $10 000, if the Bank of China's foreign exchange rate is $100 against 650 yuan, the export profit and loss rate is (   ).

   A. 50.9%
   B.33.7%
   C. 45.9%
   D. 36.7%

5. In general case, CIF shall take more (   ) into consideration than the FOB price.

   A. foreign freight, domestic expenses
   B. abroad freight, insurance premium
   C. abroad costs, domestic expenses
   D. abroad insurance premium and net profit

6. Skimming pricing strategy is designed to gain a premium from those buyers who want to take advantage of the readiness of a market. After a time, when the premium segment is saturated, the firm gradually____ prices to draw in the_____segments of the market. (   )

   A. reduces / more price sensitive
   B. increases / more price sensitive
   C. reduces / less price sensitive
   D. raises / more demand sensitive

7. Some provisions of the contract are: "$1, 000 per metric ton CIF Singapore", the price should be (   ).

   A. price set after
   B. provisional price
   C. fixed price
   D. to be determined

8. The international trade pricing method which is often used in our country is (   ).

   A. pending price
   B. provisional price
   C. price set after
   D. a fixed price

9. To solve the problem between the two sides in international trade with fixed price or a non fixed price differences, which of the following can be used? (   )
   - A. batch for
   - B. provisional price
   - C. pending price
   - D. price set after

10. The hypothesis to adopt the fixed price is (   ).
    - A. choosing the pricing time
    - B. identify the standard of pricing
    - C. provisions for adjustment of price
    - D. analysis preparation for profit and loss

11. The price which is according to the date of bill of lading or the average price for the month of shipment is (   ).
    - A. price before shipment
    - B. price upon shipment
    - C. price after shipment
    - D. price upon the goods at the port of destination

12. A dealer or buyers abroad who earns "a double-charge commission" often uses (   ).
    - A. the price adjustment provisions
    - B. discount
    - C. commission
    - D. vague commission

13. An export contract stipulated in the "1 000 us dollars per metric ton CIF Hong Kong, and 2% discount", then the seller's net income should be (   ).
    - A. $960
    - B. $1 020
    - C. $980
    - D. $1 040

II. Multiple Choices—Select more answer choices.

1. Pricing principles for China's import and export commodities include (   ).
   - A. implementation of equality and mutual benefit principle
   - B. according to the international market level
   - C. combined with national, regional policy
   - D. giving foreign preferential conditions
   - E. determining reasonable price in our business intentions

2. Based on a deal on CFR terms, the total cost of the export factors include(   ).
   - A. purchase cost
   - B. domestic expenses
   - C. export tax
   - D. import tax
   - E. insurance premium

3. If a deal is done with CIFC 3% terms, export exchange net income should be deducted from the price (   ).
   - A. purchase cost
   - B. freight
   - C. insurance premium
   - D. commission
   - E. domestic cost

4. If a deal is on the CIF terms and conditions, the seller's quotation should include (   )
   - A. purchase cost price
   - B. domestic expenses
   - C. overseas freight
   - D. foreign insurance premium
   - E. net profit

5. The international chamber of commerce, in order to adapt to the new development of international trade, has set new terms (   ).
   - A. FOB
   - B. CFR
   - C. DAP
   - D. CIF
   - E. DAT

6. CIPC3% usually involve abroad costs (   ).

    A. the overseas freight   B. foreign insurance premium

    C. commission   D. bank fees

    E. certificate fees

7. (   ) can be used in international trade as pricing methods.

    A. fixed price   B. price to be determined

    C. price set after   D. tentative price

    E. partly fixed price, partly non- fixed price

8. Standard of using a fixed price includes (   ).

    A. with typical mercantile exchange announced price shall prevail

    B. be subject to international market price

    C. combined with local market price in the international markets

    D. clinch a deal valence shall prevail by the seller to other customers

    E. both sides negotiate to determine prices

9. The basis of price amendments includes (   ).

    A. wage changes   B. management fees changes

    C. changes in prices of raw materials   D. profit changes

    E. insurance costs changes

10. The correct use of commission has an exert   (   ) role on the import and export business in China.

    A. is beneficial to mastering the price

    B. arouse the enthusiasm of middlemen in our products

    C. to expand sales

    D. to take care of the old customers

    E. to enhance the competitiveness of the goods in foreign markets

11. The price terms in the international trade contract include (   ).

    A. the measuring unit   B. the amount of unit price

    C. currency   D. trade terms

    E. total cost of the goods

III. Explain the following terms in English.

    1. 出口总成本   2. 出口换汇成本

    3. 固定价格   4. 后定价格

    5. 暂定价格   6. 待定价格

    7. 价格调整条款   8. 佣金

    9. 明佣   10. 折扣

    11. 出口成本价格   12. 出口外汇净收入

    13. 出口盈亏额

IV. Briefly answer the following questions.

    1. 简述影响商品成交价格的主要因素。

2. 简述固定价格优缺点及使用时的注意事项。

3. 简述非固定价格的利弊。

4. 简述"暗佣"及"暗扣"的含义。

5. 简述佣金与折扣的支付方法。

6. 采用非固定价格时应注意哪些问题？

7. 简述我国进出口商品的作价原则。

8. 出口成本价格与出口成交价格的区别是什么？

9. 采用非固定价格时应注意的问题有哪些？

10. 规定价格条款时应注意哪些事项？

V. Calculation.

1. 我方某公司以 CIFC3% 条件出口一批货物，外销价为每公吨 1 000 美元，支付运费 80 美元，保险费 10 美元。该公司进货成本为每公吨 4 000 元人民币，国内直接和间接费用加 15%。求该商品出口总成本、出口外汇净收入、出口换汇成本。

2. 我方某公司对外报价 FOB 价每公吨 500 美元，外商来电要求改报 CIF 纽约含佣金 3%，保险费率合计为 0.8%，国外运费每公吨 60 美元。请计算我方应报价。

3. 我方对外报价每公吨 1 000 美元 CIF 新加坡，外商来电要求改报 FOB 价中国口岸，已知保险费率为 0.85%，国外运费每公吨 75 美元，试计算我方应报价。

4. 我方某公司对外商报价为 CFR 价 1 000 美元，外商要求改报 CFRC4% 价，我方应报价多少？

5. 某合同规定：CIF 香港，每公吨 1 000 美元，折扣 2%。根据该合同成交的进出口业务中出口方每公吨净收入是多少？

6. One import and export corporation exports a batch of goods abroad. Their offer is at USD 2 000 per metric ton CIF New York. The freight for the goods is USD150 per metric ton from Tianjin to New York against all risks, premium rate is 0.4%.

Question:

How to make the offer of FOB Tianjin?

VI. Comprehension questions.

1. What are the basic terms and conditions of the contract in international business?

2. What is the most important term among the basic terms and conditions in an international business contract?

3. What are the most often used terms and conditions among the price terms and conditions?

4. How to determine the price for imports and exports?

5. What is the term when the consignment is delivered with all the charges up to arrival at the port of destination paid by the seller?

6. What is the contract term whereby the seller undertakes to pay for the cost of transport of the goods to a specific destination port?

7. What is the most appropriate term when the seller pays for the goods to be loaded on board the container ship, but does not pay freight or insurance?

8. Under which term does the seller have no obligation to contract for carriage?

VII. Please determine whether the following statements are True or False. Then put T for True or F for False in the bracket at the end of each statement.

1. An auction is a public sale of items sold to the lowest bidder. (　　)

2. Bailee is a public warehouseman considered a "bailee for hire". One person who holds or stores goods for another. (　　)

3. Bailor: The owner of goods being stored, typically a shipper. (　　)

4. Barrels are iron used for packing odd dishes, glassware, lamp bases, and anything breakable. (　　)

5. A bid is a statement of what a vendor will take for a good or service. Vendor may bid either verbally or in writing and the bid is generally good for a defined period of time. (　　)

6. A confirmed reservation exists when a supplier acknowledges, either orally or in writing, that a booking has been refused. (　　)

7. Confirming order is a type of PO used when there is a rush to place an order. (　　)

8. Declared valuation is a system for establishing the van line's minimum liability for loss or damage to shipment. (　　)

9. Direct Pay Request is a type of payment request. Used for employee reimbursement, petty cash, and other types of payments that do not require Purchasing approval. (　　)

10. Duties are taxes levied by governments on the importation, exportation, or use of goods. (　　)

VIII. Case Study.

Related studies have compared the pricing strategies of TikTok Shop and Temu, and found that TikTok Shop mainly drives the sales of domestic beauty and 3C products through the "live streaming+short video seeding" model. TikTok Shop leverages the advantages of social e-commerce to increase product exposure and user purchase intention through content marketing, while combining flexible pricing strategies to attract consumers. On the other hand, Temu has rapidly risen to become one of the top 3 e-commerce apps in North America in terms of downloads, mainly through its "full custody supply chain+ultimate cost-effectiveness" model. Moreover, research has found that Temu greatly reduces intermediate links and indirect costs by directly connecting with suppliers and manufacturing factories. Therefore, Temu offers highly competitive prices.

At the national tariff level, Mexico announced a temporary tariff of 35% temporary tariff on over 100 imported textiles effective 2025, resulting in an increase in prices for related products. Vietnam announced that from July 1, 2025, it will cancel the duty-free treatment for low-cost imported goods and increase the value-added tax rate from 8% to 10%. Taking electronic products exported by sellers as an example, if the selling price is $100, originally only $8 of value-added tax needs to be paid, but after the tax rate is increased, $10 of value-added tax needs to be paid. This adjustment has intensified the operational pressure on small and medium-sized sellers, which may force them to raise prices.

Based on the above case, analyze the factors that affect the prices of cross-border e-commerce products.

Chapter Nine

Part A Text

Delivery of Goods

The delivery of goods, in international trade, is one of the most important steps. This is because in international trade where an exporter and an importer are always far apart, the goods under the contract have to go a long distance and sometimes may change multiple carriers in transit before they reach the importer. In international business, it is one of the basic tasks for the exporter to deliver the goods to the buyer or carrier or agreed conveyance after the contract has been signed, according to the stipulated time, place, and transport methods in the contract.

The delivery of goods to the destination stipulated in the contract is a work of strong timeliness, wide involved aspects, long distance and complicated technology. So an international trader should understand and know well the basic knowledge of the delivery of the goods in order that he can make a comprehensive consideration of all the problems that will occur in transit. In this case, he can give the contract very clear, complete, reasonable and practical terms of delivery and make sure that the contract can be performed without any trouble and problems.

The delivery of the goods means that the seller delivers the contract goods at the agreed time, place and in the agreed manner to the buyer. In international sales of goods, the delivery also means to transfer the necessary documents at the stipulated time to the buyer. The essentials of a transport system embrace three elements: the route, the vehicle (including motive power unit), and the terminal. Each must have a strong interface with the other to generate efficiency and facilitate trade development.

国际货物运输是国际贸易的一个重要组成部分。这是因为买卖双方所在地相隔比较远，国际贸易中的货物从卖方国家转移到买方国家，必须通过运输来实现，有时甚至需要多次转运才能到达进口商手中。在一笔具体的进出口交易中，在买卖合同签订以后，按照合同规定的时间、地点和运输方式，将货物运交买方或承运人或指定的运输工具是卖方的基本义务之一。

国际货物运输是一项时间性强、涉及面广、线路长、环节多的复杂工作。从事国际贸易的人员必须熟悉和掌握有关国际货物运输的基本知识，才能在交易洽商和签订合同时充分考虑运输方面的问题，使合同中的装运条款订得完整、明确、合理和切实可行，以确保签订的货物买卖合同能顺利履行。

所谓交货是指卖方在合同规定的时间、地点以及按照双方同意的运输方式将合同标的物交给买方。在国际货物销售中，交货也可以被认为是在规定时间内将必需的单据交给买方。运输系统包括三个要素：路线、交通工具（包括动力装置）和终点站。各要素间需紧密衔接以提高效率，并促进贸易发展。

The delivery methods of digital trade mainly involve digital ordering trade and digital delivery trade.

(1) Digital ordering trade delivery. Digital ordering trade emphasizes the buying and selling conducted on computer networks through methods specifically designed to receive or place orders. This approach is actually an innovative digitization based on traditional goods trade methods. In digital ordering trade activities, digital ordering buyers and sellers conduct actual transactions of digital ordering trade mainly through (cross-border) e-commerce platforms or other digital platforms, Internet channels, etc. Therefore, the ordering process of goods or services involved in digital ordering trade delivery is a fully digital delivery process. Specifically, digital ordering trade buyers can browse products online, place orders (by shopping carts), and complete transactions through various digital electronic payments on e-commerce platforms or other digital platforms. Digital ordering trade sellers receive orders digitally through e-commerce platforms or other digital platform channels, process third-party platform payments, and arrange logistics for the delivery of goods or services, achieving digital ordering trade goods delivery.

(2) Digital delivery trade. Digital delivery trade is different from digital ordering trade, as it refers to "all cross-border transactions that are remotely delivered through ICT networks and in electronic downloadable formats". The digital delivery trade method belongs to the category of service trade and refers to the digitization of traditional service trade. In digital delivery trade, the main objects of transactions are digital products or services, such as common game software, electronic music, electronic reading books, online education courses, short videos, big data analysis, decision-making services, etc. The products or services involved in this digital delivery trade can be directly transmitted to buyers through Internet channels or other digital modes, that is, there is no need for physical on-site delivery. Digital delivery trade has the characteristics of efficiency and speed, that is, buyers can immediately download and use these digital products or services after purchasing.

In summary, based on the analysis of the two modes of digital ordering trade and digital delivery trade, it can be found that the delivery methods of products and services in digital trade are different from traditional goods delivery, reflected in its characteristics of high efficiency and convenience, cost reduction, and enhanced customer experience. These characteristics enable the delivery methods of digital trade to drive the digital transformation and development of global trade enterprises, greatly enabling cross-border transactions of goods and services, thereby expanding the global market scope of digital trade products and services. Enterprises in the production chain related to digital trade can promote digital trade goods or services to the global market through digital trade e-commerce platforms, attracting more potential customers.

数字贸易的交付方式主要涉及数字订购贸易和数字交付贸易。

（1）数字订购贸易。数字订购贸易强调"通过专门用于接收或下达订单的方法在计算机网络上进行的买卖"。这种方式实际上是基于传统货物贸易方式的一种创新数字化。在数字订购贸易活动中，数字订购买家和卖家之间主要通过（跨境）电子商务平台或其他数字平台、互联网渠道等进行数字订购贸易的实际交易。因此，数字订购贸易交付涉及的商品或服务的订购过程是一个完全数字化的交付过程。具体看，数字订购贸易买家可以在电子商务平台或其他数字平台进行线上浏览商品、（购物车）下单购买，并通过各种数字化电子支付方式完成交易。数字订购贸易卖家则通过电子商务平台或其他数字平台渠道进行数字化接收订单、第三方平台支付处理，并安排物流进行商品的发货或服务的提供，实现数字订购贸易货物交付。

（2）数字交付贸易。数字交付贸易与数字订购贸易不同，它指的是"通过 ICT 网络，并以电子可下载格式进行远程交付的所有跨境交易"。数字交付贸易方式属于服务贸易的范畴，指向的是传统服务贸易的数字化。在数字交付贸易中，交易的主要对象是数字产品或数字服务，比如常见的游戏软件、电子音乐、电子阅读书、在线教育课程、短视频、大数据分析、决策服务等。这些数字交付贸易涉及的产品或服务完全可以通过互联网渠道或其他数字模式直接传输给买家，无须物理上的实地交付。数字交付贸易具有高效快捷的特点，即买家购买后，可以立即下载并使用这些数字产品或服务。

综上所述，基于数字订购贸易和数字交付贸易两种模式的分析，可以发现数字贸易的产品和服务交付方式与传统货物交付方式不同，体现在其具有高效便捷、降低成本、增强客户体验等特点。这些特点使数字贸易的交付方式推动全球贸易企业的数字化转型和发展，很大程度上使得商品和服务可以实现跨越国界交易，从而拓宽了数字贸易的产品和服务的世界市场范围。数字贸易相关生产链的企业可以通过数字贸易电子商务平台将数字贸易商品或服务推向全球市场，吸引更多的潜在客户。

Section One　Methods of the Delivery（装运方式）

As to the methods of delivery in international practice, there are many methods to deliver the goods purchased, such as ocean transport, railway transport, air transport, river and lake transport, postal transport, road transport, pipeline transport, land bridge transport and international multimodal transport and so on. The buyer and seller can decide which method will be the best for goods to be transported according to goods characteristics, quantity, transit journey, value, time, the natural conditions and so on.

国际货物运输有多种方式：海洋运输、铁路运输、航空运输、江河运输、邮包运输、公路运输、管道运输、大陆桥运输以及由各种运输方式组成的国际多式联运等。买卖双方应根据商品特点、数量大小、路程远近、价值大小、时间长短、自然条件等因素商定应采用的运输方式。

1．Ocean transport（海洋运输）

Ocean transport is the most widely used form of transportation in international trade as well as the most efficient form in terms of energy. It still has the attraction of being a cheap mode of transport for delivering large quantities of goods over long distances. Before a shipment is made, the exporter has to consider many different factors influencing transport considerations such as cost, safety, speed and convenience.

So far as foreign trade is concerned, goods transport is mostly (over 80% of world trade in volume terms) done by ocean vessels. There are several features of ocean transportation.

(1) Large transport volume.

(2) Great capability of transport.

(3) Low freight.

(4) Sound adaptability to various goods.

(5) Low speed.

(6) High risk.

Because of the prominent advantages in large capacity of transport and low freight, ocean transport plays a very important role in international transportation even with its low speed and high risks. Nowadays, more than 2/3 of transport is done by ocean transportation. There are two kinds of ocean vessels: charter and liners.

海洋运输是国际贸易运输中采用最广泛的一种形式，从能源角度来讲也是最有效的形式。对于长途运送大批量货物，它还具有作为一种廉价运输方式的吸引力。在安排货物运输之前，出口商必须考虑各种不同的影响运输条件的因素，例如，费用、安全、速度和便利条件。

就货物运输来说，大多数的国际贸易运输（80%以上）都是由远洋运输船舶完成的。海洋运输有以下特点。

（1）运量大。

（2）通过能力大。

（3）运费低。

（4）对货物的适应性强。

（5）航速低。

（6）风险较大。

由于海运运量大和费用低的突出优点，尽管它存在航速低、风险大的不足，但仍在国际贸易货运中占有十分重要的地位，在国际贸易总运量中有 2/3 以上利用海运。运输船可分为租船运输和班轮运输。

1) Shipping by chartering（租船运输）

Shipping by chartering is also called tramp. Shipping by chartering refers to a freight-carrying vessel that has no regular route or fixed schedule of sailing, nor definite freight rates, or specific ports. It is first in one trade and then in another, always seeking those ports where there is a demand at the moment for shipping space. Thus, it is usually used to transport bulk cargo of low value, such as rice, minerals, oil and timber, etc. The shipper charters the ship from the shipowner and uses it to carry the goods. The owner of the cargo should sign a charter party with the shipowner. The freight is paid according to the agreement between the two parties.

Shipping by chartering falls into three types: voyage charter, time charter and demise charter.

租船运输又称不定期货船。租船运输没有固定的船期表，没有固定的航线，不定运价和不定港口。哪里有货就向哪里开航，哪里装船最好就去哪里接货。因此，通常用来运输货值较低的大宗货物，如粮食、矿石、石油、木材等。发货人从船东处租货船装运货物，货主与船主签订租船合同，按双方商定的运价收取运费。

国际上使用的租船方式主要有三种：定程租船、定期租船和光船租船。

(1) Voyage charter（定程租船）

The voyage charter is an agreement for the carriage of goods from one specified port to another, or for a round trip. It includes single voyage charter, return voyage charter, successive voyage charter, and a contract of affreightment (COA),also called quantity contract/volume contract. According to the route stipulated in the charter party, the shipowner is responsible for delivering the goods to the port of destination, for managing the ship, and bearing all expenses.

Under a voyage charter, payment by the charterer is usually based on an agreed rate per ton for a "full and complete cargo". Should the charterer fail to provide sufficient cargo to fill the ship, they are liable for what is termed dead freight, a pro rata payment for the space not used. A voyage charter also stipulates the number of days known as lay days, for loading and unloading. Should these be exceeded, the charterer is liable for a demurrage charge for each day in excess, and conversely is entitled to dispatch money for each day not taken up. The liability of the shipowner is to provide a ship that is seaworthy and to avoid unjustifiable deviation en route.

定程租船又称程租船或航次租船，是指租船人按照航程租赁全部舱位，由船舶所有人负责将货物运至指定的目的港。定程租船就其租赁方式的不同可分为单程租船（又称单航次租船）、来回航次租船、连续航次租船、包运合同/运量合同。根据租船合同规定的路线，船东负责将货物交到目的港，并负责船只管理，以及支付所有费用。

在定程租船情况下，租船人常常按议定的费率装满货物后的每吨支付费用。如果他不能使船只载满，空舱费用由租船人按载重吨支付。定程租船还规定了装卸货的受载日期。如果受载日期超过规定，租船人须支付每天超期的滞期费。反之，船方支付在受载日期内提前完成装卸每天的速谴费。船方的责任是保证船舶的适航性，并避免航途中不必要的绕航。

(2) Time charter（定期租船）

The time charter, also called transport vessel or vehicle charter, is a kind of transport based on a fixed period instead of on a certain number of voyages or trips. The charterer charters the ship for a period of time during which the ship is deployed and managed by the charterer. What concerns the charterer most is the period, not the voyage. The charter may be for a period of one year or of several years.

During the period of chartering, the ship is managed, deployed and used by the charterer. A series of work, such as loading, unloading, stowing and trimming, and the so-caused fuel expenses, port expenses, loading and unloading expenses, etc., should be borne by the charterer. The shipowner should bear the wages and board expenses of the crew, and be responsible for seaworthiness during the period of chartering and the so-caused expenses and the vessel insurance premium.

定期租船又称期限租船，是以期限为基础的租船方式，而不是以某一航线或航程为基础。船舶所有人将船舶出租给租船人使用一定期限，在此期限内由租船人自行调度和经营管理。租用时间可以是一年或数年。

在租船期间，货船的经营、管理和使用权都归承租人。同时，由于装卸货物、平仓理仓等引起的燃油费、港口费、装卸费等也都由承租人负担。船东要负责支付船员的工资，并保证在租用期间货船适合海洋运输及相关费用和货船的保险费。

(3) Demise charter（光船租船）

Demise charter, is also called bareboat charter. The charterer takes a lease of the entire ship for an agreed time. Thus, demise charter belongs to time charter, but there are some differences: as to time charter, during the period of chartering, the shipowner provides the charterer with a crew, while as to bare-boat charter, the shipowner only provides the charterer with a bareboat. The charterer shall employ the crew and pay the crew's wages and provisions, ship's maintenance and stores, etc. by themselves, apart from those expenses they are responsible for under the time charter.

光船租船也是期租的一种，所不同的是：在定期租船的方式下，船主不仅提供货船，还有船员，而在光船租船方式下，船主不提供船员，只有一条船交给租方使用，由租方自行配备船员，负责船舶的经营管理和航行各项事宜（如船舶的维护、修理及机器的正常运转等）。

(4) Charter party（租船合同）

The charter party is a contract concluded between the shipowner and the charterer when the latter charters the ship or books shipping space from the former. It stipulates the rights and obligations of the two parties. The main terms in the charter party include the interested parties, name and flag of the ship, description and quantity of the shipments, time of chartering, freight, loading and unloading expenses, time limit of loading and unloading, demurrage and dispatch money.

租船合同是租船人和船舶所有人之间所订立的载明双方权利、义务的契约。租船合同的主要条款中包括有关当事人、船名和货船标识、装运货物的名称和数量、租期、运费、装卸费、装卸时限、滞期费、速遣费。

The freight may be stipulated in the charter party as follows.

a. Freight can be paid in advance.

b. Freight can be paid after the goods have arrived at the port of destination.

c. Part of the freight is paid in advance, the rest of which is paid after the goods have arrived at the port of destination.

Before the charterer pays off freight and other charges, the shipowner is entitled to refuse to deliver the goods, this kind of right is called lien.

租船合同中有关运费的规定如下。

a. 运费预付。

b. 货到目的港时再付运费。

c. 已付部分运费，余下的货到目的港之后再付。

在租船人付清运费之前，船主有权拒绝装运货物，这称为留置权。

When discussing the problem of who will be responsible for the charges of loading and unloading, both the shipowner and the charterer should make it very clear in the charter party. There are four methods to be used to stipulate the expenses of loading and unloading:

a. The shipowner bears gross terms.

b. The shipowner is free in (FI).

c. The shipowner is free out (FO).

d. The shipowner is free in and out (FIO). When adopting this method, the interested parties shall indicate who will bear the expenses of stowing and trimming. If they agree that the charterer shall be responsible for them, then the interested parties shall stipulate "shipowner is free in and out, stowed, trimmed (FIOST)".

在签订程租船合同时，必须明确装卸费用是由租船人还是船方负担。对这个问题有四种规定方法：

a. 船方负担装货费和卸货费（Gross Terms）。

b. 船方管卸不管装 （Free In，FI）。

c. 船方管装不管卸（Free Out，FO）。

d. 船方不管装卸（Free In and Out，FIO）。如果采用这种方法，应该在租船合同中写明由谁负责平仓理仓费。如果程租船合同中规定由租船人负担这些费用，那么就必须在租船合同中订立："船主不负责货物的装卸及平仓理仓费（FIOST）。"

The time of loading and unloading will affect the turnover rate of the ship, and thus, will affect the interest of the shipowner. Therefore, it is the main clause specified in the charter party. The time limit of loading and unloading may be indicated by:

a. Fixed days.

b. Efficiency of loading and unloading.

c. Customary quick dispatch.

装卸时间影响装卸费用，进而影响船方的利益。所以，装卸时间是租船合同的主要条款，装卸时限的规定方法有：

a. 在一定天数内装卸完毕。

b. 规定装卸速度。

c. 按惯常的速度装卸。

During the time limit of loading and unloading, in case the charterer does not finish the work of loading and unloading, in order to compensate the shipowner for their losses, the charterer should pay a certain amount of fine for the exceeding time, this is the so-called demurrage.

在规定的装卸时限内，如果租船人没有完成货物的装卸工作，租船人就必须因此而向船主支付一定数目的过期费，这就是滞期费。

During the time limit of loading and unloading, in case the charterer finishes the work of loading and unloading ahead of schedule, then the shipowner shall pay a certain amount of bonus to the charterer. This is the so-called dispatch money.

在规定的装卸时限内，如果租船人提前完成了货物的装卸工作，船主就必须因此而向租船人支付一定数目的奖励费，这就是速遣费。

2) Shipping by liner（班轮运输）

A liner is a vessel with regular sailing and arrival on a stated schedule between a group of specific ports. The main features of liners usually include:

a. The liner has a regular line, port, timetable and comparatively fixed freight，which is the basic features of liners.

b. The shipowner usually leases part of shipping space instead of the whole ship.

c. The carrier is responsible for loading and unloading operations, i.e., Gross Terms.

d. The B/L drawn by the shipping company is the shipping contract between the carrier and the consignor. The rights and obligations of the carrier and the consignor are based on the B/L drawn by the shipping company.

班轮运输是指船舶在固定的航线上和港口间按事先公布的船期表航行。班轮运输主要有下列优点。

a. 有固定航线、固定港口、固定船期和相对固定的费率。这是班轮运输的基本特点。

b. 船东通常出租部分舱位，而不是全部舱位。

c. 管装管卸，有关装卸费均包括在运费内，如船方负责装卸费。

d. 承托双方的权利义务和责任豁免以签发的提单条款为依据。

3) Freight of liners（班轮运费）

Freight is the remuneration payable to the carrier for the carriage of goods. The freight paid for the carriage by a liner differs in the way of calculating from that paid under a charter party.

$$Freight = Fb + \sum S$$

Fb—Basic freight

S—Surcharge

运费是指因运输货物而付给承运人的报酬。付给班轮运输费用与付给不定期船的费用是不一样的。

$$班轮运费 = Fb + \sum S$$

Fb——基本运费

S——附加运费

4) The basic standards for calculating freight（计重标准）

(1) According to gross weight in terms of weight ton, which is indicated by "W" in the tariff.

Heavy cargo is usually charged on this basis.

Internationally, besides MT (each equaling 1 000 kg), British long tons and US short tons are also used nowadays. 1 MT is to be considered as 1 weight ton or one long ton(1 016 kg) or one short ton(907.18 kg).

按货物毛重计收，即以重量吨为计算单位计收运费，在运价表内用"W"表示。

笨重的货物一般都采用这种方法。

此外，国际上现在还有用长吨（英制）和短吨（美制）的，1 重量吨为 1 公吨（1 000 kg）或 1 长吨（1 016 kg）或 1 短吨（907.18 kg）。

(2) According to volume, i.e., measurement ton, which is indicated by "M" in the tariff. It is 40 cubic feet or one cubic meter that constitutes one measurement ton. Often light cargoes are charged on this basis.

按货物体积或尺码吨计收，在运价表内用"M"表示。1 尺码吨为 1 立方米或 40 立方英尺。通常轻型货物用这种方法。

(3) According to value of the cargo, i.e., a certain percentage of FOB price which is indicated by "A.V." (Ad Valorem) in the liner freight tariff. Usually a percentage between 1% and 4% is charged on the value of such goods as gold, silver, precious stones, and valuable drawings and paintings.

按商品的价格计收，如按 FOB 价的一定百分比计收，称从价运费，用"A.V."或"Ad-Val"表示。此项计算标准适用于贵重或高价商品，如金、银、宝石和宝贵的绘画百分比一般为 1%~4%。

(4) According to gross weight or volume, i.e., choosing the higher rate between the two, which is indicated by "W/M" in the tariff.

按货物的毛重或体积，由船公司选择其中收费高的一种计收运费，在运价中用"W/M"表示。

(5) According to gross weight or volume or A.V., i.e., at the discretion of the carrier, choosing the higher rate of the three, which is indicated by "W/M or A.V.".

In this case, it is up to the carrier to decide to charge whichever of the three that produces the highest rate of freight.

选择货物的毛重或体积或价值三者中较高的一种计收运费，在运价中用"W/M or A.V."表示。

在此方式中，由承运人从三者中选择较高的那一种计收运费。

(6) According to gross weight or volume, and then plus a certain percentage of A.V., which is indicated by "W/M plus A.V.".

按货物的毛重或体积，再加上货物价值的一定百分比，在运价中用"W/M plus A.V."表示。

(7) According to the number of the cargo. For example, a freight of so much is for one truck or one head of live animal.

按货物的件数计收。例如，卡车按每辆（Per Unit）、活牲畜按每头（Per Head）计收。

(8) According to the temporary/interim or special agreement entered into between the shipowner and the consignor.

按船主与托运人之间临时签订的协议计收运费。

Based on different draftsmen, liner freight tariffs can be divided into four kinds:

基于不同的起草人，班轮运费可分为四种：

a. Shipping Conference Freight Tariff（航运公会运价表）.

b. Liner's Company Freight Tariff（班轮公司运价表）.

c. Cargo Owner's Freight Tariff（货方运价表，如中租表）.

d. Freight Tariff of Both Parties（双边运价表，如中远表）.

The main surcharges are shown as follows:

主要特殊附加费如下：

a. Heavy lift additional（超重附加费）.

b. Long length surcharge（超长附加费）.

c. Direct additional（直航附加费）.

d. Transshipment surcharge（转船附加费）.

e. Port congestion surcharge（港口拥挤费）.

f. Port surcharge（港口附加费）.

g. Bunker surcharge or bunker adjustment factor (BAF)（燃料附加费）.

h. Optional fees（选港费）.

i. Alternation of destination surcharge（变更港口附加费）.

j. Deviation surcharge（绕航附加费）.

In addition to the above-mentioned surcharges, ice surcharge, cleaning tank surcharge, currency adjustment factor, fumigation surcharge, etc. are sometimes included.

除了上述提到的附加费，还有冷冻附加费、熏舱附加费、币值调整附加费等。

5) The way to calculate the freight（运费计算方法）

(1) First translate the English name of the commodity, find out the freight standard of calculation or the freight grade.

(2) Find out the basic freight rate in the route freight tariff according to the grades and purpose of the sea route, then the relative surcharges for the suitable route and basic port.

(3) The basic freight rate plus various additional surcharges is the freight per freight ton.

Total freight amount = [basic freight rate×(1+∑surcharge rate)+ ∑surcharges]×total freight ton

（1）首先译出托运货物的英文名称，在"货物分级表"中查出该商品所属的等级和计算标准。

（2）根据等级和目的港航线，查出基本运费率和附加费率或附加费额。

（3）商品的基本费率加各种附加费，即该商品每一运费吨的单位运价。用公式表示为

商品运费总额=[基本费率×(1+∑附加费率)+∑附加费额]×总运费吨

In addition to ocean transport, canals and inland waterways throughout the world are developing amid intermodal development driven by a logistics environment. In many countries, especially in Europe, increased road congestion and the introduction of tolls on major highways, coupled with the need for a cleaner environment, are encouraging canal and inland waterway development. The growth of containerization is also making a contribution with its adaptability to canals and inland waterways. In continental Europe, there are the most extensive inland waterway networks serving many major seaports, especially along the northern seaboard. These networks are continuously being modernized together with the vessels/barges handling both bulk cargo and containerized transshipments.

除海洋运输之外，在当今物流环境的驱动下，多种方式运输得到了发展，而全世界的运河和内陆水路也在同时发展。在很多国家，尤其是在欧洲，公路堵塞现象严重，主要的公路也开始收费，再加上对环境保护的呼声日益高涨，这一切都刺激了倾向运河和内陆水路运输的发展。集装箱化的发展也使得运河与内陆水路更加便利。在欧洲大陆，有最先进、最广泛的内陆水路

运输网络，通往很多主要的海港，尤其是北部的海港。现在，运输散装货和集装箱货物的各种船只/驳船，同内陆水路运输网络一起，在不断地更新和现代化。

2. Railway transport（铁路运输）

Railway transport is capable of attaining relatively high speeds with large quantities and is safe, low-cost, punctual, economical, and less affected by weather.

铁路运输具有货运量大、速度快、安全可靠、运输成本低、运输准确和受气候影响较小等特点。

Railway transport falls into three kinds.

(1) Railway transport at home.

(2) International railway transport between two countries.

(3) International railway transport.

铁路运输有以下三种。

（1）内地铁路运输。

（2）国与国之间的铁路运输。

（3）国际铁路货物联运。

According to the stipulations of the International Union of Railways, the International Railway Cargo Through Transport Agreement and the International Convention Concerning the Carriage of Goods by Rail, the goods originating from the export country may be transported directly to the place of destination as long as the carrier issues a railway bill of lading at the place of dispatch.

The main transport documents are the railway bill and its duplicate. The railway bill is the transportation contract and binds the consignee, the consignor and the railway department. The railway bill together with the goods is transported from the place of dispatch to the place of destination and is then delivered to the consignee after they have paid off the freight and other charges. The consignor may settle payments with the bank against the duplicate of the railway bill.

根据"国际铁路联盟""国际铁路货物联运协定"和"国际铁路货物运送公约"的规定，只要承运人在起运地签发铁路运输提单，出口货物就可以直接运往目的地。

铁路运输单据主要有铁路货运提单及其复印件。铁路货运提单实质上是约束收货人、托运人和承运人三者之间关系的一种运输合同。它随货物一起从出发地运至目的地，然后由收货人付款索单。托运人也可通过银行交换铁路货运提单的复印件。

3. Air transport（航空运输）

The advantages of air transport are high speed and quick transit, low risk of damage and pilferage with competitive insurance rates, savings in packing cost, reduced capital tied up in transit and so on; while the chief disadvantage is the limited capacity and dimensions of acceptable cargo, along with weight restrictions. It is also subject to weather conditions. However, it is suitable for goods that are of time pressing, small quantities of cargo but urgent need, light but precious. Air transport can be divided into the following kinds.

航空运输的优点是航行速度快、交货迅速、货损率低以及节省包装、储存等费用，货物可以运往世界各地而不受地面条件的限制；缺点是运量小、运价高，易受恶劣气候的影响。因此，它适用于一些时间性强、体轻而贵重、量少而急需的货物运输。航空运输可分为以下四种。

(1) Scheduled airliner（班机运输）.

(2) Chartered carrier（包机运输）.

(3) Consolidation（集中托运）.

(4) Air express（急件运送）.

The airway bill, also called an air consignment note, is a document or consignment note used for the carriage of goods by air supplied by the carrier to the consignor.

空运提单，也称为航空托运单，是用来证明货物已由承运人通过航空方式交给收货人。

The airway bill has the following features:

a. It is a transport contract signed between the consignor/shipper and the carrier/ airline.

b. It is a receipt from the airline acknowledging the receipt of the consignment from the shipper.

c. The airway bill is an internationally standardized document mostly printed in English and in the official language of the country of departure, which facilitates the on-carriage of goods going through 2 to 3 airlines in different countries to the final destination. Generally, there are usually 12 copies of each airway bill for distribution to the various parties, such as the shipper, consignee, issuing carrier, second carrier (if applicable), third carrier (if applicable), airport of destination, airport of departure, and extra copies for other purposes (if required). Copies 1, 2 and 3 are the originals.

The No.1 original airway bill is retained by the airline for filing and accounting purposes.—"For the carrier". This is signed by the consignor.

The No. 2 original airway bill is to be carried with the consignment and delivered to the consignee at the destination. — "For the consignee". This is signed by the carrier and the consignor, and is sent with the goods to the consignee.

The No. 3 original airway bill is for the shipper, who may present it to the negotiating bank as a shipping document evidencing shipment having been made. " For the consignor" . This is signed by the carrier and sent back to the consignor. See Fig.9-1 Example of Airway Bill.

空运提单有以下特性：

a．空运提单是托运人/发货人与承运人/航空公司之间签订的货物运输协定。

b．空运提单是航空公司开给托运人的托运货物的收据。

c．空运提单通常都是按国际标准用英语和起运地的语言印制的，这样方便途中经由 2~3 个不同国家转到目的地。一般来说，空运提单可以有 12 份，以便交给不同的有关当事人，如托运人、收货人、承运人、第二承运人（如果有的话）、第三承运人（如果有的话）、目的地机场、起飞机场以及其他用途（如果有的话）。每份空运提单有三份正本。

第一份由托运人签署交给承运人或其代理人保存，作为运输契约凭证。

第二份由承运人与托运人共同签署，连同货物备交收货人，作为核收货物的依据。

第三份由承运人签署，于收到货物后交付托运人，作为收到货物的运输契约的证明。

图 9-1 所示为一份空运提单实例。

AIRWAY BILL

Shipper's name and address MATSUDA TELEVISION SYSTEMS CO. LOT5, PRESIAN TENKU APUAN SITE 400 SHA ALAM SELANG DE MALAYSIA		NOT NEGOTIABLE Airway Bill Issued by Beijing Kinte World Express Co., Ltd.
Consignee's name and address MATSUDA QINGDAO CO., LTD. NO. 128 WUHAN ROAD QINGDAO CHINA		It is agreed that the goods described herein are accepted in apparent good order and condition (except as noted) for carriage SUBJECT TO THE CONDITIONS OF CONTRACT ON THE REVERSE HEREOF, ALL GOODS MAY BE CARRIED BY ANY OTHER MEANS. INCLUDING ROAD OR ANY OTHER CARRIER UNLESS SPECIFIC CONTRARY INSTRUCTIONS ARE GIVEN HEREON BY THE SHIPPER. THE SHIPPER'S ATTENTION IS DRAWN TO THE NOTICE CONCERNING CARRIER'S LIMITATION OF LIABILITY. Shipper may increase such limitation of liability by declaring a higher value of carriage and paying a supplemental charge if required.
Issuing Carrier's Agent Name and City Beijing Kinte World Express Co., Ltd.		
Agents IATA Code	Account No.	

Fig.9-1　Example of Airway Bill（空运提单实例）

Airport of Departure(Add. of First Carrier) and Requested Routing K.LUMPUR,MALAYSIA							Accounting Information FREIGHT COLLECT		
to QING DAO	By First Carrier KE855/17JUN	to	by		to	by	Currency USD	Declared Value for Carriage NVD	Declared Value for Customs NVD
Airport of Destination QINGDAO, CHINA		Flight/Date KE855/17JUN		Amount of Insurance			INSURANCE-If carrier offers insurance and such insurance is requested in accordance with the conditions thereof indicate the amount to be insured in figures in the box marked "Amount of Insurance".		
Handling Information NOTIFY PARTY-SAME AS CONSIGNEE									
No. of Pieces	Gross Weight	Rate Class		Chargeable Weight	Rate/Charge			Total	Nature and Quantity of Goods
52	510			211	AS ARRANGED				TV-PARTS 12.638M^3
Prepaid Weight Charge Collect AS ARRANGED					Other Charges				
Valuation Charge									

Tax		
Total Other Charges Due Agent		Shipper certifies that the particulars on the face hereof are correct and that insofar as any part of the consignment contains dangerous goods, such part is properly described by name and is in proper condition for carriage by air according to the applicable Dangerous Goods Regulations.
Total Other Charges Due Carrier		Signature of Shipper or his agent
Total Prepaid	Total Collect AS ARRANGED	JUN. 10th, 2009　QINGDAO　KEWQAO Executed on____ at_____ Signature of issuing Carrier or as Agent
Currency Conversion Rates	CC Charges in des. Currency	
For Carrier's Use Only at Destination	Charges at Destination	Total Collect Charges　　AIRWAY BILL NUMBER KEW-51000788

Fig.9-1　Example of Airway Bill（空运提单实例）（续）

4．Postal transport（邮包运输）

According to international trade practice, the seller fulfils the duty of delivery only if he delivers the parcel to the post office, pays off the postage, and gets the receipt. The post office is responsible for the delivery of the goods to the destination, and the consignee picks up the goods at the post office. Postal transport falls into two kinds: regular mail and air mail.

This method is simple and convenient, and delivery is made simply when a receipt of the goods posted is obtained. It is a kind of international and "door-to-door" transport. According to the postal regulations worldwide, the longest length of each parcel is limits to one meter, and the weight under 20 kilograms. The restriction of the size and weight of the parcels limits the practicality of this mode, it is only suitable for precision instruments, machinery components, bullion and ornaments, material medical and other small sized and precious goods.

邮包运输是托运人在托运地邮局办理邮件托运手续后，由邮局负责将邮件传递到目的地，收货人直接在目的地邮局提取邮件的一种运输方式。邮包分为普通邮包和航空邮包两种。

这种运输方式的特点是手续简便，费用不太高，具有广泛的国际性和"门到门"的运输性质。根据各国邮政的规定，国际邮包运输限定每件长度不能超过 1 米，重量不能超过 20 千克，所以邮包运输只适用于量轻体小的商品，如精密仪器、机器零件、金银首饰、药品以及各种样品和零星物品等。

5．International combined transport/International multimodal transport（国际多式联运）

International combined transport means the conveyance of cargo using at least two modes of transport by which the goods are carried from the place of dispatch to the destination on the basis of combined transport or a multimodal transport contract. Under this method, the container is used as an intermedium and makes up an international multimodal and joint transport mode by sea, air and land (See Fig.9-2).

国际多式联运是在集装箱运输的基础上产生和发展起来的一种综合性的连贯运输方式。它一般是以集装箱为媒介，把海、陆、空多种传统的单一运输方式有机地结合起来，组成一种国际连贯运输（见图 9-2）。

It usually includes:

(1) Train-Air (or Truck-Air, or Ship-Air). The export goods are carried to Hong Kong by train or truck or ship and then loaded into airplanes at Hong Kong.

(2) Train-Ship. The export goods from Chinese interior provinces may also be transported to Hong Kong by railway for transshipment to foreign ports by vessels.

(3) Container Transport/Containerized Traffic.

通常包括：

（1）火车、飞机的联合运输方式。出口货物先由铁路或卡车或船运往香港，然后在香港将货物装上飞机。

（2）火车、船的联合运输方式。中国内陆省份的出口货物先由铁路运往香港，然后在香港转船运往国外港口。

（3）集装箱运输方式。

鸿运船务有限公司　　　　　　　　　　**ORIGINAL**

Hongyun Shipping Co., Ltd.

BILL OF LADING

Shipper GUANGDONG MACHINERY IMPORT AND EXPORT CORP. (GROUP) 726 DONGFENG ROAD EAST, GUANGZHOU, CHINA	B/L No. COSU299120081
	Combined Transport Bill of Lading Received in apparent good order and condition except as otherwise noted the total number of containers or other packages or units enumerated below for transportation from the place of receipt to the place of delivery subject to the terms and conditions hereof.
Consignee TO ORDER OF SHIPPER	One of the Bills of Lading must be surrendered duly endorsed to the Carrier by or on behalf of the Holder of the Bills of Lading, the rights and liabilities arising in accordance with the terms and conditions hereof shall, without prejudice to any rule of common law or statue rendering them binding on the Merchant, become binding in all respects between the Carrier and the Holder of the Bills of Lading as through the contract evidenced hereby had been made between them.
Notify Address 　SHITAYA KINZHOUKU CO., LTD. 　2-217-CHOME UENO TAITO-KU TOKYO	IN WITNESS where of the number of original Bills of Lading stated under have been signed. All of this tenor and date, one of which being accompanied, the other(s) to be void.

Pre-carriage by	Place of Receipt	For delivery of goods please apply to		
Ocean Vessel Voy. No. JING AN CHENG V. 0021	Port of Loading GUANGZHOU			
Port of Discharge YORKOHAMA	Place of Delivery YORKOHAMA	Final Destination for the Merchant's Reference only		
Container, Seal No. & Marks & No. A99JP20002 SHITAYA YORKOHAMA	No. of Package & Description of Goods 500 BUNDLES RABBIT BRAND SHOVEL WITH METAL HANDLE TOTAL: FIVE HUNDRED BUNDLES ONLY	Gross Weight kgs 20 000kgs		Measurement m³ 62.152m³
Freight and Charges Freight Prepaid	Revenue Tons.	Rate Per	Prepaid	Collect
Prepaid at	Payable at	Place and Date of issue GUANGZHOU 20th,March, 2010		
Total Prepaid	No. of Original B(s)/L THREE(3)	Stamp & Signature		

LADEN ON BOARD THE VESSEL
Date

By..
(Terms continued on Back here of)

Fig.9-2　Combined Transport Bill of Lading（多式联运提单）

6. Container transport（集装箱运输）

With the expansion of international trade, the container service has become more and more popular. The use of containers provides a highly efficient form for transport by ship, by road, by rail and by air, though its fullest benefits are felt in shipping, where costs may be reduced by as much as half. Therefore, nowadays, it has become a very convenient and modern transport method in international practice. Containers are constructed of metal and have standard lengths, mostly ranging from ten to forty feet. The International Standard Organization has made 3 catena, 13 classes standard specifications from 1A to 3A, among which the mostly used is Type 1A(8 inches ×8 inches×40 inches, Type 1C(8 inches×8 inches×20 inches) and Type 1AA (8 inches×8.6 inches×40 inches) .

Container transport falls into two kinds (methods of consignment): full container load (FCL) and less than container load (LCL). As for the consignment that reaches the demand of FCL, the vanning FCL is done either by the consignor himself or the carrier at the production side or the warehouse, then it is sent to the container yard(CY) for consolidation by the carrier. As for the consignment that does not reach the demand of a full container, we call it less than container, the vanning LCL is done by the consignor himself and then send the consignment to the container freight station(CFS) or inland container depot for consolidation by the carrier, who will piece together the goods according to the nature, destination, weight and so on in the container and then send it to the container yard.

随着国际贸易的不断扩大，使用集装箱运输越来越普遍。这种成组运输因其装载量大，往往又能使船舶、火车、汽车、飞机等各种运输工具衔接在一起，从而降低近一半的成本而成为一种新型的现代化运输方式。集装箱按照标准的大小尺寸用金属制作。国际标准化组织（ISO）对集装箱的规格从 1A 到 3A 共分成 3 个系列 13 种标准规格。其中，应用最多的是 1A 型（8 英尺×8 英尺×40 英尺）、1C 型（8 英尺×8 英尺×20 英尺）和 1AA 型（8 英尺×8.6 英尺×40 英尺）。

集装箱运输分为整箱货（FCL）和拼箱货（LCL）两种。对于托运数量达到整箱要求的整箱货，可以由发货人在自己的工厂或仓库自行装箱，也可以由承运人代为装箱，装箱后直接运往设在港口码头的集装箱堆场（CY）。对于托运数量达不到一个集装箱容积或负荷量要求的拼箱货，则一般由发货人将货物交承运人码头的集装箱货运站（CFS）或内陆集装箱货运站（Inland Container Depot），由承运人根据货物的性质、流向、重量等将多个货主的货物拼装成箱，并运交集装箱堆场。

7. Land bridge transport（大陆桥运输）

Land bridge transport is a mode of transport that connects the ocean transport on the two sides of the land by the railway and land which runs across the continent, i.e., ship-train-ship. Land bridge transport uses the container as a medium, so it has all the advantages of container transport. There are three main land bridges in the world: (1) American land bridge; (2) Siberian land bridge; (3) The New European- Asia land bridge.

大陆桥运输是指使用横贯大陆的铁路或公路运输系统作为中间桥梁,是海—陆—海的连贯运输。一般以集装箱为媒介,是国际多式联运的一种形式。它具有集装箱运输的优点。目前世界上主要的大陆桥有：（1）美洲大陆桥；（2）西伯利亚大陆桥；（3）新欧亚大陆桥。

8. Pipelines transport（管道运输）

Pipelines transport is used for transporting commodities, such as crude oil and gases etc., long distances over land and under the sea. Rising fuel costs make pipelines an attractive economic alternative to other forms of transport in certain circumstances. Safety in transferring flammable commodities is another important consideration.

管道运输是利用管道输送气体、液体和粉状固体的一种运输方式，这种管道运输线路长，一般埋于海底。油价的不断上涨使得管道运输越来越受青睐，此外，对于运输易燃物品，管道运输安全可靠。

Section Two　Delivery Conditions（装运条件）

Delivery conditions include the time of delivery, and in some cases including the time of loading and unloading, and the charges resulting from loading and unloading operations, the port of shipment, the port of destination, partial shipments and transshipments, shipping documents, etc.

装运条款主要包括装运时间，有时包括装卸时间、装卸费用、装运港和目的港、分批和转船以及货运单据的规定等内容。

1．Time of delivery（装运时间）

The time of delivery refers to the time limit during which the seller shall deliver the goods to the buyer at the agreed place by the agreed methods. There are the following ways to stipulate the time of delivery in the contract.

装运时间又称装运期，通常是指货物装上指定运输工具，并在规定的时间或期限内卖方将货物交给买方。在进出口合同中对装运时间的规定方法，主要有以下几种。

(1) Stipulate the definite time of delivery. For example:

Shipment on or before March 15, 2018.

Shipment during January/February/March 2018.

Shipment on or before April 30, 2018.

明确规定具体期限。例如：

2019 年 3 月 15 日前装运。

2019 年 1/2/3 月装运。

装运期不迟于 2019 年 4 月 30 日装运。

(2) Stipulate a period of fixed time, the seller can arrange shipment during whichever date, for example:

Shipment during March 2019.

Shipment during January/February/March 2019.

Shipment within 15 days after receipt of L/C.

Shipment by first available vessel.

Shipment by first opportunity.

Shipment subject to available shipping space.

March shipment — the exporter is required to make delivery to a designated ship during the month of March, that is, on any day from March 1th to March 31th, and secure from the steamship company a B/L dated in March.

规定了某一段装运时间，卖方可以选择其中任何一天装运，例如：

2019 年 3 月装运。

2019 年 1/2/3 月装运。

收到货款后 15 天内安排装运。

由第一艘货轮装运。

第一时间安排装运。

有舱位时安排装运。

3 月安排装运，可以在 3 月，即 3 月 1 日至 31 日中的任何一天，都可安排装运。

(3) Stipulate shipment within … days after receipt of the letter of credit, for example:

Shipment within 30 days after receipt of L/C.

Shipment within 45 days after receipt of L/C.

Shipment within 3 months after receipt of L/C.

规定在收到信用证后××天内安排装运，例如：

收到信用证后 30 天内安排装运。

收到信用证后 45 天内安排装运。

收到信用证后 3 个月内安排装运。

In order to prevent the buyer from opening L/C late, when the clause "shipment within 30 days after the date of receipt of L/C" is used, it is necessarily accompanied by another clause "The relevant L/C must reach the seller not later than …". In this way a somewhat indefinite clause is made more or less definite.

在使用"收到信用证后 30 天内安排装运"条款时，还必须加上"信用证不得迟于……到达我处"。从某种意义上说，也是对装运时间的限制。

(4) Stipulate the goods shall be shipped in the near future, for example:

Immediate shipment.

Shipment as soon as possible.

Prompt shipment.

But there are not unanimous explanations about these terms in international trade, and thus, it is quite easy to result in disputes, so we should try to avoid using them.

规定即将安排装运，例如：

立即装运。

尽速装运。

即刻装运。

但这类术语在国际上并无统一的解释，极易引起争议和纠纷。因此，除非买卖双方已有统一理解，否则应避免使用这类术语。

2. Port of shipment and port of destination（装运港和目的港）

The points that we should pay attention to when stipulating the port of shipment in an export contract.

(1) The port of shipment shall be close to the origin of the goods.

(2) We should take into consideration the loading and unloading, and specific transportation conditions and the standards of freight and various charges at home and abroad.

(3) Under the FOB terms, the buyer is responsible for chartering a ship. However, when we stipulate the port of shipment, its specifications shall be suitable to the ship chartered by the buyer.

(4) In export trade, it is the usual practice to designate only one port of shipment in one transaction, but exceptionally, when large amounts of goods are involved and, in particular, the goods are stored at different places, two or more ports of shipment are also specified, such as "Shanghai and Guangzhou", "Dalian/ Qingdao/ Shanghai". Sometimes, as the port of shipment is not yet determined at the time the transaction is being concluded, a general clause like "China ports" may be used.

商定装运港时要特别注意的问题。

（1）选择靠近商品产地的装运港。

（2）要考虑国内外装运港口的装卸条件、具体的运输条件、收费标准等。

（3）在 FOB 术语下，买方负责租船，但值得注意的是，该装运港足以容纳所租船。

（4）在出口贸易中，习惯做法是只规定一个港口为装运港，并列明具体港口名称。但如果该批货物太多，特别是分放在几个地方，这时候可以破例规定两个或三个装运港，如"装运港上海和广州""装运港大连、青岛和上海"。有时在签订合同时装运港口还没有定下来，也可以规定为"在中国装运"。

The port of destination is usually proposed and determined by the buyer, which shall be convenient for reselling the goods and shall be the one at which the vessel may safely arrive and be always afloat. When we determine the port of destination, we must pay attention to the following points.

(1) We should not accept the port in a country with which our government does not permit us to do business.

(2) The stipulation on the port of destination shall be definite and specific. We should not use ambiguous terms, such as "main ports in Europe" or "main ports in Africa".

(3) If we have to choose a port which has no direct liner to stop by or the trips are few, we should stipulate "transshipment to be permitted" in the contract.

(4) The port of destination shall be the one at which the vessel may safely arrive and be always afloat.

(5) As to the business with an inland country, we usually choose a port which is nearest to the country. We usually do not accept an inland city as the place of destination unless through combined transportation for which the combined transport operator will be responsible.

(6) Facilities in the port of loading or unloading are also very important and therefore reasonable attention should be given to issues such as loading and unloading facilities, freightage and additional freightage, etc. The ports of shipment should be, in principle, ports that are close to the source of goods, while the port of destination should be ports that are near the users.

(7) In case the middleman abroad has not found a proper buyer when the contract is concluded, in order to make it convenient for him to sell the cargo afloat, the "optional port" may be accepted upon request of the foreign party, the buyer is allowed to choose one from the several ports of destination provided.

(8) Pay attention to the names of foreign ports. Many ports have the same names. For example, there are 12 "Victoria" ports around the world.

目的港一般是由买方根据使用、转售的需要而提出，经卖方同意后确定的，目的港要方便货船抵达和停靠。合同中规定目的港的方法有以下几种。

（1）如果我国政府规定不能与某个国家做外贸业务，那么，就不能选择该国的港口为目的港。

（2）对于目的港的规定必须明确具体，最好不用模棱两可的措辞，如"欧洲主要港口""非洲主要港口"等。

（3）如果我国没有直达船或直达船很少，就应该在合同中写清楚允许转船。

（4）所选择的目的港必须适合货船的停靠。

（5）如果与内陆国家的公司做业务，那么就应选择离这个国家最近的港口。除非有联合直达运输服务，否则一般不选择内陆国家为目的港。

（6）码头的装卸设备也很重要，因此，必须注意码头的装卸设备、货运条件等问题。一般地说，装运港要靠近货源，而目的港要靠近买方。

（7）如果在签订合同时，国外的中间商未能找到合适的买家，为了便于该中间商销售货物，可以根据外国客户的要求，接受买方的"选择港口"条件，但必须是合同中规定的那几个港口。

（8）应注意国外目的港的重名问题。世界上重名港很多，如维多利亚（Victoria）就有12个。

3．Partial shipment and transshipment（分批装运和转船运输）

Definition of partial shipment: In the case of an export business covering a large amount of goods, it is necessary to make shipments in several lots by several carriers sailing on different dates.

Reasons for partial shipment: It is done because of the limitation of shipping space available, poor unloading facilities at the port of destination, dull market season, or possible delay in the process of manufacturing of the goods, etc.

所谓分批装运，是指一笔成交的货物分若干批于不同航次装运。

分批装运的原因：由于舱位不够或装卸港条件以及市场销售的影响和限制，或工厂生产加工延误等而需分批装运。

Transshipment in ocean shipping, is the movement of goods in transit from one carrier to another at the ports of transshipment before the goods reach the port of destination.

Reasons for transshipment: Transshipment is necessary when ships sailing direct to the port of destination are not available, the port of destination does not tie along the sailing route of the liner, or the amount of cargo for a certain port of destination is so small that no ships would like to call at that port.

所谓转船运输，是指货物通过中途港重新装卸和转运。

转船的原因：由于没有直达船，或者货船航行的线路不经过所要到达的目的港，或者装运的货物太少而没有货船愿意驶往该目的港等而需转船。

Generally speaking, partial shipment or transshipment is favorable to the seller, which shall put the seller in a better position to perform the relevant contract. According to the relevant stipulations of the UCP600 (Uniform Customs and Practice for Documentary Credits), transport documents which appear on their face to indicate that shipment has been made on the same means of conveyance and for the same journey, provided they indicate the same destination, will not be regarded as covering partial shipments, even if the transport documents indicate different dates of issuance and/or different ports of shipment, places of taking in charge, or dispatch. If transshipment is necessary in case of no direct or suitable ship available for shipment, a clause in this regard can be included in the contract. According to the relevant stipulations of the "UCP600" unless the credit stipulates otherwise, partial shipment and transshipment are allowed. But contractual laws in some countries stipulate that: Partial shipment and transshipment, if not stipulated in the contract, shall not be deemed to be allowed. It, therefore, should be clearly stipulated in the relevant contract. In case where such a kind of clause as "transshipment is allowed" is stipulated in the contract (such as, shipment during March and April in two equal monthly lots), then, the seller should strictly follow the stipulations of the contract. According to the relevant stipulations of the "UCP600", if any installment is not shipped within the period allowed for that installment, the credit ceases to be available for that and any subsequent installments, unless otherwise stipulated in the credit.

　　一般来说，分批装运和转运对卖方有利，卖方可以争取主动。按《跟单信用证统一惯例（UCP600）》的有关规定，如果运输单据表面注明货物是使用同一运输工具并经过同一路线运输的，而且运输单据注明的目的地相同，那么即使每套运输单据注明的装运日期不同和/或装货港、接受监管地、发运地不同，也不作为分批装运。没有直达船或无合适的船舶运输而需要转运的，可以要求在合同中订立允许装船条款。按《跟单信用证统一惯例（UCP600）》的有关规定，除非信用证有相反的规定，可允许分批装运和转船。但按有些国外合同法，如果没有在合同中规定分批装运和转运条款，那么将不等于可以分批装运和转运。因此，一般应对此条款做明确规定。但如果在合同中规定了分批装运条款（例如，3月和4月两批每月平均装运），那么，卖方应严格按合同规定执行。按《跟单信用证统一惯例（UCP600）》的有关规定，除非另有规定，否则其中任何一批未按规定装运，则本批及以后各批均告失效。

4．Shipping advice（装运通知）

The usual practice of international trade under FOB terms is for the seller, after getting the goods ready for shipment, to send a notice to the buyer before the agreed shipment date (usually 30-45 days before the shipment date) so that the buyer can arrange the relevant vessel for taking delivery. The buyer, after receiving the relevant notice from the seller, should at the agreed time, notify the seller of the name of the vessel and the estimated arrival date of the vessel. And the seller, after the goods are placed on board the vessel, should at the agreed time, notify the buyer of the contract No., the name and weight of the goods, the invoice amount, the vessel's name and the date of shipment so that the buyer can make necessary arrangements for purchasing the relevant insurance and taking delivery of the goods. See Fig.9-3 Sample of Shipping Advice and Fig.9-4 Example of Shipping Advice.

SHIPPING ADVICE

FAX:　　　　　　　　　　　　INVOICE No.:_____

TELEX:　　　　　　　　　　　L/C No.:_____

TEL:　　　　　　　　　　　　S/C No.:_____

MESSRS:

DEAR SIRS,

WE HEREBY INFORM YOU THAT THE GOODS UNDER THE ABOVE MENTIONED CREDIT HAVE BEEN SHIPPED. THE DETAILS OF THE SHIPMENT ARE STATED BELOW:

SHIPPING MARKS

COMMODITY:_____

NUMBER OF BALES:_____

TOTAL G.T.:_____

OCEAN VESSEL:_____

DATE OF DEPARTURE:_____

B/L No.:_____

PORT OF LOADING:_____

DESTINATION:_____

_____

× × ×

Fig.9-3　Sample of Shipping Advice（装运通知样本）

按国际贸易的一般做法，在 FOB 条件下，卖方应在约定装船前（一般为 30~45 天）向买方发出货物备妥通知，以便买方派船接货。买方在接到卖方发出的通知后，应按约定的时间，将船名、船舶到港日期等通知卖方。卖方在货物装船后应在约定时间将合同号、货物品名、重量、发票金额、船名及装船日期等内容告知买方，以便买方办理保险并做好接卸货物的准备。图 9-3 所示为装运通知的样本，图 9-4 所示为装运通知的一个实例。

广州毛织品进出口贸易公司

GUANGZHOU KNITWEAR AND MANUFATURED GOODS

IMPORT & EXPORT TRADE CORPORATION

321, ZHONGSHAN ROAD GUANGZHOU, CHINA

SHIPPING ADVICE

FAX: 37626000 　　　　　　　　　　INVOICE No.:___NO123___

TELEX: 64042523 　　　　　　　　　L/C No.:___06/2006_____

TEL: 64042521 　　　　　　　　　　S/C No.:___WE2333_____

MESSRS:

　　YI YANG TRADE CORPORATION

　　88 MARSHALL AVE

　　DONCASTER VIC 3108

　　CANADA

DEAR SIRS,

　　WE HEREBY INFORM YOU THAT THE GOODS UNDER THE ABOVE MENTIONED CREDIT HAVE BEEN SHIPPED. THE DETAILS OF THE SHIPMENT ARE STATED BELOW:

SHIPPING MARKS

Y.Y.T.C 　　　　　　　　　COMMODITY: COTTON TEATOWLES___

MONTREAL 　　　　　　　NUMBER OF BALES: 200 BALES___

C/NO.1-367 　　　　　　　TOTAL G.T.:___19911KG___

　　　　　　　　　　　　OCEAN VESSEL: GUANGZHOU V.053

　　　　　　　　　　　　DATE OF DEPARTURE: OCT.24,2005

　　　　　　　　　　　　B/L No.: HJSHB142939

　　　　　　　　　　　　PORT OF LOADING: SHANGHAI

　　　　　　　　　　　　DESTINATION: MONTREAL

　　　　　　　　　　　　GUANGZHOU KNITWEAR AND MANUFATURED GOODS

　　　　　　　　　　　　　　IMPORT & EXPORT TRADE CORPORATION

　　　　　　　　　　　　　　　　LILY

　　　　　　　　　　　　　　　　OCT.24, 2005

Fig.9-4　Example of Shipping Advice　（装运通知实例）

Section Three　Shipping Documents（货运单据）

International trade attaches so great importance to shipping documents that, to a certain degree, it can be called documentary trade, or "symbolic" trade. This is because shipping documents represent the title to the goods. For example, under a letter of credit, the buyer cannot take delivery of the goods until he obtains the shipping documents; on the other hand, only if the seller releases the shipping documents can he receive the payment. What documents to be used and how to carefully and accurately complete them deserve our adequate attention. As a rule, every contract of sale stipulates the kinds of shipping documents required. The slightest negligence in these documents might result in serious problems, which is not infrequent in practice. It is, therefore, imperative for both the exporter and the importer to abide by such stipulations. Generally, commercial invoice, bill of lading, insurance policy or certificate, packing list, and weight memo, etc., are called shipping documents. In addition, other documents required by the buyers and related to the matter of duty to be paid on the imported goods, sometimes, are also included in shipping documents, they are the pro forma, consular invoice, certificate of origin, certificate of value, certificate of inspection. The commercial invoice, bill of lading and insurance policy constitute the chief shipping documents in international trade. They are indispensable in almost every instance of export and import consignment. This unit mainly deals with commercial invoice, pro forma invoice, bill of lading, packing list, multimodal transport document (MTD), weight memo and inspection certificate.

国际贸易对单证的要求非常高，从某种程度上讲，国际贸易是一种单证的交易，或者说是"象征性交易"，因为货运单证代表着对货物的所有权。例如，在信用证下，买方只有在获取货运单证后才能提货，而卖方也只有在交出货运单证后才能得到货款。要使用什么样的单证，以及如何仔细、准确地完成这些单证非常值得我们注意。一般来说，每一笔销售合同都要规定各种所需要的单证。忽略这些单证将会产生严重的后果，这在国际贸易中并不罕见。所以，对进出口双方来说，遵守这些规定是很必要的。商业发票、提单、保险单、装箱单、重量单等通常称为货运单证。此外，货运单证还包括买方所要求的以及与对进口货物征收关税有关的单证，如形式发票、领事发票、产地证书、价值证书、检验证书等。在国际贸易中，商业发票、提单和保险单是最主要的单证。在每一宗进出口货物中，它们都是必不可少的。本单元将主要涉及商业发票、形式发票、提单、装箱单、多式联运单据、重量单和检验证书。

1. Commercial invoice（商业发票）

1) Definition of commercial invoice（商业发票的定义）

An invoice is a statement sent by the seller to the buyer giving particulars of the goods being purchased, and showing the sum of money due. Different parties require such statements for different purposes. There are various invoices, such as commercial invoices, banker's invoices, consular invoices, customs invoices and pro forma invoices. Among these, the commercial invoice is the most common one and has to be provided for each and every consignment as one of the documents evidencing shipment. When speaking of an invoice covering a certain shipment, we usually refer to the commercial invoice. It is a document which contains identifying information about merchandise sold for which payment is to be made. All invoices should show the name and address of the debtor, terms of payment, description of items, and the price. In addition, the invoice should show the manner of delivery. See Fig.9-5 Example of Commercial Invoice.

　　发票是卖方对其所出售的货物开出的包括各项细节的清单，并作为向买方收取货款的凭证。买卖双方出于不同的目的需要这些清单。发票的形式多种多样，有商业发票、银行发票、领事发票、海关发票和形式发票。在这些发票中，商业发票使用得最为广泛，几乎每一宗货物都要求提供商业发票，作为证明货物已发送的单证之一。当我们说为发送的货物开具发票时，指的是商业发票。商业发票是一种载有买方必须付款的所售货物的识别情况的单证。所有商业发票应写明债务人的名称和地址、支付条款、商品名称、价格。此外，该发票还应写明运输方式。图 9-5 所示为商业发票实例。

COMMERCIAL INVOICE

ORIGINAL

TEL: __64042522__
FAX: __64042523__
POSTAL CODE: __200032__

INVOICE No.: 04SB200D
DATE: APR.27, 2004
S/C No.: T228855
L/C No.: AI2004166763

TO: MAGGIET CORPORATION PTY LTD.
　　101 BURWOOD HIGHWAY
　　BURWOOD VIC 3125

FROM: SHANGHAI, CHINA　　　　　　　　TO: MELBOURNE, AUSTRALIA
COMMODITY DESCRIPTIONS AND QUANTITY　　　UNIT PRICE　　AMOUNT
　　　　　　　　　　　　　　　　　　　CFR MELBOURNE, AUSTRALIA
KNITTED GARMENTS OF 92 PERCENT COTTON AND 8 PERCENT SPANDEX AS PER ORDER No. 1354 MULTISTICH CREW

1354/243023	400PCS	USD 5.20	USD 2 080.00

TOTAL:	400PCS		USD 2 080.00

SHIPPING MARKS:　　　　　　　　TOTAL QUANTITY: 400PCS
MAGGIET　　　　　　　　　　　PACKED IN: 16 CARTONS ONLY
MELBOURNE　　　　　　　　　　GROSS WEIGHT: 152.00KGS
NO. 1-16　　　　　　　　　　　NET WEIGHT: 136.00KGS
　　　　　　　　　　　　　　　COUNTRY OF ORIGIN: CHINA
SAY TOTAL US DOLLARS TWO THOUSAND AND EIGHTY ONLY
SHANGHAI IMPORT & EXPORT TRADE CORPORATION
DR. 2261 NANJING ROAD
　　　　　　　　Signature: 陈红军

Fig.9-5　Example of Commercial Invoice（商业发票实例）

2) Contents of the commercial invoice（商业发票的内容）

Commercial invoices vary in forms. However, no matter what forms they may take, the contents must fully comply with the contract. In general, a commercial invoice summarizes contract terms, and declares that shipments have been made on the basis of them. It contains, first of all, the names and addresses of the seller and the buyer; next, a full description of the goods dispatched, including the weights and numbers and marks of all the packages; thirdly, the price per unit and the total cost of the consignment. The commercial invoice will also state the port of shipment and the date, the terms of sale, such as CIF, and the terms of payment, such as by sight draft, perhaps under a letter of credit. Finally, it must be signed by an authorized employee of the seller, and may even quote import or export license numbers.

Sometimes the invoice price is broken down into such things as the cost of materials, the cost of processing and manufacture and the cost of packing and transport. The amount of detail on an invoice depends on the rules of the importing country. Some countries require a more detailed breakdown of the price. Some foreign governments have special regulations for commercial invoices, such as requiring them to be translated into the local language or requiring the use of metric weights and other measurements. Several customs authorities and other regulatory agencies also insist on complete consistency between the different documents. Thus, the numbers and marks on the commercial and consular invoices, the insurance certificate, and the bill of lading must agree exactly. Originals of commercial invoices must bear the signature of the seller, who is usually the shipper. The abbreviation "E. & O.E." standing for "Errors and Omissions Excepted" is usually printed at the foot of the invoice form. It means that the shipper is prepared to make correction in case errors and omissions are found.

商业发票的形式各不相同，但不管它们采取什么样的形式，其内容必须与合同完全相符。通常商业发票概括了合同条款，并表明货物根据合同条款已经装运。首先，商业发票包括卖方和买方的姓名和地址。其次，包括运出货物的细目：所有包件的重量、数量和唛头。再次，包括货物的单价和总价。发票也要说明装运的港口和日期以及价格条款，如到岸价和付款方式，如即期汇票或信用证项下的即期汇票。最后，发票必须由卖方授权的雇员签字，甚至还可能需要写上进出口许可证的号码。

有时发票上的价格可以分解成为诸如材料费、加工制造费和包装运输费。对发票细节的要求取决于进口国家的规章制度。有些国家要求发票提供更为详细的价格分解。有些国家政府对商业发票有特殊的规定，如要求商业发票翻译成当地使用的语言或者在重量上使用国际公制还有其他的一些计量方法，有的海关当局和一些管制机构还强调不同文件上的一致性。因此，商业发票、领事发票、保险证明和提单上的号码和标号必须绝对一致。商业发票的原件必须有卖方的签名，通常就是发货人。缩写"E. & O. E."代表着"错误和遗漏例外"，通常印在发票的页脚。它的意思是如果有错误和遗漏，发货人将随时准备修改。

3) Functions of commercial invoice（商业发票的功能）

The invoice functions mainly as a record of the export transaction for buyers, sellers and customs authorities. Copies of the invoice are used by the exporters, their bank, the paying bank, the receiving agents at the port of discharge, the customs in the exporting country and the importers. The importer needs it to check whether the goods consigned to him are in compliance with the terms and conditions of the respective contract. The banks need it together with the Bill of Lading and the Insurance Certificate to effect payment. The customs need it to calculate duties, if any. The exporters and importers need it to keep their accounts. In the absence of a draft, the commercial invoice takes its place for drawing money.

商业发票主要用作买方、卖方、海关出口交易的记录。发票副本由出口商、出口商银行、出口商付款行、卸货港接收代理人、进出口商海关使用。进口商使用商业发票核对商品是否与合同条款一致。银行使用商业发票、提单和保险凭证支付款项。海关依据商业发票征税（如果有的话）。进出口商可以依据商业发票记账。在没有开立汇票的情况下，商业发票可以代替汇票收回货款。

4) Illustrations of commercial invoice（商业发票说明）

(1) Checklist（清单）

To understand and be able to write an invoice, you should think about these points.

* Customer's name.

a. The office address.

b. The delivery address.

* The invoice number (for your records).

* The order number.

* The reference number and/or description of each item.

* The quantity.

* The price of each item.

* The total price of items and total of all items.

* The amount of discount allowed and the conditions.

* The method of freight, insurance and cost.

* The delivery address.

* The number of parcels, packages or crates.

* The markings on the parcels, packages or crates.

* Any other points.

为了理解和正确填写商业发票，必须考虑以下几点。

*顾客的姓名。

a. 办公地址。

b. 发货地址。

*发票号码（便于记录）。

*订单号码。

*参照号码和/或各项商品的货名。

*数量。

*各项商品的价格。

*各项商品的总价和所有商品的总价。

*所同意的折扣数量及条件。

*支付运费、保险费和成本的方法。

*发货地址。

*包、件或箱的数量。

*包、件或箱上的标志。

*其他事项。

(2) Format of commercial invoice（商业发票的格式）（See Fig.9-6）

××× Import and Export Co.

To: _____   Invoice No.: _____

_____   Sales Contract No.:_____

Date of Invoice:_____

From _____   To_____

Letter of Credit No.: _____   Issued by_____

Marks and Numbers	Quantity and Descriptions	Unit Price	Amount

_____ (Signed) _____

Fig.9-6   Format of Commercial Invoice   （商业发票的格式）

2．Proforma invoice（形式发票）

Proforma, in Latin, means "for the sake of form". A proforma invoice is a document such as an invoice, issued as a temporary statement, but ultimately to be replaced by a final statement which can only be issued at a later date. Outwardly, except for the marked "proforma", it is like an ordinary commercial invoice containing the general particulars, for example, marks, number of goods, descriptions, quantities, quality, prices, etc. However, in nature, it is a different form of invoice which treats "hypothetical" sales as though they had actually and contractually taken place. It is not a formal document but a document without engagement, which is binding neither on the import nor the export .

Proforma invoices are required for various reasons. Primarily the importer requires them to comply with the regulations in force in their country. Moreover, the importer can require them in advance for information, or letter of credit purposes. In many countries, especially in the developing countries of the Third World, foreign trade is under strict control. The governments of such countries usually enforce an Import License System or an Import Quota System. Importers must apply for the necessary Import License or foreign exchange and they may not import any goods without the approval of Import License or the allocation of foreign exchang. Often their application has to be supported by an informal invoice, a proforma invoice, issued by the foreign exporter showing the name of commodity, specifications, unit price, etc.

The importer who asks for a proforma invoice is in fact making an enquiry, and the expert who sends the proforma invoice is actually making an offer. If the exporter wants to make a firm offer, he must mention the term of validity in the covering letter when sending the proforma invoice（See Fig.9-7）.

广东对外贸易进出口公司
GUANGDONG IMPORT AND EXPORT CORPORATION

727EAST DONGFENG ROAD
GUANGZHOU
CHINA, 510090
TEL:86-20-37636211
FAX:86-20-37636212

形式发票
Proforma Invoice

No.: _____

Date:_____

Accountee:_____

_____

Shipped Per Steamer:_____

From _____   To _____

B/L No.: _____   Contract No.: _____

Shipping Marks & Nos. _____

Description of Goods	Quantity	Unit Price	Amount

TOTAL:

GUANGZHOU IMPORT AND EXPORT CORPORATION
727 EAST DONGFENG ROAD, GUANGZHOU, CHINA

Fig.9-7　Sample of Proforma Invoice　（形式发票样本）

Proforma 在拉丁文里是"为了形式"的意思。形式发票是指一种凭证，它只作为临时单证使用，数天后由开具的最终发票所代替。从外观上看，除注明"形式"字样外，它和一般的商业发票一样，包含一些常规项目，如唛头、货物的件数、货名、数量、质量、价格等。但是，从本质上讲，形式发票是一种不同形式的发票，因为它涉及的是一种"假设"的销售，就像签订了合同，实际发生了一样。形式发票不是正式文件，而是一种对买卖双方都无约束力的文件。

需要使用形式发票的原因有多种，其中最重要的原因是进口商需要形式发票以便适应其本国现行的规章制度。进口商还可事先要求得到形式发票来了解进口货物的有关情况，申请进口许可证或信用证。在许多国家，特别是第三世界的发展中国家，对外贸易由国家严格管制。这些国家的政府通常都实行进口许可证制度或进口配额制。进口商必须申请必要的进口许可证或外汇，未经批准进口许可证或未经配给外汇，进口商就不得进口任何货物。进口商的申请往往需提供外国出口商签发的非正式发票——以形式发票为依据，该发票需列明商品名称、规格、单价等。

进口商索取形式发票事实上是在询盘，而出口商寄送形式发票实际上是在报盘。假如出口商要报实盘，则必须在信内指明其将在有效期内寄送形式发票。形式发票样本如图 9-7 所示。

3. Bill of lading（提单）

As more than 80 percent of China's exports are carried by sea-going ships, the most import ant shipping document is the bill of lading. It is a document given by a shipping company, representing both a receipt for the goods shipped and a contract for shipment between the shipping company and the shipper. It is also a document of title to the goods, giving the holder or the assignee the right to possession of the goods. See Fig.9-8 Sample of Ocean Bill of Lading and Fig.9-9 Example of Ocean Bill of Lading.

由于我国 80%以上的出口货物是由远洋船只运输的，因此，最重要的海运单据就是提单。它是轮船公司签发的单证，既代表承运货物的收据，又代表承运人和托运人之间的运输合同。它也是代表货物所有权的证件，它给予持有人或受让人提货的权利。海运提单样本如图 9-8 所示。海运提单实例如图 9-9 所示。

1) Functions of Bill of Lading（提单的作用）

The Bill of Lading has three important functions: (1) It is a receipt for goods signed by the shipping company and given to the shippers. (2) It is also evidence of a contract of carriage between the shipping company and shippers. (3) It is a document of title because the legal owner of the Bill of Lading is the owner of the goods. For this reason the Bill of Lading can be used to transfer the goods from one owner to another. When the exporters complete it, they can write the buyer's name in the space, "consignee". This means the consignee is the legal owner of the goods, as named on Bill of Lading. Otherwise the exporters can write "to other" in the consignee space. Underneath "to order" they write the name and address of the agent. Then the agent in the importing country can endorse the bill to the buyer. In this way the importers can transfer the consignment to their customers. This means that there has to be a separate Bill of Lading for each consignee and several consignments can not be consolidated on to one bill.

From the above we can see that the Bill of Landing fulfils at least three important functions: (1) It serves as a receipt for goods signed by the shipping company (carrier) and given to the shipper (consignor). (2) It is also the evidence of a contract of carriage between the carrier and the consignor. (3) It conveys a document of title because the legal owner of the bill of lading is the owner of the goods it covers.

OCEAN BILL OF LADING

Shipper	B/L No.
Consignee or order	中国外运上海公司 SINOTRANS SHANGHAI COMPANY **OCEAN BILL OF LADING** SHIPPED on board in apparent good order and condition (unless otherwise indicated) the goods or packages specified herein and to be discharged at the mentioned port of discharge or as near there to as the vessel may safely get and be always afloat.
Notify address	

Pre-carriage by	Port of Loading	(continued right column)
Vessel	Port of Transshipment	
Port of Discharge	Final Destination	

The weight, measure, marks and numbers, quality, contents and value, being particulars furnished by the Shipper, are not checked by the Carrier on loading.

The Shipper, Consignee and the Holder of this Bill of Lading hereby expressly accept and agree to all printed, written or stamped provisions, exceptions and conditions of this Bill of Lading, including those on the back hereof.

IN WITNESS where of the number of original Bills of Lading stated below have been signed, one of which being accomplished, the other(s) to be void.

Container, Seal No. & marks & Nos.	No. and Kind of Packages & Description of Goods	Gross Weight kgs	Measurement m³

Freight and Charges	Regarding Transshipment Information Please Contact

Ex. Rate	Prepaid at	Freight Payable at	Place and Date of issue
	Total Prepaid	No. of Original Bs/L	Signed for or on behalf of the Master as Agent

Fig.9-8　Sample of Ocean Bill of Lading（海运提单样本）

OCEAN BILL OF LADING

Shipper SUZHOU KNITWEAR AND MANUFACTURED GOODS IMPORT&EXPORT TRADE CORPORATION	B/L No. 20110128
	中国外运上海公司
	SINOTRANS SHANGHAI COMPANY
	OCEAN BILL OF LADING

Consignee or order TO ORDER OF NATIONAL PARIS BANKS 24 MARSHALL VEDONCASTER MONTREAL, CANADA.	SHIPPED on board in apparent good order and condition (unless otherwise indicated) the goods or packages specified herein and to be discharged at the mentioned port of discharge or as near there to as the vessel may safely get and be always afloat.

| Notify address YI YANG TRADE CORPORATION 88 MARSHALL AVE DONCASTER VIC 3108 CANADA | The weight, measure, marks and numbers, quality, contents and value, being particulars furnished by the Shipper, are not checked by the Carrier on loading.

The Shipper, Consignee and the Holder of this Bill of Lading hereby expressly accept and agree to all printed, written or stamped provisions, exceptions and conditions of this Bill of Lading, including those on the back hereof. |
|---|---|

Pre-carriage by	Port of Loading SHANGHAI	IN WITNESS where of the number of original Bills of Lading stated below have been signed, one of which being accomplished, the other(s) to be void.
Vessel PUDONG VOY.053	Port of Transshipment	
Port of Discharge MONTREAL	Final Destination MONTREAL	

Container & Seal No. & Marks and Nos.	No and Kind of Packages & Description of Goods	Gross weight kgs	Measurement m³
Y. Y. T. C MONTREAL C/No.1-367	COTTON TEATOWLS TOTAL ONE 40'CONTAINER	19911kgs	53.06 m³

Freight and Charges FREIGHT PREPAID	Regarding Transshipment Information Please Contact

Ex. Rate	Prepaid at	Freight Payable at	Place and Date of issue
	Total Prepaid	No. of original Bs/L THREE(3)	Signed for or on behalf of the Master 王军

as Agent |

Fig.9-9 Example of Ocean Bill of Lading（海运提单实例）

提单有三个重要的作用：（1）它是轮船公司签发并交给发货人的收据；（2）它也是轮船公司和托运人之间的运输合同的证明；（3）提单还是证明货物所有权的单证，因为提单的法定拥有者即货物的拥有人。出于这个原因，提单可以用来把货物从一个拥有者手中移交到另一人手中。当出口商填单时，会在提单上的"收货人"一栏空白处写上买方的姓名。这就意味着收货人如提单上所示，是货物的法定拥有者。另外，出口商可在"收货人"一栏中填上"凭指定"。在"凭指定"下面填上代理人的姓名和地址。然后，进口国的代理人可以背书提单，把它交给买方。通过这种方法，进口商就可以把货物转交给顾客。这就意味着不同的收货人必须有分别开立的提单，并且几件货物不能同时开在一张提单上。

总结归纳如下：提单至少具有三种主要功能：（1）经船运公司（承运人）签署后，交给发货人（托运人）作为货物收据；（2）作为承运人和托运人之间运输合同的凭据；（3）因为提单的拥有人即提单项下货物的拥有人，所以提单是代表货物的所有权凭证。

2) Contents of Bill of Lading（提单的内容）

A bill of lading not only contains a full description of the consignment—numbers and weights and marks of packages—but also a lot of other information as well. It quotes the name of the shipper and the carrying vessel, the ports of shipment and destination, the freight rate, the name of the consignee(unless the B/L is "to order", like a check), and the date of shipment, which is very important from a contractual point of view. It may also contain other terms and conditions. Some bills of lading are marked "freight prepaid", when a shipper is selling CIF or CFR, others may allow transshipment, which means that the cargo may be transferred from one ship to another at some intermediate port. It is often important to a shipper that his bill of lading should be "clean" rather than "dirty", that is, the shipping company should not have made any qualification about the quantity or condition of the cargo actually shipped. This is because the shipper's Letter of Credit may insist on clean bills, just as it may insist on "on board" as opposed to "alongside" ladings. Sometimes mate's receipt is given to the shipper in advance of the B/L, which takes time to issue.

提单不只包含货物的详细说明——数量、重量和箱包的唛头，还包含许多其他情况。提单提供了发货人的姓名和运载船舶的船名、装运港及目的港、运费率、收货人姓名（除非是指示提单，同支票相像）以及装运日期，从合同的观点来看，装运日期极为重要。提单也可能包含许多其他条款。在发货人按 CIF 或 CFR 条款出售货物时，提单上注明"运费已付"。有些提单允许转船，转船的意思是货物可在一些中间港从一艘船转到另一艘船上。对发货人来说，有一点常常也很重要，那就是提单应该是"清洁"的，而不应该是"不清洁"的，也就是说，轮船公司对实际装运的货物，对其数量及情况，不应注任何条件。这是因为发货人的信用证可能一定要求清洁提单，就像要求"已装船提单"而不同意"备运提单"一样。有时在签发提单以前，先给发货人一张大副收据，因为签发提单需要花一些时间。

3) Use of Bill of Lading（提单的用途）

The B/L is the central document of a sea export transaction. The shipper fills in the form provided by the shipping company as soon as he has all the details of the goods. Then he sends the B/L to the ship where an officer of the shipping company checks that the goods are "in good order and condition" and signs the B/L when the goods are loaded on the ship's rail. The B/L must be in the hands of the shipping company or their agents by the time the consignment is ready to be loaded.

When a consignment is loaded, an officer or agent of the shipping company signs the B/L that the goods have been "received in apparent good order and condition". In other words, the consignment must be exactly as written on the B/L and not different. The cases should be undamaged, and sacks, if any, should not be torn or stained. Drums of liquid should not be dented or leaking. The number and kind of packages should be the same as on the B/L.

If there is any difference between what it says on the B/L and the actual condition of the consignment, the shipping company has to write a clause on the B/L noting the damage or loss. In this case it is no longer a clean B/L and the bank representing the importer may not accept it. So the exporters' bank may not be able to get payment for the goods. For this reason "foul" or "clauses" B/L must be avoided at all costs and exporters must make sure their goods arrive at the docks in good order and condition. Sometimes certain defects of the goods are unavoidable. For instance, timber often has "split ends". Chemicals cause discoloration of packing. In such cases the exporters must get the agreement of the importers to certain clauses on the B/L. These clauses must be agreed before the export contract is signed, and the importers should tell their bank about the agreed clauses.

A B/L is usually made out in sets of three or four originals. The shipper may ask for several extra copies for his files. One copy of the B/L is kept for the ship. The other copies are sent to the exporters or directly to their bank. These negotiable BL/s are used for payment. They pass to the buyers or their agents in the importing country. Then the BL/s and the other shipping documents are presented to the shipping company when the ship arrives. The shipping company can then compare the negotiable BL/s with their copy on the ship. In this way the importers can show their legal right to the goods and obtain them from the ship. In recent years, a considerable simplification of documentary practices has been achieved. BL/s are frequently replaced by non-negotiable documents similar to those which are used for other modes of transport than carriage by sea. These documents are called "sea waybills", "liner waybills", "freight receipts", or variants of such expressions.

提单是海运出口交易的核心文件。发货人一旦获取关于货物的所有细节，就开始填写由轮船公司提供的表格。然后将之送到船上，由轮船公司的官员核查货物是否"情况良好"，并在装运货物越过船舷时在提单上签字。在货物准备装运之前，提单必须在轮船公司或其代理人手中。

货物装船后，船运公司的职员或代理人签署提单，注明货物"收讫，表面完好无损"。换句话说，装船货物必须和提单上所写的一致，不得有丝毫差别。装货的箱子必须没有损坏，如果有包装或袋包装的话，不应有破损或脏污。装液体的桶不应碰瘪或渗漏。货物的件数和种类必须和提单上注明的相符。

如果提单上所记载的与货物的实际情况有所不同，轮船就要在提单上批注损伤或损毁。这样，提单就不再是清洁提单了，进口商银行就不会接受这样的提单，出口商银行也不能获取货款。所以，不清洁提单应极力避免，出口商必须保证其货物到达码头时"情况良好"。有时，货物的某些缺陷是难免的。例如，木材的末端开裂，化学品引起包装的掉色。在这些情况下，出口商必须同进口商在提单的某些条款上达成一致。这些条款必须在出口合同签订以前就达成共识，出口商还应该把这些达成共识的条款通知其银行。

提单通常制成一套三至四份原件。发货人可以要求多签发几份以便存档。船方保留一份提单。其他的几份送交给出口商或直接给其银行。这些可转让的提单用来获取货款。它们被送到进口国的买方和代理商手中。接下来当轮船抵达时，提单和其他货运单据就送交到轮船公司。然后轮船公司就将可转让的提单和船上的副本提单做比较。这样，进口商就可以表明其对货物的所有权并从船上提取货物。近几年来，单据的简化方面取得了很大的进展。提单经常被非海运的其他运输方式所使用的类似的、不可转让的运输单据所替代。这些单据被称为"海运单""班轮运单""货运收据"或其他名称。

4) Classification of bill of lading（提单的种类）

There are several types of Bs/L which are categorized in different ways.

根据不同的方法提单可分为如下几种类型。

(1) On board B/L and Received for shipment B/L（已装船提单和备运提单）

According to whether the goods are loaded or not, the Bs/L can be classified into on board (or shipped) B/L and received(or received for shipment) B/L. A shipped on board B/L is evidence that the goods have been loaded on board a certain steamer. It commences with the wording "Shipped in apparent good order and condition", According to general foreign trade practices, only the shipped on board B/L is accepted by banks for payment under a L/C.

A received for shipment B/L is evidence given by the ship-owner that the goods have been received, waiting for shipment but have not yet been actually loaded on a particular ship. The goods are not on board the ship, but somewhere on the docks or at the warehouse under the shipping company's control. Where payment is arranged under a L/C, the terms of credit usually do not allow the acceptance of such a bill for negotiation.

依据货物是否装船，提单可分为已装船提单和备运提单。第一个提单指货物已装上开往目的港的运输船只。在它的正面通常标有"货已装船"字样。装运提单上还有"货物装运情况良好"的条款。按照国际贸易惯例，在信用证项下，只有装运提单才被银行接受来付款。

备运提单是船方签发的表明货已收到，但还没有实际装上船的证明。因此，货物能否在比较短的时间内发运或装运上船就不可确定。它的正面通常有"货已收待运"的字样。很显然，这种提单没有装运提单的价值大。当以信用证方式付款时，信用证上的条款通常不允许接受这样的提单来议付。

(2) Clean B/L and Unclean B/L（清洁提单和不清洁提单）

According to whether there are notes on the B/L, it falls into two kinds: clean B/L and unclean B/L.

A clean B/L shows that the goods have been shipped on board, in apparent good order and condition, and there is no modification of the shipowner. This B/L is called "clean". It confirms that the goods have not suffered apparent or outside damage and there does not seem to be any defect in the packing. By issuing a clean B/L, the shipowner admits his full liability for the cargo described in the B/L under the law and his contract. This type is much favored by banks for financial settlement purpose.

An unclean B/L is generally marked "insufficiently packed", "covers old and stained", "wet by rain", "…packed in damaged condition", "unclean", "foul", etc. There are many recurring types of such clauses including inadequate packaging, unprotected machinery, wet or stained cartons, damaged crates, etc. This type of B/L is usually unacceptable to a bank. But not all B/L(s) which are noted are unclean B/L.

But the following three kinds of noted B/L are not regarded as unclean B/L:

—The notes do not indicate clearly that the goods or packing are unsatisfactory, e.g. "old carton", or "old drum", etc.

—The purpose of the note is to emphasize that the carrier shall not be responsible for the risks resulting from the quality of the goods or packing.

—The purpose of the note is only to deny that the carrier has any knowledge of the content, quantity, volume, quality or technical specifications of the goods.

根据提单上有无不良批注，提单分为两种：清洁提单和不清洁提单。

当提单标明货物"表面情况良好"并且没有船主的批注时，这样的提单就称为清洁提单。它证明货物没有受到内在或外在损伤，包装也没有任何缺陷。签发清洁提单就意味着船主承认他将按法律和合同对提单中描述的货物负完全责任。这样的提单对银行有利，因为它便于结算。

当提单被批注了某些不利于货主的批语时，如"包装不充分""覆盖物陈旧并有污点""雨淋""包装破损""不清洁""污浊"等语句时，它就称为"不清洁"提单。有关这样的语句有很多，例如，包装不合适，机械保护不当，包装箱受潮、有污点，包装箱破损等。这种提单在信用证下当然不会被银行所接受来议付。

但是，根据国际航运公司的解释，对下列性质批注的提单不应视为不清洁提单：

——批注意义未明确表示货物或包装的"不清洁"状况，如仅批注"旧箱"或"旧桶"等。

——批注意义仅在于强调承运人对货物或包装性质所引起的风险不承担责任。

——批注意义在于表明承运人不知道货物的内容、重量、容量、质量或技术规格，对所引起的风险不承担责任。

(3) Straight B/L, Order B/L and Blank B/L（记名提单、指示提单和不记名提单）

According to whether the B/L is transferable, it is divided into three kinds: straight B/L, order B/L and blank B/L.

A straight B/L is made out so that only the named consignee at the destination is entitled to take delivery of the goods under the bill. The consignee is designated by the shipper. The carrier has to hand over the cargo to the named consignee, not to any third party in possession of the bill. This kind of B/L is not transferable. The shipper cannot pass the bill to a third party by endorsement. So the bill is of very restricted application. When the goods are shipped on a non-commercial basis, such as samples or exhibits, materials in aid of other countries, or when the goods are extremely valuable, a straight B/L is generally issued.

按照提单是否可转让，提单可以分为三种：记名提单、指示提单和不记名提单。

记名提单是指在提单的收货人栏内具体填明了收货人的名称，该收货人是由托运人指定的，只能由该收货人提货，不能由第三方拥有该提单。这种提单不能背书、转让给第三方。这种提单限制严格，常用于非商业目的，如样品或展品，对外援助，或托运贵重物品时。

An order B/L indicates that the bill is made out to the order of or to order of …any person named in such a bill, which may be transferred /negotiated after endorsement. So it is sometimes called a transferable B/L. It is because of this that nowadays, it is commonly used in international practice.

指示提单（Order B/L），是指提单收货人栏内只填写"凭指定"（To order）或"凭某人指定"（To order of ××）字样，并经背书就可转让的提单，故又称为"可转让提单"。正因为如此，外贸业务中经常使用这种提单。

A blank B/L is also called an open B/L or bearer B/L. It refers to a bill in which the name of a definite consignee is not mentioned. The area in B/L calling for the name of the consignee is left blank, with neither the name of the consignee nor the phraseology of "to order" filled in. This kind of B/L can be transferred/ negotiable without endorsement. There usually appear in the box of consignee words like "to bearer" and the holder of the B/L can take delivery of the goods against the surrender of B/L, i.e., ownership of the goods passes when the bill is handed over to anyone.

不记名提单是指提单收货人栏内没有指明任何收货人，既没有收货人的名称，也没有"凭指示"，即仅填写"来人"或空着不填。这种提单不经背书即可以转让，这样，谁持有提单，谁就可以提货，承运人交货也只凭单，不凭人。因此，采用这种提单风险大，一般不予使用。

(4) Direct B/L, Transshipment B/L and Through B/L（直达提单、转船提单和联运提单）

According to the modes of transport, it can be divided into three kinds.

根据运输方式，提单可分为三种。

A direct B/L is referred to the consignment carried to the port of destination directly without transshipment.

直达提单是指轮船中途不经过换船而直接驶往目的港卸货所签发的提单。

A transshipment B/L is issued by shipping companies when there is no direct service between the port of loading and port of destination, and the ship owner arranges to tranship the cargo at an intermediate port at his expense. This kind of B/L usually bears such a clause "Transshipment to be made".

当装运港与目的港之间没有直接的运输服务，且船主准备在中间港用自己的费用将货物转船时，轮船公司就签发转船提单。这种提单通常有这样的条款"将转船……"。

A through B/L is issued when the entire voyage involves more than one carrier, where the ocean shipment forms only part of the complete journey and, subsequent thereto, the goods have to be carried by other land or sea carriers. The first carrier issues the bill and collects the freight for the entire voyage, and arranges transshipment and forwarding of the goods at the intermediate port. The shipper prefers this kind of B/L because of the trouble having been saved to deal with other carriers by himself.

联运提单是指经过海运和其他运输方式联合运输时，由第一程承运人所签发的包括全程运输的提单。联运提单的性质同转船提单一样，途中转运的手续和费用都由第一程承运人承担，但转运后的责任则由各段的承运人分别负责。

(5) Long form B/L and Short form B/L（全式提单和略式提单）

According to the contents of the B/L, it can be divided into two forms: long form B/L and short form B/L.

A long form B/L refers to the B/L on the back of which all the detailed terms and conditions about the rights and obligations of the carrier and the consignor are listed as an integral part of the bill. It is more frequently used.

A short form B/L is a document which omits the terms and conditions on the back of B/L.

根据提单内容可分为两种：全式提单和略式提单。

全式提单又称繁式提单，是指提单背面列有承运人和托运人权利、义务的详细条款的提单。

略式提单又称简式提单，是指提单上略去背面条款，而只列出提单正面的必须记载事项。

(6) Freight prepaid B/L and Freight to be collected B/L（运费预付提单和运费到付提单）

According to the time for payment of freight, it can be divided into two types.

A freight prepaid B/L means that all the freight is paid by the consignor when the B/L is issued by the carrier on which "freight prepaid" is indicated.

A freight to be collected B/L refers to the B/L on which "freight payable at destination" is indicated.

根据运费支付时间，提单可分为两种。

运费预付提单是指运费已由托运人预付，签发提单时，在提单上写明"运费预付"的字样。

运费到付提单是指提单上写有"运费到达目的港时支付"的字样。

(7) Liner B/L and Charter party B/L（班轮提单和租船提单）

According to the types of the carrying vessels, it can be classified into a liner B/L and a charter party B/L.

根据船舶营运的方式可分为班轮提单和租船提单。

(8) Other types of B/L（其他类型的提单）

Besides the above-mentioned types of B/L, there are some other types such as: container B/L; on deck B/L; stale B/L; groupage B/L; house B/L; antedated B/L and advanced B/L, etc.

除了上述提单，还有其他一些种类的提单，如集装箱提单、舱面提单、过期提单、成组提单、运输代理提单、倒签提单和预借提单等。

4. Multimodal transport document (MTD)（多式联运单据）

The multimodal transport document (or CTD for Combined Transport Documents) is a document which evidences the combined transport contract and indicates that the multimodal transport operator shall take over the goods and shall be responsible for delivering the document according to the clauses in the contract.

多式联运单据（或 Combined Transport Documents，CTD）是证明多式联运合同已订立，并证明多式联运经营人已接管货物并负责按照合同条款运送和交付货物的单据。

5. Packing list（装箱单）

A packing list is a document made out by a seller when a sale is affected in international trade. It shows numbers and kinds of packages being shipped, total of gross, legal and net weights of the packages, and marks and numbers on the packages. It is used to make up the deficiency of an invoice. It also enables the consignee to declare the goods at the customs office, distinguish and check the goods when they arrive at the port of destination, thus, facilitates the clearance of goods through customs. What's more, packing lists can facilitate settling insurance claims in case of loss or damage. See Fig. 9-10 Sample of Packing List.

装箱单是国际贸易中卖方售货时出具的单据，是说明所发运货物的数量、种类、毛重，每件货物的法定净重以及标志和号数的单证。它用于补充发票的不足之处，以便收货人在货物抵达目的港后区分和核对货物并向海关申报货物。这样可以加快货物的清关过程。并且，在货物失落或受到损坏时，可凭装箱单向保险公司索赔。图 9-10 所示为装箱单实例。

PACKING LIST

TEL: 86-21-65756156

FAX: 86-21-65756189

INV. No.: TY034

DATE: Apr. 26th,2004

PI No.: 20040329

TO: MAMUT ENTERPRISESAV, TARRAGONA 75-3ER

ANDORRA LA VELLA, PRINCIPALITY OF ANDORRA

FROM: SHANGHAI, CHINA　　　　TO: BARCELONA, SPAIN

SHIPPING MARK

N/M

DESCRIPTION	QTY Sets	CTNS	N.W. kgs	G.W. kgs	MEAS m^3
HAND TOOLS					
(1) 9pc Extra Long	1, 200	17	629	612	0.883 6
Hex Key Set	1, 200	75	1, 875	1, 800	2.309 3
(2)8pc Double Offset	800	100	2, 900	2, 800	4.295 3
Ring Spanner	1, 200	60	1, 260	1, 200	1.360 8
(3)12pc Double Offset	1, 000	67	1, 608	1, 541	1.408 4
Ring Spanner					
(4)12pc Combination					
Spanner					
(5)10pc Combination					
Spanner					
TOTAL:	5, 400	319	8, 272	7, 953	10.257 4

SAY TOTAL: PACKED IN THREE HUNDRED AND NINETEEN (319) CTNS ONLY.

SHANGHAI TIANYE TOOL IMPORT & EXPORT CO., LTD.

LILING

Fig.9-10　Sample of Packing List（装箱单实例）

6．Weight memo（重量单）

Weight memo is a document made out by a seller when a sale is affected in foreign trade. It indicates the gross weight, net weight of each package. It is used to make up the deficiency of an invoice. It is also used to facilitate the customs formalities and the general check of the goods by the consignee on their arrival at the destination. Packing list and weight memo usually come out in a combined form（See Fig.9-11）.

重量单是对外贸易中卖方售货时出具的单据，是说明每件货物的毛重和净重的证件。它用于补充发票的不足之处，以便收货人在货物到达目的港后核对货物和加快办理海关手续。装箱单和重量单通常合而为一，做成一个单证（如图 9-11 所示）。

WEIGHT MEMO

重　量　单

Name of the Company：公司名称　　　　　　　　　P/L NO.:

Address：公司地址　　　　　　　　　　　　　　　包装单号码

　　　　　　　　　　　　　　　　　　　　　　　DATE:

　　　　　　　　　　　　　　　　　　　　　　　制单日期

SHIPPER: 托运人公司资料

托运人地址

BUYER: 买方公司资料

买方地址

COMMODITY: 商品

SHIPMENT BY: 运输公司资料

SHIPPED PER: 船只资料

FROM: 出口地（港）_____

TO: 进口地（港）_____

SAILING ON OR ABOUT: 装船日

MARKS & NOS.	DESCRIPTION	QTY	N.W.	G.W.	MEASUREMENT
唛头箱号	商品名称	数量	净重	毛重	尺寸体积

总计：总数量　　总净重　　总毛重　　总尺寸体积

总箱数（英文大写）

Name of the Company 公司名称

Signature 签名

（签名英文正楷 – 职称）

SHIPPING MARKS

正侧唛资料

Fig.9-11　Sample of Weight Memo（重量单样本）

7. Inspection certificate（检验证书）

An inspection certificate or survey report is a document which shows the quality or quantity or other elements of the goods (See Fig.9-12~Fig.9-15). It is issued by the manufacturer of the goods, chambers of commerce, surveyors, or government institutions. It mainly performs two functions: firstly, as a document of quality or quantity, it can decide whether the quality or quantity of the goods shipped by the seller is in conformity with that stipulated in the contract. It is an important proof at the time of refusing payment, lodging or settling a claim. Secondly, it is one of the shipping documents used at the time of negotiating payment.

For import commodities that are subject to inspection by the inspection authorities as stipulated in the foreign trade contract, upon their arrival, the receivers, and users or forwarding agents should apply to the inspection authorities at the arrival port/station in due time. A survey report or inspection certificate shall be issued to the applicant after inspection. These commodities shall be checked and released by the customs upon presentation of the seal of the inspection authorities affixed on the customs declaration.

For export commodities which are subject to inspection as stipulated in the contract or by law, the manufacturers or suppliers should apply for inspection before shipment. If they are proved up to the standard, the inspection authorities shall issue inspection certificates for them to clear the goods through customs. If vessels and containers are used for carrying perishable goods, such as cereals, oils, foodstuffs, and frozen products for export, the carriers and container stuffing organizations should apply for inspection of the holds or tanks and containers to the inspection authorities at the port. They shall be permitted to carry the goods only after a certificate is issued after examination which proves that they conform to the technical condition for shipping.

检验证书或检查报告是表明货物的数量、质量或其他因素的单证（见图 9-12~图 9-15）。它由制造商、商会、检查人员或政府机构签发。它主要有两方面的作用：第一，作为质量和数量的单证，它可确定所运货物是否与合同中的规定相一致。它是在拒绝付款、索赔或理赔时的一个重要证明。第二，它是议付货款的货运单证之一。

按对外贸易合同规定，进口商品在抵达后必须接受检验部门的检验。收货人、用户或货运代理商应在抵达港/站及适当时间内向商检部门申请商检。商检后，将发给申请人一份检查报告或检验单。在出示附在海关申报单上盖有商检部门的印章后，海关将检查和放行这些商品。

根据合同或法律规定，出口商品必须接受检查，制造商、供应商在货物装运前应申请商检。经检查，如果货物符合标准，商检部门将为它们签发检验单为货物结关。如果用船只和集装箱运输供出口的、易腐烂的谷类食物、油、粮食和冷冻产品时，运输工具和集装箱的填装部门应向所在港的商检机构申请检验其货舱、箱和集装箱。经检验后，如果它们符合运输的技术条件，那么商检机构将签发检验单允许它们运输货物。

中华人民共和国出入境检验检疫

ENTRY-EXIT INSPECTION AND QUARANTINE

OF THE PEOPLE'S REPUBLIC OF CHINA

数量检验证书

QUANTITY CERTIFICATE

编号

No.:

发货人：

Consignor

收货人：

Consignee

品　名：

Description of Goods

标记及号码

Marks & No.

报验数量/重量：

Quantity/Weight Declared

包装种类及数量：

Number and Type of Packages

运输工具：

Means of Conveyance

检验结果：

Results of Inspection

　　我们已尽所知和最大能力实施上述检验，不能因我们签发本证书而免除卖方或其他方面根据合同和法律所承担的产品数量责任和其他责任。

　　All inspections are carried out conscientiously to the best of our knowledge and ability. This certificate does not in any respect absolve the seller and other related parties from his contractual and legal obligations especially when product quantity is concerned.

Fig.9-12　Sample of Quantity Certificate（数量检验证书样本）

申请单位（盖章）：　　　　　　　　　　　　　　　　　　　　证明书：＿＿＿＿＿＿＿＿

申请人郑重声明：　　　　　　　　　　　　　　　　　　　　　注册号：＿＿＿＿＿＿＿＿

　　本人被正式授权代表出口单位办理和签署本申请书。

　　本申请书及普惠制产地证明书格式 A 所列内容正确无误，如发现弄虚作假，冒充格式 A 所列货物，擅改证书，本人愿接受签证机关的处罚并负法律责任。现将有关情况申报如下：

生产单位		生产单位联系人电话	
商品名称 （中英文）		H. S. 税目号 （以六位数码计）	
商品（FOB）总值（以美元计）		发票号	
最终销售国		证书种类（画"√"）	加急证书
货物拟出运日期			

贸易方式和企业性质（请在适用处画"√"）

正常贸易 C	来料加工 L	补偿贸易 B	中外合资 H	中外合作 Z	外商独资 D	零售 Y	展卖 M

包装数量或毛重或其他数量	

原产地标准：

本项商品系在中国生产，完全符合该给惠国给惠方案规定，其原产地情况符合以下第　　条：

（1）"P"（完全国产，未使用任何进口原材料）；

（2）"W"其 H.S.税目号为.........................（含进口成分）

（3）"F"（对加拿大出口产品，其进口成分不超过产品出厂价值的 40%）。

本批产品系：1. 直接运输从...................到.................。

　　　　　　2. 转口运输从...................中转国（地区）..................到......................。

申请人说明	领证人（签名）
	电　话：
	日　期：　　年　　月　　日

　　现提交中国出口商业发票副本一份，普惠制产地证明书格式 A（FORM A）一正二副，以及其他附件　　份，请予审核签证。

　　注：凡含有进口成分的商品，必须按要求提交《含进口成分受惠商品成本明细单》。

商 检 局 联 系 记 录

图 9-13　普惠制产地证明书申请书

ORIGINAL

1. Goods consigned from (Exporter's business name, address, country)	Reference No.: **GENERALIZED SYSTEM OF PREFERENCES** **CERTIFICATE OF ORIGIN** **(Combined declaration and certificate)** **FORM A** **Issued in** <u>**THE PEOPLE'S REPUBLIC OF CHINA**</u> **(country)** See Notes, overleaf
2. Goods consigned to (Consignee's name, address, country)	
3. Means of transport and route (as far as known)	4. For official use

5. Item number	6. Marks and numbers of packages	7. Number and kind of packages , description of goods	8. Origin Criterion (see Notes overleaf)	9. Gross weight or other quantity	10. Number and date of invoices

11. Certification
 	
    It is hereby certified, on the basis of control carried out , that the declaration by the exporter is correct.
 	
Place and date, signature and stamp of certifying authority
	12. Declaration by the exporter
	
	    The undersigned hereby declares that the above details and statements are correct, that all the goods were produced in ....<u>**CHINA**</u>............
	                            (country)
	
	and that they comply with the origin requirement Specified for those goods in the Generalized System of Preferences for goods exporter to
	
	....
	(importing country)
	
	....
	Place and date, signature of authorized signatory

Fig.9-14   GSP Certificate of Origin FORM A（普惠制产地证明书格式 A（正面））

中华人民共和国出入境检验检疫出境货物报验单

报检单位（加盖公章）：   编号＿＿＿＿＿＿

报检单位登记号：   联系人：   电话：   报检日期：   年 月 日

发货人	（中文）				
	（外文）				
收货人	（中文）				
	（外文）				

货物名称（中/外文）	H.S.编码	产地	数/重量	货物总值	包装种类及数量

运输工具名称号码		贸易方式		货物存放地点	
合同号		信用证号		用途	
发货日期		输往国家（地区）		许可证/审批号	
启运地		到达口岸		生产单位注册号	

集装箱规格、数量及号码

合同、信用证订立的检验检疫条款或特殊要求	标记及号码	随付单据（画"√"或补填）	
		□合同 □信用证 □发票 □换证凭单 □装箱单 □厂检单	□许可/审批文件 □ □ □

需要证单名称（画"√"或补填）		检验检疫费	
□品质证书 ＿正＿副 □重量证书 ＿正＿副 □数量证书 ＿正＿副 □兽医卫生证书 ＿正＿副 □健康证书 ＿正＿副 □卫生证书 ＿正＿副 □动物卫生证书 ＿正＿副	□植物检疫证书 ＿正＿副 □熏蒸/消毒证书 ＿正＿副 □出境货物换证凭单 □ □ □ □	总金额 （人民币元）	
		计费人	
		收费人	

报检人郑重声明： 　1. 本人被授权报检。 　2. 上列填写内容正确属实，货物无伪造或冒用他人的厂名、标志、认证标志，并承担货物质量责任。 　　　　　　签名：＿＿＿＿＿	领取证单	
	日　期	
	签　名	

◆ 国家出入境检验检疫局制

图 9-15　中华人民共和国出入境检验检疫出境货物报验单

Section Four   Logistics Mode of Cross-border E-commerce（跨境电子商务的物流模式）

Currently, there are five modes for cross-border e-commerce logistics operations: express, postal packets, overseas warehouse, special courier, central railway multimodal transport. More and more cross-border logistics have adopted "cross-border e-commerce + overseas warehouse" mode, namely, the overseas buyers (enterprises) first complete online purchase of products through cross-border e-commerce sites, and then the sellers use their global layout in the localization overseas warehousing, logistics system to realize the goods transportation, and effect delivery in time.

目前，跨境电子商务的物流运作方式主要有以下五种模式：快递、邮政小包、海外仓、专线速递、中欧铁路多式联运。越来越多的跨境物流采用了"跨境电子商务+海外仓"模式。即海外买家（企业级买家）首先通过跨境电子商务网站完成产品的在线购买，然后利用卖家在全球范围内布局的本地化海外仓储、物流系统实现货品的及时运输、配送。

The newly issued e-commerce law has made new regulations for the logistics operation of cross-border e-commerce. That is, the e-commerce party can agree to use express logistics services for delivery. Express logistics service providers supply express logistics services for e-commerce, and should abide by laws and administrative regulations, as well as meeting the promised service specifications and time limits. The delivery logistics service provider shall prompt the consignee to inspect the goods on spot personally when effect delivery; if it is handed over by others, it shall be approved by the consignee. The express logistics service provider can accept the e-commerce operator's entrustment to provide the collection and payment service while rendering the express logistics service.

新颁布的电子商务法对于跨境电子商务的物流运作方式做了新的规定。即电子商务当事人可以约定采用快递物流方式交付商品。快递物流服务提供者为电子商务提供快递物流服务，应当遵守法律、行政法规，并应当符合承诺的服务规范和时限。快递物流服务提供者在交付商品时，应当提示收货人当面查验；交由他人代收的，应当经收货人同意。快递物流服务提供者在提供快递物流服务的同时，可以接受电子商务经营者的委托提供代收货款服务。

1．The international express（国际快递）

International express mainly refers to the four giants: UPS, FedEx, DHL, TNT, including UPS and FeDex headquarters located in the United States, DHL headquarters in Germany, TNT based in the Netherlands. International express has a very high demand for delivery of information, collection and management, supported by a global self-built network and international information systems.

国际快递主要是指 UPS、FedEx、DHL、TNT 这四大巨头，其中，UPS 和 FedEx 总部位于美国，DHL 总部位于德国，TNT 总部位于荷兰。国际快递对信息的提供、收集与管理有很高的要求，以全球自建网络以及国际化信息系统为支撑。

2. The postal parcel（邮政小包）

The postal network has global coverage, wider than any other logistics channels. And the post office is commonly state-run, enjoying national tax subsidies, so the price is very cheap. Generally, that the goods are wrapped in a personal way is not convenient for the customs statistics, also leading to failing to enjoy general export tax rebates. At the same time, the postal service is slower with a high rate of packet loss.

邮政网络基本覆盖全球，比其他任何物流渠道都广。而且，由于邮政一般为国营，有国家税收补贴，因此价格非常便宜。一般以私人包裹方式出境，不便于海关统计，也无法享受正常的出口退税。同时，速度较慢，丢包率高。

3. Overseas warehouse（海外仓）

Overseas warehousing service refers to logistics service providers, independently or jointly, providing the goods storage, sorting, packing, controlling and management of one-stop service, by the network trading platform in foreign trade, to the seller in a sales target. The seller tends to store the goods in the local warehouse so that when the buyer has a demand, he can make a quick response in a timely manner. The sorting, packaging, and delivery of the goods tend to be dealt with promptly. The whole process includes three parts, namely, the initial transportation, warehouse management and local distribution.

所谓海外仓储服务是指由网络外贸交易平台、物流服务商独立或共同为卖家在销售目的地提供的货品仓储、分拣、包装、派送的一站式控制与管理服务。卖家将货物存储到当地仓库，当买家有需求时，第一时间做出快速响应，及时进行货物的分拣、包装以及递送。整个流程包括头程运输、仓储管理和本地配送三个部分。

4. Multinational business of domestic express（国内快递的跨国业务）

EMS is relatively mature, and it can reach more than 60 countries around the world. SF Express (Shunfeng) also has established express service to the United States, Australia, South Korea, Japan, Singapore, Malaysia, Thailand, Vietnam and other countries, and cross-border B2C service is launched between mainland China and Russia.

由于依托着邮政渠道，EMS 的国际业务相对成熟，可以直达全球 60 多个国家。顺丰也已开通了到美国、澳大利亚、韩国、日本、新加坡、马来西亚、泰国、越南等国家的快递服务，并启动了中国大陆往俄罗斯的跨境 B2C 服务。

5. Special line logistics（专线物流）

Cross-border railway logistics refers to the transport of goods abroad by aviation package module, followed by the domestic delivery destination countries through cooperation company, which is one of the more popular ways of logistics. Special line logistics can concentrate large quantities of goods to send to the destination, by means of economies of scale to reduce costs, therefore, cheaper than commercial couriers, faster than postal packets, with a low packet loss rate. Compared with the postal packets, the freight cost is high, and the scope of domestic coverage area needs to be expanded.

跨境专线物流一般是通过航空包舱方式将货物运输到国外,再通过合作公司进行目的地国国内的派送,是比较受欢迎的一种物流方式。其集中大批量货物发往目的地,通过规模效应降低成本,因此,价格比商业快递低,速度快于邮政小包,丢包率也比较低。相比邮政小包来说,其运费成本还是高了不少,覆盖地区有待扩大。

Part B Terminology Practice

1. **Shipping documents**（装运单据）: Documents such as commercial invoices, bills of lading, policies of insurance, etc., involved in the shipping of goods.

2. **Commercial invoice**（商业发票）: A document prepared by a seller giving details of goods supplied, their price, contract terms and the total amount due to be paid by the buyer.

3. **Bill of Lading(B/L)**（提单）: A document signed by a ship's Master, acknowledging receipt of cargo. It also serves as a contract of freight, and as title to the cargo.

4. **Consignment**（托运）: A parcel of goods sent by one party to another.

5. **Consignee**（收货人）: the person, firm, or representative to whom a seller of shipper sends merchandise and who, upon presentation of the necessary documents, is recognized as the owner of the merchandise.

6. **Short weight**（短重）: A consignee makes a claim for short weight against the supplier when he finds that the quantity of goods on arrival is less than that shown in the invoice and other documents.

7. **Transshipment**（转运）: Transferring a cargo from one carrying vessel to another at an immediate port, before arrival at the ultimate port of destination.

8. **Title**（所有权）: A legal right to the ownership of goods or property.

9. **On board B/L**（已装船提单）: An on board Bill of Lading certifies that a consignment has actually been loaded on the carrying vessel; opposed to an alongside Bill of Lading.

10. **Alongside**(船边): A term applied to, e.g. a Bill of Lading, which means that the goods have not been loaded when the Bill of Lading is issued, but are on the dock awaiting loading.

11. **Mate's receipt**（大副收据）: An acknowledgement of receipt of a consignment on board a carrying vessel. It is usually given to the Master so that he may sign the Bill of Lading.

12. **Negotiable B/L**（可转让提单）: The B/L which can be transferable or assignable.

13. **Endorsement**(背书): A signature on the reverse of a negotiable instrument made primarily for the purpose of transferring the holder's rights to another person.

14. **Blank**（空白背书）: Endorsement, an endorsement of an instrument which does not specify any person to whom payment is to be made, thus making the amount named in the instrument payable to any person who presents it without further endorsement.

15. **Customs clearance**(清关): Completion of customs formalities when exporting or importing

goods.

16. **Van**（货车）：The truck used for carrying the household goods.

17. **Van operator**（货车司机）：The driver of the vehicle carrying household goods.

18. **Contract**（合同）：An agreement, either written or verbal, between two parties.

19. **Shipper**（发货人）：The person whose household goods are being moved.

20. **Irregular route carrier**（非固定线路承运人）：A carrier operating within a specified and defined territory, as set forth in the carrier's Certificate, but not over a specified route or routes between fixed termini. Our industry members are irregular route carriers.

21. **Joint rates**（联运费率）：A joint rate is a rate that applies over the lines or routes of two or more carriers and that is made by arrangement or agreement between such carriers evidenced by concurrence of power of attorney. Joint tariffs are those which contain joint rates.

22. **Packing list**（装箱单）：A list of products shipped by the vendor to be used to verify the items during the receiving process. This document does not have any pricing on it generally and should not be confused with an invoice.

23. **Individual shipper**（个人发货人）：The owner of household goods being shipped.

24. **Interchange**（货物联运交接）：The exchange of freight laden trailers from one carrier to another for further transportation of the shipments therein.

25. **Interline**（联运）：The transfer of a shipment from one carrier to another for further transportation.

26. **Interstate**（州际运输）：Move which has its origin and destination situated in different states. This also includes moves which have origin and destination in the same state, but which pass through another state on their way.

27. **Carrier**（承运人）：A company that transports passengers, freight or household goods.

28. **Cartons**（纸箱）：Containers used for packing smaller odds and ends. Breakables and non-breakables may be packed in cartons.

29. **Order number**（订单号）：The number used to identify each shipment. It appears on both the Bill of Lading and the Order for Service.

30. **S.I.T. (Storage-In-Transit)**（中转储存/运输途中的储存）：Temporary storage of household goods in the warehouse of the carrier or his agent, pending further transportation.

31. **Inventory**（库存/存货清单）：The detailed descriptive list of household goods showing number and condition of each item.

32. **Connecting flight**（库存/存货清单）：A segment of an ongoing journey that requires passengers to change aircraft, but not necessarily carriers. Under International Air Transportation Association (IATA) regulations, a flight connection becomes a stopover if the passenger is required to wait more than 24 hours for the next flight.

Part C Terms

1. ORC (Origin Receive Charges) 本地收货费用（广东省收取）

2. THC (Terminal Handling Charges) 码头操作费（香港收取）

3. BAF (Bunker Adjustment Factor) 燃油附加费

4. CAF (Currency Adjustment Factor) 货币贬值附加费

5. YAS (Yard Surcharges) 码头附加费

6. EPS (Equipment Position Surcharges) 设备位置附加费

7. DDC (Destination Delivery Charges) 目的港交货费

8. PSS (Peak Season Surcharges) 旺季附加费

9. PCS (Port Congestion Surcharges) 港口拥挤附加费

10. DOC (document charges) 文件费

11. O/F (Ocean Freight) 海运费

12. B/L (Bill of Lading) 海运提单

13. MB/L(Master Bill of Lading) 船东提单（或 Ocean Bill of Lading）

14. MTD (Multimodal Transport Document) 多式联运单据

15. S/O (Shipping Order) 装货指示书

16. W/T (Weight Ton) 重量吨（即货物收费以重量计费）

17. MT (Measurement Ton) 尺码吨（即货物收费以尺码计费）

18. W/M(Weight or Measurement ton) 即以重量吨或者尺码吨中从高收费

19. CY (Container Yard) 集装箱（货柜）堆场

20. FCL (Full Container Load) 整箱货

21. LCL (Less than Container Load) 拼箱货（散货）

22. CFS (Container Freight Station) 集装箱货运站

23. TEU (Twenty-foot Equivalent Unit) 20 英尺换算单位（用来计算货柜量的多少）

24. A/W (All Water) 全水路（主要指由美国西岸中转至东岸或内陆点的货物的运输方式）

25. MLB(Mini Land Bridge) 小陆桥（主要指由美国西岸中转至东岸或内陆点的货物的运输方式）

26. NVOCC(Non-Vessel Operating Common Carrier) 无船承运人

27. Certificate of Quality 品质证书

28. Certificate of Weight 重量证书　　　29. Certificate of Quantity 数量证书

30. Certificate of Packing 包装证书　　　31. Certificate of Health 健康证书

32. Certificate of Quarantine 检疫证书　　33. Veterinary Certificate 兽医证书

34. Sanitary Certificate 卫生证书　　　　35. Certificate of Origin 产地证书

36. Certificate of Fumigation 熏蒸证书

37. Fumigation/Disinfection Certificate 熏蒸/消毒证书

38. Animal Health Certificate 动物卫生证书　　39. Phytosanitary Certificate 植物检疫证书

40. Phytosanitary Certificate For Re-export 植物转口检疫证书

41. export licence, application 出口许可证申请表 42. export licence 出口许可证

43. exchange control declaration, export 出口结汇核销单

44. dispatch note Model T   T 出口单证（海关转运报关单）（欧盟用）

45. dispatch note Model T1   T1 出口单证（内部转运报关单）（欧盟用）

46. dispatch note Model T2   T2 出口单证（原产地证明书）

47. control document T5   T5 管理单证（退运单证）（欧盟用)

48. re-sending consignment note 铁路运输退运单

49. dispatch note Model T2L   T2L 出口单证（原产地证明书）（欧盟用）

50. goods declaration for exportation 出口货物报关单

51. cargo declaration(departure) 离港货物报关单

52. certificate of origin form GSP 普惠制原产地证书

53. goods declaration for customs transit 海关转运货物报关单

54. TIF form TIF 国际铁路运输报关单   55. TIR carnet TIR 国际公路运输报关单

56. consular invoice 领事发票   57. house waybill 全程运单

58. master B/L 主提单   59. B/L original 正本提单

60. B/L copy 副本提单   61. empty container B/L 空集装箱提单

62. tanker B/L 油轮提单   63. inland waterway B/L 内河提单

64. mate's receipt 大副收据

Part D Exercise

I. Please determine whether the following statements are True or False. Then put T for True or F for False in the bracket at the end of each statement.

1. Sometimes when the buyer cannot determine a specific port of discharge, he may require two or three ports to be written on the contract for option. (   )

2. When there are optional ports in the contract, the goods may be unloaded at any one of the ports at the shipping company's disposal. (   )

3. When importing on FOB terms, we can generally stipulate the port of discharge. (   )

4. An order B/L may be negotiable after being endorsed. (   )

5. A B/L is a transport contract in which the shipping company promises to transport the goods received to the destination. (   )

6. A letter of indemnity is issued by the seller to the buyer to certify that the goods delivered are in good condition. (   )

7. According to the UCP500, a B/L which is issued subject to a Charter Party must be accepted unless the Credit stipulates otherwise. (   )

8. When you transport your goods by a Time Charter, you have to pay for loading and unloading. (   )

9. When the shipowner speeds up his ship and arrives at the destination at an earlier date than is stipulated, he can obtain dispatch money from the shipper. (   )

10. When the charterer fails to load or unload the goods within the stipulated period of time, he has to pay demurrage to the shipowner. (   )

II. Answer the following questions in English.

1. What is a clean on board B/L?

2. What is a packing list?

3. What is a weight memo?

4. What is a commercial invoice?

5. What is an inspection certificate?

6. What is B/L?

III. Answer the following questions briefly according to what you have learnt in this unit.

1. Please explain in English what the meaning of chartering is and its character.

2. What is time of delivery and what has to be paid attention to in stipulating the time of shipment?

3. Please tell the functions of a B/L.

4. What are the main kinds of B/L in international trade?

5. What is the meaning of the sentence in the L/C from abroad: "Partial shipment permitted against prorate shipment"?

6. We often see in the foreign L/C: "Shipment to be made in two lots" and "…in two shipments". Please explain the differences of these two sentences.

7. If there is the sentence in the L/C: "Singapore PSA berth terms", what is the meaning? How to deal with it?

8. If there is the sentence in the L/C: "Shipment from Tianjin via Hong Kong to London by Container Vessel", what is the meaning? How to deal with it?

9. If there is the sentence in the L/C: "Shipment from China to Hamburg with indication of transshipment at Hong Kong on Carrier Maersk Lines", can we accept it?

10. If there is the sentence in the L/C: "Certificate issued by P&I Club", what is the meaning? Can we accept it?

11. If there is the sentence in the L/C: "Lloyds Register Shipping Certificate Required", what is the meaning? Can we accept it?

12. If there is the sentence in the L/C: "Container Shipment required, Shipment must be in full Container load and Unavoidable, if any, Spill over in to LCL Cargo", what is the meaning? How to deal with it?

IV. Case Study.

1. A ship started on its voyage after loading, but in the course of the journey a fire broke out during transit in Hold A, which had been loaded with stationary and tea. The captain ordered his

crew to pour water on the fire. It was found out, after the fire was extinguished, that part of the stationery had been burned, the remainder and all the tea had been soaked through.

Questions:

(1) What were the natures of the respective losses?

(2) What risk would you have covered if you had wanted to be compensated for the losses?

2. The ABC Company exported a consignment of silk. As the shipping marks in the relevant L/C were not clear, the person in charge thought that the L/C did not stipulate the shipping marks. He, then, made the shipping marks himself. As a result, discrepancies occurred between the made shipping marks and those stated in the L/C. The buyers, therefore, refused to pay for the documents. However, after negotiation, the buyers agreed to pay only when the ABC Company had reduced the original prices by 10 percent.

Questions:

What lessons can we learn from this case?

3. Which of the following cases belongs to digital trade delivery? And why?

a. Case description: Bookstore A is an online electronic bookstore , which is located in New York State, USA. The bookstore sells its e-books to target consumers worldwide through its self-built website. After purchasing e-books from Bookstore A, consumers can enjoy various services, such as immediately obtaining authorized e-book files through the download link provided by Bookstore A.

b. Case description: Company B is a software development company located in Canton, China, mainly providing subscription services for project management software to the global market. The user group of company B can register online on company B's electronic website platform, pay subscription fees, obtain the use rights of the software designated by company B, and access and use the paid software through the Internet during the subscription period.

c. Case description: Company C is an online education platform located in London, the UK, mainly providing online course training in multiple international languages (English, Chinese Mandarin, Japanese, Spanish, etc.). Registered students of Company C can choose language learning courses they are interested in on its online education platform and complete their purchases through online payment or third-party payment provided by Company C. After purchasing the language learning course, the students of company C can access the purchased course content online anytime and anywhere.

d. Case description: Company M is an e-commerce company located in Ontario, Canada. In 2025, the company has recently established a new digital music platform that mainly provides consumers with online sales services for massive music. Consumers can search for their favorite singer's music on company M 's music platform, pay for and download their favorite music on the platform, and enjoy music online on the company M 's music platform after purchase.

e. Case description: G Company is a cloud computing service provider located in the

Guangdong Hong Kong Macao Greater Bay Area of China, mainly providing cloud computing services such as data storage and computing resources to domestic enterprise users. Its users can also obtain the right to use cloud computing resources by registering online on the G company platform and paying a certain fee, and then can access and use these resources through the Internet.

f. Case description: KG Company is an electronic product manufacturer located in Canton, China, mainly selling KG's smartphones to consumers in the United States and Europe through cross-border e-commerce platforms. After overseas consumers place orders on cross-border e-commerce platforms, the goods are shipped from warehouses in Canton, China, and then transported and distributed through international logistics before finally reaching consumers in the United States and Europe.

g. Case description: BR Company is a fashion brand enterprise located in Paris, France. In 2025, it has marketed clothing to consumers in the European Union through cross-border e-commerce platforms. After placing an order on a cross-border e-commerce platform, the goods are shipped from a warehouse in Paris, France, through international logistics transportation and local delivery in the European Union, and finally delivered to EU consumers.

V. Please make out the Shipping Advice according to the following particulars.

买方：上海进出口贸易公司　　地址：上海市中山路 1321 号　　电话：021-56325468
卖方：日本高田商社　　　　　地址：日本东京大通町 324　　　电话：028-54872458
品名：电视机（彩色 48 英寸）　单价：1 000 美元/台 FOB 上海
数量：100 台　　　　　　　　　包装：每台装一纸箱
总价：100 000 美元　　　　　　装运时间：2009 年 8 月 16 日　　装运港：大阪
目的地：上海　　　　　　　　　合同号码：THX040831
信用证号码：HX030702　　　　重量：30kg/台
尺码：0.5m³　　　　　　　　　 船名：DONGFANG
航次：Voy.0707

SHIPPING ADVICE

Dear Sirs:　　　　　　　　　　　　　　　　　　　　　Date:_____

Re: Shipment of Contract No.
Letter of Credit No.

We wish to advise that the following stipulated vessel will arrive at _____ port, on/ about _____Vessel's name _____ Voy. No._____.

Form _____ to _____

We'll appreciate seeing that the covering goods would be on the above vessel on the date of L/C called.

C.C.

VI. Please answer the following questions according to the B/L given below.

（1）托运人   （2）收货人

（3）被通知人   （4）提单号码

（5）船名   （6）装货港

（7）目的港   （8）唛头

（9）件数和包装   （10）总毛重

（11）总尺码   （12）货物名称

（13）运费缴付方式   （14）"DDC COLLECT" 的中文意思

（15）正本提单件数   （16）提单日期及签发地点

（17）货物的装运日期

BILL of LADING

Shipper GUANGDONG TEXTILES IMP.AND WOOLEN KNITWEAR CO., LTD. 13/F, GUANGDONG TEX. MANSION NO.168 XIAOBEI RD. GUANGZHOU, CHINA		B/L NO.: KRL030523
Consignee CONSIGNAD TO CANADIAN IMPERIAL BANK OF COMMERCE.QUEEN AND SIMCOE TORONTO, ONTARIO,CANADA		**COMBINED TRANSPORT** **BILL OF LADING** **KINGROAD LOGISTICS CO., LTD.** RECEIVED in apparent good order and condition except as otherwise noted the total number of Containers or other packages or units enumerated below for transportation from the place of receipt to the place of delivery subject to the terms hereof. One of the original Bills of Lading must be surrendered duly endorsed in exchange for the Goods or Delivery Order. On of this document (duly endorsed)to the Carrier by or on behalf of the Holder, the rights and liabilities arising in accordance with the terms hereof shall (without prejudice to any rule of common law or statute rendering them binding on the Merchant) become binding in all respects between the Carrier and the Holder as though the contract evidenced hereby had been made between them. IN WITNESS whereof the number of original Bills of Lading stated have been signed. One of which being accomplished , the other(s) to be void. (Terms of Bill of Lading continued on the back hereof)
Notify Address ABC CO.		
Place of Receipt GUANGZHOU, CHINA		
Ocean Vessel REPULSE BAY V. 48E21	Port of Loading GUANGZHOU, CHINA	
Port of Discharge VANCOUVER CANADA	Place of Delivery VANCOUVER CANADA	

Marks and Numbers	Number and Kind of Packages	Description of Goods	Gross Weight	Measurement
	30CTNS	LADIES 95 PERCENT COTTON	285kgs	1.85m³

P.O.#   5 PERCENT(SPANDEX) KNITTED TOP.

STYLE#

QUANTITY   GOODS HAVE BEEN LOADED ON BOARD

PRE-PACK   VESSEL NAME: REPULSE BAY V.48E21

MADE IN CHINA   DATE: 2009/5/15

CARTON#   THE ESTIMIATED ARRIVAL DATE: 2009.06.20

                     THE L/C NO.....

                     P/O NO. 06674

                     STYLE NO. 05-168

                     SHIPPED QUANTITY OF EACH ORDER, 1 260 PCS

CFS-CFS   FREIGHT PREPAID & DDC COLLECT

          SAY TOTAL   THIRTY (30) CARTONS ONLY

According to the declaration of the merchant

For delivery of goods please apply to :

　　THE FORWARDER AGENT IN CANADA

　　WSA LINE INT'L (VANCOUVER) INC

　　#213-3889 HENNING DRIVE

　　BURNAY. BC V5C 5N5 CANADA

　　TEL: 804-2986448 FAX:804-2928834

　　　ATTN:MR. KEVIM MOK

Freight amount	Freight payable at GUANGZHOU	Place and Date of issue GUANGZHOU, MAY 15. 2009
Cargo Insurance through the undersigned not covered Covered according to attached Policy	Number of Original B/Ls THREE (3)	For and on behalf of KINGROAD LOGISTICS CO., LTD.
LADEN ON BOARD THE VESSEL 　MAY 15.2009　　BO SHI JI 282 V. 0227S Date_____　By_____ 　　KINGROAD LAGISTICS CO., LTD.		AS CARRIER

VII. Please fill in the B/L according to the following particulars.

Dongfeng Company in Shenzhen, China exported 8 000 pcs of children's toys to British Ocean Company in June, 2009, at USD6.5 per pc CFR LONDON, to be packed in 12 pcs to one carton. Each carton has a gross weight of 5.5 kilograms. The measurement for the carton is: 20cm×30cm× 30cm, and the marks are BOC/LONDONG/NOS: 500.

The goods will be shipped by S.S. Dongfeng from Shenzhen Port to London on Sept.28th, 2009.

BILL of LADING

Shipper			B/L No.		
Consignee			Combined Transport B/L		
Notify Address			For delivery of goods please apply to:		
Pre-carriage by		Place of Receipt			
Ocean Vessel Voy. No.		Port of Loading			
Port of Discharge		Port of Delivery	Final Destination for the Merchant's Reference only		
Container, Seal No. & Marks & Nos.		No. of Package & Description of Goods	Gross Weight kgs		Measurement m³
Freight & Charges		Revenue Tons	Rate Per	Prepaid	Collect
Ex. Rate		Prepaid at	Payable at		Place and Date of issue
		Total Prepaid	No. of Original B(s)/L		Stamp & Signature

VIII. Multiple Choices.

1. Before shipment, the buyers generally send their (   ) to the sellers, informing them of the
   packing and marking, mode of transportation, etc.

   A. shipping documents   B. shipping requirements

   C. shipping advice   D. shipping marks

2. If direct steamer is not available for transportation, (　　).

    A. the goods will not be shipped   B. partial shipment should be allowed

    C. the goods have to be separated   D. the goods have to be transshipped

3. Which of the following is not the mode of cross-border e-commerce logistics operation?

    (　　)

    A. postal packets   B. overseas warehouse

    C. special courier   D. high-speed train

4. Which of the following does not belong to the kind of B/L according to whether the B/L is transferable? (　　)

    A. straight B/L   B. blank B/L

    C. order B/L   D. direct B/L

5. Which of the following does not belong to the kind of B/L according to the mode of B/L?

    (　　)

    A. transshipment B/L   B. order B/L

    C. through B/L   D. direct B/L

Chapter Ten

Part A Text

Cargo Transportation Insurance

In international buying and selling of goods, there are a number of risks, which, if they occur, will involve traders in financial losses. For instance cargoes in transit may be damaged due to breakage of packing, clash or fire, etc. These hazards, and many others, may be insured against. Every year, a certain amount of cargo is destroyed or damaged by perils of the sea in transit, but whichever particular cargo it would be it can not be anticipated. All cargo owners take the risk of loss through the perils. However, foreign traders can insure themselves against many of these risks. Based on the principle that the fortunate helps the unfortunate, the industry of insurance has been developed to overcome these financial losses. Insurance is a process for spreading risk, so that the burden of any loss is borne not by the unfortunate individual directly affected but by the total body of people under consideration. In return for a payment known as a premium paid by the insured, an insurance company will agree to compensate the insured person in the event of losses during the period of insurance.

The history of insurance goes back as far as the twelfth century, when marine insurance was known to exist in Northern Italy. In the fourteenth century, Italian merchants came to Britain and brought their system of insurance to safeguard ships and cargo with them. In those days, of course, there were no insurance companies; merchants would group together and write their names under a promise to pay for ships or cargoes lost in storms or taken by pirates, and this is how the term "underwriters" came into existence. If the ship was lost, the financial loss was spread and no single merchant risked all his money.

There are a great number of insurance companies in the world. Lloyd's is a famous organization incorporated in London in 1871. It is the center of marine insurance which started in a seventeenth century coffee house. Through which, insurance brokers may place their business. In China, the People's Insurance Company (Group) of China limited, established in 1949, underwrites almost all kinds of insurance and has agents in almost all main ports and regions in the world. Since the establishment of the PICC, it has become the practice of Chinese foreign trade corporations to have their imports insured with the PICC. Insurance on China's exports may also be covered here if the foreign importers consider it appropriate.

国际贸易货物的买卖存在着各种各样的风险,这些风险的发生将会给有关的商人们带来经济损失。例如,货物在运输途中由于包装破损、碰损或火灾等原因而损坏等。这些风险以及其他一些风险都可以通过保险加以防范。虽然，每一年都有一定数目的货物在运输途中不可避免地遭受海上风险而被摧毁或受损，但是灾难会降临到哪一批货上事先是不可预知的。所有的货主都要冒货物灭失的危险。然而，从事国际贸易的商人可以通过保险防止很多危险。根据"幸运的帮助不幸的"这个原则，保险业发展起来，用于弥补这些经济上的损失。保险的目的是将风险分摊，这样风险发生时，就可以由所有的相关人员分摊而不是由直接遭遇方单独承担。当保险人交付保险费后，如在保险期内发生损失，保险公司将同意向保险人赔付该损失。

保险的历史可以追溯到 12 世纪，据说当时在意大利的北方，已经存在着海运保险。在 14 世纪，意大利商人来到了英国，随之也带来了保护他们的船只和货物的保险制度。在那个时代，当然还没有保险公司，商人们总是聚集在一起，共同保证偿付在风暴中遭受损失的或被海盗抢劫的船只或货物，并在保证书下面签字画押。这就是"underwriters"（字面的意思是"在下面签署的人"，但是，实际的意思是"保险商"或"保险公司"）一词的来源出处。如果船只沉没，经济损失由大家分摊，而不是由哪一个商人单独出资承担所有的风险。

世界上有众多的保险公司。劳埃德海上保险协会是最著名的机构之一，1871 年组建于伦敦。该公司作为海运保险中心，早在 17 世纪就在一家咖啡馆内开始营业。保险经纪人通过劳埃德保险公司进行业务活动。中国人民保险集团股份有限公司成立于 1949 年。它可以承担几乎所有险别的保险，在全世界主要港口和地区都有代理。自从中国人民保险公司成立以来，进口货物在该公司投保已经成为我国外贸公司的习惯做法了。中国的出口货物，在外方买家认为适宜的情况下，也可在人保公司投保。

Before examining the content of insurance, it is appropriate first of all to consider three concepts: risks, losses and expenses.

Marine Risks in connection with cargoes in transit can be classified into two categories: (1) Marine Risks, which are caused by Natural Calamities and Accidents; (2) Extraneous Risks which consist of General Extraneous Risks and Special Extraneous Risk.

Risks such as tsunami, earthquake or volcanic eruption, lightning and heavy weather, etc. fall into the category of Natural Calamities; while fire, explosion, sinking, grounding, stranding, collision, missing, etc. belong to Accidents. It should be noted that Marine Risks do not include all the risks at sea. For instance, freshwater and/or rainwater damage are/is not included in the Marine Risks.

Extraneous Risks are risks that are beyond the coverage of the Marine Risks mainly including General Extraneous Risks and Special Extraneous Risks. General Extraneous Risks include: pilferage, contamination, breakage, sweating and/or heating, taint of odor, rusting, fresh and/or rain water damage, shortage in weight, clashing, etc. Special Extraneous Risks: war, warlike operations, hostile acts, armed conflicts or piracy capture, seizure, arrest, restraint or detainment, etc.

It is very important to have a clear understanding of the above mentioned concepts, since some of the risks are not covered by the relevant insurance. For instance, partial losses or damages caused by Natural Calamity are not covered by F.P.A. while Special Extraneous Risks are not in the coverage of All Risks.

在了解保险的内容之前应首先了解几个概念：海洋货物运输的风险、损失和费用。

海洋货物运输的风险主要分为海上风险和外来风险两大类。（1）海上风险：由自然灾害和意外事故引起。（2）外来风险：包括一般外来风险和特殊外来风险。

自然灾害主要包括海啸、地震或火山爆发、雷电和恶劣气候等。意外事故包括火灾、爆炸、沉没、搁浅、触礁、碰撞和失踪等。值得注意的是，海上风险并不是指海上发生的一切风险，例如，淡水雨淋就不属于海上风险。

外来风险是指海上风险以外的其他外来风险，主要包括一般外来风险和特殊外来风险。一般外来风险包括偷窃、玷污、渗漏、破碎、受热受潮、串味、生锈、淡水雨淋、短少和提货不着、短量、碰损等；特殊外来风险包括战争、类似战争的行为、敌对行为、武装冲突或海盗行为，以及由此引起的捕获、拘留、逮捕、管制或扣押等。

分清楚上述这些概念很重要，因为保险承保范围并不是包括所有风险的。例如，平安险对自然灾害引起的部分损失就不赔偿；而一切险则对特殊外来风险引起的损失不赔偿。

Section One　Marine Insurance（海运保险）

At present, according to the different transportation methods, there are ocean marine transportation insurance, overland transportation insurance, air transportation insurance and parcel post transportation insurance in our country. Among these, ocean marine transportation insurance is the most widely used in international trade practical business. The ocean marine transportation insurance is also the first used insurance and so has the longest history among all. The overland transportation insurance and air transportation insurance have been developed on the basis of ocean marine transportation insurance. Even though they have different obligations, their basic principles and guarantees provided by the insurance companies are nearly the same. In this unit we are going to deal with ocean marine transportation insurance.

目前，我国办理的进出口货物运输保险业务按照运输方式的不同，主要分为海洋运输货物保险、陆上运输货物保险、航空运输货物保险和邮包运输保险等，其中业务量最大、涉及面最广的是海洋运输货物保险。海洋运输货物保险也是起源最早、历史最久的一种保险。陆上、航空等货物运输保险都是在海洋运输货物保险的基础上发展起来的。尽管各种不同货物运输保险的具体责任有所不同，但它们的基本原则、保险公司保障的范围等基本一致。本章将重点讨论海上运输保险。

Originally, insurance was only applied to losses at sea where risks were always great. What's more, ocean shipping takes up the biggest share of the volume of goods transported in international trade. Therefore, marine insurance has become the most important insurance.

Marine insurance is defined as a contract of insurance whereby the insurance in return for premium collected undertakes to indemnify the insured in a manner and to the extent thereby agreed, against marine losses, that is to say, the losses incidental to marine adventure. Such insurance involving the marine conveyance of cargo from one country to another is, then, marine cargo insurance, which is seen as an indispensable adjunct to foreign trade.

However, the term "marine insurance" is somewhat misleading because the contract of marine insurance can, by agreement of the parties or custom of the trade, be extended so as to protect the insured against losses on inland waters or land which are incidental to the sea voyage. In the export trade it is usual to arrange an extended marine insurance in order to cover the transportation of goods from the warehouse of the seller to the port of dispatch, and from the port of arrival to the warehouse of the overseas buyer.

In insurance, the party who insures others against loss or damage and undertakes to make payment in case of loss is called the insurer; the party who is insured against loss and to whom payment covering the loss will be made is the insured; the contract made between the insurer and the insured is the insurance policy; and the sum of money the insured agrees to pay the insurer for an insurance policy is the premium. In the normal course of business the exporter, who wishes to have his goods insured, does not approach the insurer directly but instructs an insurance broker to effect the insurance on his behalf.

最初，保险只应用于海上货物的损失，因为海上风险众多。并且，由于海运在国际贸易中占货运量的一大部分，因此海上保险已成为最重要的保险。

海上保险是一种保险合同，作为对所收集的被保险人的保险费的回报，它按照双方同意的方式和程度来赔偿被保险人的海上损失——海洋运输过程中偶然发生的损失。这种涉及把一国的货物经过海洋运输运到另一国的保险就称为海洋货物运输保险。它是对外贸易不可缺少的一部分。

然而，"海上保险"可能会引起误解。因为海上保险合同经双方当事人同意或贸易惯例许可后，可以扩展到保护被保险人在内河或陆地上遭遇到的像海上偶然发生的损失。在出口贸易中，经常安排扩展的海上保险从卖方的仓库运到发运港，再从抵运港运至外国买家的仓库。

在保险中，为他人保险货物免受灭失或损坏以及发生损失后负责赔偿的一方，称为保险人。被保险损失和接受赔偿损失金的一方，称为被保险人。保险人和被保险人之间订立的合同就是保险单，被保险人同意付给保险人的一笔钱称为保险金。在一般的商务过程中，想为货物保险的出口商并不直接同保险人打交道，而是请保险经纪人代表自己来安排保险。

Section Two   Risks, Losses and Expenses（风险、损失和费用）

According to the loss or damage caused by risks included in different coverage and the expenses involved, the insurance company is responsible for indemnifying the insured goods. Obviously, risk, loss and expenses are closely related to each other. In order to have a clear understanding of the contents of insurance, these three terms should be clarified.

保险公司按照不同险别包括的风险所造成的损失和发生的费用承担赔偿责任。所以在保险业务中，风险、损失和费用三者有着密切的联系。为了准确地理解保险的内容，我们有必要澄清这三个概念。

1. Risks（风险）

While the cargo is traveling to another country, it is likely to encounter various perils which may cause the goods to suffer loss of one kind or another. Marine risks in connection with cargo in transit can be classified into two types: perils of the sea and extraneous risks. Perils of the sea are caused by natural calamities and fortuitous accidents; the latter, by various extraneous reasons, including general extraneous risks and special extraneous risks.

Marine Risks

(1) Perils of the sea: Natural calamities and Fortuitous accidents.

(2) Extraneous risks: General extraneous risks and Special extraneous risks.

在货物运到另一个国家的途中，它可能要遭遇到各种各样的风险，这些风险会引起货物受到这样或那样的损失。海洋货物运输的风险主要分为海上风险和外来风险两大类。海上风险由海上发生的自然灾害和外来风险引起；外来风险由各种外来原因引起，它包括一般外来风险和特殊外来风险。

风险

（1）海上风险：自然灾害和意外事故。

（2）外来风险：一般外来风险和特殊外来风险。

1) Perils of the sea（海上风险）

Perils of the sea are those caused by natural calamities and fortuitous.

(1) Natural calamities: Disasters such as vile weather, thunder and lighting, tsunami, earthquake, floods, etc.

(2) Fortuitous accidents: Accidents such as ship stranded, striking upon the rocks, ship sinking, ship collision, colliding with icebergs or other objects, fire, explosion, ship missing, etc.

海上风险是由自然灾害和意外事故引起的风险。

（1）自然灾害：是指恶劣气候、雷电、海啸、地震、洪水等灾难。

（2）意外事故：是指船舶搁浅、触礁、沉没、船舶互撞、与流冰或其他物体相撞、起火、爆炸以及船只失踪等事故。

2) Extraneous risks（外来风险）

Extraneous risks are risks caused by extraneous reasons, consisting of general extraneous risks and special extraneous risks.

(1) General extraneous risks include: theft or pilferage, rain, shortage, contamination, leakage, breakage, train of odor, dampness, heating, rusting hooking, etc.

(2) Special extraneous risks include: war risks, strikes, non-delivery of cargo, refusal to receive cargo, etc.

外来风险由各种外来原因所引起，包括一般外来风险和特殊外来风险。

（1）一般外来风险包括：偷窃、雨淋、短量、污染、渗漏、破损、串味、受潮、受热、锈损和钩损等。

（2）特殊外来风险包括：战争、罢工、交货不到、拒绝收货等风险。

2. Losses（损失）

Marine losses are the damages or losses of the insured goods incurred by perils of the sea. Losses sustained by the insured because of the risks listed above come from not only the loss of the goods or the damage done to the goods, but also from the expenses the insured sustained in rescuing the goods in danger. According to the extent of damage, losses in marine insurance fall into two types: total loss and partial loss. The former may be subdivided into actual total loss and constructive total loss; the latter, general average and particular average.

Marine Losses

(1) Total Loss: Actual total loss and Constructive total loss.

(2) Partial Loss: General average and Particular average.

海损一般是指海运保险货物在海洋运输中由于海上风险所造成的损坏和灭失。被保险货物遭遇保险责任范围内的事故，除了使货物本身受到损毁导致损失，还会产生费用方面的损失。根据损失的不同程度可分为全部损失和部分损失。前者可再分为实际全损和推定全损。后者可分为共同海损和单独海损。

海损

（1）全部损失：实际全损、推定全损。

（2）部分损失：共同海损、单独海损。

1) Total loss（全部损失）

Total loss refers to the loss of the entire shipment caused by the occurrence of one of the perils of the sea, fire, or some other reasons.

(1) Actual total loss: The actual total loss occurs where the insured goods have been totally lost or damaged, or found to be totally valueless on arrival.

(2) Constructive total loss: Constructive total loss is found in the case where an actual total loss appears to be unavoidable or the cost to be incurred in recovering or reconditioning the goods together with the forwarding cost to the destination named in the policy would exceed their value on arrival.

全部损失是指由于海难、火灾或其他原因引起的全部运输货物的全部损失。

（1）实际全损：实际全损是指该批被保险货物完全灭失或完全变质已失去原有的使用价值。

（2）推定全损：推定全损是指该批被保险货物受损后，实际全损已经不可避免，或者恢复受损货物并将其送到保险单所注明的目的地所需的费用将超过货物的价值。

2) Partial loss（部分损失）

Partial loss refers to the loss of part of a consignment. According to different causes, partial loss can be either general average or particular average.

(1) General average

In the insurance business the term "average" typically means "loss" in most cases. It all goes back to the situation where a ship is in danger, and somebody's cargo must be abandoned. Whose should it be the captain has to make a decision, and one of the shippers will suffer. To cover this situation the concept of general average was introduced. It means that whichever shipper loses all or part of his cargo, all the others will club together to recompense him for his loss. All policies the insured take out automatically cover them against it.

(2) Particular average

A particular average means that a particular consignment is suffered by one whose goods are partly lost or damaged. When there is a particular average loss, other interests in the voyage (such as the carrier and other cargo owners whose goods were not damaged) do not contribute to the partial recovery of the one suffering the loss. An example of a particular average occurs when a storm or fire damages part of the shipper's cargo and no one else's cargo has to be sacrificed to save the voyage. The cargo owner whose goods were damaged looks to his insurance company for payment, provided, of course, his policy covers the specific type of loss suffered.

Since most losses encountered by shippers are partial, that is, of the particular average nature, it is important to know exactly what provisions for such partial losses are in the insurance policy.

部分损失是指货物的损失只是部分的。根据损失产生的原因不同，部分损失可分为共同海损和单独海损。

（1）共同海损。在保险业中，"average" 一般是 "海损" 的意思。这个词来源于船舶遇到海难时，有的货物必须抛弃入海。该抛弃谁的货物呢？船长必须做出决定，而总有一个发货人要受到损失。为应付这种情况提出了 "共同海损" 这一概念。意思是说不论哪个发货人损失了全部或部分货物，所有其他发货人都将凑钱分摊其损失。这就是共同海损，被保险人取得了保险单则自动为它们承保共同海损。

（2）单独海损。单独海损是指因货物丢失或损坏而蒙受的损失。在单独海损中，运输中的其他被保各方（如承运人和其他货物没有受到损失的货主）不必分摊受损的一方的补偿费用。例如，暴风雨或火灾将发货人的货物部分损坏，其他货主没有必要去牺牲自己的货物来挽救整个货物运输。受损的货主可根据保险单规定的险别向保险公司要求赔偿。

由于发货人遇到的大部分损失都是部分损失，所以确切地了解保险单中有关部分损失的条款是非常重要的。

3. Expenses（费用）

Losses sustained by the insured because of the risks come from not only the loss of the goods or the damage done to the goods, but also from the expenses the insured sustained in rescuing the goods in danger. Transportation insurance not only insures the losses caused by risks but also the losses of expenses. The main expenses include:

被保险货物遭遇保险责任范围内的事故，除了使货物本身受到损毁导致损失，还会产生费用方面的损失。运输保险除了保障损失，还保障费用的损失，这些费用主要有：

1) Sue and labor expense（施救费用）

These expenses are the expenses arising from measures properly taken by the insured, the employee and the assignee, etc. for minimizing or avoiding losses caused by the risks covered in the insurance policy. The insurer is held responsible to compensate for such expenses.

施救费用是指在保险范围内，由被保险人、雇佣人员和受让人等为抢救保险货物，以防止损失扩大所采取措施而支出的合理费用。

2) Salvage charges（救助费用）

Salvage charges are expenses resulting from measures properly taken by a third party other than the insured, the employee and the assignee, etc.

救助费用是指在货物保险范围内，由被保险人、雇佣人员和受让人以外的第三者采取救助行为而向其支付的报酬费用。

Section Three　Marine Insurance Coverage（海上保险险别）

The object of buying insurance is to obtain as much protection as necessary, at as low a cost as possible. To do this, one has to know what risks can be covered and decide how much coverage is needed.

According to the People's Insurance Company of China Ocean Marine Cargo Clauses, insurance is mainly classified into two groups: Basic Insurance Coverage and Additional Insurance Coverage. The applicant can purchase Basic Insurance Coverage individually. However, before purchasing Additional Insurance Coverage, they must first purchase Basic Insurance Coverage. Basic Insurance Coverage is further classified into the following three conditions: Free from Particular Average (F.P.A.), With Particular Average (W.P.A.) and All Risks. F.P.A. covers mainly Total Loss and General Average, while W.P.A. covers Particular Average in addition. All Risks cover, in addition to the scope of W.P.A., Extraneous Risks such as Shortage Risk, Intermixture and Contamination Risk, Leakage Risk, Clash and Breakage Risk, Taint of Odor Risk, Sweating and Heating Risk, Hook Damage Risk, Rust Risk, Breakage of Pacing Risk, etc. In case of F.P.A. or W.P.A., one or several kinds of these Extraneous Risks may be covered in addition.

买保险的目的就是花尽可能少的钱去购买尽可能多的和必要的保护。为此，人们必须知道哪些风险可以承保，并决定需要哪些险种。

根据《中国人民保险公司海洋运输货物保险条款》，保险可分为两大类：基本险和附加险。购买者可以单独购买基本险。然而，在购买附加险以前，他必须购买基本险。基本险可再分为平安险（F.P.A.）、水渍险（W.P.A.）和一切险。平安险主要包括全部损失和共同损失，而水渍险则再加上单独海损。一切险除水渍险的范围外，还包括诸如偷窃、提货不着险，短量险，混杂、玷污险，渗漏险，碰损、破碎险，串味险，受潮/受热险，钩损险，锈损险，包装破损险等外来风险。投保平安险或水渍险可加保这些外来风险的一种或数种。

1．Basic Insurance Coverage（基本险）

1) Free from Particular Average (F.P.A.)（平安险）

Free from particular average, basically, is a limited form of cargo insurance coverage in as much as that no partial loss or damage is recoverable from the insurers unless the actual vessel or craft is stranded, sunk or burnt. Under the latter circumstances, the F.P.A. cargo policy holder can recover any losses of the insured merchandise which was on the vessel at the time as would obtain under the more extensive W.P.A. policy. The F.P.A. policy provides coverage for total losses and general average emerging from actual "marine perils".

According to PICC's Ocean Marine Cargo Clauses revised on January 1th, 1981, F.P.A. insurance covers:

(1) Total or Constructive Total Loss of the whole consignment hereby insured caused in the course of transit by natural calamities—heavy weather, lightning, tsunami, earthquake and flood. In case a constructive total loss is claimed for, the Insured shall abandon to the Company the damage goods and all his rights and title pertaining thereto. The goods on each lighter to or from the seagoing vessel shall be deemed a separate risk. "Constructive Total Loss" refers to the loss where an actual total loss appears to be unavailable or the cost to be incurred in recovering or reconditioning the goods together with the forwarding costs to the destination named in the Policy would exceed their value on arrival.

(2) Total or Partial Loss caused by accidents—the carrying conveyance being grounded

stranded, sunk or in collision with floating ice or other objects as fire or explosion.

(3) Partial Loss of the insured goods attributable to heavy weather, lightning and/or tsunami, where the conveyance has been grounded, stranded, sunk or burnt, irrespective of whether the event or events took place before or after such accident.

(4) Partial or Total Loss consequent on falling of entire package or packages into sea during loading, transshipment or discharge.

(5) Reasonable cost incurred by the insured in salvaging the goods or averting or minimizing a loss recoverable under the Policy, provided that cost shall not exceed the sum insured of the consignment so saved.

(6) Losses attributable to discharge of the insured goods at a port of distress following a sea peril as well as special charges arising from loading, warehousing and forwarding of the goods at an intermediate port of call or refuge.

(7) Sacrifice and Contribution to General Average and Salvage Charges.

(8) Such proportion of losses sustained by the shipowners as is to be reimbursed by the Cargo Owner under the Contract of Affreightment "Both to Blame Collision" clause.

平安险，从基本上讲，是一种有限制的货物保险形式，因为承保人不会对部分损失或损坏进行赔偿，除非船舶的确遭受搁浅、沉没、失火等损失。在这种情况下，平安保险单持有人可得到船上被保险货物的损失赔偿，这与保险范围更广的水渍险一样。平安险提供由于实际海难所造成的全部损失和共同海损的保险。

根据 1981 年 1 月 1 日修订的《中国人民保险公司海洋运输货物保险条款》的规定，平安险负责赔偿：

（1）被保险货物在途中由于恶劣气候、雷电、海啸、地震、洪水自然灾害造成整批货物的全部损失或推定全损。当被保险人要求赔付推定全损时，须将受损货物及其权利委付给保险公司。被保险货物用驳船运往或运离海轮的，每一驳船所装的货物可视作一个整批。

推定全损是指被保险货物的实际全损已经不可避免，或者恢复、修复受损货物以及运送货物到原定目的地的费用超过该货物的价值。

（2）由于遭受搁浅、触礁、沉没、互撞、与流冰或其他物体碰撞以及失火、爆炸意外事故造成货物的全部或部分损失。

（3）在运输工具已经发生搁浅、触礁、沉没、焚毁意外事故的情况下，货物在此前后又在海上遭受恶劣气候、雷电、海啸等自然灾害所造成的部分损失。

（4）在装卸或转运时由于一件或数件整件货物落海造成的全部或部分损失。

（5）被保险人对遭受承保责任内危险的货物采取抢救、防止或减少货损的措施而支付的合理费用，但以不超过该批被救货物的保险金额为限。

（6）运输工具遭遇海难后，在避难港由于卸货所引起的损失，以及在中途港、避难港由于卸货、存仓以及运送货物所产生的特别费用。

（7）共同海损的牺牲、分摊和救助费用。

（8）运输契约订有"船舶互撞责任"条款，根据该条款规定应由供货方偿还船方的损失。

2) With Average/With Particular Average (W.A./W.P.A.) （水渍险）

This insurance covers wider than F.P.A. Aside from the risks covered under F.P.A. conditions as above, this insurance also covers partial losses of the insured goods caused by heavy weather, lightning, tsunami, earthquake and/or flood.

水渍险的负责赔偿范围比平安险广。除了上述平安险的各项责任，水渍险还负责被保险货物在运输途中由于恶劣气候、雷电、海啸、地震、洪水等造成的部分损失。

3) All Risks（一切险）

The cover of All Risks is the most comprehensive of the three. Aside from the risks covered under F.P.A. and W.P.A. conditions as above, this insurance also covers all risks of loss of or damage to insured goods whether partial or total, arising from external causes in the course of transit. It should be noted that "All Risks" does not, as its name suggests, really cover all risks. The "All Risks" clause excludes coverage against damage caused by war, strikes, riots, etc. These perils can be covered by a separate clause. And it covers only physical loss or damage from external causes.

在三种基本险别中，一切险承保的范围最广泛。除了包括上述平安险和水渍险的各项责任以外，该保险还负责被保险货物在运输途中由于外来因素所致的全部或部分损失。要注意的是，一切险并不是像其名称所说的那样，承保所有的风险。一切险条款排除对由于战争、罢工、动乱等因素造成的损失的赔偿。这些风险可由单独的条款来负责赔偿。并且，一切险只负责赔偿由于外来原因所造成的物理性灭失或损坏。

4) The Free Obligation of Basic Insurance Coverage（基本险的除外责任）

The three coverages, i.e. F.P.A. and W.P.A. and All Risks do not cover:

(1) Loss or damage caused by the international act or fault of the insured.

(2) Loss or damage falling under the liability of the consignor.

(3) Loss or damage arising from the inferior quality or shortage of the insured goods prior to the attachment of this insurance.

(4) Loss or damage arising from normal loss, inherent vice or nature of the insured goods, loss of market and/or delay in transit and any expenses arising therefrom.

(5) Risks and liability covered and excluded by the ocean marine cargo were risks clauses and strike, riot and civil commotion clauses of this company.

上述三种险别对下列损失不负赔偿责任：

（1）被保险人的故意行为或过失所造成的损失。

（2）属于发货人所引起的损失。

（3）在保险开始前，被保险货物已存在的由品质不良或数量短差所造成的损失。

（4）被保险货物的自然损耗、本质缺陷、特性以及市价跌落、运输延迟所引起的损失或费用。

（5）本公司海洋运输货物战争险条款和货物运输罢工险条款规定的责任范围和除外责任。

2．Additional Insurance Coverage（附加险）

According to the nature of insured goods, the cargo may choose any of the three covers mentioned above. If more protection is needed, they may further insure their goods against one or additional risks. No additional risks can be purchased to insure goods independently. Additional risks include general additional risks and special additional risks. Since the scope of cover of general additional risks is already included in that of All Risks, it is not necessary for the goods to be insured by additional risks if they are insured by All Risks.

根据被保险货物的特点，投保人可选择上述三种险别中的任何一种。如果还需要更多的保护，还可以加保一种或数种附加险。附加险不能单独投保。附加险有一般附加险和特殊附加险之别。一般附加险由于已经包含在一切险的承保范围内，所以如已投保了一切险就不需要再加保一般附加险。

1) General Additional Risks （一般附加险）

Additional risks complement the basic risks. When you ask for one or several of the additional risk coverages, you will have to ask for one of the basic risks coverages at the same time. There are general additional risks and special additional risks. General additional risks cannot be used to insure goods alone. General additional risks under CIC fall into the following eleven kinds:

(1) Theft, pilferage and non-delivery clause. To cover loss of or damage to the insured goods on the insured value caused by theft and/or pilferage; non-delivery or entire package; loss or damage for which the liability of the shipowner or other party concerned is exempted by the Contract of Carriage.

(2) Fresh water and/or rain damage clause. To cover loss of or damage to the insured goods directly caused by rain and/or fresh water.

(3) Shortage clause. To cover risk of shortage occurring during the course of transit due to breakage of outer packing, or loss of quantity and actual shortage in weight in the case of bulk cargo, but excluding normal loss.

(4) Intermixture and contamination clause. To cover risks of intermixture and contamination occurring during the course of transit.

(5) Leakage clause. To cover risk of leakage occurring during the course of transit caused by damage to the container, or deterioration of the insured goods resulting from leakage of liquid in which the insured goods are stored.

(6) Clash and breakage clause. To cover risk of breakage and clash occurring during the course of transit caused by shock, collision or press of the insured goods.

(7) Taint of odor clause. To cover risk of taint of odor of the insured edible, Chinese medicine, toilet material, etc. occurring during the course of transit effected by other goods.

(8) Sweat and heating clause. To cover risks of sweat, heating and wetting occurring during the course of transit arising from sudden change of temperature or breakdown of ventilation of the carrying vessel.

(9) Hooks damage clause. To cover hook damage to the insured goods occurring during loading or unloading including expenses of reconditioning or change of packing, if any.

(10) Breakage of packing clause. To cover loss or damage occurring during the course of transit caused by breakage of packing resulting from rough handling, loading and unloading including expenses of reconditioning and change of packages, if any, for the safe prosecution of transportation.

(11) Rust clause. To cover risk of rust occurring during the course of transit.

All the above additional risks have been included in the basic risk All Risks. Therefore, if the goods are covered with All Risks, there is no need to cover the general additional risks.

附加险是基本险的扩大和补充，被保险人只能在投保了基本险别中的一种险的基础上，根据需要选择加保一种或数种附加险别。附加险别有一般附加险和特殊附加险两类。一般附加险别不能单独投保。中国人民保险公司承保的一般附加险有下列 11 种：

（1）偷窃、提货不着险条款。本保险对被保险货物遭受下列损失，按保险价值负责赔偿：偷窃行为所致的损失；整件提货不着；根据运输契约规定船东和其他责任方免除赔偿的部分。

（2）淡水雨淋险条款。本保险对被保险货物因直接遭受雨淋或淡水所致的损失负责赔偿。

（3）短量险条款。本保险对被保险货物在运输过程中，因外包装破裂或散装货物发生数量散失和实际重量短缺的损失负责赔偿，但正常的路途损耗除外。

（4）混杂、玷污险条款。本保险对被保险货物在运输过程中，因混杂、玷污所致的损失，负责赔偿。

（5）渗漏险条款。本保险对被保险货物在运输过程中，因容器损坏而引起的渗漏损失，或用液体储藏的货物因液体的渗漏而引起的货物腐败等损失，负责赔偿。

（6）碰损、破碎险条款。本保险对被保险货物在运输过程中因震动、碰撞、受压造成的破碎和碰撞损失，负责赔偿。

（7）串味险条款。本保险对被保险食用物品、中药材、化妆品等原料等货物在运输过程中，因受其他物品的影响而引起的串味损失，负责赔偿。

（8）受潮/受热险条款。本保险对被保险货物在运输过程中因气温突然变化或由于船上通风设备失灵致使船舱内水汽凝结、发潮或发热所造成的损失，负责赔偿。

（9）钩损险条款。本保险对被保险货物在装卸过程中因遭受钩损而引起的损失，以及对包装进行修补或调换所支付的费用，均负责赔偿。

（10）包装破损险条款。本保险对被保险货物在运输途中因搬运或装卸不慎，包装破裂所造成的损失，以及为继续运输安全所需要对包装进行修补或调换所支付的费用，均负责赔偿。

（11）锈损险条款。本保险对被保险货物在运输过程中发生的锈损负责赔偿。

上述一般附加险均已包括在一切险的责任范围内，因此，凡已投保一切险的无须加保任何一种一般附加险。

2) Special Additional Risk（特殊附加险）

Special additional risk differs from general additional risk in that the former covers loss or damage caused by special extraneous reasons such as politics, law, regulations and war. On the other hand, like general additional risk, special additional risks cannot be used to insure goods alone either.

Special additional risks include:

(1) War risk

(2) Strike risk

(3) On deck risk

(4) Import duty risk clause

(5) Rejection risk

(6) Aflatoxin risk

(7) Failure to delivery clause

(8) Ocean marine cargo war risk

Fire Risk Extension Clause for Storage of Cargo at destination Hong Kong, including Kowloon or Macao.

特殊附加险承保由于政治、军事、国家政策法令以及其他特殊外来原因引起的风险所造成的损失。它同一般附加险一样，不能单独投保。

特殊附加险常见的有以下几种。

（1）战争险

（2）罢工险

（3）舱面险

（4）进口关税险

（5）拒收险

（6）黄曲霉素险

（7）交货不到险

（8）海运战争险

出口货物到香港（包括九龙）或澳门存储期间的火险责任扩展条款。

3. Insurance under other transportation methods（其他运输方式下的货运保险）

In international trade, not only goods shipped by sea must be insured, but also goods transported by land, air and parcel post should also be insured. Therefore, the insurance company has different clauses for different transportation methods.

(1) Overland transportation insurance.

(2) Air transportation insurance.

(3) Parcel Post Insurance.

在国际贸易中，不仅海洋运输的货物需办理保险，陆上运输、航空运输、邮包运输的货物也都需要办理保险。保险公司对以不同方式运输的货物都定有相应的专门条款。

（1）陆上运输货物保险。

（2）航空运输货物保险。

（3）邮运包裹保险。

4. Commencement and termination of basic insurance（保险责任期限）

The commencement and termination of basic insurance are usually stipulated by adopting the customary "Warehouse to Warehouse Clause" clause.

By the warehouse to warehouse clause, the liability of the insurer is extended to cover pre-shipment and post-shipment risks. The insured goods are covered from the time when they leave the warehouse at the place named in the policy for the commencement of the transit and continue to be covered until they are delivered to the final warehouse at the destination named in the policy, but the policy imposes an overriding time limit of 60 days after the completion of discharge of the insured goods from the seagoing vessel at the final port of discharge. Upon expiration of that time limit of 60 days the cover ceases to protect the goods even if they have not reached the final warehouse.

保险责任期限是指保险人承担保险责任的起讫时限。按照国际保险业的习惯，采用的是"仓至仓条款"。

"仓至仓条款"即保险责任自被保险货物运离保险单所载明的起运地发货人仓库或储存处所时开始生效，包括正常运输过程中的海上、陆上、内河和驳船运输在内，直至该项货物到达保险单所载明目的地收货人的仓库为止，但最长不超过被保险货物卸离海轮后 60 天。超过期限，保险公司不会赔偿损失。

5. London Insurance Institute Cargo Clauses（伦敦保险协会海运货物保险条款）

London Insurance Institute Cargo Clauses were first made in 1912. The newly revised London Insurance Institute Cargo Clauses in 1982 included six types:

(1) Institute Cargo Clauses A

(2) Institute Cargo Clauses B

(3) Institute Cargo Clauses C

(4) Institute War Clauses-Cargo

(5) Institute Strike Clauses-Cargo

(6) Malicious Damage Clauses

"协会货物条款"最早制定于 1912 年，现在适用的是 1982 年 1 月 1 日修订本，主要条款有 6 种：

（1）协会货物条款（A）。

（2）协会货物条款（B）。

（3）协会货物条款（C）。

（4）协会战争险条款（货物）。

（5）协会罢工险条款（货物）。

（6）恶意损害险条款。

1) Institute Cargo Clause A（协会货物条款（A）承保范围）

The scope of clause A is comprehensive, so the method of "all risks except exclusions" is adopted. Exclusions include:

(1) General exclusions

a. Loss or damage due to willful misconduct of the insured.

b. Natural leakage of the subject matter, natural wear and tear, or wastage of the subject matter.

c. Insufficient or improper packing.

d. Delay.

e. Inherent vice of the subject matter.

f. Insolvency of the owner of the ship, the carrier or the charterer.

g. Nuclear or atomic weapons.

(2) Exclusions of unseaworthiness and unfitness of the carrying vessel, including the containers

If the insured knows beforehand that the cargo-carrying ships are unseaworthy, the cargo-carrying ship transportation vehicle, or the container is unfit for cargo, the insurer does not cover the losses or expenses thereby.

(3) Exclusions of War

The losses caused by war, civil war, or action of hostility and so on will not be compensated by insurance companies. The losses caused by capture, detention, detainment (excluding pirates) also cannot get compensation from insurance companies.

The insurer does not cover the losses caused by war, antagonistic activities, capture, distrait.

(4) Exclusions of Strike

The insurer does not cover the losses caused by strikes, labor disturbances, civil commotion, or riot.

A 条款包括的范围很广，采用的是"一切风险减除外责任"的办法。除外责任包括：

（1）一般除外责任

a. 归因于被保险人故意的不法行为造成的损失或费用。

b. 自然渗漏、自然损耗、自然磨损。

c. 包装不足或不当所造成的损失或费用。

d. 直接由于延迟所引起的损失或费用。

e. 保险标的内在缺陷或特性所造成的损失或费用。

f. 由于船舶所有人、租船人经营破产或不履行债务所造成的损失或费用。

g. 由于使用任何原子或核武器所造成的损失或费用。

（2）不适航、不适货除外责任

指保险标的在装船时，被保险人或其受雇人已经知道船舶不适航，以及船舶、装运工具、集装箱等不适货。

（3）战争除外责任

如由于战争、内战、敌对行为等造成的损失或费用；由于捕获、拘留、扣留等（海盗除外）所造成的损失或费用。

（4）罢工除外责任

罢工者、被迫停工工人造成的损失或费用，以及由于罢工、被迫停工所造成的损失或费用等。

2) Institute Cargo Clause B（协会货物条款（B））

Clause B lists all risks covered so that the insured may choose the proper insurance cover.

其承保风险的做法是采用"列明风险"的方法，即在条款的首部开宗明义地把保险人所承保的风险一一列出。

3) Institute Cargo Clause C（协会货物条款（C））

Institute Cargo Clause C only covers major casualties.

协会货物条款（C）只承保"重大意外事故"。

6. Choosing the right coverage（选择适当的险别类型）

The clear distinction among the clauses F.P.A., W.P.A. and All Risks is of great practical significance. It may help exporters choose the right coverage.

Most exporters will probably want to have the widest form of coverage they can get "All Risks". But because of the nature of their goods, underwriters may agree to provide only a more limited form of coverage. Moreover, even though an exporter can get "All Risks" coverage, he may well decide that it is uneconomical. An experienced exporter will come to know the losses he can expect, and may find it cheaper to write them off as trade losses than to pay the relatively high All Risks premium.

Products should be insured in the appropriate category. A good rule of thumb is that an exporter should insure under the coverage accepted in his particular trade. Now let's examine which type of insurance cover an intelligent exporter would choose for the following items.

(1) A consignment of shoes

(2) Logs of wood

(3) Wooden toys

(4) Heavy machinery

(5) Plywood

(6) Bicycles

Probably, you will give the following answers: (1), (3), (4) and (6) would probably be insured "All Risks" because they are prone to being damaged in transit. Most manufactured goods fall into this category. (2) would be insured F.P.A., while it could be lost it is not likely to be damaged. (5) on the other hand would be insured W.P.A. because it could be damaged in transit, but is less prone to being damaged than the finished products mentioned. Normally the insurance company will advise the exporter in this respect.

清楚地区分平安险、水渍险和一切险具有很重要的实际意义。它能帮助出口商选择正确的险别。

大部分的出口商可能都想获得覆盖范围最广的险种，它们可以购买"一切险"。但是考虑到它们货物的性质，保险人可能只同意提供一种有限的险种。并且，即使出口商能投保"一切险"，它也需要考虑是否划算。有经验的出口商会预计可能有的损失，并会发现把损失当作生意损失而勾销比支付相对较高的一切险保险金便宜。

货物应选择适当的险种来保险。从经验的角度看，出口商应该投保所在行业接受的险种。现在，让我们来看看一个聪明的出口商是如何为下列货物投保的。

（1）鞋子

（2）原木

（3）木制玩具

（4）重型机械

（5）胶合板

（6）自行车

你可能会给出下列答案：（1）、（3）、（4）和（6）可以投保一切险，因为它们在运输途中易受损坏。大多数的制造品属于这一范畴。（2）应投保平安险，因为它可能丢失但不太可能受损。（5）则必须投保水渍险，因为在运输途中，它可能会受损，但比起上述所提到的制成品来说，又不太容易受损。通常，保险公司会建议出口商这样做。

Section Four   Insurance Value（保险价值）

Insurance value, in marine cargo insurance, is the actual value of the insurable cargo. It is generally calculated as: Insurance Value = Cost of goods + amount of freight + insurance premium +

a percentage of the total sum to represent a reasonable profit for the buyer. The insurable value is the maximum amount payable by the insurance company in case of loss, and the premium is calculated and paid on the basis of this amount.

在海洋货物运输保险中，保险价值是所保险货物的实际价值。它通常是这样计算的：保险价值=货物的价值+运费金额+保险金额+代表买方利益总额的百分比。保险价值是保险公司在货物损失时所应承担的最高赔偿金额，保险费以此为基础进行计算并付款。

Section Five　Insurance Premium（保险费用）

The insurance premium is payable to the insurer when they issue the insurance policy or certificate. The premium charged for the insurance policy is calculated according to the risks involved. A policy that protects the holder against limited risks charges a low premium, and a policy which protects against a large number of risks charges a high premium. The most frequently used trade terms which affect insurance arrangements are FOB, CFR, and CIF. Where the contract between the exporter and the foreign importer is an FOB contract, it is the importer's responsibility to insure the goods. If the goods are contracted to be sold on CIF terms, then it is the exporter's turn to take out the policy and pay the cost of insurance.

当投保人将保险费付给保险人后，保险人将签发保险单或凭证。保险单收取保险金是根据所包含的险别计算的。为持单人提供有限险别保护的保险单收取低保险金，而提供大量险别保护的保险单则收取高保险金。在国际贸易中，影响安排投保的最常用的贸易术语是 FOB、CFR 和 CIF。如果出口商与国外进口商订立的是 FOB 合同，那么将由进口商负责货物的保险。如果货物是以 CIF 术语销售的，那么出口商就负责获取保险单和支付保险费。

Section Six　Forms of Marine Insurance Contract（海运保险合同格式）

An insurance policy or an insurance certificate is issued when goods are insured. An insurance policy (or a certificate) forms part of the chief shipping documents. A policy also functions as collateral security when an exporter gets an advance against their bank credit.

货物保险后，将由保险公司签发保险单或保险凭证。保险单或保险凭证是主要的装运单证。在信用证下，保险单还可作为抵押担保从银行获得垫付贷款。

1．Insurance policy（保险单）

An insurance policy, issued by the insurer, is a legal document setting out the exact terms and conditions of an insurance transaction—the name of the insured, the name of the commodity insured, the amount insured, the name of the carrying vessel, the precise risks covered, the period of cover, and any exceptions that may exist. It also serves as a written contract of insurance between the insurer and the person taking out insurance (See Fig.10-1~Fig.10-3).

保险单是保险人签发的一种具有法律效力的单证，它严格规定了一笔保险业务的条款和条件——被保险人姓名、保险货物名称、保险金额、载货船只名称、承保险别、保险期限和可能发生的免责事项。它也是保险人和被保险人之间订立的书面契约（见图 10-1~图 10-3）。

中国人民保险公司
THE PEOPLE'S INSURANCE COMPANY OF CHINA
总公司设于北京 1949 年创立
Head Office: BEIJING　　　Established in 1949
保险单
INSURANCE POLICY

保险单次号次
POLICY No.

中　国　人　民　保　险　公　司　（　以　下　简　称　本　公　司　）
THIS POLICY OF INSURANCE WITNESSES THAT PEOPLE'S INSURANCE COMPANY OF CHINA (HEREINAFTER CALLED "THE COMPANY")

Fig.10-1　Blank Insurance Policy（空白保险单）

根　据
AT THE REQUEST OF _____
（　以　下　简　称　被　保　险　人　）　的　要　求　，　由　被　保　险　人　向　本　公　司　缴　付　约
(HEREIN AFTER CALLED"THE INSURED") AND IN CONSIDERATION OF THE AGREED PREMIUM PAID TO THE COMPANY BY THE
定　的　保　险　费　，　按　照　本　保　险　单　承　保　险　别　和　背　面　所　载　条　款　与　下　列
INSURED UNDERTAKES TO INSURE THE UNDERMENTIONED GOODS IN TRANSPORTATION SUBJECT TO THE CONDITIONS OF THIS POLICY
条　款　承　保　下　述　货　物　运　输　保　险　，　特　立　本　保　险　单　。
AS　PER　THE　CLAUSES　PRINTED　OVERLEAF　AND　OTHER　SPECIAL　CLAUSES　ATTACHED　HEREIN.

标记 MARKS & NOS.	包装及数量 PACKING & QUANTITY	保险货物项目 DESCRIPTION OF GOODS	保险金额 AMOUNT INSURED

总保险金额：
TOTAL AMOUNT INSURED: _____

保费　　　　　　费率　　　　　　　装载运输工具

PREMIUM AS ARRANGED　RATE AS ARRANGED　PER CONVEYANCE S.S. _____
开航日期　　　　　　　　自　　　　　　　　至
SLG.ON OR ABT._____　FROM _____　TO _____
承保险别：
CONDITIONS：
所　保　货　物　，　如　遇　出　险　，　本　公　司　凭　本　保　险　单　及　其　他　有　关　证　件　给　付　赔　偿　。
CLAIMS, IF ANY, PAYABLE ON　SURRENDER OF　THIS POLICY　TOGETHER　WITH　OTHER　RELEVANT　DOCUMENTS
所　保　货　物　，　如　果　发　生　本　保　险　单　项　下　负　责　赔　偿　的　损　失　或　事　故　，
IN THE EVENT OF ACCIDENT WHEREBY LOSS OR DAMAGE MAY RESULT IN A CLAIM UNDER THIS POLICY IMMEDIATE NOTICE
应　立　即　通　知　本　公　司　下　属　代　理　人　查　勘　。
APPLYING　FOR　SURVEY　MUST　BE　GIVEN　TO　THE　COMPANY'S　AGENT　AS　MENTIONED　HEREUNDER.

中国人民保险公司上海分公司
THE PEOPLE'S INSURANCE COMPANY OF CHINA, SHANGHAI BRANCH

赔款偿付地点
CLAIM PAYABLE AT/IN_____
日期
DATE_____
地址：中国上海中山东一路 23 号　　TEL: 32340532　　　TELEX:33128
Address: 23 Zhongshan Dong Yi Lu Shanghai, China Cable 42001 Shanghai

General manager　　×××

Fig.10-1　Blank Insurance Policy（空白保险单）（续）

中国人民保险公司

THE PEOPLE'S INSURANCE COMPANY OF CHINA

总公司设于北京　　　1949 年创立

Head Office: BEIJING　　　Established in 1949

保险单

INSURANCE POLICY

保险单次号次

POLICY No. SH043101984

中　国　人　民　保　险　公　司　（　以　下　简　称　本　公　司　）
THIS POLICY OF INSURANCE WITNESSES THAT PEOPLE'S INSURANCE COMPANY OF CHINA (HEREINAFTER CALLED "THE COMPANY")
根　据
AT THE REQUEST OF SUZHOU KNITWEAR AND MANUFACTURED GOODS IMPORT & EXPORT TRADE CORPORATION
（　以　下　简　称　被　保　险　人　）　的　要　求，　由　被　保　险　人　向　本　公　司　缴　付　约
(HEREIN AFTER CALLED"THE INSURED") AND IN CONSIDERATION OF THE AGREED PREMIUM PAID TO THE COMPANY BY THE
定　的　保　险　费，　按　照　本　保　险　单　承　保　险　别　和　背　面　所　载　条　款　与　下　列
INSURED UNDERTAKES TO INSURE THE UNDERMENTIONED GOODS IN TRANSPORTATION SUBJECT TO THE CONDITIONS OF THIS POLICY
条　款　承　保　下　述　货　物　运　输　保　险，　特　立　本　保　险　单　。
AS　PER　THE　CLAUSES　PRINTED　OVERLEAF　AND　OTHER　SPECIAL　CLAUSES　ATTACHED　HEREIN.

标记 MARKS & NOS.	包装及数量 PACKING & QUANTITY	保险货物项目 DESCRIPTION OF GOODS	保险金额 AMOUNT INSURED
AS PER INVOICE No.T03617	367 BALES	COTTON TEATOWELS 全棉抹布	USD 96696

保险金额:
TOTAL AMOUNT INSURED: SAY US DOLLARS NINETY SIX THOUSAND SIX HUNDRED AND NINETY SIX ONLY

保费　　　　　　　费率　　　　　　装载运输工具
PREMIUM AS ARRANGED　　RATE AS ARRANGED　　PER CONVEYANCE S.S. PUDONG VOY.053
开航日期　　　　　　　　自　　　　　　　　　至
SLG.ON OR ABT.　OCT.24th, 2010　FROM　SHANGHAI　　TO　MONTREAL
承保险别:
CONDITIONS: FOR 110% OF INVOICE VALUE COVERING ALL RISKS PER C.I.C. 1/1981

所　保　货　物，　如　遇　出　险，　本　公　司　凭　本　保　险　单　及　其　他　有　关　证　件　给　付　赔　偿　。
CLAIMS, IF ANY, PAYABLE ON SURRENDER OF THIS POLICY TOGETHER WITH OTHER RELEVANT DOCUMENTS
所　保　货　物，　如　果　发　生　本　保　险　单　项　下　负　责　赔　偿　的　损　失　或　事　故，
IN THE EVENT OF ACCIDENT WHEREBY LOSS OR DAMAGE MAY RESULT IN A CLAIM UNDER THIS POLICY IMMEDIATE NOTICE
应　立　即　通　知　本　公　司　下　属　代　理　人　查　勘　。
APPLYING　FOR　SURVEY　MUST　BE　GIVEN　TO　THE　COMPANY'S　AGENT　AS　MENTIONED　HEREUNDER.

中国人民保险公司上海分公司

THE PEOPLE'S INSURANCE COMPANY OF CHINA, SHANGHAI BRANCH

赔款偿付地点
CLAIM PAYABLE AT/IN　MONTREAL IN US DOLLARS
日期
DATE　OCT.22nd, 2010
地址: 中国上海中山东一路 23 号　　TEL:021-32340532　　　　TELEX:33128　PICC CN.
Address: 23 Zhongshan Dong Yi Lu Shanghai, China Cable 42001 Shanghai

General manager　　李强

Fig.10-2　Filled Insurance Policy　（填制好的保险单）

中国人民保险公司上海分公司

出口运输险投保单

编号＿＿0381143＿＿

兹将我处出口物资依照信用证规定拟向你处投保国外运输险计开：

（中　文）苏州毛织品进出口贸易公司			
被保险人		过户	
（英　文）SUZHOU KNITWEAR AND MANUFACTURED GOODS IMPORT&EXPORT TRADE CORPORATION			

标记或发票号码	件　数	物 资 名 称	保 险 金 额
AS PER INVOICE No.T0367	367 捆	全棉抹布 COTTON TEA TOWELS	USD 96 696
运输工具（及转载工具）	PUDONG VOY.053	约启运于 2010 年 10 月 24 日	赔款偿付地点　加拿大蒙特利尔
运输路程	自　上海　经　到 蒙特利尔	转　载 地　点	

要保险别：

FOR 110% OF INVOICE VALUE COVERING ALL RISKS AS PER

C.I.C. 1/1981

投保单位签章

苏州毛织品进出口贸易公司

李莉

2010 年 10 月 20 日

Fig.10-3　Export Transportation Insurance Policy（出口运输险投保单）

2. Insurance certificate（保险凭证）

An insurance certificate is a kind of simplified insurance policy. The insurance certificate only indicates the name of the insured, the name of the insured cargo, quantity, marks, conveyance, place of shipment, place of destination, insurance cover, and insurance amount. However, the rights and obligations of the two parties are omitted. The insurance certificate has the same legal validity as the insurance policy (See Fig.10-4).

保险凭证是一种保险证明，实际上是简化的保险单。它包含保险单上的必要项目，如品名、数量、唛头、运输工具、装运地点、目的港、保险险别、保险金额等。但它并不列出保险人和被保险人的权利和义务，保险凭证与保险单具有同样的效力（见图10-4）。

	Certificate of Insurance		
GERLING – KONZERN ALLGEMEINE VERSICHERUNGS-AKTIENGESELLECHAFT	Agency	Open Cover	Number
Address of Agency	GERLING SERVICE NEDERLAND N.V. Herengracht 520, 1017 cc Amsterdam / The Netherlands Tel: (20)5249213 Fax: (20)6268093 Telegrams: Gerlingnet		

This is to certify that under the above-named open cover insurance is granted to

ORDER

For account of whom it may concern.

Sum Insured: USD123 046(US DOLLARS ONE HUNDRED AND TWENTY THREE THOUSAND AND FORTY- SIX ONLY)

Insured goods

DEMINERALIZED WHEY POWDER

Gross Weight:	121 380.00 kgs
Net Weight:	119 000.00 kgs
Shipping Marks:	CH/99/66.908 ------------- DALIAN CHINA
Packing:	476 025kg in 4-ply paper sacks with inner polyethylene liner and big bags in 7×20' containers as per Contract NO. CH/99/66.908 and as per L/C NO. L/C8230074/99

Insured Voyage	
Place of commencement of insurance Interior of Helsinki, Finland	To Dalian, P.R.C.
Via Rotterdam, Netherlands	By means of transport With MV Sea Nordica and Lindoe Maersk Shipping date September 15, 2005

Fig.10-4　Sample of Insurance Certificate （保险凭证样本）

Conditions
1．Marine Insurance (ADS) and Special Conditions for Cargo (ADS Guterversicherung 1973).   2．Conditions of the above-mentioned open cover.   3．From the conditions overleaf the following are applicable: <div align="center">9, 10, 11</div>   4．Cover applies to the voyage between the places of commencement and termination of insurance mentioned above as per Warehouse to Warehouse of ＿＿＿ days after discharge from the ocean vessel at the port of destination.   5．In addition: claims payable in China in currency of the draft, covering Ocean Marine Transportation All Risks, War Risks.   <div align="center">Claims are payable to the bearer.</div>   <div align="center">The certificate is made out in three originals. If a claim is paid against one of them the other(s) will be void.</div>
Important instructions to be followed in case of loss or damage see overleaf.

Claims Survey Agent (to be called in when claims exceed the amount of Euro2000 or countervalue in other currency) <div align="center">Huatai Insurance Agency &</div> <div align="center">Consultants Service Ltd.</div> <div align="center">115 Sidalin Road</div> <div align="center">Dalian, China</div> <div align="center">Tel (411)2654528, 2630872</div> <div align="center">Fax: (411)2804558</div> <div align="center">Telex: 86222 PICC CN</div>	<div align="center">Date September 12, 2005</div> <div align="center">GERLING – KONZERN</div> <div align="center">ALLGEMEINE</div> <div align="center">VERSICHERUNGS-AKTIENGESELLSCHAFT</div>

Fig.10-4 Sample of Insurance Certificate（保险凭证样本）（续）

3．Open policy（预约保单）

This type of policy is of great importance for export business, it is a convenient method for insuring the goods where a number of consignments of similar export goods are intended to be covered. An open policy covers these shipments as soon as they are made, under the prior arrangement between the insured and the insurance company.

对于出口商来说，这种预约保单非常重要，如果是为一大宗货物投保的话，这种预约保单特别方便。根据投保人与保险公司签订的合同，一经起运，保险人即自动承保。

4．Combined certificate（联合凭证）

When the goods are exported to Hong Kong and some countries in Southeast Asia, the insurance company sometimes adds the coverage and insurance amount to the commercial invoice which is made out by a foreign trade company. This is a certificate that combines the invoice with the insurance policy. It is the simplest insurance certificate in use.

当货物出口香港以及部分东南亚地区时，保险公司将承保的险别、保险金额和保单号加注在出口公司开具的商业发票上。这是商业发票与保险单相结合的一种凭证，是最简单的一种保险单。

5. Endorsement（保险更改批单）

After insurance has been taken out, if the insured wants to amend or change the contents of the policy, they may apply to the company for approval. After approval by the company, another certificate indicating the relevant amendment will be issued. This certificate is called an endorsement.

在保险办完之后，如果投保人想要更改保险条款，可向保险公司提出申请。经与保险公司协商之后，发出另一份已修改过的保单，这就是保险更改批单。

When effecting insurance with the insurance company, it is advantageous for the insurance applicant to bear in mind that:

(1) He should avoid duplicate coverage of insurance. For instance, it is not right to effect insurance covering All Risks plus Risk of Odor, since Risk of Odour falls into the category of General Extraneous Risks which are actually covered by All Risks.

(2) He should purchase a Basic Insurance Condition before he purchases Additional Risks. For instance, he should purchase a F.P.A. before he purchases the insurance for the coverage of Fresh Water Rain Damage.

(3) The insured must have insurable interest in the subject of insurance.

(4) Not all losses or expenses are covered by the Basic Insurance Conditions. For instance, the following losses and expenses shall be excluded from Basic Insurance Conditions:

a. Loss or damage caused by the intentional act or fault of the insured.

b. Loss or damage falling under the liability of the consignor.

c. Loss or damage arising from the inferior quality or shortage of the insured goods prior to the attachment of this insurance.

d. Loss or damage arising from normal loss, inherent vice or nature of the insured goods, loss of market and/or delay in transit and any expenses arising therefrom.

(5) The insured should present the following documents to make claims against the Insurance Company: Original Policy, Bill of Lading, Invoice, Packing List, Tally Sheet, Weight Memo, Certificate of Loss or Damage and/or Shortage Memo, Survey Report, Statement of Claim. If any third party is involved, documents relative to pursuing recovery from such party should also be included.

(6) According to the relevant stipulations of the PICC, the validity of a claim shall not exceed a period of two years counted from the time of completion of discharge of the insured goods from the seagoing vessel at the final port of discharge.

在进行投保时应该注意：

（1）不要重复投保，如投保一切险加串味险是不正确的，因为串味险属于一般外来风险，而一切险的保险范围已包含了该风险。

（2）附加险必须在投保一种基本险的情况下才能加投，例如，只有在投保平安险的前提下，才能加保淡水雨淋险。

（3）被保险人对保险的标的应该有可保利益。

（4）基本险并不是对所有的风险损失和费用都负赔偿责任。例如，本保险对下列风险损失和费用将不负赔偿责任：

  a. 被保险人的故意或过失行为所造成的损失。

  b. 属于发货人责任所引起的损失。

  c. 在保险责任开始前，被保险货物已存在的品质不良或数量短差所造成的损失。

  d. 被保险货物的自然损耗、本质缺陷、特性以及市价跌落、运输延迟所引起的损失或费用。

  （5）在向保险人索赔时，必须提供下列单证：保险单正本、提单、发票、装箱单、磅码单、货损货差证明、检验报告及索赔清单。如涉及第三者责任，还须提供向责任方追偿的有关单证及其他必要单证或文件。

  （6）根据中国人民保险公司的有关规定，保险索赔时效从被保险货物在最后卸载港全部卸离海轮后起算，最多不超过两年。

Section Seven　Endorsement of the Insurance Policy（保险单的背书）

An insurance policy is a document which can be transferred by endorsement. According to customary practice of the international insurance industry, after endorsement by the insured person the ownership right of the insured goods would be transferred to the assignee. Before or after the endorsement, the insurance company needs not be notified. So the exporter can complete the transfer procedures by simply signing the word "endorsement" in the insurance policy.

  保险单是可以经背书转让的单据。根据国际保险行业的习惯，保险单据经被保险人背书后，即随着被保险货物的所有权转移自动转到受让人手中。背书前后均不需要通知保险公司，因此，出口方只需在保险单上背书就完成了转让手续。

Section Eight　Insurance Practice in China（我国保险实务）

1. To insure（投保）

When the imported and exported goods are transported from the port of shipment to the destination, the buyer or the seller is required to insure the goods through insurance companies. In handling the insurance, there is a need to select the appropriate insurance coverage, determine the amount of insurance, pay insurance premiums, and complete the relevant procedures. When insuring the goods, the following should be paid attention to: the choice of insurance coverage; determination of insurance amount and calculation of the insurance premiums, etc.

  进出口货物自装运港运抵目的地时，买方或卖方须向保险公司为货物投保。在办理保险时，需选择适当的险别，确定保险金额、缴纳保险费，并办理有关手续。在办理保险业务时，应注意：保险险别的选择；保险金额的确定与保险费的计算；投保业务手续；等等。

2. Insurance documents（保险单证）

Insurance documents are legal papers to testify to the setting up of the insurance contract. These documents should state the responsibilities and obligations of the insurer and the insured. They are the certificates to show that the insurer promises to insure the goods, and the insured can lodge claims against the insurer once damage or loss occurs.

保险单证是证明保险合同成立的法律文件，它列明保险人与被保险人之间的权利和义务，既是保险人承保证明，也是被保险人向保险人索赔的凭据。

3．Insurance claims（保险索赔）

The insured person or his agent should do the following when making claims to the insurer:

(1) Loss notification and cargo damage inspection;

(2) Reserve the right to make claims against the third party;

(3) Take reasonable rescue measures;

(4) Get the certificate ready for claims.

被保险人或其代理人向保险人索赔时，应做好下列几项工作：

（1）损失通知和货损检验；

（2）保留向第三者责任方的索赔权；

（3）采取合理的施救措施；

（4）备妥索赔证明。

Section Nine Digital Trade Insurance（数字贸易保险）

With the rapid development of digital trade, digital trade insurance, as a relatively new field, has also attracted increasing attention in the trade sector. The demand for insurance services in digital trade is also growing. Therefore, it is necessary to provide some basic introductions to digital trade insurance:

Firstly, there is currently no clear definition of digital trade, but it is generally believed that digital trade insurance refers to insurance products specifically designed for the special risks faced in the field of digital trade. Similar to the insurance design concept of traditional trade, the purpose of digital trade insurance is to cover various risks arising during digital trade activities. These risks include but are not limited to cargo loss during logistics distribution, data leakage, cyber hacking attacks, network payment fraud, and telecommunications fraud, etc.

随着数字贸易的快速发展，数字贸易保险作为一个相对较新的领域，也日益引起贸易领域的关注，数字贸易对保险服务的需求也日益增长，因此，有必要对数字贸易保险进行一些基本介绍：

首先，数字贸易的定义目前没有明确的界定，但一般认为数字贸易保险是指专门为数字贸易领域所面临的特殊的风险所设计出来的一系列保险产品。与传统贸易的保险设计思路类似，数字贸易保险的目的在于覆盖数字贸易活动过程中所可能出现的各种风险。这些风险包括但不限于物流配送过程的货物损失、数据泄露、网络黑客攻击、网络支付电信欺诈等。

Based on the main risk ranges mentioned above, the types of digital trade insurance can be divided into several categories:

(1) The risk of goods loss in the logistics and distribution process: In the broad process of digital trade activities, in addition to pure digital delivery, cross-border electronic goods usually require cross-border transportation and local distribution through cross-border logistics. During this process, there may be risks such as loss, damage, or delay of goods.

(2) Data leakage risk: Digital trade involves the transmission and storage of massive amounts of data, including user personal information, platform transaction records, etc. Therefore, data leakage or tampering may cause significant losses to businesses and consumers.

(3) Network security risks: Network attacks, such as hacking, malicious software, etc., are highly likely to cause damage to digital trading platforms, leading to interruptions in digital trading services or delivery, or data loss.

(4) Payment risk: The payment process in digital trade may face risks such as fraud, telecommunications fraud, and other chargebacks, which can cause economic losses to digital trade enterprises.

基于以上这些主要风险范围，数字贸易保险的类型可以划分为几大类：

（1）物流配送过程的货物损失风险：在广义的数字贸易活动过程中，除了纯粹的数字交付之外，跨境电子商品通常需要通过跨境物流进行跨国运输和本地配送。这一过程中可能面临货物丢失、损坏或延误等风险。

（2）数据泄露风险：数字贸易涉及海量数据的传输和存储，包括用户个人信息、平台交易记录等。因此，数据泄露或被篡改可能给企业和消费者带来重大损失。

（3）网络安全风险：网络攻击，如黑客入侵、恶意软件等，都极有可能对数字贸易平台造成破坏，导致数字贸易服务或数字贸易交付中断或数据丢失。

（4）支付风险：数字贸易中的支付环节可能面临欺诈、电信欺诈，以及其他拒付等风险，给数字贸易企业带来经济损失。

Part B Terminology Practice

1. **Marine insurance**（海上保险）: The insurance of ships or their cargo against specific causes of loss or damage that might be encountered at sea. The definition has been widened over the years to include the transit of cargo over land at both ends of the voyage.

2. **Peril of the sea**（海上风险）: A marine insurance term used to designate heavy weather, stranding, lightning, collision and sea water damage.

3. **Average**（平均/分摊损失）: In insurance, it means a loss, or the apportionment of a loss between different parties; general average refers to a loss incurred by one consignment, but shared by all the other consignors who use the same carrying vessel on the same voyage. Particular average refers to a partial loss of a consignment as a result of a hazard affecting only the consignment, and not a hazard affecting all the consignments on the same carrying vessel.

4. **Total loss**（全部损失）: Loss of the entire consignment.

5. **Partial loss**（部分损失）: The loss of part of the goods.

6. **F.P.A.**（平安险）: Abbreviation of "Free from Particular Average", an insurance term meaning that goods are covered only against hazards to which all the consignments on the same carrying vessel (or other means of transport) are subject, and not against hazards affecting only the insurer's consignment.

7. **W.P.A./W.A.**（水渍险）: Short for "With Particular Average", an insurance term meaning that

goods are covered against a particular average.

8. **All Risks**（一切险）：An insurance term meaning that the goods insured are covered against all the risks specified in the contract of insurance.

9. **Special risks**（特殊险）：Risks detailed in an insurance policy, over and above the normal cover afforded by that type of policy.

10. **Insurance policy**（保险单）：A written document between an insured person and an insurance company specifying the exact losses to be covered and the costs to the insured person.

11. **Insurance certificate**（保险证明）：A document issued under, e.g. an open cover policy, instead of a policy of insurance.

12. **Customs**（海关）：The federal agency charged with collecting duties (taxes) on specific items imported into the country and restricting the entry of forbidden items.

13. **Customs broker**（报关行/报关代理人）：A person or firm that specializes in international documentation and customs clearances.

Part C Terms

1. natural calamities 自然灾害
2. accidents 意外事故
3. fine print 细则
4. to provide the insurance 为……提供保险
5. premium rate 保险费率
6. ocean marine cargo insurance, marine insurance 水险（海运货物）
7. average 海损
8. particular average 单独海损
9. general average 共同海损
10. marine losses 海损
11. partial loss 部分损失
12. total loss 全部损失
13. actual total loss 实际全损
14. constructive total loss 推定全损
15. absolute total loss 绝对全损
16. Aflatoxin Risk 黄曲霉素险
17. All Risks 一切险（综合险）
18. Breakage and Packing Risk 包装破裂险
19. Clash & Breakage Risk 碰损、破碎险
20. Failure to Delivery Risk 交货不到险
21. Free from Particular Average（F.P.A.）平安险
22. Fresh and/or Rain Water Damage 淡水雨淋险
23. Damage Risks 损坏险
24. Hook Damage Risk 钩损险
25. Import Duty Risk 进口关税险
26. Intermixture & Contamination Risk 混杂、玷污险
27. Leakage Risk 渗漏险
28. On Deck Risk 舱面货物险
29. Rust Risk 锈损险
30. Shortage Risk 短量险
31. Strikes, Riots, Civil Commotions（S.R.C.C.）罢工、暴动、民变险
32. Sweating & Heating Risk 受潮受热险
33. Taint of Odor Risk 串味险
34. Theft, Pilferage & Non-delivery（T.P.N.D.）偷窃、提货不着险
35. War Risk 战争险
36. With Particular Average（W.P.A.）水渍险
37. perils of the sea 海上风险
38. extraneous risk 外来风险

39. combined certificate 联合凭证
41. insurance premium 保险费
40. insurance policy 保险单
42. insurance coverage 保险范围

Part D Exercise

I. Please determine whether the following statements are True or False. Then put T for True or F for False in the bracket at the end of each statement.

1. In China, insurance companies do not accept insurance based on Institute Cargo Clauses. (　　)

2. Institute Cargo Clauses (A) has the widest coverage among all its clauses. (　　)

3. Almost all the insurance companies provide door-to-door coverage service. (　　)

4. Insurance against FPA means that the insured cannot obtain compensation from the insurer if a particular average occurs. (　　)

5. If you have insured your goods against All Risks, you will get compensated for whatever risks occur to your goods. (　　)

6. According to China Insurance Clauses, if you want to insure your goods against WPA, you must also cover War and Strike Risks. (　　)

7. According to international trade practice, you cannot have the goods insured if you do not have insurable interest in the goods. (　　)

8. One cannot claim compensation with the insurance company if he does not have insurable interest in the goods. (　　)

9. If an insurance clause stipulates a franchise, the insurance company does not grant compensation if any damage occurs to the goods. (　　)

10. Irrespective of Percentage means that the insurance company will cover all the losses to the goods caused during transportation. (　　)

11. An insurance policy is the contract made between the insurer and the insured. (　　)

12. Hook damage, theft, taint of odour, breakage, damp are fortuitous risks. (　　)

13. Under constructive total loss, the insured can ask the insurer to cover all the losses. (　　)

14. According to international practice, the insurance policy and the insurance certificate have the same legal effect. (　　)

15. The date of the bill of lading should be earlier than the date of the insurance policy. (　　)

16. According to CIC provisions, free from Particular Average means that the insurance company is not liable to compensate for a particular average. (　　)

II. Please give the following definitions for the names in English.

1. Natural Calamity

2. Partial Loss

3. Actual Total Loss

4. Particular Average

5. Sue and Labor Expense

6. Salvage Charges

III. Choose the best answer.

1. The one who buys insurance is called (　　).
   A. an insurance company　　　　　　B. a broker
   C. the insured　　　　　　　　　　　D. an insurer

2. What is the name given to the sum of money which a person agrees to pay to an insurance company? (　　)
   A. compensation　　　　　　　　　　B. premium
   C. investment　　　　　　　　　　　D. commission

3. An insurance agreement is called an (　　).
   A. insurance policy　　　　　　　　　B. insurance contract
   C. insurance cover　　　　　　　　　D. insurance document

4. Under FOB contract, the (　　) is to arrange insurance.
   A. seller　　　　B. insurer　　　　C. buyer　　　　D. carrier

5. When the seller contracts for insurance, it is a(n) (　　) contract.
   A. CFR　　　　B. FCA　　　　C. FAS　　　　D. CIF

6. The one who lodges a claim is known as an (　　).
   A. insurer　　　B. the insured　　　C. insurance broker　　　D. claimant

7. (　　) does not have the normally accepted meaning, but means loss in the insurance business.
   A. Partial loss　　　B. Total loss　　　C. Coverage　　　D. Average

8. (　　) is the broadest kind of coverage but does not include all risks.
   A. Free from Particular Average　　　B. All Risks
   C. With Particular Average　　　　　D. T.P.N.D.

9. Risk of breakage is considered to be the (　　).
   A. Free of Particular Average　　　　B. With Average
   C. General Additional Risks　　　　　D. Special Additional Risks

10. The marine insurance term for all goods lost when the ship sank is (　　).
    A. general average loss　　　　　　B. particular average loss
    C. total loss　　　　　　　　　　　D. partial loss

11. (　　) is the most restrictive coverage.
    A. All Risks　　　　　　　　　　　B. T.P.N.D.
    C. Free from Particular Average　　　D. With Average

12. The marine insurance term for some goods thrown overboard to save a ship is (　　).
    A. total loss　　　　　　　　　　　B. general average loss
    C. particular　　　　　　　　　　　D. All Risks

13. Which of the following is included in All Risks coverage? (　　)
    A. particular loss due to cargo thrown overboard to keep afloat
    B. total loss due to the destruction of war
    C. partial loss due to the workers' strike on the dock

D. total loss due to failure to delivery

14. (　　) is covered by a basic F.P.A. policy.

    A. 10% loss caused by breakage in transit

    B. 15% loss caused by pilferage

    C. 20% loss caused by heavy rain

    D. 25% loss caused by a ship collision

15. (　　) is covered by a W.P.A. policy.

    A. Loss due to the carrying vessel's stranding

    B. Loss caused by the carrying vessel's collision

    C. Loss due to theft, pilferage and non-delivery

    D. Loss caused by heavy rain

16. S.R.C.C. is (　　).

    A. special additional risks   B. total loss

    C. general additional risks   D. All Risks

IV. Multiple Choices.

1. Insurance may be: (　　).

   (1) corporations   (2) partnerships   (3) individuals

   A. (1) only   B. (2) only   C. (1) and (3) only

   D. (2) and (3) only   E. (1), (2) and (3)

2. An insurance policy involves (　　).

   (1) financial arrangement

   (2) agreement to compensate

   (3) promise to pay if loss results from a specified event

   A. (3) only   B. (1) and (2) only   C. (1) and (3) only

   D. (2) and (3) only   E. (1), (2) and (3)

3. The insurance policy (　　).

   (1) is generally unilateral

   (2) is conditional

   (3) is of utmost good faith

   (4) includes a promise by the insured to pay premium for at least a minimum specified time

   A. (1) and (2) only   B. (3) and (4) only

   C. (1), (2), and (3) only   D. (2), (3) and (4) only

   E. (1), (2), (3) and (4)

4. Insurance policies have which of the following components? (　　).

   (1) Declarations   (2) Insurance agreements

   (3) Exclusions   (4) Conditions

   A. (1) and (2) only   B. (3) and (4) only

   C. (1), (2), and (3) only   D. (2), (3) and (4) only

   E. (1), (2), (3), and (4)

5. Insurance functions include (　　).

　　(1) reducing risks　　　　(2) sharing losses　　　(3)taking bets

　　A. (2) only　　　　　　　　　　　　B. (1) and (2) only

　　C. (1) and (3) only　　　　　　　　D. (2) and (3) only

　　E. (1), (2) and (3)

6. Lloyd's of London functions include (　　).

　　(1) obtaining information on marine and aviation risks

　　(2) maintaining a record of losses

　　(3) aiding loss settlement

　　(4) supervising salvage and repairs

　　A. (1) and (2) only　　　　　　　　B. (3) and (4) only

　　C. (1), (2) and (3) only　　　　　　D. (2), (3) and (4) only

　　E. (1), (2) (3) and (4)

V. Reading Comprehension.

In this exercise there is an insurance policy. Please read it carefully and then answer the questions given below.

If the transaction is concluded on the basis of CIF term, according to the following insurance policy, then:

Question 1:

Is this transaction a deal of export or import?（该笔交易是进口贸易还是出口贸易？）

Question 2:

Before the beneficiary goes to the bank for negotiation, does he need to endorse the transfer of the policy?（受益人到银行办理议付前，是否需要对该保单进行背书转让？）

Question 3:

The insurance amount is USD8 591.81, is it the amount of the invoice?（保险金额为 8 591.81 美元，该金额是否就是发票金额？）

中保财产保险有限公司

THE PEOPLE'S INSURANCE (PROPERTY) COMPANY OF CHINA, LTD.

Contract No. 20090930A　　　　　　　　　No. of Original: One
合同号码　　　　　　　　　　　　　　　　保险单号次

Invoice No.09-267-0136　　　　　　　　　Policy No. FC04701502101
发票号码

海　洋　货　物　运　输　保　险　单

MARINE CARGO TRANSPORTATION INSURANCE POLICY

被保险人：

Insured:　　GMG HARDWARE & TOOLS IMP. & EXP. COMPANY, LTD.

　　中保财产保险有限公司（以下简称本公司）根据被保险人的要求，及其所缴付约定的保险费，按照本保险单承担险别和背面所载条款与下列特别条款承保下列货物运输保险，特签发本保险单。

This policy of Insurance witnesses that the People's Insurance (Property) Company of China, Ltd. (hereinafter called "the Company"), at the request of the Insured and in consideration of the agreed premium paid by the Insured, undertakes to insure the undermentioned goods in transportation subject to the conditions of this Policy as per the Clauses printed overleaf and other special clauses attached hereon.

保险货物项目 Descriptions of Goods	包装 单位 数量 Packing Unit Quantity	保险金额 Amount Insured
HAND TOOLS	116 PACKAGES	USD8 591.81

货物标记

Marks of Goods

GMG

LONDON

NO.1-116

承保险别

Conditions

Covering All Risks as per Ocean Marine Cargo Clauses(1/1/1981)

(Warehouse to Warehouse Clause is included) of The People's

Insurance (Property) Company of China, Ltd.

总保险金额：

Total Amount Insured: US DOLLARS EIGHT THOUSAND FIVE HUNDRED AND NINETY ONE AND 81/100 ONLY

保费   运输工具   开航日期

Premium   AS ARRANGE   Per conveyance S.S. NING GLORY V.98/207W Slg.on or abt DEC.10,2009

起运港   目的港

From   SHANGHAI   to   LONDON

所保货物，如发生本保险单项下可能引起索赔的损失或损坏，应立即通知本公司下述代理人查勘。如有索赔，应向本公司提交保险单正本（本保险单共有_____份正本）及有关文件。如一份正本已用于索赔，其余正本则自动失效。

In the event of loss or damage which may result in a claim under this Policy, immediate notice must be given to the Company's Agent as mentioned hereunder. Claims, if any, one of the Original Policy which has been issued in _____ Original(s) together with the relevant documents shall be surrendered to the Company. If one of the Original Policies has been accomplished, the others to be void.

中保财产保险有限公司

THE PEOPLE'S INSURANCE(PROPERTY) COMPANY OF CHINA, LTD.

赔款偿付地点

Claim payable at _____ PIRAEUS

日期   在   ......

Date   DEC.10th, 2009   at   SHANGHAI   李牛（签名）

地址：

Address: 2 Daqing Road, Shanghai, China

            Fax: 83324566 Telex:410467 PICC CN

VI. Case Study.

Case Description:

A cargo ship bound from Huangpu port, Guangzhou, China, to Singapore, caught fire on the voyage. Because the fire spread to the engine room, the engine room, for the sake of common safety ordered flooding of the cabin, then the fire was quickly extinguished. However, as the main engine was damaged and unable to continue sailing, the captain hired a tug boat to tow the ship back to Huangpu port to repair and then re-bound to Singapore. The losses are: (1) 200 boxes of goods were destroyed by fire; (2) 600 boxes of goods were water-damaged, with no other losses; (3) 600 boxes of goods suffered both smoke and heat damage and water damage, but did not find any traces of fire; (4) 150 boxes of goods were burned off and there was a serious water-soaked; (5) The main engine and part of the deck were burned; (6) Towing costs; (7) Additional fuel costs and crew wages.

Question:

Please analyse the nature of these losses, and point out the type of insurance coverage required to obtain insurance compensation from the insurance company?

案情介绍：

中国有一货轮从广州黄埔港驶往新加坡，在航行途中船舶货舱起火，大火蔓延到机舱，船长为了船货的共同安全，下令往舱内灌水，火很快被扑灭。但由于主机受损，无法继续航行，于是船长雇用拖轮将船拖回新港修理，修好后重新驶往新加坡。这次造成的损失主要有：

（1）200 箱货被火烧毁。

（2）600 箱货被水浇湿，无其他损失。

（3）600 箱货既受热熏损失，又受水渍损失，但未发现任何火烧的痕迹。

（4）150 箱货被火烧过且有严重水渍。

（5）主机及部分甲板被烧坏。

（6）拖轮费用。

（7）额外增加的燃油和船上人员工资。

问题：

试分析上述损失的性质，并指出需投保何种险别，才能取得保险公司的赔偿？

Chapter Eleven

Part A Text

Payment of Goods

In international trade, how and when an exporter receives payment for the goods he sends abroad are things/issues that concern him the most. Payment in domestic trade is a fairly simple matter. It can be made either in advance or within a reasonably short period after delivery. However, these problems are magnified many times in international trade. A lot of time is unavoidably lost in correspondence, dispatch and delivery. Who is liable for this loss? Must the seller wait perhaps six months for his money or shall the buyer pay several months before he even gets his goods? What's more, in the case of non-payment, the seller will be involved in expensive legal action and possibly a total loss. Because of these problems, different methods of payment have been adopted in international trade. Generally, in every contract for the sale of goods abroad, the clause dealing with the payment of the purchase price consists of four elements: time, mode, place, and currency of payment. The various methods of financing exports represent the order and variations of these four elements.

在国际贸易中，出口商最关心的事就是怎样以及什么时候才能得到销往国外商品的货款。国内贸易的支付比较简单，它可以是先付款后交货，也可以是在交货后的一小段合情合理的时间内付款。然而，国际贸易的支付比国内贸易的支付复杂得多。在通信、发货、交货的过程中不可避免地要浪费很多时间。谁来承担这个损失？卖方难道等六个月才能收到货款？或者说买方在见到货物以前几个月就得支付货款？并且，如果买方拒绝付款，卖方就要花钱打官司，甚至是血本无归。由于这些原因，国际贸易采用不同的支付方式。一般来说，在每一笔出口合同中，涉及货款支付的条款都包括下列四点：支付时间、支付方式、支付地点和支付货币。出口融资的各种方式体现了这四个要素的排列顺序与变化形式。

Section One Instruments of Payment in International Trade（国际贸易中的支付工具）

In international sales of commodities, the main issues concerning the settlement of payment are means of payment, time and place of payment, and mode of payment, etc. Issues in this regard should be clearly specified in the contract by the parties concerned.

In international trade, the most frequently used means of payment include currencies and bills. The former is used for account, settlement and payment; the latter for settlement and payment. In practice, sellers of goods, in general, almost never insist on their rights to demand cash for payment, but readily take certain bills, such as bill of exchange(draft), promissory note, and cheque (check) as substitutes, among which draft is widely used.

A draft is an unconditional written order drawn by the drawer for the money to be paid by the drawee (payer). Drafts are negotiable instruments and may be sold.

A promissory note is a written and signed promise to pay a stated amount of money to a particular person.

A cheque is a written order to a bank to pay a certain sum of money from one's bank account to another person. The payer of a check is the drawer of the check. A cheque drawn on a bank overseas cannot be readily negotiated by the exporter. If the exporter's bank was prepared to negotiate it for him then he would receive payment right away but at the cost of the discount. Failing this, the exporter would have to ask his bank to collect the cheque for him and this would be both time-consuming and relatively expensive.

在国际贸易中，货款的结算主要涉及支付工具，付款时间、地点以及支付方式等问题，交易双方应在合同中对此做出明确的规定。

在国际贸易中，最常使用的支付工具包括货币和票据。前者用于计价、结算和支付；后者用于结算和支付。实际上，销售货物的人，总的来说，几乎从不坚持要求用现金支付的权利，而是乐意用一些票据，如汇票、本票和支票来代替现金支付，其中以使用汇票为主。

汇票是出票人要求受票人（付款人）无条件付款的书面命令。汇票可以议付，可以转卖。

本票是向某人支付一定金额款项的书面承诺。

支票是向银行开出的，要求银行从出票人自己的银行账户上向另一人支付一定金额款项的书面命令。支票的出票人就是付款人。出口商不能凭以海外银行为付款人的支票立即议付货款。如果出口商的银行愿意议付，那么出口商就可以立即得到付款，但其需要支付贴现的费用。如果出口商的银行不愿议付，那么出口商只有委托其银行收款，这既费时又费钱。

1. Bill of Exchange（汇票）

1) Definition of Bill of Exchange（汇票的定义）

A bill of exchange, also called a draft, is defined as "an unconditional order in writing, addressed by one person to another, signed by the person giving it, requiring the person to whom it is addressed to pay on demand, or at a fixed or determinable future time, a sum certain in money, to or to the order of a specified person, or to bearer". The operation process of a draft includes: drawing, presentation, acceptance, payment, endorsement, dishonour and recourse. Drafts are negotiable instruments and may be sold (See Fig.11-1, Fig.11-2 and Fig.11-3).

汇票是由一人向另一人签发的无条件的书面命令，要求接受命令的人在见票时或在指定的或可以确定的将来某一日期，支付一定的金额给特定的人或其指定的人或持票人。汇票的使用程序包括出票、提示、承兑、付款、背书、拒付及追索。汇票可以议付，可以转卖（见图 11-1、图 11-2 和图 11-3）。

Sample A

No. 1022

USD 20 000   London, 19th March, 2018

On demand, pay to Bill Green or bearer the sum of UNITED STATES DOLLARS TWENTY THOUSAND ONLY.

(Signed) Tom White

To: Mr. David Smith

New York

样本 A

编号：1022

汇票金额：20 000 美元   伦敦：2018 年 3 月 19 日

见票时付比尔·格林或持票人贰万美元整。

（签字）汤姆·怀特

此致

大卫·史密斯

纽约

Sample B

No: 123/67

Exchange for US$ 8 000   Guangzhou, China, 5th March, 2018

At 60 days sight of this FIRST of Exchange (the SECOND of the same tenor and date being unpaid) pay to or to the order of Guangzhou ABC Import and Export Corporation the sum of UNITED STATES DOLLARS EIGHT THOUSAND ONLY.

To: A&C Import and Export Co., Ltd.

23 Washington Street

New York, USA   Guangzhou ABC Import and Export Corporation

Authorized Signatory

(Signed)

样本 B

汇票号：123/67

汇票金额：8 000 美元   中国广州，2018 年 3 月 5 日

凭本汇票（副本未付）于见票后 60 天付广州 ABC 进出口公司或其指定人捌仟美元整。

此致

A&C 进出口公司

华盛顿大街 23 号   广州 ABC 进出口公司

美国纽约

（汇票号：123/67）   经理（签字）

Fig.11-1　Samples of Bill of Exchange（汇票样本）

BILL OF EXCHANGE

No._____

Exchange For

At_____.sight of THIS SECOND BILL of EXCHANGE

(the FIRST of the same tenor and date unpaid) pay to_____or order the sum of

Value received and charge the same to account of _____
_____

Drawn under_____

L/C No._____dated_____

To.

_____

_____ (Signature)_____

Fig.11-2 Blank Bill of Exchange（空白汇票）

BILL OF EXCHANGE

No.___T03617___   Date: OCT.24th,2004

For USD 89 705.50

At _____×××_____sight of THIS SECOND BILL of EXCHANGE

(the FIRST of the same tenor and date unpaid) pay to BANK OF CHINA___or order the sum of

SAY US DOLLARS EIGHTY NINE THOUSAND SEVEN HUNDRED AND FIVE POINT FIFTY ONLY

Drawn under   NATIONAL PARIS BANK (CANADA) MONTREAL

L/C No. _____TH2003_____   Dated _____OCT.6th,2004_____

To.

NATIONAL PARIS BANK_____

24 MARSHALL VEDONCASTER MONTREAL，CANADA

SUZHOU KNITWEAR AND MANUFACTURED GOODS

IMPORT & EXPORT TRADE CORPORATION

李莉

Fig.11-3   Filled Bill of Exchange（填制好的汇票）

2) Contents of Bill of Exchange (Draft)（汇票的内容）

According to the definition of bill of exchange, the two specimens of Fig.11-1 may be decomposed into the following elements.

(1) An unconditional order in writing.

(2) Addressed by one person/party (the drawer).

    Sample A: Tom White

    Sample B: Guangzhou ABC Import and Export Corporation

(3) To another (the drawee).

    Sample A: David Smith, New York

    Sample B: A&C Import and Export Co. Ltd., New York

(4) Signed by the person /party (drawer) giving it.

a. Requiring the person/party to whom it is addressed (the drawee, or the payer)

b. To Pay

c. On demand, or at a fixed or determinable future time

    Sample A: on demand

    Sample B: 60 days after sight (a determinable future time)

d. A sum certain in money

    Sample A: USD 20 000

    Sample B: USD 8 000

e. To, or to the order of, a specified person/party, or to bearer (the payee)

    Sample A: Bill Green (or bearer)

    Sample B: Guangzhou ABC Import and Export Corporation

根据汇票的定义，图 11-1 中的两张汇票可以分解成以下几个方面。

（1）无条件的书面命令。

（2）由一人/一方（出票人）签发。

    样本 A：汤姆·怀特

    样本 B：广州 ABC 进出口公司

（3）向另一人（受票人）签发。

    样本 A：大卫·史密斯，纽约

    样本 B：A&C 进出口公司，纽约

（4）由给出汇票的人/一方（出票人）签发。

a. 要求接受命令的人/一方（受票人，或付票人）

b. 支付

c. 在见票时或在指定的或可以确定的将来某一日期

    样本 A：在见票时

    样本 B：见票后 60 天（确定的将来某一日期）

d. 一定的金额

    样本 A：USD20 000

样本 B：USD8 000

e. 给特定的人/一方，或其指定的人或持票人（受票人）

样本 A：比尔·格林（或持票人）

样本 B：广州 ABC 进出口公司或其指定人

3) The Parties to a Bill of Exchange（汇票当事人）

A bill of exchange involves three parties.

Drawer: The person who writes the order and gives directions to the person to make a specific payment of money. He is usually the exporter or his banker in import and export trade; usually, he is also a creditor of the drawee.

Drawee: The person to whom the order is addressed and who is to pay the money. He is usually the importer or the appointed bank under a letter of credit in import and export trade. In addition, when a time bill has been accepted by the drawee, he becomes an acceptor who is the same person as the drawee. The drawer and the acceptor must be different persons.

Payee: The person (individual, firm, corporation, or bank) to whom the payment is ordered to be made. The drawer and payee may often be the same person. In this case, the bill may be worded "Pay to our order…". The payee is usually the exporter himself or his appointed bank in import and export trade. The payee may also be the bearer of the bill. The payee may be the original payee in the bill, or may be another party to whom the original payee has transferred the instrument. If a bill has such an instruction "Pay… Co. or order" or "Pay to the order of …Co.", it means to pay to the payee or to anyone to whom he in turn directs payment to be made. In this way, the bill should be endorsed by the payee, now the endorser, and can be passed on to a new payee, the endorsee, thus making it negotiable. A bill may have many endorsers.

The relationship among these parties in a bill of exchange may be described as a triangle (See Fig.11-4).

一张汇票的主要当事人之间的关系可以通过图 11-4 所示的三角形表示出来。

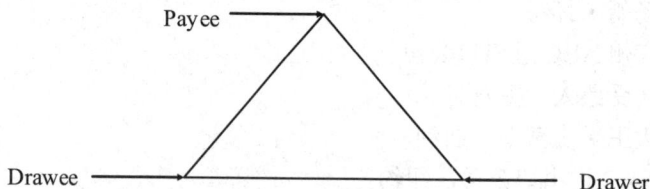

Fig.11-4　Relationship of the Concerned Parties in a Bill

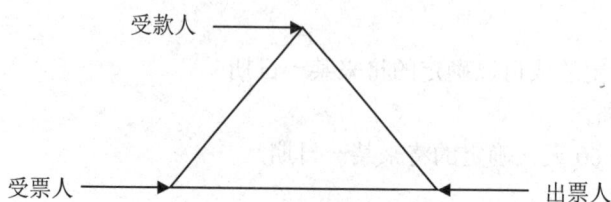

图 11-4　汇票当事人之间的关系

一张汇票中主要涉及三个当事人。

出票人：签发命令要求另一人支付一定金额的人。在进出口贸易中，其通常是出口商或出口地银行，并且经常是受票人的债权人。

受票人（付票人）：接受命令并将付款的人。在进出口贸易中，其通常是进出口商或信用证下的指定银行。还有，当受票人承兑一张远期汇票时，其就成为承兑人。出票人和承兑人必须是不同的人。

受款人：接受付款的人（个人、商号、公司或银行）。出票人和受款人通常是同一个人，在这种情况下，汇票上可能有这样的字句："付款给我们……"。在进出口贸易中，受款人经常就是出口商自己或其指定的银行。受款人也可能是持票人。受款人可以是汇票中的原有受款人，也可以是原有受款人所转让汇票的人。如果一张汇票有这样的指示："付××公司或其指定人"，意味着汇票可以经受款人（现在是背书人）而转让给新的受款人（被背书人），这样使之成为可以转让的票据。一张汇票可以有多个背书人。

4) Classification of Bill of Exchange（汇票种类）

On the basis of different criteria, bills of exchange may be classified into several types:

根据不同的标准，汇票可以分为以下几种：

(1) Commercial Bill and Banker's Bill（商业汇票和银行汇票）

According to different drawers, the bills of exchange can be classified into commercial bill and banker's bill. If the drawer is a commercial concern, the bill is called a commercial bill. It is often used in foreign trade finance. If the drawer is a bank, the bill is called a banker's bill. It is mainly used in remittance.

汇票按出票人的不同，分为商业汇票和银行汇票。商业汇票是由工商企业开出的汇票，它经常用于对外贸易的资金融通。银行汇票是由银行开出的汇票，它主要用于汇付。

(2) Clean Bill and Documentary Bill（光票和跟单汇票）

In the transfer of the bill of exchange, if the bill of exchange is accompanied by shipping documents, it is a documentary bill; if not, it is a clean bill. In international trade, mostly it is the documentary bill that is used, occasionally the clean bill is used to collect payment in small or sundry charges, such as commission, interest, sample fees and cash in advance, etc.

按汇票流通时是否随附货运单据，分为跟单汇票和光票。随附货运单据的汇票，称为跟单汇票。不随附货运单据的汇票，称为光票。在国际贸易中的货款结算大多数使用跟单汇票。如果是小额费用或杂费，如收取佣金、利息、样品费和代垫费用等时，偶尔也会使用光票。

(3) Sight (or Demand) Bill and Time (or Usance) Bill（即期汇票和远期汇票）

According to the time when the bill falls due, bills of exchange may be divided into sight (or demand) bills or time (or usance) bills. A sight bill demands immediate payment by the drawee at the sight of the bill. In case of a time bill, the drawee is required to accept it first and pay it at a fixed or determinable future time. In other words, it requires acceptance before payment. The fixed or determinable future time may be a certain number of days after acceptance: a. At … days after sight, such as "30 days sight" or "60 days after sight"; b. At … days after date of the draft, such as "90 days after date of this draft"; c. At a fixed date in the future, such as "On May 12th, 2018".

汇票按付款期限的不同，可分为即期汇票和远期汇票。汇票上规定见票后立即付款的称为即期汇票。汇票上规定受票人先承兑，然后在指定的或将来一个可确定的日期付款的，即要求先承兑后付款的称为远期汇票。在指定的或将来一个可确定的日期是承兑以后的若干天：a. 付款人见票后若干天付款，如见票后 30 天或 60 天；b. 出票后××天付款，如出票后 90 天付款；c. 将来某一指定日期，如于 2018 年 5 月 12 日付款。

(4) Commercial Acceptance Bill and Banker's Acceptance Bill（商业承兑汇票和银行承兑汇票）

In time or usance commercial bills, when the drawer is a commercial firm and the drawee is another commercial firm, the bill after acceptance by the commercial firm or the drawee is called a commercial acceptance bill; when the drawer is a commercial firm or bank and the drawee is a bank, the bill after acceptance by the bank or the drawee is called a banker's acceptance bill.

在商业汇票中，由工商企业出票而以另一工商企业为付款人的远期汇票，经付款人承兑后，就称为商业承兑汇票。如工商企业出票而以银行为付款人的远期汇票，经付款银行承兑后，就称为银行承兑汇票，由银行承担到期付款的责任。

5) Use of Bill of Exchange in foreign trade（汇票在对外贸易中的作用）

A bill of exchange (draft) is an order to pay. It is made out by an exporter and presented to an importer, usually through a bank. It may be payable immediately on presentation (a sight or demand draft), or so many days after presentation (a time draft). In the latter case, the drawee writes "ACCEPTED" across it and signs his name. The exporter can then get immediate payment by discounting the draft and supplying a letter of hypothecation. If a time draft is not honored at maturity, it will be noted and protested by a Notary Public, and presented to the drawee. Such a draft, and the corresponding payment terms, "Documents against Acceptance", obviously involve risk to the exporter or his bank.

汇票是索款的票据，由出口商开出，提示给进口商，一般都通过银行。可以是见票即付（即期汇票），也可以是提示多少天后再付款（远期汇票）。在后一种情况下，受票人在汇票上写上"承兑"并签上自己的名字。这样出口商便可以将汇票贴现，填送押汇质押书后，立即取款。如果远期汇票到期不付款，公证人就要在汇票上附注受票人拒付字样，并出具拒绝证书，然后再次提交给受票人。这种汇票以及相应的"承兑交单"付款条款显然对出口商或其银行有一定的风险。

6) Acts related to a Bill of Exchange（汇票行为）

(1) To draw（出票）

To draw is to fill in by the drawer the particulars in a bill of exchange: the date of drawing, the name of the drawee, the time and amount of the payment, etc. The draft is signed by the drawer and then sent to the payee.

There are three methods to fill in the payee:

a. Restrictive payee, such as "pay… only" or "pay … not transferable".

b. To order, such as "pay … or Order" or "Pay to the Order of …" This type requires endorsement when transferable.

c. To bearer, such as "pay bearer". This type requires no endorsement.

出票是指出票人在汇票上填写付款人、付款金额、付款日期和地点以及受款人等项目，经签字后交给受款人的行为。

在出票时，受款人一栏（俗称"抬头"）的填写方法通常有三种：

a. 限制性抬头。例如"仅付××"（Pay××only）或"付××公司不准转让"（Pay××not transferable）。这种抬头的汇票不能流通转让，只有受款人才能收取票款。

b. 指示性抬头。例如"付××或其指定人"（Pay××or Order 或 Pay to the Order of××）。这种抬头的汇票，除××可以收取票款外，也可以经过背书转让给第三者。

c. 持票人或来人抬头。例如"付给来人"（Pay Bearer）。这种抬头的汇票无须由持票人背书，仅凭交付汇票即可转让，且任何持有汇票的人都有权收取票款。

(2) Presentation（提示）

The act of taking the bill to the drawee and demanding that he make the payment or accept the bill is known as presentation. For a sight bill, payment should be made at the same time the presentation is made, and for a time bill, the drawee is required to accept the bill when presented to him.

提示是指持票人将汇票提交付款人要求承兑或付款的行为。付款人看到汇票叫见票，如是即期汇票，付款人见票后应立即付款；如是远期汇票，付款人见票后先办理承兑手续，到期时付款。

(3) Acceptance（承兑）

The formal act whereby the drawee adopts the bill as his own obligation is known as acceptance. Acceptance is the written signification by the drawee of his assent to the order of the drawer. This is accomplished in the regular manner by writing the word "ACCEPTANCE", with the date and the signature of the drawee, across the face of the bill. When the bill is accepted by the drawee, he is then known as an acceptor.

承兑是指付款人对远期汇票表示承担到期付款责任的行为。承兑手续是由付款人在远期汇票正面写上"承兑"字样，注明承兑日期，并由付款人签字，交给持票人。付款人承兑汇票后，即为承兑人。

(4) Payment（付款）

Under a sight bill, the drawee is required to make the payment when the bill is presented to him while for a time bill, the drawee is required to accept the bill when presented and make payment at maturity. When paid, the bill is retained by the payer, and a receipt is issued and signed by the holder of the bill.

对即期汇票，在持票人提示时，付款人即应付款，不需要经过承兑手续；对远期汇票，付款人经过承兑后，在汇票到期日付款。付款人付清款项后，汇票上的一切债权债务即告结束。

(5) Endorsement（背书）

The bill of exchange is negotiable and transferable as the payee on most bills is "to the order of…". Negotiation and transfer are effected with endorsement. If the payee on the bill is "to the bearer", then negotiation and transfer are done with mere delivery of the bill. Endorsement is done when the payee has signed his name on the back of the bill with or without additional words conveying instructions or qualifying liability.

Generally speaking, there are three main kinds of endorsements.

除限制性抬头的汇票外，汇票在国际市场上是一种可流通的支付工具，可以在金融市场上流通转让。汇票在转让时，除来人抬头的汇票只需交付汇票即可转让外，指示性抬头汇票转让时必须办理背书。背书是转让汇票权利的一种法定手续，是由汇票持有人在汇票背面签上自己的名字，或加上受让人的名字，注明背书日期并把汇票交给受让人的行为。

汇票背书主要有以下三种。

a. Restrictive Endorsement. The endorser may write clearly on the upper part above the signature on the back of the bill the terms to the endorsee with restrictive conditions. A restrictive endorsement is one which limits the bill for further negotiation, such as "Pay … only" or "Pay … non-transferable". Once the bill is restrictively endorsed, it cannot be transferred anymore.

a. 限制性背书。背书人在汇票背面其签字的上方写明被背书人，并加上限制性条件。例如 "仅付××" "付××不准转让"。汇票经限制性背书后，就不能再流通转让了。

b. Demonstrative Endorsement. A demonstrative endorsement is one which specifies the person to whom, or to whose order, the bill is to be payable, such as "Pay … or to order of ".

b. 指示性背书。背书人在汇票背面其签字的上方写明被背书人，但允许其继续转让。例如 "付给××或其指定人"。

c. Blank Endorsement. A blank endorsement, or endorsement in blank, is one which specifies no payee. The effect of a blank endorsement is to make the bill payable to bearer and to make delivery without additional endorsement. The bearer or holder of a bill so endorsed may sometimes be required, however, to place his endorsement upon it at the time of making a further negotiation.

c. 空白背书。它指的是背书人只在汇票背面签字而不注明被背书人的名字，故亦称 "不记名背书"。汇票经空白背书后，受让人或持票人根据情况的需要再做转让时，可通过自己的背书把汇票转成记名背书，此后的被背书人又可将其恢复为空白背书继续转让。

In international markets, after the acceptance of the time bill, if the bearer or the holder wants to get cash before the bill matures, he can go to the bank or discount house which is prepared to discount the bill by paying immediate cash for the bill at a little less than its face value, i.e. after deducting the interest based on the current rate discount, and then, will collect the full amount from the acceptor when the bill becomes due. This is called discounting.

在国际市场上，远期汇票经过承兑，持票人如需在汇票到期前取得票款，可将汇票背书转让给银行（或专业贴现公司），银行扣除利息后将票款付给持票人，这叫 "贴现"。

2. Promissory Note（本票）

A promissory note is an unconditional promise in writing made by one person to another, signed by the maker, engaging to pay, on demand or at a fixed or determinable future time, a sum certain in money, to or to the order of a specified person or to bearer.

The main difference between a promissory note and a draft lies in that there are three parties, namely drawer, drawee and payee involved in a draft but only two, the drawer and payee in a promissory note. In a promissory note, the drawer is the obligor.

Promissory notes can be made by commercial firms, called commercial promissory notes; or by bankers, called bank promissory notes. Commercial promissory notes can be sight promissory notes or time promissory notes, while bank promissory notes can only be sight. In international trade, most promissory notes are drawn by bankers, who are generally non-negotiable.

本票是一人向另一人签发的，保证在见票时或在指定的或可以确定的将来的某一日期，支付一定的金额给特定的人或其指定的人或持票人的无条件书面承诺。

本票和支票的最大区别是汇票的当事人有三个：出票人、受款人和受票人。而本票的当事人只有两个：出票人和受款人。本票的付款人即出票人本人。

本票可分为商业本票和银行本票。由工商企业或个人签发的称为商业本票，由银行签发的称为银行本票。商业本票有即期和远期之分，银行本票则都是即期的。在国际贸易结算中使用的本票，大都是银行本票。

3. Cheque (Check)（支票）

A check is an unconditional order in writing drawn on a banker signed by the drawer, requiring the banker to pay on demand a sum certain in money to or to the order of a specified person or to bearer.

The payer of a check is the drawer of the check. A cheque drawn on a bank overseas cannot be readily negotiated by the exporter. If the exporter's bank was prepared to negotiate it for him then he would receive payment right away but at the cost of the discount. Failing this, the exporter would have to ask his bank to collect the cheque for him and this would be both time-consuming and relatively expensive.

支票是银行存款户对银行签发的授权银行对特定的人或其指定人或持票人在见票时无条件支付一定金额的书面命令。

支票的出票人就是付款人。出口商不能凭以海外银行为付款人的支票立即议付货款。如果出口商的银行愿意议付，那么出口商就可以立即得到付款，但其需要支付贴现的费用。如果出口商的银行不愿议付，那么出口商只有委托其银行收款，这既费时又费钱。

Section Two　Modes of Payment in International Trade（国际贸易支付方式）

Trading with other countries is not the same as trading within one's own country. Both exporters and importers face risks in export or import transactions because they will inevitably experience the possibility that the other party may not fulfill the contract.

For exporters, they are likely to take the risks of buyer default; the customers might not pay in full for the goods. There are several reasons for this: the importers might go bankrupt; a war might break out or the importers' government might ban trade with the exporting country; or they might ban imports of certain commodities. Moreover, the importers might run into difficulties getting the foreign exchange to pay for the goods, or they are not even reliable and simply refuse to pay the agreed amount of money.

For importers, they may face the risks that the goods will be delayed and they might only receive them a long time after paying for them. This may result from port congestion or strikes. Delays in fulfillment of orders by exporters and difficult customs clearance in the importing country can cause loss of business. There is also the risk that the wrong goods might be sent.

In order to prevent such risks, different methods of payment have been developed. The modes of payment in international trade can be generally divided into three categories: remittance, collection and letter of credit.

Remittance and collection belong to commercial credit, and letter of credit belongs to banker's credit. In foreign trade, "credit" stipulates who takes the responsibility of paying money and surrendering the shipping documents that represent the title to the goods. In remittance or collection transactions, the buyer is responsible for making payment, and the seller for handing over documents. In letter of credit transactions, the banker is responsible for paying money and tendering documents on behalf of both parties.

对外贸易与国内贸易有所不同。出口商和进口商在交易中都要面对一些风险，因为它们将不可避免地遇到一方不能履行合同的情况。

对出口商来说，有买方违约和买方不支付全部货款的风险。这主要是由以下几个原因引起的：出口商破产、战争爆发、进口商所在国家的政府禁止与出口商所在国进行贸易往来，或者禁止进口某些商品。另外一个可能的原因是进口商很难获取外汇以支付货物。还有可能是进口商不可靠和根本就不想支付货款。

对进口商来说，要面临延迟交货或付款很长一段时间才能收到货的风险。这可能是由港口拥挤或罢工引起的。出口商的推迟发货以及进口国复杂的结关手续都会给生意带来损失。另外，还有发错货的风险。

为预防这种种可能的风险，人们采用了不同的支付方式。总的来说，国际贸易支付方式可以分为三大类：汇付、托收和信用证。

汇付和托收属于商业信用，信用证属于银行信用。"信用"在对外贸易中货物的交接和货款的支付上规定由谁承担付款和提供货物所有权单据的责任问题。在汇付和托收交易项下，买方负责付款，卖方负责提交装船单据。在信用证交易项下，银行代替买卖双方负责付款和提交单据。

1. Remittance（汇付）

Remittance is a process whereby the payer instructs his bank or other institutions to have a payment made to the payee. Four parties are involved in the remittance business: the remitter, the payee, the remitting bank and the paying bank. In international sales of goods, remittance service is often used for payment of advance payments, cash with order, open account, down-payment, payment in installments and commission, etc. Remittance can be made by mail transfer, telegraphic transfer and demand draft.

汇付是指付款人通过银行或其他途径将款项汇交收款人。在汇付业务中，通常有四个当事人：汇款人、收款人、汇出行和汇入行。在国际贸易中，汇付方式常用于预付货款、随订单付款和赊销、支付定金、分期付款以及佣金等费用的支付。汇付方式包括信汇、电汇和票汇三种。

1) Mail Transfer (M/T)（信汇）

Mail Transfer is a process where the remitting bank, at the request of the remitter, sends instructions by mail to the paying bank, asking it to make a specified amount of payment to the payee. The cost of this method is lower, but the speed is slower.

信汇是汇出行应汇款人的申请，将信汇委托书寄给汇入行，授权解付一定金额给收款人的一种付款方式。信汇的成本较低，但速度较慢。

2) Telegraphic Transfer (T/T)（电汇）

Telegraphic Transfer (T/T) is a process where the remitting bank, at the request of the remitter, sends a cable to its correspondent bank in the country concerned with instructions, to make a certain amount of payment to the payee. The payee can receive payment promptly, but the charges for this type of transfer are relatively high.

电汇是汇出行应汇款人的申请，电报通知另一国家的代理行指示解付一定金额给收款人的一种汇款方式。电汇方式下收款人可以迅速收到汇款，但费用较高。

3) Demand Draft (D/D)（票汇）

Demand Draft (D/D) is a process where the remitting bank, at the request of the remitter, draws a demand draft on its branch or correspondent bank, instructing them to make a specified amount of payment to the payee on behalf of the remitter.

票汇是指汇出行应汇款人的申请，代汇款人开立以其分行或代理行为解付行的银行即期汇票，支付一定金额给收款人的一种汇款方式。

4) Advantages and disadvantages of remittance（汇付的利与弊）

In international trade, most transactions are paid through M/T and T/T if remittance is used. T/T is beneficial to the seller because it enables him to obtain money promptly, accelerate the turnover of funds, increase interest income and avoid the risks of fluctuation in exchange rate. But it is disadvantageous to the buyer in that he has to bear more cable expenses and bank charges. In practice, if T/T is not definitely stipulated in transaction, the buyer had better make payment by M/T. When the amount of payment is comparatively large, or the money market fluctuates greatly, or the currency of settlement used is likely to devalue, it is wise for the buyer to use T/T. In a word, the choice of T/T or M/T should be clearly stipulated in the contract according to specific situation. As far as D/D is concerned, it is transferable, which is different from M/T and T/T.

在国际贸易中，使用汇付时，大多数交易是通过信汇和电汇完成的。电汇对卖方有利，可以使卖方较快地收到货款，加速资金周转，增加利息收入和避免汇率变动的风险，但买方却要多付电报费用和银行费用。在实际业务中，除非明确规定要使用电汇，买方最好通过信汇付款。有时，当款项的金额较大或因货币市场动荡，使用的结算货币有贬值的可能时，通过电汇付款是买方明智的选择。总之，是用电汇还是信汇要根据实际情况在合同中明确规定。就票汇来说，它是可以转让的，这一点与信汇和电汇不同。

2. Collection（托收）

When funds are not required immediately, or where bills are not sufficiently attractive to a banker for negotiation, they may be handed by an exporter to his bank for collection. The exporter asks his bank to arrange for the acceptance or payment of the bill overseas, and the bank will carry out its task through its own branch office abroad or a correspondent bank (See Fig.11-5).

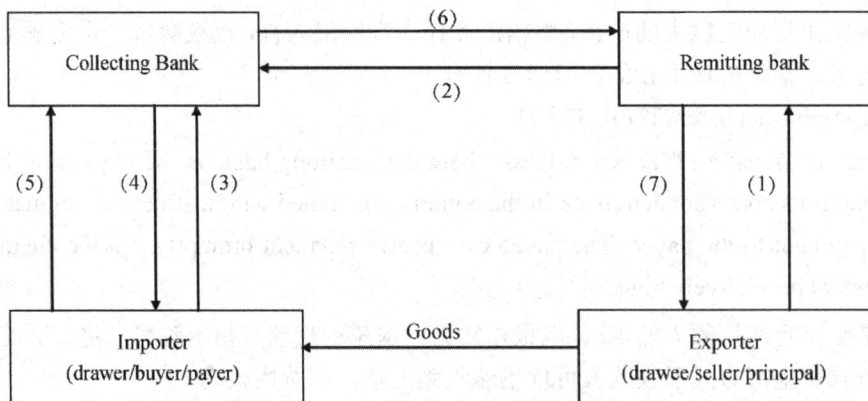

Fig.11-5　Procedures of Collection

Collection means the handling by banks, on instructions received, of documents (financial documents and/or commercial documents), in order to: (1) obtain acceptance and/or, as the case may be, payment, or (2) deliver commercial documents against acceptance and/or, as the case may be, against payment, or (3) deliver documents on other terms and conditions. There are two types of collection: clean collection and documentary collection. The parties to a collection transaction mainly include: the principal, the remitting bank, the collection bank, the presenting bank and so on. Clean collection means the collection of financial documents without being accompanied by commercial documents (Financial documents mean bills of exchange, promissory notes, checks, payment receipts or other similar instruments used for obtaining the payment of money; Commercial documents mean invoices, shipping documents, documents of title or other similar documents or any other documents whatsoever, not being financial documents).

Documentary collection means collection of: (1) financial documents accompanied by commercial documents; (2) commercial documents not accompanied by financial documents. The documentary collection is widely used in international trade. Documentary collection is divided into two types: documents against payment(D/P) and documents against acceptance(D/A). Documents against payment requires actual payment against transfer of shipping documents. Documents against acceptance requires delivery of documents against acceptance of the draft drawn by the exporter.

当出口商不急需资金，汇票的流通引不起银行的足够注意时，出口商就有可能将这些汇票交给银行托收。出口商委托银行安排汇票的接收和海外支付，然后银行再通过国外分行或代理行来办理此项业务。如图 11-5 所示为托收的程序图。

托收是指银行为了：（1）取得承兑和/或视情况给予付款；或（2）在承兑后和/或视情况在付款后交付商业单据；或（3）按其他条件交付单据，而根据所收到的指示来处理有关单据（资金单据和/或商业单据）。托收的当事人主要包括委托人、托收银行、代收行和提示行等。

托收分为光票托收和跟单托收两种。

光票托收是指资金单据的托收，不附有商业单据（资金单据是指汇票、期票、支票、付款收据或其他用于取得付款的类似凭证，商业单据是指发票、装运单据、所有权单据或其他类似的单据，或一切不属于资金单据的其他单据）。

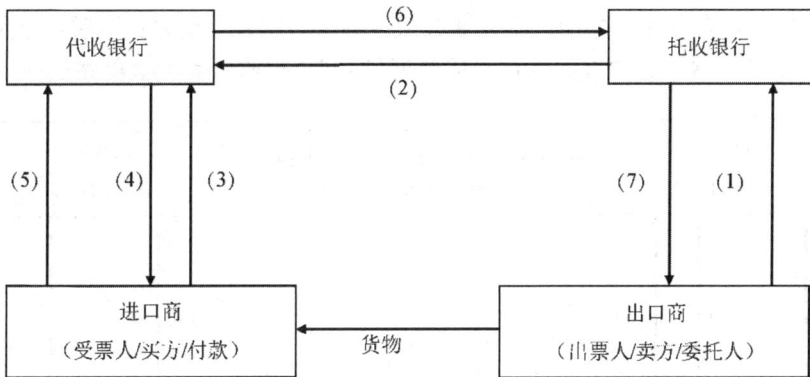

图 11-5 托收的程序

跟单托收是指：（1）资金单据的托收，附有商业单据；（2）商业单据的托收，不附有资金单据。在国际贸易中大多采用跟单托收。跟单托收又分为付款交单和承兑交单两种。付款交单要求转交货运单据即付货款，而承兑交单要求进口商承兑出口商开具的汇票时才转交货运单据。

1) Document against Payment (D/P)（付款交单）

Under D/P, the exporter is to ship the goods ordered and deliver the relevant shipping documents to the buyer abroad through the remitting bank and the collection bank with instructions not to release the documents to the buyer until the full payment is effected. According to the different time of payment, Document against Payment can be further divided into D/P at sight and D/P after sight.

在付款交单支付方式下，出口人交出单据后指示托收行和代收行在国外的买方付清货款后才交出单据。根据付款时间不同，付款交单可分为即期付款交单和远期付款交单。

(1) D/P at sight（即期付款交单）

Under this term, the seller draws a sight draft, and sends it with the shipping documents to the collecting bank. Then the collecting bank presents the sight draft and shipping documents to the buyer. When the buyer sees them, he must pay the money at once, then he can obtain the shipping documents. This method is also called "Cash Against Documents", the procedure of which can be seen in the following (See Fig.11-6).

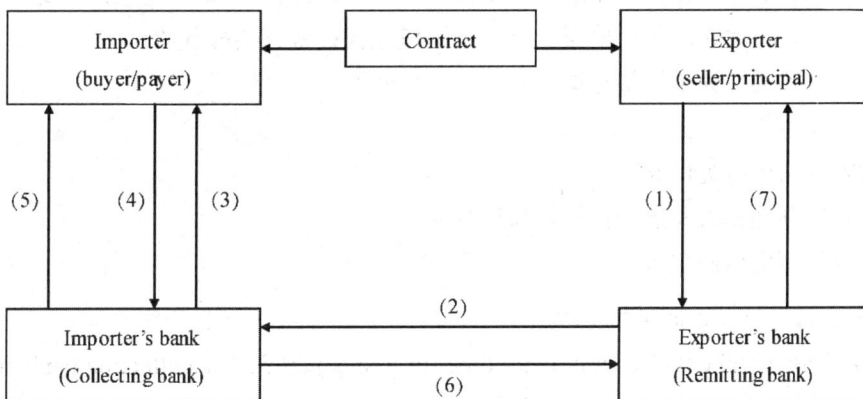

Fig.11-6　Procedures of D/P at sight

在这种方式下，卖方开具即期汇票并通过银行向买方提示，买方见票后马上付款，只有付款清货后才能领取单据。这种方式也称"凭单据付款"。即期付款交单程序如图 11-6 所示。

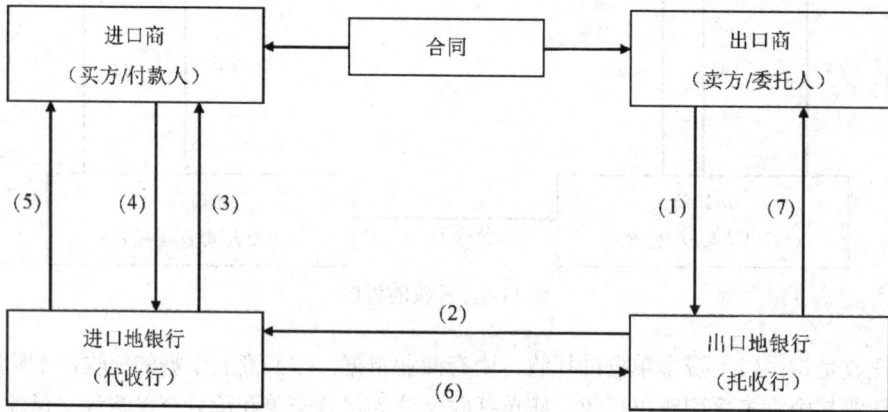

图 11-6　即期付款交单程序

Notes:

(1) According to the contract, the exporter loads the goods and draws a sight draft, then sends the draft together with shipping documents to his bank for collection a documentary bill on his behalf.

(2) The remitting bank sends the documentary bill to a correspondent bank overseas — the collecting bank — for payment collection.

(3) The collecting bank presents the bill and documents to the importer for payment.

(4) The importer effects payment.

(5) The collecting bank hands over the documents to the importer.

(6) The collecting bank notifies the remitting bank of crediting the money to their account.

(7) The remitting bank effects payment to the exporter.

说明：

（1）出口商根据合同规定装货后，开立即期汇票，连同货运单据交托收行，委托代收货款。

（2）托收行将汇票连同货运单据一起寄交进口地代办银行委托代收。

（3）代收行向买方提示汇票与单据。

（4）进口商付款。

（5）代收行交单给进口商。

（6）代收行办理转账并通知托收行款已收妥。

（7）托收行向出口商交款。

(2) D/P after sight（远期付款交单）

Under D/P after sight, the seller draws a time (or usance) draft. The collecting bank presents the time draft and shipping documents to the buyer. When the buyer sees them he just accepts the time bill and then effects payment at maturity of the draft. When receiving the money from the buyer, the collecting bank hands over the shipping documents to him. The procedure of D/P after sight is shown as follows (See Fig.11-7).

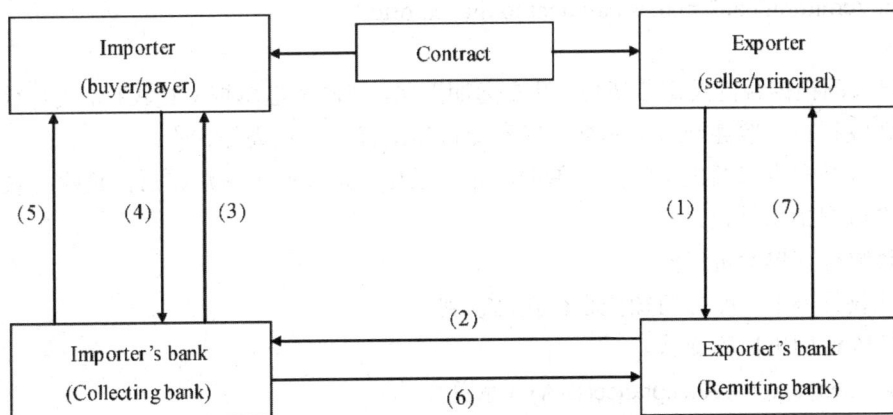

Fig.11-7　Procedures of D/P after sight

　　在远期付款交单方式下,卖方开立远期汇票。代收行将此汇票向买方提示汇票和货运单据。买方见票后仅须承兑汇票,等汇票到期支付货款。代收行收到货款后,即交付单据。远期付款交单程序如图 11-7 所示。

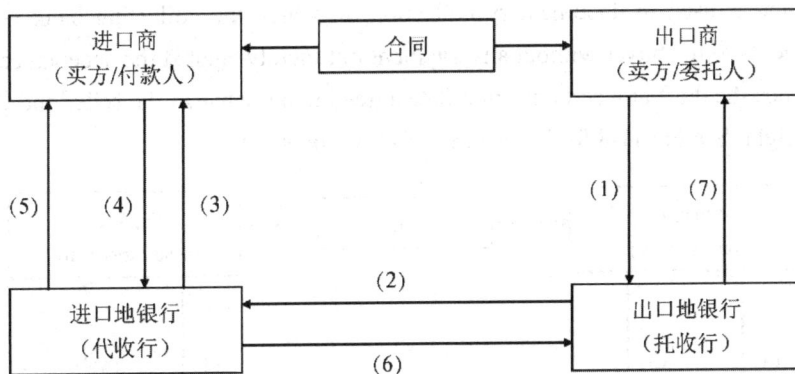

图 11-7　远期付款交单程序

Notes:

(1) According to the contract, the exporter loads the goods and draws a sight draft, then sends the draft together with shipping documents to his bank for collection of a documentary bill on his behalf.

(2) The remitting bank sends the documentary bill to a correspondent bank overseas—the collecting bank.

(3) The collecting bank presents the bill and documents to the importer for payment. After the importer accepts the draft, the collecting bank releases the draft and documents.

(4) The importer makes payment when it falls due.

(5) The collecting bank hands over the document to the importer.

(6) The collecting bank notifies the remitting bank of the crediting of the money to their account.

(7) The remitting bank makes payment to the exporter.

说明：

（1）出口商根据合同规定装货后，开立远期汇票，连同货运单据交托收行，委托代收货款。

（2）托收行将汇票连同货运单据一起寄交进口地代办银行委托代收。

（3）代收行向进口商提示汇票与单据，让其承兑。进口商承兑汇票后，代收行收回汇票。

（4）进口商到期付款。

（5）代收行交单给进口商。

（6）代收行办理转账并通知托收行款已收到。

（7）托收行向出口商交款。

2) Document against Acceptance(D/A)（承兑交单）

Under Documents against Acceptance(D/A), the exporter releases the documents on the condition that the importer has made acceptance on the draft. The exporter makes a presentation to the importer through the bank the time draft and the shipping documents after the shipment, the collecting bank will release the documents to the importer after the importer has made the acceptance, and the importer will make the payment only at the expiry of the draft. That is to say, this term of payment is applicable only to a time bill that is used in documentary collection, in which the collecting bank will release the shipping documents to the buyer without any payment but merely against the acceptance of the bill by the buyer to honor the draft at a certain future date agreed upon between the seller and the buyer. D/A is always after sight. See Fig.11-8 for Procedures of D/A after sight.

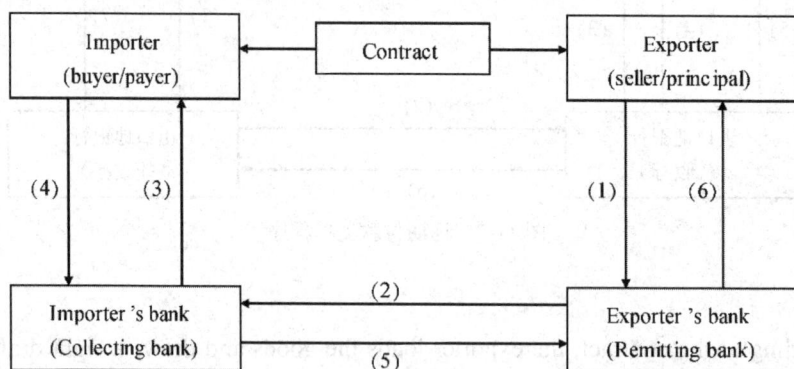

Fig.11-8　Procedures of D/A after sight

这种付款方式仅用于跟单托收中的远期汇票。在此方式下，代收行向买方交付单据不以后者付款为条件，仅以后者的承兑为条件，即买方做出的在买卖双方同意的某个将来的日期保证支付汇票款项的书面承诺。这也就是说承兑交单是指出口人的交单以进口人在汇票上承兑为条件。即出口人在装运货物后开具远期汇票连同货运单据，通过银行向进口人提示，进口人承兑汇票后，代收行即将货运单据交给进口人，进口人在汇票到期时才履行付款义务。远期承兑交单程序如图 11-8 所示。

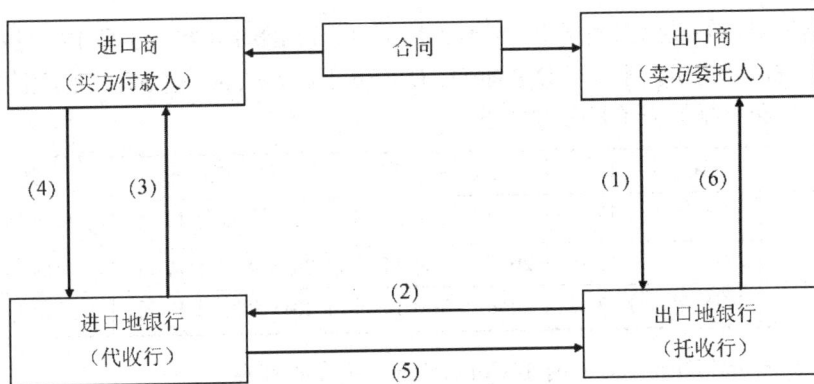

图 11-8 远期承兑交单程序

Notes:

(1) According to the contract, the exporter loads the goods and draws a time draft, then sends the draft together with shipping documents to his bank for collecting documentary bills on his behalf.

(2) The remitting bank sends the documentary bill to a correspondent bank overseas—the collecting bank.

(3) The collecting bank presents the bill and documents to the importer for acceptance, after which, the collecting bank takes back the draft and gives the shipping documents to the importer.

(4) The importer makes payment when the time falls due.

(5) The collecting bank notifies the remitting bank of crediting the money to its account.

(6) The remitting bank makes payment to the exporter.

说明：

（1）出口商根据合同规定装货后，开立远期汇票，连同货运单据交托收行，委托代收货款。

（2）托收行将汇票连同货运单据一起寄交进口地代办银行委托代收。

（3）代收行向买方提示汇票与单据，进口商在汇票上承兑。代收行收回汇票，同时将货运单据交给进口商。

（4）进口商到期付款。

（5）代收行办理转账并通知托收行款已收到。

（6）托收行向出口商交款。

Take the following as an example. Suppose the exporter drew a documentary draft on March10th, 2018, and the bank in the importer's country made the presentation to the importer on the same day when the draft was received on March17th, 2018, then under circumstances of D/P at sight, D/P at 30 days and D/A at 30 days, the presentation and acceptance dates of the draft, the date of payment, and the date of document release are as follows:

Date	Date of Presentation	Date of Acceptance	Date of Payment	Date of Documents releasing
D/P at sight	March 17th, 2018	No acceptance	March 17th, 2018	March 17th, 2018
D/P at 30 days	March 17th, 2018	March 17th, 2018	April 17th, 2018	April 17th, 2018
D/A at 30 days	March 17th, 2018	March 17th, 2018	April 17th, 2018	March 17th, 2018

下面举例说明。假设出口商于 2018 年 3 月 10 日开出跟单汇票，3 月 17 日进口地银行收到汇票当天向进口商提示，那么在 D/P 即期、D/P 30 天和 D/A 30 天的情况下，汇票的提示日、承兑日、付款日和单据的交单日分别如下：

日　　期	提　示　日	承　兑　日	付　　款　　日	交　单　日
D/P 即期	2018 年 3 月 17 日	无须承兑	2018 年 3 月 17 日	2018 年 3 月 17 日
D/P30 天	2018 年 3 月 17 日	2018 年 3 月 17 日	2018 年 4 月 17 日	2018 年 4 月 17 日
D/A30 天	2018 年 3 月 17 日	2018 年 3 月 17 日	2018 年 4 月 17 日	2018 年 3 月 17 日

3) Advantages and Disadvantages of Collection（托收的利弊）

Collection has the following advantages for the importer: (1) It facilitates the importer to get financing. Under D/P after sight, capital tie-up of the importer can be avoided or reduced; (2) The expenses are low. Under collection, the importer does not need to pay the service fee as required for the opening of L/C. At the time of market with intense competition, collection is usually used by the exporter to get customers and promote its sales.

But collection has some risks for the exporter: If the importer goes bankrupt or is not in a position to pay the debts, then the exporter will face the risk of non-payment or late payment by the importer. In case the importer refuses to make payment for the documents, the bank will not have obligations to take care of the goods for the exporter unless they have reached agreement in advance. Especially under D/A, the importer can get the shipping documents and take delivery of the goods after mere acceptance is made on the draft. Whether the exporter gets the payment or not will depend on the credit standing of the importer. Should the importer fail to make payment on the expiry of the draft, the exporter will suffer a loss.

托收对于进口商来说具有以下优点：① 有利于资金融通，如能争取到远期付款，还可不占用或少占用资金；② 费用低，进口商可以免去申请开立信用证的手续费用。在市场竞争激烈的情况下，托收常被出口商用来作为一种争夺客户、扩大销售的竞争手段。

但托收对于出口人来说却存在着一定的风险：如进口商破产或丧失清偿债务的能力，出口商则可能收不回或晚收货款。在进口人拒不付款赎单后，除非事先约定，银行没有义务代为保管货物。尤其是在承兑交单的条件下，进口商只要在汇票上办理承兑手续，即可取得货运单据，凭此提取货物，出口商收款的保障就是进口商的信用，一旦进口商到期不付款，出口商便会遭到货款全部落空的损失，所以承兑交单比付款交单的风险更大。

3. Letter of Credit(L/C)（信用证）

The methods of payment just described above are used if a buyer and a seller have gained a degree of confidence in each other. But trading partners have other alternatives. If an importer's bank is satisfied with its customer's credit rating, it will open a letter of credit in favor of and addressed to the exporter. This letter pledges to pay the exporter if the merchandise is shipped in accordance with the conditions in the letter of credit—conditions that are based on the contract between the buyer and seller. Thus, the bank backs up the business transaction between the importer and the exporter. Letters of credit has become a safer and quicker method of obtaining payment in international trade. See Fig.11-9 for Notification of Documentary Credit.

BANK OF CHINA， SHANGHAI BRANCH

信用证通知书

Notification of Documentary Credit

To:致： JINSHAN SUB-BR(U26) SHANGHAI TIANYE TOOL IMPORT & EXPORT CO., LTD. 3188 JINZHANG ROAD, GANXIANG TOWN, JINSHAN DISTRICT, SHANGHAI, CHINA	WHEN CORRESPONDING PLEASE QUOTE OUR REF. NO.558899J May 10th, 2018
Issuing Bank 开证行 CREDIT ANDORRA ANDORRA LA VELLA, ANDORRA 0786600	Transmitted to us through 转递行/转让行
L/C No. 信用证号 Dated 开证日期 OSK-04-31173 2010-04-20	Amount 金额 USD 21 892.00

Dear Sirs,

谨启者

We advise you that we have received from the bank a letter of credit, the contents of which are as per attached sheet(s).

兹通知贵公司，我行收自上述银行信用证一份，现随附通知。

This advice and the attached sheet(s) must accompany the relevant documents when presented for negotiation.

贵公司交单时，请将本通知书及信用证一并提示。

This advice does not convey any engagement or obligation on our part unless we have added our confirmation.

本通知书不构成我行对此信用证的任何责任和义务，但本行对本证加具保兑的除外。

If you find any terms and conditions in the L/C which you are unable to comply with and or any error(s), it is suggested that you contact applicant directly for necessary amendment(s) so as to avoid any difficulties which may arise when documents are presented.

如本信用证中有无法办到的条款及/或错误，请与开证申请人联系，进行必要的修改，以排除交单时可能发生的问题。

THIS L/C IS ADVISED SUBJECT TO ICC PUBLICATION NO.600.

本信用证之通知系遵循国际商会跟单信用证统一惯例第 600 号出版物办理。

This L/C consists of   sheet(s), including the cover letter and attachment(s).

本信用证连同面函及附件共   张纸。

Remarks:

备注：

Yours faithfully,

For BANK OF CHINA

Fig.11-9 Notification of Documentary Credit（跟单信用证通知书）

以上所谈论的支付方式，都是在买卖双方彼此有一定程度的信任的基础上才采用的。当然，贸易伙伴还有其他的选择。如果进口商的银行对自己的客户（进口商）的信誉感到满意，可以开出一张以出口商为受益人的信用证寄给出口商。在信用证上，银行做出如下保证：如果出口货物是按信用证条款的规定发运，本行将保证付款不误。信用证条款是以买卖双方签订的销售合约为依据的。银行用开信用证的方式支持出口商。现在，信用证已成为国际贸易中获取货款的一种较为安全和迅速的支付方式。如图 11-9 所示为信用证通知书。

Letter of credit specimen 1（信用证范例 1）

SEQUENCE OF TOTAL	*27	:1 / 1
FORM OF DOC, CREDIT	*40	A:IRREVOCABLE
DOC. CREDIT NUMBER	*20	:31173
EXPIRY	*31	D:DATE 040531 PLACE CHINA
APPLICANT	*50	:MAMUT ENTERPRISES ANDORRA LA VELLA PRINCIPALITY OF ANDORRA
BENEFICIARY	*59	:SHANGHAI TIANYE TOOL IMPORT & EXPORT CO., LTD. 3188 JINZHANG ROAD GANXIANG TOWN, JINSHAN DISTRICT SHANGHAI, CHINA
AMOUNT	*32 B:CURRENCY USD AMOUNT 21 892	
AVAILABLE WITH / BY	*41 D:ANY BANK IN CHINA BY NEGOTIATION	
DRAFTS AT…	42 C:SIGHT	
DRAWEE	42 A:CRDAADAD *CREDIT ANDORRA *ANDORRA LA VELLA	
PARTIAL SHIPMENTS	43 P:NOT ALLOWED	
TRANSSHIPMENT	43 T:ALLOWED	
LOADING IN CHARGE	44 A:SHANGHAI	
FOR TRANSPORT TO…	44 B:BARCELONA (SPAIN)	
LATEST DATE OF SHIPMENT	44 C:040510	
DESCRIPTION OF GOODS	45 A:	
TOOLS AS PER PROFORMA INVOICE NO. 20040329 DATED MARCH 29th, 2004 FOB SHANGHAI		
DOCUMENTS REQUIRED	45 A:	
+COMMERCIAL INVOICE, 1 ORIGINAL AND 4 COPIES		

+PACKING LIST, 1 ORIGINAL AND 4 COPIES

+CERTIFICATE OF ORIGIN GSP CHINA FORM A, ISSUED BY THE CHAMBER OF COMMERCE OR OTHER AUTHORITY DULY ENTITLED FOR THIS PURPOSE.

+FULL SET OF B/L, (1 ORIGINAL AND 5 COPIES) CLEAN ON BOARD, MARKED " FREIGHT COLLECT " ISSUED BY: CARGO SERVICES FAR EAST LIMITED, ROOM 13018E, ATL LOGISTICS CENTRE, BERTH 3, KWAY CHUNG CONTAINER TERMINALS, KWAI CHUNG, N. T. HONG KONG, TEL: (852) 2481 8308　　　　　FAX:(852) 2481 8401 CONSIGNED TO: MAMUT ENTERPRISES, AV, TARRAGONA 75-3ER, ANDORRA LA VELLA, PRINCIPALITY OF ANDORRA, TEL: +376 823 323 FAX: +376 860 914-860 807, CONTACT PERSON: MS, DEBORAH GUALLAR NOTIFY: BLUE WATER SHIPPING ESPAÑA, S.A., VIA LAITTANA 7, 3 ER 2NA, A, 08003 BARCELONA (SPAIN) TEL: 0034-93-295-4848 FAX: 0034-93-268-16-81, CONTACT PERSON: MS CHRISTINA

Letter of credit specimen 2（信用证范例 2）

DOCUMENTARY CREDIT
BENEFICIARY
SHANGHAI IMPORT & EXPORT TRADE CORPORATION
1321, ZHONGSHAN ROAD SHANGHAI, CHINA

DATE OF ISSUE
01/04/10

ISSUING BANK
　NATIONAL AUSTRALIA BANK LIMITED SYDNEY
　(TRADE AND INTERNATIONAL PAYMENTS)

FORM OF DOCUMENTARY CREDIT
　IRREVOCABLE

DATE AND PLACE OF EXPIRY
　17/05/10 IN COUNTRY OF BENEFICIARY

APPLICANT
　THE CLOTHING COMPANY AUSTRALIA PTY LTD.
　101 BURWOOD HIGHWAY

BURWOOD VIC 3125

CURRENCY AND AMOUNT
USD 20 800.00

POS./NEG. TOL.
10/10

AVAILABLE WITH/BY
FREELY NEGOTIABLE AT ANY BANK
BY NEGOTIATION

DRAFTS AT…
SIGHT

DRAWEE
NATIONAL AUSTRALIA BANK LIMITED SYDNEY
(TRADE AND INTERNATIONAL PAYMENTS)

PARTIAL SHIPMENTS
PERMITTED

TRANSSHIPMENT
NOT PERMITTED

LOADING ON BOARD/DISPATCH/TAKING IN CHARGE AT/FROM
ANY CHINESE PORT

FOR TRANSPORT TO
MELBOURNE AUSTRALIA

LATEST DATE OF SHIP
100503

DESCRIPTION OF GOODS
KNITTED GARMENTS OF 92 PERCENT COTTON AND 8 PERCENT
SPANDEX AS PER ORDER No.1354 MULTISTICH CREW
4 000 PCS   USD 5.20   USD 20 800.00
CFR MELBOURNE AUSTRALIA

DOCUMENTS REQUIRED (IN DUPLICATE UNLESS OTHERWISE STATED)
+FULL SET OF CLEAN ON BOARD MARINE BILL OF LADING
MADE OUT TO THE ORDER OF SHIPPER BLANK ENDORSED
AND MARKED FREIGHT PREPAID
+COMMERCIAL INVOICE
+PACKING LIST
+CERTIFICATE OF ORIGIN
+PACKING DECLARATION

ADDITIONAL CONDITIONS
+ALL DOCUMENTS IN DUPLICATE UNLESS OTHERWISE STIPULATED
+DOCUMENTS NEGOTIATED WITH OR SUBJECT TO ACCEPTANCE ANY
DISCREPANCY WILL ATTRACT A HANDLING FEE OF USD 40
THIS FEE WILL BE DEDUCTED FROM PROCEEDS REMITTED BY OURSELVES.
+CONTACT AT SUNTOR AND BLOOMING IS JIMMY ON TELEPHONE 216399001.
+ALL DOCUMENTS MUST BE IN THE NAME OF:
THE CLOTHING COMPANY AUSTRALIA PTY LTD.
101 BURWOOD HIGHWAY
BURWOOD VIC 3125
+INSTRUCTIONS FOR NEGOTIATING BANK: ON PRESENTATION OF
DOCUMENTS
UNDER THIS L/C, THE NEGOTIATING BANK'S PRESENTATION SCHEDULE
MUST INDICATE THE NUMBER AND DATE OF ANY AMENDMENTS THAT HAVE BEEN
AVAILED/REJECTED UNDER THEIR NEGOTIATION.

CHARGES
ALL BANK COMMISSIONS AND CHARGES OUTSIDE AUSTRALIA, PLUS ADVISING
AND REIMBURSING COMMISSIONS, ARE FOR ACCOUNT OF BENEFICIARY.

PERIOD FOR PRESENTATION
DOCUMENTS TO BE PRESENTED WITHIN 14 DAYS AFTER THE DATE OF
SHIPMENT INDICATED ON TRANSPORT DOCUMENT BUT WITHIN THE CREDIT
VALIDITY.

CONFIRMATION INSTRUCTIONS
ADVISING BANK IS NOT REQUESTED TO CONFIRM THE CREDIT

REIMBURSEMENT BANK
NATIONAL AUSTRALIA BANK LIMITED SYDNEY

(TRADE AND INTERNATIONAL PAYMENTS)

INSTRUCTIONS TO THE PAYING/ACCEPTING/NEGOTIATING BANK

DOCUMENTS ARE TO BE FORWARDED TO NATIONAL AUSTRALIA BANK TRADE SOLUTIONS SERVICE CENTRE P.O.BOX 9909 4/20 BOND STREET, SYDNEY, NEW

SOUTH WALES 2001 ORIGINALS BY AIR COURIER OR REGISTERED AIRMAIL. DUPLICATES BY AIRMALL.

ON RECEIPT OF DRAFT AND DOCUMENTS OF NEGOTIATION (DRAWN IN COMPLIANCE WITH THE CREDIT) WE WILL REIMBURSE NEGOTIATING BANK BY TELEGRAPHICALLY REMITTING FUNDS AS INSTRUCTED.

REIMBURSEMENT INSTRUCTIONS ARE TO INDICATE NAME OF CORRESPONDENT BANK AND NAME AND NUMBER OF ACCOUNT TO BE CREDITED.

ADVISE THROUGH BANK

AUSTRALIA AND NEW ZEALAND BANKING

SWIFT: ANZBCNSH:XXX

LEVEL 39 SHANGHAI SENMAO INTERNAL

BLDG, 101 YIN CHENG, SHANGHAI, CHINA

1) Definition of letter of credit（信用证的定义）

According to The Uniform Customs and Practice for Documentary Credits, 2007 Revision, ICC Publication No. 600 ("UCP600"), a documentary credit means any arrangement, however named or described, that is irrevocable and thereby constitutes a definite undertaking of the issuing bank to honor a complying presentation. "To honor" means. a) to pay at sight if the credit is available by sight payment, b) to incur a deferred payment undertaking and pay at maturity if the credit is available by deferred payment, and c) to accept a bill of exchange ("draft") drawn by the beneficiary and pay at maturity if the credit is available by acceptance. The payment by letter of credit refers to the credit given by banks. It is not money but a promise by the issuing bank or the bank concerned bank to make payment using the banks' credit. The issuing banks provide credit, not money.

国际商会《跟单信用证统一惯例（UCP600）》（2007 年修订版）给信用证的定义是：信用证是指一项不可撤销的安排，无论其名称或描述如何，该项安排构成开证行对相符交单予以承付的确定承诺。承付是指：a. 如果信用证为即期付款信用证，则即期付款。b. 如果信用证为延期付款信用证，则承诺延期付款并在承诺到期日付款。c. 如果信用证为承兑信用证，则承兑受益人开出汇票并在汇票到期日付款。信用证支付方式是银行的信用，而不是资金。开证行或相关银行以自己的信用做出付款保证。开证行提供的是信用，不是资金。

In UCP500, the definition of documentary credit(s) means any arrangement, however named or described, whereby a bank (the "Issuing Bank"), acting at the request and on the instructions of a customer (the "Applicant") or on its own behalf.

To make a payment to the "Beneficiary" or to the order of A THIRD PARTY (the "Beneficiary"), or to accept and pay bills of exchange (draft(s)) drawn by the Beneficiary.

To authorise another bank to effect such payment, or to accept and pay such bills of exchange (draft(s)).

To authorise another bank to negotiate, against stipulated document(s), provided that the terms and conditions of the Credit are complied with. For the purposes of these Articles, branches of a bank in different countries are considered as another bank.

根据国际商会《UCP500》的解释，信用证是指由银行（开证行）依据客户（申请人）的要求和指示或其代表，在符合信用证条款的条件下，凭规定的单据：

向第三者（受益人）或其指定的人进行付款，或承兑和（或）支付受益人所开立的汇票。

授权另一银行进行该项付款，或承兑支付该汇票。

授权另一银行议付，或者授权另一家银行凭符合信用证规定的单据进行议付。就本惯例而言，一家银行在不同国家设立的分支机构将被视为另一家银行。

Uniform Customs and Practice for Documentary Credits was first developed by the International Chamber of Commerce (ICC) in 1933. Since then it has been revised 6 times: 1951, 1962, 1974, 1983, 1993 and 2007. The current version was revised in 2007 and came into force on July 1, 2007. UCP600 has now been accepted by most banks in the world and become one of the most important documents for international traders.

Apart from the change in structure (in UCP600, there are 39 articles, while in UCP500 there are 49 articles) and wording, the UCP600 has the vital changes as below.

(1) Revocable letter of credit has been canceled.

(2) Days for document processing that changed from 7 days to 5 days. UCP600 stipulates that a nominated bank acting on its nomination, a confirming bank, if any, and the issuing bank shall each have a maximum of 5 banking days following the day of presentation to determine if a presentation is complying. This period is not curtailed or otherwise affected by the occurrence on or after the date of presentation of any expiry date or last day for presentation. Whereas UCP500 stipulates that the issuing bank, the confirming bank, if any, or a nominated bank acting on their behalf, shall each have a reasonable time, not to exceed 7 banking days following the day of receipt of the documents, to examine the documents and determine whether to take up or refuse the documents and to inform the party from which it received the documents accordingly. This is the most practical change: the reduction of time to examine documents from the previously 7 bank working days (UCP500 Article 13b) to now 5 (UCP600 Article 14b).

(3) The changes to standard for examination of documents. In UCP500, the criteria for examining documents were "All the terms in each document should be in accordance with those in the L/C, and there should be no discrepancies among the document". Therefore, when there are any discrepancies between the documents and the credit, this will lead to the discrepancies between the documents and the credit. The bank can avoid payment responsibilities. As a result, when the banks examine the documents, they implement "strict compliance" in order to avoid payment responsibilities, or even

deliberately look for non-compliance. In UCP600, the standard for examination of documents has been changed. UCP600 stipulates: "Data in a document, when read in context with the credit, the document itself and international standard banking practice, need not be identical to, but must not conflict with, data in that document, any other stipulated document or the credit."(UCP600 Article 14d). That's to say, according to UCP600 the terms in documents need not be in strict conformity with the terms in the credit, if there is no conflict with terms in documents and credit, the bank should perform payment responsibilities.

Because of the changes, it is better to note that in the L/C this credit is subject to UCP600 or subject to UCP500.

As to the details of differences between UCP600 and UCP500, please read Appendix 1 of UCP600.

《跟单信用证统一惯例》是由国际商会于 1933 年制定的，历史上共修改过 6 次：1951 年、1962 年、1974 年、1983 年、1993 年和 2007 年。目前版本是 2007 年修改并于 2007 年 7 月 1 日生效的。该惯例已被世界上大多数银行采用，成为公认的最为重要的国际贸易惯例之一。

相对于《UCP500》，《UCP600》除了在结构上和遣词造句上有变化之外，实质变化有如下几点：

（1）可撤销信用证被取消。

（2）银行处理单据天数有变化，由 7 天改为 5 天。《UCP600》规定按指定行事的指定银行、保兑行（如有的话）及开证行各有从交单次日起至多 5 个银行工作日用以确定交单是否相符。这一期限不因在交单日当天或之后信用证截止日或最迟交单日截止而受到缩减或影响。而《UCP500》规定开证行、保兑行（如有），或代其行事的指定银行，应有各自合理的审单时间——不得超过从其收到单据的翌日起第 7 个银行工作日，以便决定是接受或拒绝接受单据，并相应地通知寄单方。这是 UCP 最实际的变化之一：减少审查时间从以前 7 个银行工作日内（《UCP500》第 13 条 b 款）到现在 5 个银行工作日（《UCP600》第 14 条 b 款）。

（3）审单标准的变化。《UCP500》对银行审单的标准是"单单相符，单单不得互不一致"。因此，一旦出现单证不符、单单不一致的情况，就造成信用证的不符点，就意味着银行不需要再承担付款责任，于是，导致了银行在审核单证时，为避免付款责任，实施"严格相符"，甚至故意寻找不符点。而《UCP600》规定："单据中的数据，在与信用证、单据本身以及国际标准银行实务参照解读时，无须与该单据本身中的数据、其他要求的单据或信用证中的数据等同一致，但不得矛盾（《UCP600》第 14 条 d 款）"。也就是说，根据《UCP600》，单证不要求等同，如果单证或信用证中的数据没有矛盾，银行应履行付款责任。

由于《UCP600》的变化，在信用证中最好注明：该信用证系遵循《UCP600》或遵循《UCP500》。

2) Circulation of letter of credit（信用证的流通）

After signing, with the exporter, a contract agreeing to make payment by L/C, the importer requests their bank to issue a letter of credit in favor of the exporter. If the issuing bank accepts the importer's application, the opening bank issues a letter of credit and then informs its foreign branch or correspondent to advise the beneficiary (the exporter), who then examines the letter of credit. If it does not conform to the conditions specified in the sales contract, the exporter may request an amendment. If it is an irrevocable letter of credit, and they usually are, it cannot be changed unless all parties agree to the amendment.

After confirming the letter of credit, the exporter delivers the goods to the shipper, who then issues a bill of lading. Other documents, such as invoices and insurance documents, are prepared by the exporter. The next step occurs when the exporter draws a draft on the opening bank and presents it, with the letter of credit and documents, to their own bank. Usually, this bank will examine the documents and, if they are in order, pay the draft. The letter of credit and documents are sent to the opening bank. It is the bank's responsibility to examine the documents against the letter of credit issued. If discrepancies exist, they will have to be corrected, either by a new letter of credit, by new documents, or by amendments. If no discrepancies are found after careful checking, the opening bank will reimburse funds to the exporter's bank (negotiating bank) in accordance with the terms of the credit. The opening bank then presents the documents to the buyer for payment or acceptance. Documents are released to the buyer upon payment of the amount due or acceptance of the draft. With the documents, the buyer can take delivery of the goods. See Fig.11-10 for Circulation of Letter of Credit.

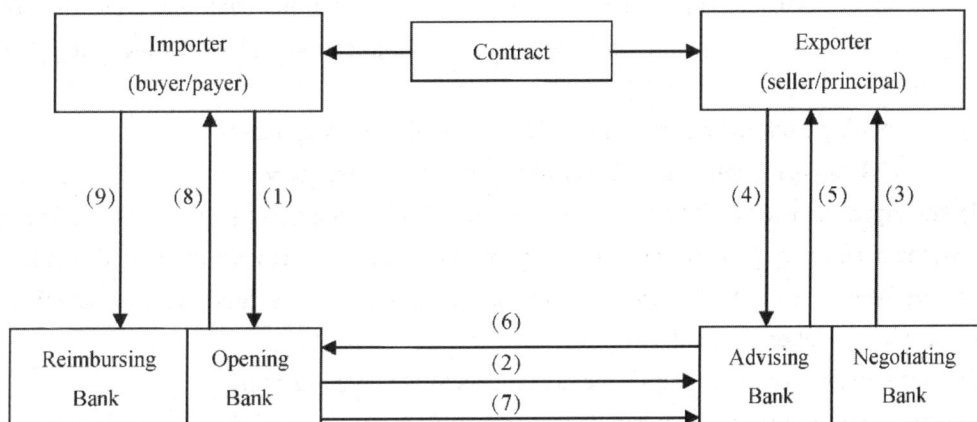

Fig.11-10　Circulation of Letter of Credit

如果买方和卖方签订合同并同意用信用证支付货款后，买方向银行申请开立信用证。如果银行同意其申请，开证行就开出信用证，然后通知其在国外的分行或代理行，让它转告信用证的受益人（即出口商）。随之受益人审查信用证的条款。如果信用证条款与销售合同中的条款不符，出口商可要求其对之修改。如果是不可撤销信用证（通常在外贸中使用的都是不可撤销信用证），那么非经有关各方同意，信用证上的条款是不能修改的。

出口商接受信用证后才把出口货物交给承运人，承运人收下货物后出具提单。其他货物单据，如商业发票和保险证明等，也由出口商办理。接着出口商开一张以开证行为付款人的汇票，连同信用证和货运单据一起交本国的银行。通常，出口方银行要审单，如单证相符，银行即凭汇票付款，再把信用证和货运单据寄给开证行。银行的责任是对照信用证的条款审单。一旦发现有不符点，则必须改正。改正的办法有：重新开立信用证、制备新单据，或者进行修改。开证行仔细核对单据无误后，按信用证条款将款项还给出口商银行（议付行）。然后，开证行向进口商出示汇票和单据要求其付款承兑，在付款人付款或承兑后将单据交给进口商，进口商便可凭单据提货。信用证的流通过程如图 11-10 所示。

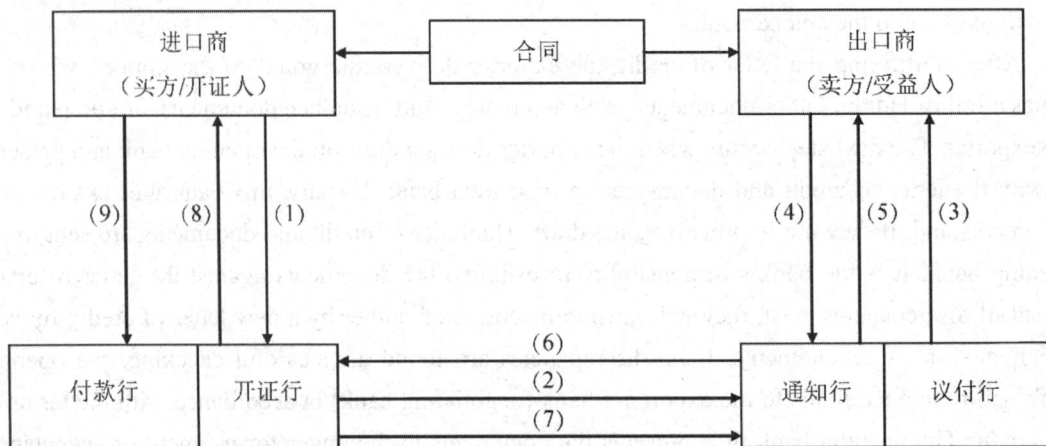

图 11-10　信用证的流通过程

Notes:

(1) The buyer makes an application for a letter of credit with his bank and signs the opening bank's agreement form. The opening bank approves the application and issues the actual letter of credit document.

(2) The opening bank forwards the letter of credit to the advising bank.

(3) The advising bank delivers the letter of credit to the beneficiary.

(4) Having examined the letter of credit, the beneficiary (seller) ships the goods to the buyer. After that, the beneficiary prepares documents, draws up a draft and presents them to his bank.

(5) The beneficiary's bank negotiates the documents and pays funds to the beneficiary in accordance with the letter of credit.

(6) The negotiating bank forwards the documents to the opening bank.

(7) The opening bank receives the documents and checks them. If the documents are in order and comply with the letter of credit, the opening bank credits the negotiating bank's account.

(8) The opening bank notifies the buyer to make payment for the documents.

(9) After making payment, the buyer receives the documents and takes delivery of the goods.

说明：

（1）进口商向当地银行（开证行）申请开立信用证，并与开证行签订协议。开证行同意其申请后开出信用证。

（2）开证行将信用证寄给通知行。

（3）通知行将信用证转递给受益人。

（4）受益人（出口商）经审核信用证认可后，即向买方发货。受益人发货后，备妥信用证规定的单据，送交当地银行议付。

（5）受益人银行（议付行）确认单据后，按照信用证规定将垫款给受益人。

（6）议付行将单据寄给开证行索款。

（7）开证行经审核单据无误后，付款给议付行。

（8）开证行通知进口人付款。

（9）进口人付款并取得货运单据后，即可提货。

3) Major Parties Involved in a Letter of Credit（信用证的当事人）

(1) The opener (buyer, applicant) applies to the bank to issue the letter of credit.

(2) The opening bank (the issuing, opening, establishing bank), which is the bank receiving the application from the applicant to issue the letter of credit and is responsible for payment. It is usually the bank at the place where the importer is located.

(3) The advising bank (notifying bank), which is the bank at the place where the exporter is located and may usually be the branch of the issuing bank or its correspondent. The advising bank hands the letter of credit to the exporter under instructions from the issuing bank. It only proves the authenticity of the letter of credit and is not responsible for anything else.

(4) The beneficiary who is empowered to use the letter of credit and is usually the exporter.

(5) The negotiating bank, which is the bank ready to pay or discount the documentary bill presented by the beneficiary under the letter of credit. The negotiating bank may be the advising bank or another appointed bank to negotiate under the letter of credit. The negotiating bank has the right of recourse against the beneficiary.

(6) The paying bank which is the bank responsible for payment mentioned in the letter of credit. It is usually the issuing bank or it may be another bank appointed by the issuing bank according to the stipulation in the letter of credit. When the paying bank makes the payment, it has no recourse against the beneficiary.

（1）开证人（买方），是指请求银行开立信用证的人。

（2）开证行，是指接受开证申请人的委托开立信用证的银行，它承担保证付款的责任。开证行一般是进口人所在地的银行。

（3）通知行，是指受开证行的委托，将信用证转交出口人的银行。它只证明信用证的真实性，并不承担其他义务。通知行一般是出口人所在地的银行，而且通常是开证行的代理行。

（4）受益人，是指信用证上所指定的有权使用该证的人，即出口人或实际供货人。

（5）议付行，是指愿意买入受益人交来的跟单汇票的银行。议付行可以是指定的银行，也可以是非指定的银行，由信用证的条款来规定。议付行对受益人有追索权。

（6）付款行，是指信用证规定的汇票付款人。它一般是开证行，也可以是它指定的另一家银行，根据信用证条款的规定决定。付款行一经付款，对受益人不得追索。

4) Types of Letter of Credit（信用证分类）

In international trade, different kinds of letter of credit are used to meet various requirements of trading and payment. According to different criteria and purposes, letters of credit may be mainly classified into the following types.

在国际贸易中，不同形式的信用证满足不同的贸易和支付需求，根据使用标准和目的，信用证主要分为如下几类。

（1）Documentary L/C and Clean L/C（跟单信用证和光票信用证）：Documentary L/C is widely used in international trade. Under a documentary L/C, the opening bank makes payment against the documentary draft or the documents alone. The documentary draft is a draft accompanied by shipping documents; these documents mean documents of title or documents certifying that the goods have been delivered, such as B/L, railway bill, air waybill and parcel receipt, etc.

Clean L/C refers to the letter of credit that requires the opening bank to make payment upon presentation of the draft without documents. When the letter of credit does not require the shipping documents, it is also called a clean letter of credit. It is often used when the letter of credit is used as pre-payment.

国际贸易中使用的信用证大多是跟单信用证，它是开证行凭跟单汇票或仅凭单据付款的信用证。跟单汇票是指附有货运单据的汇票，单据是指代表货物或证明货物已交运的单据，如提单、铁路运单、航空运单和邮包收据等。

光票信用证，是指开证行仅凭不附单据的汇票付款的信用证。有的信用证要求汇票附有非货运单据，也属光票信用证。在采用信用证方式预付货款时，通常用光票信用证。

(2) Irrevocable L/C and Revocable L/C（不可撤销信用证和可撤销信用证）：The irrevocable L/C means that once the credit is issued, it cannot be cancelled or amended before the expiry date without the agreement of the beneficiary. Under such a credit, the exporter can rely on payment being made as soon as he has shipped the goods and produced the shipping documents called for in accordance with the terms of the L/C. Because of its greater security for the exporter, it is very commonly used in international trade.

不可撤销信用证，是指信用证一经开出，在有效期内，未经受益人及有关当事人的同意，开证行不得片面修改和撤销的信用证。议付时只要受益人提供的单据符合信用证规定，开证行必须履行付款义务。这种信用证对受益人较有保障，在国际贸易中使用最为广泛。

The revocable L/C, as the name implies, can be cancelled or amended during the term of validity without notice to the beneficiary. It does not constitute a legally binding undertaking by the banks concerned. The value of this credit as security for payment is plainly doubtful, so such credit is seldom used in trading with other countries.

In UCP600, there is no revocable L/C anymore.

可撤销信用证，正如其名称所示，是指开证行对所开信用证不必征得受益人或有关当事人的同意，在议付前，有权随时修改或撤销的信用证。这种信用证对出口人的保障较少，因此在国际贸易中很少使用。

《UCP600》中可撤销信用证已经被删除。

（3）Confirmed L/C and Unconfirmed L/C（保兑信用证和不保兑信用证）：The security provided by an irrevocable credit may be further enhanced if the bank in the exporter's country(advising bank) is requested by the issuing bank to add its "confirmation", thus making it a confirmed L/C. The exporter, then, has a confirmed irrevocable L/C and is doubly guaranteed against payment by both the confirming bank and issuing bank.

If an L/C is not confirmed, it is an unconfirmed L/C, where the point of payment is the overseas issuing bank, although the advising bank would usually be prepared to negotiate the bill of exchange.

保兑信用证，是指一家银行开出的不可撤销的信用证由另一家银行加以保证兑付。在信用证上加以保兑的这家银行叫保兑行。信用证经另一家银行保兑后，对受益人来说，就取得了两家银行的付款保证。

不保兑信用证，是指未经另一家银行加具保兑的信用证，由开证行单独承担付款保证责任。

(4) Sight L/C and Usance L/C（即期信用证和远期信用证）：Sight L/C means "the L/C by draft at sight" or "L/C by sight draft". Under sight credit, the negotiating bank makes payment immediately upon the presentation of the sight draft and shipping documents as stipulated in the L/C by the seller. Similarly, when the negotiating bank delivers the sight draft and the documents to the opening bank, the latter also makes reimbursement at once.

When the seller presents a time draft together with the shipping documents stipulated in the L/C to the negotiating bank, the latter doesn't make payment immediately. It hands over the draft and the documents to the opening bank. The opening bank doesn't pay the money immediately either. It just accepts the draft and returns it to the seller. It makes payment when the time draft falls due. This kind of letter of credit is called a usance L/C.

即期信用证与"凭即期汇票付款的信用证"或"即期汇票信用证"的意思相同。当卖方按照信用证规定把即期汇票连同装船单据向议付行提示时，后者就立即付款。同样，议付行向开证行提交即期汇票和单据时，后者也应立即偿付。

当卖方向议付行提示远期汇票和信用证里规定的单据时，后者并不立即付款，而是把汇票和单据转递到开证行，开证行见票时也不立即付款，而仅仅是承兑汇票，然后，将之退还给卖方，汇票到期时开证行才付款。这种信用证就是远期信用证。

(5) Transferable and Non-transferable L/C（可转让信用证和不可转让信用证）：Transferable L/C is a credit under which the beneficiary (first beneficiary) may request the bank authorized to pay, incur a deferred payment undertaking, accept or negotiate (the transferring bank), or in the case of freely negotiable credit, the bank specifically authorized in the credit as a transferring bank, to make the credit available in whole or in part to one or more other beneficiary(-ies) (second beneficiary (-ies)). Transferable credit can only be transferred once, i.e. it can only be transferred by the first beneficiary to the second beneficiary who shall not have the right to transfer the credit to any third beneficiary. But the second beneficiary can transfer the credit back to the first beneficiary.

Non-transferable L/C is referred to as the letter of credit that the beneficiary cannot transfer the right of the letter of credit to others. If there is no "transferable", it means that this L/C is non-transferable.

可转让信用证：它是指受益人（第一受益人）可以要求授权付款、承担延期付款责任、承兑或议付的银行（转让银行）或在自由议付信用证的情况下，在信用证中特别授权的转让银行将该信用证的全部或部分转让给一个或数个受益人（第二受益人）使用。可转让信用证只能转让一次，即只能由第一受益人转让给第二受益人，第二受益人不得要求将信用证转让给其后的第三受益人。但再转让给第一受益人，不属被禁止转让的范畴。

不可转让信用证，是指受益人不能将信用证的权利转让给他人的信用证。凡信用证中未注明"可转让"者，就是不可转让信用证。

(6) Revolving L/C（循环信用证）：F-A credit is established for a certain sum and quantity of goods with a provision that, when a shipment has been made and documents presented, the credit is reinstated in its original form, and another shipment can be made until the stipulated time or total amount is reached. It is suitable for shipments in a series at intervals where the parties wish the process to proceed without interruption. By doing so, it avoids repeated opening procedures and opening limitations, thereby saving both opening charges and deposit margins.

循环信用证，是指信用证被全部或部分使用后，其金额又恢复到原金额，可再次使用，直至达到规定的次数或规定的总金额为止。循环信用证一般适用于定期分批装运、分批结汇的长期供货合同，既可避免多次开证手续上的重复及开证额度的限制，又可节省开证费用和押金。

(7) Reciprocal L/C（对开信用证）：When the two parties conclude a transaction in which they act as importers and exporters mutually and the trades are related and equal or almost-equal. The two parties open letters of credit in favor of each other. So the two L/Cs are conditioned on each other.

Features of reciprocal L/C: a. The two L/Cs must be valid simultaneously. b. The drawer and beneficiary of one L/C are usually the drawee and payer of the other L/C; c. The opening bank of one L/C is usually the advising bank of the other.

This type of L/C is often used in barter trade, compensation trade, processing trade, etc.

对开信用证：指两张信用证的开证申请人互以对方为受益人而开立的信用证。

对开信用证的特点：a. 两张信用证同时有效；b. 第一张信用证的受益人（出口人）和开证申请人（进口人）就是第二张信用证的开证申请人和受益人；c. 第一张信用证的通知行通常就是第二张信用证的开证行。

对开信用证多用于易货贸易或来料加工和补偿贸易业务。

(8) Back to back L/C（背对背信用证）：In a back to back L/C, two L/Cs are involved. One is in favor of the exporter who is not the actual supplier of goods; The other is opened by the exporter in favor of the actual supplier. It is usually used if the supplier does not want his identity known. The back to back letter of credit will show a lesser amount of the value of the goods, the difference being the profit the exporter makes. The tenor is often reduced by a few days to arrange for the substitution of invoices.

一份背对背信用证要涉及两张信用证：一张信用证的受益人是出口商，但其并不是真正的供货方；另一张信用证是出口商通过自己的往来银行开给真正的供货方，并以其为受益人。第二张信用证的金额略低，两证的金额差价就是出口商想赚的钱。两张信用证的有效期也相差若干天，目的是使出口商有充分的时间替换发票。

(9) Red Clause L/C（红条款信用证）：A red clause L/C is similar to a normal L/C except that it contains a clause(originally typed or printed in red) authorizing the negotiating bank to make clean advances to the exporter. Through this clause, the beneficiary may take advantage of the importer's credit standing. Nowadays, red clause credits are mainly used in situations where the buying company (importer) has, in the exporting country whose role is to purchase merchandise for export. To finance this purchase, the importer may arrange the opening of a red clause letter of credit.

红条款信用证与普通信用证不同的是它含有授权议付行垫付货款给出口人的条款(最初用红字打印)。通过它,受益人可利用进口人的资信情况获得好处。现在,红条款信用证主要在进口商国家有代理的情况下使用。代理人在其中起到购买出口物资的作用。进口商为提供资金往往开具红条款信用证。

(10) Standby L/C(备用信用证): It is also called the guarantee L/C, which is a guaranty issued by the opening bank on behalf of the applicant, declaring that the bank will undertake certain obligations. That's to say, the opening bank guarantees that when the applicant fails to fulfill its obligations that have to be done, the beneficiary can make a bill of exchange on the applicant according to the stipulations of the standby letter of credit, or present to the opening bank the statements or evidence papers which can certify the applicant's failure to fulfill their obligations to claim the payment.

备用信用证又称担保信用证,是指开证行根据开证申请人的请求对受益人开立的承诺承担某项义务的凭证。即开证行保证在开证申请人未能履行其应履行的义务时,受益人只要凭备用信用证的规定向开证行开具汇票(或不开汇票),并提交开证申请人未履行义务的声明或证明文件,即可取得开证行的偿付。

5) Advantages and disadvantages of L/C(使用信用证的优点和缺点)

Because under the mode of L/C, the banks promise to make payment if all the documents are in good order, both the exporter and the importer are protected. The importer has to make sure that the goods must be in strict conformity with the agreement, and the exporter is assured to be paid. The importer might be able to get better trade terms by using the L/C system, though this will be offset somewhat by the bank's charges. When he wants to open an L/C to cover his purchase from abroad, the importer may apply to his banker for an L/C for any amount. The banker usually will not ask for payment of the full amount of the L/C to be opened but will only collect a deposit, thus the importer can avoid the problem of financial shortage. In other words, the bank finances or guarantees the balance of the purchase price. As to the exporter, he knows that the goods will be paid for by the importer's bank, even if the exporter is unfamiliar with the importer's credit standing. Therefore, from what has been illustrated above, one will readily see that a banker's letter of credit for payment of the purchase is one of the most desirable payment modes.

由于使用信用证支付时,银行保证付款,所以进出口双方的利益均得到了保障。进口商能够从银行得到保证:其所订购的货物一定能符合买卖合同的规定。出口商也可以得到保证,即出口货款对方一定照付不误。此外,如果采用信用证方式付款,进口商还可以争取到较优惠的交易条件,当然,也要付出一定代价,即付给银行一定数量的业务费用。通过信用证,进口商还可以从银行那里得到资金融通的便利。当进口商想开立信用证用于支付国外的款项时,可以向其银行申请开立一定金额的信用证,而此时银行通常不要求进口商支付该信用证的全部金额,只是收取一定押金,这样一来,进口商就不会遭遇资金短缺的窘境。换句话说,开证行为货款的余额融通资金提供担保。对于出口商来说,由于有进口商银行的支付,即使对进口商的资信情况不甚了解,也不用担心付款问题。因此,银行开出的信用证是支付货款的最理想方式之一。

However, even though there are a lot of advantages to using L/C, it cannot eliminate all risks to be likely encountered by traders. This is because relevant banks deal with documents, they would make payments according to the submission of relevant documents rather than the goods themselves, there will be possibilities that importers may take risks of disputes or even suffer loss from the fraudulent acts of the exporter. The beneficiary may get payment from the bank with mock documents which are not in accordance with the physical goods, or sometimes even with documents of no goods. In addition, the wrong practice of the related personnel and importing procedures, ambiguous expressions or negligence may also bring losses or risks to the related party.

然而，尽管使用信用证有很多好处，但是信用证并不能绝对消除外贸人士可能遭遇到的所有风险。这是因为银行处理的只是单据，并非货物本身，只要提供符合要求的单证，银行就要履行付款责任。因此，进口商就有可能成为欺诈行为的受害人。受益人凭虚假的、与实际货物不相符的程序，模糊的表述或工作疏忽等都可能给有关方面带来风险和损失。

6) Attention should be paid to the following when using L/C（使用信用证时应注意的问题）

L/C removes the obstacles in international trade where importers and exporters do not trust each other, and it provides financing for both the importers and exporters. Attention should be paid to the following under payment by L/C:

(1) An L/C must bear a valid period which may be longer than the shipping period, but the shipping date should not be later than the validity date of the L/C.

(2) If validity is not stated in the L/C, the validity of the L/C shall be determined according to the shipping date.

(3) The description of commodities in the commercial invoice must correspond with that in the L/C. In all other documents, the goods may be described in general terms, provided they are not inconsistent with the description of the goods in the L/C.

(4) The words "about", "approximately", "circa" or similar expressions used in connection with the amount of the L/C, or the quantity, or the unit price stated in the credit are to be construed as allowing a difference not to exceed 10% more or less than the amount, quantity or unit price to which they refer. When the expression "on or about" or similar expressions refers to the date, it will be interpreted as a stipulation that an event is to occur during a period of five calendar days before until five calendar days after the specified date, both the start and end dates included (Article3 of UCP600).

(5) In addition to stipulating an expiry date for presentation of documents, every L/C which calls for a transport document(s) should also stipulate a specified period of time after the date of shipment during which presentation must be made in compliance with the terms and conditions of the L/C. If no such period is stipulated, banks will not accept documents presented to them later than 21 days after the date of shipment. In any event, documents must be presented not later than the expiry date of the L/C.

(6) The L/C is opened on the basis of the contract, and is independent from the contract once it is opened. The bank is only bound by and responsible for the L/C, and makes payment against documents which are fully in conformity with the L/C. L/C business is purely a business of

documents handling, under which the bank is not responsible for the goods, but only for the documents. The documents presented by the exporter must be in strict conformity with the L/C, otherwise the bank has the right to reject them.

(7) When the importer applies for credit, they should make it clear which UCP version is used, while the exporter receiving the credit, they must also read it very carefully, and pay attention to the version of the UCP. This is because when UCP600 came into force on July 1st, 2007, UCP500 did not lose efficacy automatically. If the L/C is used according to UCP500, all the terms under this credit should adhere to UCP500.

(8) In UCP600, it is stated clearly that any document mentioned in the L/C should be presented in at least one original set of copies. But in UCP500, it is not so clearly stipulated.

(9) UCP600 makes it clear that the currency used in the invoice must conform to the currency stated in the L/C.

信用证解决了进出口商人之间互不信任的矛盾，同时也为进出口商人提供了融通资金的便利。在以信用证为支付方式的情况下应注意以下几点：

（1）信用证必须有有效期，信用证的有效期可以晚于装运期，但装运期不能迟于有效期。

（2）如果信用证没有有效期，则以装运期掌握信用证的有效期。

（3）商业发票中货物的描述必须与信用证的规定相符，其他单据则可以使用货物统称，但不得与信用证规定的货物描述抵触。

（4）凡"约""大概""大约"或类似词语，用于信用证金额、数量和单价时，应解释为有关金额、数量或单价不超过10%的增减幅度。如果"在或大概在（on or about）"或类似用语用于指时间时，这一用语将被视为规定事件发生在指定日期的前后5个日历日之间，起讫日期计算在内（《UCP600》第3条）。

（5）信用证除规定一个交单到期日外，凡要求提交运输单据的信用证还须规定一个在装运日后按信用证规定必须交单的特定期限。如未规定该期限，银行将不接受迟于装运日期后21天提交的单据，但无论如何，提交单据不得迟于信用证的到期日。

（6）信用证以销售合同为基础，但一经开立则独立于销售合同。银行只受信用证的约束，只对信用证负责，只凭完全符合信用证条款的单据付款。信用证是纯单证业务，银行只管单据，不管货物。出口商提交的单据必须和信用证严格相符，否则银行可以拒付。

（7）进口商在申请开立信用证时，需注明信用证所遵循的UCP版本。同样，出口商在收到信用证后，要注意审核来证所遵循的UCP版本。因为《UCP600》于2007年7月1日生效后，《UCP500》并没有自动失效。如果信用证遵循的是《UCP500》，那么，该信用证项下所有问题依然要按照《UCP500》的规定处理。

（8）《UCP600》规定每一种单据必须至少提交一份正本，而《UCP500》中并没有十分明确的规定。

（9）《UCP600》规定发票中使用的货币必须与信用证中注明的货币一致。

7) Checks and Amendment of the L/C（审证和改证）

Once the L/C is opened, the opening bank will send the L/C either directly to the seller or to the notifying bank. Upon arrival of the L/C, the seller should check the L/C immediately. If the L/C contains unacceptable requirements, they should be rejected at once, preferably by fax, asking for amendments. Frequently, changing and unanticipated circumstances may require an L/C to be amended. The seller may, for instance, not be able to ship within a specific time limit and will require an extension. The buyer may require a large shipment due to additional demand and therefore has to increase the amount of the L/C. If the L/C is irrevocable, an amendment can be made only with the consent of all parties—the buyer, the seller and the opening bank.

信用证开立后，开证行就会将信用证直接寄给卖方或寄给通知行。卖方收到信用证后，应立即审证。如有不能接受的条款，应立即拒绝。最好用传真通知对方立即改证。常常因为情况变化或出现意想不到的情况要求改证。例如，卖方无法在信用证规定的日期内交货而要求展证；买方有可能需要增购货物，因此需增加信用证的金额。如果信用证是不可撤销的，改证须由买方、卖方、银行三方一致同意。

Sample of amendment to the L/C（改证范例）

Sales Contract

No. 91JA1002

Seller: China National Textiles Imp. & Exp. Corp., Guangzhou Branch

Buyer: Endo Trading Co. Ltd., Osaka Branch

This contract is made by and between the Buyers and the Sellers, whereby the buyers agree to buy and the Sellers agree to sell the undermentioned commodity according to the terms and conditions stipulated below:

Commodity: Men's Cotton Y/D Long Sleeve Shirts Garments Washed.

Specifications: Colors: Beige, Black, Navy Blue, Light Blue and Red equally assorted.

Size: S/4, L/4 per dozen.

Quantity: 5 000 dozen.

Unit Price: USD3.50 per pc CIFC3% Kobe/Osaka.

Total Value: USD220 500 (Say US DOLLARS TWO HUNDRED AND TWENTY THOUSAND FIVE HUNDRED ONLY).

Packing: In cartons of 50 dozen each.

Shipping Marks: At seller's option.

Insurance: To be effected by the Sellers for 110% of the invoice value against All Risks, S.R.C.C. , and War Risk as per the China Insurance Clauses of January 1st, 1981.

Time of Shipment: Not later than 25th April, 2018, with transshipment and partial shipments allowed.

Port of Shipment: China Port.

Port of Destination: Kobe/Osaka, Japan.

Terms of Payment: By irrevocable documentary sight L/C to be opened in favor of the Sellers 30 days ahead of the time of shipment.

Done and Signed in Guangzhou on 3rd of March 2018.

Endo Trading Co., Ltd.   China National Textiles

Osaka Branch   Imp. & Exp. Corp.

                                                Guangzhou Branch

(The Buyers)   (The Sellers)

....

                                                XYZ Bank

                                                Date: 20th February, 2018

To: Bank of China, Shanghai

We hereby open our Irrevocable Documentary L/C No. A50-6781-338 in favor of China National Textiles Imp. & Exp. Corp., Guangzhou Branch, for account of Endo Trading Co., Ltd., Osaka Branch up to an aggregate amount of CAD220 500 (Say CANADIAN DOLLARS TWO HUNDRED AND TWENTY THOUSAND FIVE HUNDRED ONLY), for shipment from China to Kobe/Osaka for 100% of the full invoice value covering the shipment of 500 dozen Men's Cotton Y/A Short Sleeve Shirts, Fabric Washed, as per Sales Contract No. 90Ja1002 dated March 3rd, 2018, from China.

Port: to Kobe/Tokyo

Drafts to be drawn at 45 days after sight on ourselves accompanied by the following documents marked "×" below:

(×) Signed Commercial Invoice in triplicate.

(×) Full set of Clean On Board Bills of Lading made to order, blank endorsed, marked "Freight Prepaid" and notifying the account.

(×) One Original Marine Insurance Policy or Certificate for 10% of the invoice value covering. All Risks, War Risks and TPND with claims, if any, payable in Japan in the currency of drafts. 5% more or less in quantity and invoice value is allowed.

Partial shipments are permitted.

Transshipment is prohibited.

Shipment must be made not later than 30 April, 2018.

Drafts drawn under this credit must be presented for negotiation in China on or before 16 May, 2018.

Section Three   Cross-border Payments and Process（跨境支付业务与流程）

1. Cross-border Payments（跨境支付业务）

Cross-border payment refers to the process by which Chinese consumers buy overseas products on the net with foreign merchants or foreign consumers buy Chinese products with China's dealers. Due to the different currencies, the adoption of certain settlement tools and payment systems is both required to realize the conversion of funds between two countries or regions, so as to finally complete the transaction.

通俗地讲，跨境支付就是中国消费者在网上购买国外商家产品或国外消费者购买中国商家产品时进行的支付活动。由于币种不一样，跨境支付需要通过一定的结算工具和支付系统实现两个国家或地区之间的资金转换，最终完成交易。

2. The classification of cross-border payments（跨境支付的分类）

Cross-border transfer remittance way: third-party remittance payment platforms, commercial banks, and professional companies.

Overseas offline consumption way: credit card, debit card, foreign currency cash, and RMB cash.

Cross-border network consumption way: third-party payment platform, e-bank online payment, credit card online payment, electronic remittance, mobile phone, and fixed phone payment.

跨境转账汇款途径：第三方支付平台、商业银行和专业汇款公司。

境外线下消费途径：信用卡刷卡、借记卡刷卡、外币现金和人民币现金。

跨境网络消费途径：第三方支付平台、网银线上支付、信用卡在线支付、电子汇款、移动手机支付和固定电话支付。

3. Third party cross-border payment process（第三方跨境支付流程）

Cross-border settlement methods have two types : a cross-border payment remittance method and a cross-border settlement method.

跨境电子商务的结算方式有跨境支付购汇方式和跨境收入结汇方式两种。

The foreign exchange cross-border payment business carried out by the third-party payment licensed company is mainly the bank card acquiring business, which includes two modes: offshore acquiring and foreign card acquiring.

第三方支付许可公司开展的外汇跨境支付业务主要是银行卡收单业务，包括境外收购和外国卡收购两种模式。

Among them, the overseas acquiring business of the third-party payment licensed company collects the foreign exchange payment paid by the domestic individual to the overseas website through the identity of the non-financial institution.

其中，第三方支付许可公司的海外收购业务通过非金融机构的身份将国内个人支付的外汇支付收入海外网站。

The basic process of the business is that after the domestic individual purchases the goods on the overseas website according to the displayed foreign currency quotation, the third-party pays the licensed company to pay the corresponding RMB amount, and then the third-party payment licensed company's domestic cooperative bank purchases the foreign exchange and enters the foreign exchange.

业务的基本过程是，国内个人根据显示的外币报价在海外网站上购买商品后，第三方支付许可公司支付相应的人民币金额，然后，第三方支付许可公司的国内合作银行购买外汇并进入外汇流程。

After receiving the payment success information issued by the non-financial institution, the overseas merchants will send the goods to the domestic residents by post. After receiving the goods, the domestic residents will send the clearing instructions to the third-party payment licensed company. The third-party payment licensed company remits the foreign currency payment to the overseas merchant bank settlement account through the domestic cooperative bank in accordance with the settlement agreement with the overseas merchant, and completes the cross-border settlement.

海外商家收到非金融机构发出的支付成功信息后，将货物邮寄给国内居民。收到货物后，国内居民将清算指示发送给第三方支付许可公司。第三方支付许可公司根据与境外商户的清算协议，通过境内合作银行向外国商业银行结算账户支付外币，完成跨境结算。

The foreign card acquiring business of the third-party payment licensed company is to collect the foreign exchange payment from the overseas individuals for the domestic non-financial institution on behalf of the domestic website through its status as a non-financial institution.

第三方支付许可公司的外卡收购业务旨在通过其作为非金融机构的身份，代表国内网站向海外个人收取外汇，并支付给国内非金融机构。

The business process is that after the overseas individual purchases the goods on the domestic website, the overseas payment company that cooperates with the domestic third-party payment licensed company pays the license to the domestic third-party payment company to open the foreign bank account to pay the foreign exchange payment (the payment method can be credit cards issued overseas such as Visa/MasterCard can also be T/T wire transfers).

其具体业务流程是海外个人在国内网站上购买商品后，与国内第三方支付许可公司合作的境外支付公司会向国内第三方支付公司开出支付许可，通过已开立的国外银行账户进行外汇支付（支付方式可以是 Visa/MasterCard 等海外发行的信用卡，也可以是 T/T 电汇）。

After the domestic third-party payment licensed company confirms receipt of foreign exchange payment, it notifies the domestic website to deliver the goods to overseas individuals. After receiving the goods, the overseas individual confirms and instructs the domestic third-party to pay the licensed company to transfer the payment to the domestic website. The cooperative bank of the domestic third-party payment licensed company handles the cross-border settlement of foreign exchange funds according to the instructions, and after the settlement of foreign exchange, transfers the RMB funds to the domestic website.

国内第三方支付许可证公司确认收到外汇付款后，通知国内网站将货物交付给海外个人。海外人员收到货物后，确认并指示国内第三方支付许可证公司将款项转入国内网站。国内第三方支付许可公司合作银行按照指示办理外汇资金跨境结算，结汇后，将人民币资金转入国内网站。

In the process of cross-border e-commerce, domestic consumers are accompanied by information flow in addition to commodity flow and cash flow. The details are as shown in the following eight steps.

(1) Log in to the overseas online shopping platform and purchase goods (the domestic consumers log in to the overseas website to determine the goods or services to be purchased, and place an order).

(2) Commodity information (The external e-commerce sends the consumer's order, i.e. the merchandise message, to the third-party payment).

(3) Obtain a certification letter (The third-party payment obtains the domestic consumer certification information).

(4) Enter the authentication information, select the RMB payment method, and confirm the payment (the domestic consumer inputs information and chooses the payment method).

(5) Payment information (The third-party payment sends payment information to the custodian bank).

(6) Purchasing payment information (Receives the purchase remittance information from the custodian bank).

(7) Purchasing payment information (The foreign e-commerce receives the purchase remittance information paid by the third-party).

(8) Sending goods (send products and related services to domestic consumers).

在跨境电子商务中，境内消费者在境外购物过程除了商品流和现金流，还伴随着信息流。具体如以下 8 个步骤所示。

（1）登陆境外网购平台、选购商品（境内消费者登录境外网站确定要购买的商品或服务，并下订单）。

（2）商品信息（境外电商将消费者的订单，即商品消息发送给第三方支付）。

（3）获取认证信息（第三方支付获取境内消费者认证信息）。

（4）输入认证信息，选择人民币支付方式，确认支付（境内消费者输入信息并选择支付方式）。

（5）支付信息（第三方支付将支付信息发给托管银行）。

（6）购汇付款信息（接收托管银行的购汇付款信息）。

（7）购汇付款信息（境外电商收到第三方支付的购汇付款信息）。

（8）发送货物（向境内消费者发送产品和有关服务）。

The new e-commerce law stipulates that e-commerce parties can agree to pay the payment by electronic payment. Electronic payment service providers offer electronic payment services for e-commerce. They should abide by national regulations and inform users of the functions, usage methods, precautions, related risks and charging standards of electronic payment services, and attaching unreasonable trading conditions is prohibited. Prior to issuing the payment instruction, the user should check the complete information such as the amount and payee included in the payment instruction. After the electronic payment service provider completes the electronic payment, it shall promptly and accurately provide the user with the information confirming the payment in accordance with the agreed manner.

新的电子商务法规定，电子商务当事人可以约定采用电子支付方式支付价款。电子支付服务提供者为电子商务提供电子支付服务，应当遵守国家规定，告知用户电子支付服务的功能、使用方法、注意事项、相关风险和收费标准等事项，不得附加不合理交易条件。用户在发出支付指令前，应当核对支付指令所包含的金额、收款人等完整信息。电子支付服务提供者完成电子支付后，应当及时准确地向用户提供符合约定方式的确认支付的信息。

4. Payment methods for digital trade（数字贸易的支付方式）

There are various payment methods for digital trade, which not only facilitate the transaction process but also promote the rapid development of digital trade. The following is a brief introduction to several main payment methods in digital trade:

数字贸易的支付方式多种多样，这些支付方式不仅可以提高交易过程的便捷度，还大力推动了数字贸易的快速发展。以下是对数字贸易中几种主要支付方式的简介。

1) Bank transfer（银行转账）

Digital trade also uses traditional payment methods such as bank transfers because the transaction funds transferred by banks are all circulated through the banking system, which has the characteristic of high security, but its speed is relatively slow, especially in cross-border e-commerce transactions, which may take several days to arrive. In addition, the transaction fees for bank transfers are relatively high, especially for cross-border wire transfers and cross-border e-commerce transactions, which generally require payment of intermediary transaction fees.

数字贸易也使用银行转账这种传统的支付方式，因为，银行转账的交易资金都是通过银行系统进行流转，具有安全性高的特点，但其速度相对较慢，特别是在跨境电商交易中，可能需要几天时间才能到账。此外，银行转账的手续费也相对较高，尤其是跨境电商交易中的跨境电汇，一般需要支付中转行的手续费。

2) Credit cards （信用卡）

Credit cards are one of the most common and widespread payment methods in digital trade, especially in cross-border e-commerce, especially in the European and American cross-border e-commerce markets. Due to their high acceptance in Europe and America, credit cards have a very high popularity rate. Moreover, global credit card brands can generally be used around the world. On the other hand, for sellers, credit card payments also have certain limitations, such as higher transaction fees and security risks.

信用卡是数字贸易特别是跨境电商贸易中最普遍、最常见的支付方式之一，尤其在欧美跨境电商市场，信用卡由于欧美的接受度高而使得其普及率极高。而且，全球化的信用卡品牌一般可以在全球各地使用，另一方面，对卖家而言，信用卡支付也存在一定的局限，比如较高的手续费和安全支付风险。

3) Digital payment platform（数字支付平台）

A digital payment platform is a digital payment tool specifically designed for digital trade activities, which is equipped with a global payment network technologically and can help digital trade sellers receive payments from around the world. Digital payment platforms are also widely used in emerging sectors such as cross-border e-commerce, supporting multiple payment methods including credit cards, electronic wallets, bank transfers, etc. In addition, digital payment platforms also provide functions such as funds settlement and withdrawal, offering integrated payment solutions for digital trade activities.

数字支付平台是专门针对数字贸易活动而设计的数字化支付工具，其在技术上具备全球化支付网络，因此能够帮助数字贸易卖家接收来自世界各地的付款。数字支付平台也被广泛运用到跨境电子商务等新业态中，支持多种支付方式，包含信用卡、电子钱包、银行转账等。此外，数字支付平台还提供了资金结算和提现等功能，为数字贸易活动提供了集成化的支付解决方案。

Part B Terminology Practice

1. **First of Exchange**（汇票的第一联）: The first copy of a bill of exchange.

2. **Second of Exchange**（汇票的第二联）：The second copy of a bill of exchange.

3. **Negotiable**（可转让的）：Transferable or assignable, when applied to a draft or a check, means that the value it represents can be transferred to another party, if it is endorsed by the drawer.

4. **Accepted**（承兑）：A draft is said to be accepted when the drawee signs their names on it, with the word "accepted", thus undertaking to pay the value of the draft to the drawer at a specified future date.

5. **On demand**（即期付款）：Payable as soon as a request for payment is made; a sight draft is payable on demand, and is also called a demand draft.

6. **Honored**（兑现）：A bill of exchange is said to be honored when it is paid at maturity, that is, when it is due to be paid.

7. **Maturity**（到期日）：The date when a draft is due to be paid.

8. **Notary Public**（公证员）：A legal officer whose office is of great antiquity; their chief function is the certifying of documents.

9. **Noted**（拒付注记）：A bill of exchange is said to be noted when a Notary Public inscribes on it a note to the effect that it has been dishonored at maturity, that is, that the drawee has failed to make payment against the draft when it fell due.

10. **Protest**（拒付证书）：A declaration by a Notary Public that payment or acceptance of a draft has been demanded, but refused by the drawee.

11. **Endorsed**（背书）：A draft, like a check, may be endorsed by the drawee; this amounts to a declaration that the amount payable against the draft will be received by another party, to whom the draft is given. The endorsement is usually a signature on the back of the document.

12. **Discount**（贴现）：A percentage deduction made for cash payment, e.g. against a draft before its maturity.

13. **Letter of hypothecation**（质押书）：A document giving a lien on goods in return for a cash advance.

14. **Dishonored**（拒付）：A draft is said to be dishonored when the drawee refuses to pay the amount due or to accept the draft.

15. **Presentation**（提示）：The collecting bank or the holder of a draft shows and hands it over to the drawee for acceptance or payment.

16. **Document against payment**（付款交单）：Payment terms under which a buyer receives title to a consignment against immediate payment, usually under a sight draft.

17. **Document against acceptance**（承兑交单）：Payment terms under which a buyer receives title to a consignment on undertaking to make payment at a future date by accepting a draft.

18. **Confirming bank**（保兑行）：The bank that guarantees payment under a confirmed letter of credit.

19. **Default**（违约）：To fail to meet a legal obligation, such as making the payment due under a contract or against a draft.

20. **Cash in advance**（预付货款）：Payment for goods in which the price is paid in full before shipment is made. This method is usually used only for small purchases or when the goods are built.

21. **Cash on delivery**（货到付款）：The buyer must pay for the goods when they are delivered

to him.

22. **Guaranteed payment**（保证付款）：A room set aside by the hotel, at the request of the customer, in advance of the guest's arrival. Payment for the room is guaranteed and will be paid unless an appropriate cancellation is made. The company or organization should receive a cancellation code or the name of the person accepting the cancellation from the hotel.

23. **Line Haul**（干线运输费）：The charge, based on the weight for the number of miles transported, is called the line haul.

24. **Financing**（融资）：Loan from banking services contractor for money to purchase equipment or other high priced items.

25. **Expedited service**（加急服务）：A program which, for an additional charge, allows a specific delivery date to be requested. If the date is not met, only standard charges will apply.

Part C Terms

1. applicant 开证申请人
2. beneficiary 受益人
3. opening/issuing bank 开证行
4. advising/notifying bank 通知行
5. negotiating bank 议付行
6. payment/drawee bank 付款行
7. open a credit 开立信用证
8. amend a credit 修改信用证
9. booking note 订舱单
10. shipping space 舱位
11. dead freight 空舱费
12. the freight agent 承运人
13. settle an account 清算
14. remit, send money 汇款
15. deferred payment 延期付款
16. payment in advance 预付货款
17. pay by installments 分期付款
18. cash payment 现金付款
19. deferred payment 延期付款
20. down payment 付款订金
21. extension of payment 延长付款
22. full payment 全额付款
23. non-payment 不付款
24. partial payment 部分付款
25. payment in kind 分类付款
26. payment in account 账面付款
27. account receivable 应收账
28. cash account 现金账
29. credit account 贷方账
30. D/P sight 即期付款
31. D/P after sight 远期付款
32. trust receipt 信托收据
33. discount a bill 贴现期票
34. margin 押金

Part D Exercise

I. Please determine whether the following statements are True or False. Then put T for True or F for False in the bracket at the end of each statement.

1. In international trade, it is always necessary for the seller to urge the buyer to open the covering L/C in good time. (   )

2. When the buyer fails to issue the covering L/C within the specified time of the contract, the

seller holds the right of declaring the contract avoided. (　　)

3. When the contract requires payments to be effected in US dollars, the relevant L/C may choose to effect payment in RMB. (　　)

4. If the L/C prohibits partial shipments and the goods are shipped in full quantity with the price not reduced, a short drawing of 5 percent of the amount is permissible. (　　)

5. Regarding quantity, the seller may still have the right to deliver 5 percent more or less. (　　)

6. According to the UCP500, a freely negotiable credit must stipulate a place for presentation of documents for negotiation. (　　)

7. According to Article 20 of the UCP600, when the shipment date and the expiry date of the L/C are August 30th and September 15th respectively, the beneficiary may present the documents between September 16th and 20th because these dates have not exceeded a period of 21 days.(　　)

8. When the goods are posted, the latest date of shipment refers to the date of Post Receipt. (　　)

9. If the Issuing Bank appoints the Bank of China as its Advising Bank of L/C, then the Issuing Bank may ask the Bank of Asia to advise amendments to the L/C. (　　)

10. The Beneficiary of a L/C may indicate his acceptance or rejection of the amendments when he presents the relevant documents. (　　)

11. In our country, goods for export must go through customs clearance. (　　)

12. When exporting goods on CFR, CPT or FOB terms, the seller must pay the insurance premium. (　　)

13. According to UCP600, if documents are in correspondence with L/C's stipulations, discrepancies between the documents themselves are allowed. (　　)

14. Banks will refuse to pay if the documents which are not required by the L/C are presented to them. (　　)

15. When documents are presented to the Opening Bank, they shall be examined carefully within one month. (　　)

16. As an L/C beneficiary, the buyer must act on any suggestions written in the L/C even if they are not documents. (　　)

17. If an L/C stipulates some conditions but does not require the related documents, the banks may disregard them as not stated. (　　)

18. According to the UCP500, Commercial Invoice must be issued by the beneficiary named in the L/C. (　　)

19. The beneficiary of an L/C may choose to present one copy of the Insurance Policy if it has more than one original copy. (　　)

20. A Certificate of Origin can be used only to prove the time when the export commodities were produced. (　　)

II. In each blank space, write a word that fits naturally.

1. An air waybill is a rec_____an evidence of cent_____, but not a tit_____ document. It is therefore not trans_____or neg_____and a shipper does not lose his ownership of the cargo by handing the air waybill _____the airline.

A shipper can present his copy to exercise his "right of dis_____" to stop the goods at any point of journey,to have the goods del_____to a different consignee, or to have the shipment returned, pr_____that the shipper does not exercise this right in such a way as to prejudice the carrier or other consignors and repays any ex_____occasioned by the exercise of this right.

2. The most generally used_____of payment in the_____trade is the_____of credit. It is_____for individual transactions or_____a series, makes_____with unknown buyers easy and_____protection for both seller and buyer. The process of establishing an L/C_____with the buyer. He instructs his bank to_____an L/C for the_____of the purchase_____in favor of the seller. The_____contain full details of the_____as agreed upon between the buyer and the seller. The buyer's bank_____the L/C to its_____in the seller's country. _____receiving the L/C, the_____advises the seller of the arrival of the_____. In foreign trade it is_____for the correspondent to_____the credit. This means that the correspondent_____to pay the seller the money_____to him, provided the conditions set_____in the L/C have been complied_____. The seller can now execute the buyer's order, _____that when he has done so, the_____will be paid at once by the correspondent. The buyer is equally_____, because the correspondent will pay on his _____only if the conditions of the transaction are fully _____ _____ by the seller.

III. Payment and acknowledgement.

A. Read the bill of exchange below and answer questions.

TWO COPIES

No. 80W5069-2   Date: 4th Dec., 2005

EXCHANGE FOR   USD63 162.00

At 90 DAYS sight of this FIRST OF EXCHANGE (Second of the same tenor and date unpaid) pay to the order of OURSELVES the sum of _____Value received Drawn under L/C No. 314955B OF 1st AUG. 2005 ISSUED BY YOURSELVES.

TO HORNER   HENAN NATIVE PRODUCE & ANIMAL

    TRUST CO.   BY-PRODUCTS IMP. & EXP. CO.

    PITTSBURG

                                ———————————————

                                  MANAGER

Questions:

1. Who are the drawer and drawee?

2. On which day was the draft drawn?

3. Is the bill in sole (one copy) or two?

4. How much money is involved?

5. This bill only shows the sum of money is figures. Can you write out the same amount in words? Where do you write it?

6. In a bill of exchange, the places of the sender and the receiver are fixed. Where are they respectively?

7. How long is this bill valid?

8. According to the bill, what is the mode of payment used?

9. What do the following abbreviations stand for? USD_____ No._____ L/C_____ CO._____

B. Figures and words.

Checks, bills and receipts often contain sums of money in two forms: figures and words. Spell out the following figures.

1. £ 100.00

2. USD89.50

3. ￥868 000.00

4. STG234 4s 3p

5. Euro590.00

IV. Read the following letters regarding payment terms. Identify the writer, the term proposed and the reason given. Then fill in the Information Form.

1. Thank you for S/C No.336 covering our order for your computers valued USD 988.00. As this deal is of a value of less than USD1 000.00, we shall be glad if you agree to ship the goods to us as before on Cash Against Documents basis.

2. We used to deal with you on sight draft basis. Now, we would like to propose a different way of payment, i.e. When the goods ordered by us are ready for shipment and the freight space is booked, you cable us and we will remit you the full amount by T/T. The reasons are that we can thus assure our customers of the time of delivery and save a lot of expenses on opening the L/C.

3. Thank you for your order of September 1st. We regret being unable to ship the goods to you on COD terms. Since our terms are always cash in advance. (We have no facilities for COD shipment.) We are ready to ship your order on receipt of your remittance for USD5 000.

4. In order to pave the way for your pushing the sales of our products in your market we agree to payment for this transaction under D/A terms as a special accommodation.

5. As to the modes of payment, we usually adopt confirmed, irrevocable letters of credit payable by draft at sight. However, in order to expand business, we will, as an exceptional case, accept payment for your trial order on D/P basis, provided the amount involved is less than USD2 000. In other words, we will draw on you by documentary draft at sight, through our bank, on collection basis.

6. We are very interested in your automatic blankets, for which we believe there is a good market. As we can't count on regular sales, we don't feel able to make purchase on our account. We therefore suggest you send us the goods on a consignment basis. That means we would settle accounts for sales every month and send you the payment due after deducting expenses, and commission at a rate to be agreed.

Information From

Letter No.	Buyer/Seller	Term Proposed	Reason
1			
2			
3			
4			
5			
6			

V. Identify the problems and complete the letters by suggesting a solution.

1. Thank you for your L/C.

It seems that the amount in your L/C is insufficient, as the correct total CIF value of your order comes to USD6 600, instead of 6 000. Would you kindly _____?

Problem:_____ .

2. After checking, we find that the currency used for the unit price and the total amount is not in conformity with that stated in our S/C. In your L/C the currency of payment is HKD while our contract demands USD. In view of the above, we would ask you to _____.

Problem:_____ .

3. According to the L/C we received, the payment was to be made at 120 days. But we want it to be made at sight, which was agreed upon by you in your order sheet. We should be obliged if you will _____ .

Problem: _____ .

4. We are pleased to receive your L/C No. 6689, but find that transshipment is not allowed.

As there is no direct steamer to your port at the moment, we have to ship your goods via Kobe. Otherwise, you will have to wait until the whole season before direct shipment between our ports resumes. Therefore we would like to ask you to _____ .

Problem: _____ .

VI. Read the following bill of exchange carefully, and then fill in the blanks.

Bill of Exchange

凭

Drawn under　　　Sakura Bank, Ltd., (FORMERLY MITSUI

TAIYO KOBE) TOKYO

信用证　　　　第　　　　　号

L/C　　　　　No. 201009301111

日期　　　　　年　　　　　月　　　　　日

Dated　　　　Sept. 30, 2010

按　　　　　　息　　　　　　　　付款

Payable with interest @ ....% per annum

号码　　　　　汇票金额　　　　中国　　广州　　年　月　日

No.........................Exchange for USD 24 560.00 Guangzhou, China ......20..........
见票   日后（本汇票之副本未付）   付
At...******...sight   of this FIRST of exchange (Second of exchange being unpaid) pay
to the order of ....或其指定人
金额 US DOLLARS TWENTY-FOUR THOUSAND FIVE HUNDRED AND SIXTY ONLY
the sum of
此致

　　　To <u>SAKURA BANK, LTD., (FORMERLY</u>　　　GUANGZHOU MACHINERY
　　　　　<u>MITSUI TAIYO KOBE) TOKYO</u>　　　IMP. & EXP. CORP., (GROUP)

(1) The name of the issuing bank_____
(2) The number of the credit_____
(3) The opening date of the credit_____
(4) The amount and currency of the credit _____
(5) Draft deadline _____
(6) Payee_____
(7) Drawee _____
(8) Drawer _____

VII. Make out the bill of exchange according to the information you have got from the particulars.

广州广发玩具进出口公司向美国太平洋有限公司出口玩具 3 000 件，每件 20 美元 CIF 纽约，纽约银行于 2009 年 6 月 10 日开出不可撤销即期信用证，该证号码：10-20090611-1，广州广发玩具进出口公司于 2009 年 7 月 5 日装运。请补充如下汇票。

凭　　　　　...
Drawn under　...
信用证　　　第　　　　　号
L/C　　　　...
日期　　　　年　　　　月　　　　日
Dated　　　...
按　　　　　息　　　　　付款
Payable with interest @ ....% per annum
号码　　　　汇票金额　　　中国　　广州　　年　月　日
No.........................Exchange for ...., China ......20..........
见票　　　　　　　　　　　日后（本汇票之副本未付）　　付
At...............sight   of this FIRST of exchange (Second of exchange being unpaid) pay
  to the order of ....或其指定人
金额
the sum of
此致
To

VIII. Give the right settlement method in the form according to the information you have got.

序　号	信　息　资　料	结 算 方 式
1	（1）出口的货物是库存的服装商品，且国内没有市场	
	（2）进口商是我方的长期客户，有着良好的商业信誉	
2	（1）出口的货物是为欧盟研制的新产品，首次打入该市场，不知前景如何	
	（2）为了获取更多的市场信息，改进新产品，提升品牌	
	（3）进口商是我方多年的客户，有着良好的商业信誉	
3	（1）出口的货物是一般的电器产品，在该国有一定的市场占有率	
	（2）该进口商是我方新的客户，商业信誉程度不知	
4	（1）出口的货物是一般的农作物产品，长期出口该国，具有较大的市场占有率	
	（2）该进口商是我方多年的客户，商业信誉较好	
	（3）该国最近经济状况不太好，政局有所动荡	

IX. Case Study.

1. Mr. Smith, an American businessman, sold a batch of IBM computers to a Hong Kong importer, Mr. Chen. The sales contract was concluded in the United States of America on the terms of CIF Hong Kong. During execution of this contract, disputes arose between the seller and the buyer on the form and interpretation of the contract.

Question: In such a case, did the law of the USA or the law of Hong Kong apply to the disputes? Why?

2. A Chinese export company sold 25 metric tons of Donkey Meat to a Japanese client. As stipulated in the contract, the goods were to be packed in 1 500 boxes with a net weight of 16.6 kilograms per box. If the goods were packed according to stipulations, the total weight was 24.9 metric tons, the remaining 100 kilograms might not be delivered. When the goods arrived at the Japanese port, the Japanese Customs Officers checked them and found that each box contained 20 kilograms, not 16.6 kilograms. Therefore, this shipment amounted to 30 metric tons. However, the goods totaled 24.9 MT in weight on all the documents, and the payment was also effected against 24.9 MT. Thus 5 100 kilograms of Donkey Meat were free of charge. Worst of all, because of the discrepancy between the net weight on the documents and the actual weight, Japanese Customs thought the export company helped its client to evade duties.

Question: How does the exporter deal with this issue? What lessons can the exporter draw from this case?

3. China's C Foreign Trade Company and the United States' U Company have reached an export contract for digital electronic pens in 2024. The letter of credit stipulates that the quantity will be 10 metric tons, to be shipped in batches from July to November 2024, with 2 metric tons per month. The buyer will load 2 metric tons per month from July to September 2024, and the bank has made payments in installments based on vouchers. The fourth batch of digital electronic pens was originally scheduled to be shipped for export on October 26, 2024, but due to various reasons, the shipment was delayed until November 3, 2024. The fifth batch of 2 metric tons of digital electronic pens was shipped

on November 13, 2024. When the beneficiary presents the bill of lading to the bank for negotiation of the fourth and fifth batches of payment, all payments are refused by the bank.

Question: Can the bank refuse payment in the above situation? Why?

4. Guangdong Foreign Trade Company CM and B Company in the UK have reached a deal to export RP-brand fashionable clothing in 2024. The letter of credit stipulates a quantity of 9 metric tons, to be shipped in batches from June to November in 2024, with 1.5 metric tons of RP-brand fashionable clothing to be shipped per month. Company CM will load 1.5 metric tons per month from June to October, and the bank has made payments in batches with vouchers. The fourth batch of RP-brand fashionable clothing was originally scheduled to be shipped for export on November 30th, but due to the landfall of a typhoon in Guangdong, the shipment of the fourth batch of RP-brand fashionable clothing was delayed until December 2nd. When the foreign trade company CM presented the bill of lading to the bank for negotiation, it was refused payment by the bank. Later, the foreign trade company CM requested payment from the bank on the grounds of force majeure, but was also refused by the bank.

Question: Does the bank have the right to refuse payment in the above situation? Is the requirement of CM for foreign trade companies reasonable? Why?

Chapter Twelve

Part A Text

Disputes, Claim and Arbitration

Disputes arise in international trade for many reasons. For instance, a buyer may breach a contract by wrongfully refusing to accept goods or failing to pay for the goods when payment is due. A seller may violate a contract by failing to make an agreed delivery, delivering goods that do not conform to the contract, etc. Usually a claim will be made, after the disputes, by the injured party against the other party.

国际贸易当中，常常由于这样或那样的原因而引起争议，如买方违反合同无理拒绝接受货物，或者在付款期限到期后拒绝支付货款；而卖方没有交付协定的货物，或者所交货物与合同规定不符等。往往在争议发生后合同受损害的一方要向另一方提出索赔。

The disputes involved in digital trade refer to the disputes or conflicts between trading parties caused by various reasons during the process of digital trade. This type of digital trade dispute can be classified into the following categories.

(1) Product quality disputes: In digital trade, due to the differences between online and offline, consumers may receive actual products that do not match the description on the digital platform, or there may be certain quality issues, which can lead to product quality disputes.

(2) Logistics delivery disputes: Due to the complexity, distance, and uncertainty of cross-border logistics in digital trade, cross-border goods may be lost, damaged, or delayed during transportation or regional distribution, leading to disputes between buyers and sellers.

(3) Payment disputes: There may be issues in the payment process of digital trade, such as payment failures, digital telecommunications fraud, etc., which can lead to disputes between buyers and sellers.

(4) After-sales service disputes: Consumers may need after-sales service, such as returns, exchanges, and after-sales repairs, after purchasing goods on digital trading platforms. If the after-sales service is not in place or does not meet consumer expectations, it may also lead to disputes in digital trade after-sales service.

数字贸易中所涉及的纠纷是指在数字贸易过程中，因各种原因所导致的交易双方之间的争议或冲突。这类数字贸易纠纷按照类型划分基本包括以下几类。

（1）商品质量纠纷：数字贸易中，由于线上线下的差异性，消费者可能收到的实际商品与数字平台描述的不符，或者存在某些质量问题，从而引发商品质量纠纷。

（2）物流配送纠纷：由于数字贸易中跨境物流的复杂性、远距离性和不确定性，跨境商品可能在运输过程中或地区配送过程中出现丢失、损坏或延误，导致交易双方产生纠纷。

（3）支付问题纠纷：数字贸易中的支付环节可能出现问题，比如支付失败、数字电信欺诈等，这些问题可能引发交易双方的纠纷。

（4）售后服务纠纷：消费者在数字贸易平台上购买商品后，可能需要售后服务，比如退、换货，售后维修等。如果售后服务不到位或不符合消费者期望，也可能引发数字贸易售后服务纠纷。

Section One　Disputes and Claim（纠纷和索赔）

As the previous units indicate, in order to avoid disputes or properly handle their consequences, some preventive clauses are usually included in a contract such as tolerance clause, more or less clause, commodity inspection clause, etc. In foreign trade, attention should also be paid to the matters of claim, force majeure, arbitration, etc. It is necessary that they be clearly stipulated in the sales contract.

正如前几单元所述，为预防争议或妥善处理其后果，合同中通常被纳入预防性条款，例如公差条款、溢短装条款、商品检验条款等。在外贸实务中，还应特别关注索赔事项、不可抗力情形、仲裁程序等事宜。这些内容有必要在销售合同中明确规定。

1．Breach of contract（违约）

Breach of contract means the refusal or failure by a party to a contract to fulfill an obligation imposed on him under that contract, resulting from repudiation of liability before completion, or conduct preventing proper performance, ect.

In foreign trade, it is ideal that the seller delivers the goods conforming to the contract in respect of quality, specifications, quantity and packing, and hands over the documents concerning the goods at the right time and place stipulated in the contract. And the buyer makes payment for the goods and takes delivery of them in the same manner specified in the contract. However, there always exists a gap between ideal and reality. Complaints or claims, sometimes, still arise in spite of well-planned and careful work in the performance of a contract. In practice, it is not infrequent that the exporter or the importer neglects or fails to perform any of his obligations, thus giving rise to breach of contract and various trade disputes, which, subsequently, lead to claim, arbitration, or even litigation.

违反合同的意思是合同的一方拒绝或未能完成合同中所规定的义务,造成合同完成前拒绝其责任，阻止正常的合同履行，等等。

在对外贸易中，如果卖方能按合同所规定的品质、规格、数量和包装交货，并能按规定的时间和地点提交与货物有关的单据，而买方也能按照合同的规定支付货款和提取货物的话，那就是最为理想的。然而，理想和现实之间总是存在一些差距。在履行合同的过程中，虽然计划周密，小心谨慎，但抱怨或索赔仍时有发生。在实践中经常会发生出口商和进口商忽略或不能履行其义务的情况，由此会产生违反合同和各种各样的贸易纠纷的事情发生，进而还会导致索赔、仲裁甚至诉讼。

1) Breach by the seller（卖方违约）

A seller may breach a contract as follows:

(1) By failing to make delivery according to the shipment date stated in the contract.

(2) By failing to deliver the goods.

(3) By delivering the goods that do not conform with the contract or the L/C in respect of quality, specifications, quantity and packing, etc.

(4) By presenting shipping documents that are incomplete and inadequate.

卖方可能违约的情况有：

（1）卖方不按合同规定的交货期交货。

（2）不交货。

（3）所交货物的品质、规格、数量、包装等与合同或信用证规定不符。

（4）所提供的货运单据种类不齐、份数不足等。

2) Breach by the buyer（买方违约）

A buyer may breach a contract where, under an L/C, he fails to open the relevant L/C according to the stipulated period; where he wrongly refuses to accept the goods; or where, under FOB, he fails to dispatch the vessel according to the stipulations of the contract.

买方违约的情况有：在信用证支付条件下，不按期开证或不开证；无理拒收货物；在 FOB 条件下，不按合同规定派船；等等。

3) Both parties are responsible（买卖双方均负有责任）

Both parties may be responsible due to misunderstanding or miscomprehension of the contract that has not been clearly stipulated; or due to breach of the contract by both parties. Breach of a contract occurs where any party to a contract does not follow the stipulations of the contract. The sales contract shall have a legally binding force upon the contracting parties. Any party who has violated the contract shall be legally held responsible for the breach, and the injured party is entitled to remedies according to the stipulations of the contract or the relevant laws.

例如，因合同条款规定不明确，致使双方理解或解释不统一而引起纠纷，或双方均有违约行为，等等。违约是买卖双方中的任何一方违反合同规定义务的行为。买卖合同对缔约方均具有法律约束力。任何一方违约都应该承担违约的法律责任，而受害方则有权根据合同或有关法律规定得到补救。

2．Disputes（争议）

In international trade, disputes often arise between the two parties when one party thinks that the other fails to carry out the duties stipulated in the contract wholly or partially, which very likely leads to claims, arbitration and legal action. There are many reasons for disputes, but the main reasons are the following three.

(1) Seller's breach of contract. For example, incomplete performance of delivering according to the quality, quantity, and packaging specified in the contract; failure to deliver on time or refusal to deliver; types of delivery documents provided are incomplete, the number of copies is insufficient, and there is a delay in delivery.

(2) Non-performance or incomplete performance of the contract is caused by the buyer. For instance, the buyer does not dispatch a vessel to carry the goods or does not name the carrier in time, or does not open an L/C in time or rejects the goods unreasonably.

(3) Stipulations of the contract are unclear, such as "prompt shipment", "quantity about 10 000 MT", "destination European main ports", etc., which may bring about different interpretations.

在国际贸易中，争议是指交易的一方认为另一方未能部分或全部履行合同所规定的责任与义务而引起的纠纷。争议很可能引起诉讼、仲裁或法律行为。导致争议产生的原因很多，一般可归纳为以下三种情况。

（1）卖方违约。例如，不按合同规定的品质、数量、包装交货；不按期交货或拒不交货；所提供的交货单据种类不齐、份数不足，延迟交货；等等。

（2）买方违约。例如，未能及时安排货船装货，或未及时通知货船船名，未按时开出信用证或拒不开证；无理拒收货物；等等。

（3）合同规定欠明确。例如，采用"立即装运""大约1万公吨""欧洲主要港口"之类的规定方法，造成双方对合同条款的理解和解释不一致，以致产生争议。

3. Claim（索赔）

Claim means that in international trade, one party breaks the contract and causes losses to the other party directly or indirectly, the party suffering the losses may ask for compensation for the losses. In some contracts, the two parties often stipulate clauses on settlement of claim as well as inspection and claim clauses.

In case the sellers are liable for the non-conformity of the goods with the contract and a claim is made by the buyers within the period of claim or the period of quality guarantee stipulated in the contract, the sellers may settle the claim upon the agreement of the buyers in the following ways.

(1) Agree to the rejection of the goods and refund to the buyers the value of the rejected goods in the same currency as contracted herein, and bear all direct losses and expenses incurred from the rejection, including interest, banking charges, freight, insurance premium, inspection charges, storage charges and all other necessary expenses required for the custody and protection of the rejected goods.

(2) Devalue the goods according to the degree of inferiority, extent of damage and amount of losses suffered by the buyers.

(3) Replace the defective goods with new ones which conform to the specification, quality and performance as stipulated in the contract, and bear all expenses incurred and direct losses sustained by the buyers. The sellers shall, at the same time, guarantee the quality of the replaced goods for a further agreed period.

所谓索赔，是指在国际贸易中，争议发生后，遭受损害的一方向违约方提出赔偿的要求。买卖双方通常都会在合同中写明索赔的办法以及有关商检和索赔的条款。

如果货物与合同中规定的货物不符，买方可在合同中规定的时间内或合同中的品质保证期限内向卖方提出索赔。卖方可以按照下列方法解决买方的索赔问题。

（1）同意买方拒收货物，并按合同规定退还买方货款，承担因此而遭受的一切损失，包括利率、银行费用、运费、保险费、商检费、保管费以及其他所有因此而产生的费用。

（2）根据货物的质量好坏程度、损坏的程度和买方遭受的损失大小降价处理货物。

（3）按照合同规格、品质和履行合同的要求重新更换货物，承担因此而引起的全部费用，以及买方因此而遭受的一切损失。同样，卖方要保证更换货物的质量。

Example of claim:

In case of quality discrepancy, claims should be filed by the Buyer within 30 days after the arrival of the goods at the port of destination, while for quantity discrepancy, claims should be filed by the Buyer within 15 days after the arrival of the goods at the port of destination. In all cases, claims must be accompanied by survey reports of recognized public surveyors agreed to by the Seller. If the goods have already been processed, the buyer shall thereupon lose the right to claim. Should the responsibility of the subject under claim be found to rest on the part of the seller, the seller should, within 20 days after receipt of the claim, send their reply to the buyer together with suggestions for settlement.

索赔条款实例：

品质异议须于货到目的港之日起 30 天内由买方提出，而数量异议须于货到目的港之日起 15 天内由买方提出，并均须提供经卖方同意的公证行的检验证明。如果货物已经过加工，买方即丧失索赔权利。如责任属于卖方，卖方收到异议 20 天内答复买方并提出处理意见。

Should the seller fail to make delivery on time as stipulated in the contract, the buyer shall agree to postpone the delivery on the condition that the seller agrees to pay a penalty which shall be deducted by the paying bank from the payment under negotiation, or by the buyer directly at the time of payment. The rate of penalty is charged at 0.5% of the total value of the goods whose delivery has been delayed for every seven days, with any odd days less than seven days shall be counted as seven days. However, the total amount of penalty shall not exceed 5% of the total value of the goods involved in the late delivery. In case the seller fails to make delivery ten weeks later than the time of shipment stipulated in the contract, the buyer shall have the right to cancel the contract and the seller, in spite of the cancellation, shall still pay the aforesaid penalty to the buyer without delay.

若卖方不能按合同规定如期交货,在卖方同意由付款行在议付货款中扣除罚金或由买方于支付货款时直接扣除罚金的条件下,买方应同意延期交货。罚金率是每 7 天收取延期交货部分金额的 0.5%,不足 7 天者按 7 天计算。但罚金不得超过延期交货部分总金额的 5%。在卖方延期交货超过合同规定期限 10 周时，买方有权撤销合同，但卖方仍应不延迟地按上述规定向买方支付罚金。

4．Claim related to imports（进口方索赔）

(1) Claim compensation from the seller. If the seller fails to deliver on time or refuses to deliver, or if the quantity, quality, and specifications of the goods delivered do not comply with the contract provisions, if the goods are damaged due to poor packaging, the buyer will file a claim against the seller.

(2) Claim compensation from the shipping company. The shipping company is responsible for the relevant losses or damages where the shipping company is responsible for circumstances such as the quantity of the goods is less than that stated in the relevant B/L, the goods have traces of damage under a clean B/L.

(3)Claim compensation from the insurance company. If the goods are damaged due to natural disasters, accidents, or other accidents during transportation and are covered by insurance, the insurance company should compensate for the loss.

（1）向卖方索赔。若卖方未能按时交货或拒绝交货，或所交付货物的数量、质量及规格不符合合同条款，若货物因包装不良导致损坏，买方将向卖方提出索赔。

（2）向承运公司索赔。当出现以下情况且责任在于承运公司时，其需承担相关损失或损害：货物数量少于相关提单所载数量，货物在清洁提单下出现损坏痕迹。

（3）向保险公司索赔。若货物在运输过程中因自然灾害、意外事故或其他突发事件受损，且在保险责任范围内，保险公司应赔偿损失。

5．Claim clauses（索赔条款）

Clauses in respect of claim in an import and export contract can be fixed as follows:

进出口合同中的索赔条款的规定方式如下：

1) Discrepancy and claim clauses（异议和索赔条款）

Discrepancy and claim clauses include that besides stipulating that if any party breaches a contract, the other party is entitled to lodge claims against the party in breach, other aspects in respect of proofs presented when lodging a claim and effective period for filing a claim, etc.

异议和索赔条款的内容除规定一方如违反合同，另一方有权索赔外，还包括索赔期限和赔付的金额等。

2) Proofs（索赔依据）

The clause in this respect stipulates the relevant proofs to be presented and the relevant competent authority for issuing the certificate. The proofs should be complete and clear, and the authority should be competent to issue the relevant certificate. Otherwise, claims can be rejected by the other party. Proofs include legal proof which refers to the sales contract and the relevant governing laws and regulations, and fact proof which refers to the facts and the relevant written evidence in respect of the breach.

主要规定索赔必须具备的证据和出具证明的机构。证据应齐全、清楚，出证单位应符合要求，否则将会遭到对方拒赔。索赔依据主要包括法律依据和事实依据两个方面。前者是指相关贸易合同和适用的有关法律法规。后者是指违约的事实真相及其书面证明。

3) Period for claim（索赔期限）

Period for claim refers to the effective period in which the claimant can make a claim against the party in breach. Claims beyond the agreed effective period may be refused by the party in breach. Therefore, the claim period should be reasonably fixed. Generally speaking, a period that is too long may put the seller under heavy responsibility and a period that is too short may make it impossible for the buyer to file a claim. In addition, a detailed stipulation in respect of the starting date for making a claim should also be included in the clause; For instance, "Claim should be filed by the Buyer within 15 days after the arrival of the goods at the port of destination", "Claims should be made by the Buyer within 10 days after the discharging of the goods at the port of destination", "Claim should be made within 15 days after the arrival of the goods at the business place of the Buyer", and "Claim should be made within 10 days after the inspection", etc. Most of the contracts concerning the sale of general goods include only the "Discrepancy and Claim" clause, but contracts for bulk commodities or machines and equipment will include both "Discrepancy and Claim" clause and "Penalty" clause.

索赔期限是指索赔方向违约方提出的有效时限，逾期索赔，违约方可以不予受理。因此，索赔期限应合理安排。一般来说，如果索赔期限规定过长，卖方将承担过重的责任；如果规定过短，将使买方无法进行索赔。在规定索赔期限时还应该对索赔期限的起算时间做出具体规定。例如，"买方应在货物到达目的港后 15 天内起算"；"买方应在货物到达目的港卸离海轮后 10 天起算"；"货物到达买方营业处所或用户所在地后 15 天起算"；"货物经检验后 10 天起算"；等等。在一般商品买卖合同中，大多只订立异议和索赔条款，而在买卖大宗商品和机械设备之类的商品的合同中除了订立异议和索赔条款外，还订立罚金条款。

4) Penalty（罚金条款）

A clause in respect of penalty in a contract shall stipulate that "any party who fails to perform the contract shall pay an agreed amount as penalty for compensating the other party for the damage". The penalty clause is stipulated where the seller fails to make timely delivery, the buyer fails to open the relevant L/C or the buyer fails to take delivery on time. The penalty ceiling is also included in the contract.

合同规定，当一方未履行合同义务时，应向另一方支付合同约定的金额，以补偿对方的损失。罚金条款一般适用于卖方延期交货，或买方延迟开立信用证或延期接货的情况下。合同一般还规定最高限额。

6. Problems should be paid attention to when a buyer files a claim.（进口方办理索赔时应注意的问题）

When a buyer files a claim, attention should be paid to the following.

在进口方办理索赔时，一般应注意以下事项。

1) Proofs for claiming（索赔证据）

When filing a claim against the seller, the buyer should present adequate proofs and give sufficient reasons, and documents such as a statement of claim, inspection certificate issued by the inspection authority, invoice, packing list, copies of B/L, etc. should be presented. Under an FOB or CFR contract, an insurance policy should be included. When lodging a claim against the shipping company, the buyer should also present a tally report issued and signed by the master or tally clerk of the harbor authority and a damage and/or short-landed memo issued and signed by the master. Additional documents such as combined inspection report issued and signed by the insurance company and the buyer should be included for any claim that may be filed with the insurance company.

在向卖方提出索赔时，买方应该提供索赔清单、商检局签发的检验证书、发票、装箱单、提单副本等。索赔时还应提出确切的根据和理由，如为 FOB 或 CFR 合同，还应该附保险单一份；买方在向船公司索赔时则须另附由船长及港务局理货员签证的理货报告及船长签证的短卸和/或残损证明；向保险公司索赔时，须另附保险公司与买方的联合检验报告。

2) Claim amount（索赔金额）

Claim amount should include the invoice value of the contract and incidental expenses such as inspection fees, loading and unloading expenses, bank charges, storage charges, and interest, etc.

索赔金额除了合同规定的商品价值，还可以提出有关的费用索赔，如商品检验费、装卸费、银行手续费、仓租、利息等。

3) Claim period（索赔期限）

Claim should be made within the validity of the contract. If an extension of the validity is necessary for commodity inspection, then the claim period can be extended after obtaining approval from the other party.

索赔应该在合同规定的索赔有效期内提出。如因商检工作可能需要更长的时间，那么可以向对方要求延长索赔期限。

4) Seller's responsibility for settlement（卖方的理赔责任）

If the goods incur losses or damage that are caused by the shipping company, the insurance company or the seller, then the buyer can file a claim against the responsible party. If losses or damage are caused directly by the seller, then the buyer shall lodge a claim directly with the seller.

如果进口货物发生损失，而这种损失是船运公司、保险公司或卖方的责任，那么买方可以向责任方索赔，如属卖方必须直接承担的责任，应直接向卖方要求索赔。

Section Two　Force Majeure（不可抗力）

In international trade, after the conclusion of the contract, occasionally some events beyond the parties' control may take place, which makes it impossible to fulfill the contract. In order to safeguard their interests, the parties of a contract usually stipulate the force majeure clause in the contract.

Force majeure means that the frustration of the contract by the party in question results from natural or social forces including flood, earthquake, typhoon, fire, war and government decrees of prohibition beyond the control of man. This party shall be free from liability for performance, or be given an option of prolonging the performance of the contract owing to the above-mentioned event or series of events.

According to international practice, the party that is free from liability according to the force majeure clause should satisfy the following two requirements. First, the party should promptly inform the other party right after the accident so that the latter is able to take necessary remedial measures. Otherwise, the former will still be held responsible for the loss or extended loss thus caused. Second, the party that failed to perform the contract should provide effective documentation describing the force majeure events and their consequences. If it is to do this, or if the facts identified are not in conformity with his descriptions, the liability of his failure to perform the contract will not be exempted or fully exempted.

A contract may be suspended or terminated because of the consequence of a force majeure event. If the performance of the contract is just delayed by a force majeure case temporarily or for a short time, the contract may be suspended. After the force majeure accident ends, the contract should be resumed. For example, if there is a delayed shipment because of an industrial strike, the contract will be suspended. But when the strike is over, the contract should continue and the seller must proceed with shipment. If the force majeure accident has damaged or destroyed the basis of the contract, for example, the flood has damaged or destroyed the goods ready for shipment, then the contract must terminate.

There are different interpretations of this term among countries in the world. But, in most cases, it refers to those accidents caused by natural phenomena or social factors, such as earthquake, flood, tempest, war, and governmental prohibition on import/export of certain commodities. In order to clarify what the term of force majeure covers under a particular contract, different approaches are adopted.

在国际贸易中，合同签订后会发生一些不为人类所能控制的意外事件，这使得合同方不能履行合同。为了维护自己的利益，合同的双方通常规定不可抗力的合同条款。

在国际贸易中，不可抗力又称人力不可抗拒，是指在合同签订后，由于一些自然因素或社会因素而引发的诸如洪水、地震、台风、火灾、战争等不为人类所能控制的意外事件，以致合同不能履行或不能按期履行时，遭受意外事件的当事人可免除其不履行或不按期履行合同的责任，而另一方不得要求赔偿损失，这些意外事件称为不可抗力。

按照国际惯例，当发生不可抗力影响合同履行时，当事人要想取得免责权利，就必须做到以下两点：第一，必须在意外发生后及时通知对方，以便对方能够采取补救措施，否则，当事人仍然要对意外事故的后果负责。第二，当一方援引不可抗力条款要求免责时，必须向对方提交证明文件作为证据。如果当事人未能提供证明文件作为证据，或者所提交的证明文件不符合所陈述的事实，那么，当事人就不能部分或全部免责。

由于不可抗力事件的影响，合同可以暂缓执行或终止。如果合同的执行只是由于不可抗力的缘故受到暂时的或短时间的影响，合同将暂缓执行。不可抗力事件结束后，合同应恢复执行。例如，由于罢工而迟延的发货，待罢工结束以后，应按合同继续发运货物。如果不可抗力事故损坏或摧毁了合同的基础，如所发运的货物被洪水完全毁灭，那么合同就不得不终止了。

但是，不同的国家对于"不可抗力"这个术语的解释是不同的。虽然在大多数情况下，它指的是自然现象或社会因素所引起的事故，例如地震、洪水、暴风雨、战争以及政府禁止进出口某些货物。为了明确地界定"不可抗力"这个术语在某一特定合同中的所指范围，通常采取以下几种方式。

1. Stipulate the force majeure clause in a general way（概括式）

If the shipment of the contract goods is prevented or delayed in whole or in part due to force majeure, the seller shall not be liable for non-shipment or late shipment of the goods of this contract. However, the seller shall notify the buyer by cable or telex and furnish the buyer within 15 days by registered airmail with a certificate issued by the China Council for the Promotion of International Trade attesting such event or events.

若由于不可抗力的原因，致使卖方不能全部或部分装运或延迟装运合同货物，卖方对于这种不能装运或延迟装运本合同货物不负有责任。但卖方须用电报或电传通知买方，并须在 15 天内以航空挂号信向买方提交由中国国际贸易促进委员会出具的证明此类事故的证明书。

2. Stipulate the force majeure clause in a way to list the contents（列举式）

If the seller is unable to fully or partially ship or delay the shipment of the contracted goods due to war, earthquake, flood, fire, typhoon, or snow disaster, the seller shall not be liable for such inability or delay in shipping the contracted goods. But the seller shall notify the buyer by telegram or telex and shall submit a certificate issued by the China Council for the Promotion of International Trade to the buyer by registered airmail within 15 days to prove such events.

若因战争、地震、洪水、火灾、台风、雪灾等不可抗力，导致卖方无法全部或部分装运或延迟交付合同货物，卖方对该不能装运或延迟装运合同货物不负责任。但卖方须以电报或电传通知买方，并在 15 天内以航空挂号信向买方提交由中国国际贸易促进委员会出具的事件证明书。

3. Stipulate the force majeure clause in a way to colligation（综合式）

The seller shall not be held responsible for failure or delay to perform all or any part of this contract due to war, earthquake, flood, fire, storm, heavy snow or other causes of force majeure. However, the seller shall advise the buyer immediately of such occurrence, and within 15 days thereafter, shall send by registered airmail to the buyer for their acceptance a certificate issued by the competent government authorities of the place where the accident occurs as evidence thereof. Under such circumstances, the seller however, is still under the obligation to take all necessary measures to hasten the delivery of the goods. In case the accident lasts for more than 3 weeks, the buyer shall have the right to cancel the contract.

由于战争、地震、洪水、火灾、台风、雪灾或其他不可抗力的原因，致使卖方不能全部或部分装运或延迟装运合同货物，卖方可不负责任。但卖方应立即将事件通知买方，并于事件发生后 15 天内将事件发生地政府主管当局出具的事件证明书用航空挂号邮寄买方为证，并取得买方认可。在上述情况下，卖方仍有责任采取一切必要措施从速交货。如果事件持续超过 3 个星期，买方有权撤销合同。

Among these three ways, the last one is the best, because it has some flexibility. If a contingency not stipulated in the contract occurs, the way will be useful and helpful for the parties involved to solve the problem. It is better to use this way in the contract.

在三种方法中，最后这种方法既明确又有一定的灵活性，若发生了合同未列明的意外事故，有利于双方当事人协商处理，合同中的不可抗力条款最好采用这种方法。

Section Three　Arbitration（仲裁）

In international trade practice, in case of disputes, the two parties shall try to settle the disputes through amicable negotiations. In case no settlement can be reached through negotiation, the case shall then be settled through conciliation, arbitration, or even litigation.

Settlement of disputes through negotiation is, therefore, even more attractive than going to court. It would be better for the businesspeople to settle the disputes by themselves through friendly negotiation. However, many attorneys are skilled negotiators, therefore, having a competent third party to speak as an intermediary is often more effective than speaking for oneself. A voluntary process that is sometimes used when negotiation seems to be failing is mediation. The parties to the dispute choose a third party to assist them in settling it. The mediator often tries first to communicate the position of the parties to each other, and then usually proposes a basis or several bases for settlement. Mediation merely facilitates negotiation, no award or opinion or the merits of the disputes are given. Mediation is especially useful in situations where the parties have some continuing relationship, because it allows them to compromise and to reach a solution themselves. Arbitration is another widely used alternative to settling disputes. Arbitration differs from mediation in that the third party to whom the dispute is submitted decides the outcome. Arbitration is often provided for in a contract, parties who have not so provided can choose to have their dispute arbitrated after it has arisen.

在国际贸易中，买卖双方发生了贸易纠纷，应当采用友好的协商办法来解决纠纷。但当双方当事人不能经协商解决问题时，就不得不采用调解、仲裁甚至诉讼解决问题。

通过友好协商解决争议比诉诸法庭更为可取。贸易双方最好通过友好协商自行解决争议。如果协商不能解决时就通过调解的方式解决。调解员只是促成双方协商解决，不对争议做任何评论或裁决。目前，在国际贸易中广泛使用的另一种解决争议的方法就是仲裁。与调解不同，仲裁则对争议做出裁决。如果希望通过仲裁解决争议，一般由合同当事人于争议发生前，在合同中订立仲裁条款，或在争议发生后经双方同意后提交仲裁。

The main ways to resolve disputes encountered in the process of digital trade are platform mediation, third-party arbitration, and legal litigation. Generally speaking, most digital trade platforms have dedicated customer service teams and digital trade dispute mediation mechanisms, which are particularly prominent in large cross-border e-commerce platforms. Both parties to a transaction can first submit a dispute through a cross-border e-commerce platform, which will be mediated and arbitrated by the platform's customer service. If the cross-border e-commerce platform cannot resolve the dispute through mediation, both parties to the transaction can choose a third-party arbitration institution for arbitration. These institutions usually have professional legal backgrounds and arbitration experience, and can fairly resolve disputes. In extremely special circumstances, if the dispute involves significant interests or complex legal issues, both parties to the transaction may need to resolve the dispute through legal means. This usually includes filing a lawsuit or applying for an arbitration award in court.

数字贸易过程中遇到的纠纷解决途径主要是平台调解、第三方仲裁和法律诉讼。一般来说，大多数的数字贸易平台都是设有专门的客服团队和数字贸易纠纷调解机制的，这一点在大型跨境电商平台很明显。交易双方遇到纠纷首先可以通过跨境电商平台提交纠纷，由跨境电商平台客服进行调解和仲裁。如果跨境电商平台调解无法解决纠纷，交易双方则可以选择第三方仲裁机构进行仲裁。这些机构通常具有专业的法律背景和仲裁经验，能够公正地解决纠纷。在极特殊的情况下，如果纠纷涉及重大利益或复杂法律问题，交易双方可能需要通过法律途径解决纠纷。这通常包括向法院提起诉讼或申请仲裁裁决。

1. The definition of arbitration（仲裁的定义）

Arbitration means that the two parties, before or after the disputes arise, reach a written agreement that they will submit the disputes which cannot be settled through amicable negotiations to a third party for arbitration.

Normally, a board of arbitration consists of three arbitrators. Firstly, the plaintiff and the defendant choose one arbitrator respectively. Then, the two arbitrators so chosen by the plaintiff and defendant choose a third arbitrator. If the parties of a contract have agreed to submit the dispute for arbitration, then a court will not review the wisdom of the decision of an arbitrator. But it may hold that the dispute was not arbitrable under the agreement of the parties, or that the arbitrator exceeded their authority, or acted arbitrarily, or in a discriminatory manner.

仲裁又称公断，是指交易双方在争议发生前或争议发生后达成书面协议，自愿将他们的争议提交双方同意的仲裁机构裁决，以解决争议的一种方式。

通常仲裁庭由三位仲裁员组成。首先，原告和被告各选一位仲裁员，然后由这两位仲裁员再选第三位仲裁员。如果双方当事人同意将争议提交仲裁，那么法院就无权对仲裁员的裁定做出评论。当然，如果双方有协议规定不通过仲裁解决争议，或仲裁员超过仲裁权限，仲裁时武断且带有偏见，那么这种仲裁将不再有效。

2. Characteristics of arbitration（仲裁的特点）

Compared with a court trial, arbitration has the following advantages.

(1) An arbitrator who is familiar with the technical or social settling of the dispute may be chosen.

(2) There is less delay in disposing of the dispute through arbitration, while a trial, may sometimes take several years to get the disputes settled in court.

(3) Since the procedure is more informal than in court, the parties may choose not to be represented by lawyers.

(4) Privacy can be maintained in both the arbitration hearing and the award.

(5) The parties concerned may choose the arbitrator from the arbitration organization.

(6) The arbitration procedure is simpler and the cost of arbitration is cheaper.

(7) The arbitration award is final and has binding force upon the parties concerned.

同诉讼相比，仲裁有以下几个优势。

（1）可以选择熟悉争议处理技巧、争议社会背景的仲裁员。

（2）通过仲裁处理争议比较迅速，而法院审理有时则可能要几年才能将争议解决。

（3）仲裁程序不如诉讼正式，当事人可以不请律师。

（4）仲裁的审理和裁决可以不公开。

（5）双方均有在仲裁机构中推选仲裁员的自由。

（6）仲裁程序比诉讼简单，费用也较低。

（7）裁决一般是终局的，对双方当事人都有约束力。

3. The differences between arbitration and legal actions（仲裁与诉讼的不同）

The differences between arbitration and legal actions can be generalized as follows.

(1) The legal action has jurisdiction, while arbitration does not.

(2) Arbitration is based on the two parties' own will, in case no agreement can be reached, any party cannot force the other party to submit to arbitration, whereas in judicial proceedings the plaintiff may take a unilateral action against the defendant without agreement between the two parties in advance.

(3) The arbitration organization is not an official one, which has no jurisdiction. The parties involved can appoint their own arbitrators, and the third one will be appointed by the arbitration institution. Arbitrators are appointed by the two parties, while judges are appointed by the government.

(4) Arbitration can be handled according to commercial practices, so arbitration is more flexible and permissive; thus, in international trade, in case no settlement can be reached through amicable negotiations, the two parties would like to submit to arbitration, while a case is tried in accordance with law if it is brought to a court. According to international commercial practices, an arbitration agreement is a prior arrangement and a precondition.

仲裁与诉讼的不同之处有以下几点。

（1）诉讼具有管辖权，而仲裁没有。

（2）仲裁是建立在双方自愿的基础上的，当事人通过仲裁解决争议时，必须先签订仲裁协议，仲裁机构只有收到当事人提交的仲裁协议才可受理。

（3）仲裁机构一般是民间性机构，不具有强制管辖权，仲裁的双方当事人有权各指定一名仲裁员，另外再由仲裁机构指定一名首席仲裁员组成仲裁庭审理案件；而诉讼机构法院是国家机构，法官由国家任命，不能由诉讼当事人选定。

（4）仲裁的办理可以按照商业习惯来进行，因而仲裁更具有灵活性和可执行性。因此，在国际贸易实务中，当买卖双方未能通过协商达成解决问题的协议时，一般更愿意通过仲裁解决问题，如果上法庭，就必须按照法律条款执行。按照国际贸易惯例，买卖双方应先签订仲裁协议。

4. Issues should be considered in arbitration（仲裁中应注意的问题）

1) Place of arbitration（仲裁地点）

Since applicable laws concerning arbitration differ from country to country, and different applicable laws differ in their interpretations in respect of the rights and obligations of the parties concerned, therefore parties concerned are always making efforts to choose an arbitration place they trust and know quite well. For instance, Chinese traders will always hope that any disputes arising from or in connection with the contract shall be referred to the China International Economic and Trade Arbitration Commission for arbitration which they are familiar with. But things are not always as one wishes, therefore, in China's foreign trade, arbitration is sometimes made either in the country of the other party (other than in China) or in a third country.

仲裁地点不同，适用的法律可能不同，对双方当事人的权利、义务的解释就会有差异。因此，交易双方都会争取在自己比较了解和信任的地方仲裁。例如，如果可能，中国商人总希望将合同的有关争议提交他们熟悉的中国国际经济贸易仲裁委员会仲裁。但事情并不总能遂人愿，所以在中国的对外贸易中，有时仲裁选择在对方（而不是在中国）所在国或双方同意的第三国。

2) Arbitration body（仲裁机构）

Disputes in international trade can be either referred to a permanent arbitration organization for arbitration as stipulated in the arbitration agreement by the parties concerned or submitted for arbitration to an interim arbitration tribunal formed by the arbitrators agreed upon by the two parties. At present, most countries and some international organizations in the world have their permanent arbitration organizations specialized in the settlement of commercial disputes. In China, the China International Economic and the Trade Arbitration Commission and Maritime Arbitration Commission are permanent arbitration organizations. When including arbitration clauses in the sales contract, Chinese companies of foreign trade, if possible, are usually fixing an arbitration clause in their contract to stipulate that any disputes arising from or in connection with the contract shall be referred to the China International Economic and Trade Arbitration Commission for arbitration. An interim arbitration tribunal is specially formed and composed of the arbitrators appointed by the parties concerned for the purpose of hearing the case of disputes and shall be automatically dismissed after the hearing of the case is finished. Under such a circumstance, the two parties should make it clear in the arbitration clause with respect to the manner of arbitration, number of arbitrators, etc.

在国际贸易当中，争议可由当事人在仲裁协议中规定在常设仲裁机构进行，也可以由当事人双方共同指定仲裁员组成临时仲裁庭进行仲裁。目前在国际上许多国家和一些国际组织都设有专门处理商事纠纷的常设仲裁机构。我国的常设机构是中国国际经济贸易仲裁委员会和海事仲裁委员会。我国各外贸公司在买卖合同中订立仲裁条款时，如可能的话，一般都在合同的仲裁条款中订明与合同有关的争议将在中国国际经济贸易仲裁委员会仲裁。临时仲裁庭是专门为审理争议案件而由当事人指定的仲裁员组成的，案件处理完毕即自动解散。在这种情况下，双方当事人应在仲裁条款中就双方指定的仲裁员的人数、办法等做明确规定。

3) Applicable arbitration rules（仲裁规则的适用）

The country where the arbitration is going to be conducted and the relevant applicable arbitration rules should be conducted clear in the sales contract. If Chinese arbitration rules are applicable, then China International Economic and Trade Arbitration Commission Rules shall apply. It should be noted that arbitration rules do not always align with the arbitration place. According to the usual international practice of arbitration, the arbitration rules in the arbitration place shall in principle apply, but it is legal for the parties concerned to agree in their contract that the arbitration rules of the arbitration organization in other countries (regions), other than the arbitration rules of the country where the arbitration is going to be conducted, shall apply.

在买卖合同中，应注明进行仲裁的所在国以及适用的仲裁规则。适用我国的仲裁规则，是指适用《中国国际经济贸易仲裁委员会仲裁规则》。应注意，所采用的仲裁规则与仲裁地并非绝对一致，按国际仲裁的一般做法，原则上采用仲裁所在地的仲裁规则，但有的法律也允许双方当事人在合同中约定，采用仲裁地点以外的其他国家（地区）仲裁机构的仲裁规则进行仲裁。

4) Arbitral award（仲裁的裁决）

The arbitral award is usually final. But it is still important to stipulate in the contract that "The arbitration award is final and shall have binding force upon the two parties."

仲裁的裁决一般是终局的。但仍应规定：仲裁裁决是终局的，对双方都有约束力。

5．Examples of Arbitration Clauses（仲裁实例）

The arbitral award is final and binding upon both parties.

The following are some examples of arbitration clauses in the contract of our import and export business.

仲裁裁决是终局的，对双方都有约束力。

以下是我国进出口合同中仲裁条款订法的实例。

(1) The arbitration clause stipulated in our country: All disputes arising out of the performance of, or relating to this contract, shall be settled amicably through friendly negotiation. In case no settlement can be reached through negotiation, the case shall then be submitted to the China International Economic and Trade Arbitration Commission, Beijing, China, for arbitration in accordance with its Arbitration Rules. The arbitral award is final and binding upon both parties.

规定在我国仲裁的条款：凡因执行本合同所发生的或与本合同有关的一切争议，双方应通过友好协商解决。如果协商不能解决，应提交北京中国国际经济贸易仲裁委员会，根据该会仲裁规则进行仲裁。仲裁裁决是终局的，对双方都有约束力。

(2) The clause stipulating arbitration in the country where the defendant is located: All disputes arising out of the performance of, or relating to this contract, shall be settled amicably through friendly negotiation. If no settlement can be reached through negotiation, the case shall then be submitted for arbitration. The location of arbitration shall be in the country of the domicile of the defendant. If in China, the arbitration shall be conducted by the China International Economic and Trade Arbitration Commission in Beijing in accordance with its Arbitration Rules. If in ××, the arbitration shall be conducted by ×× in accordance with its Arbitration Rules. The arbitral award is final and binding upon both parties.

规定在被诉方所在国仲裁的条款：凡因执行本合同所发生的或与本合同有关的一切争议，双方应通过友好协商解决。如果协商不能解决，应提交仲裁。仲裁在被诉方所在国进行。如果在中国，由中国国际经济贸易仲裁委员会根据其仲裁规则进行仲裁。如果在××国，则由××（对方所在国仲裁机构名称）根据其仲裁规则进行仲裁。仲裁裁决是终局的，对双方都有约束力。

(3) Provisions for arbitration in a third country: All disputes arising out of the performance of, or relating to this contract, shall be settled amicably through friendly negotiation. In case no settlement can be reached through negotiation, the case shall then be submitted to ×× for arbitration, in accordance with its rules of arbitration. The arbitral award is final and binding upon both parties.

规定在第三国仲裁的条款：凡因执行本合同所发生的或与本合同有关的一切争议，双方应通过友好协商解决。如果协商不能解决，应提交××（某第三国某地及某仲裁机构的名称）根据其仲裁规则进行仲裁。仲裁裁决是终局的，对双方都有约束力。

Part B Terminology Practice

1. **Dispute**（纠纷）：A conflict of claims or rights. Whenever one party to a contract requests something from the other party under the terms of their contract and that request is not complied with, there is a dispute.

2. **Claim**（索赔）：The demand or assertion of a right. In international trade, it refers to the claim for losses.

3. **Litigation**（诉讼）：Court action.

4. **Parties to a contract**（合同当事人）：People who sign a contract and are responsible for carrying it out.

5. **Arbitration**（仲裁）：Adjudication by a third, impartial party between two other disputing parties, without involving legal action.

6. **Arbitration clause**（仲裁条款）：Statement in a contract which indicates that both parties agree to arbitration in case of a dispute.

7. **Arbitration agreement**（仲裁协议）：Agreement in a contract by which parties agree that they will take disputes to an arbitrator before they pursue other legal recourses.

8. **Penalty clause**（罚款条款）：A contractual stipulation that a supplier must forfeit a portion of payment due if a consignment is delivered late, is damaged, or is deemed unsatisfactory in some other manners by the purchaser.

9. **Force majeure**（不可抗力）：An event that can generally be neither anticipated nor reduced to control, e.g. , an earthquake which leads to the damage of the shipment.

10. **Arbitral award**（仲裁裁决）：In this context, the decision of arbitrators; the payment of an amount of money to settle a dispute.

11. **Arbitral tribunal**（仲裁庭）：A group of people who meet to settle a dispute between others.

12. **Review**（审查）：In this sense, a check by a court to see that the decision of an arbitration tribunal is carried out.

13. **Guarantee**（担保/保证人数）：The number of persons to be served at a function. This number is provided to the hotel at least 48 hours before the function. Most hotels are prepared to

serve at least 5% more than the guaranteed figure. Payment is made on the basis of the guaranteed number or total number served, whichever is greater.

14. **Manifest**（载货清单）：Document listing all the contents of a shipment being transported by rail, air, truck or boat.

15. **Warehouse receipt**（仓单）：A receipt issued by a person engaged in the business of storing goods for hire, having all important and necessary information on it.

16. **Warranty**（保证书）：A written guarantee of the integrity of a product and of the supplier's responsibility for the repair or replacement of defective parts.

17. **Standard requisition**（标准请购单）：A document that requisitioning departments utilize to communicate to purchase what, when, and how many products or services are needed.

Part C Terms

1. ACP（African, Caribbean and Pacific Group）非洲、加勒比和太平洋国家集团（洛美协定）

2. actionable subsidy（补贴协议）可诉补贴

3. amber box measures（农产品国内支持）黄箱措施

4. appeal（解决争端）上诉　　　　　　　　5. appeal body　上诉机构

6. Basel Convention《巴塞尔公约》（有关危险废弃物的多边环境协定）

7. Berne Convention《伯尔尼公约》（有关保护文学和艺术作品版权的公约）

8. base tariff level　基础税率

9. Blue Box Measures（农产品国内支持）蓝箱措施

10. BOP(Balance-of-payments) provisions　国际收支条款

11. built-in agenda　既定日程　　　　　　12. bound level　约束水平

13. common agriculture policy（欧盟）共同农业政策

14. CBD (Convention on Biological Diversity)《生物多样性公约》

15. circumvention　规避

16. Convention on International Trade in Endangered Species《濒危物种国际贸易公约》

17. commercial presence（服务贸易）商业存在

18. consumption abroad（服务贸易）境外消费

19. cross border supply（服务贸易）跨境交付

20. complaint（解决争端）申诉方　　　　21. defendant（解决争端）被诉方

22. countervailing duty　反补贴税　　　　23. counter-notification　反向通知

24. cross retaliation　交叉报复

25. CTG(Council for Trade in Goods)　货物贸易理事会

26. currency retention scheme　货币留成制度

27. customs value　海关完税价值　　　　28. customs valuation　海关估价

29. quota-free products　非配额产品　　　30. findings（解决争端）调查结果

31. geographical indications（知识产权）地理标识

32. GMOs (genetically modified organisms) 转基因生物

33. government procurement 政府采购   34. grey area measures 灰色区域措施

35. GRULAC 拉美国家在 WTO 中的非正式集团

36. HS (Harmonized Commodity and Coding System) 协调制度（商品名称及编码协调制度）

37. booking confirmation 订舱确认   38. calling forward notice 要求交货通知

39. freight invoice 运费发票   40. arrival notice (goods) 货物到达通知

41. notice of circumstances preventing delivery (goods) 无法交货通知

42. notice of circumstances preventing transport (goods) 无法运货通知

43. delivery notice (goods) 交货通知   44. cargo manifest 载货清单

45. freight manifest 载货运费清单   46. bordereau 公路运输货物清单

47. container manifest (unit packing list) 集装箱载货清单

48. charges note 铁路费用单   49. short delivery 短交

50. short unloaded 短卸   51. lost in transit 短失

52. survey report 公证报告   53. damage report 破损证书

54. marine protest 海难报告

55. E.& O.E.(Errors and Omissions Excepted) 有错当查

Part D Exercise

I. Determine whether the following statements are True or False. Then put T for True or F for False in the bracket at the end of each statement.

1. According to the Commodity Law, if one party has a "breach of warranty", the injured party may rescind the contract and claim for damages. ( )

2. The Foreign Economic Contract Law of the People's Republic of China stipulates that the party who has breached the contract cannot take any remedial measures. ( )

3. The Commercial Code of the USA applies "fundamental breach of contract" to explaining the consequences of the breach of contract. ( )

4. The CISG states that if one party's breach of contract deprives the other party or the injured party of the main economic interests in the contract, the injured party may declare the contract avoided. ( )

5. According to usual international trade practice, buyers lose the right to claim for damages if they have processed or resold the goods. ( )

6. One of the best ways to avoid performing contractual obligations in international trade is to declare a force majeure event. ( )

7. Once a force majeure event happens, the party who fails to perform its obligations must inform the other party of the event. ( )

8. The party who incurs a force majeure event may delay the performance of the contract if this party is able to continue the contract. ( )

9. When settling disputes, the conciliator may force the parties in disputes to act on his advice.
( )

10. Usually the parties who require arbitration in settlement of claims may not appeal to the court. ( )

11. A penalty clause is a contractual stipulation that a supplier must forfeit a portion of payment due if a consignment is delivered late, is damaged, or is deemed unsatisfactory in some other manners by the purchaser.( )

12. Force majeure refers to an event that can generally be either anticipated or controlled, e.g. , an earthquake which leads to the damage of the shipment. ( )

13. An arbitral tribunal is a group of people who meet to resolve a dispute between others. ( )

14. Review is a check by a competent authority to see that the decision of an arbitration tribunal is carried out. ( )

15. Claim refers to a statement of loss or damage to any household goods while in the charge of the carrier or his agent. ( )

II. Fill in the blanks with proper words and expressions.

1. There is a _____ between the contents of Case No. 68 and those _____ .

2. This delay had placed us in an _____ position.

3. The cartons appear to have been very _____ at some time during loading and unloading, but the contents have not suffered any _____ .

4. The _____ of returning the defective goods will, of course, be _____ by us.

5. It is obvious that through an _____ some straw ropes were not cleared out of the packages.

6. We were sorry to receive your complaints that the goods _____ to you are not of the _____ .

7. We are extremely sorry about the delay, which you will realize was due to circumstances _____ .

8. The buyer lodged _____ the shipment _____ USD500_____short weight.

III. Explain the following terms in English.

1. 违约   2. 留置权
3. 索赔   4. 理赔
5. 救济方法   6. 恢复原状
7. 实际损失   8. 交货

IV. Briefly answer the following questions.

1. 各国法律对实际履行作为一种救济方法的规定有何不同？

2. 大陆法、英美法和《联合国国际货物销售合同公约》对损害赔偿责任的确立各有什么规定？

3. 各国法律对损害赔偿范围的规定有何不同？

4. 各国法律对构成解决合同的条件的规定有何不同？我国又是怎样规定的？

5. 处理理赔工作时应该注意哪些问题？

6. 按英国法规定，卖方行使停运权有几种方法？行使停运权时应注意哪几个条件？

7. 按《英国货物买卖法》的规定，所交货物与合同不符违反要件的情况有几种？

V. Case study.

1. A Chinese international trade company exported a batch of walnuts to the British customers on CIF terms, payable by an irrevocable sight letter of credit. As it was a seasonal commodity, it was stipulated in the contract that "To effect shipment from China port in October. The seller should guarantee that the vessel would reach the port of destination no later than December 2nd. If the vessel reaches the port of destination later than that date, the buyer is entitled to cancel the contract. In case the payment has been made, the seller should return the payment to the buyer".

After the conclusion of the contract, the Chinese company shipped the cargo in the middle of October. The Chinese company received the payment from the bank on the basis of the documents (the commercial invoice, the bill of lading, and the insurance policy) provided under the L/C. Unfortunately, during the voyage, the main parts of the machine were damaged, and the ship stopped sailing. In order to ensure timely arrival at the port of destination, the Chinese company rented a powerful tugboat at a high price for tugging the freighter to move on. Then, rough weather attacked the ship, so the ship was late for hours as regulated. It happened that the market price of walnut fell. Most of the company's clients requested to cancel the contract. The Chinese company suffered heavy economic losses.

Question: Is it a real contract based on CIF terms that the Chinese international trade company concluded with the English clients? Tell the reasons.

2. A merchant in South America placed an order with a Chinese export company for a certain commodity on CFR Asuncion terms. With a view to developing new markets, the export company immediately made an offer abroad on the basis of CFR Asuncion, and the transaction was soon concluded. When shipping the goods, however, this company came to realize that Asuncion is an inland city. As was the case, if the company had the goods transported to Asuncion, it had to, first of all, have the goods transported by sea to a seaport in Argentina or some other South American neighboring country. After that, the goods might be transported to Asuncion through river transportation or inland transportation. As a result, this company had to pay a considerable sum of freight charges.

Question: What can we learn from this case?

3. Our company made an offer with an Italian buyer, which is valid before 10th of this month. Because of the post office's late delivery, we received the acceptance on 11th. At this moment, we found the price of these goods on the market was rising.

Question: How can we do?

4. A French buyer visited a Chinese trading company to buy some goods in the morning. When the Chinese seller offered the price, he didn't say anything. But in the afternoon, the French buyer visited again and accepted the morning's offer. At this moment, the Chinese company found the price of this goods on the international market was rising.

Question: How could the Chinese trading company deal with? Why?

5. 上海一家伞厂与意大利客户签订了雨伞出口合同。买方开来的信用证规定，10 月份装运交货，不料 9 月初，该伞厂仓库失火，成品、半成品全部烧毁，以致无法交货。

问题：卖方可否援引不可抗力条款要求免交货物？

6. 广州一家进出口公司于 1990 年 11 月 2 日与伊朗签订了一份进口合同，交易条件为 FOB。后因海湾战争爆发，我方接货货轮无法驶抵伊朗，到 1991 年 4 月海湾战争结束后，我方方能派船接货，而外商以我方未能按时派船接货为由，要求我方赔偿其仓储费。

问题：外商这一要求是否合理？

7. 北京一研究所与日本客户签订一份进口合同，欲引进一精密仪器，合同规定 2 月底交货。2 月 10 日，日本政府宣布该仪器为高科技产品，禁止出口。该禁令自公布之日起 20 日后生效。日商来电以不可抗力为由要求解除合同。

问题：日商的要求是否合理？我方应如何妥善处理？

8. 甲公司与乙公司签订了购销棉麻纺织品的合同，约定由甲公司于 2009 年 12 月月底之前交付 200 公吨棉麻纺织品给乙公司，而当乙公司收到 100 公吨货物后，于 2009 年 5 月明确通知甲公司由于棉麻纺织品销路不畅，不会接收甲公司的继续供货。这时甲公司仓库下存棉麻纺织品 10 公吨。甲公司为了盈利，在收到乙公司通知后，继续按双方合同约定为乙公司运送了其余的 90 公吨棉麻纺织品。后因乙公司拒绝接收后 100 公吨棉麻纺织品，酿成纠纷。

问题：本案谁违约？属于哪种违约行为？本案应如何处理？

Chapter Thirteen

Part A Text

A Brief Introduction to Cross-border E-commerce

Cross-border e-commerce is developed based on the network. The network space is a new space, relatively speaking, to the physical space, and is a virtual reality of network address and password. Cyberspace's unique values and behavior patterns profoundly affect cross-border e-commerce, making it different from the traditional way to trade and showing its own characteristics.

跨境电子商务是基于网络发展起来的，网络空间相对于物理空间来说是一个新空间，是一个由网址和密码组成的虚拟但客观存在的世界。网络空间独特的价值标准和行为模式深刻地影响着跨境电子商务，使其不同于传统的交易方式而呈现出自己的特点。

Cross-border e-commerce is a new-type mode of trade that the digitalization and electronization of exhibition, negotiation and conclusion of business of the traditional trade by Chinese production and trade enterprises through e-commerce means. It finally realizes the import and export of products and is at the same time also an effective way to broaden overseas marketing channels, promote China's brand competitiveness and realize the transformation and upgrading of China's foreign trade.

跨境电子商务是我国生产和贸易企业通过电子商务手段将传统贸易中的展示、洽谈和成交环节数字化、电子化，最终实现产品进出口的新型贸易方式；同时，也是扩大海外营销渠道，提升我国品牌竞争力，实现我国外贸转型升级的有效途径。

Section One　Features of Cross-border E-commerce（跨境电子商务的特征）

1．Global forum（全球性）

Network is a medium-body with no boundaries, sharing the characteristics of globalization and decentralization. Cross-border e-commerce, attached to the network, also has the characteristics of globalization and decentralization. E-commerce, compared with the traditional way of trade, boasts its important feature: borderless trade, losing the geographical factors brought by the traditional exchanges. Internet users do convey products, especially high-value-added products, and services to the market without crossing borders. The positive effect brought by features of the network is the greatest sharing degree of information, whilst its negative impact is that the users confront risks due to different cultural, political and legal factors. Anyone, who has a certain technical means, can put information into the network, connecting with each other, at any time and in any place.

网络是一个没有边界的媒介体，具有全球性和非中心化的特征。依附于网络发生的跨境电子商务也因此具有了全球性和非中心化的特性。电子商务与传统的交易方式相比，其一个重要特点在于电子商务是一种无边界交易，丧失了传统交易所具有的地理因素。互联网用户无须跨越国界就可以把产品，尤其是高附加值产品和服务提交到市场。网络的全球性特征带来的积极影响是信息的最大程度的共享，消极影响是用户必须面临因文化、政治和法律的不同而产生的风险。任何人只要具备了一定的技术手段，在任何时候、任何地方都可以让信息进入网络，相互联系进行交易。

2．Intangibility（无形性）

The development of the network promotes the transmission of digital products and services. And digital transmission is done through different types of media, such as data, voice and image in the global context of the network environment. Since the media in the network are in the form of computer data code; they are invisible. Digital products and services on the basis of the characteristics of digital transmission activities also have the feature of intangibility, although traditional trade in kind is given priority to physical objects, in electronic commerce, intangible products can replace physical objects.

网络的发展使数字化产品和服务的传输盛行。而数字化传输是通过不同类型的媒介，例如数据、声音和图像在全球化网络环境中集中进行的，这些媒介在网络中是以计算机数据代码的形式出现的，因而是无形的。数字化产品和服务基于数字传输活动的特性也必然具有无形性，传统交易以实物交易为主，而在电子商务中，无形产品却可以替代实物成为交易的对象。

3．Anonymity（匿名性）

Due to the decentralization of cross-border e-commerce and its global features, it is difficult to identify e-commerce users' identities and their geographical location. Online transactions of consumers often do not show their real identities and their geographical location. What's important is that this doesn't affect trade. Network anonymity also allows consumers to act anonymously. In the virtual society, the convenience of concealing identities quickly leads to asymmetry between freedom and responsibility. People here can enjoy the greatest freedom, but only bear the smallest responsibility, or even simply evade responsibility.

由于跨境电子商务的非中心化和全球性的特性，因此很难识别电子商务用户的身份和其所处的地理位置。在线交易的消费者往往不显示自己的真实身份和自己的地理位置，重要的是这丝毫不影响交易的进行，网络的匿名性也允许消费者这样做。在虚拟社会里，隐匿身份的便利迅即导致自由与责任的不对称。人们在这里可以享受最大的自由，却只承担最小的责任，甚至干脆逃避责任。

4．Real-time（即时性）

For the network, the transmission speed is irrelevant to geographical distance. Traditional trading patterns, information communication such as letters, telegraphs, faxes, etc., between the sending and receiving of information, involve different time lengths. With regard to the information exchange in e-commerce, regardless of the actual distance of time and space, one party sends a message to the other party who receives that information almost at the same time, just like talking face to face in person. Some digital products (such as audio and video products, software, etc.), can also have instant settlement, ordering, payment, delivery done in a flash.

对于网络而言，传输的速度和地理距离无关。传统交易模式，信息交流方式如信函、电报、传真等，在信息的发送与接收间，存在着长短不同的时间差。而电子商务中的信息交流，无论实际时空距离远近，一方发送信息与另一方接收信息几乎是同时的，就如同生活中面对面交谈。某些数字化产品（如音像制品、软件等）的交易，还可以即时清结，订货、付款、交货都可以在瞬间完成。

5. Paperlessness（无纸化）

Electronic commerce mainly takes the way of paperless operation, which serves as a main characteristic of trade in the form of e-commerce. In e-commerce, electronic computer communication records utilize electronic information instead of a series of paper-based trading. Users send or receive electronic information. Since the electronic information exists in the form of bits and transmission, the whole process is realized through paperless information. Paperlessness brings positive effects in terms of making information transferred without the limitation of paper, however, many specifications of the traditional law are with the standard "paper trades" as the starting point. Therefore, paperlessness brings chaos in the legal system to a certain extent.

电子商务主要采取无纸化操作的方式，这是以电子商务形式进行交易的主要特征。在电子商务中，电子计算机通信记录取代了一系列的纸面交易文件。用户发送或接收电子信息。由于电子信息以比特的形式存在和传送，整个信息发送和接收过程实现了无纸化。无纸化带来的积极影响是使信息传递摆脱了纸张的限制，但由于传统法律的许多规范是以规范"有纸交易"为出发点的，因此，无纸化在一定程度上造成了法律的混乱。

Section Two　Current Situations and Features of China's Cross-border E-commerce Development （我国跨境电子商务的发展现状与特征）

According to a report by *Economic Daily* in 2025, in recent years, the scale and quality of cross-border e-commerce in China have grown from small to large, becoming a new highlight in China's foreign trade and global economic and trade fields. According to statistics, China's cross-border e-commerce imports and exports reached 2.63 trillion yuan in 2024, an increase of 10.8% year-on-year. In the past 5 years, the scale of cross-border e-commerce trade in China has grown by more than 10 times. As of February 2025, the number of cross-border e-commerce enterprises in China had exceeded 120,000, and cross-border e-commerce enterprises had registered over 30000 trademarks overseas. The potential of cross-border e-commerce in "selling globally" is further unleashed, and its advantages in "buying globally" are also continuously being utilized.

2025 年《经济日报》报道，近年来，我国跨境电商规模从小到大，质量做强做优，已成为我国对外贸易和全球经贸领域的新亮点。据统计，2024 年我国跨境电商进出口 2.63 万亿元，增长 10.8%。过去 5 年，我国跨境电商贸易规模增长超过 10 倍。截至 2025 年 2 月，我国跨境电商企业数量已超 12 万家，跨境电商企业累计在海外注册商标超过 3 万个。跨境电商在"卖全球"方面的潜力进一步释放，在"买全球"方面的优势也在持续发挥。

Currently, China's cross-border e-commerce is developing rapidly with outstanding features. Firstly, new business subjects spring up. Secondly, the trade scale is expanding rapidly. Thirdly, the threshold for small and medium-sized enterprises conducting cross-border trade lowers. Fourthly, emerging markets have become the highlights. Turnover with emerging markets such as Brazil, Russia and India has soared, making important contributions to the rapid development of domestic cross-border e-commerce retail and export platforms. Fifthly, the import size is small, but the export one develops to the contrary. Imported goods mainly include food such as milk powder, and luxuries like cosmetics on a small scale. Exported goods are mainly goods for everyday consumption such as clothes, accessories, small household appliances, and digital products with a large scale and a yearly fast growth rate.

当前，我国跨境电子商务发展迅速，特征突出。一是新的经营主体大量涌现。二是贸易规模迅速扩张。三是中小企业从事跨境贸易的门槛降低。中小企业建立直接面向国外买家的国际营销渠道，降低交易成本，缩短运营周期。四是新兴市场成为亮点。巴西、俄罗斯、印度等新兴市场交易额大幅提升，为境内众多跨境电子商务零售出口平台的快速发展做出重要贡献。五是进口规模小，出口规模大。进口商品主要包括奶粉等食品和化妆品等奢侈品，规模较小；出口商品主要包括服装、饰品、小家电、数码产品等日用消费品，规模较大，每年增速很快。

Section Three　Regulations on Cross-border E-commerce（我国的跨境电子商务法律法规）

In recent years, the term "cross-border e-commerce" has been repeatedly mentioned in government work reports and statements, and simultaneously the policy support at the national level has been constantly increasing. All of this essentially shows that the emerging foreign trade model of "cross-border e-commerce" has been truly recognized by the government. On August 31, 2018, the *Electronic Commerce Law* was reviewed and approved by the National People's Congress and came into effect on January 1, 2019, becoming the first comprehensive law in the field of e-commerce in China.

近年来，政府工作报告多次提及"跨境电子商务"，国家层面的政策支持力度也在不断加码。这一切都从本质上说明"跨境电子商务"这一新兴外贸模式已经被政府真正认可。2018 年 8 月 31 日，《电子商务法》经全国人民代表大会审议并通过，于 2019 年 1 月 1 日起施行，成为我国电子商务领域的首部综合性法律。

The Electronic Commerce Law of the People's Republic of China is a government regulation, enterprises and individuals using data messages as a means of trading, generated through information networks. It is the general term for the legal norms of social relations and government management relations concerning various commercial transaction relationships caused by transaction forms, and closely related to such commercial transactions.

《中华人民共和国电子商务法》是一项政府法规，规范企业和个人以数据电文为交易手段，通过信息网络所产生的，因交易形式所引起的各种商事交易关系，以及与这种商事交易关系密切相关的社会关系、政府管理关系的法律规范的总称。

Other than clearly stipulating that cross-border e-commerce practitioners should abide by the legal provisions of import and export supervision, the E-commerce Law also strengthens the legal basis for solutions to hot issues in cross-border import consumption complaints, and promotes the cross-border e-commerce industry from multiple perspectives to facilitate healthy growth. The regulation of cross-border e-commerce by e-commerce legislation is a major landmark event in cross-border e-commerce in China.

《电子商务法》除了明确规定跨境电子商务从业者应该遵守进出口监管的法律规定外，更加强了跨境进口消费投诉热点问题的解决方案的法律依据，多角度促进跨境电子商务行业良好健康发展。电子商务立法对跨境电子商务的规范是我国跨境电子商务的一个重大标志性事件。

Compared with domestic e-commerce, cross-border e-commerce bears numerous links, including taxation, customs clearance, intellectual property rights, and data security. Therefore, government supervision and guidance function as the core link of future cross-border e-commerce. In the future, cross-border e-commerce regulations are likely to be more specific and detailed, and new regulations are most likely to be made to keep pace with the times, so as to adapt to the continuous development of cross-border e-commerce, improve the operability of real cross-border e-commerce trade, and truly solve the relevant problems in the practice of e-commerce.

相对于国内电子商务，跨境电子商务环节多，涉及面更多，包括税收、通关、知识产权、数据安全等。所以，政府监管和引导是未来跨境电子商务的核心环节。未来跨境电子商务的法规将会更为具体详细和做出与时俱进的新规定，以适应跨境电子商务的不断发展，提高实际跨境电子商务贸易中的可操作性，真正解决跨境电子商务实践中的难题。

The present *E-commerce Law* regulates cross-border e-commerce issues in a legal form. It shows its supportive attitude in a clear tone: the authorities not only facilitate cross-border e-commerce, but also require legal compliance. For a long time, cross-border e-commerce has had two business models: bonded and direct mail. Because the legal relationship is not clear, the contract relationship or the entrusted relationship lead to different responsibilities, resulting in a series of disputes. In addition, cross-border transactions still have issues like tax evasion, smuggling, etc.. Some cross-border dealers sell counterfeits, or do not provide after-sales services. Some issues like private transactions, cash transactions to evade supervision and infringement of intellectual property rights still exist. Article 26 of the *E-commerce Law* stipulates that "e-commerce operators engaged in cross-border e-commerce shall abide by the laws, administrative regulations and relevant state regulations of import and export supervision and management." Clearly, regardless of the mode of cross-border e-commerce, both import and export laws and domestic laws must be strictly observed.

现行《电子商务法》以法律形式规范了跨境电子商务问题，支持态度很明确：不仅为跨境电子商务提供便利，同时也要求其合法合规。长期以来，跨境电子商务存在两种业务模式：保税和直邮，由于法律关系不明确，合同关系还是委托关系导致的责任也不同，因此产生了一系列纠纷。此外，跨境交易还存在逃税避税、涉嫌走私；部分跨境经销商真假掺卖、不提供售后；

私下交易、现金交易以逃避监管以及侵犯知识产权等问题。现行《电子商务法》第二十六条确定，"电子商务经营者从事跨境电子商务，应当遵守进出口监督管理的法律、行政法规和国家有关规定。"明确了跨境电子商务无论何种模式，必须遵守进出口以及国内法律。

The *E-commerce Law* has pioneered China's e-commerce legislation and has exemplary significance for e-commerce legislation worldwide.

《电子商务法》开创了我国电子商务立法的先河，对世界范围内的电子商务立法具有示范意义。

Section Four Pattern of Trade（贸易模式）

The basic pattern of trade of cross-border e-commerce in China is mainly divided into business to business (B2B) and business to consumer (B2C). With B2B mode, enterprises apply e-commerce with priority given to the use of advertisement and information release, due to the fact that its deals and customs clearance processes are fulfilled in an offline manner, it is still essentially   traditional trade, and is incorporated into the customs statistics of general trade. With the B2C mode, China's enterprises, directly facing overseas customers, are mainly involved with sales of personal consumer goods;   logistics is mainly carried out by aviation packets, mail, express way, and its declaration entity is postal or courier services, which are not included in the customs registration at present. (Fig.13-1)

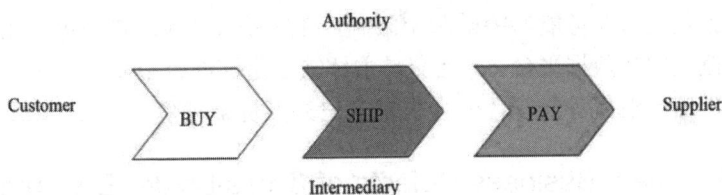

Fig.13-1   A Brief Graph to Cross-border E-commerce Procedure（跨境电子商务流程简图）

我国跨境电子商务主要分为企业对企业（即 B2B）和企业对消费者（即 B2C）的贸易模式。B2B 模式下，企业运用电子商务以广告和信息发布为主，成交和通关流程基本在线下完成，本质上仍属传统贸易，已纳入海关一般贸易统计。B2C 模式下，我国企业直接面对国外消费者，以销售个人消费品为主，物流方面主要采用航空小包、邮寄、快递等方式，其报关主体是邮政或快递公司，目前大多未纳入海关登记（见图 13-1）。

Section Five   Policy Defects of Cross-border E-commerce（跨境电子商务面临的政策缺陷）

1. The ownership management issues of e-commerce transactions（电子商务交易归属管理问题）

Based on the analysis of e-commerce transaction mode, pure electronic trading, to a great extent, belongs to the category of service trade, which is under the rules of GATS rules according to the trade in services. Those orders via electronic commerce, contract, etc., which are transported by the traditional mode of transportation, are classified as the trade in goods category, which belongs to the category of the management of the GATT. In addition, for special types of e-commerce, trade in services is neither service trade nor goods trade, such as electronic products provided by means of electronic commerce (such as cultural products, software, entertainment, etc.), whether this kind of e-commerce trade belongs to service trade or trade in goods is still under discussion.

从电子商务交易形式上分析，纯粹的电子交易在很大程度上属于服务贸易范畴，国际普遍认可归入 GATS 的规则中按服务贸易进行管理。对于只是通过电子商务方式完成定购、签约等，但要通过传统的运输方式运送至购买人所在地，则归入货物贸易范畴，属于 GATT 的管理范畴。此外，对于特殊的电子商务种类，既非明显的服务贸易也非明显的货物贸易，如通过电子商务手段提供电子类产品（如文化、软件、娱乐产品等），国际上对此类电子商务交易归属服务贸易或货物贸易仍存在较大分歧。

2. The market access issue of trading body（交易主体市场准入问题）

Cross-border e-commerce and payment business can break through space and time limits, making the business reach every corner of the world, the economic and financial information and capital chain are increasingly focused on the data platform. Once the trading body lacks adequate financial strength or faces problems such as irregular operations, credit crisis, system failures, information leakage, it will cause the risk of customer foreign exchange funds.

跨境电子商务及支付业务能够突破时空限制，将商务辐射到世界的每个角落，使经济金融信息和资金链日益集中在数据平台。一旦交易主体缺乏足够的资金实力或出现违规经营、信用危机、系统故障、信息泄露等问题，便会引发客户外汇资金风险。

Section Six　Payment Business Defects of Cross-border E-commerce（跨境电子商务支付业务的管理缺陷）

1. Difficulty in auditing the trade authenticity（交易真实性难以审核）

The virtuality of e-commerce is directly responsible for the difficulty in auditing trade authenticity for the Supervision Department of the Foreign Exchange when it comes to the authenticity of cross-border e-commerce transactions, and the legitimacy of the money; this provides a way for both domestic and overseas abnormal funds to deal with the balance of payments through cross-border e-commerce.

电子商务的虚拟性直接导致外汇监管部门对跨境电子商务交易的真实性、支付资金的合法性难以审核，为境内外异常资金通过跨境电子商务办理收支提供了途径。

2. Difficulties of the balance of payments（国际收支申报存在困难）

On the one hand, through the electronic payment platform, domestic e-commerce business bank account is not directly involved with the cross-border capital flows, and it usually takes 7 to 10 days for the payment platform to complete the real trading fund settlement, so it is more difficult for the trading main body to implement the provisions of the declaration. On the other hand, different transaction modes of international payment declaration also produce certain effects. Payment institutions, serving as the actual remittance body of offline payment unified purchase, can declare payment institution as the main body of the international balance of payments, but it is difficult for this declaration mode to reflect each transaction essence of funds, adding the difficulties of foreign exchange supervision.

一方面，通过电子支付平台，境内外电子商务的银行账户并不直接发生跨境资金流动，且支付平台完成实质交易资金清算常需要 7～10 天，因此由交易主体办理对外收付款申报的规定较难实施。另一方面，不同的交易方式下对国际收支申报主体也产生一定的影响。线下统一购汇支付方式实际购汇人为支付机构，可以支付机构为主体进行国际收支申报，但此种申报方式难以体现每笔交易资金实质，增加外汇监管难度。

Section Seven　Rights Protection Regulations of Cross-border E-commerce（跨境电子商务的保护权益法规）

The newly passed *E-commerce Law* in 2018 has added a number of clear regulations on consumer protection rights.

2018 年新通过的《电子商务法》增加了许多相关消费者保护权益的明确规定。

1. "Tying sales" must have significant marks and prompts（搭售须有显著提示）

In response to the annoying "tying sales" problem, the E-commerce Law has added provisions: if e-commerce operators provide "tying sales" goods or services, they should be brought to the attention of consumers in a significant way, and "tying sales" goods or services should not be the default consent option.

针对恼人的"搭售"问题，《电子商务法》增加规定：电子商务经营者搭售商品或服务，应当以显著方式提请消费者注意，不得将搭售商品或者服务作为默认同意的选项。

2. Deposit is guaranteed to be refunded smoothly（保证押金顺利退还）

In response to the difficulty of refunding the deposit, the E-commerce Law has added the following provisions: if the e-commerce operator receives a deposit from the relevant consumer, it shall clearly indicate the manner and procedure for refunding the deposit, and may not set unreasonable conditions for the refund of the deposit. If the consumer applies for the refund of the deposit and meets the conditions for the refund of the deposit, the e-commerce operator shall return it in time.

针对押金退还难的问题，《电子商务法》增加了如下规定：电子商务经营者按照约定向消费者收取押金的，应当明示押金退还的方式、程序，不得对押金退还设置不合理条件。消费者申请退还押金，符合押金退还条件的，电子商务经营者应当及时退还。

3. Protect personal information and privacy（保护个人信息和隐私）

The e-commerce law adds provisions: e-commerce operators who collect and use personal information of their users shall abide by the personal information protection rules stipulated by relevant laws and administrative regulations. When e-commerce operators sell goods or services to consumers according to their hobbies, and consumption habits, etc., they should also provide consumers with options that do not target their personal characteristics, so as to respect and equally protect the legitimate rights and interests of consumers.

《电子商务法》增加规定：电子商务经营者收集、使用其用户的个人信息，应当遵守有关法律、行政法规规定的个人信息保护规则。电子商务经营者根据消费者的兴趣爱好、消费习惯等特征向其推销商品或者服务，应当同时向该消费者提供不针对其个人特征的选项，尊重和平等保护消费者合法权益。

Part B Terminology Practice

1. **Cross-border e-commerce**（跨境电子商务）：a new-type mode of trade that the digitalization and electronization of exhibition, negotiation and conclusion of a business of the traditional trade by Chinese production and trade enterprises through e-commerce means to finally realize the import and export of products.

2. **Network space**（网络空间）：a virtual reality of network address and password.

3. **B2B**（企业对企业）：business-to-business, commerce transactions between businesses, such as between a manufacturer and a wholesaler, or between a wholesaler and a retailer.

4. **B2C**（企业对消费者）：business-to-consumer, is the type of commerce transaction in which businesses sell products or services to consumers.

5. **TOT**（贸易条件）：terms of trade, refers to the relative price of exports in terms of imports and is defined as the ratio of export prices to import prices. It can be interpreted as the amount of import goods an economy can purchase per unit of export goods.

6. **International trade**（国际贸易）：the exchange of capital, goods, and services across international borders or territories, which could involve the activities of the government and individuals.

7. **Globalization**（全球化）：the worldwide movement toward economic, financial, trade, and communications integration.

8. **Decentralization**（去中心化）：the process of redistributing or dispersing functions, powers, people or things away from a central location or authority.

9. **Intangibility**（无形性）：used in marketing to describe the inability to assess the value gained from engaging in an activity using any tangible evidence. It is often used to describe services where there isn't a tangible product that the customer can purchase, that can be seen, tasted or touched.

10. **Turnover**（周转率）：a financial ratio that measures the efficiency of a company's use of its assets in generating sales revenue.

11. **Virtual Reality (VR)**（虚拟现实）：immersive multimedia or computer-simulated reality, replicates an environment that simulates physical presence in places in the real world or imagined worlds and lets the user interact in that world.

12. **Electronic money**（电子货币）：the money balance recorded electronically on a

stored-value card. These cards have microprocessors embedded which can be loaded with a monetary value.

Part C Terms

1. based on 基于
2. profoundly affect 深远影响
3. traditional way of trade 传统贸易模式
4. a new-type mode of trade 新贸易模式
5. at the same time 即时性
6. brand competitiveness 品牌竞争力
7. realize the transformation 实现转型
8. upgrading of foreign trade 外贸升级
9. sharing the characteristics of 有……特征
10. digital products and services 数字化产品和服务
11. physical objects 实物
12. is given priority to 以……为主
13. due to 由于……
14. brings positive effects 积极影响
15. in terms of 以……形式
16. has attracted great attention from 引起……高度重视
17. is mainly divided into 主要分为
18. trading body 交易主体
19. accounted for 占……比例
20. an increasing number of 越来越多
21. the national level 国家层面
22. National People's Congress 全国人民代表大会
23. the core link of ……的核心环节
24. are most likely to 可能……
25. abide by 遵守……
26. be strictly observed 严格遵守

Part D Exercise

I. Answer the following questions according to the information you have got.

1. What is the definition of "Cross-border e-commerce"?

2. What is "Network Space"?

3. What is B2B?

4. What is B2C?

5. What are the features of Cross-border E-commerce?

6. Why is it difficult to identify the e-commerce user's identity and their geographical location?

7. What is the definition of Globalization?

8. What is Decentralization?

9. What are the features of China's Cross-border E-commerce Development?

10. What are the Policy Defects of Cross-border E-commerce?

11. What is Virtual Reality?

12. What are Payment Business Defects of Cross-border E-commerce?

13. What is Electronic money?

14. What is TOT?

15. What does Intangibility mean?

16. What essentially shows that the emerging foreign trade model of "cross-border e-commerce" has been truly recognized by the government?

17. What is the significance of e-commerce legislation?

18. Why does government supervision and guidance function as the core link of future cross-border e-commerce?

19. How does the newly passed e-commerce law solve the "Tying sales" problem in a legal form?

II. Match each one on the left with its correct meaning on the right.

1. turnover   A. the exchange of capital goods, and services across international borders

2. network space   B. the digitalization and electronization of a business

3. E-money   C. redistributing or dispersing functions away from a central location

4. terms of trade   D. the worldwide movement toward economic, financial, trade, and communications integration

5. B2B   E. businesses sell products or services to consumers

6. B2C   F. commerce transactions between businesses

7. globalization   G. the amount of import goods an economy can purchase

8. decentralization   H. the money balance recorded electronically on a stored-value card

9. cross-border e-commerce   I. a virtual reality of network address and password

10. International trade   J. financial ratio that measures the efficiency of a company's use of its assets in generating sales revenue

1. (   ) 2. (   ) 3. (   ) 4. (   ) 5. (   )
6. (   ) 7. (   ) 8. (   ) 9. (   ) 10. (   )

III. Translate the following phrases into Chinese.

1. profoundly affect

2. traditional way of trade

3. a new-type mode of trade

4. at the same time

5. brand competitiveness

6. realize the transformation

7. upgrading of foreign trade

8. sharing the characteristics of

9. digital products and services

10. physical objects

11. is given priority to

12. brings positive effects

13. in terms of

14. has attracted great attention from

15. trading body

IV. Case Study.

Bicycles named "Giant Dragon" exported from China were very popular in Asia, but in Europe and North America, this item enjoyed no popularity. How come?

V. Find out some cases about policy defects in doing cross-border e-commerce.

VI. Determine whether the following statements are True or False. Then put T for True or F for False in the bracket at the end of each statement.

1. Cross-border e-commerce is developed based on the network. (   )

2. Network is a medium with boundaries, sharing the characteristics of globalization and decentralization. (   )

3. The positive effect brought by features of network is the greatest sharing degree of information, whilst its negative impact is that the users confront risks. (   )

4. Due to the decentralization of cross-border e-commerce and global features, it is easy to identify the e-commerce user's identity and their geographical location. (   )

5. For the network, the transmission speed is irrelevant to geographical distance. (   )

6. The rapid development of cross-border e-commerce has attracted little attention from the government and business circles. (   )

7. The basic patterns of trade of cross-border e-commerce in China are mainly divided into business to business (B2B) and business to consumer (B2C). (   )

8. Those orders by electronic commerce, contracts, etc., which are transported by the traditional mode of transportation, are classified as trade in goods category, which does not belong to the category of the management of the GATT. (   )

VII. Translate the following paragraphs into English.

1. 近年来，政府工作报告多次提及"跨境电子商务"，国家层面的政策支持力度也在不断加码。这一切都从本质上说明"跨境电子商务"这一新兴外贸模式已经被政府真正认可。2018年8月31日，《电子商务法》经全国人民代表大会审议并通过，将于2019年1月1日起施行，成为我国电子商务领域的首部综合性法律。

2. 中国政府对外汇实行严格的管制，授权外管局逐一审批贸易和投资中的外汇交易。但是跨境电子商务中，交易金额小、交易频繁，如果外管局坚持以前的监管方式，就会给支付造成很大障碍。

3. 外管局颁发跨境支付牌照后，用户可以通过支付宝等第三方支付工具使用人民币进行支付，支付宝负责向境外电子商务网站支付美元、英镑、欧元、日元、韩币等本地货币，再由境外电子商务网站或者支付宝合作的转运公司将商品运送至国内。

4. 《电子商务法》增加规定：电子商务经营者收集、使用其用户的个人信息，应当遵守有关法律、行政法规规定的个人信息保护规则。电子商务经营者根据消费者的兴趣爱好、消费习惯等特征向其推销商品或者服务，应当同时向该消费者提供不针对其个人特征的选项，尊重和平等保护消费者合法权益。

VIII. Multiple Choices.

1. The word methods to describe quality includes (   ).

A. sale by specification standard

B. sale by brand trademark

C. sale by the name of origin

D. sale by specification and design

E. sale by sample

2. The classification of e-commerce is (　　).

　　A. business to business e-commerce (B2B)

　　B. business to consumer e-commerce (B2C)

　　C. business institutions to administrative agencies e-commerce (B2A)

　　D. consumer to administrative agencies e-commerce (C2A)

3. Marine bill of lading is a document that consignee should present when taking the goods at the port of destination, it is (　　).

　　A. the cargo receipt issued by the ship or its agent upon receipt of the carriage of goods

　　B. stipulating rights and obligations of the contract between the shipper and consignor

　　C. the contract of carriage between the carrier and the shipper

　　D. the legal property rights certificate

　　E. important document for exporters to get payment or negotiation from the bank

4. Regulation method for Usance draft payment is (　　).

　　A. payable at sight　　　　　　　　　　B. several days after sight

　　C. pay several days after drawing　　　　D. pay several days from date of B/L

5. Parties of collection include (　　).

　　A. the principal　　　　　　　　　　　B. entrusting bank

　　C. the collecting bank　　　　　　　　　D. the payer

　　E. remittance bank

6. According to the economic development of all countries to participate in the international division of labor, the international division of labor can be divided into (　　).

　　A. vertical division

　　B. horizontal division

　　C. three tiers in the international industrial division

　　D. hybrid division

　　E. technology division

7. With the development of international division of labor, the international commodity structure and national import and export commodity structure will change constantly, in (　　).

　　A. the rising proportion of industrial manufactured goods in international trade

　　B. export growth in developing countries

　　C. the rising proportion of intermediate mechanical products

　　D. rapid development of service trade

　　E. the rising proportion of trade in goods

8. Natural condition is the foundation of international division of production and the development, and the conditions include (　　).

　　A. population distribution　　　　　　　B. geographical geological conditions

　　C. climate conditions　　　　　　　　　D. natural resources

　　E. land area

9. Factor endowment theory argues that between countries in labor productivity under the same conditions, formation of cost differences between countries is due to (　　).

A. the differences of factor endowments

B. national differences in the economies of scale

C. the different elements combination ratio

D. the different trade policies

E. product prices

10. If Germany and Britain produce 8 yards of cloth, 15 yards of linen and 10 yards of cloth, 20 yards of linen respectively in the same labor time, then based on the principle of division of labor, the pattern of comparative advantage is (　　).

A. Britain will do production and export cloth

B. Britain will do production and export linen

C. Germany will do production and export cloth

D. Germany will do production and export linen

E. Two products are produced by Germany and exported

Appendix   Model Test

Model Test 1

I. Translate the following terms. (20%)

A. From English into Chinese. (1 for 1, 10%)

1. Visible Trade
2. Cash Discount
3. Pro Forma Invoice
4. Joint Venture
5. Open Policy
6. Letter of Credit
7. CIF
8. Representative Sample
9. More-or-less clause
10. Bill of Lading

B. From Chinese into English. (1 for 1, 10%)

1. 世界银行
2. 毛重
3. 托运人
4. 进口许可证
5. 国际商会
6. 发票
7. 共同海损
8. 商业合同
9. 贸易术语
10. 海洋运输

II. Choose the best answer for each of the following questions. (1 for 1, 10%)

1. Contracts must be renewed one week (   ) their expiration.

   A. on   B. against   C. the moment of   D. before

2. The commodities you offered are (   ) line with the business scope of our clients.

   A. outside   B. out of   C. out   D. without

3. We are arranging for an inspection tour of (   ) the material was processed.

   A. place   B. the place   C. where   D. there

4. We are reconsidering those trade terms (   ) might be adverse to the interest of our principals.

   A. what   B. that   C. when   D. where

5. We find that there is no stipulation of transshipment (   ) in the relevant L/C.

   A. allowing   B. which allows
   C. which allowed   D. being allowed

6. After unpacking the case we found that the goods did not (   ) with the original sample.

   A. match   B. come up   C. agree   D. measure

7. If the first shipment (   ), we guarantee that we will send you many repeat orders.

   A. match   B. come up   C. agree   D. measure

8. It is necessary that an arbitration clause (   ) in the contract.

   A. will be included   B. must be included
   C. be included   D. has been included

9. Please see that your written confirmation (　　) by the end of this month, otherwise we will be free from the obligation for this offer.

    A. reaches us   B. will reach us   C. reach us   D. reached us

10. That helps to explain (　　) businesses are setting up Net sites even though profits aren't yet very big.

    A. that   B. the reason for   C. why   D. why that

III. Give the English definition of the following terms. (4 for 1, 20%)

1. Importing

2. Offer

3. Nude Cargo

4. Net weight

5. Marine Losses

IV. Judge the following statements, and mark T (True) or F (False). (1 for 1, 25%)

1. Price terms are mainly applied to determining the prices of commodities in international trade. (　　)

2. Warsaw-Oxford Rules clearly explain the thirteen kinds of trade terms in current use. (　　)

3. As an exporter, you concluded a deal with an American on the basis of EXW; then your transaction risk is reduced to the minimum degree. (　　)

4. According to the interpretation of the Revised American Foreign Trade Definitions, FAS is suitable for all kinds of transportation. (　　)

5. On CIP terms, the seller must pay the freight and insurance premium as well as bear all the risks until the goods have arrived at the destination. (　　)

6. A letter of indemnity is issued by the seller to the buyer to certify that the goods delivered are in good condition. (　　)

7. Trade facilitation is a term of international trade. Its basic spirit is to simplify and coordinate trade procedures and accelerate the flow of elements across borders. (　　)

8. When you transport your goods by a Time Charter, you have to pay for loading and unloading. (　　)

9. When the shipowner speeds up his ship and arrives at the destination at an earlier date than is stipulated, he can obtain dispatch money from the shipper. (　　)

10. When the charterer fails to load or unload the goods within the stipulated period of time, he has to pay demurrage to the shipowner. (　　)

11. Sometimes when the buyer cannot determine a specific port of discharge, he may require two or three ports to be written on the contract for option. (　　)

12. When there are optional ports in the contract, the goods may be unloaded at any one of the ports at the shipping company's disposal. (　　)

13. When importing on FOB terms, we can generally stipulate the port of discharge. (　　)

14. An order bill of lading may be negotiable after being endorsed. (　　)

15. A bill of lading is a transport contract in which the shipping company promises to transport the goods received to the destination. (　　)

16. In China, insurance companies do not accept insurance based on Institute Cargo Clauses. (　　)

17. Institute Cargo Clauses (A) has the widest coverage among all its clauses. (　　)

18. Almost all the insurance companies provide door-to-door coverage service. (　　)

19. Insurance against F.P.A. means that the insured cannot obtain compensation from the insurer if a particular average occurs. (　　)

20. If you have insured your goods against All Risks, you will get compensated for whatever risks occur to your goods. (　　)

21. The quantity terms of goods is one of the conditions of an effective sales contract. (　　)

22. In international trade, only the Metric System is allowed to indicate the quantity of goods. (　　)

23. If the parties to a sales contract do not in advance agree upon whether the quantity of goods is determined by gross weight or net weight, it will be determined by gross weight. (　　)

24. Net weight refers to the actual tare of all the packing materials. (　　)

25. Conditioned weight is, in fact, the actual weight of the moisture of a certain commodity. (　　)

V. Case Analysis. In this part there are 5 cases, three of which are in Chinese, two in English. Please analyze the cases. If the case is in Chinese, you can answer in Chinese. If it is in English, you should answer in English. (5 for 1, 25%)

1. 我国某出口公司向法国出口货物一批，合同中的贸易术语是 CIF 马赛，卖方在合同规定的时间和装运港装船，货船离港后不久便触礁沉没。次日，当卖方凭提单、保险单以及发票等有关单据通过银行向买方要求付款时，买方以未收到合同中规定的货物为由，拒绝接受单据和付款。

问题：我方应该如何处理？

2. 某公司向国外出口一批仪器，合同规定由买方提供唛头，但截至买方提供时间届满为止，仍未见其通知设计情况，而该公司货已备好。

问题：该公司应如何处理此事？

3. 某公司以 FOB 条件出口一批茶具，买方要求公司代为租船，费用由买方负担。由于公司在约定日期无法租到合适的船，且买方不同意更换条件，以致延误了装运期，买方以此为由提出撤销合同。

问题：买方的要求是否合理？

4. In 2018, a certain export company in China sent a group of businessmen to the United States for the purchase of equipment. In New York both parties reached an oral agreement on such items as specifications, unit price, and quantity. Upon leaving, the group indicated to the other party that, when they got back to Beijing, they would draft a contract, which would become effective after being signed by both parties. After going back to Beijing, the group found that the clients withdrew their import of the equipment, and thus the contract was not signed and the L/C was not opened, either. The US side urged the Chinese side to perform the contract; otherwise they would lodge a claim with the Chinese side in the US.

Question: Please analyze the case and give an opinion on how the Chinese export company was to deal with this case, and why?

5. A Chinese trading company A concluded a transaction in steel with a Hong Kong company B on the basis of FOB China Port. Company B immediately resold the steel to Company H in Libya on the terms of CFR Liberia. The L/C from B required the price terms to be FOB China Port and the goods to be directly delivered to Liberia. The L/C also required "Freight Prepaid" to be indicated on the Bill of Lading.

Question: Why did Company B perform so? What should we do about it?

Model Test 2

I. Give the definitions of the following terms. （5%×3=15%）

1. Offer
2. Duplicate sample
3. Draft

II. Judge the following statements, and mark T (True) or F (False). （1%×20=20%）

1. An offer may not indicate the terms of payment. (   )
2. The price-list and catalogues sent to some companies are also offers with binding effect. (   )
3. According to the United Nations Convention on Contracts for the International Sale of Goods, an acceptance with non-material alterations or additions can still constitute a valid acceptance. (   )
4. According to the CISG, a late acceptance caused by abnormal transmission of the post office is nevertheless effective unless the offer or shows objection without delay. (   )
5. Landed quality refers to the quality of the goods re-inspected upon their arrival at the port of destination. (   )
6. After issuance of the letter of credit, the Issuing Bank may refuse payment if the applicant becomes bankrupt. (   )
7. After the negotiating bank negotiates the documents, which are refused by the opening bank later, the negotiating bank may ask the beneficiary for repayment. (   )
8. In response to the annoying "tying sales" problem, the 2018 e-commerce law has added provisions: if e-commerce operators provide "tying sales" goods or services, they should be brought to the attention of consumers in a significant way, and "tying sales" goods or services should not be the default consent option. (   )
9. If the L/C prohibits partial shipments and the goods are shipped in full quantity with the price not reduced, a short drawing of 5 percent of the amount is permissible. (   )
10. If the Issuing Bank appoints the Bank of China as its Advising Bank of L/C, then the Issuing Bank may ask the Bank of Asia to advise amendments to the L/C. (   )
11. A bank will only accept a clean transport document. A clean transport document is one bearing no clause or notation expressly declaring a defective condition of the goods or their packaging. The word "clean" need not appear on a transport document, even if a credit has a requirement for that transport document to be "clean on board". (   )
12. If a letter of credit stipulates some conditions but does not require the related documents the banks may disregard them as not stated. (   )
13. The date of the insurance document must be no later than the date of shipment, unless it appears from the insurance document that the cover is effective from a date not later than the date of shipment. (   )

14. The war risks both under CIC and ICC can be covered independently. (　　)

15. Insurance against F.P.A. means that the insured cannot obtain compensation from the insurer if a particular average occurs. (　　)

16. The insurance endorsement cannot be used as an independent document. It is only a supplementary document attached to the insurance policy or certificate. (　　)

17. Warsaw-Oxford Rules clearly explain the thirteen kinds of trade terms in current use. (　　)

18. According to Incoterms2010, FCA is suitable for all kinds of transportation. (　　)

19. The main difference between a CIF contract and a DDU contract lies in the fact that the former is a symbolic delivery of goods, whereas the latter is a physical delivery of goods. (　　)

20. In general, soft currency should be chosen for exports and hard currency for imports. (　　)

III. Make the best choice. (1%×15=15%)

1. The international uniform customs practice in written for documentary collection is (　　).

   A. UCP600　　　B. ISP98　　　　　C. Incoterms 2000　　　D. URC522

2. The payer of a promissory note is the (　　).

   A. drawer　　　B. drawee　　　　C. payee　　　　　　　　D. creditor

3. (　　) needn't draft generally.

   A. Open Negotiation L/C　　　　　B. Sight Payment L/C

   C. Deferred Payment L/C　　　　　D. Restricted Negotiation L/C

4. The Opening Banks of L/C deal with (　　).

   A. services　　　　　　　　　　　B. goods

   C. documents　　　　　　　　　　D. performance to which the documents may relate

5. Which of the followings does not belong to the classification of e-commerce? (　　).

   A. B2B　　　　　B. B2C　　　　　C. B2A　　　　　　　　D. C2B

6. If the cargoes are not discharged from the ship or lighter, then the time of insurance liability under war risks shall be limited to (　　) days counting from the midnight of the day when the vessel arrives at the port of destination.

   A. 15 days　　　B. 30 days　　　C. 60 days　　　　　　D. 2 years

7. W.P.A. is (　　) in Chinese.

   A. 平安险　　　B. 水渍险　　　C. 一切险　　　　　　D. 战争险

8. The Ad Val. standard for liner freight is calculated on the basis of (　　).

   A. CIF price　　　　　　　　　　B. FCA price

   C. CFR price　　　　　　　　　　D. FOB price

9. Unless the L/C stipulates otherwise, (　　).

   A. Partial shipments and transshipments are allowed

   B. Partial shipments and transshipments are not allowed

   C. transshipments are not allowed, but partial shipments are allowed

   D. transshipments are allowed, but partial shipments are not allowed

10. The net weight and gross weight for some goods is 28kgs per piece and 30kgs respectively. Its measurement is 45cm×35cm×22cm per piece. If the calculation standard for liner's freight tariff is W/M10, the shipping company will calculate the freight (   ).

    A. on the basis of net weight

    B. at the shipper's option

    C. on the basis of measurement

    D. at the carrier's option

11. The most frequently used pricing methods is (   ).

    A. fixed pricing

    B. flexible pricing

    C. partial fixed price and partial unfixed price

    D. floating pricing

12. In international export practice, in case we conclude a FOB or CFR contract with the buyer abroad, unless otherwise agreed, we must give the buyer notice that the goods have been delivered on board the vessel, so as to enable him to (   ) in time.

    A. arrange shipment   B. cover insurance

    C. take delivery   D. open L/C

13. The CIF contract is a typical "document transaction" or "(   )".

    A. dependent transaction   B. physical delivery

    C. symbolic delivery   D. arrival contract

14. The variations of CFR involve only the problem of who is to pay (   ) charges, with nothing to do with the place of delivery or the place of risk separation.

    A. loading   B. demurrage   C. freight   D. unloading

15. (   ) is covered by a W.P.A. policy.

    A. Loss due to the carrying vessel's stranding

    B. Loss caused by heavy rain

    C. Loss due to theft, pilferage and non-delivery

    D. Loss caused by the carrying vessel's collision

IV. Make suitable choices. (2%×6=12%)

1. According to CISG Article 19, additional or different terms relating, among other things, to the (   ), quality of the goods, extent of one party's liability to the other or are considered to alter the terms of the offer materially.

    A. price   B. payment   C. the settlement of disputes

    D. quantity   E. place and time of delivery

2. According to CISG Article 20, a period of time for acceptance fixed by the offeror in a telegram or a letter begins to run from (   ).

    A. the moment that the offer reaches the offeree

    B. the date shown on the letter

C. the date shown on the envelope

D. the moment the telegram is handed in for dispatch

3. The parties involved in collection include: (　　　)

A. Principal   B. Payee   C. Remitting Bank

D. Paying Bank   E. Collecting Bank   F. Payer

4. Under D/D, the draft in use is (　　　).

A. draft at sight   B. time draft   C. banker's draft

D. commercial draft   E. banker's acceptance bill   F. commercial acceptance bill

5. The commencement and termination of (　　　) are usually stipulated by adopting the customary "W/W" clause under CIC.

A. F.P.A.   B. General Additional Risk   C. W.P.A.

D. All Risks   E. War risks   F. Strike risks

6. Disasters such as (　　) are Natural Calamities.

A. vile weather   B. tsunami   C. ship stranded

D. dampness and heat   E. Explosion

V. Fill in the blanks. (1%×10=10%)

1. There are 3 kinds of expression of the Payee on the draft: (1) (　　　); (2) (　　　); (3) (　　　).

2. If the date of payment is later than the date of receipt of cargo, in order to grasp a favorable time to resale the goods, the buyer can adopt the following way: (1) (　　　); (2) (　　　).

3. Partial loss refers to the loss of part of a consignment. According to different causes, partial loss can be either (　　) or (　　　).

4. According to the relevant stipulations of the PICC, the validity of a claim shall not exceed a period of (　　　) years counting from the time of completion of discharge of the insured goods from the seagoing vessel at the final port of discharge.

5. If we offered USD1 500 Per MT FOB QINDAO, now the client wants us to quote at a price including 10% commission. To keep our profit at the primary level, we should quote: USD (　　) (　　　).

VI. Case Study. (6%×3=18%)

1. A company concludes a contract under CIF term. It receives the L/C issued abroad on 1st July. The opening date of the L/C is 20th June and the validity of the L/C is 15th August. Suppose that:

(1) the L/C stipulates "Prompt Shipment", then the latest date of shipment is (　　　).

(2) the L/C stipulates "Shipment on or about 20th July", then the date of shipment is (　　　).

(3) the beneficiary starts the shipment on 10th July and finishes it on 12th July. The ship arrives at the port of destination on 20th August. The buyer takes delivery of the goods also on 20th August. Then, the date of B/L should be (　　　). The date of insurance policy should be (　　　). The time of document presentation should be not later than (　　　). The time of delivery for the seller is (　　　).

2. 我国某外贸公司向日本商人以 D/P 见票即付方式推销某商品，对方答复如我方接受 D/P 见票后 90 天付款条件，并通过他指定的 A 银行代收货款则可接受。

请分析日方提出此项要求的出发点。（该题可用中文作答）

3. 一载货船在航行途中不慎搁浅，事后船长下令反复开倒车，强行起浮，但船上轮机受损并且船底划破，致使海水渗进货舱，造成船货部分受损。该船驶进附近的一港口修理并暂卸大部分货物，共花一周时间，增加了各项费用支出，包括船员工资共 8 000 美元。船修复后装上原货重新启航后不久，A 舱起火，船长下令灌水灭火。A 舱原载有儿童玩具、茶叶等，灭火后发现儿童玩具一部分被烧毁，另一部分儿童玩具和全部茶叶被水浸湿。

试分析上述各项损失的性质，并说明在投保何种险别的情况下，保险公司方负责赔偿？（该题可用中文作答）

VII. Calculation. (10%×1=10%)

Company A in China exports some goods in carton to the UK. They quote: USD50 PER CARTON CFR LONDON. But the businessman in the UK requires FOBC2 price. To meet his requirement, how much should the Chinese exporter offer then? (Suppose: the measurement of the carton is 45cm × 40cm × 25cm; the gross weight for one carton of goods is 35kgs; the calculation standard for freight tariff is W/M; the basic freight rate is USD120 per freight ton; the BAF is 20% and the port surcharge is10%.)

Model Test 3

本试卷分两部分，满分 100 分，考试时间 150 分钟。

1. 第一部分为选择题，应考者必须在答题卡上按要求填涂，不能答在试卷上。2. 第二部分为非选择题，应考者必须在答题卡上直接答题，答在试卷上无效。3. 请按照试题题号顺序在答题区域内作答。

I. Multiple Choices. (1%×10 = 10%)

Directions: In this part, there are items 1~10. For each item, there are four choices marked A,B, C, and D. Choose the best letter from A, B, C, or D and blacken the correspondent letter on the Answer Sheet.

1. Because it represents the title to the goods, (   ) must be handled carefully.

   A. bill of lading   B. letter of credit

   C. advice of shipment   D. international sanction

2. Please inform us (   ) the tendency of your market.

   A. for   B. in

   C.of   D.with

3. After you have received a (n) (   ) check the customer's credit standing again if necessary.

   A. sales contract   B. order

   C. invoice   D. proposal

4. When an importer is buying through his agent from the exporter, the importer can open a TLC (   ) the agent for transfer to the exporter.

   A. in accordance with   B. regarding

   C. with respect to   D. in favor of

5. They can be binding on buyers or sellers (   ) the sales contract specifies that a particular Incoterms will apply.

   A. provided   B. as soon as

   C. as well as   D. as

6. When is a bill of lading issued?

   A. When the shipper ships up the order

   B. When the goods remain at the port of shipment

   C. When the carrier receives the goods

   D. When the carrier delivers the goods to the consignee

7. (   ) can be used for all kinds of mode of transport.

   A. CIF   B. CFR

   C. FOB   D. FCA

8. As a general rule, the exported goods are always inspected by the (   ) before shipment.

   A. shipper   B. buyer   C. agent   D. distributor

9. The bank in the buyer's country in collection arrangement is (   ).

   A. remitting bank   B. collecting bank

   C. opening bank   D. confirming bank

10. (   ) represents higher risks for the cargo and is not accepted unless expressly permitted by the consignee.

A. A clean B/L   B. On deck B/L

C. On board B/L   D. Order B/L

II. Gap-Filling. (1%×10=10%)

Directions：Fill in each of the following blanks with an appropriate word (some words are given the first letter or letters).

11. An air waybill is a (1) rec_____an evidence of (2) cent_____, but not a (3) tit_____document. It is therefore not (4) trans_____ or (5) neg _____and a shipper does not lose his ownership of the cargo by handing the air waybill (6) _____the airline.

A shipper can present his copy to exercise his "right of (7) dis _____" to stop the goods at any point of journey, to have the goods (8) del_____to a different consignee, or to have the shipment returned, (9) pr_____that the shipper does not exercise this right in such a way as to prejudice the carrier or other consignors and repays any (10) ex _____occasioned by the exercise of this right.

III. Term Definition. (3% × 5 = 15%)

Directions: Briefly define or explain terms 12~16.

12. acceptance

13. clean draft

14. import license

15. general cargo vessel

16. economies of scale

IV. Short Answered Questions. (5% × 4 = 20%)

Directions: Briefly answer questions 17~20.

17. What are the fundamental principles of insurance that firms must follow when they seek cover for goods?

18. What are the three types of inspection agency?

19. Please list at least three essential constituents of a definite offer.

20. What factors need to be considered in arranging for transportation?

V. Case Study. (10%)

21.Company A made an offer for a farm product to Company B stating: "Packing in sound bags". Within the validity, Company B replied "Refer to your telex first accepted, packing in new bags". On receiving the reply, Company A began to purchase the goods for export. Days later, as the market price of the commodity was falling, Company B wrote to Company A "No contract is entered between us, as you failed to confirm our changing of the packing requirement." Company A argued that Company B's acceptance was effective and the contract was established then.

Questions:

(1) What is your opinion? Give the reasons to support your opinion.

(2) How can such disputes be presented?

VI. Term Translation. (2% ×5 = 10%)

Directions: Translate terms 22~26, into Chinese.

22. Ro-Ro ship

23. DWT

24. Transferable L/C

25. endorsement

26. VAT

参 考 文 献

[1] 盛洪昌. 国际贸易实务[M]. 北京：清华大学出版社，2020.

[2] 周瑞琪，王小鸥，徐月芳. 国际贸易实务（英文版）[M]. 北京：对外经贸大学出版社，2020.

[3] 黎孝先，王健. 国际贸易实务[M]. 北京：对外经贸大学出版社，2020.

[4] 张燕芳，史俊红. 国际贸易实务[M]. 北京：人民邮电出版社，2024.

[5] 冷柏军，李洋. 国际贸易实务双语教程[M]. 北京：中国人民大学出版社，2021.

[6] 余庆瑜. 国际贸易实务：原理与案例[M]. 北京：中国人民大学出版社，2021.

[7] 鲁丹萍. 国际贸易实务[M]. 北京：高等教育出版社，2025.

[8] 周敏倩，竺杏月. 国际贸易实务与案例[M]. 南京：东南大学出版社，2025.

[9] 覃娜，符白薇. 国际贸易实务中英双语教程[M]. 杭州：浙江大学出版社，2025.

[10] 魏雪莲，彭虹. 国际贸易实务与单证操作[M]. 北京：北京师范大学出版社，2025.

[11] 任丽萍. 国际贸易理论与实务[M]. 北京：清华大学出版社，2016.

[12] 杨春梅，赵宏，吴国新. 国际贸易实务（英文版）[M]. 北京：清华大学出版社，2021.

[13] 易露霞，尤彧聪. 跨境电子商务双语教程[M]. 北京：清华大学出版社，2019.